PRIMA Official Game Guide

Written by:

David S.J. Hodgson

Prima Games
An Imprint of Random House, Inc.
3000 Lava Ridge Court, Suite 100
Roseville, CA 95661
www.primagames.com

Prima Games

Senior Product Manager: Mario De Govia
Associate Product Manager: Shaida Boroumand
Assistant Editor: Jenkey Hu
Copy Editor: Carrie Andrews
Design & Layout: Bryan Neff & Jody Seltzer
Manufacturing: Stephanie Sanchez & Suzanne Goodwin

ISBN: 978-07615-6288-7
Library of Congress Catalog Card Number: 2009904714
Printed in the United States of America

09 10 11 12 LL 10 9 8 7 6 5 4 3 2 1

About the Author

Originally hailing from the English city of Manchester, David began his career in 1995, writing for numerous classic British gaming magazines from a rusting, condemned, bohemian dry-docked German fishing trawler floating on the River Thames. Fleeing the United Kingdom, he joined the crew at the part-fraternity, part-sanitarium known as *GameFan* magazine. David helped launch GameFan Books and form Gamers' Republic, was partly responsible for the wildly unsuccessful *incite* Video Gaming and Gamers.com. He began authoring guides for Prima in 2000. He has written over 60 strategy guides, including: *The Legend of Zelda: Twilight Princess*, *Assassin's Creed*, *Half-Life: Orange Box*, *Mario Kart Wii*, and *Fallout 3*. He lives in the Pacific Northwest with his wife Melanie, and an eight-foot statue of Great Cthulhu.

We want to hear from you! E-mail comments and feedback to dhodgson@primagames.com.

Multiplayer Credits

PMS CLAN
play like a girl

Pandora's Mighty Soldiers
www.pmsclan.com

Division Leader
PMS UT Princess/Aundrea Haddad
Division Co-Leader
PMS Solincia/Myra Noland

Contributors:
Athena AzMADEUS—Roster Manager
PMS Dark Ivory/Sarah McLaughlin—Community Manager
PMS Doom/Liz Sarver—Battles/Small Teams Co-Manager
PMS Eclipse/Kayla Hansen—Practice Co-Manager
PMS ElektraFox/Misty Baragar—Recruitment Manager
PMS Heartbreakr/Megan Baisley—Practice Manager
PMS Ruin/Desiree Mott—Recruitment Co-Manager
Strawberry Boo/Olivia Hannah—Community Co-Manager
PMS Unforgiven/Felisha Piña—Battles/Small Teams Manager
PMS Deception/Ashley Trevino
PMS Disco/Olivia Denai
PMS Jezabelle
PMS Miz Lulu/Allison Jensen
PMS Ovaryacting
PMS Pip Sq3ak
PMS Serenity yo/Marlene Taypaywaykejick
PMS Shadowleet/Mariah Farrar
Righty Is Law/Lauren Woodward
PMS Arkathia/Destinie Rogers
PMS Nitemare/Ebony Winston
PMS Padme/Alexandria Bybee
PMS Meow/Amanda Godfrey-Wilson

Author Thanks and Acknowledgements

To my loving wife Melanie; Bryn, Rachel, Samuel and Ben; Mum, Dad, and Ian; The Moon Wiring Club, Boards of Canada, Laibach, Kraftwerk, and The Knife, Ron Bennington and Fez Marie Whatley (and the rest); and G for Gol-Goroth. Who lives where it's cold as December, Who is worshipped by Shantaks but is also forgotten, For reasons I cannot remember.

Thanks to Shaida Boroumand, Mario de Govia, Jody Seltzer, Bryan Neff, all at 99 Lives, Clan PMS, and all at Prima for their tremendous help and support on this project.

This project would not have been possible without the help and dedication from Alicia Brattin, Jonathan Goff, Carlos Naranjo, everyone at the Halo 3: ODST Test department, and all at Bungie. One thousand thanks.

INTRODUCTION

Welcome to This Guide

How to Utilize This Book

Welcome to the official guide to *Halo 3: ODST*. Months in the making and involving copious and meticulous tactical advisement from both Microsoft and Bungie, this guide has many aspects that can help your battles through New Mombasa and beyond. The following breakdown of each chapter showcases what to expect.

Basic Training

pg. 4

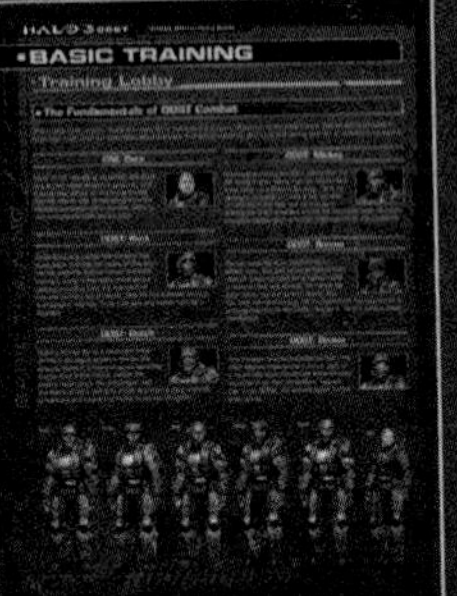

The chapter you're currently reading. After you meet the ODST strike team selected for Campaign and Firefight missions, a basic primer (covering different elements of this game compared to *Halo 3*) is revealed, as well as some general tactical knowledge.

Arms and Equipment

pg. 10

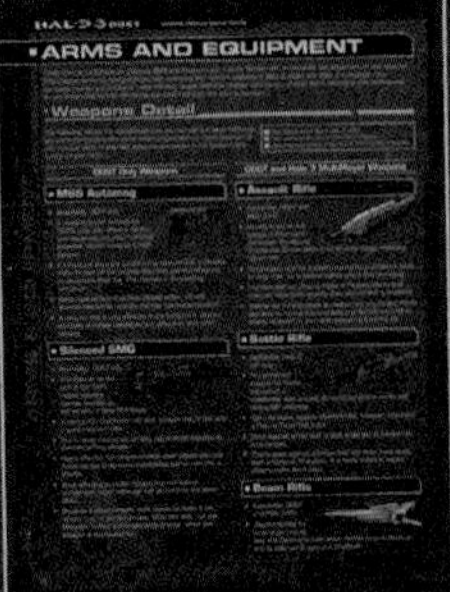

Every available piece of UNSC or Covenant machinery, whether a weapon, Turret, Grenade, vehicle, or other piece of equipment, is inspected. Notes on availability and overall takedown tactics, where appropriate, are shown, along with a visual reference.

Know Your Enemy

pg. 20

The Covenant is amassing forces in the vicinity of New Mombasa. Knowing what they are and how to effectively fight them is your key to success. Tried-and-tested tactics for defeating Grunts, Jackals, Brutes of all types, Hunters, Drones, and Engineers are revealed here.

Campaign Missions

pg. 28

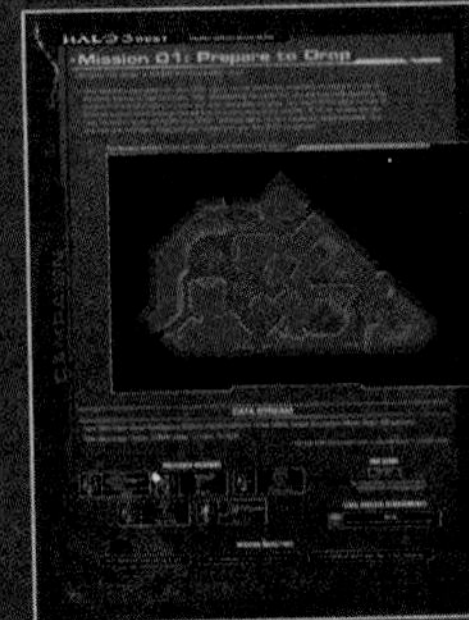

Chronicling the campaign undertaken by your ODST squadmates, this chapter features a walkthrough of every mission. Preferred weapon combos, maps, and every choke point is revealed, and strategies to survive are showcased, no matter what difficulty you're playing on.

Firefight Missions

pg. 132

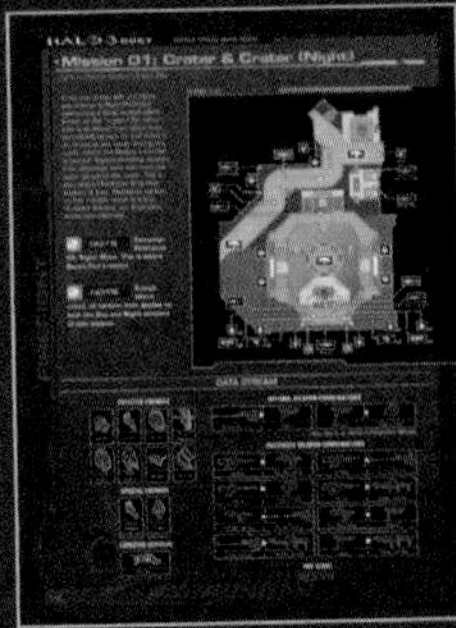

Engaging countless Covenant squads with up to four players presents can be a fearsome proposition. This takes you through all ten of the available Firefight Maps, giving thorough and tailored tactics to each of them. Need to survive longer? Digest this chapter.

Halo 3 Multiplayer Maps

pg. 170

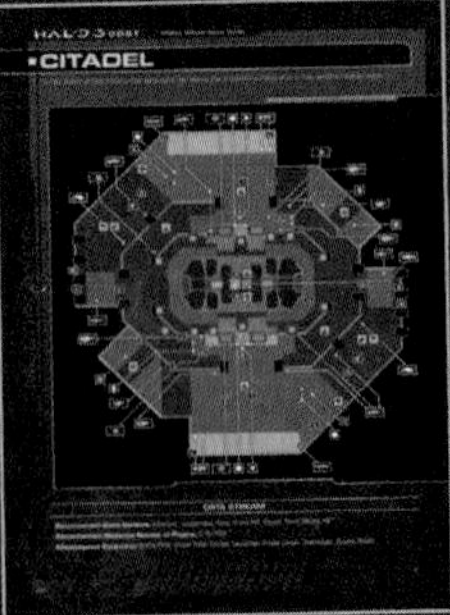

Employing the talents of an infamous clan filled with Tournament-level players, all 24 *Halo 3* multiplayer maps offer masses of tactical information, including full item placement, gameplay strategies, and many sniping and ambush spots.

Appendices

pg. 303

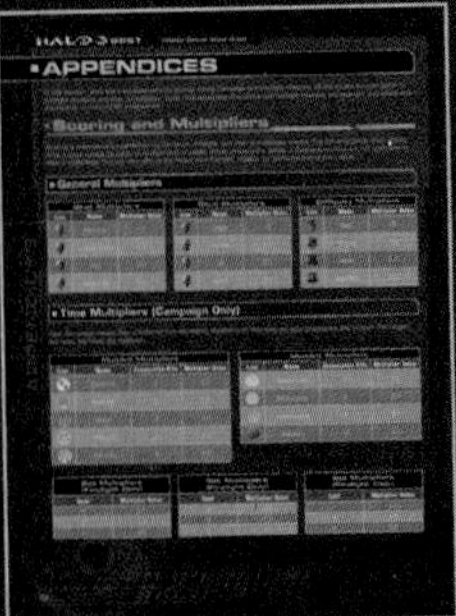

Whether you need to know the Skull or score multipliers, medals, or game unlockables, this chapter has everything you need, all in one place. Every Achievement is also detailed, with tactical advice on obtaining every one, including the infamous Vidmaster Challenges.

Map Legend

Icon	Name
	Assault Rifle
	Battle Rifle
	Beam Rifle
	Brute Shot
	Carbine
	Energy Sword
	Fuel Rod Gun
	Gravity Hammer
	Magnum
	Mauler
	Needler
	Plasma Pistol
	Plasma Rifle
	Rocket Launcher
	Sentinel Beam
	Shotgun
	SMG
	Sniper Rifle
	Spartan Laser
	Spiker
	Machine Gun Turret
	Plasma Turret
	Missile Pod
	Flamethrower
	Gauss Cannon
	Frag Grenade
	Plasma Grenade
	Spike Grenade
	Incendiary Grenade

Icon	Name
	Detonator Charge
	Deployable Cover
	Bubble Shield
	Grav Lift
	Power Drain
	Regenerator
	Flare
	Radar Jammer
	Trip Mine
	Cloaking
	Invincibility
	Auto Turret
	Overshield
	Active Camo
	Warthog
	Mongoose
	Banshee
	Ghost
	Wraith
	Scorpion
	Hornet
	Chopper
	Prowler
	Behemoth
	Pelican
	Scarab
	Phantom
	Overturned Warthog
	Overturned Ghost

Icon	Name
	Overturned Banshee
	Wrecked Warthog
	Elevator/Gravity Lift
	Health Pack
	Dead Marine
V	Wreckage
	Data Terminal
	Weapon Cache
	Building Door/Tunnel Gate
	Dead Zebras
	Shade Turret
	District Gate
	Building Door
	Energy Wall Barrier
	Monster Closet
	Phantom Drop
	Pelican Landing Pad
	Watch-Tower
	Covenant Barricade
	Covenant Landing Pad
	Covenant Beacon Antenna
	Covenant Crate
	Drop Pod
	Drone Hive
S	Stack Shaft
E	Engineer Housing
1	Choke Point
1	Waypoint (multiplayer)

Icon	Name
A	Sniper/Ambush Position (multiplayer)
	Light Enemy Presence
	Medium Enemy Presence
	Heavy Enemy Presence
9.02	Landmark
	Dare
	Virgil
	CLUE: Dare's Helmet
	CLUE: Drone Fighter Optics
	CLUE: Gauss Turret
	CLUE: Remote Detonator
	CLUE: Bent Sniper Rifle
	CLUE: Bio-Foam Cannister
	Possible Entrance to Data Have
	Oddball (multiplayer)
	Flag/Flag Base (multiplayer)
	Bomb (multiplayer)
	Bomb Base (multiplayer)
	Neutral Bomb (multiplayer)
	Hill (multiplayer)
	Territory (multiplayer)
	Active Camo (multiplayer)
	Overshield (multiplayer)

NOTE

Pleae note the color coding of icons, each color represents the level on which you will find the corresponding icon:

Below Ground *Ground* *Above Ground*

BASIC TRAINING

Training Lobby

The Fundamentals of ODST Combat

This is your ODST squad. There are many like it, but this one is yours: Welcome to the Helljumpers. Before you're dropped in from high orbit, read the main facts about the team that will be watching your back and saving your life on numerous occasions.

ONI: Dare

Most of her dossier is classified, but Dare is a known Naval Academy graduate and former intel officer on the heavy frigate *Say My Name*, one of two ships from the Harvest campaign still in service. Dare is now assigned to ONI Section One.

ODST: Buck

Eddie Buck is a career Marine who has seen more than his fair share of this war. He has had the dubious honor of participating in many of the wars' most vicious battles, including both the liberation of Harvest and the fall of Reach. That he has survived through it all speaks volumes. Truly, if he was any better, he'd be a Spartan.

ODST: Dutch

Dutch's former life as a road-train driver on Mars did well to prepare him for the arduous tasks of a heavy-weapons specialist and to drive in the ODSTs. Behind the death's head rictus, the Jolly Roger, and the layers of black and gray armor is a man of deep spiritual convictions and respect for those he serves alongside.

ODST: Mickey

Mickey loves being an ODST. More than he did being a pilot. More than he did being a crew chief on a Pelican gunship. He is no stranger to battle and has a fair number of notches in his belt, but he is unique among his ODST brothers in that he has never seen absolute ruination visited upon a human colony-world by the Covenant.

ODST: Romeo

Romeo sees his true vocation as a ladies' man. But just because he's a lover doesn't mean he can't be a fighter—and a damned fine one at that. He keeps his gear clean, his suit looking sharp, and his body lean and strong. Off the battlefield, he may not be a shining example of the UNSC, but on it, he is a consummate combatant.

ODST: Rookie

This trooper recently transferred from the 26th Marine Expeditionary Force, part of a Rapid Offensive Picket that suffered near annihilation at New Jerusalem, Cygnus. Like most ODSTs, his actions speak louder than words.

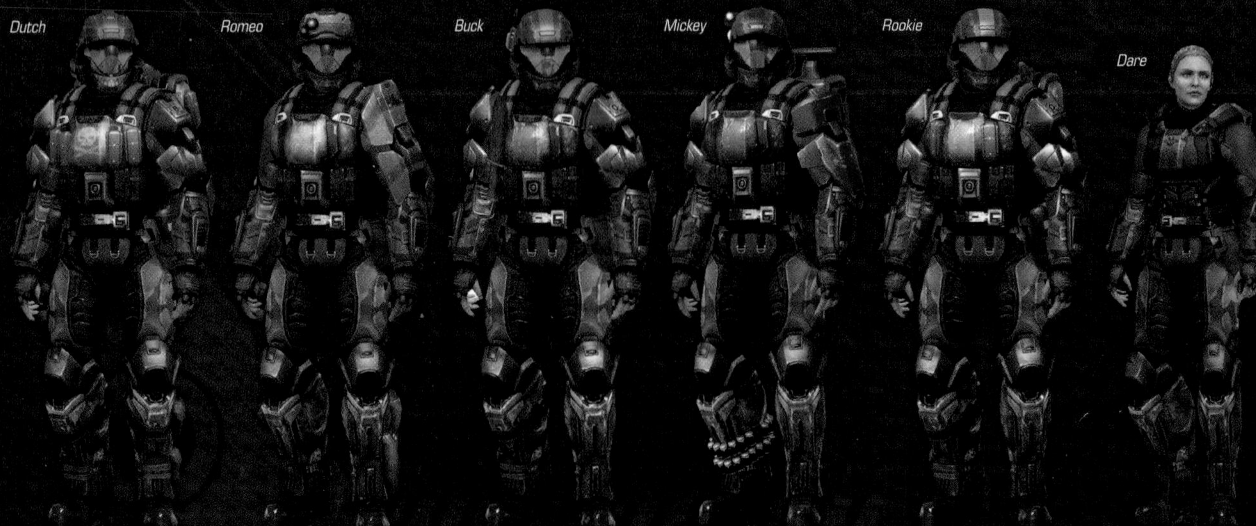

■ ODST Uniform Capabilities

Navigating the menu system and learning how to control your ODST squadmates are succinctly covered in your instruction manual. For advice on settings, sharing files, Theater mode, and other elements, check this section before continuing. The following is an enhanced view of the advice you garner during your Campaign sorties.

ODST Heads-Up Display

By now, you may have realized that you're not invincible and are actually susceptible to sharp projectiles—or even to blunt ones. However, the UNSC have crafted a uniform that helps you overcome the inherent design flaws of the human body—namely, your soft and squishy skin—as much as possible. Here's a little more knowledge on the HUDs and some advice on basic survival.

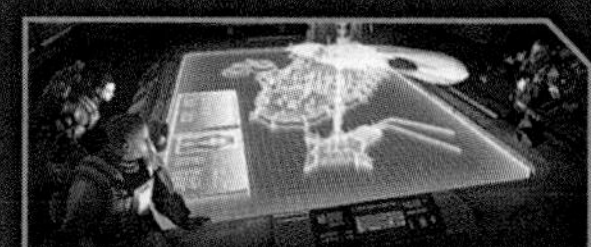

This is an example of in-game action during the Campaign (a Firefight variation is shown at the beginning of that chapter). Here's how all the information is fed into your brain, and how it can help you:

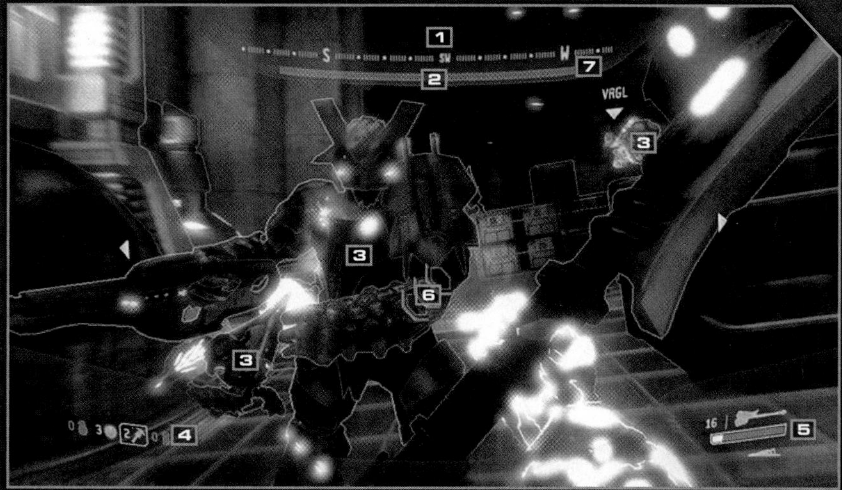

1 **Compass readout:** When this guide refers to a compass direction, check this compass. It also displays objective navigation marker waypoints (blue diamonds) and waypoints you or your friends have flagged (green pointers).

2 **VISR readout:** Underneath the compass is your health, represented by a horizontal yellow strip. This gradually turns red the more you're wounded, so be ever vigilant and locate a Health Pack before this is completely diminished. Underneath that is an area that appears only to inform you of new objectives when they are triggered, so you don't have to access your VISR database.

3 **Friends and foes:** Turn on your VISR Enhanced Vision (recommended in all low-light situations). Enemies are outlined in red, friends are outlined in green, and clues and Data Terminals are outlined in yellow. This is excellent for finding snipers at long range or watching (and counting) foes to plan an attack before you engage them. The general rule is, don't fire at anything green!

4 **Grenade inventory:** Don't simply use up the Frag Grenades, which are first on your inventory list of four Grenade types; cycle through them using LB to select the best Grenade for a particular situation. Frag Grenades bounce on impact. Plasma and Sticky Grenades stick to most targets. Flame Grenades set a target on fire. All Grenades are found via scavenging.

5 **Primary and reserve weapon ("weapon combo"):** This shows the weapon you're using (top), the remaining ammunition, and your other weapon (bottom); swap between the two using Y. Consult the "Arms and Equipment," "Campaign Missions," and "Firefight" chapters for tactics on preferred weapons and weapon combos.

6 **Target reticle:** This changes from yellow to red when an enemy is in your crosshairs. Remember that some weapons are instant-hit (and you should fire when the reticle is red) and some weapons arc into their targets, meaning you should fire at where you think your foe will be, not where they are now.

7 **Stamina risk assessment:** The tinge of red around your screen that gradually becomes more pronounced appears when you're low on Stamina. Simply locate cover and rest to restore your Stamina, or find a Health Pack to restore your Health and Stamina.

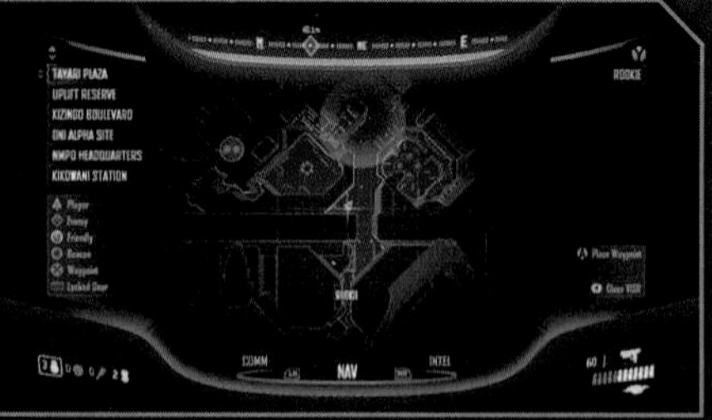

Your VISR database is a wealth of topographical knowledge, and after reading up on it in the instructions manual, you'll soon understand how best to utilize it. One of the most useful features is the waypoint (pictured) that you can flag yourself. This appears on your compass (in green) and on your map (as a green reticle). This is the most useful of your NAV system's inventory because you can use it (especially in Mombasa Streets) to flag a place you've already been, so you don't get lost in the maze of sloping sidewalks and mezzanines. Even better, human teammates can flag areas for you to explore, which may have a particular enemy you want to face, a terminal you wish to interact with, or a cache of weapons to find.

VISR onscreen prompts (such as in the example shown) are a vital help to your cause, so don't ignore them. When a weapon prompt appears in the middle of your screen, it means you're standing near a weapon you can swap. Do so depending on the situation. When your VISR updates an objective, that appears, too, but you don't need to enter your Database menu immediately; the objective appears under your compass a second later. Always look for your HUD to display when you've reached a check point so you know that when you die, you return to this location. Finally, your sense of hearing is important; from the hiss of a primed Plasma Grenade to the chatter of Grunts, you really need to listen more; it adds to your tactical knowledge of a particular choke point.

Differences in Control

As you'll discover on page 24 of your instruction manual, when playing as an ODST, much of the controller functionality is identical to that of previous Halo games played as a Spartan. However, there are a few differences you should be aware of:

VISR mode (X): Instead of deploying equipment (Spartan), you engage the VISR; think of this as an enhanced flashlight.

Throwing Grenades (LT): ODSTs do not have the skill to dual-wield, so this control is taken up by Grenade Throwing, which allows immediate lobbing of your selected projectile.

Select Grenade Type (LB): Instead of swapping weapons or reloading, LB now cycles through your Grenades. Swapping between your two main weapons is achieved by pressing Y now.

VISR Database (BACK): Also a Carnage Report in ODST Firefight mode, this database (Map menu) in the Campaign allows you to check where you are, where your goal is, waypoints you or your teammates have flagged, what your objectives are, and what information you've collected from terminals.

View Waypoints (D-pad): Your VISR negates the need for a Flashlight, so this allows you to bring up waypoints as a visual, onscreen reference complete with distance-to-target data. If you're lost, simply bring this up and you won't be.

User Preview and Preamble

Moving and Stamina

▲ **Facing down a foe at this range is usually frowned upon; no unnecessary risks, trooper!**

▲ **There are no medics here; that increasingly red glow around your helmet vision is telling you something....**

The basics you've learned before apply when traversing New Mombasa; you should keep moving to avoid becoming prone and targeted by multiple foes. You should seek cover opportunities and tactical hiding spots if you're low on Stamina. In addition, you should seek higher ground, as it is easier to target foes looking down on them than peering up. Also, learn to sidestep and strafe, moving from left to right while keeping your target reticle pinned on a particular enemy. Step this up with circle-strafing (moving around a foe at a constant distance while aiming at them). Finally, it is worth backing up if you're badly wounded and returning to the last Health Pack you didn't use. A methodical approach to alien takedowns is better than a reckless and ultimately suicidal one.

Packing Health

ike Spartans, ODSTs do not carry additional equipment with them, aside from rets, but they do access a new type of item: the Health Pack (aka the Medikit). pensed by Optican Medigel Dispensary Kiosks controlled by a friendly Superin-dent throughout New Mombasa or found scattered on the ground, Health Packs tore lost Health and Stamina so you don't die. However, your Stamina (a regen-ting attribute that acts as a buffer between taking damage and losing Health) lenishes if you wait a few moments (unless the Black Eye Skull is active); this offers same modicum of protection as it did previously, despite your lower Health, as alth does not regenerate like Stamina does. Therefore, you may continue fighting, urning to claim a Health Pack after a subsequent bout of violence, as Health Packs a finite resource. Health Pack etiquette is a key tenet of Firefight missions, too.

Know Your Environment

Certain areas have unused Turrets that may be advantageous to use instead of depleting your inventory. Learn which plazas are likely to be more active with snipers. Remember that stepping near Grenades that are about to explode is the best way to achieve an unwanted death. Note that you can enter some buildings and access upper balconies; this is better than struggling on the ground. New Mombasa has secret weapon caches, filled with UNSC-approved hardware.

Enemy Scum and Difficulty Levels

e Covenant scum you'll be cutting down in a blaze of high-velocity culling are numerous and relenting, but there is a method to their madness. Consult the "Know Your Enemy" chapter specifics on taking down each enemy type, but know the following general tactics:

ENEMY ICON During Rookie missions (which take place primarily in Mombasa Streets), enemy placement is somewhat randomized and usually takes place in the form of a Covenant Patrol (Grunts or Jackals and a Brute or two), Jackal Snipers (embedded on a balcony or rooftop, which are sometimes inaccessible), roaming Hunters, or airdrops by Phantoms. During "Flashback" missions (which take place in a variety of locales), enemy placement is in the locations detailed in this guide's walkthrough.

LEGENDARY ICON The difficulty level you choose should reflect your competence and desire for completing Achievements. Experienced soldiers should attempt the Campaign mode on Heroic and Firefight on Normal to begin with. The differences between Easy, Normal, Heroic, and Legendary all lie in the damage enemies and yourself take, how accurate your foes are, how prone they are to making mistakes, and available ammunition and items. Legendary difficulty is almost mind-snappingly hard: In order to even partially complete a mission on this setting, you must heed the following advice:

- Utilize cover almost constantly, meaning you need an adept knowledge of an area after numerous previous playthroughs.
- You must keep calm and be patient, waiting for an opportunity to strike. If you're dying, you're not waiting for a correct opportunity.
- Check points play a key here, too. Knowing when they are triggered allows you to reach one, and ever if you die, you're resurrected there instead of earlier in the mission.
- Stealth is advisable. Attacking from the sides is better than from the front, as you won't be caught by as many bullets and die.
- Headshots are a necessity in order to conserve ammunition and remove threats as quickly as possible. Throughout the Campaign chapters, we've flagged preferred weapon combinations to help you achieve this goal.
- The correct weapon combo is a must, and it is usually a variation on the Plasma Pistol (for taking out enemy shields) and the Magnum (for ending an unshielded Covenant's life with a headshot).
- Finally, guidance is golden; the tactics presented in this book have been play-tested and where flagged are preferable during playthroughs on Legendary.

TIP

It is also worth having a working knowledge of Achievements. Some are general, but some are specific to a particular mission (these are tagged in the walkthrough as such). However, some Achievements require you to perform a particular activity, such as shooting foes with a certain weapon. In addition, check this guide's Appendix for the Achievements list so you don't forget to attempt an Achievement you're not aware of.

Weapons and Grenades

oosing the correct weapon for the job is incredibly important, which is why this guide owcases every available weapon's strengths and weaknesses, and the walkthrough lists eferred weapons for each specific mission. Generally, ODSTs are not as skilled as Spartans. STs cannot dual-wield weapons (one in each hand). An ODST can theoretically carry up to ee weapons at once: two regular weapons and one classified as "Support," which slows down and must be dropped in order to use either of the other weapons. Throughout the

Reloading your weapon prior to finishing a magazine or clip is a straightforward but often overlooked tactic that simply lets you live longer. Reloading with ® when there's a temporal lull in the action allows you to start your subsequent attack with as many bullets as possible. Failure to complete this results in you automatically reloading, usually while you're being cut to ribbons.

▲ Staggering around with a heavy Turret sacrifices speed and agility in favor of massive firepower.

▲ When there's something on your target viewfinder as big as this, targeted shots are preferred over inaccurate spraying.

Accuracy is a key tactic, too, especially on harder difficulties. Unless you're firing a mounted turret, the "spray and pray" method of raking the general area where you saw a foe and hoping some of your bullets hit is an incredibly poor way to play. Short, quick, targeted bursts conserve your ammunition, make you more accurate, and don't result in an embarrassing death gurgle. Also, it is sometimes difficult to discern when to utilize a powerful weapon (such as a Rocket Launcher). Many players have ended their days as a twitching corpse still hanging on to a fully loaded Spartan Laser, so don't be afraid to fire. Heed the specific mission advice for the best times to do so.

TIP **Remember, you can walk over bullet-based weaponry that is lying around and instantly receive ammunition, instead of scavenging and swapping out ordnance. This isn't true of plasma-based weapons (such as the Plasma Rifle, Plasma Pistol, or Beam Rifle), which have ammunition that cannot be cannibalized from scavenged parts. In those cases, you must find a new weapon or one with more ammunition than your current one.**

▲ Incoming! Cycle through your Grenades so you're using projectiles most suitable for a certain situation.

Grenades and weapons with splash damage—those that cause destruction in a wider radius—are also key to your ongoing quest to stay alive. You can carry up to 12 Grenades (three of each type), and all are found when you scavenge enemy bodies or locate UNSC equipment. Note that some Grenades (Frag) bounce off foes, while others (Plasma) stick to them. Some foes (Brute Chieftains) are immune to being "stuck," so use these weapons wisely. Grenades and rockets are fantastic for killing clusters of foes, such as those just landing from a Phantom drop, and larger entities, such as Hunters or Wraiths. They are a great addition to your regular gunfire and for stopping enemies chasing you.

CAUTION **If you're collecting Grenades, don't use explosives to kill foes, as this is more likely to discharge their own Grenade supplies.**

Allies and Vehicles

◀ Meet up with a team of friendly Marines and they're ready and willing to follow you, even into certain death!

Friends with Benefits

Non-human-controlled Allies are a key advantage during frantic, street-by-street combat sorties. Marines offer help periodically, and although they tend to die easily, when fighting alongside you in a vehicle, they are worth their weight in Plasma Grenades. Depending on the storyline, ODSTs are even better friends, as technically they don't die, allowing you to step back and let them absorb all the enemy fire—if your pride and points accumulation can handle it, of course.

TIP

Remember, you can swap weapons with Marines and ODST squadmates but not with fellow human players. This has specific benefits, such as non-human-controlled teammates have infinite ammunition when carrying weapons, and general benefits outlined in the Campaigh walkthrough.

Friends with Pulses

▲ Knowing who's facing down a Brute Chieftain and who's behind them firing a Turret is the key to effective combat.

Actual human friends can be an even more vital source of help. Key cooperative tactics are displayed prominently throughout all gameplay modes contained in this guide. Completing a Campaign with one or more friends unlocks specific Achievements and essentially halves the work you have to do, enables you to outflank (attack from two or more angles) enemies so they split their fire, and makes finishing the Campaign (even on Legendary) much easier. They can also flag areas with their own waypoints, allowing you to, for example, find weapon caches they may have discovered.

Vehicular Manslaughter

▲ A Wraith falls to a mixture of dogged determination and well-placed Plasma Grenades.

At numerous points during the Campaign and in certain Firefight situations, accessing a vehicle becomes important, if not vital. Aside from enabling you to travel at speed and offering protection, vehicles are incredibly useful, as their weapons have infinite ammunition. Obviously, larger Scorpion Tanks sometimes need to be left behind due to road blockages, but smaller vehicles such as the Mongoose are ideal for driving around Mombasa Streets—if you can find one!

In general, there are three maneuvers, aside from firing, you need to know when in a vehicle: steering, which occurs using one thumbstick; accelerating and reversing, which occurs using the other thumbstick; and Boosting, which some vehicles have, and this allows you to ram foes with even more force. Note that grav vehicles such as the Ghost strafe instead of turn.

TIP

Boarding vehicles is an excellent plan, whether you or your allies do it. You can board an enemy vehicle that's in use, such as a Wraith, struggle to open a hatch, and then Grenade or melee attack it. When you're in a vehicle that can carry more than one person, such as a Warthog, but sure to wait for any Marines or ODST to join you.

▪ Preparation Complete

You are now ready to meet your combat brethren for the drop over New Mombasa. Study up on the weapons, equipment, and enemies you face before your Campaign begins. Good luck out there, trooper.

ARMS AND EQUIPMENT

Aside from an *ODST*-specific Silenced SMG and Magnum, you may be familiar with armaments and equipment at your disposal. This chapter seeks to reacquaint you with ordnance and vehicles available in *Halo 3: ODST* and *Halo 3* multiplayer. Your complete inventory is displayed in the following pages, and this chapter informs you of each item's strengths and weaknesses, so you know what specific situations are most useful for the item in question.

Weapons Detail

The following details the armaments that you can carry in twos (although you can't carry two of the same weapon type) and can swap between at will. Icons of each of your two weapons are shown in the bottom-right corner of your HUD.

- *These weapons are only found in Halo 3: ODST*
- *These weapons are found exclusively in Halo 3 Multiplayer*
- *These weapons are available in both Halo 3: ODST and Halo 3 Multiplayer*

ODST Only Weapons

M6S Automag

- Availability: *ODST* only
- A newly acquired weapon for ODSTs only; this offers a zoom-in and extremely accurate headshot potential. Worth using as a main weapon.
- Professional troopers combine this weapon with a Plasma Pistol to take off the shields; then they use the Magnum to decapitate their foe. The ultimate in Brute-killing ordnance.
- Weak against foes that have shields active. Do not attempt headshots until the foe has lost this protection!
- A weapon that is only effective in the hands of a veteran, as highly accurate headshots are difficult to land while moving.

Silenced SMG

- Availability: *ODST* only
- The silencer on the end of this SMG makes stealthy combat feasible on the streets of New Mombasa.
- A reasonably impressive clip size, a rapid rate of fire, and a quick respawn rate.
- Fire in controlled bursts to take out shielded enemies at medium to long ranges.
- Highly effective for ranged combat when paired with the Automag due to its zoom capabilities and no need for a charge.
- Most effective at closer ranges and can have a problematic recoil, although not as much as the other SMG.
- Because it takes multiple quick bursts to down a foe, others may be alerted anyway. Drop this first, not the Magnum, unless you're attacking Drones, which this weapon is best-suited for.

ODST and Halo 3 MultiPlayer Weapons

Assault Rifle

- Availability: *ODST* and *Halo 3* MP
- Usually found by the bodies of Marines in Campaign. Semistuns Grunts and Brutes when fired at close range, reducing return fire.
- Problematic against shielded opponents and takes a while to drop foes, as individual bullets aren't that damaging.
- Combine with the Plasma Pistol or Plasma Rifle to take down an opponent's shields, then execute with a headshot.
- Reliable but not impressive at medium and long ranges. You're also likely to run out of ammunition in a clip before you fell an enemy, so switch to your other weapon to finish the job.

Battle Rifle

- Availability: *Halo 3* MP only
- The preferred weapon for those interested in headshots, with a quick, three-hit burst that works well during MP matches.
- Not impressive against shielded foes; however, employing a Plasma Pistol first helps.
- Good against armor and is best employed at medium to long ranges.
- This is weak against shielded foes and fires more slowly than a Carbine. Therefore, it is more suited to expert players—who don't miss!

Beam Rifle

- Availability: *ODST* and *Halo 3* MP
- Recommended for long-range sniping over the Carbine to take down Jackals from a distance and to take out Brutes and Chieftains.

- Make every shot count, as this weapon, like other Plasma-based firearms, overheats quickly. Stagger your shots to prevent this.
- A greater supply of ammunition than a Sniper Rifle and easier to use without a scope.
- Prone to overheating, respawns slowly, and leaves a contrail that shows your position.

■ Brute Shot

- Availability: *ODST* and *Halo 3* MP
- A great weapon to lay down suppressing fire against the enemy; the quicker you fire, the more projectiles you shoot.
- Covenant enemies seem to shrug off the fire reasonably easily, meaning you run out of ammunition very quickly. A last-ditch effort.
- Employ this at close or medium ranges to take advantage of its splash damage radius. Great against small vehicles, and the blade means a lethal melee attack.
- The best weapon to use when "Grenade jumping," allowing you to launch yourself up into otherwise unreachable areas.
- Horrible reload time and easily dodged projectiles when your foes are at long range.
- Direct hits can be difficult; aiming for the feet is often a more reliable plan.

■ Carbine

- Availability: *ODST* and *Halo 3* MP
- With a quicker rate of fire than a Beam Rifle and Battle Rifle, this is another thoroughly recommended sniping weapon.
- Damage isn't as severe as a Beam Rifle's shot, and it should be supplemented with a Plasma Pistol for taking out shields.
- Usually gathered and used consistently, as this is an excellent regular weapon to employ in numerous combat situations.
- For best results, use at medium to long range, but better to switch to another weapon at close range.

■ Energy Sword

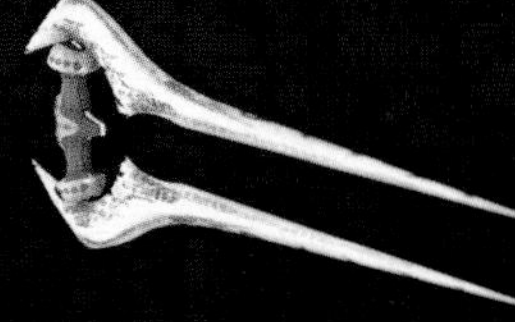

- Availability: *Halo 3* MP only
- Offers exceptionally lethal damage at exceptionally close ranges. Usually a weapon everyone gravitates toward.
- The lack of range is obviously a problem, so back this up with a preferred weapon that fires bullets or other projectile slugs.
- The attacks are quick and usually result in a kill, but they can be parried by foes armed with Energy Swords.
- Easy to conceal when not in use, making it easier to surprise a foe with it compared to the Gravity Hammer.
- Placed in areas on a map that many foes may be heading toward; this means obtaining one is more difficult than usual.
- See a foe with an Energy Sword? Back up and fire on them, lobbing Grenades to prevent them from reaching you.

■ Fuel Rod Cannon

- Availability: *ODST* and *Halo 3* MP
- Excellent damage potential when it hits; should be saved for larger enemies and vehicles, especially those on land.
- Fire at medium range only, as the arcing projectile is easily dodged at long distance.
- Offer this to a Marine or ODST friend (not a human player) to use, as they have infinite ammunition and provide excellent backup.
- This weapon has few limitations (except perhaps limited ammunition) and is an excellent way to defeat multiple foes.

■ Gravity Hammer

- Availability: *ODST* and *Halo 3* MP
- Devastating against clusters of enemies; you're able to defeat multiple Grunts and Jackals with a single pound.
- You don't need a direct hit to inflict pain, and the Hammer can wound enemies through some barriers, such as energy walls.
- The attack launches foes into the air, which can cause them to fall to their deaths.
- You can also strike with a regular melee attack, without depleting the Hammer's ammunition; do this instead of wasting swipes.
- Also recommended against Brutes, Hunters, and Chieftains if you have cover opportunities as you approach.
- Each strike takes an extremely long time to land, meaning you may be cut down in between attacks, unless you dodge.
- **MP:** Your foes can see what you're armed with and plan their attacks accordingly. This weapon is slower to strike than the Energy Sword and has limited range.

■ M6G

- Availability: *Halo 3* MP only
- A weapon to dual-wield in *Halo 3* multiplayer and to use if you wish to try quick, accurate headshots.
- Less than impressive on any armored adversary with shields, this must be paired with a Plasma-type weapon for best results.
- A weapon that is only effective in the hands of a veteran, as highly accurate headshots are difficult to land while moving.

Mauler

- Availability: *ODST* and *Halo 3* MP
- Excellent strength when blasting foes at close range and has a much faster rate of fire than other close-assault weapons, such as the Shotgun.
- **MP:** This can be dual-wielded, adding even more to the devastating nature of the attack.
- Extremely poor range and lack of availability means close-combat weapons are a preferred option.
- Devastating at extremely close range, but almost useless if your target is farther away.

Needler

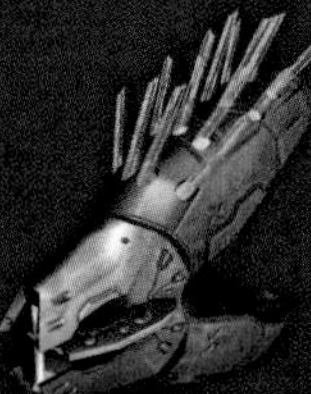

- Availability: *ODST* and *Halo 3* MP
- With a Needle swarm, you can shoot a collection of homing needles into a foe, all of which explode, killing them. This works well on Brutes and on opposing players at medium to close range.
- Relatively useless when encountering foes with shields, such as Engineers, Shield Jackals, Hunters, and Brute Chieftains.
- Ammunition is easily depleted, as the chamber of this weapon holds only a few needles.
- This cannot be used to set off explosive items, and your foe must be neither too far or too close, or the entire attack misses.

Plasma Pistol

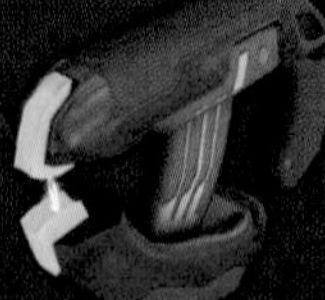

- Availability: *ODST* and *Halo 3* MP
- The ultimate "assist" weapon; it must be paired with another firearm. An overcharged shot removes shields of foes and slightly stuns them, and it destroys the engines of vehicles.
- **MP:** Excellent when dual-wielded with a weapon that is bullet-based and designed for headshots. Respawns quickly. Unfortunately, the hum it emits enables foes to listen for this attack. Plus, this attack drains your weapon's battery.
- Excellent for removing shields from Brutes and incapacitating Wraiths. Headshot a Brute afterward or hijack the Wraith.
- Combine with a ranged weapon (such as the Beam Rifle, Carbine, Magnum, or Sniper Rifle) for the ultimate weapon combo.
- Do not use the primary fire; it is very weak. Employ only overcharge shots on shielded foes. This also takes a lot of practice!

Plasma Rifle

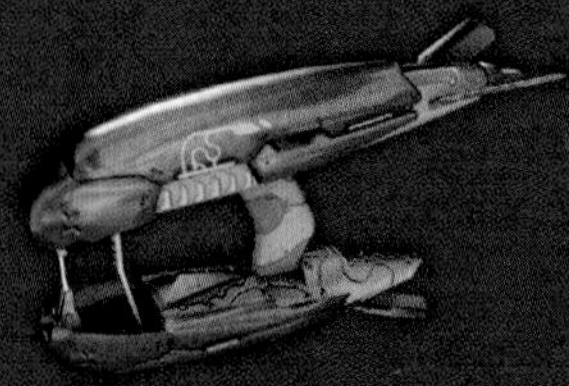

- Availability: *ODST* and *Halo 3* MP
- The next best weapon to a Plasma Pistol for taking down enemy armor; employ it in exactly the same way. Fast rate of fire.
- Recommended to use against Brutes or Hunters to knock their shields off, after which you should switch to a ranged or bullet-based weapon.
- **MP:** Excellent when dual-wielded with a weapon that is bullet-based and designed for headshots. Respawns quickly.
- Unimpressive against objects that don't require energy to function, such as Covenant skin. Overheats, so use quick bursts. Plasma bolts can be inaccurate at range.

Rocket Launcher

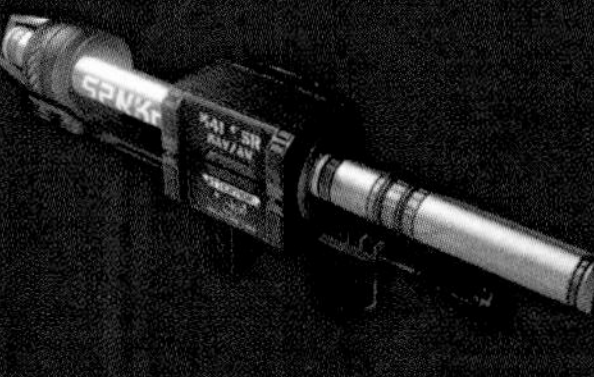

- Availability: *ODST* and *Halo 3* MP
- A feared and extremely dangerous weapon, capable of defeating anything up to a large vehicle with a single shot.
- Best used against one single, terrifying enemy (such as a Chieftain or Wraith); a cluster of foes before they disperse; or an airborne foe.
- Only a few Rockets can be carried, they are easily dodged at long distances, there's a long reload period, and they are found infrequently.
- You can easily get caught in the splash damage area surrounding the impact site of the Rocket.

Sentinel Beam

- Availability: *Halo 3* MP only
- Impressive at consistently damaging armor on an enemy. Powerful beam-emitting weapon that ODSTs do not have access to.
- A weapon more rarely encountered than a Rocket Launcher, and other armaments are usually easier to utilize effectively.
- Prone to overheating when fired repeatedly, unimpressive against armor, and accessible only via Forge.

Shotgun

- Availability: *ODST* and *Halo 3* MP
- If there's one weapon you can use at close range to massively impact a foe's health, this is it. Follow it with a melee strike.
- This suffers from a long reload time, but this can be interrupted once the initial slug has been loaded into the chamber.
- This defeats lesser foes with a single blast, but it may take too long to deliver death to Brutes. Very poor range.
- **MP:** The lack of range means veteran players usually retreat when they see you carrying one, so hide it until you're close.

SMG

- Availability: *Halo 3* MP only
- Extremely powerful when shot at foes close to you and when dual-wielded with another weapon.
- A reasonably impressive clip size, a rapid rate of fire, and a quick respawn rate. It is good when shields are no longer on a foe.
- Most effective at closer ranges and has a problematic recoil, which is exacerbated when dual-wielded. Not advisable to use on shielded foes.
- There are simply too many other weapons that offer a better rate of fire or damage compared to this.

Sniper Rifle

- Availability: *ODST* and *Halo 3* MP
- This offers a non-Plasma alternative to the Beam Rifle and is an excellent weapon when tackling all manner of Brutes.

- It will kill most enemies with a single headshot. At higher difficulty levels, certain enemies may require multiple headshots. You can rattle off the four shots in quick succession, too.
- There are only four bullets to fire before a lengthy reload; however, they impact with such damage that this quartet of pain should kill anything.
- As expected, this is terrible at close range and should be shelved for your other weapon if foes are charging you. It respawns slowly, too.
- Close-range attacks mean firing this without a zoom or melee attacks. Your shots also emit contrails, alerting foes.

Spartan Laser

- Availability: *ODST* and *Halo 3* MP
- When a shot connects, your opponent dies, no matter how big it is (Phantoms excluded).
- You can ease off the shot during the buildup time with no penalty. Good to fire over long distances, ideally before you're spotted.
- A massively powerful weapon but one with pinpoint accuracy. It should be used on Chieftains, Wraiths, Shade Turrets, and Banshees.
- Banshees make particularly fine targets, as the weapon is almost silent until it strikes.
- A better plan is to hand this over to a Marine who can wield this without worrying about ammunition loss.
- It is slow to fire. Put it away when you're engaged in mid- to close-range combat.
- It is also heavily contested during most Firefight and multiplayer matches, and you need to dodge incoming fire when building up the power.
- Although challenging, it is possible to hit multiple foes at once. If you succeed, you'll earn the Two for One Multi-player Achievement.

Spiker

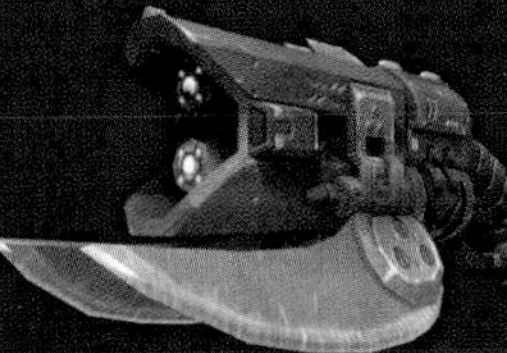

- Availability: *ODST* and *Halo 3* MP
- **MP:** Able to be dual-wielded and offers severe damage over short distances when employed in this manner.
- The speed of fire and number of ammunition shots in this weapon's chamber are both good.
- Offers a possibility of a takedown against a wide variety of foes but isn't ideally suited to killing any of them.
- Employ in closer-combat situations, ideally in walled areas where you can ambush a foe.
- A limited range, low bullet speed, and the accessibility of other, more potent weapons means this weapon is rarely recommended.

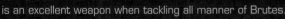

Grenades Detail

This shows the four types of Grenades that ODSTs (and Spartans in *Halo 3* multiplayer) can carry. ODSTs can carry three of each Grenade type; Spartans only have room for two of each. Remember to cycle through the available Grenades for the type that is best suited to your current combat threats. Additional Grenades are available through scavenging.

Flame Grenade

- Availability: *ODST* and *Halo 3* MP
- If successful, the Flame Grenade (aka Incendiary Grenade) instantly kills its infantry victim, except for a Brute Chieftain.
- It also inflicts additional damage on nearby enemies as the flames continue to burn. The fire is sticky, allowing you to block entrances or corridors with it.
- Rarely collected from Active Camo Brutes, they are worth saving and using against a large entity, such as a Hunter or Chieftain.

Frag Grenade

- Availability: *ODST* and *Halo 3* MP
- You begin with this Grenade type, which is excellent for lobbing into clusters of weaker enemies, like Jackals or Grunts.
- Although deemed wasteful, you can lob these Grenades to flush out foes into your line of fire, or weaken Brutes before you finish them with other ordnance.
- These Grenades don't stick; they bounce. Learn how to bounce them into an enemy's path for maximum effectiveness.

Plasma Grenade

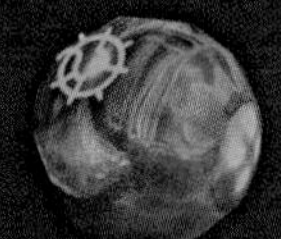

- Availability: *ODST* and *Halo 3* MP
- Incredibly useful and well worth collecting, especially on Legendary difficulty; harvest them from the corpses of dead Grunts.
- Vary your lobbing range; you can throw them farther than you think. They are fantastic for taking down Brutes.
- Favor Frag Grenades for lobbing at the ground under a foe; the Plasma Grenade has small splash damage and needs to be stuck on a foe.
- Plasma Grenades are a favorite among ODSTs when used to take out small vehicles and Shade Turrets.
- Also known as Sticky Grenades, these will adhere to any living target (except Brute Chieftains) that they hit.

Spike Grenade

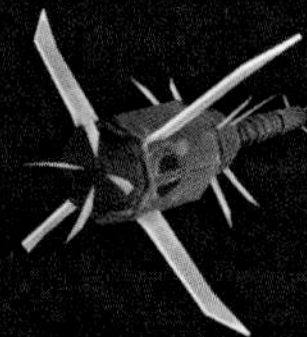

- Availability: *ODST* and *Halo 3* MP
- Spike Grenades will stick to anything they touch. A popular strategy is to attach one to a wall adjacent to your target to blast and enemy, rather than trying to hit it directly.
- Due to their shape, they are much less suited to long-range combat compared to the Plasma Grenade.
- Instead, use them to remove a Jackal's shield or to severely weaken a nearby Brute. Gather these from Brute corpses.

Support Weapons Detail

The term "Support weapon" applies to any device that, when carried, switches your camera to a third-person perspective. All Support weapons except the Flamethrower appear on stands and can be detached. However, carrying a Support weapon slows you down. Firing an attached Support weapon limits your movement, but you have infinite ammunition.

Chaingun Turret

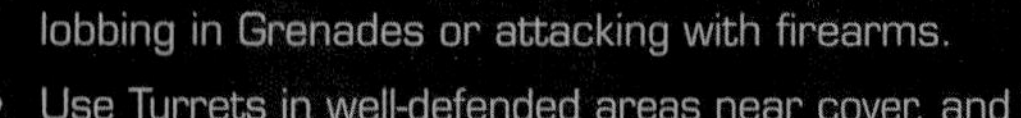

- Availability: *ODST* and *Halo 3* MP
- Also known as the Machinegun Turret, you move more slowly and are vulnerable to foes lobbing in Grenades or attacking with firearms.
- Use Turrets in well-defended areas near cover, and if you go on an offensive charge, have a second player back you up.
- You are a prone target when using a Turret; stay here during *Halo 3* multiplayer and risk a headshot. However, Turrets have infinite ammunition when on their stands, but don't if you detach them.
- Use this Turret to watch the flanks of your base or team, or to provide covering fire.
- Great to use against multiple foes such as Drones, Grunts, and Jackals.

Flamethrower

- Availability: *ODST* and *Halo 3* MP
- The only weapon that isn't already mounted on its target, this is a rarely seen but extremely devastating short-range weapon.
- This is arguably the most devastating close-attack weapon available. It burns enemies to death easily and in seconds.
- Save this for enclosed areas; outdoor locations or large chambers where foes can retreat limit the effectiveness of this weapon.
- You are slow and cannot throw Grenades when carrying this weapon, and there's no additional ammunition for it.

■ Plasma Turret

- Availability: *ODST* and *Halo 3* MP
- Used during ODST Campaigns and Firefights as the main defenses on Phantoms; you can knock these down and use them. Chieftains also occasionally use them.
- Cuts through armor and shielding amazingly quickly but less effective at piercing flesh. Still a devastating weapon, though.
- Grunts appear to be particularly resilient to Plasma Turrets, especially on higher difficulty levels.

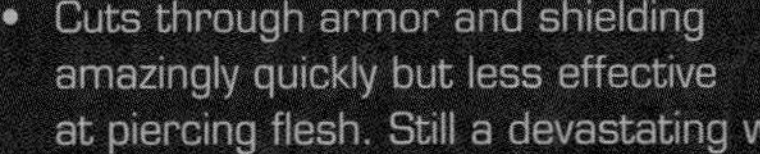

■ Missile Pod

- Availability: *ODST* and *Halo 3* MP
- Not a weapon to use on infantry, as the lineup can take a while, and a direct strike defeats a foe, which are sometimes hard to achieve.
- This isn't a mounted Rocket Launcher; the splash damage is far less impressive.
- However, it is incredibly devastating when fired on vehicles, both on the ground and in the air. This is by far the best way to strike a vehicle.

■ Shade Turret

- Availability: *ODST* only
- Not technically a portable Turret, but one that can provide devastating and reasonably accurate plasma fire. This is usually manned by a Grunt or Brute.
- The biggest problem with the Shade Turret is its fixed position, making it a magnet for enemy fire, with little chance of protection if you're using it.
- If a Shade Turret is protected, it can provide supporting fire. However, other weapons are more flexible, portable, and useful in most combat situations.

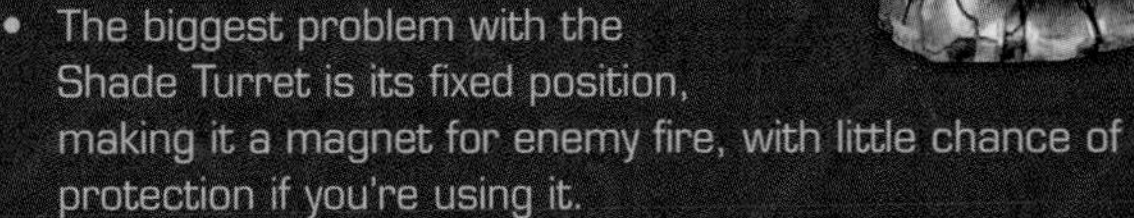

TIP **There are some general tips for detaching and moving turrets: If you want to remove a Turret from its stand, throw a Grenade at it, as wrenching it off leaves you standing still and susceptible to enemy fire. You can also constantly drop and pick up the Turret as you move, increasing the speed in which you travel, although you may end up picking another weapon if any are close by. These tactics help during *Halo 3* multiplayer.**

Equipment Detail

There is a vast array of equipment for the Spartan warrior, which is related to elements of *Halo 3* multiplayer. ODSTs cannot use Bubble Shields or Flares; these are used by the Covenant. ODSTs are able to use Health Packs, as well as individual "clues" that Rookie encounters (which are not included in this list).

■ Deployable Cover

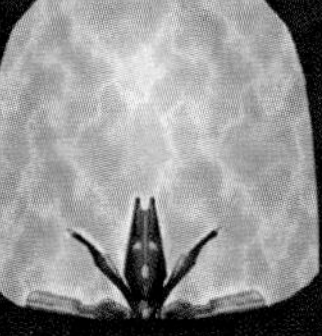

- Availability: *Halo 3* MP only
- Employed to act as additional cover, but it doesn't last long (especially on Legendary), deactivating sooner rather than later.
- Use it to block doorways near defenses you are attempting to hold. Destroy it with a simple melee attack.
- Otherwise, consistent fire from either your Plasma Pistol (overcharge) or Plasma Rifle removes this obstacle.

■ Bubble Shield

- Availability: *ODST* and *Halo 3* MP
- Creates a bubble and a smaller, central bubble within it; stand within either bubble or outside it if fire is coming directly at the bubble.
- Rush the bubble and melee attack foes inside it, or strike the base of the Shield to destroy it.

■ Grav Lift

- Availability: *Halo 3* MP only
- As you don't need to use it to deflect Covenant troops, this item's primary function is to locate otherwise-inaccessible hiding spots.
- If you leave the item behind, foes will know where you are, so shoot it to destroy it. Don't get trapped if you stand on it and shoot upward into a ceiling, either!

■ Health Pack

- Availability: *ODST* only
- Only available on the mean streets of New Mombasa, throughout the Campaign, and in Firefight missions.
- Health Packs can be found scattered near fallen Marines, and in Optican Kiosks and wall dispensers.
- Use only when absolutely necessary; if you have only light damage, return to claim one when you're more badly wounded.

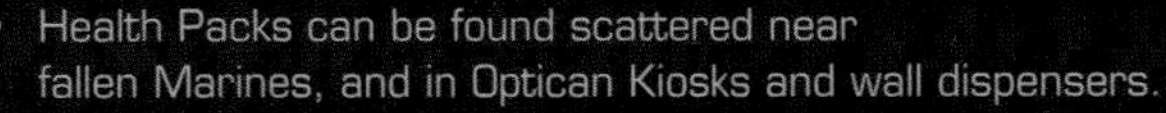

- You cannot carry these items; they are used the instant you grab one.
- During Firefight missions, conserve Health Packs so that each teammate has a chance to take one per round.

Power Drain

- Availability: *Halo 3* MP only
- The Power Drain activates even in the air and lasts for around seven seconds.
- Removes all shielding when activated, making foes quick, one-shotkills. It also briefly disables vehicles, making them vulnerable to attack.
- Target the device to destroy it, or back away if you wish.

Regenerator

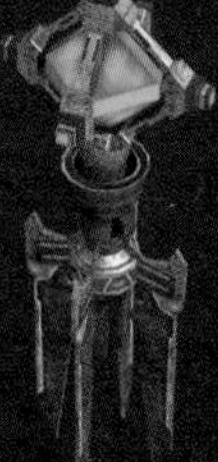

- Availability: *Halo 3* MP only
- This quickens the speed at which your shields recharge, but you're still able to die!
- Use it when you have enough cover to take a few seconds out of a fight. The device lasts around 15 seconds.

Flare

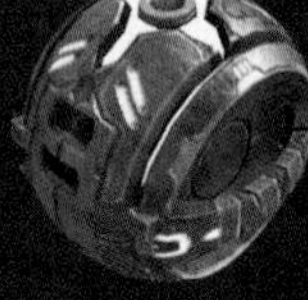

- Availability: *Halo 3* MP only
- Flares are useful to signal to teammates for a specific attack, action, or respawning weapon. They are also used to blind enemies at extremely close range.
- However, they are more of a distraction than a useful strategic device.

Radar Jammer

- Availability: *Halo 3* MP only
- This scrambles your Motion Tracker for around 20 seconds. It must be shot to be deactivated during this time.
- Without radar, you can sneak up and melee attack foes that aren't fully aware of their surroundings.

Trip Mine

- Availability: *Halo 3* MP only
- Lasting one and a half minutes before they self-detonate, place these mines around corners to annoy and destroy your foes.
- They are easy to spot due to the sounds they emit, meaning you shouldn't ever be surprised by one.

Overshield

- Availability: *Halo 3* MP only
- After a three-second period of invincibility after pickup, this charges your shields to 200 percent efficiency, which gradually disperses over time.
- This is excellent for protecting you against Rocket, Fuel Rod, Sniper, and Frag or Plasma Grenade attacks. However, you are susceptible to an assassination (melee from behind) during the shield charge.
- The Overshield is a powerful help during multiplayer, so the pickup itself may be booby-trapped with a Frag Grenade or a Trip Mine.
- This bathes you in a light, making you much more visible. This shield can be neutralized with an overcharged Plasma Pistol shot.

Active Camo

- Availability: *Halo 3* MP only
- This refracts light around the user, giving them a cloud of partial invisibility. You become more visible when you fire a weapon.
- You also leave footprints and become easier to spot the closer you are to an enemy.
- Employ one-hit kill weaponry, such as the Flamethrower, Shotgun, or Rocket Launcher so your foe isn't able to retaliate at all.

NOTE **Note that Cloaking and Invincibility are not available to ODST or Spartan Troopers; they are used by Brute Stalkers and Chieftains, respectively. The Auto Turret is not available on *ODST* or *Halo 3* multiplayer maps.**

Vehicle Detail

You have access to a wide variety of vehicles, built by both the UNSC and Covenant, which allows you to travel at speed, endure more damage thanks to the protection they provide, and ram or strafe foes with unlimited ordnance. Naturally, you're a bigger target, too. Note that many of the vehicles are enemies and are not utilized by you.

Brute Chopper

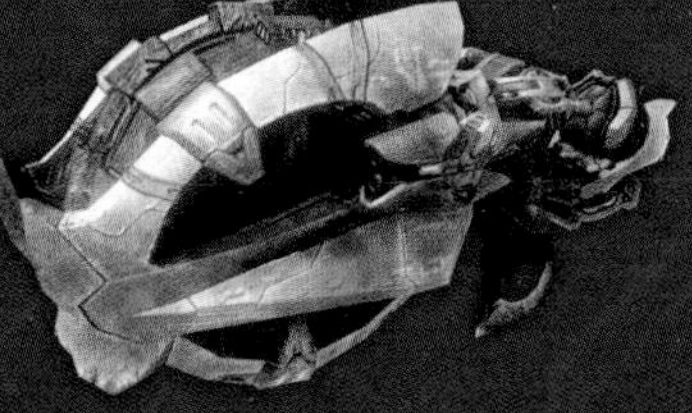

- Availability: *ODST* and *Halo 3* MP
- A mass of spikes and a huge front tire, the Chopper's role is to splatter its way through infantry units and smaller vehicles. The Boost accomplishes this with much more gusto; however, it lasts for only a second, so time your Boosts carefully.
- Lob a Grenade under or onto the driver and the Chopper usually explodes. However, this isn't a wise plan if you want to drive it; so snipe or rake the driver with gunfire, dodging to the side to avoid getting rammed.
- Make sure your front wheel is between you and foes firing on you; the Chopper's armor is concentrated to the front, and you are exposed on the sides and rear.
- The Chopper's dual cannons offer heavy, sustained, and infinite firepower; it is so dangerous that you should attack this craft from the sides or rear, even when you're in a small vehicle.

Banshee

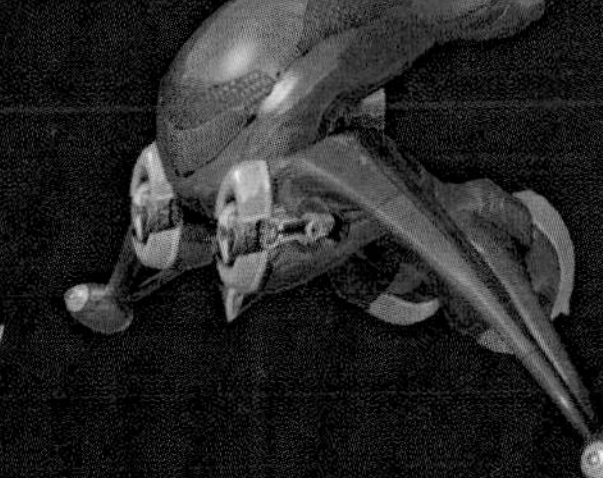

- Availability: *ODST* and *Halo 3* MP
- **MP:** This aircraft is lightweight and offers only limited protection from infantry fire, which the pilot should stay away from.
- **MP:** The Banshee is armed with twin Plasma Cannons that are excellent for engaging enemy aircraft in close-range dogfighting but are inaccurate at range. There is a Fuel Rod Cannon as well, but this is slow to fire and takes considerable wrangling to aim effectively.
- **MP:** Remember that this craft is built for speed and features a permanent boost, allowing very rapid movement at the expense of active weapons systems.
- **MP:** Be aware that you can barrel-roll this craft in an attempt to dodge incoming missiles and other small-arms fire.
- Banshees can be attacked in *ODST* but cannot be piloted.

Behemoth

- Availability: *ODST* only
- Large troop-carrying vehicles, usually with an officer aboard, these offer considerable armored protection and can sometimes transform into a mobile deployment station.
- The smaller, civilian variant of the Behemoth, known as the Olifant (pictured), is principally used for waste disposal. One is commandeered during Campaign Mission 09: Coastal Highway and used as an improvised troop carrier, but it is never driven by you.

Drop Pod

- Availability: *ODST* only
- The Single-Occupant, Exoatmospheric Insertion Vehicle (SOEIV) is used to drop troopers from orbit and has extremely limited maneuverability in transit.
- They are unavailable on *Halo 3* multi-player maps. During *ODST* Campaign missions, they are utilized during Mission 01 and cannot be manually operated.

Ghost

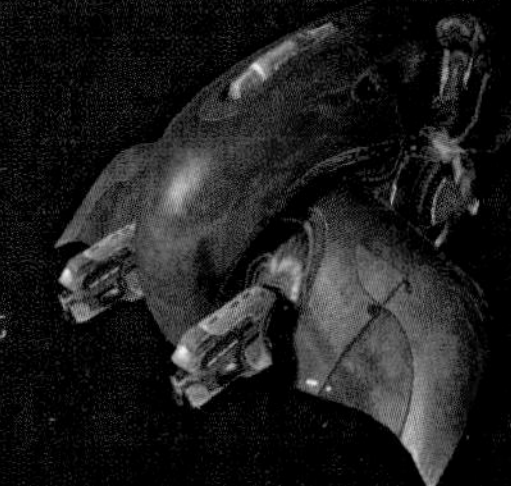

- Availability: *ODST* and *Halo 3* MP
- Until the Ghost is struck by enough fire to become damaged (that you can see), the front and wings of this craft offer good protection to the driver.
- The ability to drive this at extremely high speeds, "strafe" in all directions, and quickly dart from cover to cover means this can be a troublesome craft to face. Its dual Plasma Cannons offer rapid but reasonably weak fire. Concentrate on infantry, not larger vehicles, with it.
- Don't forget to Boost! This allows you to escape incoming fire or foes, or ram into them for certain enemy death. You can also remove a Ghost's wings if you wish, allowing you into narrower spaces. However, this is pointless, unless you're a really determined sniper.

Hornet

- Availability: *Halo 3* MP only
- Available occasionally on multiplayer maps, this lightweight and lightly armored aircraft is spectacularly maneuverable.
- Be sure you fire your Rockets when the target reticle is red so they home in on their foes at shorter ranges.
- The craft switches to manual (not homing) fire at longer ranges, enabling you to fire on ground troops and vehicles, but this is ineffective against aircraft.
- Although the craft is able to carry a pilot and two passengers, all are very exposed to enemies, especially as foes tend to favor the pilot to bring the entire trio and craft down. However, the passengers can be dropped to outflank foes or hijack enemy vehicles.
- Play with the weapons your passengers are holding; turn the Hornet into a heavy-weapons craft with two Spartan Laser–wielding Spartans or into a mobile sniping platform. Try activating a Bubble Shield just before a major enemy strike to save the craft, too.
- The common transport version of the Hornet has no homing missiles, only its mounted turrets. It's primarily used as support and troop transport.

Mongoose

- Availability: *ODST* and *Halo 3* MP
- Available on some *Halo 3* maps and hidden inside certain UNSC weapon caches dotted throughout New Mombasa. Rookie is able to utilize them to quicken the exploration in this area.
- This vehicle is useful for covering distances at speed and has room for two. You receive only slightly less damage than when on foot. Erratic and defensive driving is required using this small four-wheeled vehicle.
- **MP:** If you're riding behind the driver, there's no damage from attacks ahead of you. Not so from all other directions! Fire back as often as you can; you're much more of a problem if there are two of you to deal with, but you're also more of a target.
- The Mongoose can roll over easily, so either jump early and melee the vehicle at speed, or wait for it to come to a rest, which may actually be right-side up.

Pelican (NMPD)

- Availability: *ODST* only
- The Vertical Take-off and Landing (VTOL) vehicle of choice for the New Mombasa Police Department.
- Commandeered by ODST Mickey during the Campaign. This craft is never piloted by you.

Phantom

- Availability: *ODST* only
- The choice for Covenant forces wishing to quickly deploy in zones fortified by ODST forces. The incoming Plasma fire can be deadly. This craft is never piloted by you.
- Features a nose and two possible side Plasma Turrets manned by Grunts that, under heavy bombardment, can be detached and picked up by the ODSTs.
- This craft deposits enemies from a base opening or from either side hatch and then leaves the scene. It can be destroyed, ideally by a Scorpion.
- However, a far better plan is to lob Grenades into the open hatches or at the dropping enemies, killing them all before they can disperse.

Prowler

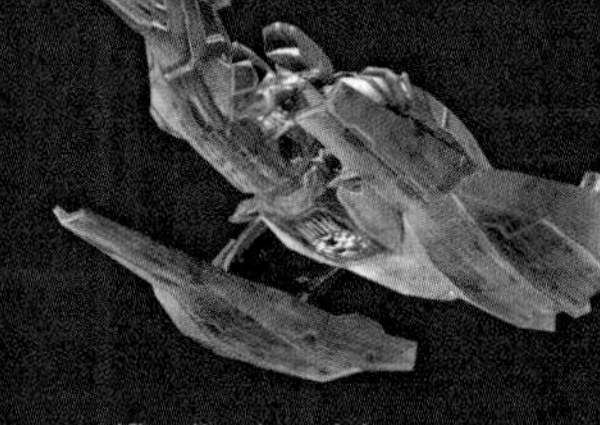

- Availability: *Halo 3* MP only
- **MP:** With similar attributes to the Chopper, the Prowler has a well-armored front that protects the driver from most small-arms fire. However, Plasma or Spike Grenades are effective on those inside this vessel, but specifically the driver.
- **MP:** The turret features a complete 360-degree swivel functionality, which can be used to lay down impressive and deadly fire.
- **MP:** Much like the Hornet, this craft can carry two passengers, who are exposed to enemy fire. Fight this with a competent driver and a heavy arsenal for the crew.

Scarab Type-47

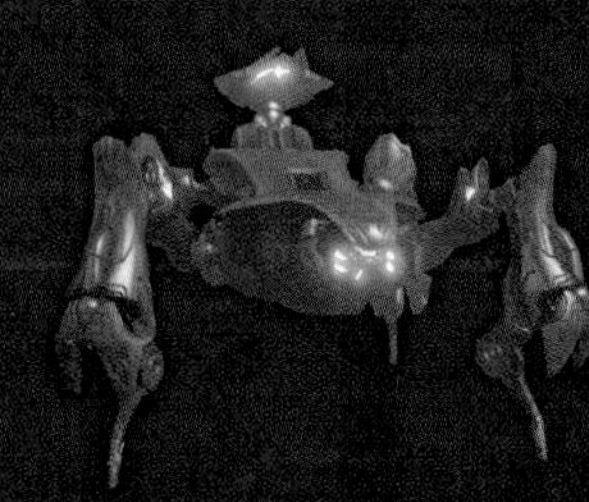

- Availability: *ODST* only
- A massive heavy-assault platform that is encountered only during *ODST* Campaign "Mission 07: Kikowani Station."
- This foe requires a precise strategy, which is detailed in the walkthrough for that mission. To summarize, you must attack the Scarab's leg joints.
- This gradually immobilizes the foe, allowing you to tackle the main Turret on the entity's thorax and then the exposed exhaust point on its rear section, which eventually destroys it.

Scorpion

- Availability: *ODST* and *Halo 3* MP
- Ignore all incoming fire from smaller weapons; it usually bounces off the Scorpion's heavy armor.
- Aside from Brutes leaping on the vehicle (which a side gunner should take care of) and Brutes with Fuel Rod Cannons, your main threats are from vehicles, specifically Banshees, Ghosts, Shade Turrets, and Wraiths.
- You can see how close your Scorpion Tank is to exploding by its general wear and tear, which (in *Halo 3*) affects your Spartan shields.
- The Scorpion's main cannon is impressive and takes down most targets in one shot, with the possible exception of Chieftains. It also has good splash damage, so fire as often as possible; aiming is important but secondary!
- Man the separate side cannon with a Marine, leaving him to deal with foes that aren't an immediate threat to the tank. Another can ride on the side; equip him with a preferred weapon.

Warthog M12 LRV

- Availability: *ODST* and *Halo 3* MP
- The front hood and windshield protect you from frontal attacks but not those from the side. You can also accelerate and ram foes constantly, which is recommended.
- The windshield can shatter, extending the expected damage from head-on collisions to the passengers on both front seats.
- Arm your Marine colleagues with better weaponry, such as the Spartan Laser, Rocket Launcher, Fuel Rod Cannon, or Sniper Rifle; their ammo is infinite, and they prove to be exceptional help.
- This particular model is armed with a Machinegun Turret, similar to the ground-mounted version, which is excellent at rapidly killing off lightly shielded or unshielded enemies. Ram the rest or keep on firing!

Warthog M12 LAAV: Gauss Cannon

The Gauss Cannon Warthog is available for *Halo 3* multiplayer matches and is briefly utilized during "Mission 09: Coastal Highway." This is tailored for enemy vehicle destruction, although it is still vicious against infantry.

Warthog: M831 TT

Able to carry Marines or ODST squadmates on Campaign Mission 09: Coastal Highway, aggressive driving and comrades armed with the best weaponry can still take down many enemies, despite no on-board weaponry.

Wraith

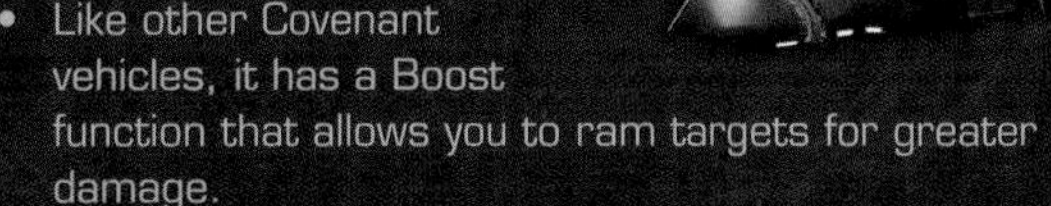

- Availability: *ODST* and *Halo 3* MP
- Offers good protection but slow movement, making it a large and easily struck target.
- Like other Covenant vehicles, it has a Boost function that allows you to ram targets for greater damage.
- You can hijack this craft, rip open the hatch, and lob in a Grenade, effectively destroying it. In *ODST*, you cannot drive this vehicle; you can only defeat it.
- The Wraith fires Plasma Mortar, which is incredibly powerful but easily dodged.
- The Wraith has a lesser Turret, too, which is used to rake nearby infantry and prevent hijacks. Snipe the driver to negate this function; he is fully visible.
- If you're driving, face the enemy as often as possible. If attacking a Wraith, circle around the back of it, destroy its shield, and devastate its exhaust port to quickly destroy it.

Wraith: Antiaircraft

This is the antiaircraft version of a Wraith, which is employed to take down enemy aircraft and is seen briefly on "Mission 07: Kikowani Station." It fires dual Fuel Rod Cannons, making it highly dangerous at close range.

KNOW YOUR ENEMY

The alien conglomerate known as the Covenant employ a wide variety of entities (mainly vicious and subhuman) that are sent to cull all humans. To retaliate, you must have a deeper understanding of each enemy type, along with knowledge of their attack patterns, strengths, and weaknesses, and the weapons they are susceptible to. This information is contained in the following pages and applies to enemies faced during Campaign and Firefight modes.

GRUNTS/UNGGOY

The least impressive Covenant adversary but one that can still cause trouble when suicidal or in large numbers, the Grunt should not be taken lightly, as groups of them can be just as deadly as their large brethren.

- Grunts are relatively weak, so save higher power weaponry (such as the Sniper Rifle) for use against tougher targets. Use a Magnum or SMG to waste the Grunts, then turn the bigger guns on their leaders.
- Grunts are usually found in groups of three to five, sometimes accompanying a Brute leader. You can encounter them manning Plasma Turrets on Watch-towers, during Phantom drops, or even while they are sleeping.
- The basic takedown tactic for any Grunt is to tag each Grunt, one at a time, with a headshot from your Magnum or other one-shot-kill weapon. Back this up with quick Assault Rifle or Silenced SMG blasts to the head if you run out of primary weapon ammunition.
- Grunt encounters are so plentiful that it is wise to keep a Magnum or SMG as one of your weapons throughout your mission.
- You can also pepper them in the head with a favored weapon as you close in, and then melee attack them to finish them off.
- During situations in which you should conserve ammunition, it is wise to simply rush and melee a group of Grunts; assassination (melee from behind) attacks and stealthy play is encouraged on higher difficulties.
- Grunts are sometimes spotted in close formation, making them susceptible to Rocket or Grenade fire.
- Plasma Grenades usually produce "Grunt freak-out" responses, with them scattering and yelling, usually when a Grenade sticks to a Grunt. Back away from any potential damage from the explosion, and hope the Grunt charges into other enemies before exploding.
- Grunts enjoy throwing Plasma Grenades, too; in fact, they are known for it during Firefight missions. To avoid a sticky and deadly situation, quickly sidestep or retreat while listening for the hiss of a primed Plasma Grenade. Keep moving so you aren't tagged by these Grenades, and always stoop to grab dropped Grenades—ones that aren't about to explode! Grunts provide your main source of Plasma Grenades.
- Although cowardly, Grunts fight until they drop if you corner them. It is better to take out their Brute leader, watch the Grunts flee, and then pick them off with SMG or rapid fire; save your Magnum or Carbine shots for Grunts that require precision killing.
- Plasma-based weapons, such as the Pistol or Rifle, are less impressive when used on Grunts; save these weapons for other enemies. Grunts are also more resistant to Assault Rifles, Silenced SMGs, and Spikers (on Legendary difficulty), making headshots from other weapons even more important.
- Grunts carry Plasma Pistols; Needlers; and, on higher difficulties, occasionally Fuel Rod Cannons. Target Cannon wielders first, then focus on Needler-carrying Grunts and finally those with Plasma Pistols.
- After a fight, grab the Fuel Rod Cannon for future encounters. The Plasma Pistol and Needler are good to utilize against the Brutes, which is handy, as you'll almost always encounter the two enemy types together.

SUICIDE GRUNTS

When the leader of a Grunt patrol (usually the Brute leader) submits to a particularly gruesome demise at your hands (such as exploding after being stuck by a Grenade), a nearby Grunt usually turns suicidal. The following techniques are deemed necessary for your survival:

- Look and listen; the screams and the glowing Plasma Grenades held in each claw alert you to a Suicide Grunt attack.
- Simply aim, and use a headshot to dispatch the charging Grunt before it reaches close-combat range.

- Turn this attack to your advantage by waiting until the Grunt moves into contact with other enemies, then drop it; the explosion can badly damage other foes without you needing to attack them.

- Try not to drop the Grunt on the ground near Grenades you wish to scavenge, as the Plasma Grenades the Grunt carries can trigger a chain reaction that can be deadly if you're close by.

GRUNT VARIANTS

Recent investigation of Grunt corpses has revealed a ranking system among these infantry troops, although most Grunts clad in different-colored armor feature the same shortfalls, and you can attack them using basic battlefield tenets. You may find gray Grunt Ultras during Legendary missions; these battle-hardened foes are a little tougher than their younger brethren.

JACKALS/KIG-YAR

A thin and wiry mercenary race with a vicious disposition and dexterity with long-range weaponry, Jackals are used as scouts and snipers due to their exceptional senses. During battles in New Mombasa, they come in two varieties; Shield and Sniper Jackals.

- Favored methods of dispatch: Beam Rifle, Carbine, Gravity Hammer, Chaingun Turret, Magnum, Plasma Pistol, Plasma Rifle, Shotgun
- Shield Jackals are armed with an almost impenetrable energy shield and carry primarily Plasma Pistols or Rifles. These aren't particularly worrisome, unless a Jackal is charging a Plasma Pistol (look for the green glow and attack before it is charged and fired).
- Jackal Snipers forgo the shield for either a Carbine or Beam Rifle and are usually situated on high balconies or rooftops, sometimes physically out of reach from you. Identify them by the telltale purple light emitted from their optics.
- Shield Jackals are difficult to tackle when they are in a defensive posture. They are susceptible to melee attacks, but normal, rapid-fire weapons hitting the shields simply glances off. However, melee attacks are not practical if you're engaging multiple foes.
- Shield Jackal takedowns involve you shooting at them with a rapid-fire weapon such as the Silenced SMG, Plasma Rifle, Magnum, or Assault Rifle; traveling through the gap in the shield, known as the "firing embrasure," on either side; and making the Jackal flinch for a second. Immediately follow that up with a headshot from any distance, using the Magnum, Carbine, Beam Rifle, or Sniper Rifle.
- You can also throw Grenades at Shield Jackals. When they leap away from the explosion, they expose their heads long enough so you can finish them off.
- Although a rarely used technique, you can lob Grenades at a Jackal's shield with the intention of the projectile bouncing off and into a cluster of other foes nearby.
- A preferred way to remove a Jackal's shield defenses is to strike them with a charged Plasma Pistol bolt or a series of Plasma Rifle blasts; they usually retreat and attempt to secure cover. Your Pistol-packing is rewarded with a clear shot of their prone forms, which you should hit with a sniping weapon unless the Jackal is sprinting and therefore difficult to hit. Should this occur, target another enemy and return to your initial target once it slows down (or rake it with bullets from a more rapid-fire gun).
- Be prepared to slow down as Jackals appear ahead of you; you need time to tackle each one, regardless of whether they're shield carriers or snipers.
- As Sniper Jackals are usually holed up some distance away and are difficult to spot (especially during nighttime missions), be sure to use your VISR Enhanced Vision to gain an outline of the entity you're about to execute; this helps immensely with your accuracy.
- Sniper Jackals have one major shortfall: they are highly susceptible to sniping. Especially on Legendary difficulty, you must methodically tag each Jackal that you see pop up from their sniping position, hitting them in the head before they spot you and retaliate.
- All other weapon types are not really an option; use your ranged weapon's zoom to finalize a target, if your manual aiming isn't spectacular.
- In Cooperative missions, one player (ideally the marksman of the team with patience to match their aim) should stay back and methodically drop all the Jackal Snipers while the rest secure other objectives.

BRUTES/JIRALHANAE

Powerful and sinewy apelike entities, Brutes have a hatred of Elites (which explains the lack of these foes in New Mombasa) and sport a variety of weapons and equipment as the situation dictates. The shock troops of a Covenant army, facing Brutes in combat can always be problematic. Some of the many varieties of Brute are detailed in this section.

- Favored methods of dispatch (Brute): Beam Rifle, Carbine, Chaingun Turret, Flamethrower, Gravity Hammer, Magnum, Needler, Plasma Pistol, Plasma Rifle, Shotgun, Sniper Rifle.
- Favored methods of dispatch (Chieftain): Beam Rifle, Carbine, Chaingun Turret, Flamethrower, Fuel Rod Cannon, Gravity Hammer, Missile Pod, Rocket Launcher, Sniper Rifle, Spartan Laser
- In addition to wielding a variety of weapons, Brutes drive Choppers, Wraiths, Ghosts, and Banshees, and command squads of Grunts. They also siphon off Overshield-like armor energy from nearby Engineers they have enslaved. They are experienced hunters and offer no rest when attacking you, attempting to outflank you at every turn.
- Expect Brutes to be armed with a variety of Covenant-only weapons, not just those that bear the Brute's name. They are also adept at rushing in with a heavy-handed melee strike.
- There are two stages to Brute combat: removing their armor and executing them. The former involves the use of various weaponry, although Plasma Pistols (overcharged shots) or Plasma Rifles are great choices. Look for splinters and sections of armor to fall from a Brute as its armor disintegrates.
- With the armor removed, the only optimal strategy is a quick headshot execution. Therefore, the combination of a Plasma Pistol and a Magnum is fantastic, as it allows you to cull Brutes in only two shots (if you're skilled enough), and you won't need to resort to Grenades, which can explode any Grenades Brutes drop.
- Be accurate with your headshots; hitting a Brute's shoulder causes the beast to spin around, making subsequent headshot attempts more difficult.
- With this in mind, a second option is to bring out a long-range weapon like the Beam Rifle, Sniper Rifle, or Carbine, and plug away at a Brute's head, ignoring all other body parts; this is their weak spot, and you must take advantage of it!
- If a Brute is leading a group of Grunts or Jackals, targeting the Brute first usually leaves the weaker foes milling about in confusion or fleeing to cover, allowing for an easy mop-up.
- As you encounter Brutes throughout your missions and headshots become a necessity, it is imperative that you always carry a Magnum, a Beam Rifle, or a Carbine (and alternatively, a Sniper Rifle). Striking Brutes on their body wastes ammunition and time, as they are tough.
- When facing a Brute, check the weapon it is carrying, and follow a defensive posture based on the strengths of that particular weapon. Brutes commonly carry Spikers and Brute Shots, but some use Carbines, Maulers, or Plasma Rifles. They prefer Spiked Grenades, and they use them to remove you from any cover you're hiding behind.
- Some (nonberserking) Brutes feature lower body sections that are or can be uncovered. With a Magnum, Shotgun, or Sniper Rifle shot to the legs, you can drop a Brute temporarily; a Shotgun blast at close range can achieve this even if the Brute has armor activated. Finish off the Brute with a Grenade or a melee strike.
- Melee attacks are important, both when you're giving and receiving them: Remember that a single melee attack to the back of a Brute (even a Chieftain) results in a one-strike kill for you! However, if you're smashed by a Brute's melee blow, expect a severe drop in Stamina. Find cover or health immediately.

BRUTE MINORS AND CAPTAINS

- Brute squads are usually made up of different types of this enemy but also include Minors and Captains. Minors are distinguished by their lack of horned headgear and their light blue armor. They are susceptible to all the previous Brute takedown tactics, and will succumb to Frag Grenades tossed in their general direction.
- Brute Captains are distinguished by their more ornate headgear and golden armor. They are also more aggressive and fly into a rage with less provocation. They can withstand a Plasma Grenade (on Legendary difficulty) too.
- Brute Captains sometimes deploy a Bubble Shield for protection, too, which you can either ignore and remain at a distance until the shield disperses, or rush in and use Grenades or a Shotgun to drop them. A blast with the Shotgun with a quick melee attack to finish works well. Otherwise, the usual Brute attack plans work well against Captains.

■ BRUTE BERSERKERS

- Brutes and Captains are prone to a final bout of berserker rage, usually when one of the following occurs: when their brethren have been slain, when their Chieftain is defeated, when the Brute is the last one standing, when a Grenade hits them, or when wounded after their armor is removed.
- They pause, then race toward you, screaming and brandishing weapons as bludgeoning instruments and firing like crazy. Simply shoot them in the head before they reach you. It takes only one shot, and that head is certainly big enough.

■ JUMP-PACK BRUTES

- Jump-Pack Brutes are airborne for much of their combat, using their jets to land en masse; they usually descend from Phantoms. They are challenging in large numbers, especially since they can descend on your location without warning and from multiple directions, but they are less problematic than you might think, given their equipment's shortfalls.
- There's a variety of options to defeat this Brute type; the most cunning of which is to listen for the sounds of their Jump Packs or view them sailing through the air, then tag them with a sniped shot from a Beam or Sniper Rifle while they are airborne.
- After being sniped out of the air or being struck by a melee attack, Jump Packs usually malfunction, sending a Brute into the air. You can then run up and launch an overcharged Plasma Pistol shot at them to stun them, and then melee attack them; or, simply time your melee attack, which allows you to easily kill this entity.
- Tracking a Jump-Pack Brute's trajectory as they sail through the air allows you to fire on them with little return fire. When they land, it takes a second for them to continue moving, which is their main weakness. Lob in a Grenade on their landing point, or cut them down before they transition from air to ground.

■ BRUTE STALKERS

- Stalkers have Active Camo abilities and lurk in shadows or behind scenery, waiting to ambush you. Fortunately, your VISR Enhanced Vision mode enables you to see their outline instead of oddly distorted air patterns in the subtle shape of a Brute, allowing you to attack them as if they were normal Brutes.
- If you're fighting a Stalker, it is worth attempting a melee attack, or pepper them with gunfire so their shield short-circuits for a moment, and the Brute appears. Continuous melee strikes are a good way to bring one down.
- Spikers are also an option, as the projectiles stick out of the entity, rendering their camo less effective. You should also try lobbing Grenades at them; this allows for an easy kill, at the expense of the Flame Grenades they drop, which is the principle prize for defeating them using nonexplosive means.
- Other homing weaponry, such as the Plasma Pistol or Needler, sometimes fails when shot at Brute Stalkers. Choose a direct Plasma Pistol strike to remove the Camo entirely, after which you can finish this Brute as normal.
- The lack of visuals means a retreat to cover is usually the best way to combat a Stalker threat, followed up by short, sharp strikes as Stalkers come into view to remove their shields as quickly as possible.
- Stalkers are equipped with Brute Maulers and Flame Grenades. It's a good idea to tackle these foes at range...if you can spot them.

■ BRUTE CHIEFTAINS

- Brute Chieftains are the largest, most devastating, and feature the most damaging weapons and elaborate headgear of all the Brute types. They are among the most dangerous foes you'll face and have toughened armor, which rebounds Needler fire. They shrug off Sticky Grenades, too, which merely bounce off their carapace armor.
- Chieftains sport one of three weapon types: a Gravity Hammer, a Fuel Rod Cannon, and a Plasma Turret. They usually send in their lower Brute brethren to soften you up first, allowing them to attack you when you're already combat-weary. Cunning!
- However, Plasma and Sticky Grenades do adhere to the weapon a Chieftain is holding. If you can expertly lob a Grenade so it sticks to a Gravity Hammer, Fuel Rod Cannon, or Plasma Turret, the Chieftain can fall in one impressive explosion!

- For any of the three Chieftain variants, range is your key to success; tag the Chieftain's helmet with a sniper rifle, then strike the exposed head again and again until he falls. Using a Chieftain's own weapons against it is also a great plan. Shoot this foe with a Turret, Rockets, a Fuel Rod, a Spartan Laser, or any other large long-reload weapon.
- Another weapon with which to shoot a helmet is an overcharged Plasma Pistol. Other weapons with which to shoot an exposed Chieftain head is a Magnum, a Carbine, or a Beam Rifle. Drop the Needler; its spines do almost no damage to these beasts!
- Grenades are good for removing some of the Chieftain's armor, although the foe usually dodges them with side dives. The armor in question is toughened compared to normal Brute armor, so attacks anywhere other than the head result in combat that can last a long time.

Gravity Hammer Chieftain

This beast waits for a lull in the action, then charges you without pause. Even on Normal difficulty, one successful Hammer strike crushes you and removes most of your Stamina, and even a glancing blow is harmful due to the splash damage the Hammer inflicts. Remain at a distance, ideally higher than this foe.

Plasma Turret Chieftain

The rapid fire from this heavy weapon often makes obtaining a clear shot improbable. Elongated battles are the norm here, so prepare to be patient. Of course, a heavy weapon to counter the Brute's is always an option.

Fuel Rod Cannon Chieftain

Offering the range of a Plasma Turret and splash damage potential of its own, this is an extremely dangerous foe; seek cover and be thankful the Fuel Rod shots arc through the air, allowing you to dodge them.

TIP **Don't forget to flee; there's nothing embarrassing about a tactical retreat, and it's better than being underpowered and overzealous.**

HUNTERS/MGALEKGOLO

A collection of thousands of orange, wormlike creatures called Lekgolo, pressed into one giant suit of unyielding armor, Hunters generally work in pairs and employ devastating cannon fire at range and crushing lunges and shield-battering during closer assaults.

- Favored methods of dispatch: Vehicle, Chaingun Turret, Plasma Rifle, Rocket Launcher, Silenced SMG, Sticky Grenades
- At long range, Hunters fire their mounted Fuel Rod Cannon, which cannot be removed from their body and shoots arcing green bolts at you. Dodge these by strafing or retreating as swiftly as possible.
- At close range, Hunters lunge in with a devastating shield strike that can cripple or kill you in seconds.
- Though rare, when encountering a pair of Hunters, it is usually better to remain at range, unseen by these fearsome foes. If a Hunter hasn't seen you yet, you can quickly weaken it with Sniper Rifle shots, Fuel Rod Cannon bolts, and Plasma or Spike Grenades.
- A Rocket Launcher or Spartan Laser can knock down a Hunter with a single strike. Check that there are no other enemies you wish to use these weapons on (such as Wraiths), and drop it with a massive shot.
- If Hunters have spotted you, and you have access to a nearby vehicle, use the vehicle to dispatch the foe rather than waste your personal ammunition during combat. Locate a Chopper, Ghost, or Warthog, and Boost into the Hunter with a single ram at high speed. This can take out a Hunter.
- If Hunters have spotted you and you have only the weaponry you're carrying, you must attempt to kill it with a mixture of careful strafing as the Hunter closes, followed up by Sticky Grenades (Frag Grenades are easily dodged), and Plasma Rifle, SMG, or Carbine shots to the Hunter's weakened spots.
- The largest weak spot is on a Hunter's back; aim for the exposed writhing flesh. Uncover more of this flesh by attaching Sticky Grenades and blasting off sections of the Hunter's carapace armor.
- Viewing a Hunter's back can be problematic; you must wait for it to lunge, then sidestep and circle-strafe so you're behind it before opening fire. Step away from the inevitable follow-up attack, too. Always dodge left; the Hunter attacks with its shield arm every time.
- Save your Grenades for protracted Hunter battles, as you may utilize a full complement of them when trying to down these monstrous hosts.

- There is a specific plan to follow during cooperative play; one of your team should attract a Hunter into close combat, while the other circles around to strike the Hunter's weak spot from behind.
- Listen! Can you hear the Hunter's cannon warming up? This allows you to predict when a Hunter (or the second of a pair) is about to fire a weapon, and you can react to it accordingly; find cover or line up the Hunters so one strikes the other with cannon fire..

HUNTER VARIANTS

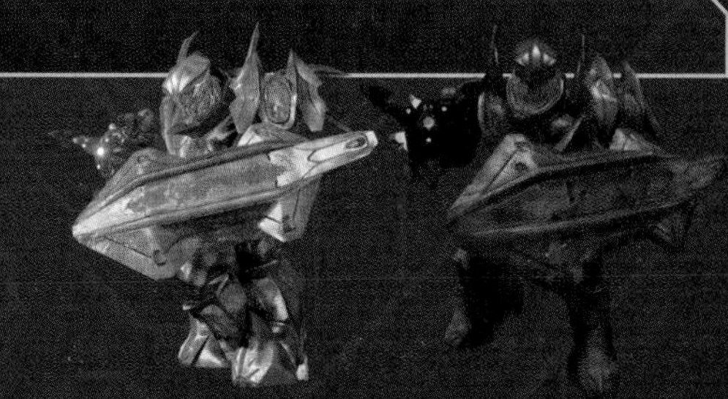

Recent combat has revealed gold-armored variants in addition to the usual dark blue hue of a Hunter's armor, which, while visually impressive, doesn't seem to yield any additional benefits to the Hunter's already awe-inspiring combat prowess. Golden Hunters attack with fuel rod shots, while blue Hunters fire streams of energy; both are equally damaging.

DRONES/YANME'E

Known colloquially by UNSC Marines as "buggers," these hive-based swarms of insectoid aliens rely on sheer numbers to annoy and finally overwhelm their foes. Individual Drones are easily dispatched, but multiple Drones can cause real consternation.

- Favored methods of dispatch: Assault Rifle, Beam Rifle, Carbine, Chaingun Turret, Flamethrower, Gravity Hammer, Magnum, Needler, Silenced SMG
- You encounter Drones only once during the Campaign (in Mission 08), but they provide constant trouble during Firefight missions.
- When you first spot an incoming swarm, quickly ascertain whether you can see where they are emerging from, such as a Hive or a Phantom.
- If a swarm entrance is available, concentrate your firepower (such as Sticky Grenades or a single rocket strike) on it so you can defeat multiple Drones before they disperse.
- Drones are difficult to target while they are airborne; seek cover to prevent yourself from being both shot and overrun.
- The key to dropping Drones that have spread out is to man a Chaingun Turret, and cut them down with rapid-fire ordnance. This is especially true during Firefights.
- Without a Turret, switch to an instant-hit, single-shot weapon such as Carbines or Beam Rifles. Homing weapons such as the Needler also offer advantages, as they can take down foes with quick bursts of fire.
- Rapid, continuous fire is never a good idea, as it wastes your ammunition. Track a Drone, fire short, sharp bursts, and target those closest to you.
- Drones usually attack using Needlers and Plasma Pistols; Needlers can be a real problem, as their shots home in on you. React by diving behind cover and sidestepping out to tag targets a few at a time before you're swarmed.
- Drones can land and attack, which is always great for you; Drones on the ground are easily dispatched, because they move far more slowly and are extremely weak. They are also easily dispatched with a melee attack, which can be done during airborne attacks, if you're close enough.

DRONE VARIANTS

Generally, Drones have been spotted with greenish hues to their light plates of carapace armor. However, there are red and yellow variations as well. Red Drones are leaders and are slightly tougher than normal. Yellow Drones are in the pupal stage, and can be spotted by their glow in nighttime Missions and Firefight levels.

ENGINEERS/HURAGOK

Enslaved by Covenant Prophets to maintain the search for Forerunner antiquities, Engineers have recently been pressed into service as unwilling living shields. Never aggressive, Engineers act as protection for other Covenant forces, which can seriously hamper your takedowns.

- Favored methods of dispatch: Chaingun Turret, Fuel Rod Cannon, Needler, Plasma Pistol, Rocket Launcher, Spartan Laser
- Engineers are only encountered floating in the air; they do not use the ground as a method of transportation.
- Engineers are docile and are never a threat when encountered singly or in pairs.
- However, Engineers are usually fitted with explosive clamping devices by Brutes and follow a group of Covenant ground infantry to provide shielded backup. It is unknown whether this is against their will.
- There are specific Achievements that involve the culling or saving of Engineers, so read up on them in the Appendices prior to attempting combat.
- Engineers offer any Covenant troops additional armor, which crackles with bluish, almost white electricity. If you encounter Brutes with this type of armor, you can be sure an Engineer is close by.
- Depending on your moral standards, you should engage an Engineer first (always during Firefight missions). As the Engineer provides protection for multiple foes, it must be removed so you don't waste ammunition taking out ground forces.
- When encountering two Engineers close to each other, many of your weapons are completely ineffective, as they pepper and reduce one Engineer's shields, which the other one promptly recharges.
- By far the most proficient way of slaying an Engineer is with an overcharged Plasma Pistol shot. If you don't have this weapon, rake Chaingun Turret fire on the beast. Otherwise, hard-hitting, single-firing weaponry is reasonable.

Recommended Weaponry: Campaign and Firefight

The following table is designed to tailor your Covenant takedown tactics to appropriate weaponry. Each available weapon is paired against a foe, on both Easy/Normal and Heroic/Legendary difficulties. The results reveal how effective a specific weapon is against a particular enemy. This chart assumes you are firing at the weapon's preferred range and that you're striking a weak point, usually the head. Note that certain weaponry, such as the Plasma Pistol, is rated low; however, this belies its true nature (for example, a single charged shot is weak against most foes but takes off their armor). Any weapon rated 💀💀💀 or higher is considered a recommended implement of destruction against that particular foe.

How to Read the Chart

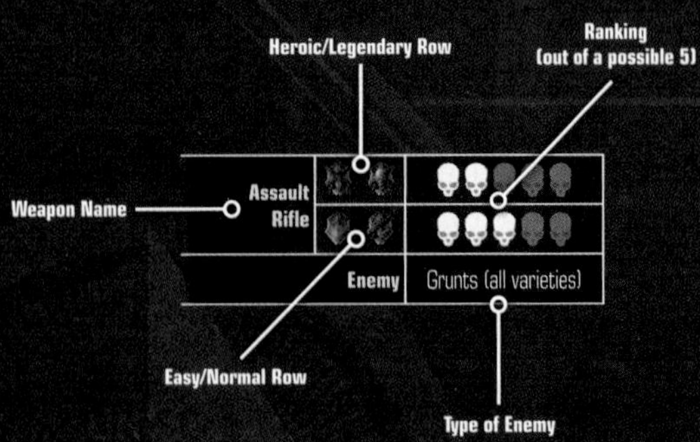

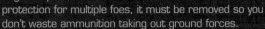

Weapon	Grunts (all varieties)	Jackals (all varieties)	Brutes	Brute Chieftains	Hunters (all varieties)	Drones (all varieties)	Engineers
Spike Grenade	5	5	5	3	4	2	3
	5	5	5	3	4	2	3
Plasma Grenade	4	5	5	3	4	2	3
	4	5	5	3	4	3	3
Frag Grenade	4	4	4	1	2	1	1
	4	4	4	1	3	2	1
Flame Grenade	5	4	5	2	3	1	1
	5	4	5	2	4	2	1
Spiker	2	2	2	2	3	2	1
	3	3	3	3	3	2	1
Spartan Laser	4	4	4	5	4	1	5
	4	4	4	5	4	2	5
Sniper Rifle	3	2	5	5	2	2	3
	3	3	5	5	3	2	4
Silenced SMG	3	1	2	1	2	3	2
	3	2	3	2	2	3	2
Shotgun	3	2	3	2	1	2	2
	4	3	4	3	2	2	2
Rocket Launcher	4	4	4	5	5	1	4
	4	4	4	5	5	1	4
Plasma Turret	4	4	5	4	5	4	5
	4	4	5	5	5	4	5
Plasma Rifle	2	3	4	1	5	3	3
	3	4	5	2	5	3	3
Plasma Pistol	1	5	5	1	1	2	5
	1	5	5	1	1	2	5
Needler	3	1	5	1	1	4	1
	3	2	5	1	1	4	1
Missile Pod	4	4	4	3	4	2	4
	4	4	4	4	4	2	4
Mauler	4	2	2	1	1	2	2
	4	3	3	2	2	2	2
Magnum	5	5	4	1	1	3	2
	5	5	5	1	2	4	3
Chaingun Turret	5	5	5	4	4	5	5
	5	5	5	5	5	5	5
Gravity Hammer	4	4	3	3	2	4	2
	4	4	4	4	3	4	3
Fuel Rod Cannon	4	4	3	4	4	1	3
	4	4	4	5	4	1	3
Flamethrower	5	5	5	5	4	4	1
	5	5	5	5	4	4	1
Carbine	5	5	4	3	2	3	2
	5	5	5	4	2	4	2
Brute Shot	2	2	2	2	2	2	1
	3	3	3	3	3	2	1
Beam Rifle	4	3	5	5	1	5	2
	4	3	5	5	2	5	3
Assault Rifle	2	2	2	1	1	5	1
	3	2	3	1	1	5	1
Enemy	Grunts (all varieties)	Jackals (all varieties)	Brutes	Brute Chieftains	Hunters (all varieties)	Drones (all varieties)	Engineers

CAMPAIGN MISSIONS

The Basics of Campaign Missions

The Training section of this guide revealed the basic tenets of Campaign mode, along with a labeled screenshot and basic movement and weapon functionality. The following introduces the structure of the Campaign Walkthrough, which provides countless effective strategies for achieving impressive results in this main gameplay mode.

1 **Overview:** Provides the mission name and a quick overview of the flashback portion of the mission.

2 **Squad Data:** This gives verbal and visual representation of who you are playing as, where you are, and how long after the drop the mission takes place.

3 **Data Stream:** The time, given as a percentage, you should expect to activate your VISR Enhanced Vision (aka "Target Acquisition") mode. Basically, this shows you how dark the mission is!

3 **Comm Data Stream (not shown):** There are two specific unlockable actions that occur only if you are playing Rookie sections; the location of 30 COMM Terminals, which in turn open eight weapon caches throughout New Mombasa (and unlock Achievements in the process). The "Tour of New Mombasa" section at the back of this walkthrough reveals more information regarding this.

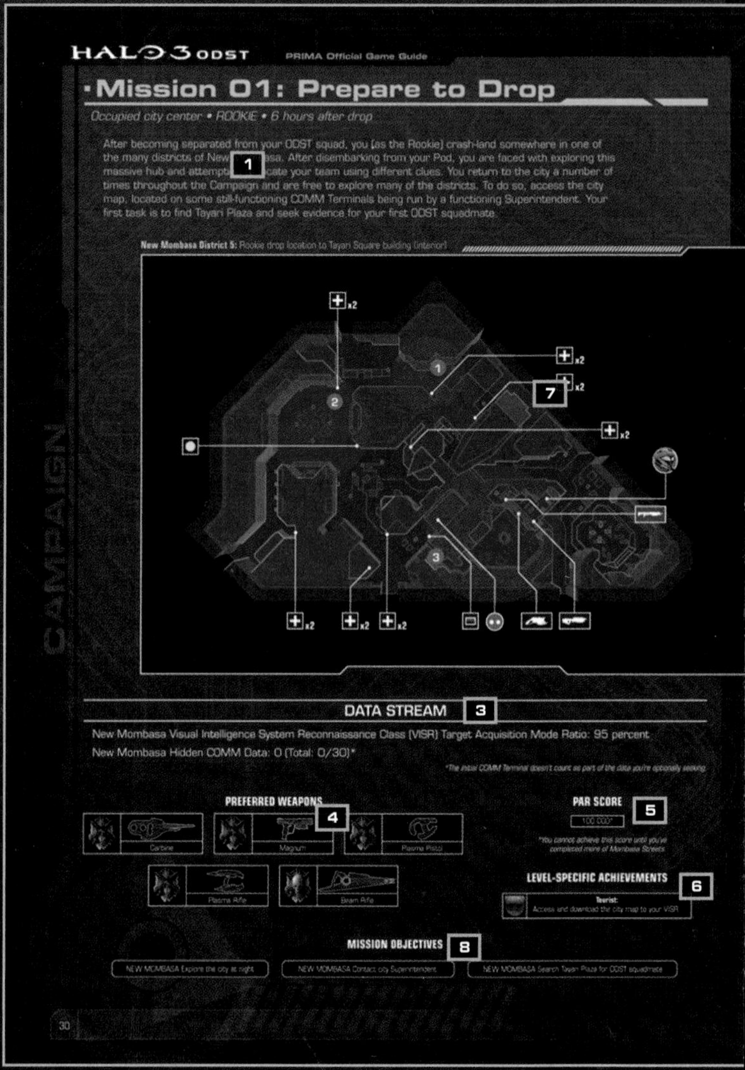

4 **Preferred Weapons:** With the wide variety of ordnance you are given or can scavenge, you may be wondering which type is tailored to your current situation. This lists the top five, along with any other pertinent data. Consult the "Weapons Detail" chapter for specific, in-game examples of weapon usage.

5 **Par Score:** The expected "Par" (or average) score for each mission is noted here, after which you can consider yourself a true master of this map!

6 **Level-Specific Achievements:** Each mission has some Achievements that you can complete only in that particular section; these are duly noted so you never need worry about missing particular goals. Refer to the "Appendices" at the back of this book for specific advice for obtaining every Achievement, mission-related or not.

HALO 3 ODST PRIMA Official Game Guide

Mission 01: Prepare to Drop

Occupied city center • ROOKIE • 6 hours after drop

After becoming separated from your ODST squad, you (as the Rookie) crash-land somewhere in one of the many districts of New[1]asa. After disembarking from your Pod, you are faced with exploring this massive hub and attempt[...]cate your team using different clues. You return to the city a number of times throughout the Campaign and are free to explore many of the districts. To do so, access the city map, located on some still-functioning COMM Terminals being run by a functioning Superintendent. Your first task is to find Tayari Plaza and seek evidence for your first ODST squadmate.

New Mombasa District 5: Rookie drop location to Tayari Square building (interior)

7

DATA STREAM 3

New Mombasa Visual Intelligence System Reconnaissance Class (VISR) Target Acquisition Mode Ratio: 95 percent

New Mombasa Hidden COMM Data: 0 (Total: 0/30)*

*The initial COMM Terminal doesn't count as part of the data you're optionally seeking.

PREFERRED WEAPONS 4

Carbine · Magnum · Plasma Pistol · Plasma Rifle · Beam Rifle

PAR SCORE 5

100,000*

*You cannot achieve this score until you've completed more of Mombasa Streets.

LEVEL-SPECIFIC ACHIEVEMENTS 6

Tourist: Access and download the city map to your VISR

MISSION OBJECTIVES 8

NEW MOMBASA Explore the city at night

NEW MOMBASA Contact city Superintendent

NEW MOMBASA Search Tayari Plaza for ODST squadmate

30

7 **Map:** Each Campaign section receives its own highly detailed map, showing the location of major weapon drops, choke points, and goals to find.

8 **Objectives:** Your HUD periodically updates with new objectives. This list, which also appears as you are given a new objective, details the tasks you are given for this section of the mission.

User Preview and Preamble

There are nine Campaign missions and a tenth additional outing, once you've completed the Campaign for the first time. Aside from the first, eighth, and ninth mission, each mission is separated into two different sections: (1) the first is a flashback to a series of battles undertaken by various members of your ODST squad, with Buck, Dutch, Mickey, and Romeo on their general quest to locate Dare and complete her secretive sortie; and (2) after these "flashbacks," the action moves to the New Mombasa city streets at night, and you play the role of Rookie, whose landing was so severe, it knocked him out for six hours. He must piece together what happened for the rest of the ODST team by finding a series of clues scattered throughout the city, which directly react to the flashback sections of the next mission.

The "tenth" mission simply grants you access to all the New Mombasa streets and allows you to thoroughly explore the city, ideally to complete your collection of supersecret COMM Terminal data locations. A tour of New Mombasa is showcased after the walkthrough to help you navigate this sprawling metropolis.

The flashback sections take place between 0 and 6 hours after drop, in a variety of locales (including New Mombasa streets). The Rookie sections take place six or more hours after drop. All missions have been thoroughly play-tested, and the optimal tactics have been recorded in the remainder of this chapter. As the Rookie sections allow you to access subsequent missions in different orders, the safest chronological path is shown. Here's how the information breaks down:

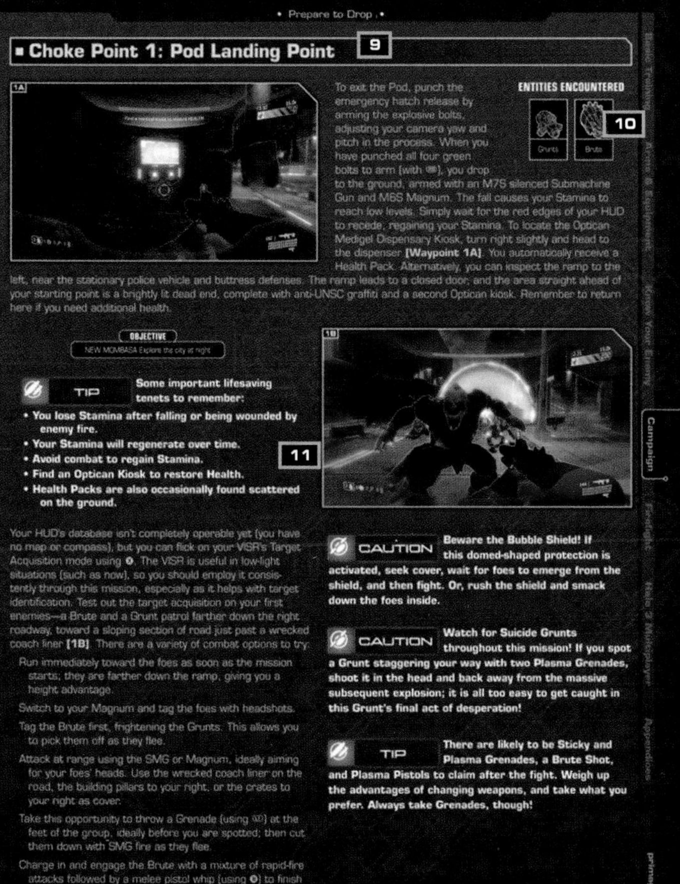
• Prepare to Drop •

■ Choke Point 1: Pod Landing Point 9

1A

To exit the Pod, punch the emergency hatch release by arming the explosive bolts, adjusting your camera yaw and pitch in the process. When you have punched all four green bolts to arm (with ⓇⒷ), you drop to the ground, armed with an M7S silenced Submachine Gun and M6S Magnum. The fall causes your Stamina to reach low levels. Simply wait for the red edges of your HUD to recede, regaining your Stamina. To locate the Optican Medigel Dispensary Kiosk, turn right slightly and head to the dispenser **[Waypoint 1A]**. You automatically receive a Health Pack. Alternatively, you can inspect the ramp to the left, near the stationary police vehicle and buttress defenses. The ramp leads to a closed door, and the area straight ahead of your starting point is a brightly lit dead end, complete with anti-UNSC graffiti and a second Optican kiosk. Remember to return here if you need additional health.

ENTITIES ENCOUNTERED 10

Grunts | Brute

OBJECTIVE

NEW MOMBASA Explore the city at night

TIP **Some important lifesaving tenets to remember:**

- **You lose Stamina after falling or being wounded by enemy fire.**
- **Your Stamina will regenerate over time.**
- **Avoid combat to regain Stamina.**
- **Find an Optican Kiosk to restore Health.**
- **Health Packs are also occasionally found scattered on the ground.**

11

1B

Your HUD's database isn't completely operable yet (you have no map or compass), but you can flick on your VISR's Target Acquisition mode using ⓨ. The VISR is useful in low-light situations (such as now), so you should employ it consistently through this mission, especially as it helps with target identification. Test out the target acquisition on your first enemies—a Brute and a Grunt patrol farther down the right roadway, toward a sloping section of road just past a wrecked coach liner **[1B]**. There are a variety of combat options to try:

Run immediately toward the foes as soon as the mission starts; they are farther down the ramp, giving you a height advantage.

Switch to your Magnum and tag the foes with headshots.

Tag the Brute first, frightening the Grunts. This allows you to pick them off as they flee.

Attack at range using the SMG or Magnum, ideally aiming for your foes' heads. Use the wrecked coach liner on the road, the building pillars to your right, or the crates to your right as cover.

Take this opportunity to throw a Grenade (using ⓁⓉ) at the feet of the group, ideally before you are spotted; then cut them down with SMG fire as they flee.

Charge in and engage the Brute with a mixture of rapid-fire attacks followed by a melee pistol whip (using Ⓑ) to finish him off.

Afterward, you can return to the Optican Kiosk and grab the other Health Pack, or access the Optican Kiosk back at the dead-end side street.

CAUTION **Beware the Bubble Shield! If this domed-shaped protection is activated, seek cover, wait for foes to emerge from the shield, and then fight. Or, rush the shield and smack down the foes inside.**

CAUTION **Watch for Suicide Grunts throughout this mission! If you spot a Grunt staggering your way with two Plasma Grenades, shoot it in the head and back away from the massive subsequent explosion; it is all too easy to get caught in this Grunt's final act of desperation!**

TIP **There are likely to be Sticky and Plasma Grenades, a Brute Shot, and Plasma Pistols to claim after the fight. Weigh up the advantages of changing weapons, and take what you prefer. Always take Grenades, though!**

2

Occupied city center • ROOKIE

31

11 Tactical Advice: Each choke point receives in-depth analysis and advice. There is copious general information, designed to help you regardless of your difficulty setting. In addition, there are specific callouts designed to help with particular issues.

Cautions, Notes, and Tips: These flag specific elements of a choke point that are dangerous (Cautions), interesting (Notes), or helpful (Tips).

Certain choke points require information designed specifically for a particular difficulty level. Look for the Normal, Heroic, or Legendary icons; the associated tactical advice is written precisely for this difficulty level. For example, if you see a "Heroic" icon, the advice will help you the most if you are playing on this difficulty, although it is still helpful for other difficulties, too.

Co-operative

Generally, the advice shown can be applied when you play through with up to three other people on your team. However, there are certain tactics that you can attempt only with multiple squadmates, and these are duly revealed.

10 Entities: It is important to know the type of foes you're about to face before you engage them. This offers a quick view of UNSC and Covenant entities you should expect, so you can plan appropriate action.

9 Choke Points: Using a mixture of common sense, the NAV map data, and this guide's maps, you should be able to navigate through each of the missions without reading directional commands (although major routes are recommended). However, the main areas where you should expect problems, clusters of enemies, or specific and highly valuable advice are listed.

Choke points appear on the in-guide map and are divided into lists (1A, 1B, 1C, etc.), all of which are related to areas on the map and your mission. Simply refer to the labeled screenshot for visual representation of each choke-point location. When you reach a location, it is flagged in the text (for example, **[1A]**).

Mission 01: Prepare to Drop

Occupied city center • ROOKIE • 6 hours after drop

After becoming separated from your ODST squad, you (as the Rookie) crash-land somewhere in one of the many districts of New Mombasa. After disembarking from your Pod, you are faced with exploring this massive hub and attempting to locate your team using different clues. You return to the city a number of times throughout the Campaign and are free to explore many of the districts. To do so, access the city map, located on some still-functioning COMM Terminals being run by a functioning Superintendent. Your first task is to find Tayari Plaza and seek evidence for your first ODST squadmate.

New Mombasa District 5: Rookie drop location to Tayari Square building (interior)

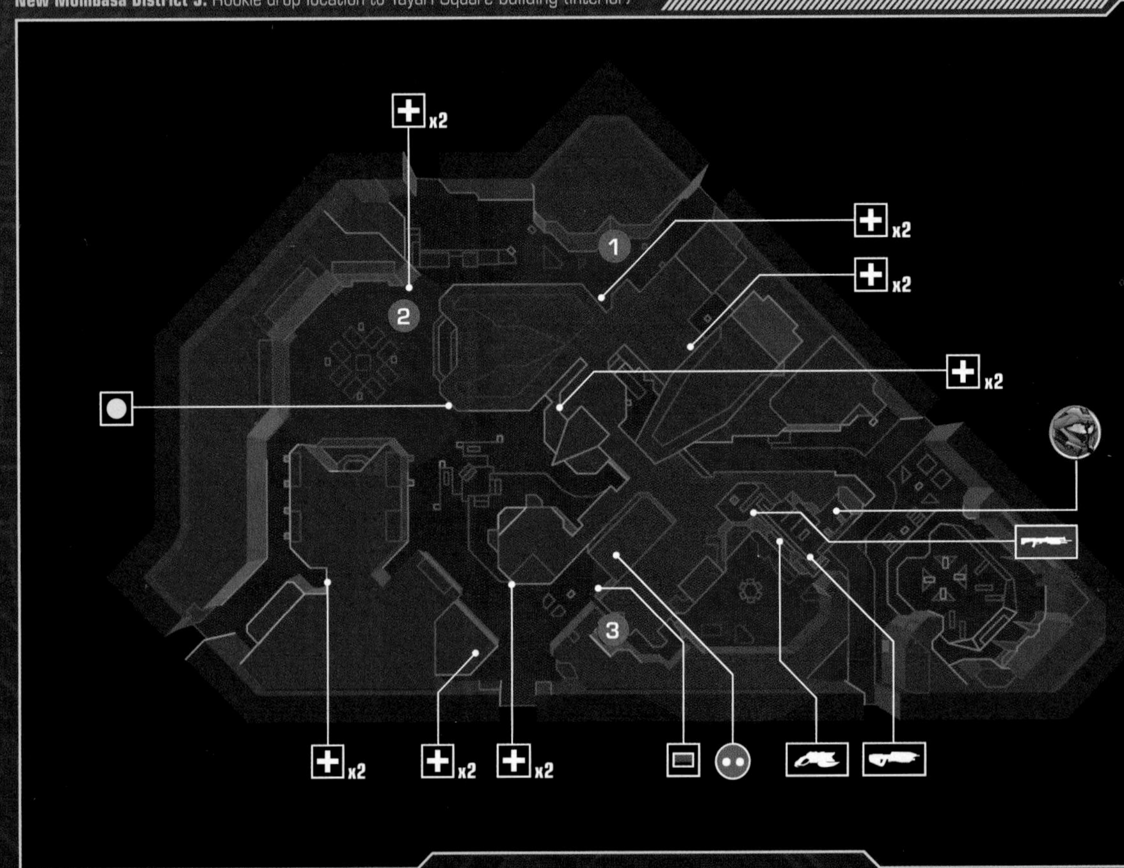

CAMPAIGN

DATA STREAM

New Mombasa Visual Intelligence System Reconnaissance Class (VISR) Target Acquisition Mode Ratio: 95 percent

New Mombasa Hidden COMM Data: 0 (Total: 0/30)*

*The initial COMM Terminal doesn't count as part of the data you're optionally seeking.

PREFERRED WEAPONS

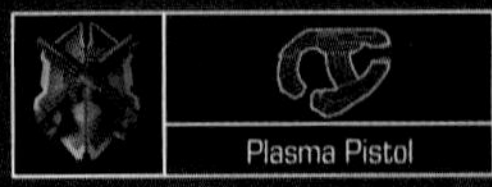

Plasma Rifle

PAR SCORE

100,000*

*You cannot achieve this score until you've completed more of Mombasa Streets.

LEVEL-SPECIFIC ACHIEVEMENTS

Tourist: Access and download the city map to your VISR.

MISSION OBJECTIVES

NEW MOMBASA Explore the city at night

NEW MOMBASA Contact city Superintendent

NEW MOMBASA Search Tayari Plaza for ODST squadmate

■ Choke Point 1: Pod Landing Point

1A

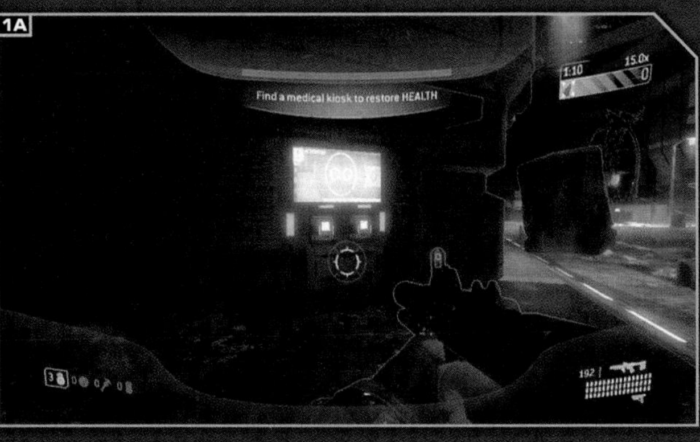

ENTITIES ENCOUNTERED

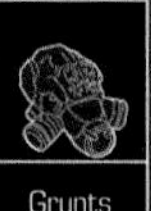
Grunts

Brute

To exit the Pod, punch the emergency hatch release by arming the explosive bolts, adjusting your camera yaw and pitch in the process. When you have punched all four green bolts to arm (with RB), you drop to the ground, armed with an M7S silenced Submachine Gun and M6S Magnum. The fall causes your Stamina to reach low levels. Simply wait for the red edges of your HUD to recede, regaining your Stamina. To locate the Optican Medigel Dispensary Kiosk, turn right slightly and head to the dispenser **[Waypoint 1A]**. You automatically receive a Health Pack. Alternatively, you can inspect the ramp to the left, near the stationary police vehicle and buttress defenses. The ramp leads to a closed door, and the area straight ahead of your starting point is a brightly lit dead end, complete with anti-UNSC graffiti and a second Optican kiosk. Remember to return here if you need additional health.

OBJECTIVE

NEW MOMBASA Explore the city at night

TIP

Some important lifesaving tenets to remember:

- **You lose Stamina after falling or being wounded by enemy fire.**
- **Your Stamina will regenerate over time.**
- **Avoid combat to regain Stamina.**
- **Find an Optican Kiosk to restore Health.**
- **Health Packs are also occasionally found scattered on the ground.**

Your HUD's database isn't completely operable yet (you have no map or compass), but you can flick on your VISR's Target Acquisition mode using Ⓧ. The VISR is useful in low-light situations (such as now), so you should employ it consistently through this mission, especially as it helps with target identification. Test out the target acquisition on your first enemies—a Brute and a Grunt patrol farther down the right roadway, toward a sloping section of road just past a wrecked coach liner **[1B]**. There are a variety of combat options to try:

- Run immediately toward the foes as soon as the mission starts; they are farther down the ramp, giving you a height advantage.
- Switch to your Magnum and tag the foes with headshots.
- Tag the Brute first, frightening the Grunts. This allows you to pick them off as they flee.
- Attack at range using the SMG or Magnum, ideally aiming for your foes' heads. Use the wrecked coach liner on the road, the building pillars to your right, or the crates to your right as cover.
- Take this opportunity to throw a Grenade (using LT) at the feet of the group, ideally before you are spotted; then cut them down with SMG fire as they flee.
- Charge in and engage the Brute with a mixture of rapid-fire attacks followed by a melee pistol whip (using Ⓑ) to finish him off.
- Afterward, you can return to the Optican Kiosk and grab the other Health Pack, or access the Optican Kiosk back at the dead-end side street.

1B

CAUTION

Beware the Bubble Shield! If this domed-shaped protection is activated, seek cover, wait for foes to emerge from the shield, and then fight. Or, rush the shield and smack down the foes inside.

CAUTION

Watch for Suicide Grunts throughout this mission! If you spot a Grunt staggering your way with two Plasma Grenades, shoot it in the head and back away from the massive subsequent explosion; it is all too easy to get caught in this Grunt's final act of desperation!

TIP

There are likely to be Sticky and Plasma Grenades, a Brute Shot, and Plasma Pistols to claim after the fight. Weigh up the advantages of changing weapons, and take what you prefer. Always take Grenades, though!

Occupied city center • ROOKIE

Tactic: Pistol Packing

By far the most proficient way of dealing with this initial encounter is to switch to your Magnum, and tag the three Grunts patrolling in your direction with headshots. Wait a few moments so the squad moves closer, and you can inspect their corpses more easily, then grab a Plasma Pistol. Use overcharged shots from this weapon to devastate the Brute's shields, and swap between the Plasma Pistol and Magnum to dominate (always end with a Magnum headshot); this combo is great for taking down otherwise armored targets. Use this tactic at Choke Point 2, too.

NOTE

Refer to the "Know Your Enemy" chapter to find more combat options when dealing with Brutes and Grunts.

Choke Point 2: Accessing the Superintendent

If you're quick enough, once you've nullified the initial Grunt and Brute patrol, you can spot two Phantoms pulling away from the roundabout and plaza at the ramp's base. Use the upper ramp (leading to a locked door) for a great overview of the next area, which has seen heavy fighting from New Mombasa's civil defense forces. Expect to face two Brutes and at least six Grunts in the lower roundabout area **[2A]** and a Brute and at least four Grunts on the higher left and right sloping roads of the plaza. In addition to the previously listed tactics, try any of the following combat techniques when attempting to secure the area:

ENTITIES ENCOUNTERED

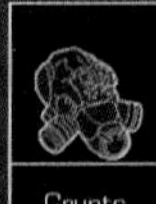

Grunts

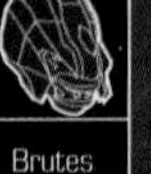

Brutes

- Prior to entering the roundabout, stand on the upper ramp at the top of the steps and use zoomed Magnum shots (press Ⓐ, then RT repeatedly) to decapitate foes from extreme range. Let the enemies come to you!
- Enter the roundabout road, skirting the edges and using the building pillars (on the left) or the vehicles or metal defense shields (to the right) as cover, tagging foes on the roundabout island.
- Flush foes on the roundabout island by lobbing in well-placed Grenades, but watch for returning projectiles from this location.
- Rush the island, using the low concrete walls and palm trees as cover while constantly strafing so you aren't an easy target to hit.
- Well-placed Plasma Grenades are a great way to end a Brute's life. Remember, you can cycle through your Grenade types using LB.
- Brute Shots are great at hammering into defenses. You can also try the familiar tactic of using a charged Plasma Pistol shot to remove Brute armor and using another to finish it off.
- During combat at the roundabout, expect to find Covenant weapons like the Needler, Carbine, and Plasma Rifle, all of which make great offensive weapons, depending on your combat style.

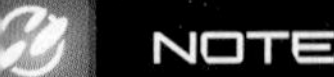

NOTE

Certain weapons, such as the Needler, grant you special Achievements if you kill a certain number of foes with it. Consult the "Achievements" section of the appendix for more information. Note that particularly rare weapons must be used in specific missions to complete associated Achievements.

Tactic: Ground Control

For a most proficient takedown, perform the Plasma Pistol overcharge on Brutes, followed by a headshot. Use simple headshots for the Grunts. This works on any difficulty and uses only two shots (one from each weapon). If you want to damage a cluster of enemies, race to the Phantom dropping off the foes, and lob a Grenade at the ground where they drop to. You'll have to ignore the foes in Choke Point 1 to reach this location in time, but this can severely damage multiple enemies with a single well-placed Grenade.

2A

2B

OBJECTIVE

NEW MOMBASA Contact city Superintendent

When the final Covenant falls in this area, your HUD updates, letting you know you are separated from your ODST squad and must contact the city Superintendent for assistance. After inspecting Covenant corpses for additional ordnance (especially Grenades), flick to your VISR mode, if you haven't already, and look for the Data Terminal with the yellow outline **[2B]**. This is very difficult to spot without your VISR on. Hold RB to access the Data Terminal, and the City Map is downloaded into your VISR. Your VISR database is now accessible by pressing . Follow the NAV menu instructions for moving and zooming in on your map and placing a Waypoint, and notice that your compass has now appeared on your HUD, along with the location of Tayari Plaza—the last known location of an ODST squadmate. Check the Intel Data in your menu for your next objective.

TIP **This grants you the Tourist Achievement. After you've made contact, the Superintendent begins to subtly manipulate the signs in your general area, giving you a series of neon bread crumbs to follow: signs stating "Detour" or "Keep Left" or voices instructing you to "Please walk" are all from the Superintendent, who guides you in the correct direction. As your Enhanced Vision doesn't allow you to spot the images on the brightly lit signs, you may need to temporarily turn off your VISR. Covenant glyphs also hint at the direction you must take.**

NOTE **Although it isn't immediately obvious, you're in District 5 of New Mombasa. This becomes increasingly clear as you return to the city repeatedly throughout the Campaign. To quickly ascertain where you generally are, consult the "Mission Hub: Mombasa Streets" section at the back of this walkthrough, which has a district map. Notice the giant numbers on some of the walls? Those are clues as to the district you're in.**

OBJECTIVE

NEW MOMBASA Search Tayari Plaza for ODST squadmate.

TIP **Your HUD now has an Assistance capability. By pressing either ♁ or , you can reveal a cursor pointing in the general direction of your next objective point. This is extremely useful, although a direct route sometimes isn't accessible.**

NOTE **This Data Terminal is an example of what 30 pieces of COMM Data look like, which are hidden in the city. Although this guide doesn't give precise locations to each piece of data, the number you can locate in each mission is listed at the start of the mission, along with the weapon caches they unlock.**

NOTE **Tayari Plaza has appeared on your compass and is approximately 170 meters from the Data Terminal. Use the blue diamond on your compass to correct your direction when attempting to reach this and future objectives.**

Choke Point 3: Building Infiltration

3A

ENTITIES ENCOUNTERED

Grunts

Brutes

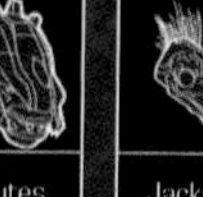

Jackals

Aside from dead defense forces, the area is devoid of human life. Collect any dropped weapons, optionally heading through the smoking remains of vehicles to reach an Optican Kiosk to the south before taking a southeasterly route toward a side door. You'll pass a second Optican Kiosk along the way. A side door is near the "Slow Down" signs in the middle of the road. Your VISR shows interesting Covenant hieroglyphs on the wall, hinting this is the correct way to go. Face southeast, and hold RB to open the security door **[3A]**.

NOTE **Look left just before entering the door, and you'll see a wall with a horizontal line of illuminated orange lights. This is a Superintendent Supply Cache, but it is currently sealed. If you find your way back here later, you can access the cache, which first opens once you begin a new game after fully unlocking Mission 10: Mombasa Streets. This one has two Mongoose vehicles, four Silenced SMGs, four Pistols, and four Frag Grenades. You can't access these items yet**

The dark corridors ahead are difficult to explore without HUD aid, so flick on VISR before continuing into the building, past the "Glass This!" graffiti. Follow the corridor (and hieroglyphs) to a second security door to the northeast. Open this and enter a courtyard. A sleeping Grunt should easily fall to your preferred weapon, after which you have around four more Grunts to defeat. Standing on the upper pavement and lobbing Grenades **[3B]** is a better plan than wading into the long grass, as the Grunts like to fire their Plasma Pistols at you, and it is difficult to aim back at them with the grass in the way. Methodically massacre the Grunts, then locate and open the security door opposite the one you came from.

TIP **Remember you can assassinate (melee attack from behind) a sleeping Grunt without waking up his brethren. Or, simply sprint across to the door opposite to escape this grassy courtyard.**

3B

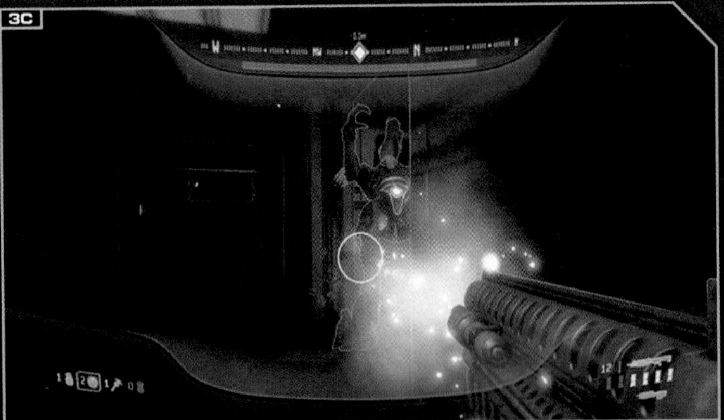
3C

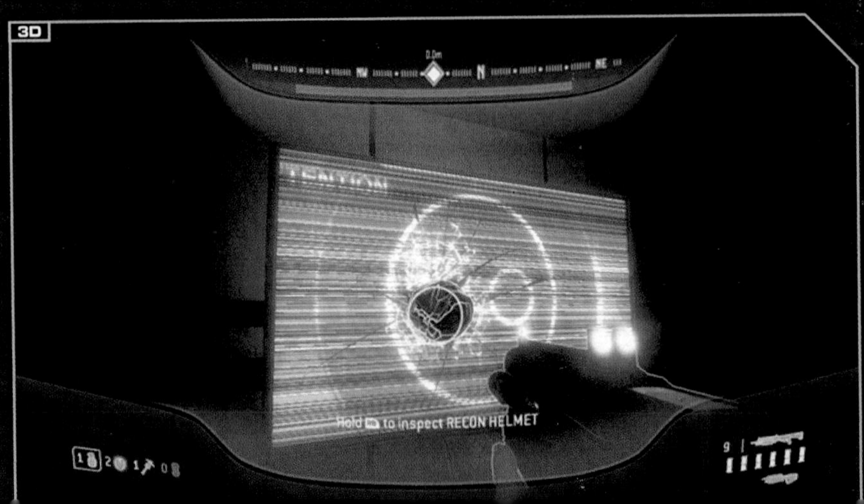

3D

Enter the next building, which was the scene of a recent massacre. Step over the Grunt and Brute bodies, although you may wish to check out the ground floor; there's an Assault Rifle if you want it. Then head west, under the pulsing light and up the stairs, brandishing a close-combat weapon. If you don't have a suitable one, stop at the top of the stairs and turn right (southwest), and step into the dead-end corridor. At this corridor's northwest end is a dead Marine. Grab the Shotgun from the corpse, and return to the main passage. Head up the stairs (marked "2" on the wall) to the next floor, and check the open door on the right (north). Execute the two **Jackals** lurking here **[3C]**, using two quick Shotgun blasts from the main passage doorway.

Alternatively, you can sidestep and face the doorway, lob in a Grenade, and back away. Or, fire a shot to attract a Jackal, then execute it (ideally with a headshot) as it ventures into the main passage. You can also step into the chamber and strafe the Jackals with Assault Rifle (or Covenant weapon) fire.

Tactic: Strafe of Death

For a truly professional Jackal takedown, look for the dead Marine being illuminated by the flashing light. Strafe past the door opposite, which auto-opens, and throw in a Grenade. The door closes, and the Jackals are ripped apart in the ensuing, contained explosion.

There may be a Carbine and Beam Rifle to grab if you want them. Now continue up the stairs (marked "3" on the wall) to the upper floor, and maneuver straight along the passage; the rooms to each side are empty. You appear in a debris-strewn office with a window to your right (southeast) that offers impressive views of Tayari Plaza. However, of greater interest is the Recon Helmet half-embedded in the flicking info screen to your left **[3D]**. Hold ® to inspect the Helmet.

▪Mission 02: Tayari Plaza

BUCK • Tayari Plaza • Immediately after drop

After a less-than-perfect landing, Buck disembarks from his Pod and immediately launches an assault on the Covenant, attempting to locate Dare's Drop-Pod before the Covenant can reach it. Storming through a Phantom's dropped forces, Buck meets up with a group of Marines; outwits a group of Brutes; pushes farther northwest, engaging in street-by-street combat; acquires a Plasma Turret but forgoes it for some sharpshooting to tackle a Watchtower and numerous Covenant Snipers; and finally faces down a pair of Hunters. This mission must not be compromised.

Buck Drop-Pod location to Tayari Plaza

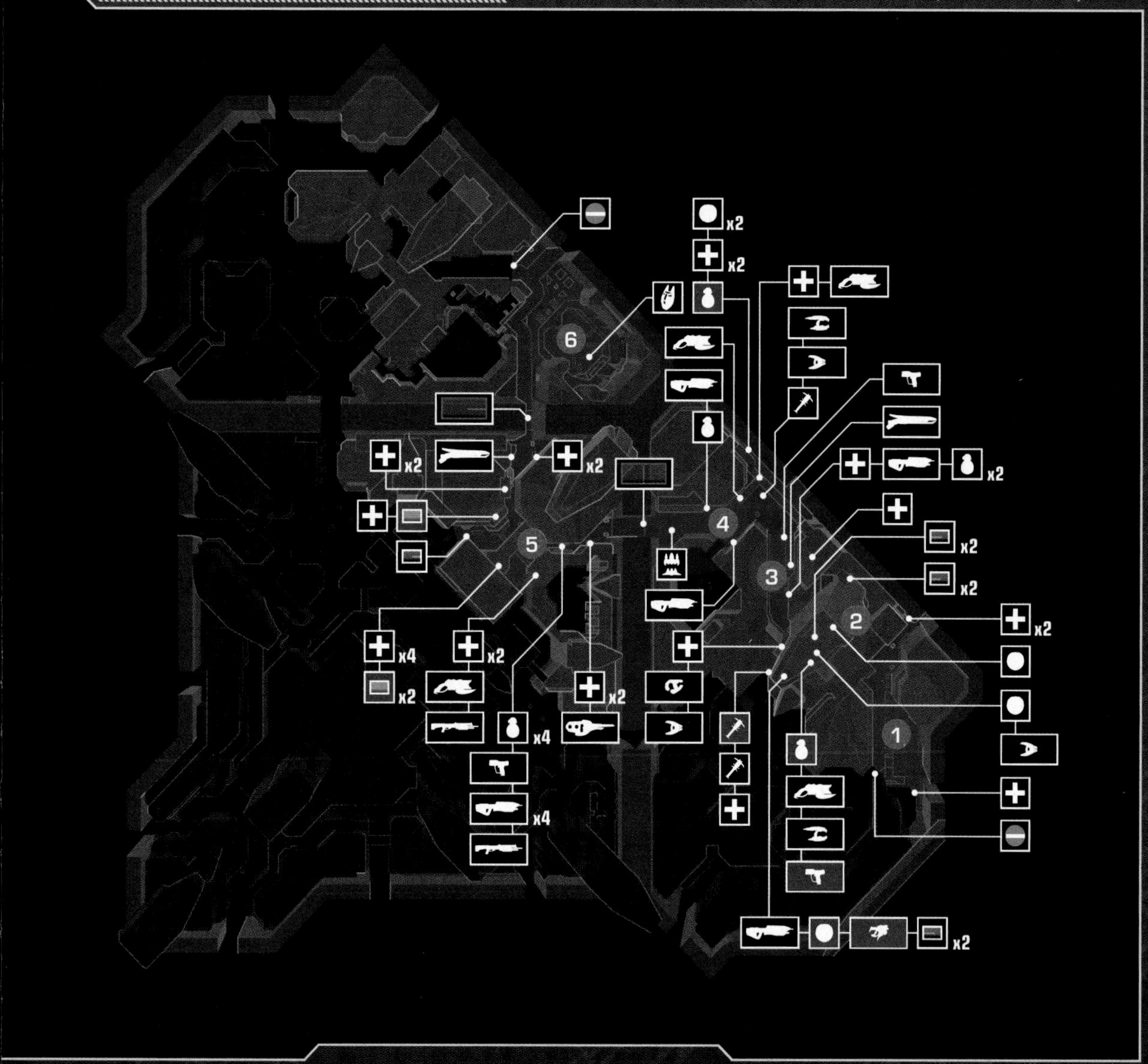

DATA STREAM

Tayari Plaza VISR Target Acquisition Mode Ratio: 10 percent*

*COMM Data Terminals are available only during Rookie missions.

PREFERRED WEAPONS

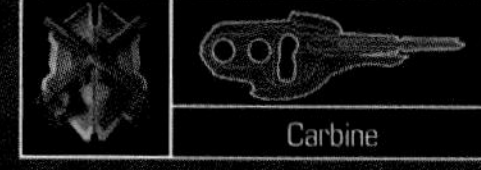
Carbine

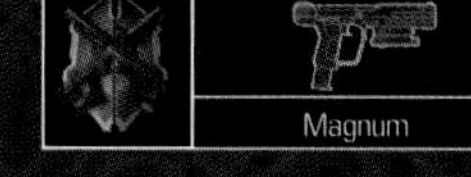
Magnum

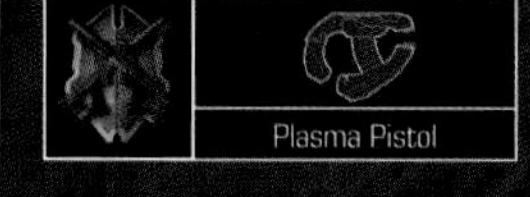
Plasma Pistol

Plasma Rifle

Beam Rifle

PAR SCORE

25,000

MISSION OBJECTIVES

TAYARI PLAZA Beat the Covenant to Dare's crash site

TAYARI PLAZA Find Dare's crash site

TAYARI PLAZA Open crashed Drop-Pod

■ Choke Point 1: Phantom Airdrop

OBJECTIVE

TAYARI PLAZA Beat the Covenant to Dare's crash site

Although you are instructed to open your VISR Intel Data (using BACK), which shows Tayari Plaza (and Dare's crash site several city blocks to the northwest), it is better to ignore this command and concentrate on the enemies dropping out of the hovering Phantom ahead (north) of you **[1A]**. These Grunts and a couple of Brutes are easy pickings.

ENTITIES ENCOUNTERED

Phantom	Grunts	Brutes

Tactic: Rooftop Camping

You have the Assault Rifle and Magnum and can easily shoot your foes' heads using either firearm (although single, zoomed Magnum shots are by far the best method). Stay on the upper plateau, which has multiple Health Packs and sandbags **[1A]** that provide excellent cover. Duck back behind the sandbags if you're struck by incoming fire, allowing your Stamina to recharge in a place where the Covenant cannot physically reach you. Continue this lengthy, long-range sniping until the enemies begin pulling back toward the building pillars to the right and the beacon **[1B]** in the distance.

Tactic: Left-Flank Charge

This involves maximizing your speed and Grenade-throwing prowess and takes some practice. Immediately jump down from the rooftop, and sprint down the stairs to your left (near the energy wall to the west that blocks your route). Move up along the road, closing in on the Phantom and watching its exit chute intently. As each Covenant squad disembarks, throw a Frag Grenade at the clustered foes; with careful aiming, you kill the Grunts and seriously wound the Brutes. This wipes out the majority of the foes before they can spread out, severely impeding their combat effectiveness.

Tactic: Additional Options

If you want to save your Magnum's ammunition, short bursts from the Assault Rifle can also work. If you've decided to wait, take any Health Packs you need from the plateau (as you can't return here), then drop down to the top of the road ramp, where a ruined Warthog is located. Check the ground for Grenades, and use the remains of the Warthog to gaze north, down the curved road ramp to some Covenant defenses and the beacon **[1B]**. If you're too slow, Grunts may try to outflank you on the left, especially if you remain in cover for too long.

As foes begin pulling back, concentrate on clearing the right side of the street and the building. The cover itself is plentiful, with both concrete barriers and vehicles providing protection. You must advance carefully. Single Magnum shots or short Rifle bursts, along with optional Grenades lobbed at Brutes dug in behind the pillars, allow you to clear the right side. Move under the building, using the pillars as cover, then clear the left side of the street and the beacon. Keep strafing to avoid being targeted and struck by foes. There's likely to be a Brute Shot or two to optionally grab before you continue.

1A

1B

 TIP

The VISR Mode isn't advisable during daylight operations, as the glare is too intense. However, it helps locate enemies and dropped weapons before and after combat; flick it on for a few seconds at a time if you need more precise target locating.

 TIP

Note the giant numbers painted on the walls near open and closed routes. For example, the zone you're currently in is "6." Familiarity with the numbering system across New Mombasa will help you during the Rookie's labyrinthine exploration missions.

■ Choke Point 2: Brute Force

Pass the S-27 sanitation truck and look northwest to the road barrier, and look northeast up a sloped road to a sealed tunnel. There is an Optican Kiosk up here. The only available route is to the northwest, where you meet two Marines who saw your crash landing **[2A]**. They haven't seen your squad, but they do offer some advice on the incoming Covenant: There are buildings you can enter to outflank the Covenant roaming the streets. You can put this advice into practice almost immediately, as the two Marines set off down the side street to the southwest. Ready yourself for combat as soon as possible. The main roadway to the northwest dead end has an Optican Kiosk, but come back to that later; the Marines need immediate backup against a quartet of Brutes heading into this area.

ENTITIES ENCOUNTERED

UNSC Marines

Brutes

2A

2B

2C

Tactic: Heeding the Marine

The Marine mentioned exploring building interiors, and the door on the left (eastern) side of the side street **[2B]** is unlocked. Head inside and move up the stairs, pausing to retrieve any dropped weapons you want and to gather all Grenades. Look closer at the bodies and you can see Brutes and Elites have been fighting each other; interspecies animosity is always helpful to your cause. Step out onto the exit overlooking the street below, and begin defeating Brutes using your preferred weaponry; your foes are unable to physically reach you. If their attacks are trained on this location, step back into cover. Continue this peekaboo takedown until the Brutes fall.

TIP **Did you notice the Spike Grenade and Mauler on the upper balcony? Grab both, or at least the Spike Grenade; there's a Watchtower later in your reconnaissance that's easily nullified with this projectile.**

Tactic: Stick It to Them

Cycle through your available (and previously collected) Grenades, picking either Plasma or Spike Grenades as you head around the corner **[2C]** at the end of the side street (assuming you didn't wait for the Marines to go on ahead). If you're fast enough, the Brutes are surprised that humans are still in this area, and you can use these few seconds of incredulity to expertly lob sticky projectiles onto them. Immediately fall back, switching to a favored firearm to finish the remaining Brutes. Utilize the two Marines now; they can draw fire away from you, allowing you to sneak up and melee or lob more Grenades at the remaining foes.

TIP **If you have a trio of Frag Grenades, use them all against these Brutes, as there are numerous additional Grenades to gather farther along this street.**

Tactic: Other Antics

Try staying behind the two Marines, using them to soak up damage while you pepper the Brutes with headshots, using the side-street pillar (**[2B]**) as cover. Or, wait halfway down the side street and launch ordnance at the Brutes using, for example, the Brute Shot; this can damage Marines just as easily as enemies, so watch your aim. Alternatively, dash in, moving around the concrete palm tree planter, and use the vehicles, pillars, and steps as cover, circling your foes while blasting them with your favored weapon. This ground-flanking maneuver is dangerous but allows you and your Marine buddies to cross fire on foes.

NOTE **These two Marines are expendable and fall during this or subsequent battles, either by Covenant or your hands; it matters not.**

CAUTION **If you stay up in the interior for too long during combat, the Brutes will chase after you and try to flank you. Keep an eye out for this!**

Choke Point 3: Plasma Turret Blockade

ENTITIES ENCOUNTERED

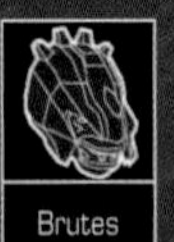
Brutes

Grunts

Whether you utilized the side door into the building or not, head in there to secure additional weaponry, optionally returning to Optican Kiosks if necessary or investigating the steps to your left (west) for a Health Pack near a dead Marine. Then drop to the main street, heading north around the corner **[3A]**. Ready yourself for combat with four to six Grunts and a couple of Brutes stationed along the ground, using vehicles, concrete, and sandbag barricades as cover. The biggest problem, however, is a Grunt manning a Plasma Turret on the upper alcove to the right of the far stairs **[3B]**. Use the trash bin or concrete barricades and sidestep out, plugging Grunts with your Pistol while lobbing Grenades at them. Continue this until the remaining foes retreat up the sloping road. Now turn your attention to the Turret.

3A

3B

Tactic: Long-Range Lobbing

Leaving the Turret until last enables you to use the right street wall and nearby scenery as cover as you tag Grunts and force any Brutes to retreat. Now step out into the street **[3A]** and carefully aim one Frag Grenade so it lands at the feet of the Grunt manning the Turret. Check the ground for additional dropped Grenades if you need another attempt. However, projectiles are needed in combat to come, so don't waste your Grenades. The Grunt usually dies, and the Turret falls to the ground on the corner of the alcove. If you fail in your lobbing, try the following tactic.

TIP **A fully loaded Plasma Turret is an effective instrument of death, especially against the Shield Jackals you are about to face. Pick up this heavy weapon and carry it with you.**

Tactic: Close-Assault Charging

With your foes in retreat, dart from cover to cover, then dive behind the pillar to the right of the sandbags, in front of the Turret. Recover your Stamina, then sprint to the low wall ahead, beneath the Turret. The Grunt can't aim at you from this low angle, allowing you to stroll up the steps **[3B]** and melee or shoot the Grunt from behind or as it flees. Beware of any enemy stragglers near the stairs and the wrecked fuel truck as you secure the area.

Choke Point 4: Watchtower Assault

4A

4B

ENTITIES ENCOUNTERED

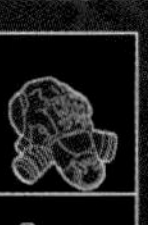
Grunts

Jackals

Advance in a westerly direction, using the left wall, street defenses, or walkway pillars as cover, and zoom in to scan the area ahead if you haven't been attacked yet. To the west is an enclosed street with several Grunts, Shield Jackals, and a few Jackal Snipers stationed on or near a Watchtower; there are also the bodies of fallen Brutes and Elites from a previous firefight. Before going any farther, stop before you pass the parked container truck **[4A]**, across from the stairs that lead northeast, up to the pedestrian walkway directly opposite the Watchtower **[4C]**. Your optimal tactical choices change, depending on your difficulty level:

Tactic: Beam Rifle Hunt

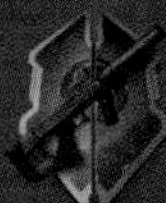

On Easy and Normal difficulty, you can obtain the devastating Beam Rifle by heading up the stairs and moving southeast along the pedestrian walkway. The Beam Rifle lies next to a dead Jackal **[4B]** (the weapon is missing on higher difficulty levels). Now take a position behind any available cover (or back up to extreme range), ideally after you deal with the Shield Jackals and other nearby nuisances, and tag the Jackal Snipers on top and around the base of the Watchtower **[4C]**; this makes a subsequent charge-in a little easier. Then search the remaining walkway area for Health Packs if you need them.

4C

Tactic: Magnum Decapitations

On Heroic and Legendary difficulty, the only Beam Rifles available are being carried by Sniper Jackals on and around the Watchtower **[4C]**, which is the biggest threat. Be sure nearer foes aren't targeting you, and use your trusty Magnum in place of the Beam Rifle, tagging usually three Sniper Jackals on or near the Watchtower. As soon as you've done this, immediately retreat to the road's right side to avoid incoming Grunt Grenades or ordnance. You can afford to lose a little Health; there's a Pack next to the stairs and two more (plus a Frag Grenade) at the walkway's northwest end.

TIP **Take your Beam Rifle or Magnum shots from extreme distance, such as from underneath the road defenses near the pedestrian walkway.**

Tactic: A Sticky Situation

Don't have a Magnum or an expert throwing arm? Then use a Spike Grenade you should have gathered from previously downed Brutes or the building exploration. Lob it down the street so it sticks to the Watchtower, watching as the ensuing explosion rocks the structure and defeats foes standing on it. However, beware of other Sniper Jackals still prowling the ground level.

Tactic: Shield Jackal and Grunt Takedowns

With Brutes and Elites lying defeated, you should move to the ground by, on, and under the stairs, where you can expect to find a Spiker, a Plasma Rifle, and a Mauler. You can use any of these (ideally, an energy weapon like the Plasma Rifle) to shoot through the side gap in the Jackals' Shields, after which you should attempt headshots. Or, you can lay down fire with the Brute Shot. Remember, the vehicles offer good cover you can move around, and crouching by the container truck and striking Jackals and Grunts from under the flatbed is another option. You can also saunter in using the heavy Plasma Turret you just appropriated; this is ideal for removing Jackal shields. As you move forward, stay on the right side as you close in on the Watchtower so you can use the building pillars as cover, allowing your Stamina to recharge. Execute Grunts with whatever weapons you have at hand, using the remaining charge of the Plasma Turret, Magnum headshots, or other violence. When the area is cleared, open the gate at the west end of the street.

Co-op Tactic: Shields Down

With a wide road and numerous cover positions, you can easily split your team to encroach along the street on both sides, giving you an advantage; the Shield Jackals can't block fire from both directions, allowing for easier takedowns.

TIP **The next area of heavy fighting can prove arduous if you haven't brought two ideal weapons with you: collect the Beam Rifle the Jackals drop for an advantage in the next locale. Conserving Grenades is a good idea, too.**

Tayari Plaza • BUCK

■ Choke Point 5: Snipers' Walkway (Hunter Patrol)

5A

5B

ENTITIES ENCOUNTERED

UNSC Marines

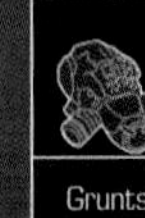
Grunts

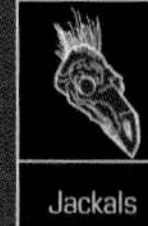
Jackals

Brutes

Hunters

The gate opens, allowing access into Zone 8, a road sloping down and west into an open plaza with a long walkway bisecting it. Ahead, you may see Marines fighting valiantly against Covenant forces by a wrecked Warthog; you can't save them, and sprinting down into the plaza is futile, as the area has numerous enemies. Instead, head along the left sidewalk, passing an Optican Kiosk (which is useful to return to, as a Carbine is lying near it that you can pick up if you don't have a long-range weapon), until you reach the Marine crouching by the concrete planter **[5A]**. She yells some sage advice: you should definitely cut through the building, and hit the forces from behind. The "forces" in question are:

Jackal Snipers on various upper balconies.

A Grunt manning a Plasma Turret **[5C]** directly opposite the Marine's position.

Shield Jackals and Grunts milling around the walkway and plaza.

Brutes on the central walkway **[5B]** and lower plaza.

This is the optimal order you should attempt to defeat these enemies.

Tactic: View from the Bridge

On greater difficulty settings, tagging the Jackal Snipers is the first plan of attack. Head through the doorway left of the crouched Marine. This leads to a two-story building. At the entrance is a dead Marine, near a weapon cache of Assault Rifles, Shotguns, and some Pistol ammo. Armed with a Beam Rifle and a secondary weapon with ranged capabilities, enter the building. There's a dead Marine, a dead Brute, and steps leading down. No weapon (the Shotgun and Spiker) or location is strategically safe, as the ground level is teeming with foes; however, there are two Health Packs to grab.

Instead, move to the doorway joining the central walkway **[5B]**, and use it as cover. Scan and drop any foes at close range before poking your head out of the doorway cover just long enough to tag the three or four Jackal Snipers. These mill around the walkway structure and are on balconies to your left and right. Make sure you nullify them all before aiming at the Grunt behind the Plasma Turret on the opposite balcony. Now edge out onto the bridge, and pick off the milling Grunts and Jackals below using your Carbine or Pistol. If you have the Carbine, use that from this vantage point to dispatch the Brutes. Resist the temptation to lob Grenades; save them for the Hunter battle that occurs after you kill all Covenant in the area.

Tactic: Ground Combat

On lesser difficulty settings, you can opt to head downstairs from the building or even down from the road (which isn't recommended when Snipers are lurking, as you have limited line of sight), and begin to engage foes at closer quarters. Naturally, the Brute Shot and Shotgun, coupled with circle-strafing, are your techniques to master. However, do this only after the Snipers and Plasma Turret are down.

5C

5D

Tactic: Exceptional Hunter Combat

A variation on the "View from the Bridge" tactic allows you to tackle foes at range and from cover for longer. Utilize the Carbine at the building doorway, until you nullify all long-range enemies. Then head out onto the walkway and across to the balconies where a Jackal was; pick up its Beam Rifle to punish the majority of remaining enemies from the cover of a balcony or building.

Hunter Tactic: Flight!

Two lolloping Hunters appear from the north gate and can seriously thwart your progress. Running away doesn't gain you any points or bravery medals, but it keeps you alive and with minimal damage from their devastating Fuel Rod Cannons. Follow this route: Move across the walkway, then jump along the platforms by the left wall, heading north toward the recently opened gate. The Hunters are circumvented, and your Stamina can easily recover.

Hunter Tactic: Fight!

Facing the Hunters in the ground-level area **[5D]** is a more thrilling tactic. Move in close but not within their melee range. Produce either the Plasma or Spike Grenades you saved from earlier encounters, and precisely lob them onto each Hunter; this brings them down in moments. If you run out of Grenades or you're inaccurate, dash across the walkway to the Plasma Turret **[5C]**, wrenching it off its base so you aren't a prone target, and lay waste with it.

TIP

With speed (plus luck and using planters and pillars as cover), you can sprint along the right side of this area, past the Plasma Turret [5C] toward the gate. Two Hunters come thundering out of the gate; simply pass them, as they won't follow you into Tayari Plaza.

Choke Point 6: Tayari Plaza Crash Site

6A

6B

ENTITY ENCOUNTERED

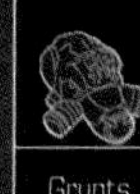

Grunts

OBJECTIVE

TAYARI PLAZA Open crashed Drop-Pod

Head north through the gate and quickly head forward, looking right (east) to see a Phantom departing Tayari Plaza. Peer below; around four or five Grunts **[6A]** are shooting Dare's Pod **[6B]**! As soon as you spot the Pod, your intel objective updates. Tactically, there's little to worry about; tag their heads from this upper roadway overlooking the plaza, or wade in with closer-ranged weapons to stop the ones bombarding the Pod. Aside from the Pod itself **[6B]**, the area is empty but is worth exploring (mainly because it's the setting for Firefight location Crater and Crater Night). When you're ready, pry open the Pod with RB.

Mission 02: Mombasa Streets

Occupied city center • ROOKIE • 6 hours after drop

Rookie sets Dare's helmet aside and attempts to locate a squadmate by journeying through New Mombasa's streets and plazas to the Uplift entrance. Along the way, you discover and tackle a new type of Covenant force—a floating, shield-deploying entity known as an Engineer. Facing numerous Covenant patrols, the Rookie pushes onward, encountering the first Brute Stalker and pondering whether to venture down numerous auxiliary streets en route to an initial weapons cache and a second clue to the ODST team's status.

DATA STREAM

New Mombasa VISR Target Acquisition Mode Ratio: 95 percent

PREFERRED WEAPONS

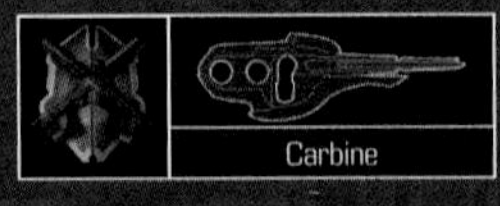

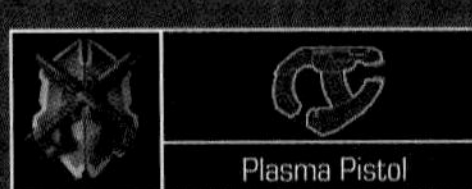

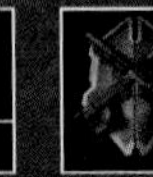

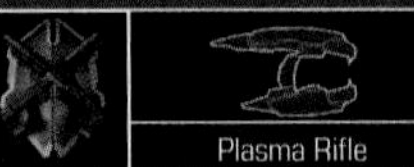

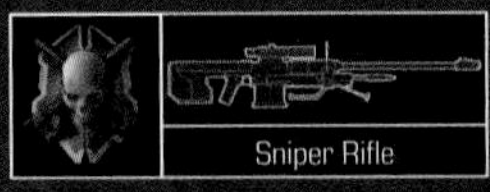

PAR SCORE

100,000

COMM DATA STREAM

After "Mission 01: Prepare to Drop": Hidden COMM Data—7 (Total: 7/30)*

After 4 of 7 COMM Data Found: Supply Cache Set 1 Opens (Total: 1/3 Sets)**

Total Caches Opened: 2/8**

Set 1 Cache Contents: Sniper Rifle (2), Sniper Ammo (2), Magnum (4), Silenced SMG (4), Frag Grenade (4)

*COMM Data Terminals are available only during Rookie missions. These terminals have been deemed "supersecret" and cannot be shown on the Mombasa Streets map.

**Although Set 1 opens two caches, the second cache is not accessible until "Mission 03: Uplift Reserve" begins or unless you repeat this mission.

LEVEL-SPECIFIC ACHIEVEMENTS

Good Samaritan: Killing things that are new and different is bad, alone or with another ODST.

Naughty Naughty: Killing things that are new and different is good, alone or with another ODST.

MISSION OBJECTIVES

NEW MOMBASA Search Uplift Reserve for ODST squadmate

Tayari Plaza to Uplift Reserve

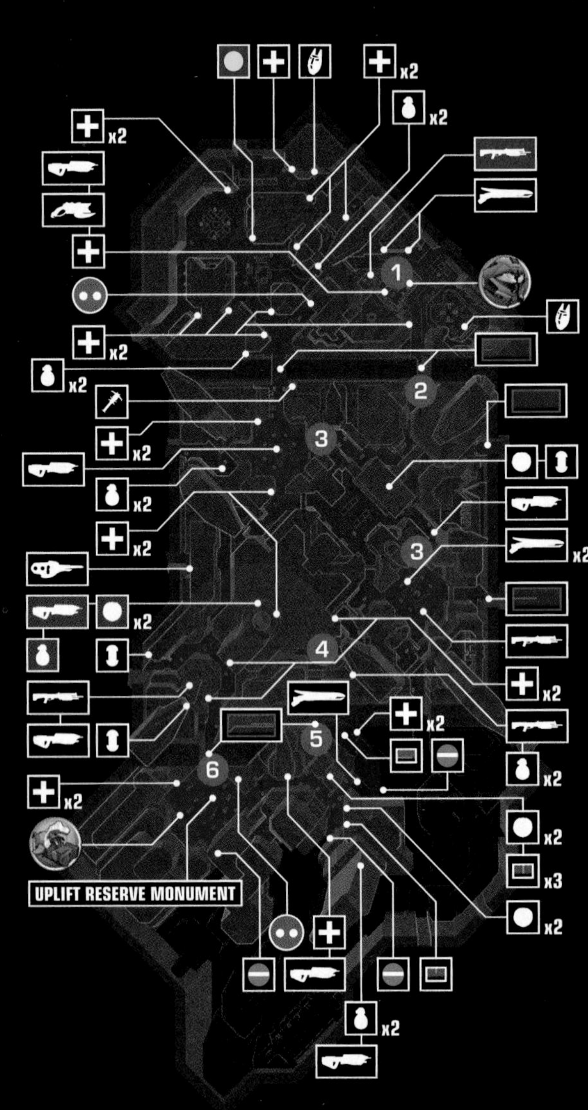

Choke Point 1: Tayari Plaza Crash Site

OBJECTIVE

NEW MOMBASA Search Uplift Reserve for ODST squadmate

ENTITY ENCOUNTERED

Grunts

NOTE **The enemies you encounter during the collective Rookie missions, known as "Mombasa Streets," arrive in random configurations of Grunts, Brutes, and Jackals. You may also chance upon patrols (usually of Brutes and Grunts) throughout this area. Therefore, you may encounter more or fewer enemies compared to the optimal path detailed below. Also note this is a continuation of "Mission 01: Prepare to Drop."**

NOTE **For general combat information, which is useful if you wish to wander off into optional street locations, consult the "Know Your Enemy" and "Weapons Detail" chapters.**

The second and every subsequent time you access this part of the mission, you are able to travel to any of the objectives and therefore begin any of the subsequent missions up to, but not including, "Mission 08: Data Hive." For general knowledge on what enemies to expect, consult the "Mission Hub: Mombasa Streets" section at the end of this chapter.

The action switches to Rookie, back at the building where you found Dare's helmet embedded into the screen. With that oddity solved, you can retrace your steps back through the structure you're inside, ideally following the optimal path toward the Uplift Reserve, located to the southwest of your present location. Head back down the steps, blasting a few Grunts in the corridors of this building, preferably with a Shotgun **[1A]**. Reach the ground floor, taking what you need from near the fallen Marine. Exit via the door to the southeast, which leads into Tayari Plaza **[1B]**. Note the Optican Kiosk on the wall to your right (west) as you head south toward the gate and into Zone 8, where Buck fought a pair of Hunters six hours ago.

Search the Grunt corpses for a dropped Plasma Pistol; depending on your preferences, this may come in very handy during the next combat fracas.

1A

1B

▪ Choke Point 2: Snipers' Walkway (Brute Patrol)

2A

ENTITIES ENCOUNTERED

Engineer

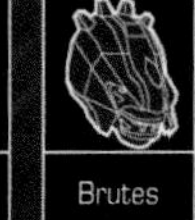
Brutes

Brute Captain

The gate opens, and you can prowl the suspiciously empty lower plaza for a moment, until you hear Brute voices. Stay in cover on the right and listen, or move along the upper balconies right of the gate, toward the walkway, and peer south to this cluster of foes **[2A]**. The Brutes are muttering about placing an explosive device inside an odd floating creature known as the Huragok, or Engineer. If you have your wits about you, you realize this creature is probably an innocent slave to the Brutes, but engage the foes in combat, and you'll discover the Engineer provides troublesome additional shielding, making the ensuing battle much more frantic.

Occupied city center • ROOKIE

Tactic: Naughty or Nice

If you're going for the Good Samaritan Achievement, you cannot harm the Engineer. Concentrate entirely on killing the Brutes. The Engineer still explodes afterward, but that isn't your fault, so you can still access the Achievement.

If you're attempting the Naughty, Naughty Achievement (you can't attempt both), you can kill any Covenant entity with impunity. However, as parts of New Mombasa with more Engineers are currently locked down, you cannot complete this Achievement and must begin it again in a future Rookie mission.

You can defeat Engineers in one of two ways: when you blast them to death, or when you defeat the Brute Captain (clad in armor that gives off a golden hue of electrical discharge when struck). Either way, it's a miserable and short-lived existence!

NOTE **Two Achievements may be referenced during the following combat: Good Samaritan and Naughty, Naughty. For complete knowledge of the Achievements, refer to the "Achievements" section of the appendix.**

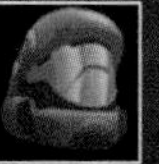
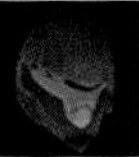

Tactic: Walkway Projectiles

Move onto the Walkway vantage point **[2A]** without being spotted. This gives you the height advantage, as you can easily spot the Brute Captain, which is underneath the Engineer before the enemies start moving. Now you can get in one or two free shots, either by firing a charged Plasma Pistol shot to shatter the Engineer or Brute's shields or by lobbing Plasma or Sticky Grenades onto your chosen foe before continuing with your favored other weapon (such as the Magnum, or the Shotgun at closer quarters on lower difficulty levels). Concentrate on the Brute Captain **[2B]**, as he's tougher and usually armed with a more devastating weapon, such as the Brute Shot.

Tactic: Close-Quarter Mayhem

Thanks to a mixture of ground-level pillars, strafing, and scampering back to the Tayari Plaza for Health Packs, you can survive standing toe-to-claw with the Brute Captain **[2B]**. Punish each foe with a mixture of armor-sapping Grenades and peppering fire. Naturally, a safer alternative is to creep around to a balcony or doorway and snipe if you have the correct equipment.

Whatever your choice, once combat is over, you must head either west (optimal) or southeast, into completely unexplored areas. Follow the debris-strewn road around to the left (south), ignoring the sloping road to your right. Enter a four-sided plaza with steps in the middle **[2C]**, with planters on either side and a pedestrian crossing at the top (southwest). Maintain the critical path by heading down the left (southeast) road from here.

■ Choke Point 3: Optional Areas

TIP **Why explore unnecessary areas? To increase your combat worthiness and collect additional points, to attack foes for weapons you'd rather use, and to continue your search for COMM Data Terminals and a Superintendent Supply Cache!**

ENTITIES ENCOUNTERED

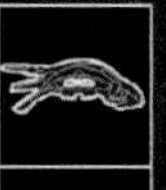
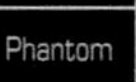
Phantom

Grunts

Jackals

Brutes

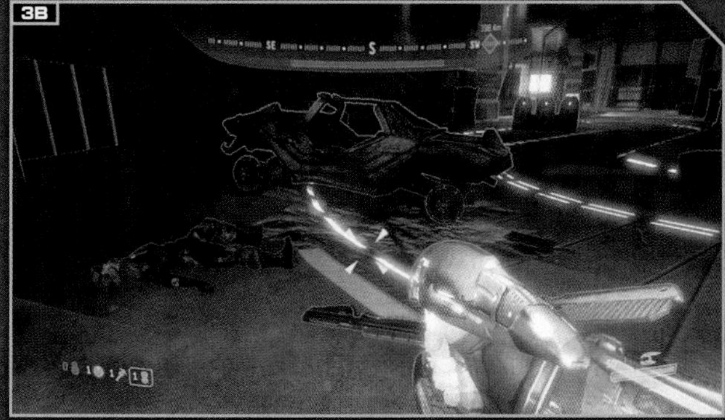
3B

3C

There are two plazas on either side of your critical path and stepped area **[2C]**. The circular plaza to the northwest **[3A]** features a random assortment of foes hopping down from a Phantom and a fierce ensuing firefight. Venture here if you dare. There's an Optican Kiosk here, as well as scattered Grenades and weapons from the fallen foes you slay. In addition, there is a passage back to your initial stomping grounds, which are completely optional to venture through.

To the southeast **[3B]** are two connecting streets and a wrecked Warthog with an Assault Rifle to claim. There is also a compact plaza with a central, hexagonal stone pergola **[3C]** with a phone cluster in the middle of it. This area is usually devoid of life. You can scrounge a few UNSC weapons from ruined Warthogs if you're lucky.

■ Choke Point 4: Brute Stalker Ambush

4A

4B

ENTITIES ENCOUNTERED

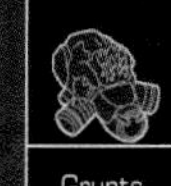
Grunts

Brutes

Brute Stalker

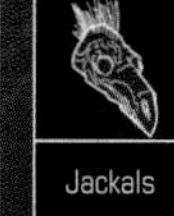
Jackals

Follow the road from the stepped plaza **2C** in a southerly direction, passing an Optican Kiosk (handy for later!), and head around a corner until you're facing west. Use the flickering low video wall as cover, and check for a small Covenant squad, usually a couple of Grunts and a Brute standing near a T-junction **[4A]**. A spot of Carbine firing or any other favored combat technique easily rids you of these foes, allowing you to advance to the junction. The road up the slope to the south is open (leading to **Chokepoint 5**), but the optimal path is east, toward a partially covered plaza where you must tackle a sizable Covenant presence.

The plaza features a protruding roof with numerous giant pillars supporting it to the southwest, under which there are various concrete planters and steps and an Optican Kiosk. Of considerably more interest is a Brute waiting near the kiosk; be sure your VISR's Enhanced Vision is on to easily spot him. He is your first Brute Stalker, and there are two takedown options for him and the Grunts milling about the stairs to the southwest.

Tactic: On Patrol

Immediately seek cover near the sloping road near the barricades **[4B]** outside the central plaza area so you aren't spotted. The following requires both skill and patience, and a good understanding of your Map menu. Flick over to this display, and note the red square showing the Brute's location. Now carefully and silently move toward the Brute, but continuously use your NAV to spot any potential enemies in the vicinity of the Brute's patrol pattern. Learn this pattern, then sneak up and melee the Brute Stalker to death without raising the alarm.

Tactic: Failure Is an Option

If you blow your cover or fire a shot from a weapon that cannot completely kill the Brute (such as from the Carbine), the Brute immediately engages his Active Camo ability, making him difficult to pin down. Use your VISR's vision and carefully scan the area between where you last saw the Brute and your current location. Lay down some fire when you spot the Brute's faint yellow outline. Then finish with your favored, Brute-killing attacks. Try to stay near the barricades **[4B]** to avoid being swarmed by additional Covenant to the southwest and west.

It is now worth maneuvering toward the central Optican Kiosk to take care of any random Covenant patrols; there are likely to be two—one to the west and the other to the southwest, at the top of the stairs behind some defenses **[4C]**. Head up the left (south) road ramp, hugging the low concrete wall on your right to minimize Stamina damage, and attack while you're closer to the second Optican Kiosk. A mixture of Brutes, Grunts, and Jackals greet you in this area, so be prepared. Use the available cover to your advantage, wiping out all foes, then gather the weapons you wish. There are dead Marines under the overhang behind the defenses you can take Assault Rifles from.

Once this area is completely devoid of foes, heal up and optionally head northeast to check an underground, circular roadway complete with a variety of weapons and a terminal of interest. However, be aware that you might run into another small Covenant patrol in the plaza as you exit. There is a dead end to the west, close to the top of the steps **[4C]**. Check there. By now, you should be peering down every dark dead-end alley on either side of each gate for possible Grenades. Now you can continue to the Uplift Reserve entrance or optionally check a winding street to Dead-End Plaza.

■ Choke Point 5: Zone 9, Dead-End Plaza (Optional)

ENTITIES ENCOUNTERED

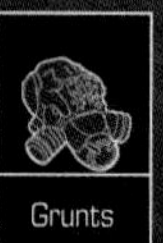
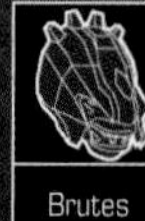
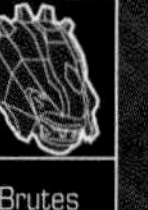

Grunts	Brutes	Jackals

If you're thoroughly scanning the area for COMM Terminals, enter the gate south of **Waypoint 4A**: Behind is a thin, winding road and a balcony on your left **[5A]** that a Jackal is sometimes patrolling. Defeat him, and set up a camping spot here if you wish. The Grunts and Brutes you can tag from this recommended cover have erected an impenetrable energy wall, which doesn't allow you eastward; however, you can take the road that curves around to the northwest, eventually allowing you into the final area, or you can head south toward the open area itself.

The second way of entering here is via Choke Point 6. From the weapons cache **[6A]**, you can venture down the curved road to the east **[5B]**, tagging a Shield Jackal, ideally using ordnance appropriated from the cache. There's also a balcony to your left (north) along the road, with a dead Marine near a weapon and a Health Pack. This allows you to enter the plaza itself **[5C]**, which has Covenant defenses dotted around and low concrete walls for perfect cover. No matter from which direction you've entered this dead end, there's a Grunt manning a Plasma Turret that needs defeating. Use a long-range Grenade lob or a sniped shot. Beware of armored Brutes roaming here, although the Plasma Turret is an excellent way to rid yourself of them.

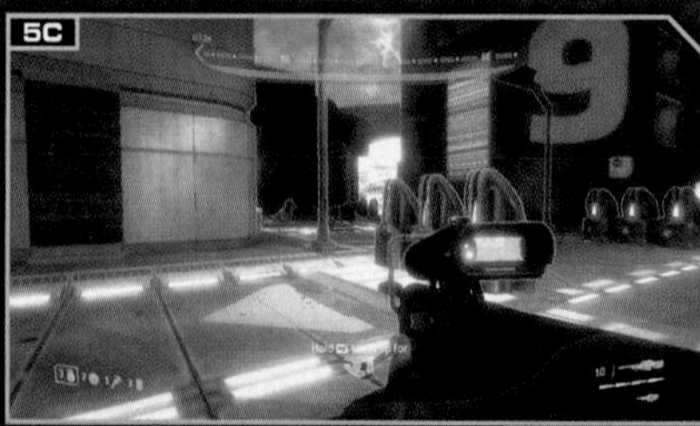

■ Choke Point 6: Uplift Reserve Entrance

6A

The optimal way to access this final area (also in Zone 9) is via a road and a gate leading south from the top of the stepped defenses area **[4C]** or via the road you can access from the optional area **[5A]**. Either way, you appear to one side of a weapons cache **[6A]**. If you followed the COMM Terminal hints at the beginning of this section, this should be open, allowing you access to it; this is one of two in the general vicinity. The other cache is located near the initial plaza you tore through during "Mission 01: Prepare to Drop" and is available only from "Mission 03: Uplift Reserve" and subsequent missions. Grab what you require. There are Sniper Rifles, ammunition, Magnums, Silenced SMGs, and Frag Grenades in each cache. These are all particularly helpful for clearing the optional enemies at Choke Point 5.

6B

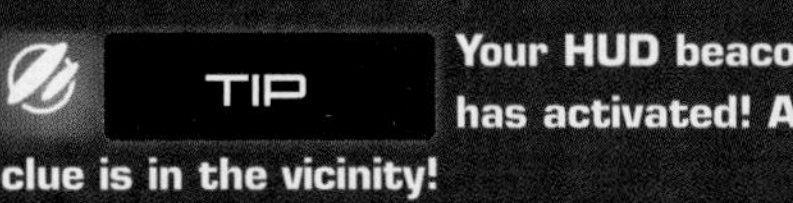

Your HUD beacon has activated! A clue is in the vicinity!

Now face southwest, checking the nearby upper (and inaccessible) balconies for Sniper Jackals. Tag any you see using a ranged weapon. Finish any remaining patrols as you work your way around the badly damaged Uplift monument **[6B]** in the middle of the entrance plaza. Retrieve a Health Pack from the Optican Kiosk to the north before checking the foot of the curved stairs to the southwest **[6C]** for a piece of machinery that shows up yellow in VISR Enhanced Vision: Drone Fighter Optics.

6C

Tactic: On Patrol (Again)

Attempting to attack this location or the Dead-End Plaza on a higher difficulty involves stopping to take cover (such as close to the weapons cache or on an upper balcony that isn't being swarmed by foes) and learning your foes' patrol patterns. When one moves into your line of sight, tag it from extreme range or outflank the Grunts and assassinate them silently.

Mission 03: Uplift Reserve

DUTCH • Uplift Nature Reserve • 30 minutes after drop

Landing on the outskirts of the Uplift Reserve (a giant savannah-type nature reserve close to a suborbital space elevator), you (as Dutch) begin with a Spartan Laser and several nearby UNSC Marines with whom to rendezvous. After locating a Warthog, you defeat several Covenant pockets of resistance as you drive across the undulating terrain, attempting to locate a lost platoon of soldiers. Once you find the remains of these forces, you cull additional Covenant until you're able to head across a bridge; witness the epic destruction of the elevator; and fight to the edge of New Mombasa, where you face your toughest concentration of foes and find a way into the city streets.

Dutch Drop-Pod Location to New Mombasa Perimeter

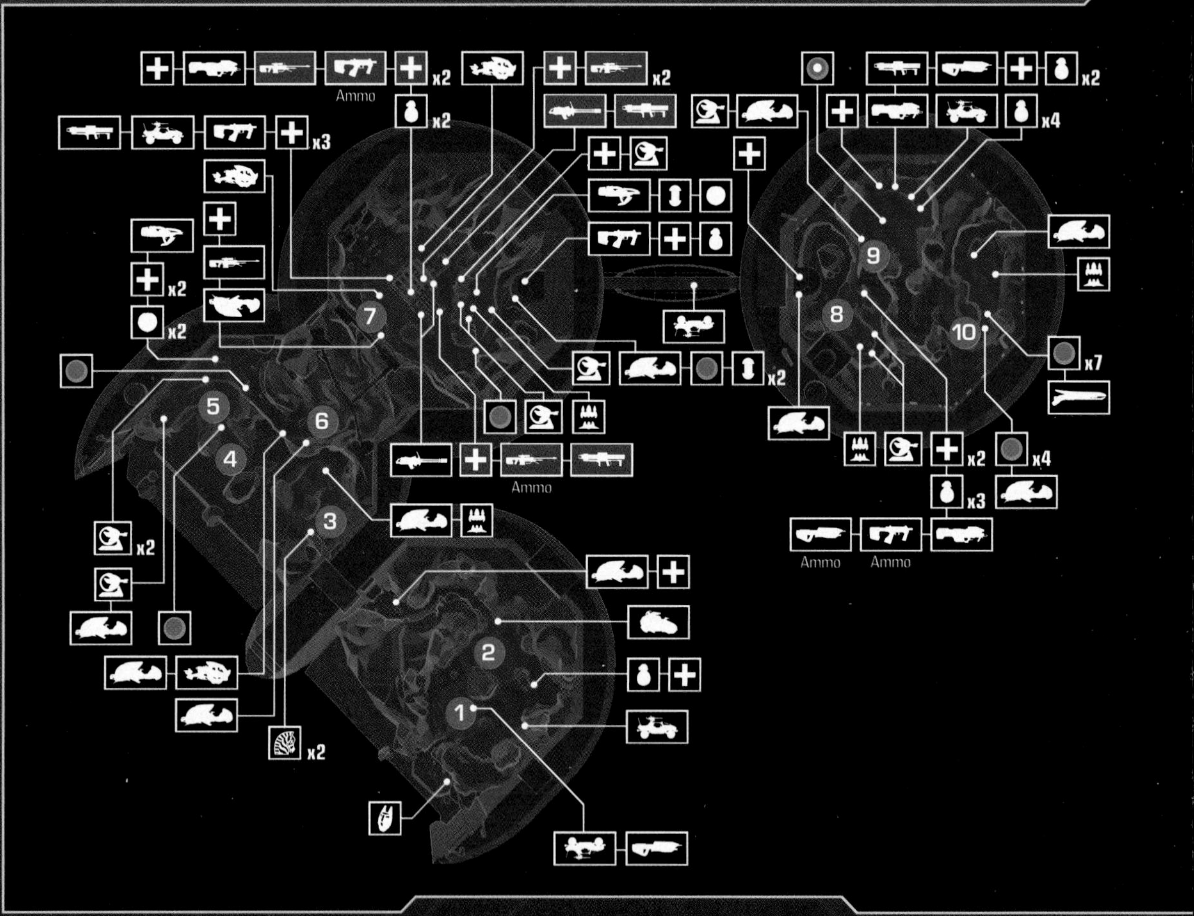

DATA STREAM

Uplift Reserve VISR Target Acquisition Mode Ratio: 5 percent*

*COMM Data Terminals are available only during Rookie missions.

PREFERRED WEAPONS

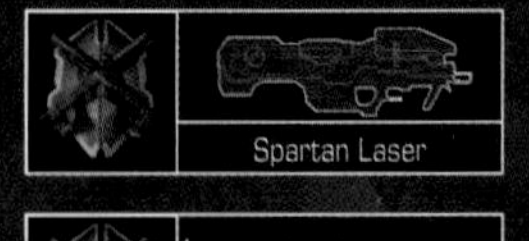

Spartan Laser

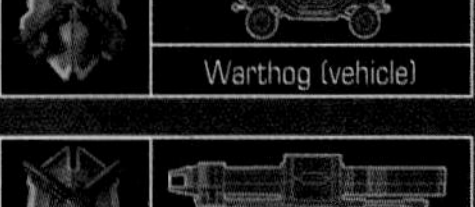

Warthog (vehicle)

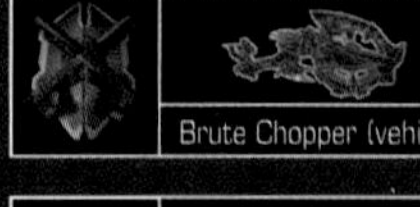

Brute Chopper (vehicle)

Sniper Rifle

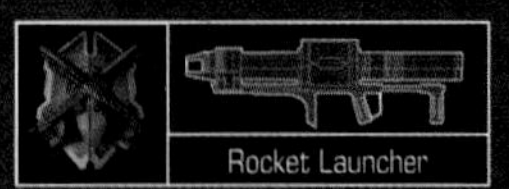

Rocket Launcher

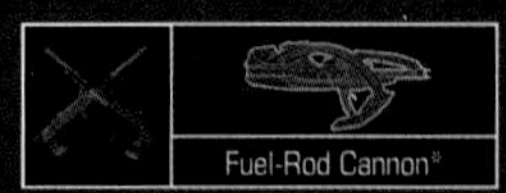

Fuel-Rod Cannon*

*Hand this weapon to a Marine in the passenger seat of a Warthog you're in.

MISSION OBJECTIVES

- UPLIFT RESERVE Link up with friendly forces
- UPLIFT RESERVE Find Marine Second Platoon
- UPLIFT RESERVE Find Colonel across bridge
- UPLIFT RESERVE Drive up and out of park

PAR SCORE

60,000

LEVEL-SPECIFIC ACHIEVEMENTS

Wraith Killer: Kill all Wraiths in Uplift Reserve

Vidmaster Challenge: Classic—Finish any level solo on Legendary, on LIVE, with no shots fired or grenades thrown.*

*This Vidmaster Challenge can be attempted on any Campaign mission; this is simply the easiest one to achieve it on.

NOTE

For cunning methods of completing these Achievements, consult the Appendices.

■ Choke Point 1: Overturned Warthog

ENTITIES ENCOUNTERED

UNSC Marines

UNSC Warthogs

Grunts

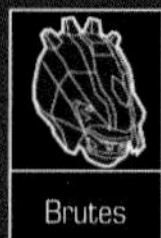
Brutes

OBJECTIVE

UPLIFT RESERVE-Link up with friendly forces

From your smoking escape Pod, check your available weaponry (a Silenced SMG and a devastating Spartan Laser), and trek northeast up a trail, passing the remains of a reserve map (which is far less detailed than your NAV map, which reveals a series of massive, outdoor bowl-shaped clearings linked with winding trails). Rendezvous with a squad of Marines as they locate an overturned Warthog **[1A]**, and fire on a group of Grunts and an armored Brute. Look to the northwest to engage the enemy.

CAUTION **UNSC Trooper armor isn't known for its buoyancy, as you'll discover if you wade too far out into the water; keep your feet or vehicle on dry land to avoid that sinking feeling.**

Tactic: A Short, Sharp Shock

As you engage the Covenant squad on the slightly higher ground **[1B]**, you should employ short, controlled Silenced SMG blasts to knock down the Grunts nearest to you and any about to throw Grenades; then tackle the armored Brute using the same weapon. You can use the Spartan Laser, but lining up the shot isn't the easiest plan, and dealing with suicide Grunts can be a pain. With the Marines backing you up (as long as you're attacking the Covenant near the UNSC forces), you can destroy them in seconds. Quickly flip the overturned Warthog and enter the driver's seat. Wait for two Marines to occupy the passenger and Turret locations; you'll need them both for the incoming mechanized enemies.

CAUTION **You can take the passenger or Turret positions in this Warthog, but these are far more problematic for your ongoing survival; you're just wasting ammunition if you take the passenger side. However, if you have control of your Warthog, you can drive out of dangerous situations, and Marines make more proficient Turret gunners than drivers.**

Tactic: Laser of Death

Your Spartan Laser is a truly devastating weapon in the right hands. And in this case, the "right hands" means your Marine passenger. Hand the Spartan Laser to him while you drive; he has the luxury of unlimited ammunition while he holds this weapon, allowing him to destroy far more foes than you're able to.

■ Choke Point 2: Covenant Drop Zone

ENTITIES ENCOUNTERED

Phantom

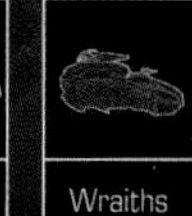
Wraiths

Brute Choppers

Ghosts

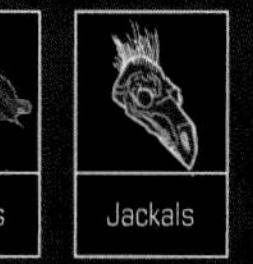
Jackals

There's a violent confrontation playing out among the undulating scrubland. With the space elevator in the distance, head northeast. You must clear this expansive area of enemy vehicles. You'll almost immediately encounter a Wraith, a Ghost, a Chopper, and a group of Jackals **[2A]**.

Tactic: Laser Strikes

f you're after the Wraith kill for personal reasons, ou can opt to park the Warthog behind cover (this is specially important, as your Marines become prone if ou don't), and quickly aim your Spartan Laser on the Wraith. The weapon takes a few seconds to warm up, o make sure you have a clear shot but aren't being fired upon by foes. Once the Laser strikes, dash back to your Warthog.

Tactic: Warthog of Courage

With no room for mistakes, it is imperative you deal with the Wraith as early as possible. The easiest way to complete this is to drive as close to the Wraith as you can without being instantly destroyed by its mortar, and then circle around the grav-tank until your Marine cohorts bombard it with enough firepower o destroy it. The key here is continuous movement; if you slow or stop for even a second, the Wraith launches an attack on you.

CAUTION **You can leap from your vehicle, jump onto the Wraith, and melee attack it until it explodes. This is a last-ditch effort, as this plan is dangerous both to yourself and the squadmates you've left driverless.**

A few moments later, a Phantom descends from the sky while a second Wraith enters the northwest corner of the initial scrubland clearing **[2B]**. The tactic for finishing this tank is the same as detailed previously. By now, your crew should have easily defeated any Jackals in the area (you can help by e-braking over them, splattering them across the grass). However, you can now either hijack the Ghost or Chopper, or drive toward them as the Marines on your Warthog blast them to bits. There are advantages and disadvantages of using a Covenant vehicle over your trusty Warthog: The Chopper and Ghost allow you to drive and shoot at the same time; the Warthog requires a separate Turret gunner. However, the Warthog is well built and able to absorb more damage than a Ghost or Chopper. There's no "wrong" choice here; choose your preferred method of transportation.

TIP **It might be wise to take a Chopper or a Ghost (if you want to vary your firepower or want a different handling vehicle), as the UNSC Marines usually send a Warthog to accompany you anyway. If your Warthog was badly damaged in the attacks against the Wraiths, move to the clearing, where you can obtain an undamaged Warthog and any Health Packs you need.**

When there's more than one of you attacking the Covenant, it makes most sense to have one player in a Warthog with Marines, while other members take a second Warthog, Chopper, and Ghost (if you manage to hijack all the available vehicles instead of destroying them).

Wraith Killer Achievement

There are six Wraiths throughout this mission. Instead of fleeing from them, you must eliminate them. Note that when a UNSC teammate or a cooperative player engages a Wraith, you must damage a Wraith in order for the kill to be counted toward this Achievement. If you don't help with the kill, and the Wraith is destroyed, your Achievement becomes untenable.

■ Choke Point 3: Endangered Species

Exit Choke Point 2 by heading along the trail to the northwest, which winds around to a humped tunnel interior. En route, UNSC aircraft are seen in the sky, and your objective updates: you must reach the Marine Second Platoon immediately. There's a parked Ghost at the entrance to the humped tunnel; this tunnel leads out to Zone 3, where you'll immediately encounter light resistance.

UPLIFT RESERVE Find Marine Second Platoon

ENTITIES ENCOUNTERED

Jackals | Grunts | Brutes

Tactic: Angles of Attack

Emerge from the short tunnel and let your gunner strafe the Jackals in front (northwest) of you, behind the hastily erected barricades **[3A]**. Of greater threat is a Grunt and a couple of Brutes on a ridge top slightly right (north) of you; one of the Grunts has a Fuel Rod Cannon, which can damage or destroy your vehicle very easily. Combat this by moving continuously and allowing your gunner a clear line of sight. Then drive west, over the hump by the dead zebra, to the shore. Move around a pond and head to the ridge, which has a Watchtower and a parked Ghost **[3B]**. Keep driving and firing on the foes; pick off the Brutes in the Watchtower first, then the Ghost drivers, but watch for incoming Grenades.

Tactic: Cannon of Carnage

If you're driving the Warthog, it is wise to disembark after combat, collect the Fuel Rod Cannon from the Grunt your squadmate recently shot, and hand it off to the Marine in the passenger seat. Do this even if he has the Spartan Laser, as the Fuel Rod Cannon has a much faster rate of fire, and the Marines are more accurate with it, compared to the Laser. The Cannon has unlimited ammo in the hands of the Marine, making your vehicle a real threat to the Covenant squads operating in this theater of war.

By now, you should have vehicles for each member of your squad; tackling foes from four different directions spreads out your enemy's fire, preventing them from concentrating on you and enabling you to assault the forthcoming choke points with ease.

Choke Point 4: Banshee Bombardment

ENTITY ENCOUNTERED

Banshees

Close to the ridge where you destroyed Brutes on a Watchtower at the previous choke point, there is a pond. Skirt this area and face east; multiple Banshees are visible in the sky and begin to swoop down, bombarding you with their energy bolts. You have two decisions to make: stand and fight, or flee to Choke Point 5. The former plan is preferable, as it makes the subsequent encounter significantly less dangerous. Try not to flee, especially since you need to destroy only one Banshee: the rest flee once one of them is downed.

Tactic: Plasma-Pistol Packing

Taking down a Banshee effectively depends on the vehicle you're driving. The weapon systems on a Ghost or a Brute Chopper aren't designed to take down a swooping Banshee, and you'll need to face uphill to even stand a chance of hitting one. Don't waste time with this tactic; instead, grab a Plasma Pistol from a Grunt corpse back at Choke Point 3, and fire a charged shot at the Banshee; this knocks it out of the sky intact. You can't pilot it, though. If you don't have a Plasma Pistol, then a well-aimed Spartan Laser shot works, too, as does a rapid-fire weapon that hits instantly.

Tactic: Gunner Earning His Pay

If you're using the UNSC Warthog, your Marine buddies make short work of the nearest Banshee as soon as they spot the flying fiends. Simply let the Gunner (or passenger) do their job, then carry on to Choke Point 5. This is preferable to stopping the Warthog and aiming the Turret yourself; you're simply making the Banshee's attacks a guaranteed success, as you're now stationary and prone.

You are driving a vehicle and not plodding through this massive terrain on foot, right?!

■ Choke Point 5: Zone 3 Perimeter Bluff

ENTITIES ENCOUNTERED

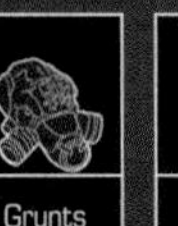
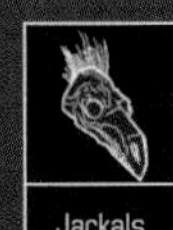

Grunts | Jackals | Brutes

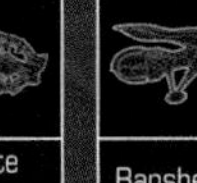

Shade Turrets | Brute Choppers | Banshees

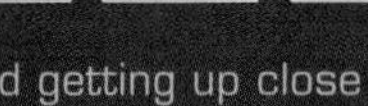

Continue across the rocky terrain to a trail leading north. You encroach on a heavily defended bluff with a variety of foes dug in, including three Shade Turrets and vehicles that intercept you as you near the curved slope that leads left (southwest) to the top plateau. Although there's an overabundance of foes to tackle at once, there are two surefire ways of minimizing your chances of death: ranged warfare and getting up close and personal (see tactics below).

CAUTION **Did you send the flying Banshees away at the previous choke point? If you didn't, they also attack you, severely impeding your chances of survival. It is imperative you strike down one or more before you reach this choke point.**

Tactic: Ranged Warfare

Better safe than sorry: The rocky terrain below the bluff, where you approach from, has numerous boulders and trees you can use as cover, either in or out of a vehicle **[5A]**. Coax a Chopper down and take it out (either by waiting for it or zooming forward to the bluff before quickly retreating). Managing your takedowns one at a time, at your own pace, is safer and reveals the limitations of the Covenant's defenses (e.g., the Shade Turrets can't move from their stationary position). You, however, are highly mobile, and the Shade Turrets are located in very visible places, allowing you to use your favored ranged weapon (Sniper Rifle, Fuel Rod Cannon, Rocket Launcher, or Magnum) to tag the Turret user from distance. Then take pot shots at the infantry on the bluff; you can easily defeat the majority of the Covenant before you drive up and onto the bluff.

Tactic: Up Close and Personal

Or, you can use your vehicle and drive up and around the ramped area to the bluff's top, shooting (or watching your Marines shoot) as you go. Continuous movement is crucial to your safety. Quickly take down the Shade Turrets **[5B]**, driving straight into them, and circle them at close range so they can't target you. Destroy these first, then splatter, ram, and e-brake (or Boost) your way through the remaining stragglers.

TIP **If you're not worried about the Marines in your Warthog, or if you're driving a Covenant vehicle, park it near an empty Shade Turret, then man the Turret and lay waste to the remaining troops along the bluff, ideally from either end of the bluff so you aren't outflanked.**

Tactic: The Bypass Boost

Hate extra points but love living? Then use a Brute Chopper to head northeast, toward the sloped ground below the bluff, and then quickly Boost up the otherwise-too-steep cliff wall and onto the end of the bluff. Speed away to Choke Point 6. You'll bypass this choke point entirely, which quickens your time and keeps you safe.

If you attempted either of the first two tactics, you can inspect the Covenant bodies for equipment, including a Fuel Rod Cannon. Unfortunately, if you do this, you may miss the Brute on a Ghost that speeds away from this confrontation to warn the forces ahead.

Choke Point 6: Shooting the Messenger

ENTITY ENCOUNTERED

Ghost

If you're mopping up Covenant stragglers at the bluff as you begin taking control of this area, you may miss a Brute fleeing the scene on a Ghost, with the express intention of warning the forces ahead. If you let this lone Brute escape, Wraiths at Choke Point 7 are alerted to your presence and are ready for you. Tackle the Ghost rider by driving alongside it using the Warthog and letting your Turret gunner do his rapid-fire job. If you're driving a Chopper or Ghost yourself, you need to both fire and drive to catch up to the Ghost. The trail through the rocky terrain to the platoon outpost branches left and right **[6]**. Both paths merge again before the large expansive platoon area, so take the considerably shorter left route so you can meet your fleeing foe (who always takes the right path) and demolish him efficiently.

■ Choke Point 7: Lost Platoon Outpost

ENTITIES ENCOUNTERED

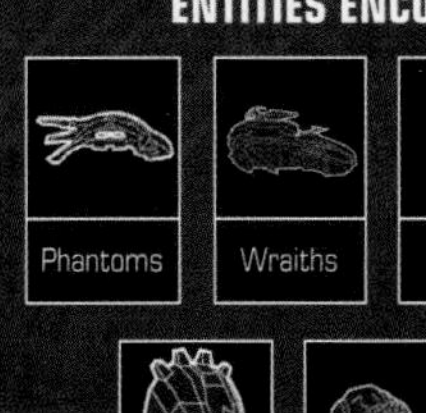

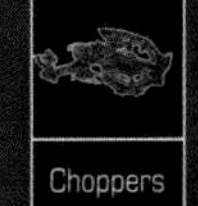

Phantoms · Wraiths · Shade Turrets · Choppers

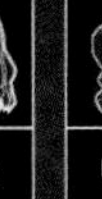

Brutes · Grunts · Jackals

Whether you caught the fleeing Ghost or not, enter the Lost Platoon Outpost heading northeast. Enter a large roundabout and observation plateau **[7A]**. Back up as a Phantom is hovering overhead; it moves on after a few seconds, and you don't want to be struck by its Plasma Turret fire. The roundabout has an upturned Ghost, Health Pack, and Sniper Rifle near a small metal barrier to the right (east). Your tactics in this area can vary wildly, but the optimal ones are shown below, based on whether the Covenant knows you're inbound or not.

Tactic: A Sniper Surprise

If you destroyed the Ghost before it reached the roundabout plateau, then it's a great idea to disembark from your vehicle and take the Sniper Rifle. Now peer northeast toward a rocky hill **[7F]** on the opposite side of this expansive location. On the hill are two Wraiths, but they are silent and not forewarned. The Covenant are slowly patrolling but are unaware of you; this makes headshots an excellent way to drop some otherwise-hardened targets and makes the subsequent fight a lot easier. The enemy type you aim for is crucial here; tag a Chopper-riding Brute in the head, then take down the Shade Turrets in this area. This galvanizes the Covenant into action!

Tactic: An Incoming Mortar

Did you leave the Ghost to warn the assembled Covenant in this choke point? Then expect the Ghost and a Chopper to be patrolling the general area and the Wraiths on the far hill to be active, launching volleys of plasma mortar that spells instant doom if it engulfs you. You can still grab the Sniper Rifle and try to get a few shots off, but nowhere near as many as you'd like; flee to the outpost building a few seconds later.

NOTE

This section of Uplift Reserve is the "Firefight Mission: Lost Platoon." You can drive around this Firefight Map at your leisure to pinpoint the topography. Of course, the weapon drops are completely different.

Uplift Nature Reserve • DUTCH

OBJECTIVE
UPLIFT RESERVE Find Colonel across bridge

Assuming you have the time and accuracy, you should drive your vehicle down the ramp to the left (northwest), to the flat ground to the north. Drive toward the opening in the north wall of the building **[7B]**, and rendezvous with the lost platoon in the process—a ragtag group of Marines who have a variety of equipment to purloin! Your objective updates as you quickly sift through the items: There's an undamaged Warthog, Health Packs, and ammunition, and on the ground there's a Marine carrying a Spartan Laser. On the open-air roof mezzanine level of the building are Sniper Rifles, more Health Packs, a second Marine wielding a Spartan Laser, and a couple of Rocket Launchers. You can access these immediately, although it is better to catch the Covenant by surprise as quickly as possible, and return here to grab these items. You now have multiple ways to finish this fight; two of the best are detailed here.

7C

7D

7E

Tactic: Vehicular Bruteslaughter

Ready to cause mass havoc and hopefully not destroy your vehicle in the process? Then run to the driver's seat of the undamaged Warthog (or, if you don't trust anyone but yourself, grab a Ghost), and wait for two Marines to join you. Furnish the passenger with a Spartan Laser, a Fuel Rod Cannon, or a Rocket Launcher if he doesn't have one. When you're tooled up, drive around either side of the building, heading for combat with several Brute Choppers and Ghosts patrolling the area **[7C]**. Lay waste to both vehicle types, circling them. Do not leave a Brute Chopper open to line itself up with you, as it has a highly damaging ram and weapon attack!

Your next focus should be on the two Wraiths that are floating down the slope from the hill to the rocky gully at this area's southern end. On higher difficulties, you must be much more cautious, but generally, you want to temporarily stop your vehicle on the flat roundabout, where it is hidden by the edge of the bluff of this plateau **[7A]**. Edge southeast, so you or your Marines have a clear view of the first Wraith at the bottom of the slope **[7E]** (this shows where the Wraith is; your Warthog should be parked on the plateau), and begin firing. When the Wraith launches its mortar, drive closer still, using the edge of the roundabout as cover, and continue to rake the Wraith with fire. Then do the same with the second Wraith to easily and quickly dispatch them. Of course, you could try circling them at **[7E]**, but this is much more dangerous and is not recommended on higher difficulties.

Once you've defeated both Wraiths, you can move toward their smoking husks and up the slope to the hill **[7F]** to begin mopping up the Covenant stragglers. You did take care of the Shade Turret at the rear of the hill, didn't you? Or if you're playing it extra safe, you can let the Marines do this job. They should have dealt with the Jackals on the central building, too. Stop and grab any equipment you want, then head toward the tunnel to the bridge **[7G]**.

Tactic: Bringing Out the Big Guns

Move your vehicle to the north side of the outpost structure **[7B]**, pausing to check the room behind the parked Warthog for any equipment you may need; then bound up the stairs to the open second floor of this structure **[7D]**. If you've arrived here early enough, the open area isn't swarming with Jackals, so you can turn right (west) and take a Sniper Rifle. Then swing around and run toward the overhang section of the building with a Turret on it. Use the wall as cover before peering out at the enemies on the hill **[7F]** and tagging the foe operating a Shade Turret. Aim for the head to take down the foe in a single shot. Aim wisely: When he fires back, you have a second or two to finish him off before his plasma shots reach you. Use the wall as cover so you aren't struck. Your fighting attracts Jackals, and they head up to this roof space from the side stairs. Mow them down quickly, and then continue to shoot all Shade Turret operators; these devices should all be empty. Follow this up with any other infantry foes on the hill.

When this occurs, peer down to ground level, stay on the roof, and locate any patrolling Choppers or Ghosts. These must be destroyed, ideally when the vehicles are moving directly toward or away from you, to aid you in lining up the shot. You can tag the driver's head with your Sniper Rifle or try a less subtle approach—taking a Rocket Launcher, using a Fuel Rod Cannon you found earlier, or swapping weapons with a Marine carrying a Spartan Laser. Remember that some projectile weapons (such as the Rocket Launcher) arc their missiles, so fire at where you think your targeted vehicle will be, not where it is when you fire. When all the vehicles except the two Wraiths are neutralized, move toward the hill. Locate the bus stop and move up the metal steps embedded into the hillside; the Wraiths are usually behind the hill if you haven't attracted too much attention yet. Edge forward with your Rocket Launcher or Spartan Laser, and when you spot part of a Wraith near the bridge entrance **[7G]**, blast the vehicle. With both destroyed, locate a favorite vehicle (and Marines armed with your favored weapons if you wish), and head to the bridge entrance.

> **TIP** **When executing Shade Turret operators from a distance, be mindful that other Brutes move into the Turret operator's chair. This makes them easy targets! Ignore the Brutes near the Shade Turrets, and tag the operator instead; it stops the Brutes berserking if you get a torso strike on one standing around.**

Enter the bridge tunnel entrance, passing a parked Ghost and an overturned but undamaged Warthog; as you try and locate the Colonel, the elevator collapses. During this time, the Colonel drops radio contact after the tether disengages, and he dies. Your objective updates. Cross the bridge, passing another parked Ghost at the eastern end.

OBJECTIVE

UPLIFT RESERVE Drive up and out of park

▪ Choke Point 8: Forward Encampment

ENTITIES ENCOUNTERED

Grunts

Jackals

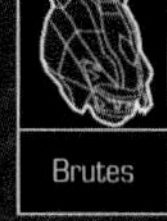
Brutes

Shade Turrets

Wind your way up the dusty trail until you spot a small Covenant forward encampment **[8A]**. There are Jackals and Grunts milling around a beacon and a small set of defenses, with a Brute in the Watchtower behind them and two Shade Turrets on the continuation of the cliff path. There are two ways to minimize these threats, detailed here.

Tactic: Circle-Strafing

Drive your vehicle around the clump of rocks and trees near the small hill in the encampment; keep moving so the Shade Turrets don't strike you. On each circular pass of the camp, cut down, ram, or otherwise dispose of more Covenant. Take out only a few enemies each time before retreating behind the rock clump to recharge your Stamina. When the foes at ground level have met their maker, drive up the cliff-side path to the right (south) and defeat the foes inside the Shade Turrets **[8B]**, either by gunfire or by ramming them (the latter is recommended).

Tactic: Shade Turret Strafing

Turn the Covenant's own weaponry on the ground troops by immediately driving your vehicle along the right cliff-side wall and up around the cliff-side path to the Shade Turrets **[8B]**. Defeat the operator of one, then the other (or ram into the other one). Next, park your vehicle so the foes below can't damage it, step into the Shade Turret, and rake the encampment and all the infantry troops with Turret fire: Revenge is a dish best served with rapid-fire Plasma Bolts.

■ Choke Point 9: Covenant Landing Site

Drive the rest of the way up the cliff-side path, pausing near the small building near the destroyed Warthog if you require a Health Pack or two. Remember to return here if you need more Health during or after this next choke point. Over the rise of the hill ahead (northeast) **[9A]** is a heavily defended plateau. You'll immediately notice a Covenant Carrier grav lift **[9B]**, with Grunts, Jackals, and Brutes milling on and around it. Left of the site is a Shade Turret, and there's a Wraith **[9C]** on the right. Immediately formulate a safe tactic to defeat them all.

ENTITIES ENCOUNTERED

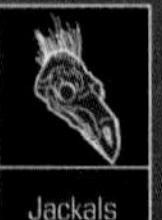

Jackals

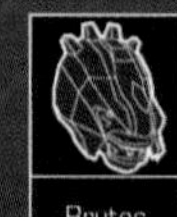

Brutes

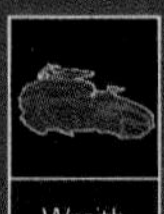

Wraith

Shade Turret

Tactic: Optimal Fallback Position

This tactic provides a manageable, extremely safe, but rather lengthy way to tackle the foes you immediately spot. Fall back to the top of the cliff-side path you just ascended **[9A]**, remaining by the rise and using the protection of the ground; creep forward over the rise, firing at any nearby enemies, starting with the Shade Turret and the Ghost (which usually heads toward you on the cliff-side path). Next, pepper the infantry on the landing platform until all local hostiles are down. As soon as you need to recover Stamina, retreat so the rise protects you. Repeat this tactic as you cut down all the nearby foes.

When only the Wraith remains, you can move into the plateau toward the landing site **[9B]** and begin firing at the Wraith **[9C]**. If you're worried about damage, creep forward on the rise instead, and dart back just as before when the Wraith fires on you. Quickly accelerate or Boost if the Wraith fires on you, and fire on the tank until it explodes. The area should be clear, allowing you to rendezvous with the Marines on the other side of the landing site. Sift through the available equipment if you want any.

TIP

The Warthog is the preferred vehicle to use at the fallback position, mainly because you can park it just behind the lip of the hill. This enables your gunner to fire on the enemies, but the Covenant's aiming is off, as they are aiming for the Warthog's lower armor. As this armor is hidden by the rise of the hill, all their fire strikes the ground instead, effectively making you temporarily invincible!

Tactic: Pride of the UNSC

Instead of a timid strategy, try a more direct approach, driving along the plateau's left edge, past the Shade Turret, and rendezvous with the Marine pinned down behind the landing site structure. There are a few seconds to gather the supplies he has collected, including Frag Grenades, Health Packs, a Spartan Laser, and a Warthog. The Marine is carrying a Rocket Launcher, and this extra firepower soon becomes extremely useful. Exit your vehicle, and maneuver along the left wall until you spot some crates and a recently deceased Marine. If you don't have a Spartan Laser, there's one here. Quickly use it on the Wraith bearing down on you. Return to your Warthog, wait for a couple of Marines to join you, and clear the rest of the Covenant from this area, using the landing site as partial cover.

Tactic: Landing Site Massacre

Constant vehicular movement is key to not being struck by foes. If you're driving a Warthog with a gunner, simply accelerate straight ahead as you reach the top of the cliff-side path, straight onto and over the landing-site platform, splattering any Covenant in your way. Drive down the other side, skid around, and enter the landing site again; do this repeatedly until your Gunner delivers killing blows to everything not Wraith-shaped in the area. You can opt to ram the Shade Turret, too. The Wraith itself can't get an accurate shot on you if you're continuously moving. Now your Gunner turns his attention to the Wraith, which can be destroyed by circling it in your vehicle, waiting for your passenger Marine (who should be armed with a Spartan Laser or other heavy weapon) to score a direct hit, or employing either of the previous Wraith-takedown tactics.

With the landing site cleared of all adversaries, locate the nearby Marines at the equipment cache, and dive into a new Warthog. On closer inspection, the dead Marine at the crates is the recently deceased Colonel mentioned in your objectives. Continue up the hill trail, but only after you've listened to an amusing conversation between a wounded Marine and a medic in this area.

9A

9B

9C

■ Choke Point 10: Hilltop Attack

10A

10B

10C

10D

10E

ENTITIES ENCOUNTERED

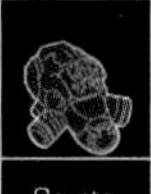
Grunts

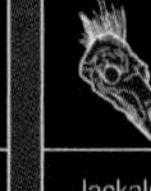
Jackals

Brutes

Brute Chieftain[F]

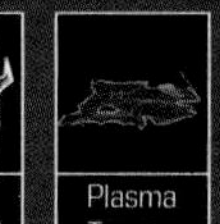
Plasma Turrets

Wraith

[F](Fuel Rod Cannon)

Slow down considerably as you near the crest of the hill and the last major choke point between the Uplift Reserve and New Mombasa's streets. Ahead, a giant section of the elevator has crushed much of a Covenant attack force, but the remaining enemies are still a considerable threat. As you close on the crest of the hill, you may spot two retreating Brutes; try running them over as you ascend. You soon reach the first line of defenses **[10A]**—several Grunts hidden behind a line of Covenant barriers. There's no rush; you don't need to drift to the side of the defenses to defeat them; simply drop any Grunts that show their heads, then disembark from your vehicle and toss a Grenade over the barriers to flush out the rest. There's an empty Ghost here if you want it.

Along the left side of the narrow opening to the crest of the hill are additional defenses: a row of barriers with more Grunts behind them and two Brutes manning Plasma Turrets **[10B]**. Employ the same tactics here, lobbing a Grenade in and tagging Grunts and Brutes with headshots. However, ignore the Brutes in favor of the real threat in this locale: the Chieftain wielding the Fuel Rod Cannon. You'll know which Brute he is; you can't quickly shake off his attack! Approach this cluster of foes and the incoming Wraith, using one of the following optimal tactics.

Tactic: Pedestrian Pulverizing

After tackling the Grunts at the first two sets of defenses, park your vehicle out of range of enemy fire (basically, at the neck of the second set of barriers), and back up until the Phantom leaves the scene. While on foot, rush out along the left wall, using the defenses near the Brute Plasma Turrets for cover if a Chieftain **[10C]** fires on you; then utilize any long-range weapon (Sniper Rifle, Rocket Launcher, Spartan Laser, or Fuel Rod Cannon) to take out the Chieftain first. Next, quickly sidle right, aiming a heavy weapon of your choice at the Wraith to the northwest **[10D]**; make sure it's the one that's still functioning; there's a smoldering Wraith near the small rocky outcrop close to the Brutes. With the Wraith out of commission, lob a couple of well-placed Grenades at the Brutes with the Plasma Turrets, then retreat to your vehicle. Use it to mop up the remaining Brutes near the body of the Chieftain and anything left standing.

Tactic: Hitting and Running

While remaining firmly planted on the ground, drive your vehicle forward so that you or your gunner can get a shot off on the Chieftain **[10C]** before immediately retreating to avoid Fuel Rod fire and the Wraith's mortar. Depending on the vehicle you're using and the competence of the Marine Turret gunner, you may need to repeat the forward-and-back tactic numerous times. When the Chieftain finally falls, and you've edged back so nearby wreckage or rocks are protecting you, focus on any remaining Grunts and Brutes behind the second barrier **[10B]**; you don't want Sticky Grenades landing on your craft. With the left side of this narrow opening cleared, choose any of the previous Wraith-tackling tactics, blasting it repeatedly as you strafe around its shots. Then escape heading north.

Tactic: Less Hitting, More Running

Pushing past the Covenant's defenses and fleeing this choke point is another sound plan; it won't win you any medals of bravery, but you won't need to worry about them being awarded posthumously, either. With some adeptness at driving, you can push straight past the Covenant defenses before they have a chance to react; this means hitting this choke-point entrance hard from the trail, without stopping or slowing. Skid around the corner, and drive straight through the middle of the camp (northwest), aiming for the small rocky bump to the right of the Wraith, flying across the foes, skidding down the exit route, turning right, and heading for the opening in the wall **[10E]** and your escape.

Hit the rocky bump head-on, and try not to flip your vehicle, as you'll be the recipient of Covenant fire from all angles, including the Fuel Rod Cannon–wielding Chieftain and the Wraith.

Uplift Nature Reserve • DUTCH

Mission 03: Mombasa Streets

ROOKIE • After midnight • Occupied city center

Uplift Reserve to Kizingo Boulevard

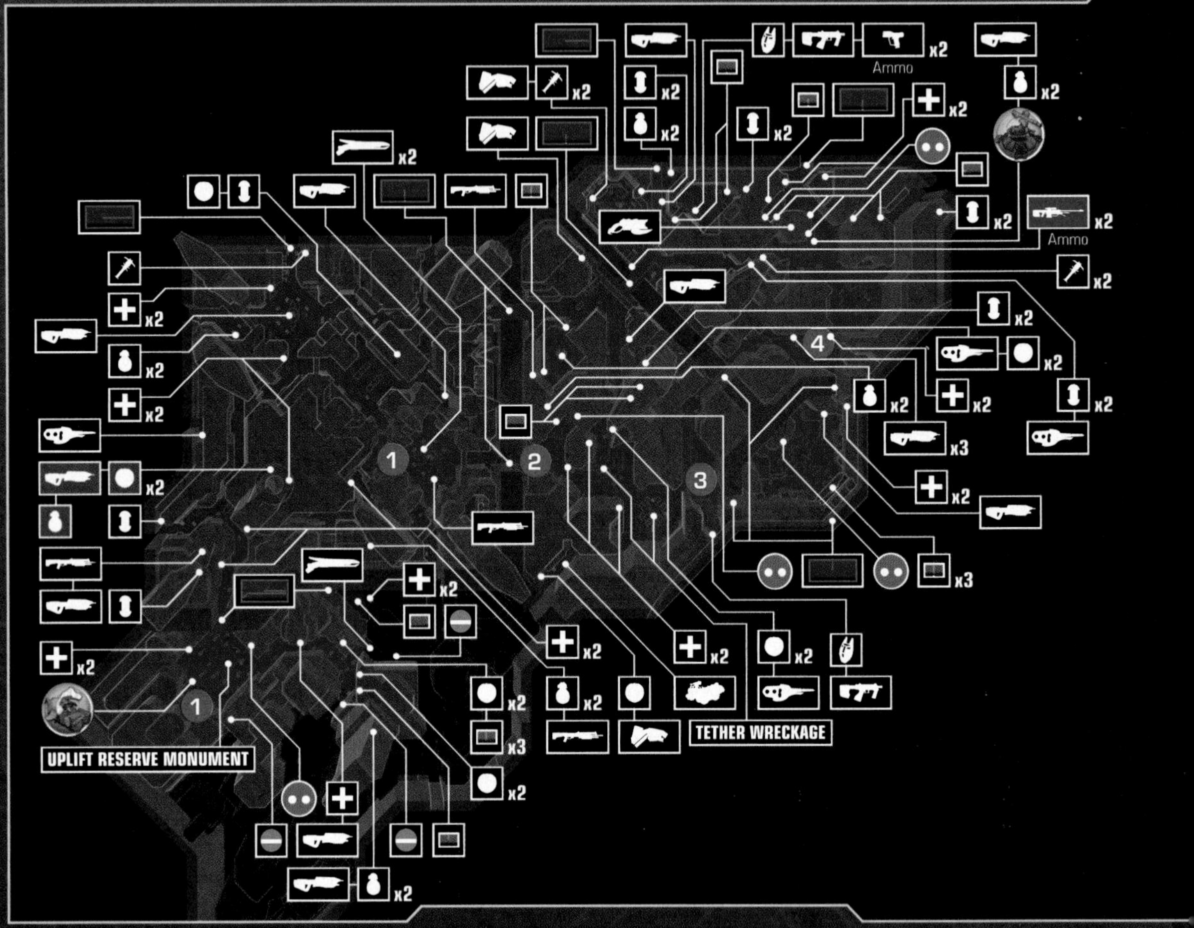

UPLIFT RESERVE MONUMENT

TETHER WRECKAGE

DATA STREAM

New Mombasa VISR Target Acquisition Mode Ratio: 95 percent

PREFERRED WEAPONS

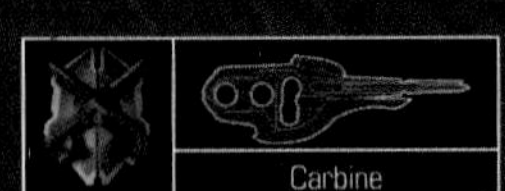
Carbine

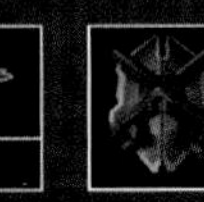

Magnum

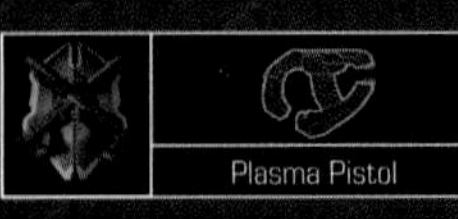
Plasma Pistol

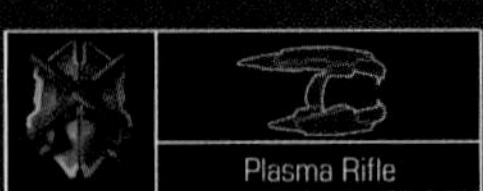
Plasma Rifle

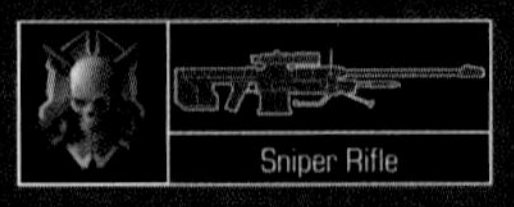
Sniper Rifle

PAR SCORE

MISSION OBJECTIVES

NEW MOMBASA Search Kizingo Boulevard for ODST squadmate

COMM DATA STREAM

After "Mission 01: Prepare to Drop": Hidden COMM Data—7 (Total: 7/30)*

After any three completed missions: Hidden COMM Data—13 (Total: 20/30)*

After any four completed missions: Hidden COMM Data—9 (Total: 29/30)*

After 4 of 7 COMM Data Found: Supply Cache Set 1 Opens (Total: 1/3 Sets)**

After 8 of 20 COMM Data Found: Supply Cache Set 2 Opens (Total: 2/3 Sets)**

After 16 of 29 COMM Data Found: Supply Cache Set 3 Opens (Total: 3/3 Sets)**

Total Caches Available: 8/8**

Set 1 cache contents: Sniper Rifle (2), Sniper Ammo (2), Magnum (4), Silenced SMG (4), Frag Grenade (4)

Set 2 cache contents: Magnum (4), Silenced SMG (4), Frag Grenade (4), Mongoose (2)

Set 3 cache contents: Rocket Launcher (2), Rocket Launcher Ammo (2), Magnum (4), Silenced SMG (4), Frag Grenade (4)

*COMM Data Terminals are available only during Rookie missions. These terminals have been deemed "supersecret" and cannot be shown on the Mombasa Streets map.

**Depending on how many COMM Terminals you have found, between 0 and 8 caches are now available and appear on your in-game map.

NOTE

This mission takes place in Districts 9, 8, 6, and 4. However, depending on when you exit the Uplift Reserve, all accessible Districts of New Mombasa (Districts 0, 3, 4, 5, 6, 8, 9, and 10) could be available to search through. You can optionally locate clues near Kizingo Boulevard, ONI Alpha Site, NMPD Headquarters, and Kikowani Station. The following walkthrough assumes you wish to play through this Campaign in chronological order, and the quickest ways to Kizingo Boulevard are shown. For a full tour of New Mombasa, check the end of this walkthrough.

TIP

Trekking through this maze of streets is much easier if you can locate a Mongoose; these small, fast vehicles are parked inside two of the eight available weapon caches. Their exact locations are shown on the guide map; unfortunately, both caches are on the other side of the city and open only after you discover eight COMM Terminals.

■ Choke Point 1: Uplift Reserve Entrance into Plasma Turret Plaza

ENTITIES ENCOUNTERED

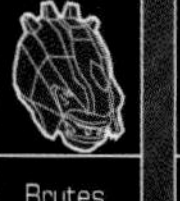
Brutes

Grunts

Jackals

If you need to, stock up on UNSC weaponry from the nearby cache as you head out from the Uplift Reserve Plaza **[A]**, which is strangely silent. Take either the northern or eastern street from this plaza, moving around to either of the perimeter gates to the north, which allow you into District 8. Step into this district and move north (via either of the two streets) until the streets merge at a junction **[1B]**. At the junction, head east, pausing only to visit an L-shaped dead-end alleyway, where you can collect an Assault Rifle and Grenades from a fallen Marine.

The street continues to wind around to the northeast, and you pass an Optican Kiosk; head up the sloping roadway, but slow down as you reach a series of barricades and a possible Covenant patrol at the entrance to a plaza **[1C]**. Back up and snipe these foes; you don't want to attract the enemies inside the plaza, too. Beware of Suicide Grunts as you continue to blast away at a Brute, then finish his smaller friends. Enter the Plasma Turret plaza **[1D]**, ideally hanging back and locating each Grunt manning a different Plasma Turret around the middle of a central gazebo, and plug them with a headshot so you don't face the terrifying prospect of Turret fire *and* Brute combat. When you have secured the Turrets, move farther into the plaza, checking for a Jackal Sniper (use your NAV Menu map to locate enemy traces) and bringing him down. The rest of the plaza has dropped Covenant armaments to gather. When you're ready, move out of District 8, heading west (and possibly confronting a couple more Grunts) to the gate to District 6.

1A

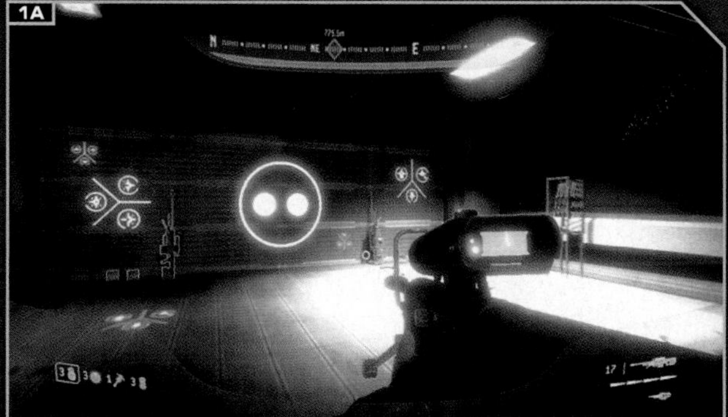

1B

1C

1D

■ Choke Point 2: Engineers' Courtyard to Wrecked Plaza to Lower Plaza

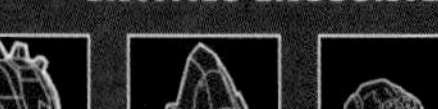

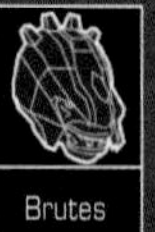
Brutes

Engineers

Grunts

Jackals

2A

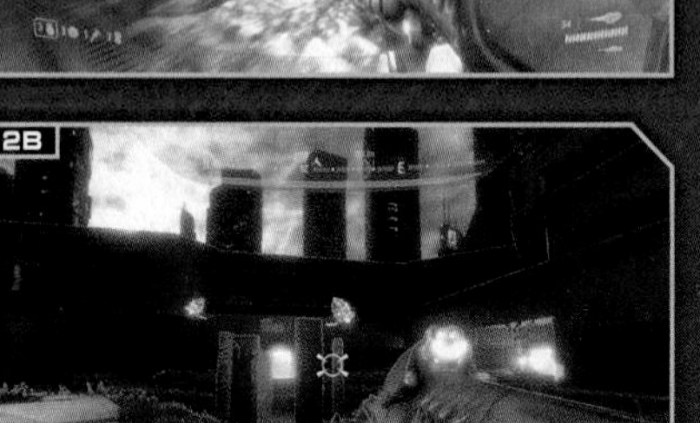
2B

2C

Ahead, to the west, you can just make out the form of a Brute and some crackling debris from the fallen elevator **[2C]**. Investigate that area in a moment, but for now, head northeast, to a weapons cache **[2A]** at the end of the street to your left. Aside from the goods you can grab from the cache (assuming it is unlocked), there's a doorway to your left, allowing you to pass through a building interior, where you can grab Grenades and a Shotgun. Go into an inner outdoor courtyard, where you'll discover two floating Engineers **[2B]**. Don't waste your non-Plasma weaponry on these creatures; their overshield style of protection makes them almost invulnerable; besides, these two aren't aggressive. Either knock both out with a charged Plasma Pistol shot, or simply ignore them, grabbing more Grenades and heading back to the street you just came from.

Move west, plugging the patrolling Brute and his Grunt friends with headshots from your favored weapon, and clamber through the wreckage of this small, stepped plaza **[2C]**. There's some scattered Covenant gear to claim and more Grunts to tag from the stepped concrete planters, which are difficult to navigate, even with your VISR Enhanced Vision constantly active. Move southeast, into a lower plaza, which may have a Jackal to take down **[2D]**. Move northeast, across the stepped area, to a sloping street heading north **[2E]**, where you have a choice of paths; you can optionally enter District 10 via the gate to the east and head into the Rally Point, or you can skirt the perimeter of District 10, moving north along the sloping street.

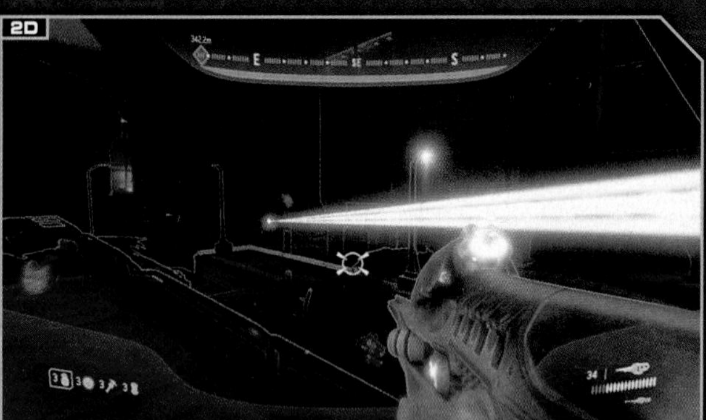
2D

2E

■ Choke Point 3: Street Battles

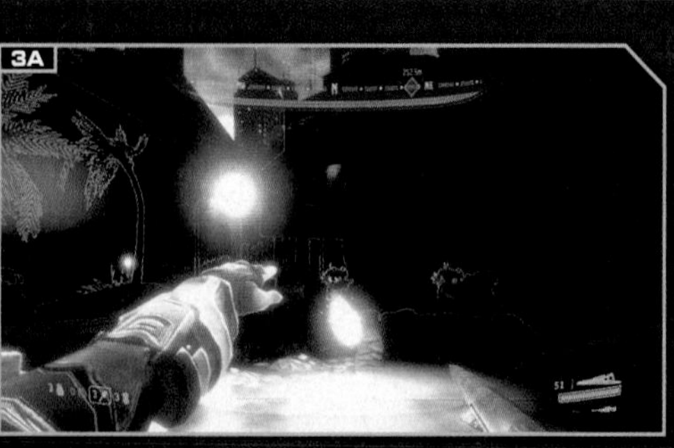
3A

3B

ENTITIES ENCOUNTERED

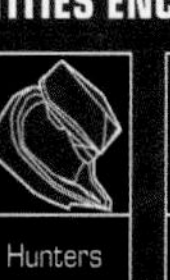
Hunters

Grunts

Jackals

Brutes

Peer ahead and you'll see a stepped area leading down to a sloping road with two hulking Hunters prowling this section **[3A]**. Astute navigators may recognize this as the starting area for Buck's previous mission ("Mission 02: Tayari Plaza"). A mixture of lobbed Grenades and accurate long-range sniping allows you to drop these beasts. Remember you can then return to the previous weapons cache if you need more ordnance. From this point, you can move northeast, attacking a Brute and a Grunt group **[3B]**, or open a district gate using this shortcut, heading straight into the lower portion of the Kizingo Boulevard plaza in District 4 (and Choke Point 4).

Assuming you moved down the side street, attacking the Brute and Grunts **[3B]**, continue to follow the path Buck took in the previous mission, heading north up a narrow street with foes at the far end. Attack the Brute, Jackals, and Grunts **[3C]**, defeating them as you push up the sloped road or adjacent stairs, tagging a Jackal on the walkway ahead of you. Then pass through into District 4 at the gate just northeast of the walkway. Push east, ignoring the sunken plaza to the north; instead, move along the narrow street, looking for Jackal Snipers on low staircase balconies **[3D]**. Check the area for dropped Grenades and other items. This street leads to a sidewalk, which takes you to another district gate—the shortcut you could have taken earlier. Either pathway leads to the Kizingo Boulevard plaza.

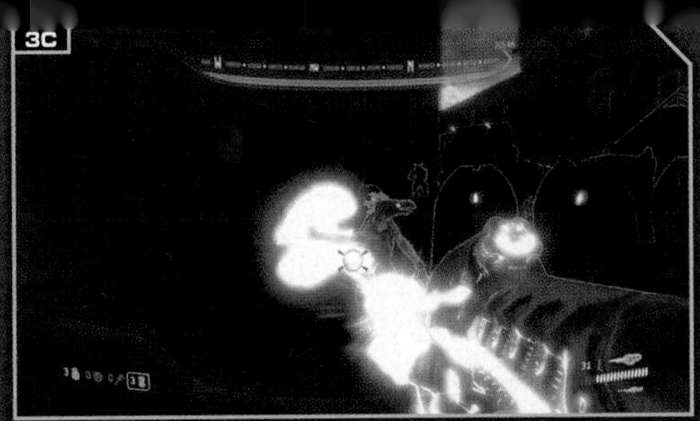
3C

3D

TIP **Enter District 10 from this point, accessing the weapons cache, and ride a Mongoose out of there, back to the Kizingo Boulevard area. Use Mongoose vehicles for quicker exploration from this point on.**

■ Choke Point 4: Kizingo Boulevard Plaza

Drive to the lower circular plaza **[4A]**, and engage a patrol (usually consisting of Brutes). There's a nearby Optican Kiosk if you need it. Then push your Mongoose to the upper stepped plaza **[4B]**, where a still-burning Banshee reminds you of previous battles. The area should be relatively quiet, although there's a Jackal Sniper to the southwest that tries to execute you as you reach your clue; therefore, grab more Health Packs from the Optican Kiosk to the northeast before locating a door that allows access into the building at the top of the stepped plaza, which holds the clue you're searching for. Follow the winding interior passage until you reach the open balcony overlooking both plazas **[4C]**. Watch out for that sniper! Gather any Grenades, and then inspect the Gauss Turret. The tale of your colleagues continues to be revealed...

ENTITIES ENCOUNTERED

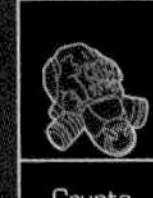
Grunts

Jackals

Brutes

4A

4B

4C

4D

▪Mission 04: Kizingo Boulevard

MICKEY • 90 minutes after drop • Kizingo Boulevard

After landing in New Mombasa's maze of streets, Mickey is fortunate enough to encounter a group of Marines. This fortune changes as a Covenant Wraith hovers into view. It is part of a mechanized division the Covenant has sent to shore up the city and wipe out any remaining defenses. You must locate one of two UNSC Scorpion Main Battle Tanks. Once you have it powered up (with optional Marines hitching a ride), you must carefully and methodically roll through the streets, engaging heavy Covenant forces at numerous plazas throughout Districts 3 and 4. You then meet up with Dutch, holding off two final waves of foes in District 10 and gaining entrance to the ONI Building.

DATA STREAM

Data Hive VISR Target Acquisition Mode Ratio: 15 percent*

*COMM Data Terminals are available only during Rookie missions.

PREFERRED WEAPONS

Rocket Launcher
Scorpion Tank (Vehicle)
Plasma Pistol
Magnum
Carbine
Rocket Launcher or Fuel Rod*

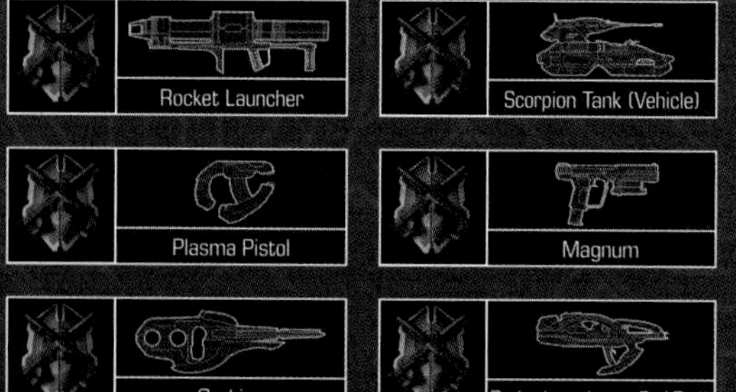

*When handed to Marines, with them positioned on the side of your Scorpion

PAR SCORE

75,000

LEVEL-SPECIFIC ACHIEVEMENTS

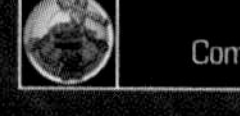

Kizingo Boulevard: Complete this mission to unlock Mickey in Firefight.

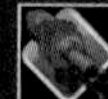

Both Tubes: Get 10 Rocket Launcher kills on Kizingo Boulevard

MISSION OBJECTIVES

- KIZINGO BOULEVARD Save Marines and Scorpion Tank
- KIZINGO BOULEVARD Drive tank to Rally Point
- KIZINGO BOULEVARD Rescue Dutch
- KIZINGO BOULEVARD Help Dutch defend Rally Point

Kizingo Boulevard: Scorpion Tank acquisition point to ONI Building Rally Point

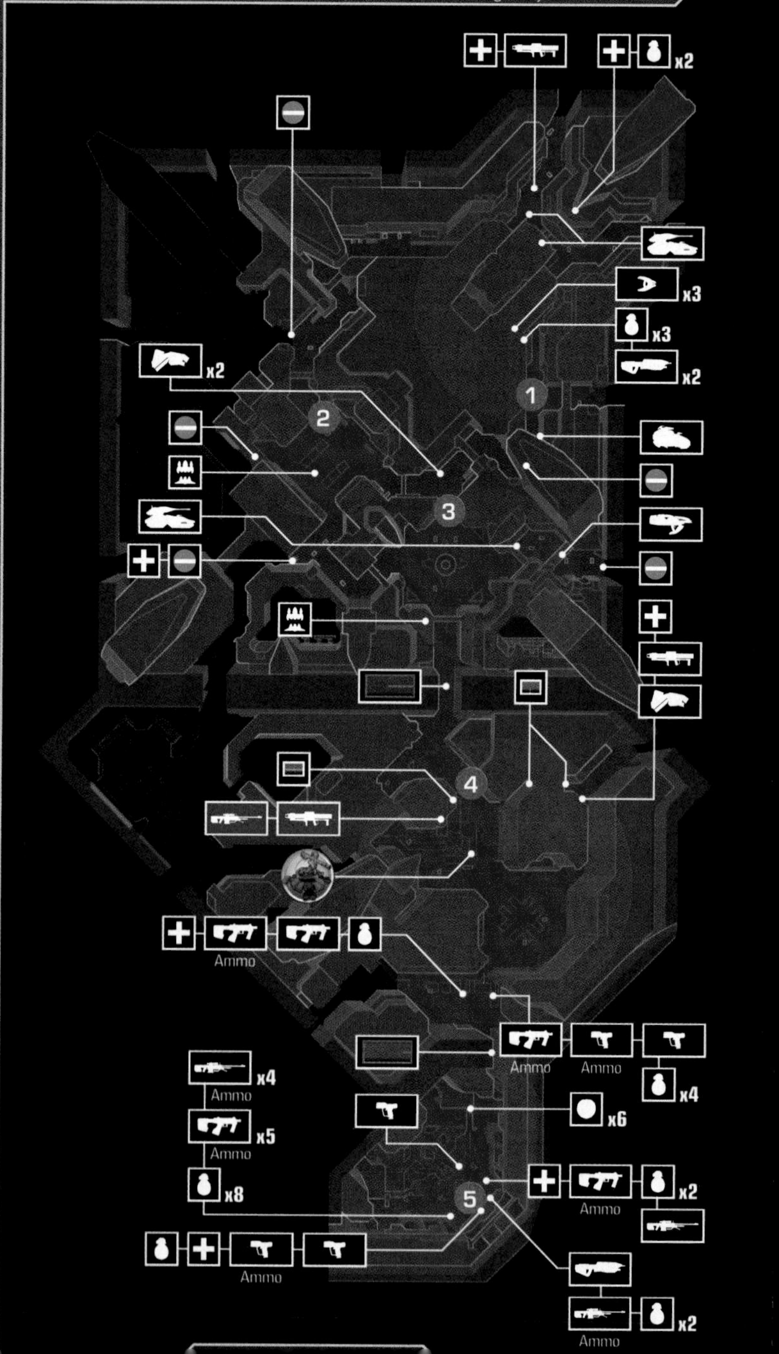

x2
x3
x3
x2
x2
1
2
3
4
Ammo
x4
Ammo
Ammo
x4
Ammo
x5
x6
Ammo
x8
5
x2
Ammo
Ammo
x2
Ammo

Choke Point 1: Covered Plaza and Scorpion Acquisition

1A

1B

ENTITIES ENCOUNTERED

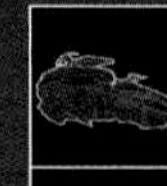

Wraith

Jackals

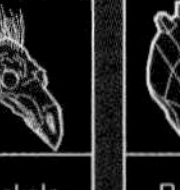

Brutes

Grunts

Phantom

Scorpions

OBJECTIVE

KIZINGO BOULEVARD Save Marines and Scorpion Tank

NOTE **This mission takes place in New Mombasa, beginning in District 3, moving into District 4, and ending at District 10. Refer to the New Mombasa Districts map at the end of this walkthrough to see how this area relates to the entire accessible city that Rookie is investigating.**

You begin under heavy fire from a Covenant Wraith grav-tank **[1A]** to the south of you. Being struck by its mortar fire seriously damages you, so use the cover and quickly switch to your Rocket Launcher. A single shot is occasionally enough to destroy it, so fire more than one shot and ensure the Wraith explodes; then switch to your Silenced SMG, and charge the Wraith's smoking husk—there are two Jackals to kill off here. Keep one Rocket remaining in your Launcher; it's a gift for a Marine you'll soon meet. From here, there's one foolish and one recommended tactic to try.

Tactic: On Foot and Outgunned

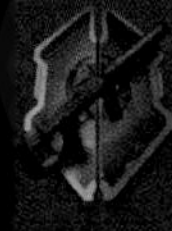

Stay close to the left wall where you spawned. You can move in a general northwest direction into a large overhanging plaza **[1B]**. Here you face several Grunts, Jackals, and armored Brutes on foot. Of particular importance are Brutes with Brute Shot weapons. Expect Brutes to activate their bubble shields, further complicating your attacks. With a Ghost to face and a large population of foes milling about this area, confronting these enemies on foot is an unwise proposition. You can hijack and board the Ghost, but there's a much better vehicle to take command of....

Tactic: On Board and Awesome

There are two vehicles to take command of! Check your NAV (or guide) map for the locations of two Scorpion Tanks **[1C]**, both fueled and ready for you to take control. Both have a Marine driving it (he'll hop out once he knows you're going to control the vehicle). Choose either of the tanks, and wait for any UNSC forces to move alongside your Scorpion; have a Marine sit on the tank's side to provide fire support, especially if you give him your Rocket Launcher or allow him to man your tank's machine-gun turret. Giving him the Rocket Launcher is important to an Achievement, while allowing him to man the turret allows you to shrug off any Brutes that attempt to assault the tank physically.

1C

Tactic: Bringing Down Brutes

This tactic applies throughout this mission; aside from Wraiths and other large targets, Brutes should be your primary focus. Not only do they tend to leap onto your Scorpion, but also they carry an antitank weapon, the Brute Shot. This damages your vehicle more than any other infantry weapon, so react immediately if you see Brutes, whether they're carrying Brute Shots or not!

TIP **If a Brute leaps onto your Scorpion, you can hope your machine-gunner Marine deals with them, or you can physically stop the Scorpion and shoot the foes off yourself when you're in a safer**

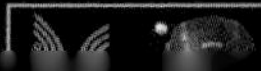

1D

1E

With only a limited amount of ammunition, it may seem tricky to complete the "Both Tubes" Achievement, which is available only on this mission. There are two methods for obtaining this Achievement. The first is to target large clusters of enemies, so each Rocket kills multiple enemies at once. Wraiths count as three enemies. There's additional Rocket ammo at the inactive Gauss Turret at Choke Point 4 (which you should access first) and at the Rally Point. Better yet, give the Rocket Launcher to a Marine who sits on your tank and blasts away; any kills he makes are added to your Achievement total, too!

Now that you're controlling a deadly piece of UNSC hardware, it's time to use it effectively: Head west, watching a Phantom deposit a Wraith in the distance. Optionally blast the Phantom out of the sky **[1D]**, tracking it with your Turret as you rumble forward; then quickly launch Cannon strikes on a pesky Ghost and any Brutes to your left (southwest) in the covered plaza. Maintain your speed as you head up the ramp **[1E]**. Destroy the Wraith on the road ahead, tagging it before it hits you with a mortar. Keep moving so the mortar passes overhead as you close. After you deal with the Wraith, check the dead-end road to the north, and blast the Brute up there. Your objective updates.

OBJECTIVE

KIZINGO BOULEVARD Drive tank to Rally Point

NOTE

The Rocket Launcher, Assault Rifle, Silenced SMG Plasma Pistol, Plasma Rifle, Plasma Turret, Brute Shot, Spiker, and Needler are all available in this general area. There are also two Frag Grenades and a Health Pack in the small, open-air plaza to the east, at the top of the steps.

Tactic: A Scorpion's Sting Operation

With two or four players, having two Scorpions rumbling through New Mombasa is always an excellent idea, as long as one of the tanks doesn't block the path of the other. However, on more savage difficulty levels, it is wise to split up your team, with one player rushing for the tank while the other engages the enemy, keeping them occupied (especially Brutes with Brute Shots, which can make it difficult to reach a tank) until the tank can pick them up.

▪ Choke Point 2: Stepped Plaza

2A

2B

TIP

From this point on, you might wish to flick on your VISR Enhanced Vision from time to time, despite the glare problems. Drive into a new area, ascertain the shapes and locations of the enemies, then attack them in normal daylight.

ENTITIES ENCOUNTERED

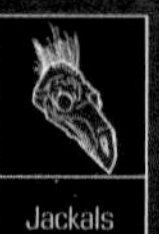
Jackals

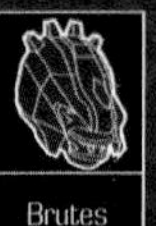
Brutes

Ghost

Phantom

Shade Turrets

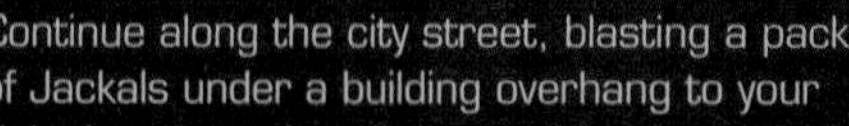
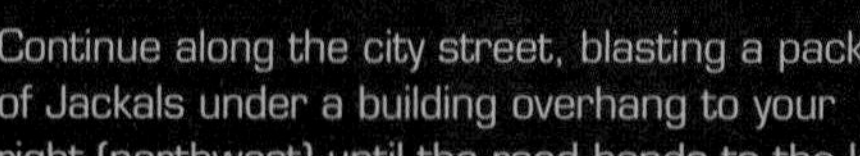

Continue along the city street, blasting a pack of Jackals under a building overhang to your right (northwest) until the road bends to the left (south). Blast the open window across from you (next to the "355" on the wall), and immediately launch a second Cannon strike on an incoming Ghost **[2A]**. Remember, hit the Ghost, not the lampposts! Continue along the winding road as it slopes up to a Y-junction **[2B]**, keeping close to the left wall. Pivot your Cannon right, dropping a Brute on the rooftop next to a beacon; then edge into the Y-junction and fire on the open skywalk, where you must defeat some Brutes. Shrug off any Grenades that are thrown. Deal with a Ghost immediately afterward. An energy wall blocks the right fork, so head left (southeast). This road leads to a stepped plaza and a cluster of enemies

2C

CAUTION

Shade Turrets spit purple-hued plasma at you; this is deadly. If your tank is being bombarded by this type of fire, locate its source and destroy it first, or risk Scorpion destruction!

2D

The stepped plaza has two Shade Turrets, a Covenant Watchtower, and a cluster of foes to the left, the right, and at the base of the stairs to your right. There is also a Shade Turret on a building balcony to your right. In addition, a Phantom descends above the top of the stepped area directly ahead of you **[2C]** and drops infantry out of its right-side Pod door. Obviously, a measured approach is called for here. Learn which enemies are likely to destroy your tank in the fastest time and make them your primary targets: Take down the Shade Turret located on the left-side building ahead of you **[2D]** from the safety of the road entrance with the buildings on each side; those buildings are your cover. Then bombard the Phantom with three direct Cannon strikes (aim for one of the engines) until it explodes.

2E

TIP

Leaving your vehicle is not recommended, as you have much less protection and your weaponry has a finite amount of ammunition. Only disembark from a Scorpion if it is badly damaged and you've found a new vehicle, or you've cleared a choke point and want to pick up a few new weapons or search for a wayward Health Pack.

As you fire your main Cannon into the building alcove at ground level to your left (culling multiple infantry), edge into the plaza so your right flank is exposed; this allows the enemies at the base of the stepped area, the Shade Turret on the building balcony to the southwest **[2E]**, and a sniper on the southeast building roof to attack you. Quick aiming is needed here. Demolish the Shade Turret first, blast the Watchtower, fire at the sniper, and then pick off remaining infantry that are milling around.

This area has taken a pounding from the fallen space elevator, and massive skeletal sections of it drape from the half-crushed building on which the second Shade Turret sat. Progress southeast in your tank. There are two exits: one at the bottom of the steps that lead to a secondary entrance to Choke Point 3, with a barrier with a Health Pack on the road before you reach the next plaza. However, it makes more tactical sense to stay in the Scorpion and head along the road from the top of the steps to the nearer exit; you won't need to rumble through the wreckage of the Watchtower, which takes longer.

TIP

There are Magnums, Shotguns, Assault Rifles, Plasma Pistols, Needlers, Brute Shots, Assault Rifles, and a Plasma Turret accessible in this choke point. There are also two Marines you can tool up with your favored armaments and have sitting on your tank to provide extra protection.

Kizingo Bouldvard • MICKEY

■ Choke Point 3: Roundabout Plaza

Drive southeast along the road from the top of the stepped plaza, following the road east and immediately halting at the junction **[3A]**. Swing your Cannon around to the right. Ideally, halt before you reach the junction itself, or face bombardment from three Shade Turrets in the center of a roundabout plaza with a gazebo in the middle of it. These Turrets are extremely nasty; it is better to peek out and take down the one on the left, then the middle one, and finally the one on the right, edging farther out each time so only one Shade Turret can fire on you. The threats don't end there, however!

Turn the corner so your Scorpion is facing the center of the plaza, and blast away at the Covenant's ground defenses and Brutes in front of you, to the right. Then pick off a Ghost before checking the skies for an incoming Phantom **[3B]**. Even if you destroy it (with three, well-placed shots to one of the Phantom's engines), it still has time to drop in a second Ghost. This isn't the biggest threat; there are a couple of Grunts on the balcony just right of the rooftop Watchtower, and they're armed with Fuel Rod Cannons **[3C]**. There are also a couple of other foes on the skywalks up there. Back up from that highly damaging green plasma, and target them immediately. There are two more Jackal Snipers: One is sniping you from the northeast roof **[3D]** just left of a parked Scorpion, and the other is on a rooftop on the west side. Make a circle, tagging any remaining foes, before parking. You may find the odd Grunt straggler as you inspect the area.

TIP

Your Scorpion can easily be destroyed in this next plaza, so stealthily peeking out and tagging foes from cover is almost imperative, especially at higher difficulty levels.

ENTITIES ENCOUNTERED

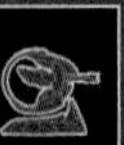
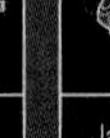

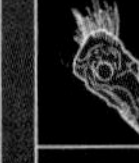
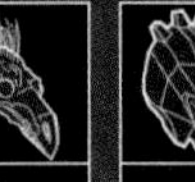

Shade Turrets	Jackals	Brutes
Ghost	Phantom	Scorpion

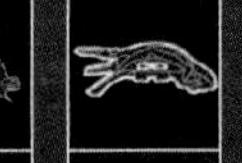
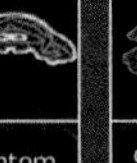

3A

3B

3C

Tactic: Outflanked and Outgunned

With two or four players attempting to secure this plaza, you have the additional help of a second Scorpion Tank. Even better, the southern road at the base of the stepped plaza (Choke Point 2) accesses this area. Radio each other to time your attack precisely. Aim at the forces in the order presented previously, but attack from two directions, causing confusion among the Covenant.

TIP

There are Plasma Pistols, Needlers, Brute Shots, Fuel Rod Cannons, Carbines (including one by the Jackal Sniper if you tagged him), Shade Turrets, and Plasma Turrets accessible in this choke point. But running over on foot and sitting in a Shade Turret is the very definition of suicide; stay inside your armored tank for more pleasing results.

3D

3E

The area is suspiciously quiet but isn't secured yet. Investigate the undamaged Scorpion [3E], parked on a road to the northeast, and use it as cover as you engage a squad of Grunts behind some defenses between the Scorpion and the dead-end energy wall. One of these enemies has a Fuel Rod Cannon—the perfect gift to any surviving Marines riding with you. You can gather a variety of ammunition from this area or from the scattered bodies of Covenant in the plaza. You're picking up Dutch's signal from the south. Exit the plaza, traveling in this direction and heading through from District 3 to 4. Your objective updates.

OBJECTIVE

KIZINGO BOULEVARD Rescue Dutch

■ Choke Point 4: Kizingo Plaza

NOTE **If you've thoroughly inspected this choke point during Rookie's nocturnal investigations, you may recognize it as Kizingo Boulevard, where you found the inactive Gauss Turret, prior to starting this mission.**

ENTITIES ENCOUNTERED

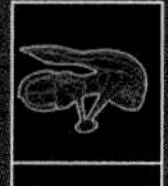
Banshees

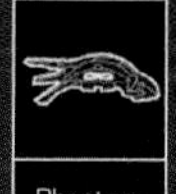
Phantom

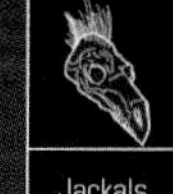
Jackals

Brutes

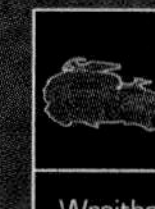
Wraiths

Ghost

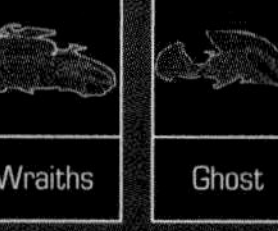

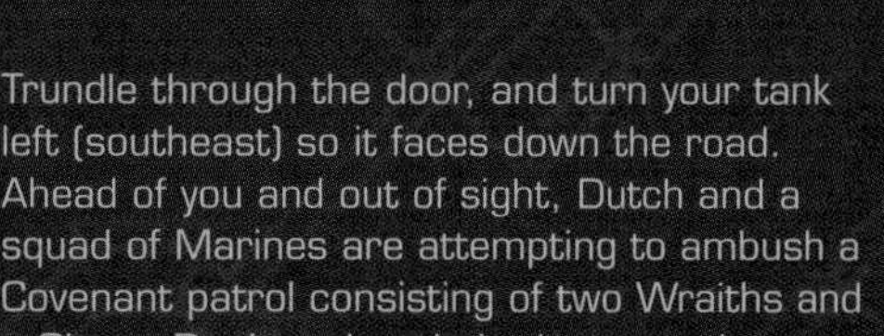

4A

Trundle through the door, and turn your tank left (southeast) so it faces down the road. Ahead of you and out of sight, Dutch and a squad of Marines are attempting to ambush a Covenant patrol consisting of two Wraiths and a Ghost. Don't rush to help them; you have closer enemies to worry about. A Marine with Dutch prematurely engages the patrol, and two Banshees swoop down to help their forces. Remain inside your Scorpion, and track the two Banshees **[4A]** as they head your way. Blow them apart with your Cannon. Trundle down the street, firing at the infantry behind cover on your left as the road turns right; then immediately swing your Turret around to the right (southwest). A Phantom is about to deposit Jackals and Brutes on the raised concrete balconies **[4B]** near a Gauss Turret; target the Phantom as it swoops down, and blast the ship out of the sky before the foes can disembark. If you're too slow, stop and blast at the infantry before continuing to the base of the sloped road.

4B

Quickly move down to the junction and roundabout area, where two Wraiths approach you from the south **[4C]**, and a Phantom drops off a Ghost. There's no need to blast the Phantom; concentrate your firepower on the Wraith that is moving toward you. In the distance to the south, you can make out Dutch's HUD insignia and a large "4"; the second Wraith is attacking Dutch and his Marines, but they can handle the attack. There's no need to rush to their aid. Instead, take out the Ghost and a possible second Ghost that another Phantom drops off at the junction. Then slowly take out any Jackals or Brutes lurking behind building pillars dotted around the perimeter of the roundabout. Move in and tag the second Wraith **[4D]** with a cannon shot, coaxing it away from Dutch and into the roundabout area, where you should finish it off. This allows you to easily aim at a final Phantom that tries dropping infantry where you defeated the first one, by the concrete balconies. This concludes the portion of this battle that you'll fight in a Scorpion.

4C

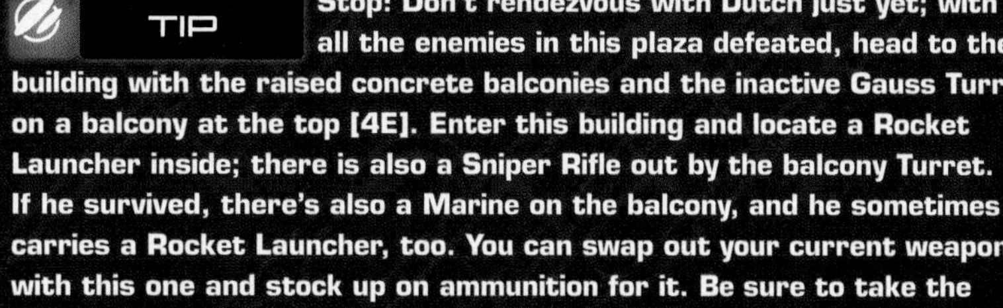

TIP **Stop! Don't rendezvous with Dutch just yet; with all the enemies in this plaza defeated, head to the building with the raised concrete balconies and the inactive Gauss Turret on a balcony at the top [4E]. Enter this building and locate a Rocket Launcher inside; there is also a Sniper Rifle out by the balcony Turret. If he survived, there's also a Marine on the balcony, and he sometimes carries a Rocket Launcher, too. You can swap out your current weapon with this one and stock up on ammunition for it. Be sure to take the Rocket Launcher (and optionally, the Sniper Rifle) before heading to Dutch.**

4D

4E

Tactic: Superior Firepower

When assaulting with a teammate, it is wise to approach along the road in two separate Scorpion Tanks. When the Banshees swoop in, fire at them in tandem so they never reach you to execute a bombing run. With the Banshees defeated, have one player move their Scorpion into the roundabout (as described previously) to challenge the Wraiths and Ghosts while the other (or another player) stays in the tank, by the building with the Gauss Turret, to blast away at incoming Phantoms and any troops escaping. If your team has three or four members, make sure each teammate knows their role; the third player can bring in another Scorpion for additional firepower, while the fourth mans the Gauss Turret and gathers Rocket Launcher ammunition for combat in Choke Point 5.

NOTE **There are Assault Rifles, a Sniper Rifle, Plasma Pistols, Plasma Turrets, Brute Shots, Needlers, Rocket Launchers, a Gauss Turret, and a Silenced SMG in the ordnance scattered throughout this choke point.**

■ Choke Point 5: ONI Building Rally Point

TIP **This section of the mission plays very similarly to the Firefight mission "Rally Point or Rally (Night)." You may wish to read up on various methods of repelling Covenant enemies during that gameplay mode and then apply it here. Or, follow any of the advice shown below.**

ENTITIES ENCOUNTERED

Jackals

Brutes

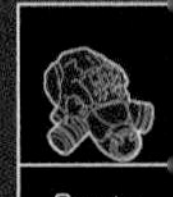

Grunts

Phantoms

Wraith

OBJECTIVE

KIZINGO BOULEVARD Help Dutch defend Rally Point

The ramp on which Dutch is standing **[5A]** leads to the Rally Point and cannot be accessed by vehicle. Head up the ramp to meet Dutch, but there's little time for pleasantries; as you reach the ONI facility entrance door, it opens and a group of Covenant infantry rush you. React with a single rocket attack before they disperse. You can take out most of them with this attack and hopefully complete the Both Tubes Achievement in the process. If not, a mixture of sniping and Grenades removes the threats from the street. Head south down the street, with Dutch running with you or ahead of you. Quickly sprint up the sloped ramp to a group of Marines behind some UNSC barricades **[5B]**. Save your Rockets and assist the Marines, checking near the building entrance (east of you) and the barricades for Grenades, Health Packs, and supplies.

TIP **Wraiths are transported in by Phantoms, and you can see the Wraiths attached to the underside of the Phantoms. This means you know which Phantoms are dropping infantry and which have weightier cargo in addition to Covenant foot soldiers.**

A Phantom appears from the north, flying down to deposit a Wraith and a group of infantry (usually Jackals and Brutes) with quick efficiency. It lands in the center of the lower road **[5C]**, and the enemies stream out. Some foes begin attacking you by heading up the sloping road on either side of the central concrete stepped area, but others are more cunning and attempt to outflank you by heading up the stairs in the southwest and northeast corners of this locale and over the narrow footbridges. They try to tag you from the upper balcony above which the Marines are dug in. You can try the following tactics no matter where the enemies are.

Tactic: Early Execution

Load up both tubes of your Rocket Launcher, and move to a position (such as the top of the stepped area or one of the footbridges overlooking the middle of the road) as the Phantom descends. You must be quick to react, or you don't have time to complete this mass execution. As the Phantom deploys its troops, throw Grenades (or fire Rockets) at the ground where the foes are landing; the ensuing explosion severely thins their numbers. Then finish off any stragglers with your Rocket Launcher, which can also take out multiple foes. Any other weapon is decent for picking off fleeing foes, too.

5A

5B

Tactic: Better Late Than Never

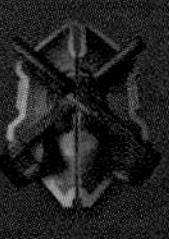

If the Phantom arrives, deposits its infantry, and then leaves, you have a more prolonged and tactical battle to plan. Stay on higher ground. You can retreat to the upper balconies on either side of the area and fire sniped shots at the Jackals and Brutes as they roam the streets. On higher difficulties, use a mixture of a Plasma Pistol (to wear down any shielded foe's protection) and a Magnum, a Carbine, or a Sniper Rifle (to finish the foe with a headshot) for most of your kills, or use any other weaponry you find lying about. This is a good time to pick up a Needler and attempt to complete the Pink and Deadly Achievement.

Tactic: Rocket Wrath for the Wraith

While you're grenading the ground under the Phantom's drop point, the Wraith is deposited on the ground **[5D]**. However, assuming you've armed yourself with a Rocket Launcher, you can simply fire on it as soon as the Phantom drops it, so it explodes a few moments after touching down on the road below. This offers an easy victory and one that helps net your Both Tubes Achievement.

Tactic: Manual Hijacking

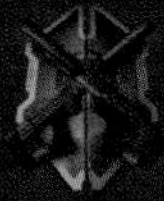

If you don't have Rockets or aren't fast enough to quickly destroy the Wraith when it drops into play, you can always lob Grenades at its structure, ideally from the balconies behind and above the vehicle. However, a better plan is to approach the Wraith from the side so you aren't destroyed by its weapons or ramming, and leap onto the Wraith, boarding it **[5D]** and then wedging a Grenade into it, so it explodes.

Tactic: Sniping and Savagery

Note the Sniper Rifle and Health Packs by the stationed Marines. Have one of your team grab the Rifle and move to a covered area, such as the balconies above the action. Your teammate can access these via the sloped roads behind the Marine's barricades. This sniper can then tag enemies from afar and pick up any foes trying to outflank you by heading up onto these balconies or up the sloping road below. With three players, have a second sniper on the opposite balcony. The other player (or players, if you have four) should head straight for closer combat, leading with the enemies encroaching via the central steps and using Grenades to weaken them as these foes fall from their Phantoms.

After the first Phantom has deposited its troops, heal up, grab ammunition and Grenades, and be ready for a second ship to hover into view. Just like before, don't waste time targeting the Phantom's hull; the problems lie with the Wraith, as well as a squad of Brutes **[5E]** and the usual Jackals and Grunts. With this second wave, use the same techniques previously outlined, lobbing well-placed Grenades at the drop-off points, and launch another single rocket at the Wraith. More importantly, a carefully fired rocket can destroy most, if not all, of the Brute squad as they exit the Phantom. Then finish off any stragglers before linking up with Dutch and gaining entry to the ONI Building.

CAUTION **On higher difficulties, one of the Grunts that disembarks from the second Phantom is carrying a Fuel Rod Cannon. Take additional cover opportunities, and be wary of the tremendous power of this weapon.**

NOTE **There are Plasma Pistols, Plasma Turrets (if you knock them off the Phantoms), Magnums, Assault Rifles, Silenced SMGs, Brute Shots, Needlers, Sniper Rifles, a Fuel Rod Cannon, and Carbines scattered throughout this choke point.**

Mission 04: Mombasa Streets

ROOKIE • 6 hours after drop • Occupied city center

DATA STREAM

New Mombasa VISR Target Acquisition Mode Ratio: 95 percent

PREFERRED WEAPONS

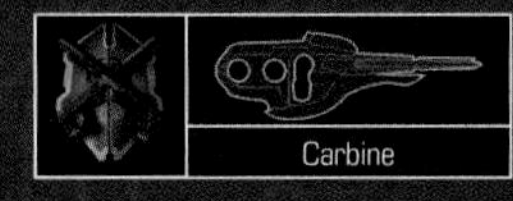
Carbine

Magnum

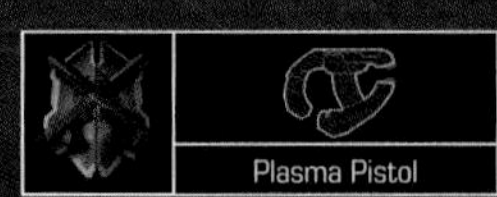
Plasma Pistol

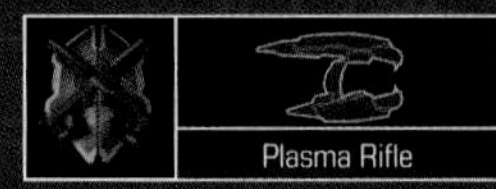
Plasma Rifle

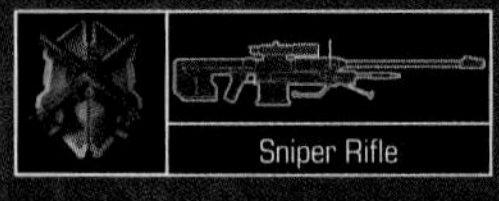
Sniper Rifle

PAR SCORE

100,000

MISSION OBJECTIVES

NEW MOMBASA Search ONI Alpha Site for ODST squadmate

Kizingo Boulevard to ONI Alpha Site

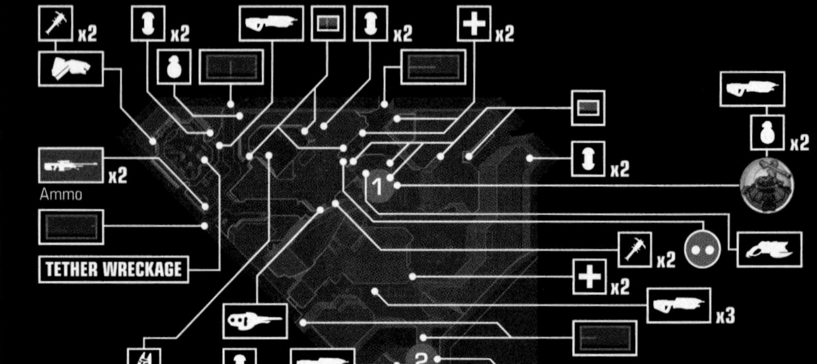

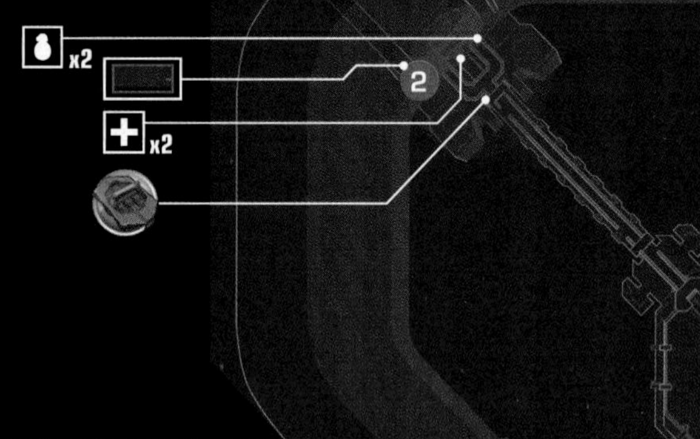

COMM DATA STREAM

After "Mission 01: Prepare to Drop": Hidden COMM Data—7 (Total: 7/30)*

After completing any three missions: Hidden COMM Data—13 (Total: 20/30)*

After completing any four missions: Hidden COMM Data—9 (Total: 29/30)*

After 4 of 7 COMM Data Found: Supply Cache Set 1 Opens (Total: 1/3 Sets)**

After 8 of 20 COMM Data Found: Supply Cache Set 2 Opens (Total: 2/3 Sets)**

After 16 of 29 COMM Data Found: Supply Cache Set 3 Opens (Total: 3/3 Sets)**

Total Caches Available: 8/8**

Set 1 Cache Contents: Sniper Rifle (2), Sniper Ammo (2), Magnum (4), Silenced SMG (4), Frag Grenade (4)

Set 2 Cache Contents: Magnum (4), Silenced SMG (4), Frag Grenade (4), Mongoose (2)

Set 3 Cache Contents: Rocket Launcher (2), Rocket Launcher Ammo (2), Magnum (4), Silenced SMG (4), Frag Grenade (4)

*COMM Data Terminals are available only during Rookie missions. These terminals have been deemed "supersecret" and cannot be shown on the Mombasa Streets map.

**Depending on how many COMM Terminals you have found, between 0 and 8 caches are now available and appear on your in-game map.

NOTE **This mission takes place within Districts 4 and 10, in the eastern and southeastern areas of New Mombasa. All accessible districts of New Mombasa (Districts 0, 3, 4, 5, 6, 8, 9, and 10) are available to search through. The following walkthrough details the quickest path to the ONI Alpha Site clue.**

NOTE **Remember! You can elect to head off across this city and locate any other clue you wish, in any order. If you do, consult the Tour of New Mombasa at the end of this chapter.**

OBJECTIVE

NEW MOMBASA Search ONI Alpha Site for ODST squadmate

■ Choke Point 1: Kizingo Boulevard Plaza

ENTITIES ENCOUNTERED

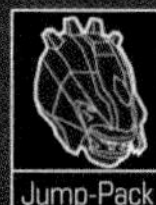
Jump-Pack Brutes

Jackals

As you finish examining the inactive Gauss Turret, a Phantom swoops down and deposits a group of Jump-Pack Brutes to the southeast of you, on the ground near the roundabout plaza **[1A]**. You can snipe them from this balcony, or exit via the building using the corridors you came in from or via dropping to the concrete stepped planter area below. Expect Brute attacks as you emerge from the building. At this point, if you've found 16 COMM Terminals, you can access a weapons cache just northwest of this exit, which contains Set 3 equipment. Take what you need, or scavenge the fallen foes for armaments, and then eliminate troublesome Jackals in the general area across the road from you, to the east **[1B]**. Behind the sniper is a building interior you can scavenge for more items. Should you need health, there's an Optican Kiosk to the northeast, near the exit into District 3 (which is the wrong direction to travel if you're completing the Campaign in chronological order). Now drive your Mongoose—which you should have kept from your previous expedition—up the steps to the gate **[1C]** leading into the Rally Point, to the south.

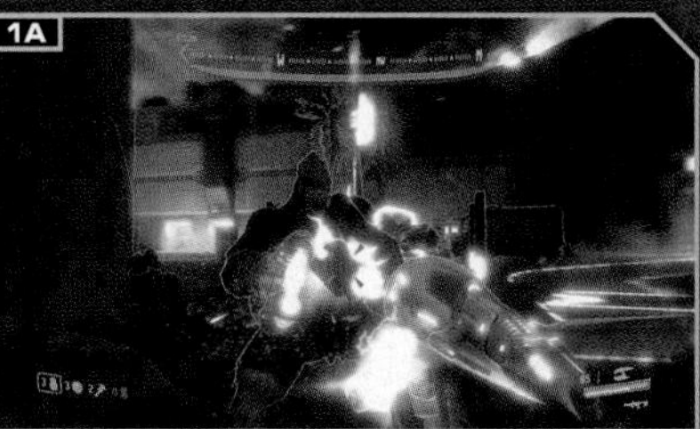

■ Choke Point 2: Rally Point (Revisited) and ONI Clue

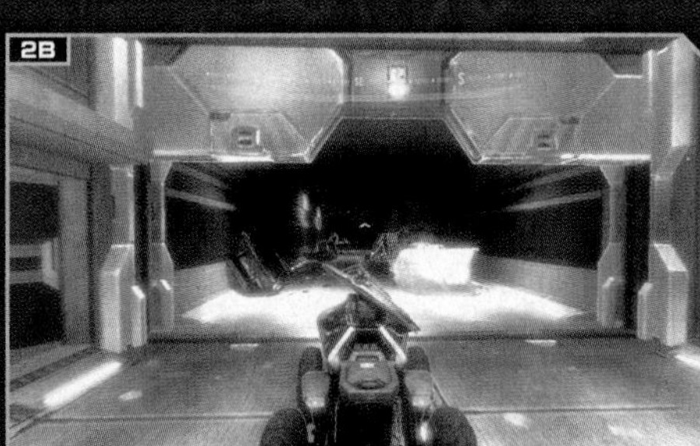

ENTITIES ENCOUNTERED

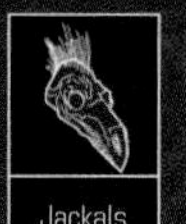
Jackals

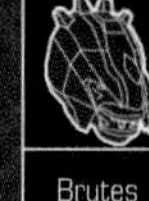
Brutes

Grunts

Enter the District 10 Rally Point, which, much like the previous choke point, you just tore through earlier in this mission when you were playing as Mickey. Sprint along the road and into the expansive stepped area. Be aware of Jackal snipers on the rooftops. Assuming the weapons cache is open **[2A]**, retrieve any preferred equipment you need (this cache opens after you find eight COMM Terminals and contains Set 2 equipment). Take a new Mongoose and give this entire area a thorough inspection. When you're done, drive up the ramp on the right side, behind the UNSC barricades, and locate the large door marked with the UNSC logo **[2B]**.

Disembark and creep forward into a tunnel, where a couple of Brutes and some Grunts are waiting behind cover **[2C]**. Lob in Grenades, as there's little lateral room for enemies to dodge your incoming projectiles; then mop up the Brutes with headshots or your favored killing techniques. When the area is secure, drive to the door at the opposite (southeast) end of the tunnel, open it, and head to an outside platform. Ahead, a Phantom peels away in the distance, but there are no close threats, allowing you to inspect the area. Drive up to ground level, checking the doorway behind you (there are Health Packs) and the locked door to an inaccessible tunnel that leads back to Rally Point; there are two Frag Grenades there. Of greater importance are the remains of a large bridge, now completely destroyed. Edge forward and locate the Remote Detonator **[2D]** to find the clue.

Mission 05: ONI Alpha Site

DUTCH • 2 Hours after drop • ONI Alpha Site

With Covenant forces massing throughout the streets of New Mombasa, there is little point defending the location. Instead, a tactical withdrawal is called for, ideally with as many large explosions (that you're at least partially responsible for) as possible. Back up from the bridge after arming it with explosives, then detonate the structure from a Watchtower. Fall back to the ONI building courtyard, where you must repel a series of Covenant waves before you retreat farther into the ONI building lobby. After holding off more Covenant inside the building, the only wise option is escaping from the building rooftop, accessed via the elevator.

ONI Facility: Entrance Bridge to ONI Interior

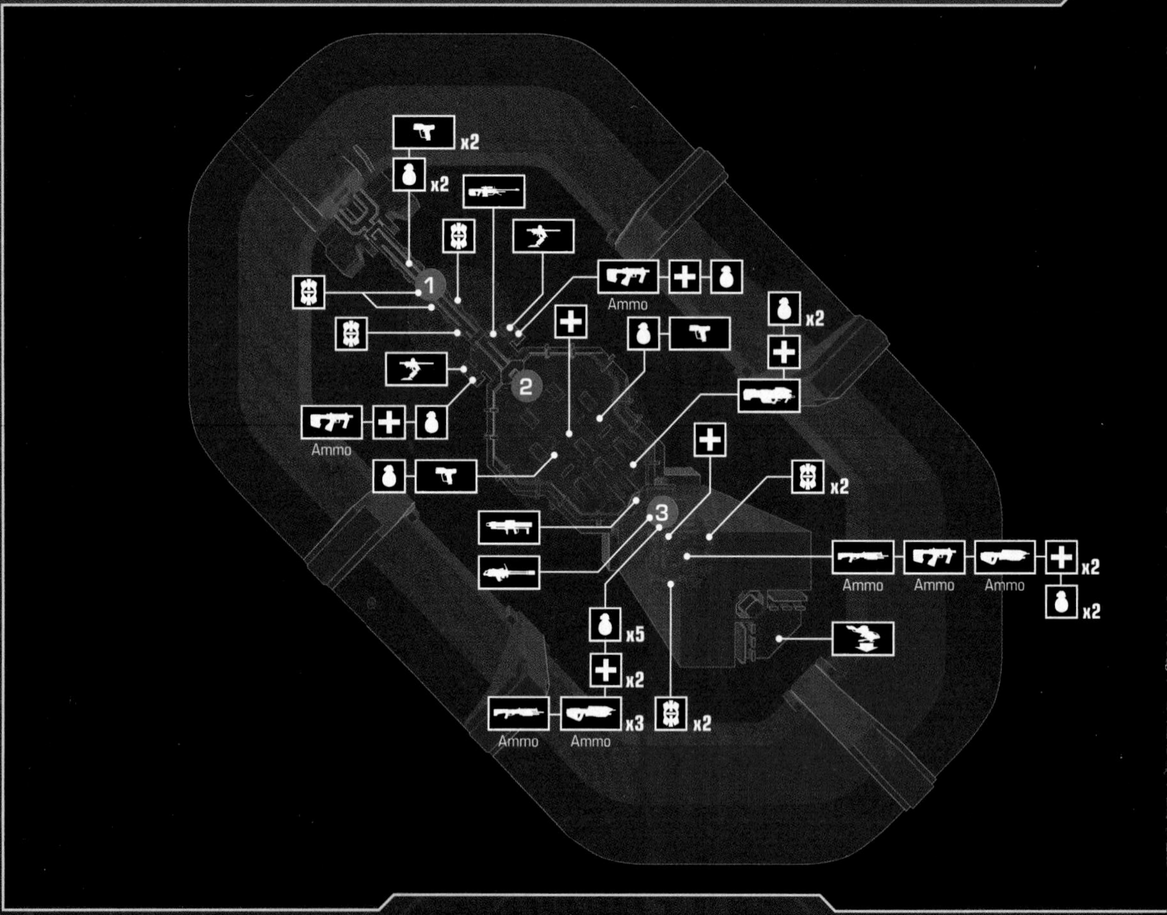

DATA STREAM

Data Hive VISR Target Acquisition Mode Ratio: 10 percent*

*COMM Data Terminals are available only during Rookie missions.

PREFERRED WEAPONS

Spartan Laser

Sniper Rifle

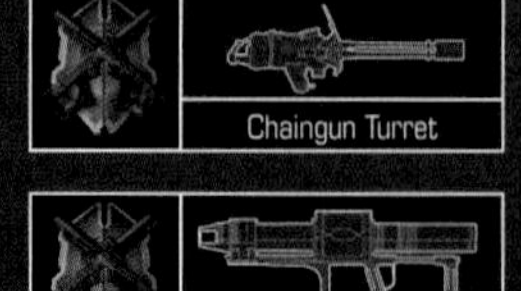
Chaingun Turret

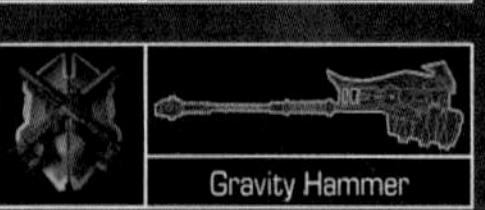
Gravity Hammer

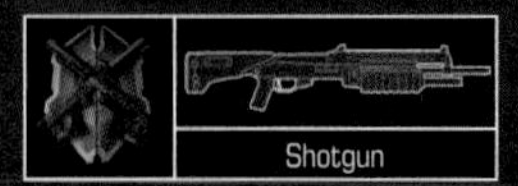
Shotgun

Rocket Launcher*

*When handed to Mickey in the ONI Building Lobby

PAR SCORE

60,000

LEVEL-SPECIFIC ACHIEVEMENTS

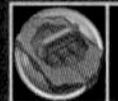
ONI Alpha Site—complete this mission to unlock "Firefight Mission: Alpha Site"

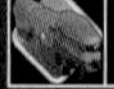
Laser Blaster: Get 10 Spartan Laser kills on ONI Alpha Site

MISSION OBJECTIVES

- ONI ALPHA SITE Arm all charges on bridge
- ONI ALPHA SITE Use detonator in Watchtower
- ONI ALPHA SITE Fall back, defend inner courtyard
- ONI ALPHA SITE Retreat, defend ONI Building interior
- ONI ALPHA SITE Take elevator to roof for evac

■ Choke Point 1: ONI Bridge (Demolition)

OBJECTIVE
ONI ALPHA SITE Arm all charges on bridge

You're given the order to arm all the charges on the bridge, as the Covenant are gaining ground and threaten to swamp the ONI Building in minutes. Their ground forces need to be waylaid with a spot of demolition. Each set of explosives **[1A]** is on a separate support pillar, clearly visible. When all three are activated, rush to the end of the bridge, where the UNSC barricades have been hastily erected. Leave the Covenant incursions (a huge group of Grunts and Brutes, plus three Wraiths) to the defenders; you have a more important responsibility: the objective that just updated.

ENTITIES ENCOUNTERED

Mickey

NMPD Officers

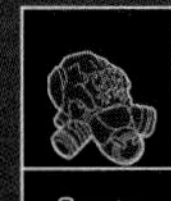
Grunts

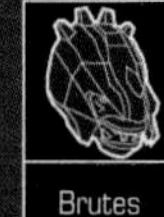
Brutes

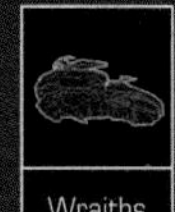
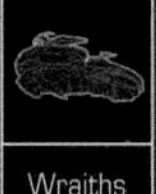
Wraiths

Phantoms

Banshees

OBJECTIVE
ONI ALPHA SITE Use detonator in Watchtower

CAUTION

Failure to destroy the bridge results in your location being overrun. You also don't have enough firepower to repel the Covenant by any other means. If you take too long, the Superintendent will detonate the charges.

As soon as the objective updates, turn to the left (northeast) and locate the UNSC Watchtower **[1B]**. Climb the ladder embedded in the structure. Once atop the Watchtower, you can take the Sniper Rifle you find there and optionally zoom in on the advancing Covenant on the bridge; there's no point tagging them, as this simply wastes ammunition. Instead, move to the terminal and immediately power it up. This sets off the detonation program, and the Superintendent unlocks the keypad and sets off a massive explosion, completely devastating the bridge and the Covenant ground forces on it. Drop to the ground below the Watchtower. There are Health Packs and Gauss Turrets on the concrete overlooks on either side of the Watchtower, but you shouldn't need to use either of these. Follow Mickey's plan and tactically withdraw, heading southeast toward the massive, cube-shaped ONI Building.

1B

Tactic: Culling the Covenant

This tactic is not recommended for those on higher difficulty levels, because one hit from a foe can make this tactic fail. At lower difficulties, however, those skilled with weaponry can easily dispatch most (if not all) of the advancing squads of Grunts and Brutes. Headshots from the barricades or Watchtower is the best plan. The only drawback is listening to Mickey yell at you to get on with arming the charges.

Tactic: Flee from the Covenant

On higher difficulty levels, Mickey's advice is sage: You have little to no chance of repelling the Covenant squads before they overrun and kill you, unless there are four players on your team (even then, the challenge is almost insurmountable). The Covenant brings in yet another Wraith, additional Brutes and Grunts, and two Banshees. It is time to retreat....

NOTE

There are numerous dropped or available weapons in this area; you begin with a Spartan Laser, which you should save for the next choke point; a Silenced SMG; a Sniper Rifle; an Assault Rifle; and a host of Covenant hardware, including the Brute Spiker, Needler, Plasma Pistol, and Brute Shot.

While one of your team scales the Watchtower to detonate the explosives on the bridge, the others can access an impressive Gauss Turret on either side of the defenses **[1C]**, and cut down the Covenant prior to the detonation. This isn't mandatory but adds to your score. Unfortunately, you can't detach the Gauss Cannon.

OBJECTIVE
ONI ALPHA SITE Fall back, defend inner courtyard

ONI Alpha Site • DUTCH

■ Choke Point 2: ONI Courtyard—Security Zone

2A

2B

ENTITIES ENCOUNTERED

Hunters

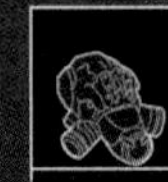
Grunts

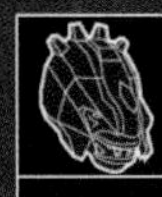
Brutes

Jackals

Phantoms

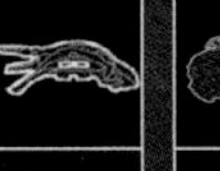

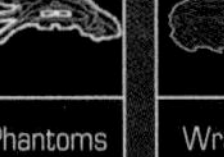
Wraiths

TIP **This section of the mission plays very similarly to "Firefight Mission: Security Zone." You may wish to read up on various methods of repelling Covenant enemies during that gameplay mode and apply it here. Or, follow any of the advice shown below:**

After dashing into the courtyard, you are instantly set upon by a couple of Hunters, Brutes, and Grunts **[2A]** that a Phantom has dropped in. The open space and limited cover (unless you dive behind the large concrete platforms and planters on either side of the stepped area) means you are an easy target, and there are more Covenant on the way. Stand firm and tackle these foes, or, if you're playing on a higher difficulty, flee to the top of the steps, toward the ONI Building. Retreating to this fallback position **[2B]** allows you to locate more cover, gain help from the local police who are holed up behind barriers in this area, and rearm yourself, as there's a variety of scattered weapons and Grenades around the defenses. You also gain a height advantage, shooting down on the enemy. Now plan for the incoming waves—around four or five Phantom drops, each with masses of Brutes, Grunts, and Jackals to face. Jackals are a particular problem, as they feature prominently and can strike you from long range; react with sniping of your own, and move from cover to cover as the opportunity arises. There will be three Wraiths **[2C]** dropped at the open (northwest) end of the courtyard, and these can decimate you if you're caught by their plasma mortar. You can tell when the last wave of foes arrives, as a Brute Chieftain **[2D]** appears. As soon as the next objective appears, follow Mickey's advice and descend into the ONI Building interior.

Tactic: Close-Combat Engagement

On lower difficulties, you can take the fight to the enemy, heading down the steps and waiting for the Phantoms to drop off their cargo before charging in with guns blazing. While not subtle, this tactic allows you to quickly drop foes before they disperse and attack you from multiple angles. If you can arc a Grenade into the opening Phantom cargo doors from which the foes descend, or drop a Grenade on the ground where they all land, you can remove multiple threats with a single strike.

Tactic: Cover-to-Cover Situations

On higher difficulties, it is vitally important to remain behind cover and as high as possible along the flat paved section at the top of the steps. This allows you to snipe at foes from long range as they ascend up to you, but not at the expense of leaving yourself open to attack; the concrete planters and barricades are useful as cover. Continuous movement and "Phantom-scanning" is also helpful. Stay mobile so you aren't outflanked, and remain at the sides of this courtyard to remain safe. Always check the skies for incoming Phantoms; they drop foes in the central, left, or right sides of the base of the courtyard steps. Knowing where the enemies have dropped in allows you to pinpoint them as they run into view.

Tactic: Turrets and Lookout Platforms

Generally, the more difficult your task is, the less time you should spend on the stepped platforms overlooking the courtyard. Although some have Turrets, you're a prone target who can be cut down from multiple angles and by multiple foes. The Turret, however, does have its uses if you wrench it off its stand. This stops the ammunition from being infinite but does allow you to avoid incoming mortar fire. Now move along the upper pavement, cutting down multiple foes until the ammo runs out, and secure another Turret you can run around with.

2C

2D

TIP Remaining on the upper pavement also allows you to spot more dangerous threats, such as armored Brutes or Hunters, as your allies are likely to be shouting for help or helping you defeat enemies. The more cross-fire opportunities you can create, the less chance you have of being hit.

At the top of the courtyard, at the base of the steps that lead into the Oni Building, you can secure a Rocket Launcher, which is an optional method of dealing with the Wraiths. Better yet, handing this weapon (or the spare Spartan Laser) over to Mickey helps your fight, as Mickey never runs out of ammunition.

Tactic: The Laser Blaster

Couple your Wraith takedowns with the Laser Blaster Achievement. Taking down all three Wraiths, one at a time once the Phantom drops them, nets you points and a quick Achievement, although the progress is hard-fought. Because there's a chance you might miss if you fire at the Wraith from extreme range, it is better to head along either perimeter side of the courtyard to a Wraith drop-off position before heating up your Spartan Laser and demolishing it with a single strike. Don't wait and watch the pretty explosion; enemies will already be heading to intercept. Instead, retreat back to cover, continue the fighting against the Covenant infantry, and check for more Wraiths being deposited by Phantoms to repeat this tactic.

CAUTION **Do you spend a disproportionate amount of time sprawled on the ground in a death spasm? Then you're being too cavalier about the Covenant's deadly attacks; seek cover, keep moving, and retreat as soon as you're instructed.**

OBJECTIVE

ONI ALPHA SITE Retreat, defend ONI Building interior

TIP **Each Wraith counts as three of the ten kills you need, so defeat each of the three tanks during this battle, and then tag any final foe to claim this Achievement. If you used up your Spartan Laser ammunition too soon (in Choke Point 1, for example), there's a second Spartan Laser on a bench up at the higher (southeast) end of this courtyard. The other available weapons include UNSC-issued hardware (Rocket Launcher, Silenced SMG, Assault Rifle, Magnum) and dropped Covenant ordnance (Brute Spiker, Needler, Plasma Pistol, and the Brute Shot). Also remember that if you don't want to risk taking down a Wraith, shooting a line of foes with a single shot is just as productive.**

■ Choke Point 3: ONI Interior: Lobby

TIP **This section of the mission plays very similarly to "Firefight Mission: Alpha Site." You may wish to read up on various methods of repelling Covenant enemies during that gameplay mode and apply it here. Or, follow any of the advice shown below.**

ENTITIES ENCOUNTERED

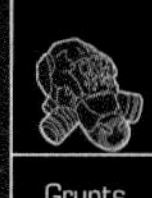
Grunts

Brutes

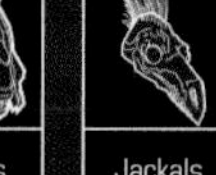
Jackals

Phantom

The Covenant continue to overwhelm the city defense forces, and you have no choice but to enter the ONI Building lobby. Follow Mickey, ideally giving him the Rocket Launcher so he can lay waste to the incoming Covenant and help you out with impressive kill counts. Move down the entrance corridor, then go south into the stepped lobby area. Pass the large UNSC pillar to the central lobby area **[3A]**, where minimal sandbag defenses are augmented with a Chaingun Turret, Grenades, and SMGs. The enemies, consisting of waves of Grunts, Jackals, and Brutes, are about to appear from either of the two doorways **[3B]**, which have energy walls that don't allow you to head back to Choke Point 2. However, the signs, pillar, and the sides of the staircases allow you to set up sniping or ambush positions to help your cause.

Tactic: Up Close and Personal

The Turret in the middle of this lobby is the perfect piece of killing equipment; keep it on its stand so you have infinite ammunition and an easy, 90-degree urn when aiming at either of the enemy incursion oints. Then let rip as soon as foes start to infiltrate he premises. This usually isn't an issue on lower lifficulties, but if you're being struck by enemies, vrench the Turret off its stand and become mobile vith it. Remember, you have Mickey and the police on our side, so don't expect to lay waste to the entire ncursion yourself. You can follow up combat with a Shotgun, stepping around corners to blast foes before neading around cover to blast again.

Tactic: Far Away and Impersonal

On higher difficulties, it becomes more problematic to wield the Turret without being injured, as you're slow and almost always compromised if you keep the Turret attached to its stand. Instead of employing the Turret which can still be effective), if you have a Sniper Rifle (or any ranged weapon), you can stay behind cover, even heading up the stairs to the southeast to gain extra lefense from more sandbags and additional height. Tag oes with headshots as they appear, and move from cover-to-cover opportunities if you're in danger.

Tactic: Up Close and Enraged

If you have a more aggressive attitude at higher difficulties, correct positioning and aiming is crucial. When you hear Mickey mention an incoming enemy wave, run with your Gravity Hammer (sometimes secured from the Brute Chieftain in the previous choke point) at the ready, toward the base of the energy walls blocking your path, and wait for the enemies to start streaming out. Lob a Grenade in there so it catches multiple foes, ambushing them when they are grouped together before they have an opportunity to spread out. Continue this tactic until you're out of Grenades, or the foes manage to struggle through your projectile bombardment; then finish them with the Hammer or Shotgun.

After a few waves of foes emerge from the doors, the action ceases, allowing you to regroup in the central area and rearm. There is the usual assortment of Covenant gear to take, too. Then be ready for a Phantom to drop off several Brutes and Jackals from the exterior platforms to the south. These foes usually infiltrate the upper lobby area **[3C]**, but the numerous pillars provide many cover opportunities. Choose any of the previous tactics to nullify the threats. Remember that if you're fast enough, you can lob a Grenade at the ground where the foes drop to from the Phantom, on the outside platform, severely impeding the enemy forces.

As soon as you've slain the last of the enemies, the elevator near the central lobby area becomes operational; access the door and you receive a new objective. Step into the elevator and activate the termina inside. The elevator ascends to the ONI Building's roof access.

OBJECTIVE

ONI ALPHA SITE Take elevator to roof for evac

TIP **Stop! Before you start the elevator, check your available weapons; it is wise to carry your favored Drone-tagging hardware (such as the Carbine) and any of the other preferred weapons (or the Brute Shot) before engaging Choke Point 4.**

Choke Point 4: ONI Interior—Elevator and Escape

ENTITIES ENCOUNTERED

Drones

Grunts

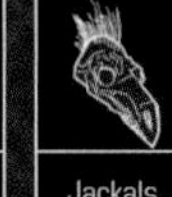

Jackals

Jump-Pack Brutes

NMPD Pelican

As you ascend in the elevator, flick on your VISR Enhanced Vision, and arm yourself for combat with Drones; a swarm heads up from underneath the rising elevator **[4A]** and flits about, annoying ou and your team. You can optionally tag each of them using your skill, or simply cower behind he elevator door, crouching until you reach the top of the shaft, where the Drones are no longer a threat. This saves ammunition, at the expense of points and pride. When you reach the roof access, follow the floor markings, passing a Health Pack, and move outside.

A Police Pelican will eventually meet the team on the pad outside, but the landing zone ("LZ" n-game) isn't safe yet; there are Jackals and Brutes to wipe off the rooftop before you can be extracted. Face off with Jump-Pack Brutes, Brutes, Grunts, and Jackals **[4B]**. Remember that ou can duck back into the roof-access corridor if you need to rest and regain Stamina. Otherwise, a series of sniped takedowns is always appropriate. On lower difficulties, wading in with a close-assault weapon (like the Shotgun or Brute Shot) can quickly clear the area. There aren't enough enemies to make this a particularly harrowing escape, and you can always load Mickey up with your favorite weapon and watch him rampage through he foes. You can even take the Turret from Choke Point 3 with you if you wish. A few moments later, with the remnants of your oes still active, the Pelican hovers on the pad **[4C]**; extricate yourself as soon as you wish. Your team has prepared a special surprise for the Covenant forces still inside the ONI Building.

4A

4B

4C

Mission 05: Mombasa Streets

ROOKIE • 6 hours after drop • Occupied city center

ONI Alpha Site to NMPD Headquarters

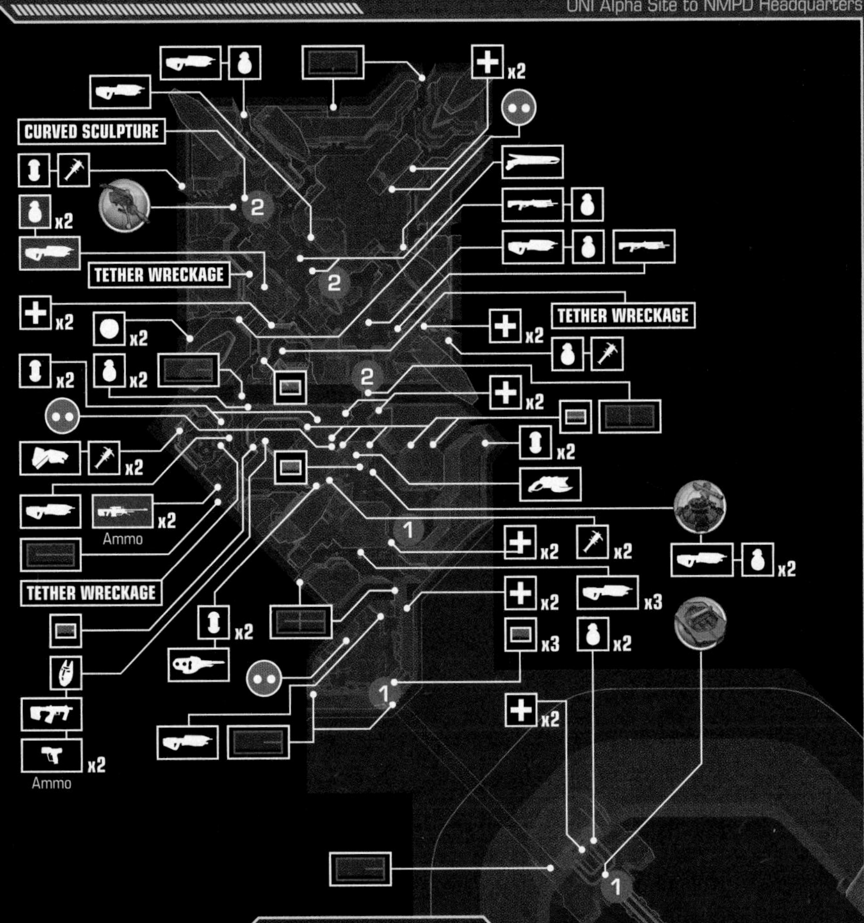

NOTE

This mission takes place in Districts 10, 4, and 3. All accessible districts of New Mombasa (Districts 0, 3, 4, 5, 6, 8, 9, and 10) are available to search through. The following walkthrough details the quickest path from the ONI Alpha Site to the NMPD HQ; you can head to any of the mission objectives you haven't discovered yet, though.

DATA STREAM

New Mombasa VISR Target Acquisition Mode Ratio: 95 percent

PAR SCORE

100,000

PREFERRED WEAPONS

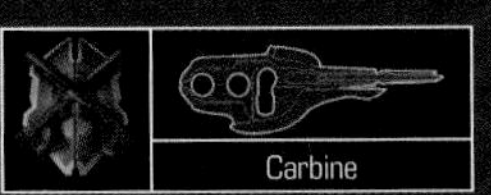
Carbine

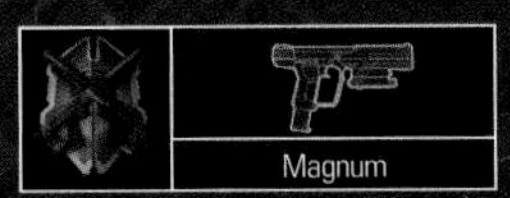
Magnum

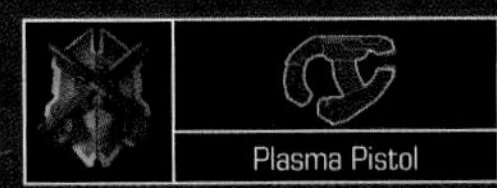
Plasma Pistol

Plasma Rifle

Sniper Rifle

COMM DATA STREAM

After "Mission 01: Prepare to Drop": Hidden COMM Data—7 (Total: 7/30)*

After completing any three missions: Hidden COMM Data—13 (Total: 20/30)*

After completing any four missions: Hidden COMM Data—9 (Total: 29/30)*

After 4 of 7 COMM Data Found: Supply Cache Set 1 Opens (Total: 1/3 Sets)**

After 8 of 20 COMM Data Found: Supply Cache Set 2 Opens (Total: 2/3 Sets)**

After 16 of 29 COMM Data Found: Supply Cache Set 3 Opens (Total: 3/3 Sets)**

Total Caches Available: 8/8**

Set 1 Cache Contents: Sniper Rifle (2), Sniper Ammo (2), Magnum (4), Silenced SMG (4), Frag Grenade (4)

Set 2 Cache Contents: Magnum (4), Silenced SMG (4), Frag Grenade (4), Mongoose (2)

Set 3 Cache Contents: Rocket Launcher (2), Rocket Launcher Ammo (2), Magnum (4), Silenced SMG (4), Frag Grenade (4)

COMM Data Terminals are available only during Rookie missions. These terminals have been deemed "supersecret" and cannot be shown on the Mombasa Streets map.

***Depending on how many COMM Terminals you have found, between 0 and 8 caches are now available and appear on your in-game map.*

MISSION OBJECTIVES

NEW MOMBASA Search NMPD HEADQUARTERS for ODST squadmate

OBJECTIVE

NEW MOMBASA Search NMPD HEADQUARTERS for ODST squadmate

■ Choke Point 1: Rally Point and Kizingo Boulevard Revisited

Hop back on the Mongoose, which you should have used to reach the ONI Alpha Site, and return northwest, into the ramped tunnel and back out to the Rally Point you fought through to reach your previous clue. A few Jump-Pack Brutes are likely roaming the interior of the building you exit close to **[1A]**, so prepare to fight them. However, stay close to cover opportunities, as there's a nasty Jackal Sniper on the rooftop to the east. Tag this annoyance when the coast is clear, but duck back into cover as you attempt to reach the northern exit heading out into District 4; the Rally Point has additional Jackals on the upper balconies to the southwest and northwest **[1B]**. When you've cleared the area or wish to flee, travel north to the gate leading to District 4.

ENTITIES ENCOUNTERED

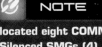

Jackals

Jump-Pack Brutes

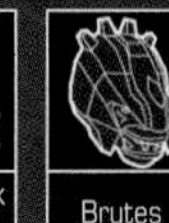
Brutes

Engineer

Grunts

NOTE

There's a weapons cache to the northwest, adjacent to the main road, opposite the base of the stepped area. You need to have located eight COMM Terminals for this to be accessible. Inside are Magnums (4), Silenced SMGs (4), Frag Grenades (4), and Mongoose vehicles (2).

Head down the ramp and go north, into the Kizingo Boulevard area where you drove the Scorpion Tank. Enter the small plaza with the circular planter island in the middle of it **[1C]**, pausing to grab a Health Pack from an Optican Kiosk to the south if necessary. There's likely to be a Covenant patrol in the area; watch for the extra protection an Engineer might offer your foes. You're following a path that's taking you north, toward the stepped concrete planters with the building you can enter. This is where you found the disabled Gauss Turret previously (if you're locating clues chronologically). Deal with a small group of Grunts and a Brute as you drive north **[1D]**, disembarking from your vehicle to grab Health Packs from an Optican Kiosk just to the right (east) of the gate to District 3.

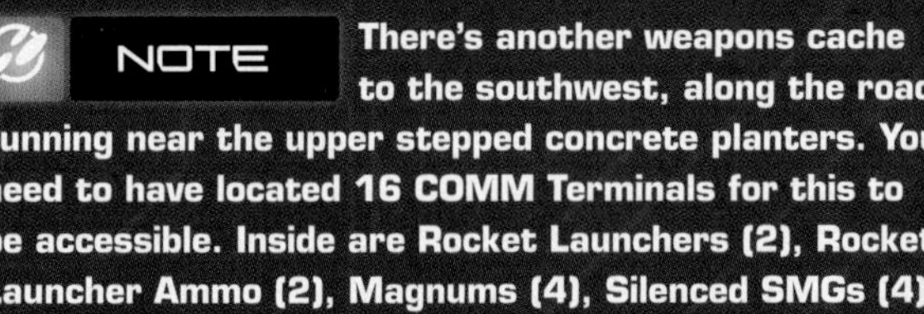
NOTE

There's another weapons cache to the southwest, along the road running near the upper stepped concrete planters. You need to have located 16 COMM Terminals for this to be accessible. Inside are Rocket Launchers (2), Rocket Launcher Ammo (2), Magnums (4), Silenced SMGs (4), and Frag Grenades (4).

1A

1B

1C

1D

■ Choke Point 2: Roundabout and Stepped Plaza Revisited, to NMPD HQ Entrance

ENTITIES ENCOUNTERED

Hunter

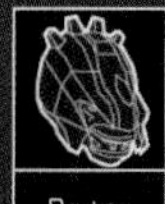
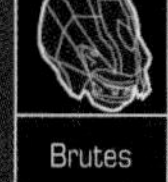
Brutes

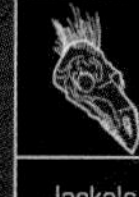
Jackals

Grunts

Drive north to the gazebo area, where the signs of the Scorpion Tank battle are still noticeable. There's a dead Marine inside the gazebo, near an Assault Rifle you can take. Of greater importance is the likelihood of a Hunter prowling this zone **[2A]**; prepare your Grenades and sidestepping capabilities, and tackle (or flee from) this foe before you're struck by its Fuel Rod Cannon. Then check the dead-end street to the northeast for a special Optican Kiosk. You can also rummage through alleyway alcoves near sealed district gates for extra Grenades. From here, you should head northwest, toward the Speed Plaza, although you can take a small detour to the northeast, driving to another weapons cache (this is a Set 2 cache), now guarded by Jump-Pack Brutes and Jackals **[2B]**, and head toward the Covered Plaza where you first found a Scorpion Tank. However, this area is guarded by Jackal Snipers on upper balconies and well-armed and armored Grunts, Brutes, and an Engineer and is out of your way.

Instead, head northeast into the stepped plaza **[2C]**, watching out for Jackal Snipers on the rooftop of the building to the northeast and a ground patrol of Brutes on the stepped area itself. Afterward, you can optionally head southwest, to the base of the steps, and check out an underground roundabout **[2D]**, collecting Grenades, Health Packs, and ammunition, and scaring a group of sleeping Grunts as you go. Continue northwest, taking care not to miss the turn left (west) into the NMPD Plaza, which has a swooping sculpture in the middle of the roundabout **[2E]**. Inspect the area closely; a bent Sniper Rifle hanging from a wire is the next clue to find.

NOTE

Expect more Brute and Engineer patrols as you lollygag in this district. Unless you're looking for COMM Terminals, press on to the NMPD Plaza to the northwest.

Mission 06: NMPD HQ

ROMEO • NMPD Headquarters • 3 hours after drop

Romeo and Buck are about to rendezvous with Dutch and Mickey, but an annoying Covenant Banshee ambush splits up half the team as they fly out of view, crash-landing atop a nearby building. As Romeo, you must trek through the rooftop of the New Mombasa Police Department Headquarters, which has already seen heavy fighting, with numerous officers down. Tactically shuffling through several exterior tiered areas near the Pelican landing platforms and through lobbies, you eventually locate a crane spanning a chasm below, which leads to the rest of your team. An escape is possible only after repelling masses of Covenant aircraft.

DATA STREAM

Data Hive VISR Target Acquisition Mode Ratio: 20 percent*

*COMM Data Terminals are available only during Rookie missions.

PREFERRED WEAPONS

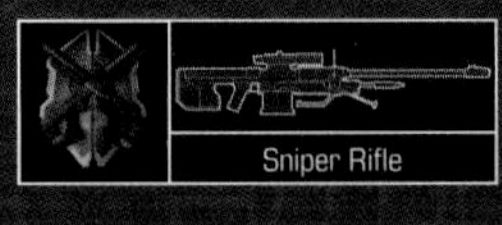
Sniper Rifle

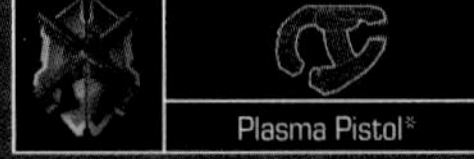
Plasma Pistol*

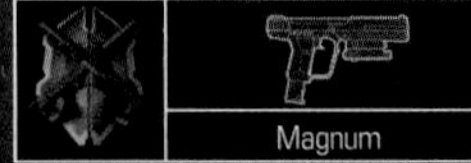
Magnum

Beam Rifle

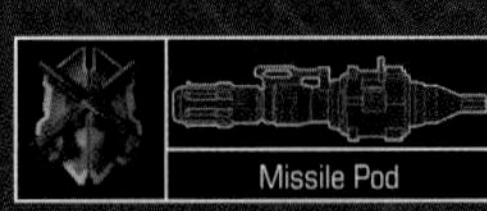
Missile Pod

*Used to remove enemy armor and take down Banshees with a single charged shot

PAR SCORE

40,000

LEVEL-SPECIFIC ACHIEVEMENTS

NMPD: Complete this mission to unlock Romeo in Firefight mission.

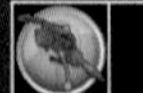
Dome Inspector: Get 15 headshot kills on NMPD HQ.

MISSION OBJECTIVES

NMPD HQ Find Mickey and Dutch's Pelican

NMPD HQ Defend Pelican crash site

New Mombasa Police Department Headquarters:
Lobbies to Pelican platforms to escape defenses

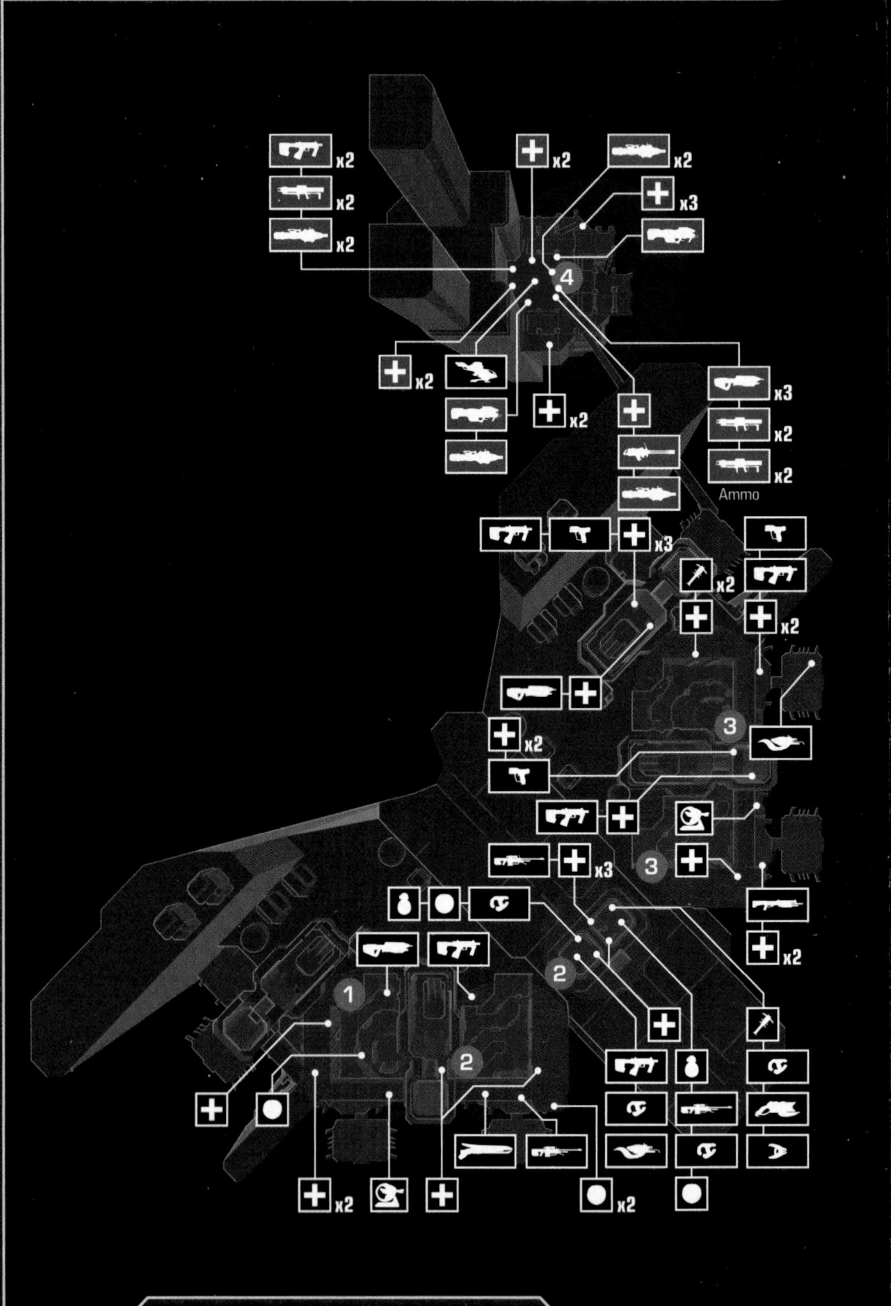

x2 x2 x2 x2 x2 x3 4 x2 x2 x3 x2 x2 Ammo x3 x2 x2 3 x2 x3 3 x2 2 1 2 x2 x2

■ Choke Point 1: Lobby and Tiered Exterior 1 (West)

OBJECTIVE

NMPD HQ Find Mickey and Dutch's Pelican

ENTITIES ENCOUNTERED

Buck

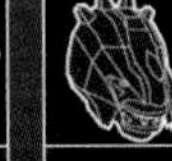
Brutes

Grunts

Jackals

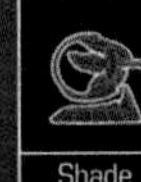
Shade Turret

Phantoms

TIP **These first two sections of the mission play very similarly to "Firefight Mission: Windward." You may wish to read up on various methods of repelling Covenant enemies during that gameplay mode and apply it here. Or, follow any of the advice shown below.**

With Mickey and Dutch fending off Covenant air attacks, you must move through the HQ building to find them from your current position, atop the HQ. Simply follow Buck into the lobby, up the steps, and to the door he opens **[1A]**. This leads to a tiered exterior that drops down to empty Pelican platforms to the south. There are some Grunts and a Brute wandering this concourse. Bring out your Sniper Rifle for this series of takedowns, ensuring it is reloaded before you zoom in on the foes. Aim at the Brute's head, and get a couple of headshots off. Watch the Grunts panic before continuing to tag them with headshots from the cover of the low concrete walls as you advance to the steps. Switch to your Magnum (or your weapon of choice), popping more heads. There's a Shade Turret on the edge of this area **[1B]**, to the left (southeast); use a Grenade or a Sniper Rifle (or other ranged weapon) to extricate the Grunt from inside the Turret, as this is a useful offensive weapon to sit in yourself. Now ready yourself for multiple threats, thanks to two Phantom drops taking place on the exterior platforms. Concentrate on the one in your specific area first, using any of the following tactics.

TIP **Sniping foes in this area isn't just recommended from a tactical standpoint; it also helps you complete the Dome Inspector Achievement that is available only to this mission.**

1A

1B

1C

Tactic: Into the Shade

During the time it takes to defeat the initial group of Grunts and a Brute, you should be able to spot a Phantom flying overhead and touching down on the platform ahead (south) of you. If you've expertly removed the Grunt from the Shade Turret, step into and man this device as early as possible, swinging it around to the right (southwest). This allows you to spot the foes disembarking from the Phantom and running into a connecting corridor **[1C]**, which leads up a ramp to your current location. Fire at will, cutting down multiple foes with the Turret so that nothing can encroach up through the corridor. Keep doing this until everything not named "Buck" is dead.

Tactic: Out Come the Grenades

An alternative plan, which doesn't leave you stationary, is to stand by the Shade Turret and throw Grenades down the sloping corridor that leads to the Phantom platform exterior, catching all the foes as they stumble out toward you. Then mop up with your favored weapon. If you're extremely quick, you can drop the Brute, then head to the top balcony overlooking the Phantom. Lob Grenades at the foes' landing spot when they disembark from the Phantom, which catches them before they can disperse. Finally, don't forget there's a door on the right (west) that connects to the interior corridor; this has a dead Marine with two Health Packs nearby.

Tactic: Minimum Encroachment

With additional firepower and warm bodies, you can really take control of this set of exterior platforms; while one player is on sniper duty (ensuring the Shade Turret is neutralized quickly, too), the second should rush the balcony and lob Grenades at the descending Phantom, dodging any Plasma Turret fire from the vessel. With additional players, you can catch more foes with Grenades or even knock Plasma Turrets off the Phantom, picking them up if they fall on the platform. Have another teammate patrol the interior corridor with a Brute Shot, pounding foes

TIP If you're not impressed with Buck's weaponry, hand him a weapon you're sure will help you both out, such as a Carbine, a Beam Rifle, or any other powerful piece of killing ordnance.

■ Choke Point 2: Tiered Exterior 2 (East)

2A

2B

ENTITIES ENCOUNTERED

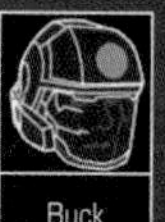
Buck

Brutes

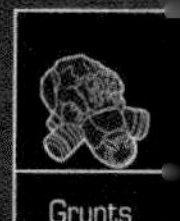
Grunts

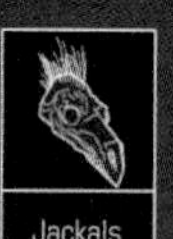
Jackals

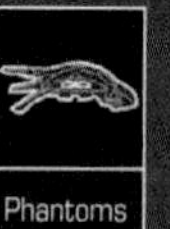
Phantoms

With the western exterior cleared of foes, you must head east, through the lower lobby door (where you can access a Health Pack if necessary) and into an identical tiered exterior location. This area has foes you must battle through from the base of the structure to the top.

Tactic: Taking out the Turret

The biggest threat to your survival is a Grunt manning a Plasma Turret **[2B]**, which is targeting the exit door from the thoroughfare you're in **[2A]**. Stay in the cover afforded by this chamber, and snipe the Turret operator before stepping out. Another excellent location to stand is back in the previous exterior area, close to the door, where the Shade Turret is; snipe any foes on the balcony edge, across the chasm gap you can fire across. You could employ the Shade Turret for this purpose. Now take cover on this raised balcony, using the nearby cover as you begin sniping foes on the tiered area north of your position. Clear away any Jackals or Grunts in this location first.

A second Phantom drops off troops on the platform to the south, behind the balcony. You can ignore these foes for the moment, as you have Jackals armed with Carbines firing on your position. If you zigzag up the stairs on the tiered area, you risk being cut down or badly wounded; instead, remain in cover and tag them with your Sniper Rifle or other favorite ranged weapon. Check the balconies on and above the tiered area **[2C]**, and continue to punish any foes you see.

Tactic: Just Taking the Turret

If you want a closer and more brutal combat, detach the Plasma Turret from its mounting, and rush to the top of the tiered area, cutting down Brutes, Jackals, and Grunts as you go. Mowing down foes is exceptionally effective and is much better than lobbing Grenades up or being cornered on the stairs halfway to the top tier **[2C]**. Don't rest until you've massacred all the Brutes and other foes. Then quickly check the area and easily hunt down and kill any stragglers for the additional points. When the area is secure, swiftly move east, toward a second lobby that has opened **[2D]**. There's a wide variety of UNSC and Covenant weapons, Grenades, and Health Packs to pick up.

The enemies streaming out of the Phantom are usually cut down with the Plasma Turret during your ascension of the tiered area, but you can always use the ramp entrance under the balcony or the side door, which leads to an interior corridor that wraps around to the exterior platform entrance and ramp. Grab a Health Pack along here if you need it.

NOTE **Between the mission commencement and the inspection of the second lobby at the end of Choke Point 2, you can pick up Assault Rifles, a Plasma Turret, a Plasma Pistol, a Plasma Rifle, a Spiker, a Needler, a Brute Shot, a Carbine, a Sniper Rifle, and a Magnum, and you can use a Shade Turret.**

2C

2D

■ Choke Point 3: Tiered Exteriors 3 and 4 (North)

3A

3B

ENTITIES ENCOUNTERED

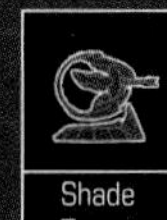

Jackals

Shade Turret

Jump-Pack Brutes

Grunts

Brutes

Brute Chieftain

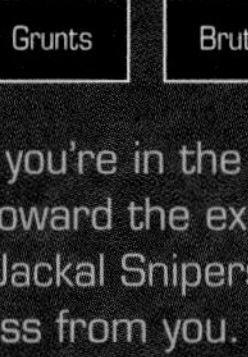
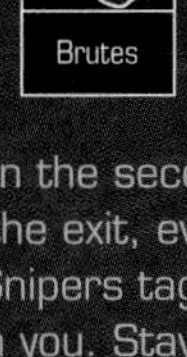

3C

3D

3E

3F

Choose your favorite sniping weapon while you're in the second lobby, and then carefully creep northeast toward the exit, ever mindful that rushing out usually results in Jackal Snipers tagging you from the balconies of the building across from you. Stay to the shaded right side while you're in the lobby so you aren't spotted immediately, and then move to the lobby's edge, by the center pillar that offers protection when you sidestep behind it **[3A]**. Peer around the left side of the pillar to locate three or four Jackals patrolling the balconies. Quickly pick off any Jackal you spot before it can react, knowing the remaining Jackals are now actively looking for you. Stay on the pillar's left side and continue spotting and tagging Jackals one by one with well-aimed headshots. Then step out slightly, facing right (east) and tackling any remaining Jackals on the skybridge above the tiered area.

TIP **You may wish to return to the lobby at this point and stock up on more wide-ranging weapons to augment your sniping ordnance. You should also be close to completing your Dome Inspector Achievement by now.**

The far balcony on the edge (east) of the tiered area has a Shade Turret and a few Jump-Pack Brutes to take care of **[3B]**, and they are firing on your location. Remain armed with a sniping weapon, and attempt to drop the Grunt in the Shade Turret. If this fails or becomes too difficult, try a well-aimed Grenade; that Grunt is a sitting target—literally. When the Turret is no longer a threat, move out into the open and begin tagging Jump-Pack Brutes, using any of your favored Brute-culling weapons. The Carbine is a good example, especially as the Brutes can fly, making ground-favorable Grenades and other weapons (such as the Brute Shot) less effective. Don't head too close to these Brutes, because they frequently attempt to arm the Shade Turret if it is still functioning. There are two ways to solve this problem: blow up the Turret with a Grenade, or snipe Brutes as they head for the turret.

When you've defeated (or run past, although this isn't recommended) the Jump-Pack Brutes, head toward another lobby door at the area's lower-left (northeast) corner. There's an interior corridor like the previous locations, but it is empty except for a Health Pack on a wall; grab it if you need it. Then step into the lobby's connecting thoroughfare **[3C]**, where you can obtain additional Health Packs and scattered weaponry.

The fourth tiered exterior **[3D]** to the north features several groups of Jackals, Grunts, a Brute, a Jackal Sniper, and an armed Plasma Turret. The majority of the more dangerous enemies are to your left (west), at the top of the tiered area. From the lobby doorway, kill any Grunts milling about nearby, but quickly dash across to the northeast, heading up the steps toward the search lights **[3E]**.

and cut down a group of Jackals up there. Use the scenery as cover, and lob Grenades down at the remaining foes in the central tiered area to the west. The Plasma Turret **[3F]** and Jackal Sniper now open up on you; either snipe or dash and lob Grenades or fire on the enemy manning this Turret before turning your attention to the sniper. Make sure you defeat all foes in the area before you reach the top tiered floor. As usual, there's a side corridor that runs from the northern perimeter wall of the tiered area to a ramp under the searchlights. Head in there for additional cover or Health Packs.

When you reach the top tiered floor, a Chieftain armed with a Plasma Turret and two more Brutes exit from the lobby door on this level to the northwest. You should already have detached your own Plasma Turret and be raking their armor with it. Cut down all remaining foes in a hail of plasma before exiting via the lobby door.

Tactic: Maximum Coefficients

If you have the luxury of teammate support, this choke point becomes much more straightforward, as you can each take out a Jackal Sniper. Pick teammates to take down the Shade Turret while the others focus on the Jump-Pack Brutes. You can storm the fourth tiered area using the stairs on either side, while a sniper or two stay by the searchlights, tagging the Plasma Turret and enemy snipers.

NOTE **Choke Point 3 has a Silenced SMG, a Magnum, a Plasma Pistol, a Plasma Rifle, a Plasma Turret, a Beam Rifle, a Carbine, a Spiker, a Needler, a Shade Turret, a Mauler, and a Brute Shot to take.**

■ Choke Point 4: Pelican Crash Site

4A

4B

4C

4D

ENTITIES ENCOUNTERED

Grunts

Jackals

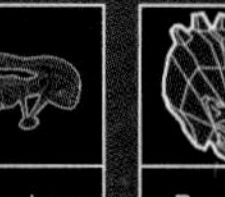
Banshees

Brutes

Mickey

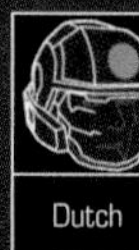
Dutch

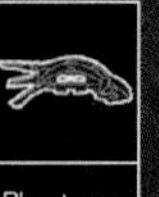
Phantoms

Jump-Pack Brutes

Enter the lobby **[4A]**, and rake the fleeing Grunts with the Plasma Turret or with a fast-firing weapon as you head northeast down the stairs, to the chamber's main exit. Before you head back outside, inspect the dead police officers. There are UNSC-rated SMGs and Health Packs to gather if you need them. Follow Buck outside, peering down to a Pelican platform **[4B]**, where a Grunt with a Fuel Rod Cannon and two Jackals are patrolling. Bring them down with headshots before the foes see you, beginning with the Grunt (as his weapon is the most devastating). Quickly deal with any Jackals, grab a Beam Rifle, and head north, carefully dropping down onto the makeshift crane bridge **[4C]** that spans from the Pelican platform to the crash site where Mickey and Dutch are waiting for you.

CAUTION **Take more care than normal when crossing this bridge; when you're halfway across, two Banshees swoop in and shake the bridge with their fire. If you're carrying a Plasma or Spike Grenade, a superbly timed throw lodges the Grenade into one of them, destroying it as the Banshee passes.**

When you reach the lower of the crash site's two floors **[4D]**, you are met with moderate threats thanks to a group of Grunts and a couple Brutes. Help Mickey and Dutch kill these enemies first; by far, the most proficient way is to bring the Beam Rifle from one of the dead Jackals you found before you dropped onto the bridge. You can attack these foes as you finish crossing the bridge, thinning their number significantly before ascending via either set of steps to the upper platform, where your teammates are already repelling Covenant attacks. Your objective updates.

OBJECTIVE
NMPD HQ Defend Pelican crash site

You must now defend the crash site against waves of Banshees **[4E]** and Phantoms **[4F]** flying toward your position. These Phantoms also deposit Covenant infantry. There's a slight feeling of panic as you decide which weapons to use, where to stand, and who to target first. Here are some optimal tactics, based on the following preferred antivehicle weaponry you should obtain:

TIP There are two Spartan Lasers, several Rocket Launchers, Missile Pods, and two Missile Pod Turrets scattered around the upper platform near the parked Pelican. Obtain at least one of these weapons to aid you in forthcoming combat. In addition, Choke Point 3 has Assault Rifles, Plasma Pistols, Plasma Rifles, Beam Rifles, Needlers, a Fuel Rod Cannon, Silenced SMGs, and Spikers to take.

Tactic: Mayhem with the Missile Pod

If you attempt to arm a Missile Pod Turret, locate the one on the Pelican's right (northwest) side (if you're facing the Pelican). The Turret on this side has a much greater firing range than the one on the other side; choosing the latter can severely impede your takedowns. Assuming you have a wide targeting area, keep the Turret attached to its base so you have infinite ammunition, and begin firing at Banshees and Phantoms as soon as they appear. On harder difficulties, it is vital that the Banshees do not move within their firing range, as their weapons can kill you with a few strikes. There's also the added problem of being struck by falling Banshee wreckage when you destroy one near your position. When attacking a Phantom with a Missile Pod Turret, blast them before they can drop off their troops to contain the Covenant in the air only. Launch several (at least three) missiles at one of the Phantom's engines to destroy it quickly.

Tactic: Other Favorable Options

If both Missile Pods have been destroyed or occupied, you can locate a Chaingun Turret. These inflict an excellent amount of damage on Banshees, dropping them easily. They are also good at strafing hostiles lingering in the area, including infantry dropped off by Phantom. However, if Banshees are getting through and bombarding you, take a Rocket Launcher or a Spartan Laser and aim either one at a Banshee; it takes only one strike to destroy one. You have six scattered Missile Pods you can use to take down a couple of Phantoms or Banshees too.

Tactic: If All Else Fails...

If you've run out of the larger weapons, there's always a charged Plasma Pistol shot to try; this disables Banshees after a single strike, after which they plummet into the streets below. For best results, get a Banshee pilot's attention by firing a couple Plasma Pistol shots at or near the Banshee. The pilot usually flies straight at you, allowing you to easily hit it with the charged Plasma Pistol shot.

Tactic: Incoming Infantry!

You should have the hardware, the team, and the skill to keep the Phantom infantry drops to zero, or at least to a minimum. If Covenant foes begin spreading out from the drop-off points on the lower level, Buck, Mickey, and Dutch do an admirable job at stopping them from reaching the Pelican, allowing you to continue firing on the airborne foes—which you should never stop attacking. The only time to ever ignore the Banshees and Phantoms is if the infantry are physically assaulting your specific location (you can leap in to help at any time, at your discretion, but there's one less teammate training weapons on the main airborne enemies).

Tactic: Not Panicking at the Pelican

With two or four players, this tactic offers the best chance at victory. Have two of your team occupy both of the Missile Pod Turrets. These two players can destroy pretty much every foe that floats into view, from across the opposite side of the chasm. Keep in radio contact, and team up on the Phantoms, each firing at the same engine at the same time to down these ships as fast as possible. Dutch, Mickey, and Buck take care of foes that manage to leave these Phantoms, so concentrate only on airborne foes. With more than two players, the remaining teammates should arm themselves with antivehicle weapons (such as the Rocket Launcher or the Spartan Laser) and should destroy the Banshees, pausing occasionally to help Dutch, Mickey, and Buck with any infantry incursions.

The waves of Banshees and Phantoms keep coming until a group of Jump-Pack Brutes eventually manages to land on the platform. Detach the Missile Pod Turret or launch any weapons you may have been saving (Sticky Grenades offer very entertaining airborne Brute deaths!). Finish them off to complete the mission.

Mission 06: Mombasa Streets

ROOKIE • 6 hours after drop • Occupied city center

NMPD HQ Plaza to Kikowani Station Plaza

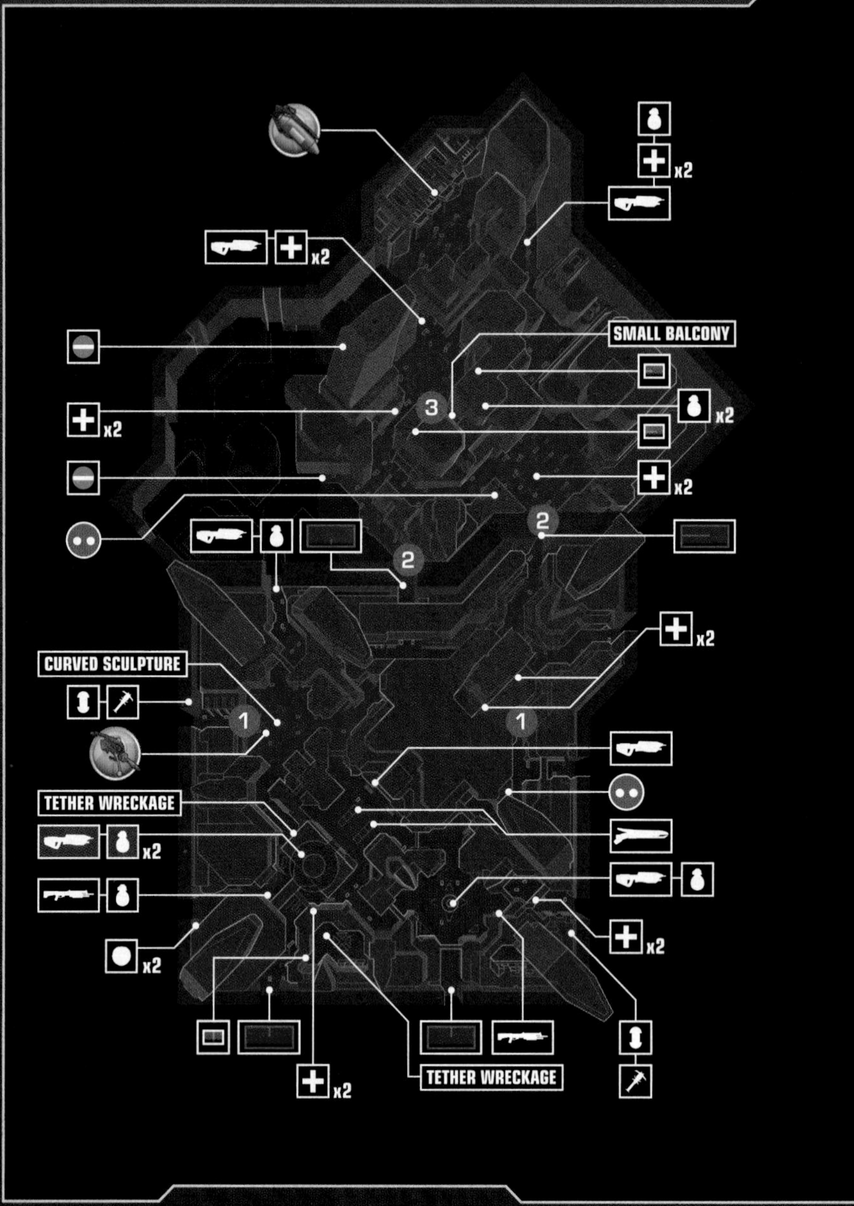

SMALL BALCONY

CURVED SCULPTURE

TETHER WRECKAGE

TETHER WRECKAGE

DATA STREAM

New Mombasa VISR Target Acquisition Mode Ratio: 95 percent

PREFERRED WEAPONS

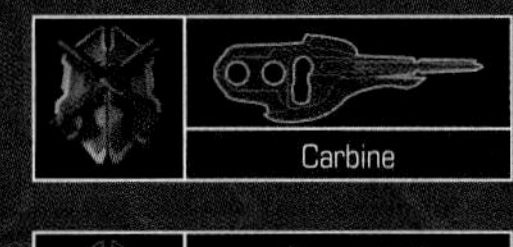
Carbine

Magnum

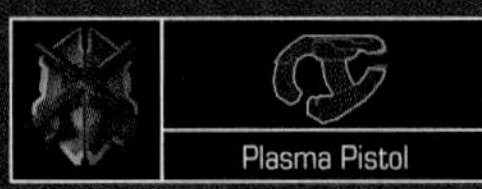
Plasma Pistol

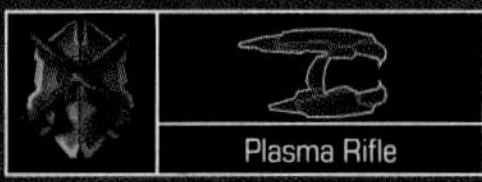
Plasma Rifle

Sniper Rifle

PAR SCORE

100,000

MISSION OBJECTIVES

NEW MOMBASA Search Kikowani Station for ODST squadmate

COMM DATA STREAM

After "Mission 01: Prepare to Drop": Hidden COMM Data—7 (Total: 7/30)*

After completing any three missions: Hidden COMM Data—13 (Total: 20/30)*

After completing any four missions: Hidden COMM Data—9 (Total: 29/30)*

After 4 of 7 COMM Data Found: Supply Cache Set 1 Opens (Total: 1/3 Sets)**

After 8 of 20 COMM Data Found: Supply Cache Set 2 Opens (Total: 2/3 Sets)**

After 16 of 29 COMM Data Found: Supply Cache Set 3 Opens (Total: 3/3 Sets)**

Total Caches Available: 7/7**

Set 1 Cache Contents: Sniper Rifle (2), Sniper Ammo (2), Magnum (4), Silenced SMG (4), Frag Grenade (4)

Set 2 Cache Contents: Magnum (4), Silenced SMG (4), Frag Grenade (4), Mongoose (2)

Set 3 Cache Contents: Rocket Launcher (2), Rocket Launcher Ammo (2), Magnum (4), Silenced SMG (4), Frag Grenade (4)

**COMM Data Terminals are available only during Rookie missions. These terminals have been deemed "supersecret" and cannot be shown on the Mombasa Streets map.*

***Depending on how many COMM Terminals you have found and whether you started your game from the fully unlocked Mombasa Streets after beating the game, between 0 and 7 Caches are now*

NOTE This mission takes place within Districts 3 and 0, in the northwestern zones of New Mombasa. All accessible districts of New Mombasa (Districts 0, 3, 4, 5, 6, 8, 9, and 10) are available to search through. The following walkthrough details the quickest path to Kikowani Station.

OBJECTIVE

NEW MOMBASA Search Kikowani Station for ODST squadmate

■ Choke Point 1: NMPD Plaza to Covered Plaza (Revisited)

1A

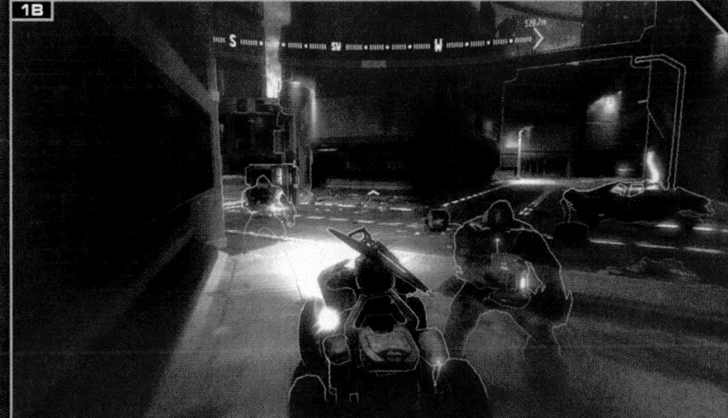
1B

1C

ENTITIES ENCOUNTERED

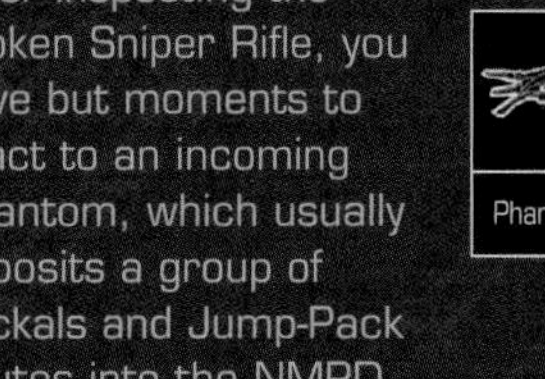
Phantom

Jackals

Jump-Pack Brutes

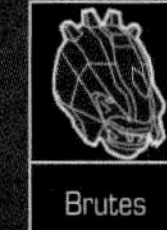
Brutes

Brute Stalkers

After inspecting the broken Sniper Rifle, you have but moments to react to an incoming Phantom, which usually deposits a group of Jackals and Jump-Pack Brutes into the NMPD Plaza **[1A]**. Use your best sniping weapon to deal with these airborne menaces, and use your favored Jackal-culling equipment before returning to your Mongoose and heading east out of this plaza. There's a road to the north and west, but these are blocked. The road to the south leads away from where you should be headed, so ignore that unless you're off to locate more COMM Terminals or you're playing through Rookie's missions out of order.

Immediately east of the NMPD plaza, you can elect to turn left (northeast) or right (southeast). The left route takes you east along a narrow road, with a gate to a western road in District 0 **[2C]** and a possible Covenant patrol. Head right to return to the Stepped Plaza, and continue around to a junction, where a Covenant patrol is likely (this could include Brute Stalkers, so be sure your VISR Enhanced Vision is active). Head north at the junction, driving around to the Covered Plaza (where you began the Kizingo Boulevard mission by locating a Scorpion) and the cache here. The cache contains Set 1 equipment and opens when you've found eight COMM Terminals. This area **[1B]** is guarded by Brutes and Brute Stalkers, so remain alert. Cross the western side of the Covered Plaza. Both routes meet up, allowing you to drive north up a ramped road, past an overturned truck **[1C]**. This road leads to a gate you must open, accessing District 0 at the very northern edge of New Mombasa city.

Choke Point 2: Optican Roundabout and Exit Roads

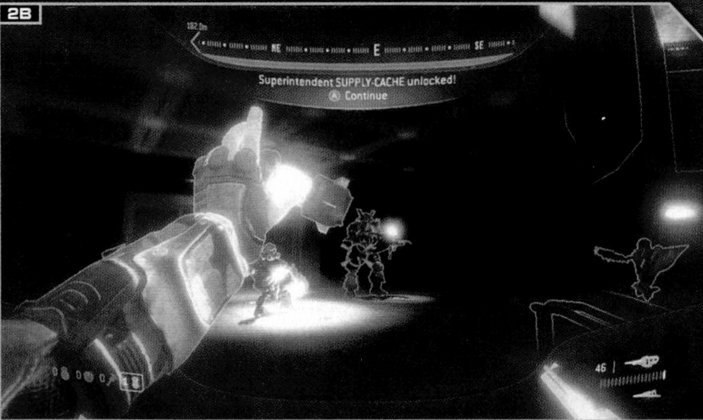

ENTITIES ENCOUNTERED

Brutes

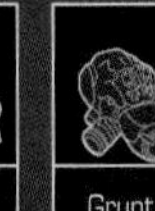
Grunts

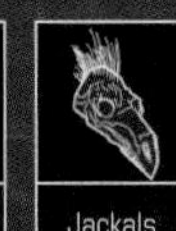
Jackals

This is likely to be an unexplored area, so press north into a new plaza **[2A]** with an Optican Kiosk in the middle of it. Grab the Health Packs you need. There's also a weapons cache that opens after you've found 16 COMM Terminals and contains Set 3 equipment. The plaza is quiet, except for a small Brute and Grunt patrol near or on the steps leading to the inaccessible WST Building to the northeast **[2B]**. Beat down these opponents (those Grunts can be suicidal, so long-range sniping is a good option) before tooling up at the cache if it's accessible. Drive out of the plaza via the northern or western road.

The road to the west **[2C]** is a sniper's alley; check your in-game NAV to locate Jackals on the rooftops. There are two or three to tackle, and there's a Covenant patrol as you round the corner, with Brutes, Jackals, and Grunts to dispose of. Move to the junction and optionally take the road heading south to a gate leading back into District 3. Or, continue north, around to Kikowani Plaza **[3A]**.

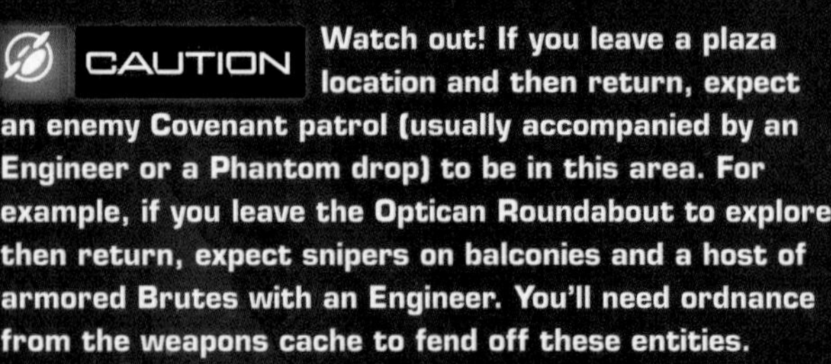

CAUTION **Watch out! If you leave a plaza location and then return, expect an enemy Covenant patrol (usually accompanied by an Engineer or a Phantom drop) to be in this area. For example, if you leave the Optican Roundabout to explore, then return, expect snipers on balconies and a host of armored Brutes with an Engineer. You'll need ordnance from the weapons cache to fend off these entities.**

■ Choke Point 3: Kikowani Plaza and Bus Terminal

Grunts

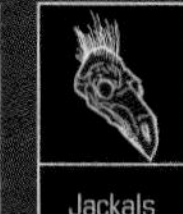
Jackals

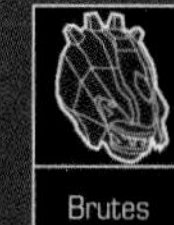
Brutes

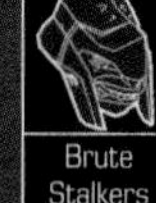
Brute Stalkers

Accessed easily via the western route from the Optican Plaza or from the western gate in District 3, the plaza **[3A]** has a building interior entrance that leads up to a balcony **[3B].** This offers excellent sniping views across the central concrete planters and pedestrian area, where there's likely to be Covenant activity. You can exit down some steps and gather a few Grenades along the way, too. Return to your Mongoose and fend off an attack **[3C]** by Jackals, Grunts, Brutes, and Brute Stalkers. There are also Jackal Snipers on rooftops in this area. From here, you can exit to the north and go directly to your goal, the Bus Terminal, or you can head east.

3A

If you go east, or travel north from the Optican Plaza, you access a ramped road winding through a covered part of the map, partially obscured on your NAV Menu. Drive into a small plaza (known as "Brutal Plaza" during Mission 07), and expect a Jackal Sniper confrontation **[3D]**. The road winds around to the Bus Terminal **[3D]**. The Bus Terminal is eerily quiet, unless you head away from this area and then return again, in which case expect a Covenant patrol nearby. Use your NAV to locate the pulsing beacon icon, driving to the sidewalk entrance to inspect a Bio-Foam Canister **[3E]**—the next clue in your investigative assault on New Mombasa's streets.

3B

3C

3D

3E

Mission 07: Kikowani Station

BUCK • Kikowani Station • 5 hours after drop

After stabilizing Romeo as much as possible, the ODSTs venture into the Kikowani Station complex, a series of gigantic hangars and buildings connected by giant hallways. After advancing on a group of Covenant near some parked vehicles, your crew manages to steal a Phantom, which picks up the other two squadmates while you appropriate a Banshee. Weaving through the heavily defended station complex, you encounter multiple Wraiths and Engineer Housing Pods; destroying these is paramount. The battle continues to a final chamber, where you must face a massive, four-legged Scarab. After fleeing the station, the Rookie must locate a nearby entrance to an Underground Hive, en route to a possible rendezvous with Dare.

Station insertion point to exterior passage.

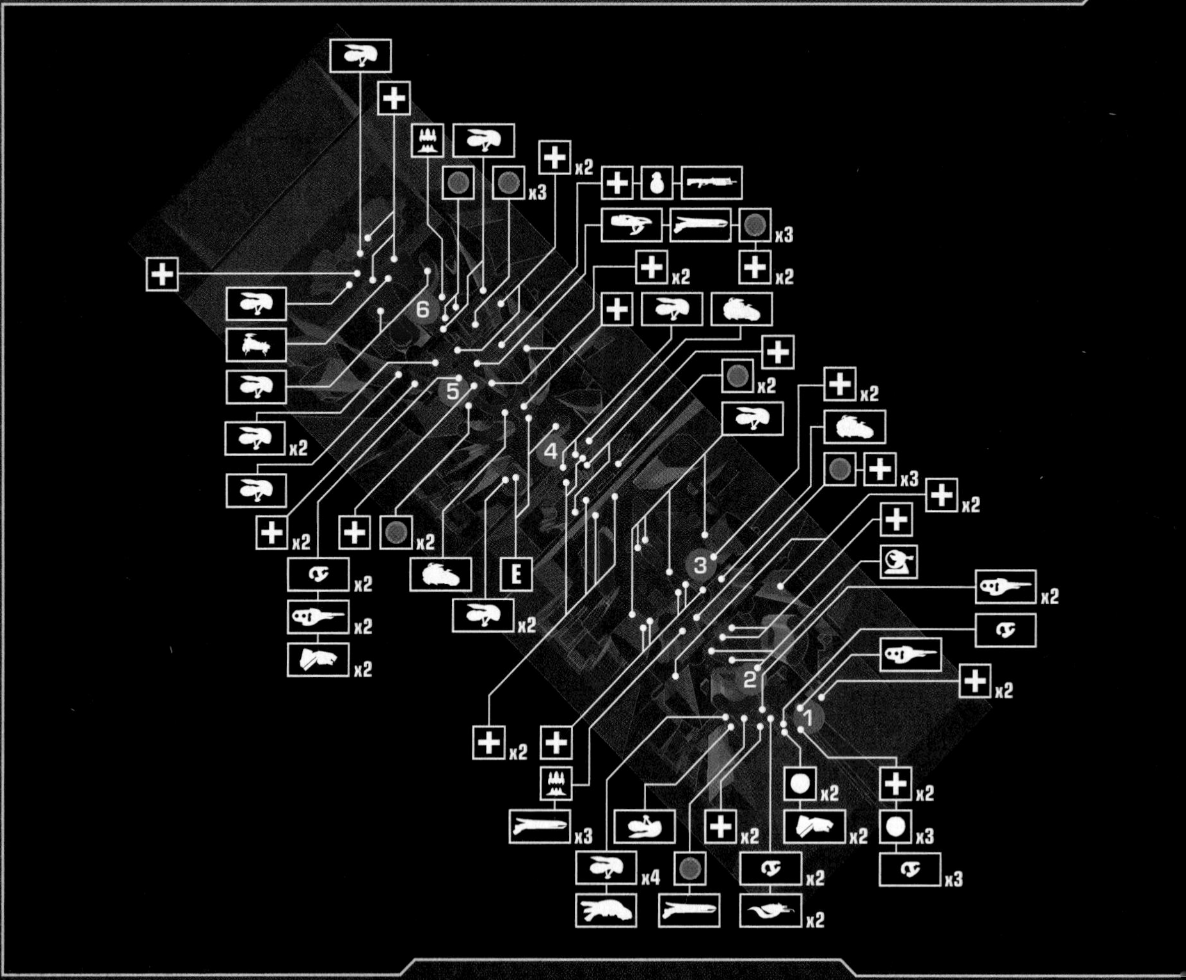

DATA STREAM

Uplift Reserve VISR Target Acquisition Mode Ratio: 100 percent*

COMM Data Terminals are available only during Rookie missions.

PAR SCORE

50,000

PREFERRED WEAPONS

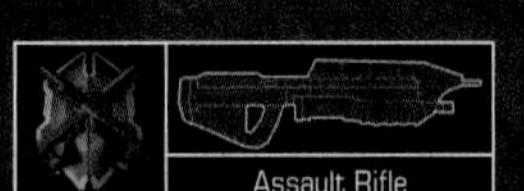
Assault Rifle

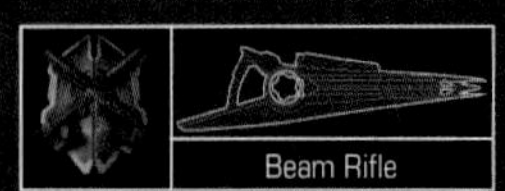
Beam Rifle

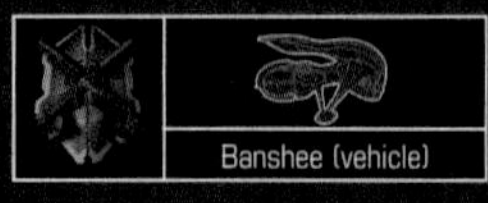
Banshee (vehicle)

Fuel Rod Cannon

Magnum

LEVEL-SPECIFIC ACHIEVEMENTS

Kikowani Station: Complete Kikowani Station on Normal, Heroic, or Legendary

NOTE

For cunning methods of completing these Achievements, consult the Appendices.

MISSION OBJECTIVES

- KIKOWANI STATION Capture Phantom dropship
- KIKOWANI STATION Escort Phantom in a Banshee
- KIKOWANI STATION Open all blocking doors
- KIKOWANI STATION Evade or destroy Scarab

■ Choke Point 1: Kikowani Tramway

1A

1B

ENTITIES ENCOUNTERED

Grunts

Jackals

Brutes

Engineer

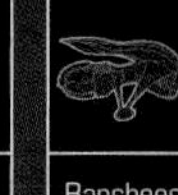
Banshees

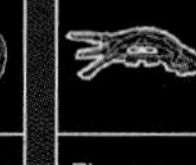
Phantoms

1C

While Romeo continues his wheezing, ignore the right-side concourse and empty tramway, and head down the stairs, following Mickey's lead. You almost immediately run into a small group of Grunts **[1A]**. Switch to your Magnum, and tag their heads easily, or lob in a Grenade, which is less subtle but gets the job done. When the immediate threats have abated, drop onto the tramway line and head west, past the first stationary carriage **[1B]**. Look southwest to check out a plaza **[1C]** and Phantom landing area with several Brutes and Jackals milling about. There are two optimal plans to try here.

OBJECTIVE

KIKOWANI STATION Capture Phantom dropship

TIP

This mission requires you to flick on your VISR Enhanced Vision. It is advisable you keep this vision mode active for the entire mission, as flying in low light without being able to see the outlines of enemies is a grim proposition.

Tactic: Up Close and Personal

If you're confident of your circle-strafing abilities, load up your Assault Rifle and continue along the tramway. Turn left when you spot the sloped entrance to the plaza. Mickey provides covering fire while you either remain at the top of the ramp (for height superiority) or dash into the plaza **[1C]**. The plaza is dotted with Grunts, Jackals, and a couple nasty Brutes, and an Engineer is helping your foes maintain their shields. Optionally tag the Engineer from the sloping entrance, then locate the Plasma Turret on the plaza ground; use it to lay waste to all the Covenant forces you want. You need to cut a route west, toward the Phantom hovering on the right side, which Mickey runs toward. Any foes on the plaza's left side are optional targets.

Tactic: A Long Way Away and Hidden

A mass of Covenant is guarding the vehicles in the plaza, which you need to continue your mission. Stop after the first tram carriage and check the Covenant weapon caches in this location. There are Plasma Pistols and, more importantly, Beam Rifles to take. Grab a Beam Rifle and begin to rapidly headshot all the Grunts; then tag the Jackals through the gap in their shields and headshot them. Deal with the Brutes next. If the Engineer floating about is causing you problems, fire a charged Plasma Pistol shot at it. If the shot hits, the Engineer explodes, removing all Covenant shields on the infantry below. Once you've defeated the majority of the plaza foes, sprint toward the Phantom on the right side.

Mickey boards the vessel; your orders are to appropriate a Banshee; there are four of these parked on the upper plaza section. Board one of these craft immediately. As soon as you take to the skies, your objective updates.

OBJECTIVE

KIKOWANI STATION Escort Phantom in a Banshee

■ Choke Point 2: Raised Platforms and Roadway

Mickey swings his Phantom around to pick up Dutch and Romeo, and then slowly makes his way north in the Phantom. Although you can follow him and guard the Phantom, this isn't wise, as you must try and clear the northern side of this giant hangar as quickly as possible. For this to occur, there's only one real attack strategy: methodically cull the most threatening Covenant forces first, before the Phantom arrives and can help you mop up the remaining forces.

ENTITIES ENCOUNTERED

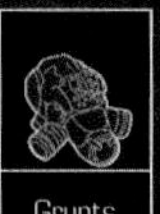
Grunts

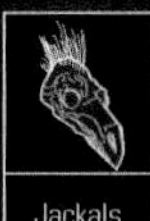
Jackals

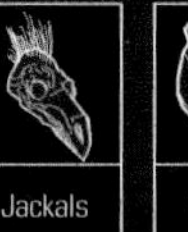
Brutes

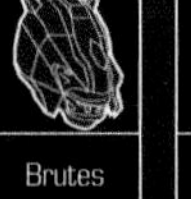
Shade Turrets

Banshees

From your Banshee pickup point, fly north, along the left (western) side of this gigantic hangar, toward a closed hangar door. Ahead should be a Shade Turret. It isn't likely to be manned yet, allowing you to quickly destroy it, then strafe from left to right, blasting the Covenant infantry on this raised roadway **[2A]**. Take out a second Shade Turret before turning east, flying down to the small "island" with three circular generators and two Shade Turrets guarding the roadway nearby. Take down these Shade Turrets, too. This should leave only the foes on the upper balconies overlooking the road. You can ascend and blast the Brutes here before quickly flying northwest, toward the hangar door **[2C]** that is opening.

TIP

Maintain a low-level flight path. You don't need to be much higher than the raised roadway. If you do this, the Covenant on the upper balconies can't effectively aim at your craft.

The hangar door opens **[2C]**, and two Banshees fly out. Behind them in the next area is a Watchtower. Ignore that for the moment, and make sure you're hovering to the side and slightly above the opening hangar door. That way, when the two Banshees fly out, they don't ram or shoot you, which can spell instant doom for your craft. Instead, angle yourself so you're firing accurate shots at their sides, and then follow one Banshee, blasting it out of the sky. Mickey and company usually deal with the other one.

CAUTION

You can simply leave the Banshees to fly around and investigate the area behind the open hangar door, although your points total (and pride) may suffer.

TIP

Remember, your Banshee's Boost capabilities are critical for maintaining an evasive (and constantly moving) posture.

TIP

Before leaving this area, especially on higher difficulties, return your craft to the group of parked Banshees, and choose another, undamaged one. You should also collect a fully loaded Beam Rifle before continuing.

■ Choke Point 3: Engineer Hangar

ENTITIES ENCOUNTERED

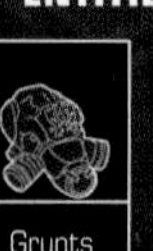
Grunts

Wraith

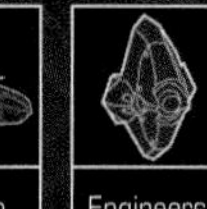
Engineers

Banshees

Ghost

Head into the hallway **[3A]** behind the hangar door and swing right (northeast), quickly blasting the foes off the Watchtower. Mickey is en route here as well, so expect a little additional firepower as you head northeast to the hallway's opposite end and the exit hangar door. There are a few Grunt infantry to easily strafe, as well as an Engineer that slowly floats up, near a Wraith that begins firing at you. You can circle-strafe around the Wraith, bombarding it with fire until it explodes, or ignore it and fly through the opening hangar door. The optimal plan is to speed toward and blast the Engineer, then deal with the Wraith.

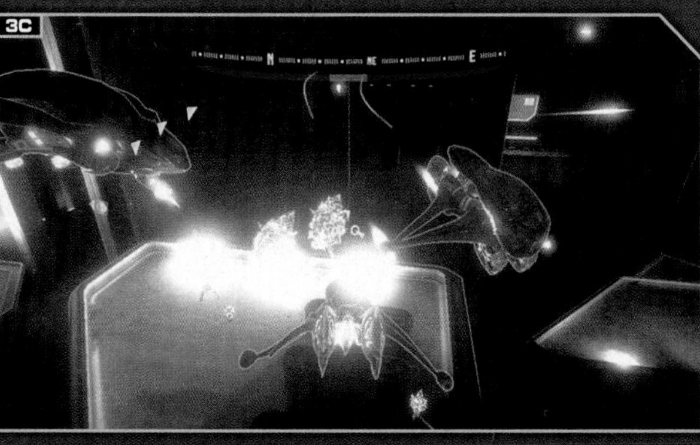

You can also land and attack the Covenant on foot, but this causes you to waste time and leaves Mickey's Phantom to deal with Covenant incursions in the next giant hangar area. If you do drop to the ground, run outside the second hangar door to procure a new Banshee; there's one parked on either side of the door.

Head into a second, giant hangar **[3B]**, and catch up to Mickey's Phantom if you wish; they are bombarding an Engineer Housing Pod atop the largest tower in the middle of this huge chamber. This is an easy target; your task is to avoid a head-on attack with up to five Banshees flying about this location, and engage them in a spot of dogfighting so they don't overwhelm the Phantom with your brethren aboard. Meanwhile, the Phantom fires on remaining clusters of Engineers, which you can target, too. However, as the Banshees are aggressive, take care of them first.

As soon as Mickey's Phantom has finished destroying the Engineer housing area, he requests your presence to open a hangar door on this chamber's northwest wall **[3C]**. The door hasn't opened and must be manually operated. Unless you're aiming for a phenomenally fast Par Score, finish off the Banshee threats in this chamber first, then drop down and secure an undamaged Banshee for yourself, before heading to the closed hangar door. Don't open the door yet if you require health; there's an Optican Kiosk to the left (west), on the pedestrian balcony you're on. Then return to the door, open it, and choose one of two options for clearing out the hallway behind the door with the enemy Phantom and Engineer Housing Pod **[3D]**.

OBJECTIVE

KIKOWANI STATION Open all blocking doors

TIP

Can't find this pesky hangar door? Remember, you can use your HUD's Assistance capability to ascertain the exact location of the door switch.

Tactic: The Dashing Banshee

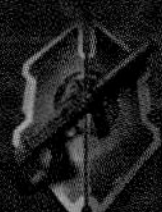

If enemy deaths aren't your concern, simply fly quickly into the hallway and turn right (southwest). Boost quickly toward the enemy Phantom, ignoring its Turret fire before turning right (northwest) and escaping out into the next gigantic area.

Tactic: On-Foot Antics

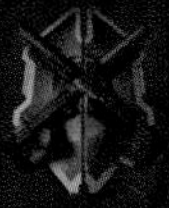

This tactic allows you to stretch your legs and rampage through the hallway on foot. You don't need to be cautious, as Mickey's Phantom executes Grunts for you. Instead of heading back to your Banshee, ignore it and keep to the left as you head down the hallway ramp, tagging Grunts as you go. Turn left (southwest), and avoid any incoming fire from the enemy Phantom at the Engineer Housing. Wait for it to depart, then launch an attack on the power coupling with Mickey. Next, hit the Ghost patrolling the exit area. You can snipe the Brute driver with your Beam Rifle or even throw caution to the wind and attempt a hijack. A better plan is to secure one of the parked (and undamaged) Banshees, and finish the vehicle with Banshee fire before heading into the following area.

Tactic: Mickey's Got Your Back

A measured, airborne response with additional help from Mickey is the safest way to maneuver through this second hallway structure. Head back to your Banshee, and stay close to the left (southwest) interior hallway wall as you strafe the running Grunts. Mickey soon shows up, flying his Phantom down the hallway, and you can both destroy the Engineer Housing together. Afterward, circle-strafe around the Ghost, or simply ignore it, as it can't follow you into this next zone.

Kikowani Station • BUCK

Choke Point 4: Kikowani Towers

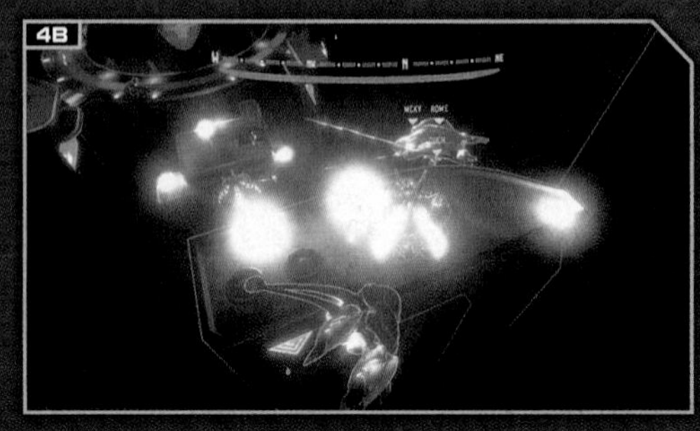

ENTITIES ENCOUNTERED

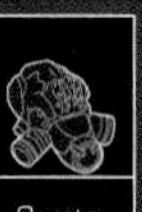
Grunts

Brutes

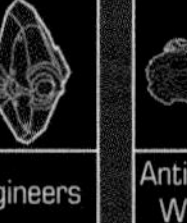
Engineers

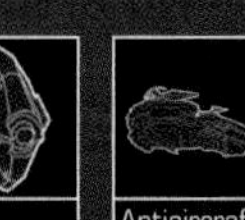
Antiaircraft Wraiths

You enter an open-air area of the station complex with three separate Engineer Housing Pods **[4A, 4B, 4C]** that you must take care of; Mickey's Phantom is doing this job, and it's wise to help him out. There are a couple ways to ensure your attacks aren't doomed, prior to escaping this massive firefight zone.

Tactic: Wrath of the Wraiths

The biggest concern comes from ground targets, as there are no enemy Banshees to strike from the sky. With this in mind, you should be aware of two big problems: a Wraith patrolling the balcony to your right (northeast) as you enter this zone, and another along the curved roadway on the opposite (northwest) side of this area, near the exit hangar door **[4D]**. These Wraiths are notoriously difficult to damage, as you must have pinpoint accuracy in taking down the Brute drivers or must circle-strafe to hit the Wraiths from behind.

For the first Wraith, you can disembark (ideally using the hangar door as cover) and then launch long-range attacks, sniping the Brutes to power down the Wraith. Or make a reckless charge and melee the Wraith by leaping on it. However, this usually ends in death by Fuel Rod Cannons, which are mounted on the Wraiths. After you defeat the first Wraith, help Mickey destroy the three Engineer Housing Pods, which are easily taken out. Park on the buildings that have undamaged Banshees; take one if you need it. Then continue toward the northwest Wraith on the road, circling around it and peppering it with accurate gunfire until it explodes. By this time, Mickey and the team should have cleared the Covenant infantry on the balconies to the left (southwest) and right (northeast).

Tactic: Engineer Housing Demolition

The three Engineer Housing Pods are Mickey's main targets, and he eventually takes them all down. You can help him destroy them in order, as shown on the map. If you help, you can escape this zone much more quickly, which is excellent if you're choosing to ignore the incoming Wraith fire. Basically, the projectile green bolts of Fuel Rod Cannons, plus the sniping and attacks from the balconies, should be avoided at all costs. You can easily see the arcing Fuel Rod shots and can Boost past or strafe around them. Stay low to avoid balcony fire. Then optionally help Mickey take down the Wraith on the roadway.

Your squadmates request your presence along the northwest wall of this zone **[4D]**. The hangar door is shut completely, and the door cannot fully open. This means you must use either of the pedestrian doorways and investigate the hallway beyond to locate a method of opening the main hangar door properly. Enter this area when you're prepared for a frantic fight.

TIP

On higher difficulties, you may wish to retreat back to secure previous Health Packs, or land on the balconies where the Covenant infantry were sniping at you and pick up any of their dropped weapons for the upcoming hallway combat. This isn't imperative, as there's ordnance and health in there, too.

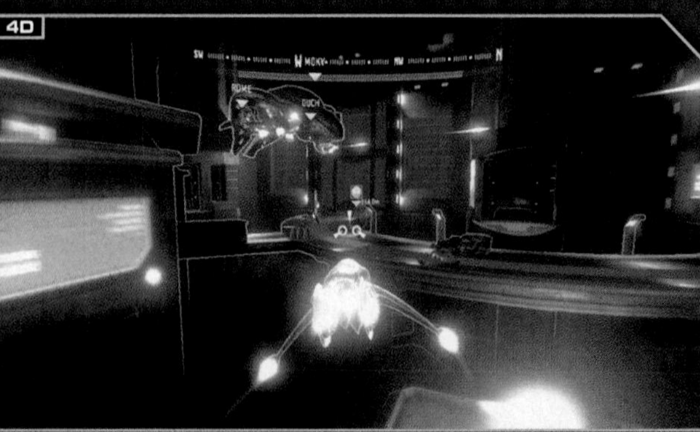

■ Choke Point 5: Chieftain's Hallway

5A

5B

Grunts

Jackals

Brutes (Stalker)

Brute Chieftains*

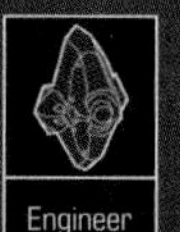
Engineer

*(Gravity Hammer)

Enter this hallway on foot (the only method of maneuvering through here), and immediately take an offensive posture. On the low concrete area is a Covenant supply crate with two Carbines in it, and there is one in the corner with a Beam Rifle. Ahead (northeast) of you is a set of steps, and on either side is a planter and a courtyard. Investigate the right one; it has a crate with Plasma Pistols in it. To your right (east) is an entrance to a controller's room, complete with a dead Marine, two dropped Frag Grenades, and a Health Pack. Here, you are relatively safe from the real threat—a group of Covenant infantry prowling the central section of the courtyard **[5A]**. You can see a Brute near a Plasma Turret facing the steps, a set of Plasma Batteries, and Grunts and Jackals on patrol. In the distance, you may spot an Engineer floating about. Above you, at the end of the hallway, are two Engineer Housing Pods clamped to the walls. Time for some attack tactics!

Tactic: Ruthless Aggression

Head up the steps on the right side, near the entrance to the controller's room. When you spot the enemy in the central area **[5A]**, lob in a Grenade so the Plasma Turret is rendered inoperable, and the set of batteries explode in a writhing ball of plasma. This should take out some of the Brutes, Jackals, and Grunts. Wade in, lobbing Grenades and use a Plasma Pistol or Rifle (grabbed from a Brute's corpse) to reduce the Stalker Brutes' shields. If you can charge a Plasma Pistol shot and down the Engineer, then do so, but this is almost impossible because you'll need to wade through the assembled foes to reach it; try this when you get a break in the fighting, before the Brute Chieftain charges in.

Instead, back down the steps **[5B]**, forcing Brutes down with you. The stairs are narrow enough for you to lob Grenades up. Watch them damage Brutes even if they attempt to dodge. Move into the central area **[5A]**, quickly grabbing health from an Optican Kiosk on your right if necessary. You now have Brute Stalkers and the Chieftain **[5C]** to deal with, and all are likely to be using overshields thanks to the Engineer. If the Engineer is dead, attack them where they stand. If the Engineer is still floating about, back up and tackle the Brutes on the staircase and the lower concrete entrance. Circle around this area, continuously moving and firing, grabbing dropped weapons if you need them. Plasma weaponry is a good choice to whittle down shields, followed by Grenades or Brute Shots.

TIP **Don't forget there's a Plasma Turret in the central area, as well as another Covenant crate with a Fuel Rod Cannon in it. Grab either of these, and laying waste to the Engineer or Brute Chieftain becomes a little easier.**

Tactic: Measured Mayhem

It is simply too dangerous to wade into the courtyard at higher difficulty levels, so you need a more measured approach. This involves remaining silent as you take a Beam Rifle from the Covenant crate on the concrete base platform near the entrance, then line up a shot to explode several Plasma Barricades and perform headshots on the Brutes you can see. Remain where you are, with the understanding that foes are likely to swarm you by heading down the stairs and around the right side of the courtyard. Keep up your Beam Rifle tagging, attempting as many headshots as possible. When foes begin to encroach, back them up with Grenades. This is a lengthy battle. If you're about to be overrun, sprint into the controller's room, where you'll be somewhat safe if you can keep foes from the doorway.

5C

5D

Kikowani Station • BUCK

During a break in the battle, step back out and around to the concrete area, optionally taking a Plasma Pistol with you, and launch a charged shot on any Brute Stalkers or the Brute Chieftain, removing their shields before finishing them with a Beam Rifle headshot and Grenades. When only one or two Brutes remain, you can sprint to this hall's center, grabbing a Fuel Rod Cannon, health, or the Plasma Turret, and dealing final blows to your foes, including that troublesome Engineer.

To open the door and allow Mickey to fly through, you must press a button located inside a booth on the left, near the hall's end. Once you do that, you may return to your Banshee or proceed forward without it. There is another Banshee available if you keep moving forward. Head left out of the hallway and then take your first right to find it.

 TIP **Pick up the Fuel Rod Cannon and Gravity Hammer before continuing; you may need these fearsome weapons when you engage the final main obstacle in this mission.**

Choke Point 6: Scarab Sentry

OBJECTIVE

KIKOWANI STATION Evade or destroy Scarab

Enter the final chamber in the station complex **[6A]**, and immediately take evasive action, flying to the side of an incoming plasma mortar that is coming from a gigantic, four-legged behemoth of a vehicle known as a Scarab **[6B]**. This is by far the most difficult foe to attack in this area, and you must focus on it in a moment. To begin with, though, it helps your cause to dodge the Phantoms' plasma fire as they ascend and depart, before destroying the Engineer Housing Pods under them. There are also Grunts milling around to your left (southwest) at an undamaged Banshee. Ignore that unless you need to swap vehicles. Also ignore the Banshee flying around and concentrate entirely on the Scarab; your continuous movements usually allow you to ignore the Banshee, as it consistently misses you. Now try one of the following takedown options.

ENTITIES ENCOUNTERED

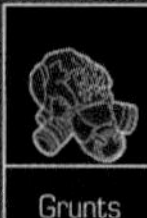
Grunts

Jackals

Brutes

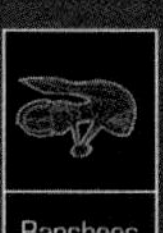
Banshees

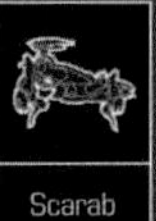
Scarab

Tactic: Immobilization

Facing off with the Scarab **[6B]** is a terrifying affair but is made a little easier if you follow Mickey's shouted instructions. Approach the Scarab and destroy the three Engineer Housing Pods surrounding it before you engage the Scarab properly. The trick to quickly nullify this enemy is to fire on its leg joints when your Banshee's targeting reticle turns red. Blast away until you see an explosion. You must vary your speed and strafing as you circle the Scarab, or its main mortar or thorax turret will strike you. Do this by weaving and Boosting across and swinging around to circle again.

When the Scarab's legs are crippled, boost so you're at the vehicle's rear and bombard its weakened rear **[6B]** with ordnance until the rear hull panel is destroyed, exposing a small energy shield. Direct your fire here until the Scarab is destroyed. If you didn't move fast enough, repeat this tactic until the Scarab sinks to the ground, and victory is assured! Note the two parked Banshees on either side of the platform the Scarab is standing on. Quickly change Banshees if you're close to wrecking your current vehicle.

Tactic: Doing the Legwork Yourself

An alternate method of taking down the Scarab is to fly your Banshee toward and hover directly above the Scarab itself. Then leap out of your Banshee, landing on the Scarab's thorax. You can simply walk around to the back of the Scarab and destroy the core once you've landed on it. You don't need to take out the legs or hop off the Scarab once you are on it to kill it. Just stay on it, walk around to its backside, and destroy the core. Any weapon or melee works for this.

Tactic: Fly and Be Free

There's actually no need to fight the Scarab; as soon as you enter this chamber, you can simply fly to the door on the opposite (west) wall, in the corner of the large platform the Scarab is standing on, and exit your Banshee. Quickly flip the switch to open the hangar door, and then dash inside and secure one of the parked Banshees on the southeast balcony. This is much safer than returning to the Banshee you just discarded, as Scarab fire can kill you instantly.

Escape time! Whether you defeated the Scarab or not, open the hangar door, Mickey flies the Phantom into this exit hallway, and you should follow, toward the cluster of Engineer Housing Pods ahead (northeast). Hit a Pod with gunfire to finally flee the Station.

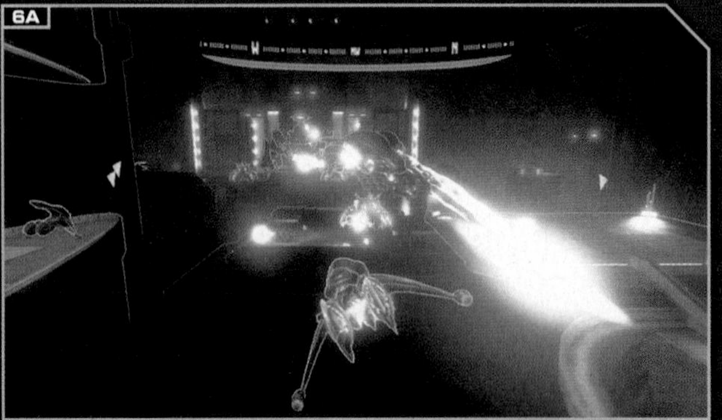
6A

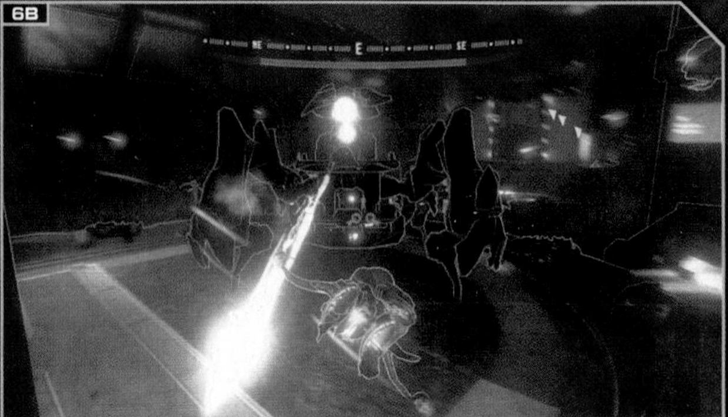
6B

Mission 07: Mombasa Streets

ROOKIE • After midnight • Occupied city center

Kikowani Station to Underground Entrance

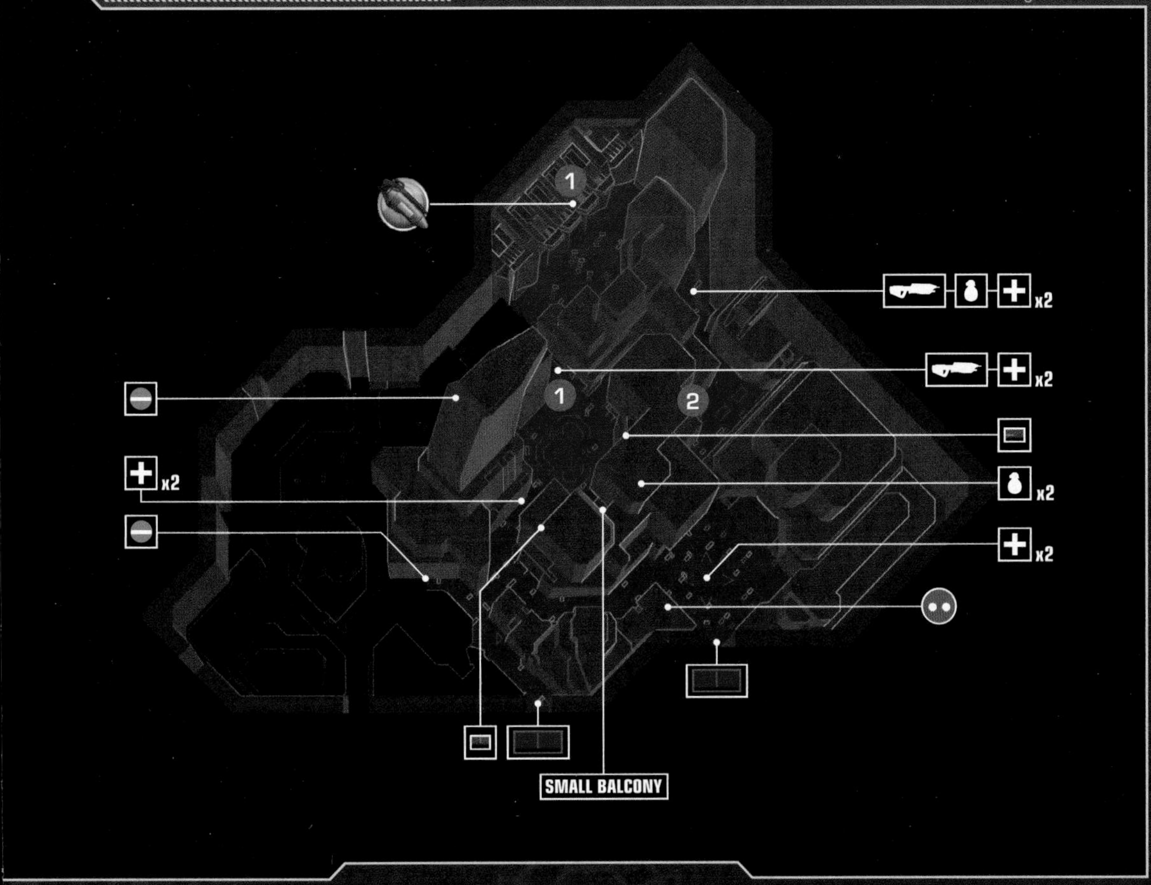

SMALL BALCONY

DATA STREAM

New Mombasa VISR Target Acquisition Mode Ratio: 95 percent

PREFERRED WEAPONS

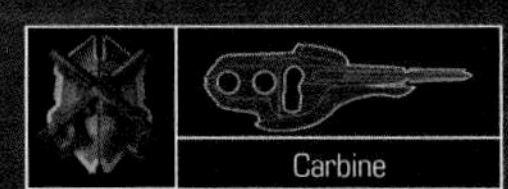
Carbine

Magnum

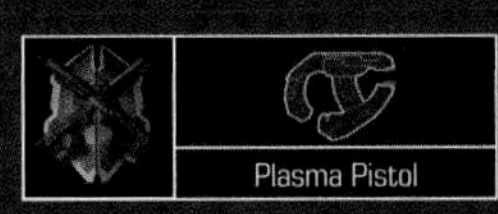
Plasma Pistol

Plasma Rifle

Sniper Rifle

PAR SCORE

100,000

MISSION OBJECTIVES

NEW MOMBASA Locate underground entrance to search for Captain Dare

COMM DATA STREAM

After "Mission 01: Prepare to Drop": Hidden COMM Data—7 (Total: 7/30)*

After completing any three missions complete: Hidden COMM Data—13 (Total: 20/30)*

After completing any four missions: Hidden COMM Data—9 (Total: 29/30)*

After 4 of 7 COMM Data Found: Supply Cache Set 1 Opens (Total: 1/3 Sets)**

After 8 of 20 COMM Data Found: Supply Cache Set 2 Opens (Total: 2/3 Sets)**

After 16 of 29 COMM Data Found: Supply Cache Set 3 Opens (Total: 3/3 Sets)**

Total Caches Available: 7/7**

Set 1 Cache Contents: Sniper Rifle (2), Sniper Ammo (2), Magnum (4), Silenced SMG (4), Frag Grenade (4)

Set 2 Cache Contents: Magnum (4), Silenced SMG (4), Frag Grenade (4), Mongoose (2)

Set 3 Cache Contents: Rocket Launcher (2), Rocket Launcher Ammo (2), Magnum (4), Silenced SMG (4), Frag Grenade (4)

**COMM Data Terminals are available only during Rookie missions. These terminals have been deemed "supersecret" and cannot be shown on the Mombasa Streets map.*

***Depending on how many COMM Terminals you have found, between 0 and 7 caches are now available and appear on your in-game map.*

NOTE

This mission takes place entirely within District 0, at the far northern edge of New Mombasa. All accessible districts of New Mombasa (Districts 0, 3, 4, 5, 6, 8, 9, and 10) are available to search through. The following walkthrough details the quickest path to the underground entrance.

NOTE

This walkthrough assumes you've collected clues in chronological order. If you haven't, the underground entrance to "Mission 08: Data Hive" will be about one block away from where you picked up your last clue, regardless of which district you are in: There are multiple elevator shafts that lead to Mission 08's starting point of Sublevel 7. For the locations of the five other underground entrances, consult the "Tour of Mombasa Streets" section at the end of this walkthrough.

OBJECTIVE

NEW MOMBASA Locate underground entrance to search for Captain Dare

Choke Point 1: Kikowani Bus Terminal and Plaza

ENTITIES ENCOUNTERED

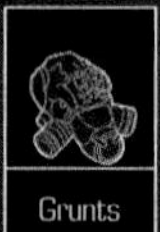

Grunts

Hunters

You appear at the bus terminal streets **[1A]**, where you last found evidence of your squadmates. Expect a few Grunts; they shouldn't cause you any trouble. Return to the Mongoose you used to get here (if you opened up a Cache earlier in your expedition, and used one for swift access through the city streets), and drive to the ramped road heading southeast, into a small plaza littered with debris. There's a dead Marine near two Health Packs, some empty buses, and two fearsome Hunters **[1B]**! Use your speed and the Mongoose to get some distance between you and these beasts, optionally checking an open building to the southeast; inside are some steps leading up to a Frag Grenade and a small balcony allowing views across the plaza. Opt for sniping from here, or use the usual Hunter-takedown tactics on the ground near their lumbering forms. Or, you can flee the area, although this isn't a wise plan; the second choke point is difficult enough to secure without Hunters rampaging up from behind!

1A

1B

Choke Point 2: Brutal Plaza

NOTE

This next section is unfortunately covered on your in-game NAV map. It is a well-guarded entrance to an Underground Hive.

TIP

It might be wise to access a weapons cache; there's one in this district if you've accessed enough COMM Terminals: You need a sizable arsenal for this choke point.

ENTITIES ENCOUNTERED

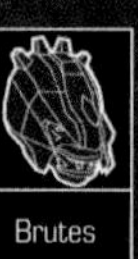

Brutes

Jump-Pack Brutes

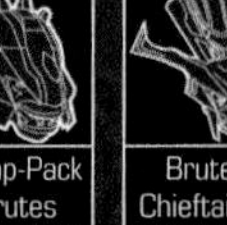

Brute Chieftain*

*(Fuel Rod Cannon)

Drive your Mongoose to the sloping road heading northeast **[2A]**, away from Choke Point 1. Or, travel southwest, following the U-shaped road to the bus roundabout area **[2B]**, which is usually empty of foes. The roundabout gives you a height advantage as you're descending a sloped road compared to **[2A]**, which has a road you must ascend. Take the exit road to the northwest. From either of these locations, you reach a small plaza area **[2C]** with around six Brutes waiting to demolish you. To add to the problems, there's also a Fuel Rod Cannon–wielding Brute Chieftain! Try one of the two following tactics.

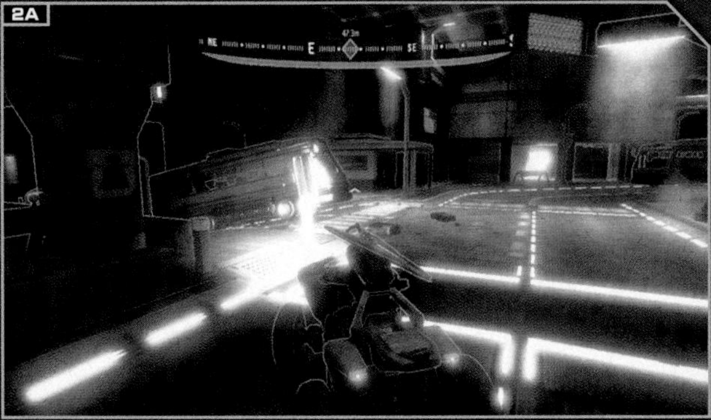
2A

2B

Tactic: War of Attrition

Wading in with your guns blazing or attempting to drive into the Brutes on your Mongoose almost always results in an embarrassingly messy death for you. Therefore, it is wise to approach this heavily defended area with extreme caution. From either access street, concentrate on dropping the Jump-Pack Brutes, lobbing in Sticky Grenades before they take flight, cutting them down with a quick sidestepped headshot, and then quickly returning to cover (such as overturned vehicles or the corners of buildings).

As each Brute comes to investigate whether you're dead or not, quickly prove you're very much alive, and grab the Brute's weapon if you're low on your own ordnance. Keep this up until you've slain all the Brutes. Then concentrate on the Chieftain; he loves to dodge your thrown Grenades, but he's susceptible to Plasma Rifle fire that whittles down his shields. Grab Rifles from slain Brutes, and take extra care to avoid that Fuel Rod Cannon's blasts! Keep a concrete planter between you and the Chieftain, and strafe around it, lobbing in Brute Shot Grenades or Plasma fire, or tag his head with a Carbine or Magnum. If you're wounded, quickly retreat to cover; the foe usually doesn't follow you. There's an Optican Kiosk back at Choke Point 1 (the entrance to the road leading southwest, away from the plaza).

Tactic: Battle Omission

Fighting Brutes that are both excitable and led by a massive foe clad in heavy armor may not be your idea of a good time. In fact, you can stay close to the southwest wall and search for the glass door just to the right of a long, yellow-illuminated panel. This is the entrance to the Underground Hive, and scrambling in here avoids combat with the Brutes entirely. Sacrificing bravery for cunning can be a worthwhile strategy. Now enter the elevator shaft and explore Sublevel 07.

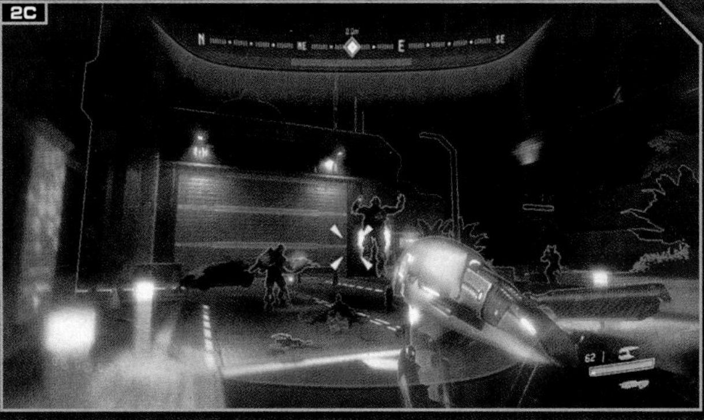
2C

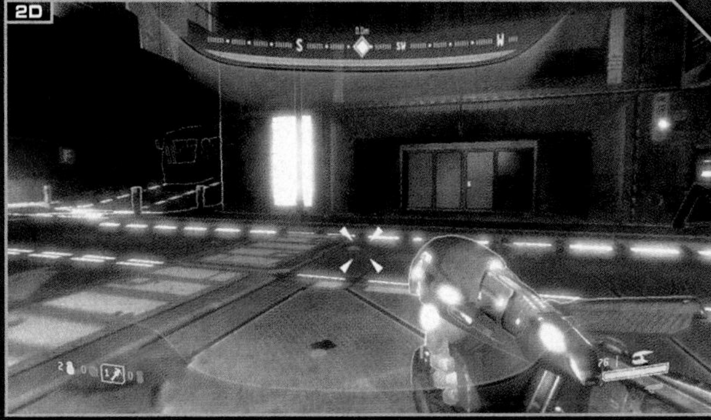
2D

TIP

Although you can return to Mombasa Streets to fully explore this location after you've completed each level, if you are searching for COMM Terminal information, be sure you've found 29 of the 30 entries before you enter the elevator shaft so you can fully access the Data Hive's hidden secret.

Mission 08: Data Hive

ROOKIE • After Midnight • Superintendent Data Center

After a thorough inspection of the New Mombasa Streets, you finally locate the Superintendent Data Center and descend to Sublevel 7. Working your way through the corridors, you soon reach a series of octagonal chambers known as data stacks. You can activate one of these stacks, allowing you and your new police buddy down to Sublevel 8. Investigate this area and locate the data stacks to gain entrance to Sublevel 9, where the temperature drops, but the enemies become much more ferocious. Heat them up with a Flamethrower, then rendezvous with Dare, who leads you through the Data Hive, now home to swarms of Drones. Battle through to the Data Center, then escort Vergil back to the surface.

Data Center Entrance to Hive and Vergil Location Point

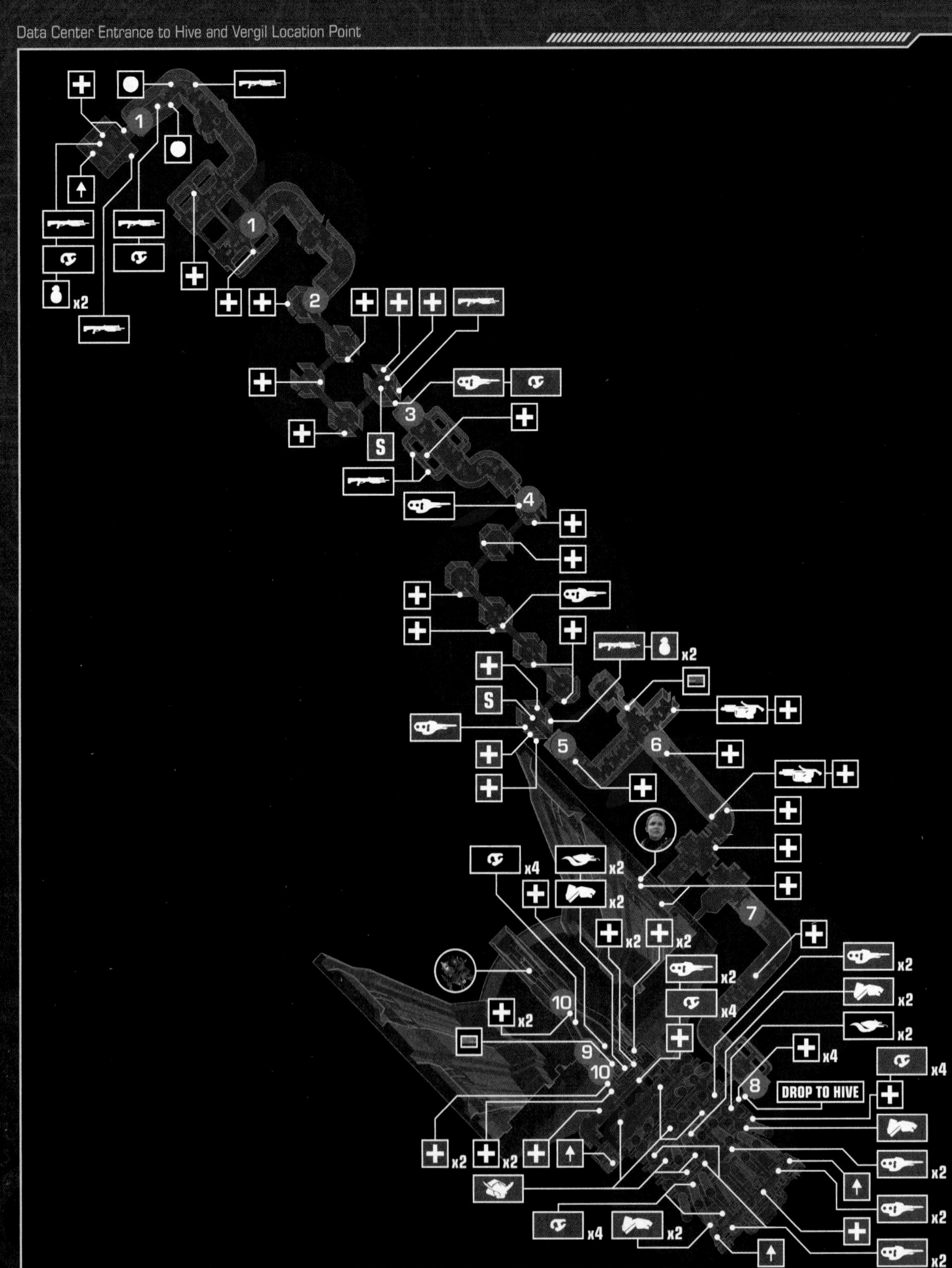

DATA STREAM

Data Hive VISR Target Acquisition Mode Ratio: 95 percent

After "Mission 07: Kikowani Station": Hidden COMM Data—1 (Total: 30/30)*

*This terminal is only accessible after you have located the previous 29 in New Mombasa Streets.

PAR SCORE

50,000

PREFERRED WEAPONS

Flamethrower | Magnum | Beam Rifle | Carbine | Gravity Hammer

LEVEL-SPECIFIC ACHIEVEMENTS

Data Hive: Complete this mission to unlock "Firefight Mission: Chasm Ten."

I Like Fire: Kill 10 enemies with the Flamethrower on Data Hive.

Audiophile: Find all Audio Logs, alone or with another ODST.

MISSION OBJECTIVES

DATA HIVE Find Dare on Sublevel 9

DATA HIVE Fight through Hive to Data Center

DATA HIVE Rescue Superintendent

DATA HIVE Escort Engineer to safety

■ Choke Point 1: Sublevel 7 Corridors

1A

1B

ENTITIES ENCOUNTERED

Grunts

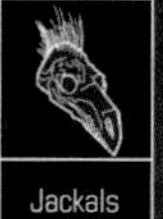

Jackals

1C

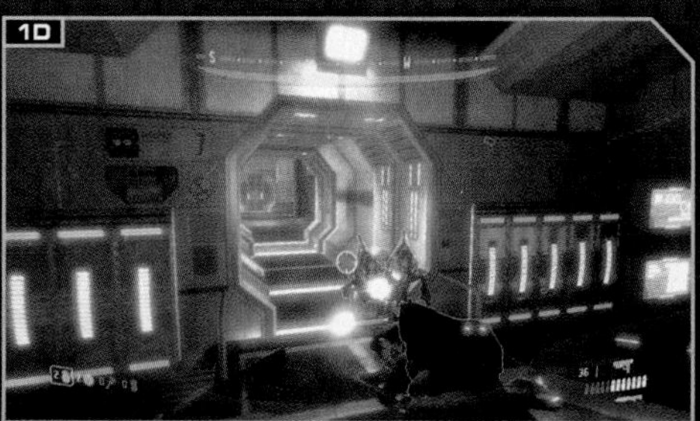

1D

You begin at the base of the elevator shaft on Sublevel 7, and you need to locate and meet up with Dare, who is on Sublevel 9. Descending two levels requires you to navigate several corridors and "stack shafts"—data-storage rooms with access to lower-level locations. From the initial chamber, you can look for weaponry (such as a Shotgun or a Plasma Pistol) before heading northeast, through the sliding doors to a sloping corridor **[1A]**. There's evidence of a recent battle between Grunts and Marines, and more Shotguns are available. Turn the corner, heading southeast; continue down the corridor toward a Grunt you can melee from behind, then turn right (southwest) again. This leads to a corridor full of Grunts **[1B]**.

OBJECTIVE

DATA HIVE Find Dare on Sublevel 9

By far the best way to deal with these Grunts is to bring out your Silenced SMG or Magnum that you began this mission with. If you're playing this mission for the first time and have weapons from the previous mission, use a ranged weapon. A mixture of headshots and quick bursts of SMG fire on panicked Grunts does the trick. Use the data processors (large computer units in this corridor section) and the plastic sides as cover. You'll reach a dead end if you continue forward, so turn southeast, and choose any of the three side doors. They lead down to a subsequent corridor **[1C]** that looks similar to the one where you fought the Grunts. This corridor has both Grunts and Jackals to take out; take them down with headshots from the Magnum; snipe from cover. Head northeast down this corridor, passing the Needler, and take a Plasma Pistol to back up your Magnum if you wish.

The corridor turns to the right (southeast) and slopes down. Be ready to headshot more Grunts, charging in to melee them when there's only one or two left. The corridor turns right (southwest) again, sloping down to a center terminal and a doorway ahead **[1D]**. There are likely to be Grunts trotting out of here; shoot them in the head, and tool up with any ammo or Grenades you find on their corpses. Enter the narrow passage the Grunts were guarding, stepping into the first in a series of octagonal stack-shaft chambers.

Superintendant Data Center • ROOKIE

▪ Choke Point 2: Sublevel 7 Stack-Shaft Chambers

ENTITIES ENCOUNTERED

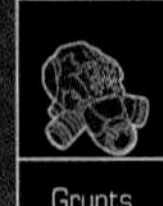
Grunts

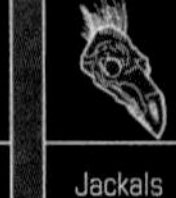
Jackals

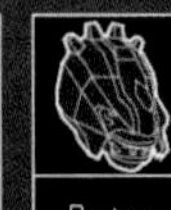
Brutes

Police Officer

Drones

Step into the first stack-shaft chamber, and make a quick inspection. There is an unusable computer terminal in the central shaft, and the sockets around the perimeter are designed to hold Health Packs (but these are empty). Remember this for later. Head down the connecting passage to the next shaft chamber **[2A]**, where a Brute and a group of Jackals accosts you. You should have saved your Grenades up until this point, as tackling the Brutes in these chambers involves either or both of the following tactics.

Tactic: Guns for Show, Plasma for a Pro

Although the shotgun makes a pleasing spray of damage, a more proficient way of removing armor from any of the Brutes in this series of corridors is to step in brandishing the Plasma Pistol, charging a shot so you can release it just before the Brute takes evasive action. The bolt knocks the Brutes' shields down. Then finish them with a headshot from your other weapon (ideally your Magnum) or with thrown Grenades. Employ headshots or Grenades (or both) on the two other enemy types in this series of rooms: Grunts and Jackals.

Tactic: Fusion Coils for a Killing Blow

This tactic is a little more dangerous if you're too close to the ensuing explosion, but be mindful of the fusion coils that are lying around these chambers; shoot at them instead of the enemies as your foes close in and are close to the coils. The coil explodes, severely damaging or killing multiple enemies in the process.

There is a group of Jackals with a Brute bodyguard **[2A]**, and there is a group of Grunts with a Brute **[2B]** in this quartet of stack shafts. After you've neutralized all foes, move to the last shaft chamber **[2C]** to the northeast, and rendezvous with a highly agitated New Mombasa police officer. Before continuing, you may scour the previous chambers for Shotguns, Plasma Pistols, Plasma Rifles, and Needlers. The shaft with the police officer has a Health Pack on one of the walls. The officer is having difficulty raising the stack in this room, but you have the necessary expertise. Locate the Data Stack Terminal **[2D]** on the central structure in this room, and raise the stack. Then prepare to repel a Drone attack **[2D]**!

Tactic: Raining Spiky Death

As soon as you open the data stack, have a Sticky Grenade chosen on your HUD's Grenade menu, and then throw the Grenade at the underside of the rising stack base. The Grenade's spikes then rain down on the Drones ascending from the floor below, killing them all if you've timed the throw right and positioned the Grenade correctly. Use this technique on all future stacks for immediate and safe Drone disposal.

TIP

Your police escort is a battle-hardened sort and does not yield to the Covenant. You can use this to your advantage, leaving the officer in a chamber that you're having difficulty with and letting him conquer your foes. Only your points and pride suffer.

Tactic: Manually Acquiring Targets

If you don't have a Sticky Grenade or lack the timing, you'll face a swarm of Drones the old-fashioned way: by manually targeting and defeating them. Use any and all cover, such as the wall alcoves or central pillars, and then pop out for a well-aimed headshot or burst of Rifle fire, and return to cover. You can even retreat to previous stack chambers if you're part-ODST, part-coward.

When you've minimized the Drone threat, or as soon as the data stack is released and there's a hole in the ground, drop down to Sublevel 8. The police officer will follow you. The Drones follow you, too, so it's better to deal with them on this sublevel.

CAUTION

If you require more of a challenge, make sure the Catch Skull is active. This makes the narrow corridors of the Data Hive much more difficult, as there is little room to dodge any incoming Grenades thrown by the Covenant.

■ Choke Point 3: Sublevel 8 Dark Corridor

3A

3B

ENTITIES ENCOUNTERED

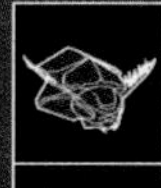
Drones

Grunts

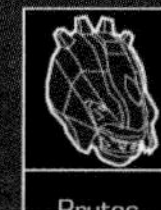
Brutes

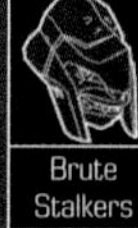
Brute Stalkers

3C

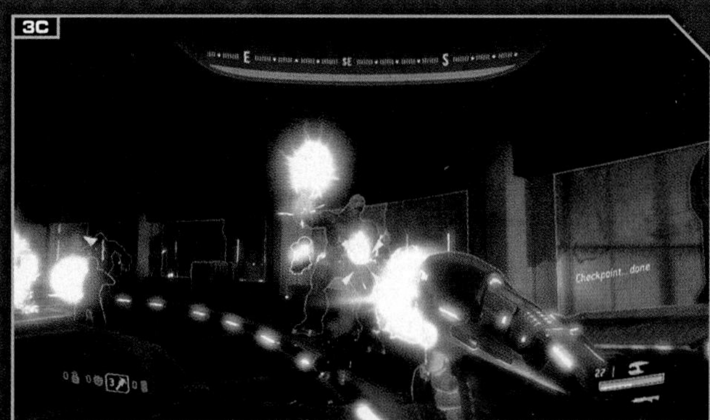

If you haven't done so already, switch on your VISR Enhanced Vision to make out all the enemies lurking in this long stretch of unlit corridor. The initial section **[3A]** features a few Drones and Grunts, with Brutes appearing at the far end. "Appearing" is an apt term, as these are Brute Stalkers **[3C]**, which are almost invisible if you don't have your vision set to Enhanced. Methodically cull the enemies using any weapon you see fit, winding your way down the corridor to the far, southeast end, where a door allows you access to a second series of data stack–shaft chambers (Choke Point 4). Midway along the corridor, you can investigate a narrow subcorridor **[3B]** that runs along either side of the main corridor; here you find multiple Marine bodies, along with Health Packs and Shotguns. Grab what you need before continuing; this is a good way to sneak around and surprise a Brute from the side.

Tactic: Optimal Equipment

Wading through this corridor is still possible on greater difficulty settings, but to survive in future areas, it is wise to utilize a specific weapon set. This corridor should be the place for you to load up on Grenades and swap a weapon for the Carbine. Stay at the corridor entrance or edge forward to the server units on either side of the corridor, remaining near the walls and slowly progressing, sniping foes expertly in the head. When you reach Brute Stalkers, bring their shields down with a charged Plasma Pistol shot, then decapitate them with the Carbine. Don't use Sticky Grenades to take out Brutes; this makes their Grenades explode, and you then won't be able to collect them. Instead, tag Brutes with your Carbine, so you can collect the Flame Grenades they were carrying.

TIP

There's no need to worry about your new friend; the police officer can simply work as an entity to draw your opponents' fire away from you. Concentrate on your own tactics.

■ Choke Point 4: Sublevel 8 Stack-Shaft Chambers

4A

ENTITIES ENCOUNTERED

Drones

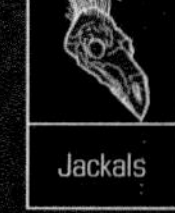
Jackals

Brutes

Move into a second series of octagon stack rooms. The first chamber has some Drones on which to test your reflexes; using the Carbine is a surefire way to defeat them easily. Check the Plasma Pistols and Needlers they drop if you wish; there's also a Health Pack on one of the alcove walls. Head southwest, where you and your police officer colleague can make short work of the Jackals roaming the room. The third chamber is empty save for a Health Pack on the wall, but foes are heading up toward you from the corridor to the southeast **[4A]**. In this corridor and the stack room beyond **[4B]**, expect close combat with Brutes. Throwing Flame Grenades so they stick to these Brutes, especially when they are in the narrow corridors, makes takedowns more straightforward. If you don't have Flame Grenades, you can lob other Grenade types down the corridors, or use your usual Brute-killing ordnance. Continue this tactic as you progress to the final stack chamber on this sublevel **[4C]**.

Inspect the alcoves for Health Packs, and then trigger the console to raise the data stack. Drop down into Sublevel 9, either before or after you coax a group of Drones up from below. Dare has to be around here somewhere....

4B

4C

Tactic: Throw and Blow

Navigating this area with a partner means making critical decisions that don't involve burning your friend to death. As the corridors are narrow and dangerous, make sure one of you loads up with Grenades during Choke Point 2. Have your Grenade carrier prime their favored Grenades and lob them at enemies coming at you both through the corridors. The other player can stand to the side, with a good view of the corridor, and finish off any foes "lucky" enough to survive the Grenade blast.

NOTE **Throughout Choke Points 2, 3, and 4, there are Carbines, Shotguns, Needlers, Maulers, Plasma Pistols, Brute Shots, and Plasma Rifles to pick up.**

TIP **Once you jump down the stack shaft, the police officer remains on Sublevel 8. Well, until his screams subside; then you suppose he's "resting." If, however, you've collected 29 COMM Terminal data entries, the officer jumps down with you. It is up to you at this point to work out why!**

TIP **Whoa, there! Before you drop down to Sublevel 9, inspect your weaponry. There's a whole clan of Brutes waiting to rip you apart, and the correct (and fully loaded) weaponry is a key requirement. You should also be at full health before dropping down the stack hole.**

■ Choke Point 5: Sublevel 9—Cold Storage Brutes

5A

5B

ENTITIES ENCOUNTERED

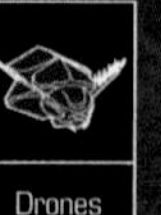

Drones

Grunts

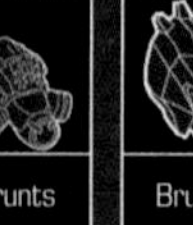

Brutes

Brute Stalker

Brute Chieftain

S (Plasma Turret)

As the corridors begin to crystallize with ice particles, deal with the Drones in the base of the stack shaft if you haven't already, and note the Health Pack in one of the wall alcoves. However, don't grab it yet; you'll need to return here to take it during the subsequent Brute battle. Head out the corridor, going southeast, and maneuver quietly down the sloping hall **[5A]** to a small group of Grunts and an armored Brute. From this point, there are a few ways to emerge victorious from the battle with the incoming Brutes.

Tactic: Shields Down, Head Off

The preferred way to tackle all the Brutes in this corner corridor choke point **[5B]** is to arm yourself with the preferred weapon combination for this encounter: pair up a Plasma Pistol with a Magnum or a Carbine. Tag the Grunts in the head with the Carbine, then use a charged Plasma Pistol shot to remove the Brute's shields before switching back again to the Carbine or Magnum to finish the Brute with a headshot. Do all of this before you actually turn the corner, and then slowly edge around the corner, coaxing as few Brutes into combat with you as possible. Repeat this tactic, re[illegible]ating to the cover of the pillars, side servers, or sloping ground while you charge your Plasma Pistol.

Tactic: Charge Down, Head in

If you've mistakenly arrived at this section of corridor without the proper weapon combo, then your available arsenal will have to do. However, the Brutes drop Plasma Rifles, which are also excellent at removing their shields. Follow this up with your other weapon (such as the Brute Shot, Needler, or Shotgun), but conserve ammunition by using the Plasma Rifle strictly for stripping Brute shields. Grenades are also excellent, although the stickier ones don't allow you to pick up any Grenades from a Brute corpse.

5C

Tactic: Watch Out, Chieftain Here!

By the time you've defeated four or five Brutes, the leader of the pack makes an appearance: a Brute Chieftain armed with a terrifyingly powerful Plasma Turret! The takedown tactics here depend on your available weaponry, but the Plasma Pistol/Carbine combination is optimal. Attempt to snipe the Chieftain's head with a Carbine and keep your distance; circle-strafe around this fearsome foe, using the server structures along this corridor section **[5C]** as cover.

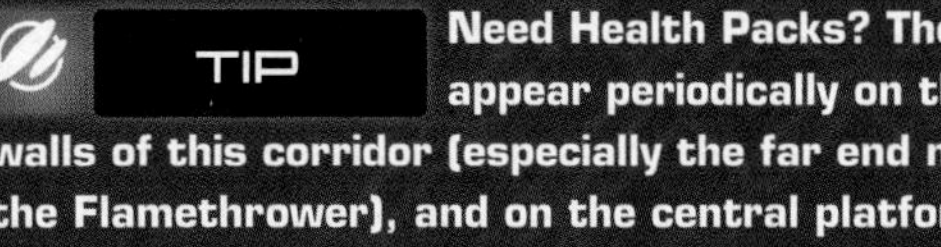

TIP

Need Health Packs? They appear periodically on the walls of this corridor (especially the far end near the Flamethrower), and on the central platform near Choke Point 5A. Brutes also drop Spikers and Brute Shots, so take these if you need them.

Tactic: Chieftain Down, Flame On

Having constant trouble from this lumbering brute as it cuts you apart with its Plasma Turret? There's a way to even the score; sprint to the northeast end of this corridor, ignoring the ice buildup on the walls, and search the right (eastern) corner, where you'll discover the mighty Flamethrower! Use the corridor structure as cover, and advance on the Chieftain. Bring him down with a deluge of napalm fire. This sorts him out in no time!

Tactic: A Little Help Here?

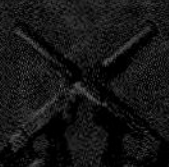

Have one player maneuvering slightly ahead of the rest of the team, and let him draw the Brutes' fire. The remaining team should stay back, draining Brutes with charged Plasma Pistol shots or sniping at them with the Carbine. When the Plasma Turret–wielding Chieftain makes his appearance, one of the team needs to draw his fire while the other slips by him and locates the Flamethrower, only to return and finish off the Chieftain.

■ Choke Point 6: Sublevel 9—Captain Dare Rendezvous

6A

6B

ENTITIES ENCOUNTERED

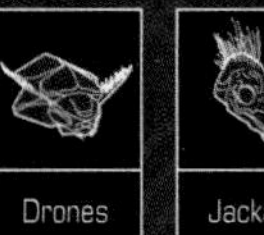
Drones

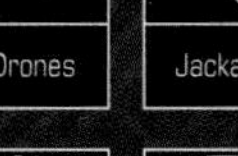
Jackals

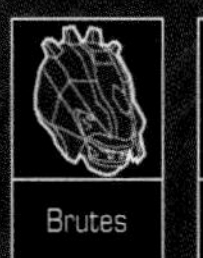
Brutes

Captain Dare

TIP

The I Like Fire Achievement (killing 10 enemies with the Flamethrower on Data Hive) is now available. This is the only opportunity to claim it, as this is the only available Flamethrower. Make sure the next ten enemies you defeat burn to death; complete this Achievement immediately in the enclosed corridors, where foes are easy and near enough to hit.

As soon as you clear Choke Point 5, return to the corridor in which you faced the Brutes, and collect any and all weapons you want. Be sure to take the Flamethrower if you want the Achievement, or take the Plasma Turret the Brute Chieftain was carrying (or better yet, complete the I Like Fire Achievement throughout this choke point, drop the empty Flamethrower, then return for the Plasma Turret), and head down the sloping corridor to the southeast. There are dead Drones scattered around here—that looks like ODST-issued Marine fire! Continue through the doors, around another bend, and through two more doors, into a darkened corridor section **[6A]**.

This area has Drones, Jackals, and a Brute or two to drop. Your optimal tactic is to engulf them all in flame, and complete the Achievement while using the server structures and glass walls for cover. Another recommended plan is to instead use the Carbine on all but the Brutes, punishing them instead with a Plasma Pistol before switching to the Carbine. Or, cull the Covenant any way you want in this reasonably enclosed space. Afterward, optionally pick up the Plasma Turret, and walk southwest to a connecting corridor. At the end of this well-lit corridor is a locked door. Knock on it, and Dare lets you through **[6B]**. Your objective updates.

OBJECTIVE

DATA HIVE Fight through Hive to Data Center

For extra points, you can turn on the Tilt and Mythic Skulls; Choke Points 5 and 6 aren't really affected, as long as you always have the Plasma Pistol for troublesome shield removal.

Choke Point 7: Sublevel 9—Lower Hallways

A Few Words About a Woman of Few Words: Captain Dare

Dare meets you carrying a Magnum, which is an excellent weapon when you wield it, but Dare's strengths lie in her using either the Carbine or (better yet) the Beam Rifle. Stumble upon either armament, and give it to her (or use it yourself). She drops Drones amazingly well with her new long-range ordnance.

Let Dare attract the enemies' attention. She doesn't die from enemy fire, allowing you to let her soak up the damage in many, but not all, situations. However, this comes at the expense of both points and professional pride.

ENTITIES ENCOUNTERED

Captain Dare

Grunts

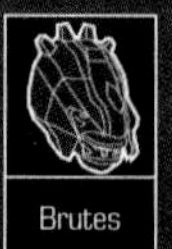
Brutes

Drones

After meeting Dare, follow her through the winding narrow passage and into a dark, wider corridor. Turn southeast and head down a sloping path **[7A]**, where a group of Grunts and a Brute are no match for Dare's wicked aim. You should move along by the wall servers, using them as cover and attempting headshots on the Grunts and Brutes if any remain. Round the corner, and face several Drones, Grunts, and a Brute. Again, the Carbine is extremely useful for one-shot kills.

At this point, it is worth breaking convention and arming yourself with a Brute Shot (or Needler if you haven't acquired that Achievement yet), which is a no-nonsense foe-disposal device that works well on this slope. There's also Magnums, Plasma Pistols, Plasma Rifles, Carbines, Brute Shots, Spikers, and Needlers scattered about. Methodically tag all the foes along this sloping path, pausing at any middle platform to secure a Health Pack. When you reach the Jackals and the Brutes down this corridor **[7B]**, and finally some Drones, employ any of the previous tactics. Soon afterward, Dare leads you past some Health Packs to an airlift down to the Drone Hive.

TIP

A good way for you to easily dispatch Brutes along this stretch of corridor is to let Dare go on ahead and attract the attention of a Brute; then sidle up and assassinate (melee attack from behind) it when it has its back to you.

7A

7B

7C

Drop down the hole and continue southwest, through the narrow corridor hatch doors and out into a wider corridor. After passing four Health Packs, choose the Brute Shot from the Covenant crate and methodically destroy the Jackals and Grunts you see near or behind the cover. As you progress along this curved corridor **[7C]**, continue to pummel Brutes with the Shot. You don't need to save the ammunition; let it rip! Soon afterward, you'll reach an opening to the east, leading into the Data Hive itself. There are four more Health Packs on the doorway here; return to these if combat goes awry in Choke Point 8. Stop and swap out your weaponry.

■ Choke Point 8: Data Hive

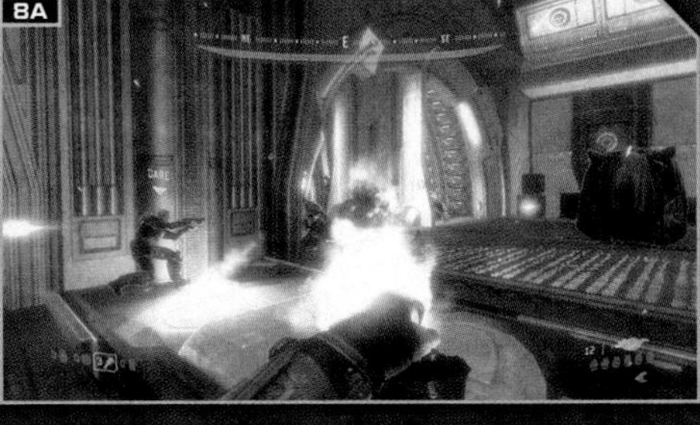
8A

TIP

The biggest threat is being surrounded by Drones while advancing through this area. A slow methodical approach is key.

Drones

NOTE

This section of the map is also "Firefight Mission: Chasm Ten," which unlocks once you finish this mission on any difficulty level.

8B

Step out into the Data Hive, grabbing a Plasma Pistol and a Beam Rifle from the nearby Covenant crates **[8A]**; these are by far the best weapons to utilize here. Stop Dare and hand her a Beam Rifle if you haven't already. It helps if she can use this to tag the incoming Drones, as she's an impressive shot, and the attacks are one-hit kills. Follow Dare up the ramp to the southeast (the remainder of this lower level has little to take except a couple Carbines). Quicken the pace and keep up with Dare as she reaches an elevator, and activate it to ride to the upper walkways. Follow Dare out onto the catwalks. As soon as she nears the center of the catwalk **[8B]**, you are flooded with Drones from a massive hive they've built inside this Data Center!

Tactic: Bugger Off

8C

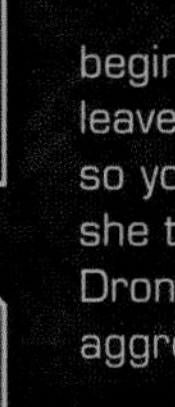

These buggers are notoriously annoying and hard to kill due to their sporadic movements, so it is imperative you are proactive with your culling. Don't wait around for your friend to begin firing; train your Beam Rifle on the hive holes the Drones begin streaming out of. When the Drones are clustered together as they leave their holes, let rip with your ranged weapon, and stay at a distance so you're not attacked from all sides. There's no need to follow Dare; she takes care of herself! You must pace yourself and take down every Drone in a wave before slowly advancing and checking the hive for further aggressive activity.

8D

TIP The Drones appear from the giant, pendulous hives hanging from the chamber's ceiling. There's more than one, so look for these growths when aiming at Drones yet to appear.

CAUTION Of course, you could simply flee through here once you've memorized the path, but this cowardly act only works on lower difficulties.

Follow Dare around to the northwest, to a Covenant crate with Carbines in it; these provide additional ammunition you may need if you're running low on Beam Rifle shots. Turn right (northeast), avoiding dropping down to the floor below, and stay on the catwalk, tagging more Drones as they appear from another Hive **[8C]**; then continue north to the exit door that lies between and behind two large hives **[8D],** where the most ferocious fighting occurs. Remember, you can retreat to claim more ammunition for your Carbine or Beam Rifle. Stay at a distance, although Drones drop Plasma Rifles and Needlers, and there are more crates with Plasma Pistols. Your weapons of choice are the Carbine and Beam Rifle. Exit into the narrow corridor, and your objective updates. Follow Dare and drop down another shaft.

OBJECTIVE
DATA HIVE Rescue Superintendent

Choke Point 9: Data Center (Entrance)

9A

Dare lives up to her name as you exit into a large underground chamber **[9A]**. She drops down in front (northwest) of you, racing toward the nearest threat: two Brute Captains **[9B]** and a Chieftain armed with a frightening Gravity Hammer **[9C]**. Survey your tactics below.

ENTITIES ENCOUNTERED

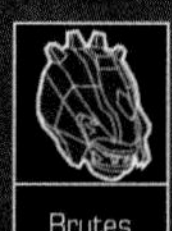

Brutes | Brute Captain[a]

[a](Gravity Hammer)

Tactic: A Brutal Shot

9B

While Dare makes a decision to tactically hide, turn right (northeast) from your balcony and drop down. Turn right (southeast) again, and secure a Beam Rifle and Brute Shot from the Covenant crates in the dead-end corridor here. Then spin around and advance on the trio of Brutes. Throw caution to the wind and advance up the right side of the sloping platform toward the door the three Brutes are guarding. Lob in a Grenade (Sticky or otherwise) of your choosing; this usually bounces off the Chieftain, but if you aim correctly, the Grenade falls right in the middle of the trio, ripping shields apart. The Brutes shouldn't have time to react, though. You should have almost depleted your Brute Shot's ammunition, laying multiple slugs into the Chieftain. Then finish off the Brute stragglers with more Brute Shots. This is simple, violent, and your enemies don't usually even get a shot off at you!

Tactic: A Sniper's Lot

9C

There's no need to drop down and have the Brutes on the same level as you, especially if you've enough ammunition in your Carbine or Beam Rifle. Instead, stay on the balcony and carefully aim at the enemies with zoomed-in targeting before beginning a series of sniped headshots. If the Brutes are pummeling your balcony, simply step back out of danger.

Tactic: Giving It Everything You've Got

The ground floor is wide enough for you to dodge most of the Hammer Chieftain's swipes. If you're not careful, you'll fly off the sides into the water below after a hammer strike. As the Chieftain's bodyguards are armed only with Spikers, these aren't as much of a threat. Using a Carbine or Beam Rifle, head to the Chieftain, and lure him into single combat. When he charges, use a Carbine, a Beam Rifle, or a Plasma Pistol to remove his shields. If he becomes invulnerable, stay at a distance and dodge his lunges. When the invulnerability wears off, tag the Chieftain in the head. Then pick up his Hammer and bludgeon the remaining foes to death with it.

Tactic: A Multiplayer Plot

Approach this area with a similar plan to the one executed when you encountered the Plasma Turret–wielding Chieftain early in this mission: One player maneuvers slightly ahead of the team and draws the Brutes' fire. The remaining team should stay back, draining Brutes with charged Plasma Pistol shots or sniping at them with the Carbine.

Once the Brute threats are nullified, head northwest, through the door the Brutes were guarding, and through a narrow corridor and into the Data Center itself. The rendezvous with the Superintendent occurs here.

OBJECTIVE
DATA HIVE Escort Engineer to safety

▪ Choke Point 10: Data Center (Escape)

With Vergil and Dare behind you, take point and retrace your steps back to the sloping platform Data Center entrance, where a trio of Jump-Pack Brutes **[10A]** land and attempt to slaughter the Engineer. Get rid of them with swift, well-timed bludgeons of your Gravity Hammer. Prepare for further combat as two Phantoms drop off Covenant squads on each side of the platform; there are Grunts, Jackals, and a couple of Brutes **[10B]**. Introduce them all to your Hammer. If you're quick enough, you can slaughter them all at the Phantom's drop-off point, although you will need to watch for the Phantom's turret fire, which can really rip through your Stamina. When you have fewer enemies to take down, switch to your Beam Rifle and plug their heads.

ENTITIES ENCOUNTERED

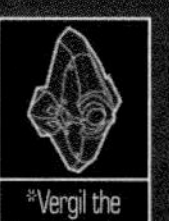
*Vergil the Superintendent

Jump-Pack Brutes

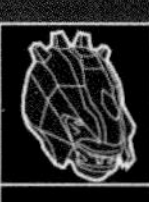
Brutes

Jackals

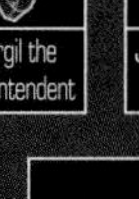

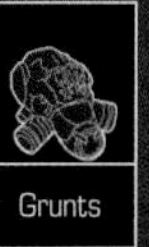

Grunts

Buck

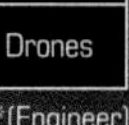
Drones

*(Engineer)

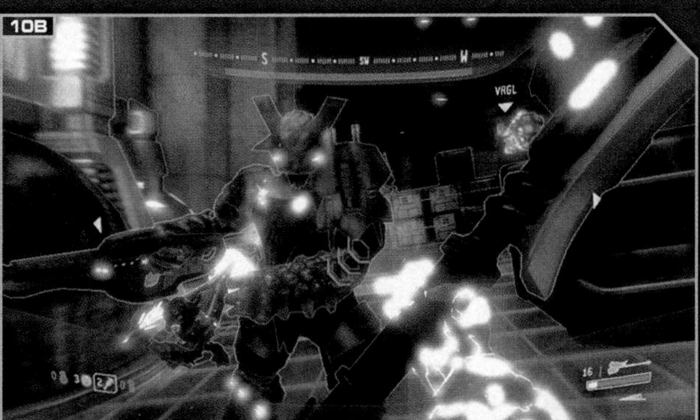

CAUTION **Pay attention to the Engineer! He is of paramount importance, and unlike Dare, he can die. Prevent this by killing first any enemy firing at the Engineer.**

Tactic: On Point

Buck finally makes an appearance, so move to the exit door he's just created, and head southwest down it. Make sure you're the first one to drop down the shaft; you don't want the Engineer to head down there before you, as there are sleeping Drones on the dark corridor's ceiling ahead (northeast) of you **[10C]**. You can handle these in one of four ways (listed in order of preference):

1. Take a weapon and assassinate them; jump up and melee attack each one.
2. Bring out your Brute Shot and blast clusters of them, continuing the bombardment until all are dead. Rapid fire and accurate shelling yields quick Drone deaths in seconds.
3. Run up and bludgeon them with your Gravity Hammer; this wakes them up earlier.
4. You can leave the Drones undisturbed, and slip past without engaging them at all.

CAUTION **When using the Hammer, don't confuse bludgeoning (your main attack) with a melee attack; the melee attack doesn't take up any power and can be used with any weapon.**

You can take Health Packs at the end of this corridor. Now wait for the Engineer to open the locked side door (to the southeast). Head through first, waiting for your crew to appear behind you, then head southwest, to a second door that the Engineer must open. Once through there, quicken your pace as you reach a corner **[10D]** with more sleeping Drones. Perform executions using any of the previous three tactics, securing the area before the Engineer arrives. Then follow the corridor to the exterior elevator.

Mission 09: Coastal Highway

ROOKIE • New Mombasa Streets • After Data Hive Extraction

With the Superintendent's data now safe in Dare's new floating friend, the time has come to rendezvous with the rest of your team and flee New Mombasa as the Covenant's overwhelming presence decimates this conurbation. Fleeing out onto the city streets, you must clear a path for Dare and the Engineer, locating an elevator that takes you to the city's coastal highway. After obtaining appropriate transportation, you have to drive more than 12 exits along the highway, nullifying threats to Dare's Olifant before holding up at the Uplift Reserve entrance. There, you must fend off final waves of the Covenant's shock troops before the rest of the team finally locates and extracts you.

Data Hive Exit to Highway to Uplift Reserve Entrance and Extraction Point

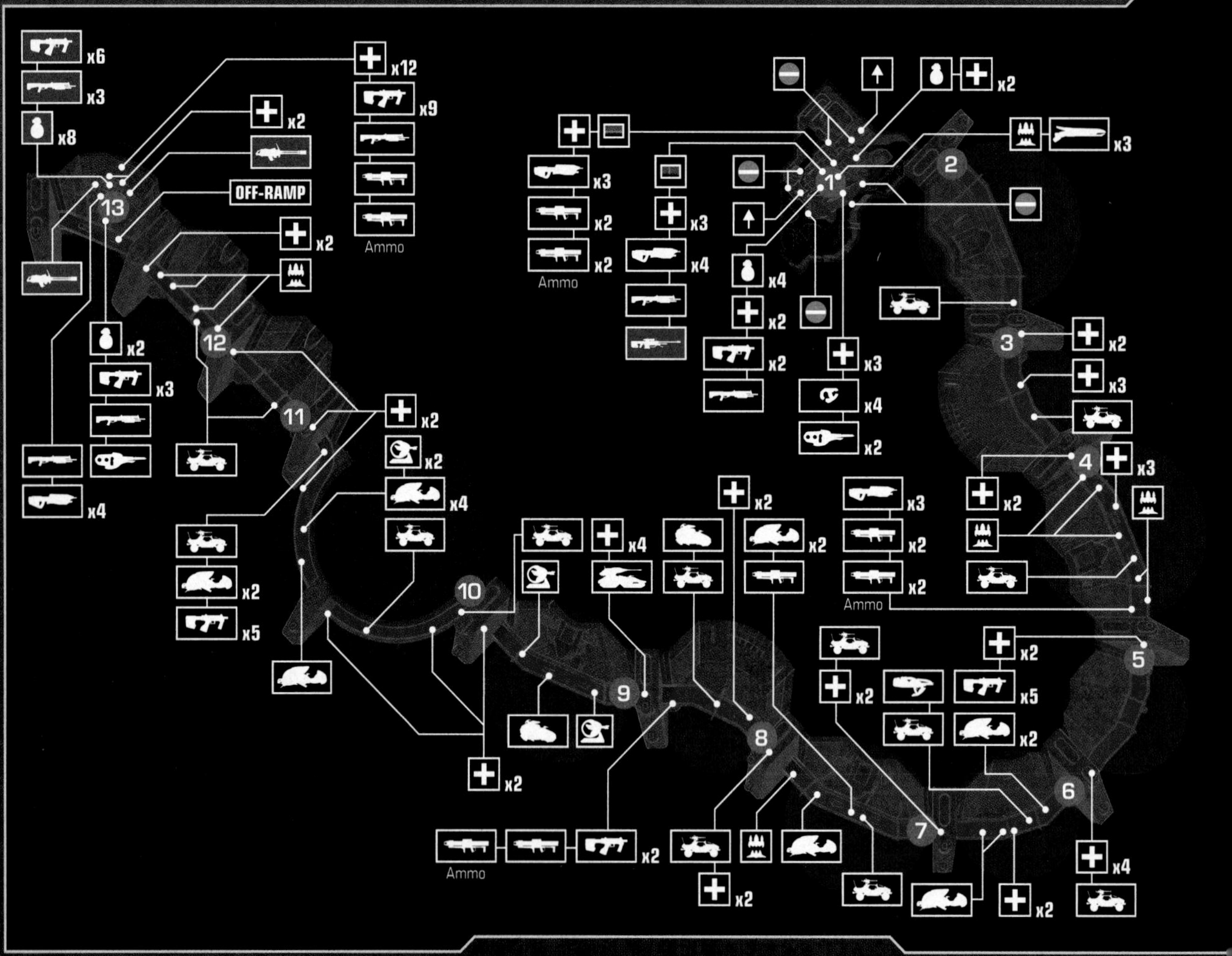

DATA STREAM

Data Hive VISR Target Acquisition Mode Ratio: 5 percent*

**COMM Data Terminals are not available during this mission.*

PREFERRED WEAPONS

Sniper Rifle

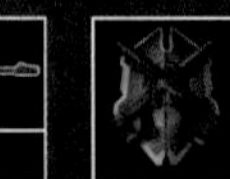
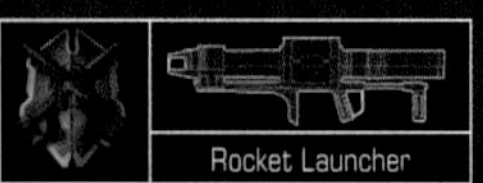
Rocket Launcher

Warthog (Vehicle w/ Gunner)

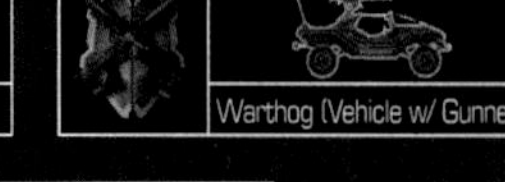
Gauss Hog (Vehicle w/ Gunner)

Scorpion (Vehicle with Gunner)

MISSION OBJECTIVES

COASTAL HIGHWAY Find elevator to highway

COASTAL HIGHWAY Escort and protect Dare's vehicle

COASTAL HIGHWAY Defend Engineer until friendly Phantom arrives

PAR SCORE

60,000

LEVEL-SPECIFIC ACHIEVEMENTS

Coastal Highway: Complete this mission to unlock "Firefight Mission: Last Exit."

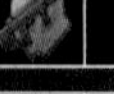
Campaign Complete (Normal): Complete the Campaign on Normal, Heroic, or Legendary.

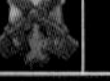
Campaign Complete (Heroic): Complete the Campaign on Heroic or Legendary.

Campaign Complete (Legendary): Complete the Campaign on Legendary.

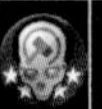
Vidmaster Challenge—Déjà Vu: Complete this mission on four-player Legendary LIVE co-op, with the Iron Skull active and no Warthog or Scorpion used.

■ Choke Point 1: Watchtower Courtyard

As the Engineer continues to bath you in semiprotective shielding when you're close to the creature, exit the Data Hive structure and head out onto the New Mombasa Streets, turning left and heading east, toward the building marked with the "1." Other streets are sealed by energy walls. Pass by sandbags on your left, pausing to claim any equipment you deem useful (there's a Shotgun, three Silenced SMGs, four Frag Grenades, and two Health Packs here), or return here if you need these items before you exit the city. Ahead (northeast) of you is a wrecked truck and a heavily defended courtyard with a Watchtower manned by Grunts with Plasma Turrets. Precision planning is called for.

ENTITIES ENCOUNTERED

Superintendent Engineer

Dare

Buck

Grunts

Jackals

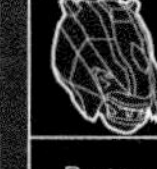
Brutes

OBJECTIVE

COASTAL HIGHWAY Find elevator to highway

Tactic: Sniping Support

The safest, most proficient use of your skills involves turning left (northwest) just before you reach the ruined truck and stepping into the covered corridor that also leads to the courtyard and has a door you can enter. There are yet more items just right of the door (a Shotgun, three Assault Rifles, and three Health Packs). Move quickly into the building, up the staircase, and out to a balcony overlooking the courtyard **[1A]**. There's a Sniper Rifle near a dead Marine here. Appropriate it and aim southeast, tagging as many enemies in the head as possible. Pay particular attention to foes that are near to Dare and the Engineer, as it is vital to keep them healthy. As soon as you tackle the ground enemies below, bring your weapon up and aim at the four Grunts on the Watchtower **[1B]**; they must be nullified, because their Plasma Turrets are incredibly damaging against your team.

TIP **When you kill a Brute with your sniper fire, he drops a Spike Grenade; save your Rifle ammo and utilize the Grenade to destroy the Watchtower with a single, well-aimed lob.**

With the Watchtower empty, drop down and work your way around the left side of the low-walled planters in the courtyard; there are some Covenant foes behind defenses near a parked flatbed truck **[1C]** to finish off. Behind the sandbags under the building, close to the Covenant Brutes, is a cache with two Rocket Launchers, two Rocket Ammo Packs, a Health Pack, and three Assault Rifles. The Launcher is particularly useful at carving a path out of the courtyard; use it to demolish the assembled Brutes and the Chieftain behind these defenses.

1A

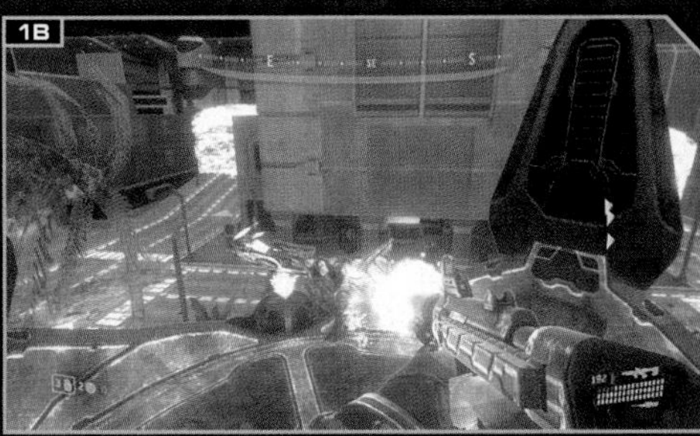

1B

1C

Tactic: Turret Takedowns

Although somewhat dangerous, if you have a solid spatial knowledge of the courtyard, you can sprint straight over to the Watchtower **[1B]** before the Covenant patrols react, and rise up to tag the Grunts manning the Plasma Turrets with quick headshots. Before you're shot at, wrench a Plasma Turret off its base, and drop to the ground. Then proceed to mow down the Covenant on the ground below where the Sniper Rifle is located **[1A]**, and finish off the Brutes behind their defenses **[1C]**.

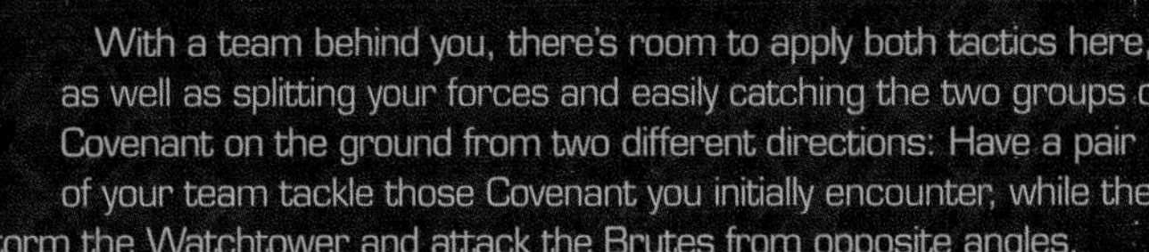

With a team behind you, there's room to apply both tactics here, as well as splitting your forces and easily catching the two groups of Covenant on the ground from two different directions: Have a pair of your team tackle those Covenant you initially encounter, while the others storm the Watchtower and attack the Brutes from opposite angles.

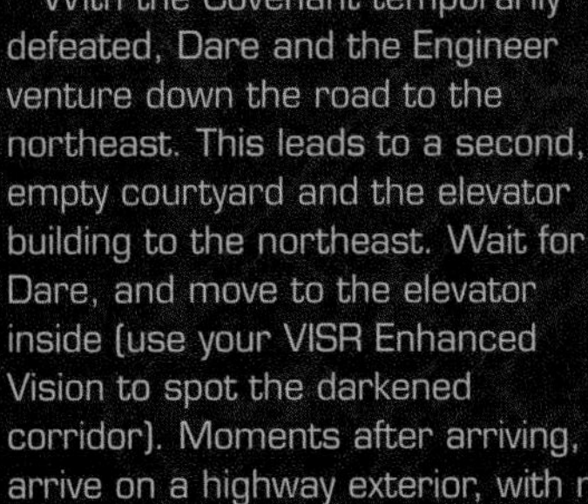

With the Covenant temporarily defeated, Dare and the Engineer venture down the road to the northeast. This leads to a second, empty courtyard and the elevator building to the northeast. Wait for Dare, and move to the elevator inside (use your VISR Enhanced Vision to spot the darkened corridor). Moments after arriving, the Engineer grants you access. You arrive on a highway exterior, with major Covenant activity. After a somewhat heated discussion, your objective updates:

OBJECTIVE

COASTAL HIGHWAY Escort and protect Dare's vehicle

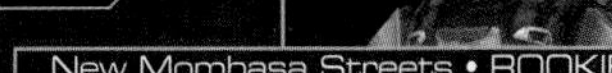

■ Highway Drive: Preparation

Dare and the Engineer have taken refuge in the armored Olifant, and it's up to you and Buck to ensure their safety as you progress along the Coastal Highway. The highway consists of sections of road that are separated by two sets of large blast doors. The first set of doors do not open until the Olifant reaches it. The second set, which allows access to the next section of highway, doesn't open until both your vehicle and the Olifant approach the door. Use this knowledge to your advantage; you may wish to park your Warthog away from the second door so you can hop out and acquire health or weapons without the Olifant setting off into the next section of highway without you guarding it.

When driving the Warthog, pay close attention to the Olifant's location. Keep it close to your current location, as the Olifant has sizable shield generators. However, these can be depleted and the Olifant destroyed, sending you back to the previous check point. Also, drive on the highway's left side, as the Olifant doesn't stop for anything—even for you if you cut in front of it! Stay away from the central median of the highway unless you want to use the sloped ground for ramps and impromptu stunts that usually flip your Warthog and waste your time.

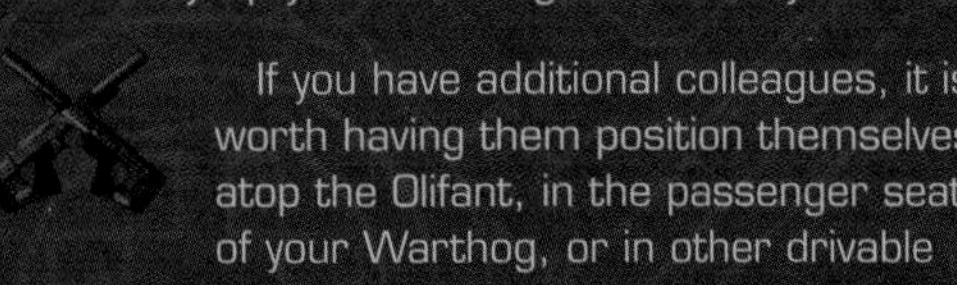

If you have additional colleagues, it is worth having them position themselves atop the Olifant, in the passenger seat of your Warthog, or in other drivable vehicles you may come across.

CAUTION

Your role is specific: You are to drive, and Buck is the gunner. If you ignore this and set off on foot or grab the Warthog Turret, the Olifant will set off without you, eventually succumbing to enemy fire if you don't catch up.

NOTE

The "section" numbers reflect those on the blast doorways, which you can see on the right exterior wall of the structure at the section's end.

■ Choke Point 2: Highway Section 99

ENTITY ENCOUNTERED

Grunts

As soon as you sit on the driver's seat of the Warthog, wait for Buck to join you and begin racing along the highway's left side, dodging strewn wreckage and passing the entrance to an off-ramp in the middle of the road. If you need to replenish your shields, you can retreat back to this entrance and drive into a lower dead end. Otherwise, ram a swarm of Grunts milling around the latter half of this section. Use your e-brake for quick turns that shunt clusters of Grunts at a time, and make sure Buck has clear shots of all his targets. When the Olifant reaches the first set of blast doors, slow down and pick up the Rocket Launcher by the dead Marine in the middle of the road, in front of the doors. There's Health here, too, and an overturned Warthog to flip back over if your current one is damaged. There's also an Optican Kiosk between the two doors.

■ Choke Point 3: Highway Section 98

ENTITIES ENCOUNTERED

Grunts

Jackals

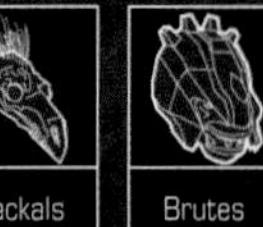

Brutes

This section winds a little sharper than the previous one and has no off-ramp to head down if your Stamina needs recharging; this means you must use the wrecked and abandoned vehicles as cover. Employ the same ramming-splatter technique, using the e-brake to skid into any stragglers while helping Buck get a good angle for his Turret. If you want to risk the Olifant's shields, always head back to the previous section for Health; it allows you to keep this section's Optican Kiosk full in case you need to retreat back to it when you encounter Highway Section 97. If you've lost your Warthog or if it is heavily damaged, there is another one on the long left

▪ Choke Point 4: Highway Section 97

4A

4B

ENTITIES ENCOUNTERED

Grunts

Drones

Tactic: Watchtower Takedowns

Use wreckage as cover, and replenish your Stamina down the off-ramp. Furthermore, this section becomes very dangerous due to the number of Grunts equipped with Fuel Rod Cannons standing atop one of four Covenant Watchtowers **[4A]**. Which Watchtower the Cannon-equipped Grunts stand on is randomly determined, so quickly drive to the first, and if you're not fired upon with the green-hued shots, drive to the second, third, or fourth and tackle the Fuel Rod Cannon Grunts there; they are your primary target, because they can devastate the Olifant's shields. A better plan is to disembark from your Warthog as you enter this stretch of highway, and shoot the first Watchtower with the Rocket Launcher you just picked up. Try this at subsequent Watchtowers, too, if you wish, then swap the Rocket Launcher for a dropped Fuel Rod Cannon; this becomes advantageous as you progress.

With death possible at any moment, equip the Rocket Launcher before the second blast door slides open, and use your Warthog as partial cover. As the doors open, take out the first Watchtower with a Rocket. If you simply wait to see whether you're attacked with Fuel Rod ordnance, it will be too late to save the Olifant. With the first Watchtower exploding, drive to the next Watchtower and repeat the plan.

With more than one player, you have separate vehicles to drive and have access to more than one Rocket Launcher. Quickly designate one person to aim at the first Watchtower as soon as the doors open, and fire a rocket before immediately entering a Warthog and progressing. The other player (or pair) should ignore the Watchtower, accelerate to the second Watchtower, exit the Warthog, and blast the Watchtower with a single well-aimed rocket. By this time, the first player or pair should zip past, heading for the next Watchtower, and so on.

Tactic: Engaging Drone Swarm

As you pass the last Watchtower and can see the exit blast doors at the end of this section of highway, stay at some distance away from the door; a large swarm of Drones flies out toward you as the doors open **[4B]**. With adept driving, give Buck some excellent shooting angles so he always has Drones targeted; he can demolish this wave of foes. Or, you can exit the Warthog, grab more Rocket Launcher ammunition or an Assault Rifle (both are in a UNSC supply crate positioned between you and the door), and help defeat them. Once the area is free from foes, head toward the Optican Kiosk if you require healing.

Dealing with Drones becomes problematic unless you reach the blast doors before the Olifant. Park the Warthog on the raised central median section just prior to the doors, and exit the vehicle. Grab the Assault Rifle and Rocket Launcher from the supply crate and retreat back behind your vehicle. When the Olifant activates the door, Buck begins to rain death on the Drones, while you back him up with Assault Rifle or Rocket fire. The raised median, wrecked vehicles, and your Warthog make good cover.

TIP

With supreme skill, you can actually take out all the Drones with a single, phenomenally timed Rocket blast as soon as the doors open, before the Drones expand their swarm. Nice work, Killionaire!

New Mombasa Streets • ROOKIE

Choke Point 5: Highway Section 96

ENTITIES ENCOUNTERED

Grunts

Jackals

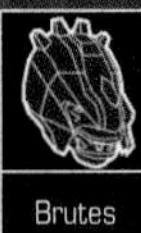
Brutes

This section of highway does not feature an off-ramp, so use the wreckage as cover if you need to replenish your Stamina by resting. Aside from the larger number of ruined vehicles, your tactical takedowns consist of using your Warthog as a splattering device, ramming all the Covenant infantry you can while allowing Buck the best possible aiming angles. Continue to the end of the section, where an undamaged Warthog is available, if needed. As always, an Optican Kiosk allows you to replenish your health.

Choke Point 6: Highway Section 95

ENTITIES ENCOUNTERED

Grunts

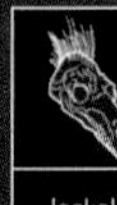
Jackals

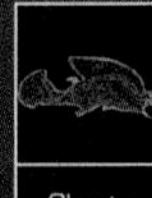
Ghosts

As you enter this section, you'll see a Covenant cruiser and a Phantom maneuvering about the skies. However, focus on the ground, as there's a group of five Ghosts ready to attack in the middle of this section, close to a fallen Phantom and an empty and fully functional Warthog, along with a dropped Fuel Rod Cannon. Since there is no off-ramp in this section, you must regain Stamina behind cover. Accelerate quickly so you're well in front of the Olifant, and the Ghosts attack you instead of the Engineer. When you reach the destroyed Phantom, drive behind and then to the front of it, so Buck has a good aiming arc, and grab the dropped Fuel Rod Cannon (if you didn't collect one earlier). Return and let Buck tag Ghosts from the cover of the Phantom. Quicken this by disembarking, and fire your Cannon at the Ghosts. Once the battle is over, search the area a little in front (southwest) of the empty Warthog for Health Packs. When you reach the next set of blast doors, disembark and enter the Gauss Warthog, a vehicle with a more powerful turret for Buck to use. There's an adjacent Optican Kiosk too.

Choke Point 7: Highway Section 94

ENTITIES ENCOUNTERED

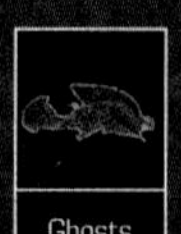
Ghosts

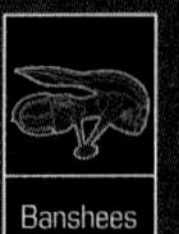
Banshees

There is an off-ramp that you can drive down to replenish shields, but only after you've dealt with a Covenant threat on the ground and in the air. However, with Buck manning the Warthog's Gauss Turret, you can slowly move forward along the highway, allowing Buck to blast Banshees out of the sky. When the Banshees begin to head your way, you can increase your speed, heading to the off-ramp entrance but not into it; use it as cover, driving in and out while Buck shoots the remaining Banshees and any Ghosts. Easily deal with any stragglers as you continue to the next blast door set. As always, there's an Optican Kiosk here.

Choke Point 8: Highway Section 93

ENTITIES ENCOUNTERED

Banshees

Wraith

Ignore the Scarab in the distance; it is too far away to attack. Instead, speed forward, giving Buck some excellent angles (usually straight and lessen your more erratic or sharp turning) so he can quickly destroy the Banshees swooping about. Drive to the midway point of this highway section, and watch as Buck focuses his attention on targeting the Wraith. This is important, as the Wraith is a primary target that can devastate the Olifant's shields with its Plasma Mortar. Keep moving around the Wraith so the Gauss Warthog isn't struck. Or park the vehicle, then leap onto the Wraith and attack it yourself. After the Wraith battle, there's likely to be some remaining Banshees to take care of; use the overturned bus toward the end of this highway section as cover, and wait for Buck to do his job. Disembark, collecting Health from the Optican Kiosk if you need it, and then enter the parked Scorpion Tank for the remainder of this outing.

▪ Choke Point 9: Highway Section 92

ENTITIES ENCOUNTERED

Shade Turrets

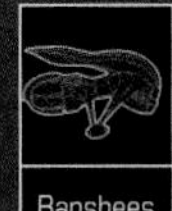
Banshees

Antiaircraft Wraith

Quickly emerge from the blast doors, and storm ahead of the Olifant in your Scorpion: Your foes' powerful weapons in this highway section can easily destroy the Olifant's shields. You have control over the Scorpion's main cannon and should use it to aim at and destroy Shade Turrets as early as possible. Blast them from a distance, then move toward the off-ramp entrance, but don't enter the underpass. Strafe to the side, using the off-ramp as cover, and shoot the Wraith before it can target the Olifant. You cannot board this type of Wraith, so destroy it from range. Finish your patrol at the far end of the highway section with another Shade Turret takedown. Between Shade Turret and Wraith takedowns, Buck deals with the Banshees, so concentrate on the other enemy types yourself. You'll reach the next blast-door set, and another Optican Kiosk, but it is wise to ignore the Health Packs and accelerate into Highway Section 91 well ahead of the Olifant.

▪ Choke Point 10: Highway Section 91

ENTITY ENCOUNTERED

Phantoms

Head out of the blast doors first, immediately turning your Scorpion's cannon 90 degrees to the right (north), and track the first of four Phantoms hoving into view above you. As soon as you have a red target reticle, begin to fire on them, maintaining the same speed as the Phantoms; slowing down or stopping allows them to escape or drift behind the curved overhang of the highway section you're on. Maintain speed and pepper the Phantom's structure until it explodes, then move to the next one. Any you miss will disappear over the blast doors and land, depositing two Ghosts at Choke Point 11. At the blast doors, take the Health from the Optican Kiosk if you need it.

TIP

It takes four shots to destroy each Phantom; don't wait around to see it explode. Target and blow apart the next one now! Also, in the middle of this section of highway is a Gauss Warthog. This offers far less protection and weaponry than the Scorpion, so ignore it. However, you can retreat to use it if your Scorpion suffers catastrophic damage on a highway section to come.

While one player (or pair) inflicts massive damage on the Phantoms using the Scorpion's main cannon, the other player (or pair) should quickly race to secure the Gauss Warthog and use its Turret to assist in Phantom destruction. This ensures a tactical advantage for the next choke point.

▪ Choke Point 11: Highway Section 90 (Unmarked)

ENTITIES ENCOUNTERED

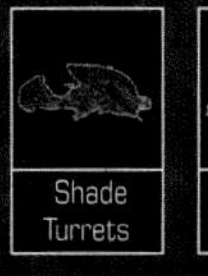
Shade Turrets

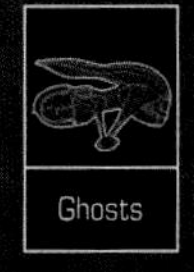
Ghosts

Ready your Scorpion's cannon as the blast doors open, and tackle the Shade Turret you can immediately spot. Prevent damage to your vehicle by checking the road ahead; there are more Shade Turrets in the central median of this highway. Simply fire on them and trundle toward the exit blast doors. If you missed one or more Phantoms back at Choke Point 10, expect to encounter between two and eight Ghosts as well. Buck helps blast at these, but they are secondary targets compared to the Shade Turrets. However, blast anything that moves, that isn't an Olifant, and that has a Covenant manning it! Near the blast doors is a regular Warthog with a Turret and five Silenced SMGs, as well as the usual Optican Kiosk. Ignore the Warthog unless you have no current vehicle.

JOTUN

New Mombasa Streets • ROOKIE

▪ Choke Point 12: Highway Sections 89 and 88 (Unmarked)

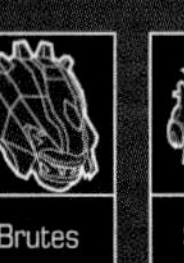

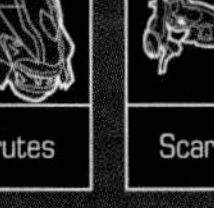

Since the Covenant continues to burn this entire city using its carrier's gargantuan excavation beam, you should be looking ahead. Ignore the Scarab pacing about in the distance. The first of two straight sections **[12A]** has a large number of infantry units to run over, usually without any problems, although there is a Brute Chieftain with a Fuel Rod Cannon midway through this first section; make it your primary target and train your cannon on it. Then turn your attention to the Jump-Pack Brutes. These Brutes enjoy landing on your vehicle and bashing it, so hop off when you're near the blast doors, and tag them with your weapon, or let Buck do his job. Then grab the Health Packs from the Optican Kiosk if you wish.

The last section of highway is completely devoid of enemies, aside from empty Watchtowers and a giant Scarab that you don't have the firepower to destroy **[12B]**. The latter stands atop the opposite blast doors and drains the Olifant's remaining shields before continuing north into the city. Fortunately, the Olifant survives this attack and enters the last blast doors. Catch up, head inside, and secure Health one last time from the Optican Kiosk. Venture through into a third highway section, with an off-ramp immediately visible. Drive your vehicle down this off-ramp **[12C]** and park, following ODST instructions to get out.

You've arrived at the rendezvous point, the entrance to the Uplift Reserve, which consists of two upper parking lots and the entrance itself up ahead (north). This entrance is an excellent defensive position, since the Engineer shields any nearby players. With Buck (or your teammates) providing covering support, head north across the roundabout with the bus stop gazebo in the middle of it. There's a suspiciously low amount of enemy activity. Check the gazebo for two Frag Grenades; you can take them now or grab them during combat later. There's also a nearby Covenant supply crate with two Carbine Rifles. Grab one if you are lacking a sniping weapon, and quickly execute the two sleeping Grunts at the entrance.

> **NOTE**
>
> **The entrance area has a wealth of supplies for you to grab if and when you need them; near the front doors is a UNSC supply crate with four Assault Rifles and a Shotgun in it. On the ground floor of the entrance building are a few more crates with Silenced SMGs, Shotguns, a Rocket Launcher, Rocket Launcher Ammo, and numerous Health Packs. On the upper mezzanine, there are two Sniper Rifles, eight Frag Grenades, and two supply crates with SMGs and Shotguns. Nestled on the upper planters on either side of the entrance, overlooking the parking lot, is a Turret. This is a not-so-subtle hint at the final round of carnage to come!**

OBJECTIVE

COASTAL HIGHWAY Defend Engineer until friendly Phantom arrives

12A

12B

12C

▪ Choke Point 13: Uplift Reserve Entrance—Extraction Point

ENTITIES ENCOUNTERED

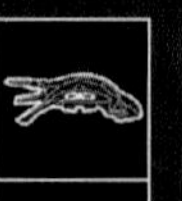

Phantoms | Grunts | Jackals | Brutes | Wraiths | Hunters

The area remains secure as Dare and the Engineer follow you into the safety of the Uplift Reserve entrance, which is an excellent place to hold out, as the Covenant is now sending several waves of enemies to attempt to kill the Engineer. This is your last stand at the Last Exit, and you must survive the following waves of foes!

> **TIP**
>
> **Although the waves have different enemies and many weapons are positioned differently, perfecting your knowledge of the "Firefight Mission: Last Exit" can help with this final fracas on subsequent playthroughs.**

The following five waves of enemies now attack your fortified entrance position:

Wave 1: Phantom dropping Grunts and Brutes **[13A]**.

Wave 2: Phantom dropping Jackals **[13B]**.

Wave 3: Phantom dropping Hunters **[13C]**.

Wave 4: Wraiths on the upper highway.

Wave 5: Phantom dropping Brutes and Brute Chieftain with Gravity Hammer **[13D]**.

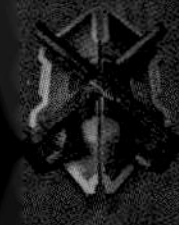

With each wave, a Phantom flies above the central roundabout courtyard and drops off its payload of foes on the south side of the gazebo bus stop. The enemies then work their way north across the courtyard, up the steps, a into the building entrance before attacking the Engineer. You must destroy them before they make contact with the Engineer. Spend some of your time checking that no foes have entered the building (listen for calls from your eammates if this occurs).

Wave 1 [13A]

Your optimal tactical plan is to utilize the high ground above the entrance or around the inner perimeter wall of either parking lot to peer over and blast away at foes. A truly proficient trooper uses the Turrets to rake enemies as they emerge from the Phantoms, or fires a well-aimed Rocket at the cluster of enemies as they first reach the ground under the Phantom to deliver multiple kills; mop up the rest with a Sniper Rifle, paying close attention to the Brutes.

Wave 2 [13B]

A clan of Jackals drops out of a Phantom, and some of them are real trouble, as they're armed with Beam Rifles. They land in the same area as Wave 1, so you can thin them out easily with a well-placed Grenade thrown just before they scatter. Then employ the same long-range sniping as before. Between Waves 2 and 3, search the area for a Beam Rifle, and make sure you're in full health.

Wave 3 [13C]

A few Hunters roaming the area aren't as problematic as you'd expect, since they can't chase you down easily due to the large amount of low-walled, stepped scenery. Rake the Hunters with Turret fire (either fixed or after you take the Turret from its base), and attempt cross-fire opportunities with Buck. Naturally, staying on the high ground and emplo Wave 1 tactics is also recommended, as the Hunters' atta are easily avoided at height.

Wave 4

When the two Wraiths appear on the upper highway, rainir down mortar shots on you and your team, the higher parki lot area becomes more of a hindrance than an advantage, retreat behind cover, avoiding the landing spots of the mort themselves. Ignore the Wraiths for the rest of this mission.

Wave 5 [13D]

The final group of foes includes Jump-Pack Brutes and a dreaded Chieftain armed with a Gravity Hammer. The upper ground isn't as defensible this time, due to the Jump-Pack Brutes, but it still means the Chieftain has to navigate up to that location to face you. Choose your favored weapon, and make sure there's a pillar, staircase, planter, ticket counter, or other structure between you and the Chieftain to minimiz being bludgeoned by his Hammer.

13B

Tactic: Cluster Bombing

This battle is arguably the toughest challenge in your expeditio but there are ways to improve your survival chances on Legendary difficulty. The first plan is to grab and hoard the Rocket Launcher and Sniper Rifle (perhaps near a Turret), and save these two ranged weapons for the Hunters and the final wave with the Brute Chieftain. This makes tackling those waves more straightforward Position yourself on either side of the upper parking lot, and rain Grenades, Rockets, or Fuel Rod blasts into the clusters of enemies as they drop dowr from the Phantom. This won't kill off everything, but it wounds or removes shields of many foes, which is extremely useful under these circumstances

After Wave 5, Mickey, Romeo, and Dutch finally make an appearance to destroy the two Wraiths that have been lobbing mortar shots at you since Wave 4. Move southwest through the parking lot, toward the Phantom—don't fire on it!—and finally rendezvous with your team. This concludes this mission and the Campaign.

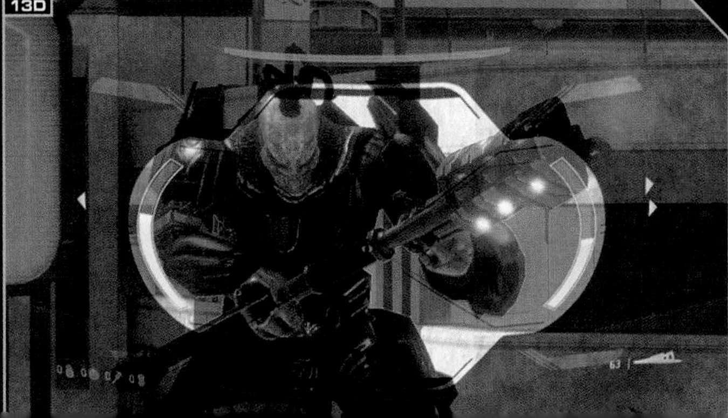

Mission 10: Mombasa Streets

ROOKIE • Occupied City Center • 6 hours after drop

This special mission unlocks once you finish "Mission 09: Coastal Highway" for the first time. This is essentially the entirety of New Mombasa Streets, accessible by you playing as Rookie. You begin in your Pod after you crash-land, just as you did during "Mission 01: Prepare to Drop." You are then free to maneuver about New Mombasa, defeating enemies and finding clues just as you did previously.

What to Do, and Why You Do It

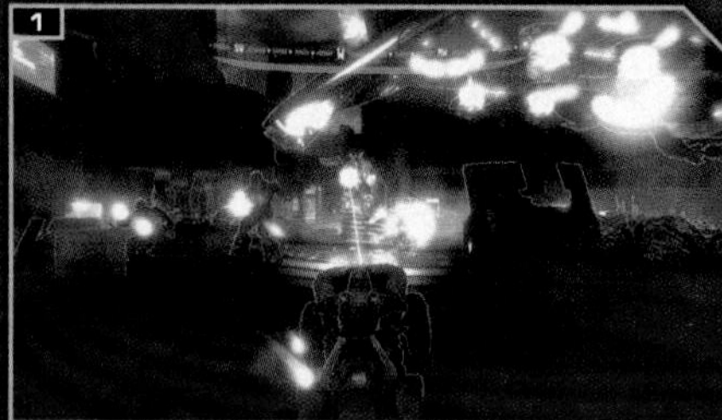

This mission allows you to attempt any or all of the following: You can prowl the streets, effectively dealing with Covenant threats **[1]**. You can find out-of-the-way alleyways or building interiors, gathering scavenged items you may find in these locations **[2]**. You can trek to Tayari Plaza, Uplift Reserve, Kizingo Boulevard, ONI Alpha Site, NMPD Headquarters, or Kikowani Station, and find the clue there **[3]**. Most importantly, you can continue your search for the 29 available COMM Terminals with hidden data on them **[4]**, before retrying "Mission 09: Data Hive" to locate the 30th terminal and complete this collectible hunt.

As you begin Mission 10, all of the previously found COMM Terminals and caches are added and appear in your inventory. This mission is simply the easiest way to finish up your collection. Find and activate any clue objects and the appropriate mission replays.

The following Tour of New Mombasa Streets can be helpful at any point in the Campaign, as you have the freedom to ignore the previous walkthrough tactics (which showed the optimal paths to clue locations in the order you are supposed to unlock them), and go off on your own, exploring plazas and roadways you haven't seen yet.

TIP

Think of New Mombasa as a hub, where you can access the majority of your other missions.

Mombasa Streets: District & Beacons

• see map on next page •

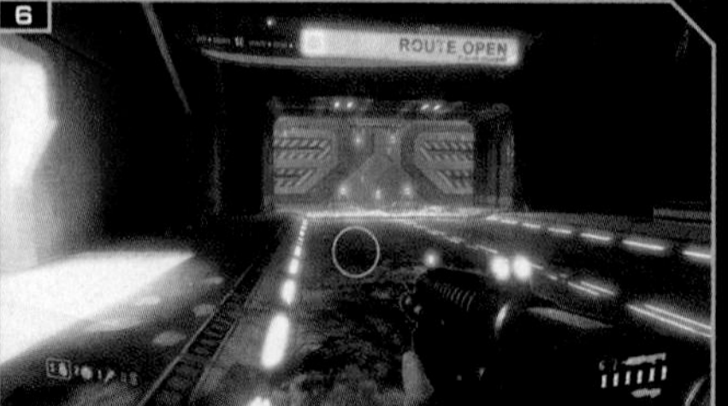

One of the easiest ways to get lost and overrun by the Covenant is not knowing where you are in this dark labyrinth of concrete and neon. Obviously, the easiest way to ascertain where you are is by locating landmarks. Aside from the main locations shown in the Tour, Mombasa Streets are separated into different districts, as shown on the nearby map. Fortunately, the numbers of these districts are shown in massive digits on the walls of the area you're in **[5]**. In addition, each perimeter gate **[6]** always takes you from one district to another. Once you know your general district, you are better suited at predicting what areas are in your general vicinity.

NOTE

There are eight districts in New Mombasa Streets: 0, 3, 4, 5, 6, 8, 9, and 10. However, you don't visit them in this order. You start in District 5, for example. The entrance to "Mission 08: Data Hive" is in District 0. The area of New Mombasa where you chaperone the Superintendent in "Mission 09: Coastal Highway" is District 1, which is only accessible on that mission.

New Mombasa Districts & Beacons

A

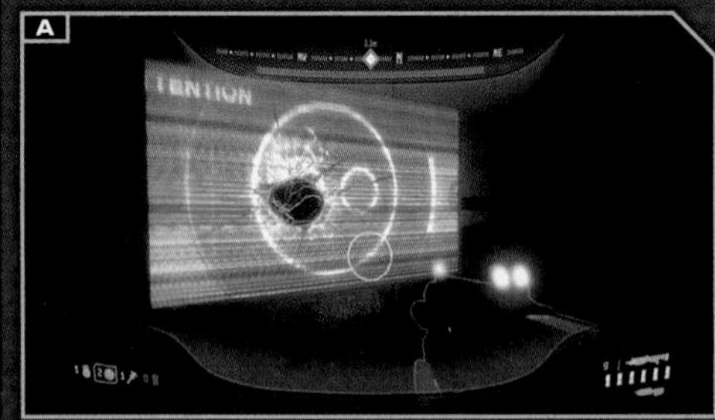

B

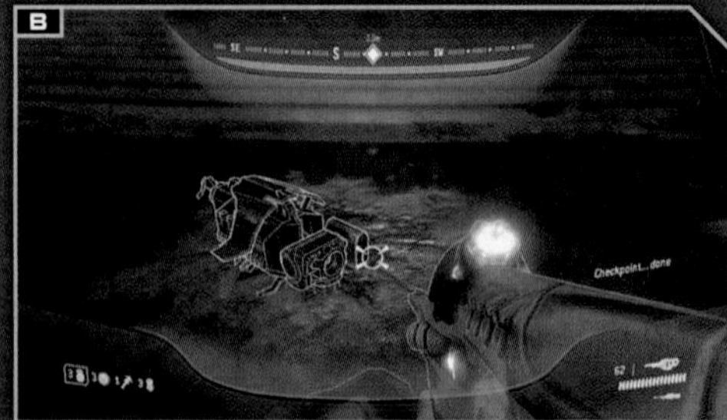

C

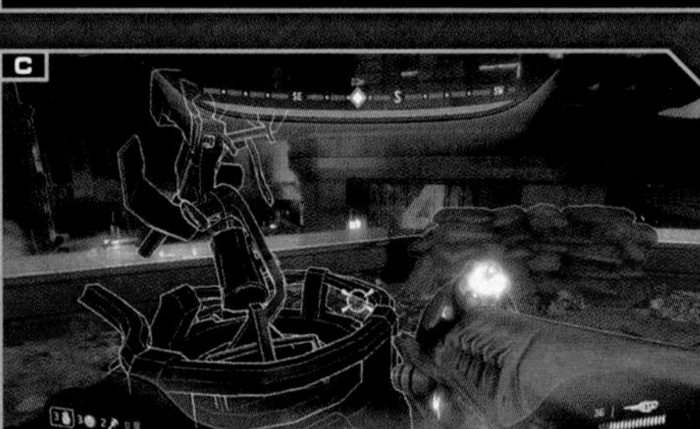

D

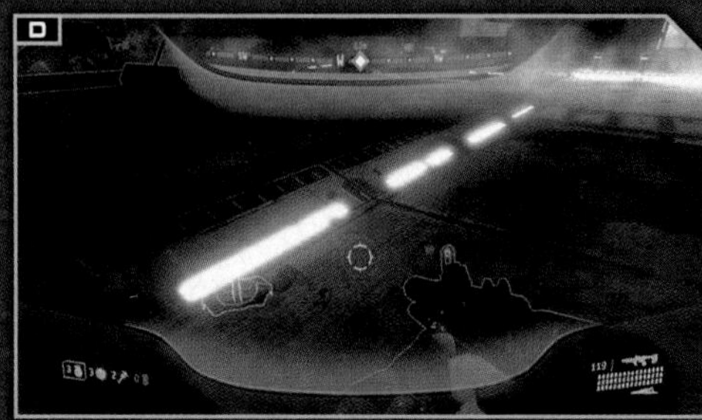

E

F

A
Tayari Plaza Clue:
Dare's Helmet

B
Uplift Reserve Clue:
Drone Fighter Optics

C
Kizingo Boulevard Clue:
Gauss Turret

D
ONI Alpha Site Clue:
Remote Detonator

E
NMPD Headquarters Clue:
Bent Sniper Rifle

F
Kikowani Station Clue:
Bio-Foam Canister

NOTE

The location of these Clues are shown on the District and Beacons Map, on the previous page.

Access Denied?

You can't just dash about the entirety of New Mombasa Streets from the get-go. Or can you? It is important to learn when you can access different districts. Naturally, if you're playing this for the first time, early in the Campaign, the districts you can visit are limited. Progress further and everything becomes available. Here's how it all breaks down:

Initial Playthrough (First Time Playing the Campaign)

You remain and cannot leave District 5 during "Mission 01: Prepare to Drop." Locate the Tayari Plaza clue and begin Mission 02.

Complete Buck's section of "Mission 02: Tayari Plaza." When the action switches back to Rookie, you can only reach the Uplift Reserve clue and begin Mission 03.

Complete Dutch's section of "Mission 03: Uplift Reserve." When you're playing as Rookie, you can now attempt to find any of the following clues, in any order: Kizingo Boulevard, ONI Alpha Site, NMPD Headquarters, and Kikowani Station.

When you've found all four clues, in any order, you can access the Data Hive via a doorway beacon that appears close to the last clue you found. This means there are four possible entrances to "Mission 08: Data Hive," depending on where you found your last clue.

NOTE

The only reason to complete the missions in the order presented in the walkthrough is that the distance traveled is less.

Mission 02 Playthrough Anomaly

If you replay Mission 02 (by finishing the flashback section, begin Rookie's section, then save and quit before selecting the mission from the Campaign menu), you change the accessibility of New Mombasa. Now all five Beacon clues are available, although "Mission 08: Data Hive" is still inaccessible until you've found all five clues.

Mission 10 Playthrough

Once "Mission 10: Mombasa Streets" becomes available, you are dropped into District 5 as if you've just begun "Mission 01: Prepare to Drop." However, the entire map is accessible, enabling you to find all six Beacon clues (Tayari Plaza's clue doesn't need to be collected first). "Mission 08: Data Hive" becomes accessible when you've found all six of them.

TIP

The exact location of the six different entrances to "Mission 08: Data Hive" are shown in the Tour at the end of this Chapter.

Mombasa Streets: Hostiles

7

The streets of New Mombasa have numerous enemies wandering around, ready to attack. Most of these attackers fall into the categories you expect, so carry armaments (or the preferred weapons) that allow for general combat. The Tour doesn't specify which enemies appear, as Covenant patrols are mostly random or change during the course of the Campaign. In fact, if you leave an area and return again (even during the same expedition), expect different adversaries. These can be, but aren't limited to, the following:

- A Phantom dropping out foes
- Grunts and a Brute [7]
- Grunts and a Brute, with Jackals
- Jackal snipers on accessible or inaccessible balconies or rooftops
- Ghosts
- A pair of Hunters
- Stalker Brutes or Jump-Pack Brutes
- Occasional Chieftains, sometimes with Engineers accompanying them
- Engineers offering patrols extra protection

TIP

Consult the "Know Your Enemy" chapter (or the walkthrough) for takedown tactics.

Mombasa Streets: COMM Data Stream

8

9

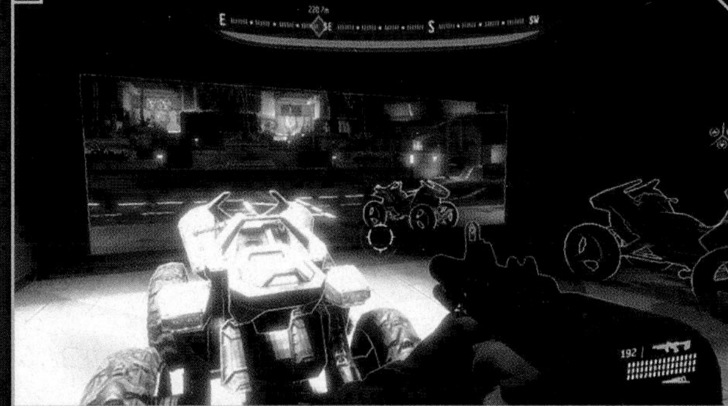

CAUTION

Warning! This information has been deemed "Most Classified," and the COMM Terminal Data locations can only be obliquely referenced. This guide hints at the districts in which you can find terminals, but not their specific location.

By now, you should have some knowledge that somebody has left a series of clues that provide information about the events leading up to the Covenant's attack on this city. The following provides specific information on how these terminals **[8]** unlock and how many of them (and the caches **[9]** they open) are available in each district.

■ COMM Terminals Overview

COMM Terminals take the form of access points, Optican Kiosks, and other scenery. However, when your VISR Enhanced Vision is switched on, they are outlined in yellow **[8]**. Go up to each one and access them to download the information to your HUD menu. This information is kept throughout the Campaign, so you only need to find each terminal once. The following table shows when the terminals become available and hints to their locations.

COMM Terminal Accessibility		
Completed Missions	**Unlocked Hidden COMM Data**	**Districts (and number of COMM Terminals available)**
02: Tayari Plaza	7/29	0 (0), 3 (0), 4 (0), 5 (1), 6 (0), 8 (5), 9 (1), 10 (0)
03: Uplift Reserve	13/29	0 (1), 3 (3), 4 (2), 5 (0), 6 (4), 8 (2), 9 (1), 10 (0)
04: (any third mission)	9/29	0 (1), 3 (3), 4 (3), 5 (0), 6 (0), 8 (0), 9 (0), 10 (2)*
08: Data Hive	1/1	During Mission 08, only after previous 29 collected
New Mombasa Total	29/29	0 (2), 3 (6), 4 (5), 5 (1), 6 (4), 8 (7), 9 (2), 10 (2)

**Once your third mission is complete, all 29 terminals in New Mombasa become available.*

The first terminal you access during "Mission 01: Prepare to Drop," when you download your city map, is not counted toward this total of 30.

■ Weapons Cache Overview

Shown on the previous map, there are seven weapon caches available in New Mombasa. They have a particular "set" noted by their location, which refers to the equipment stored inside. Use weapon caches during your battles in New Mombasa to aid in your fighting and maneuverability, thanks to certain caches containing Mongoose vehicles.

Cache Availability			
Number of COMM Terminals Found/ Available COMM Terminals	**Weapon Caches Set**	**Number of Caches/ Number of Items**	**Districts Available**
4/7	1 of 3	2/8	6, 9
13/20	2 of 3	4/8	0, 3, 4, 10
16/29	3 of 3	2/8	5

Tour of Mombasa Streets: Major Landmarks

The remainder of this walkthrough showcases the major landmarks of each district. These include plazas, Beacon clues, and weapon caches. These are designed so you can pinpoint a district you're in and read about the topography in the vicinity. There are other smaller courtyards and nooks and crannies in which you must be more thorough, and these usually result in you locating additional weapons or a COMM Terminal. The districts are listed in numerical order. If you want to know where you start, try District 5.

District 0

Number of COMM Terminals: 2 **Mirror Image of:** District 9

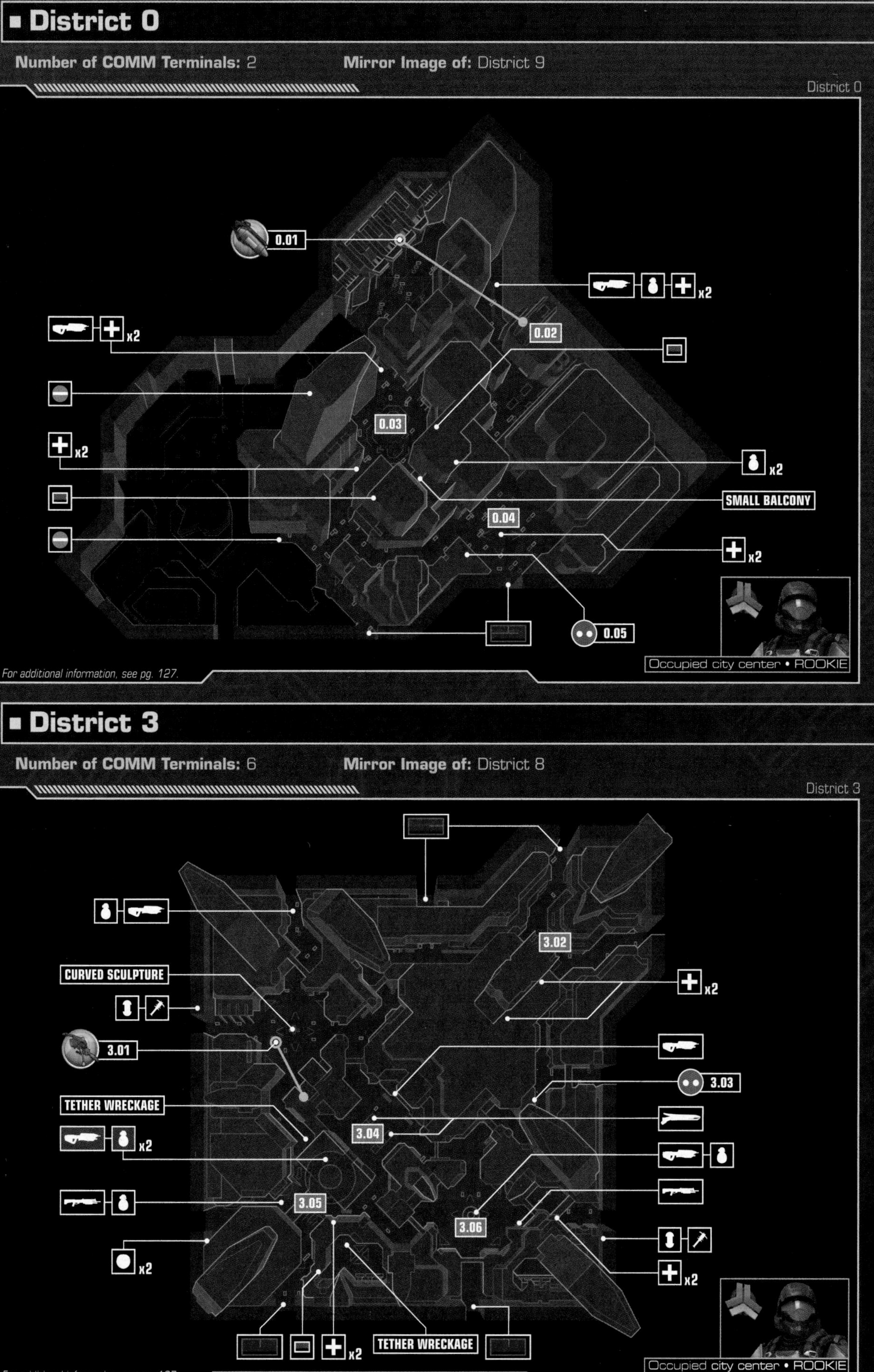

For additional information, see pg. 127.

District 3

Number of COMM Terminals: 6 **Mirror Image of:** District 8

For additional information, see pg. 127.

District 4

Number of COMM Terminals: 5 **Mirror Image of:** District 6

District 4

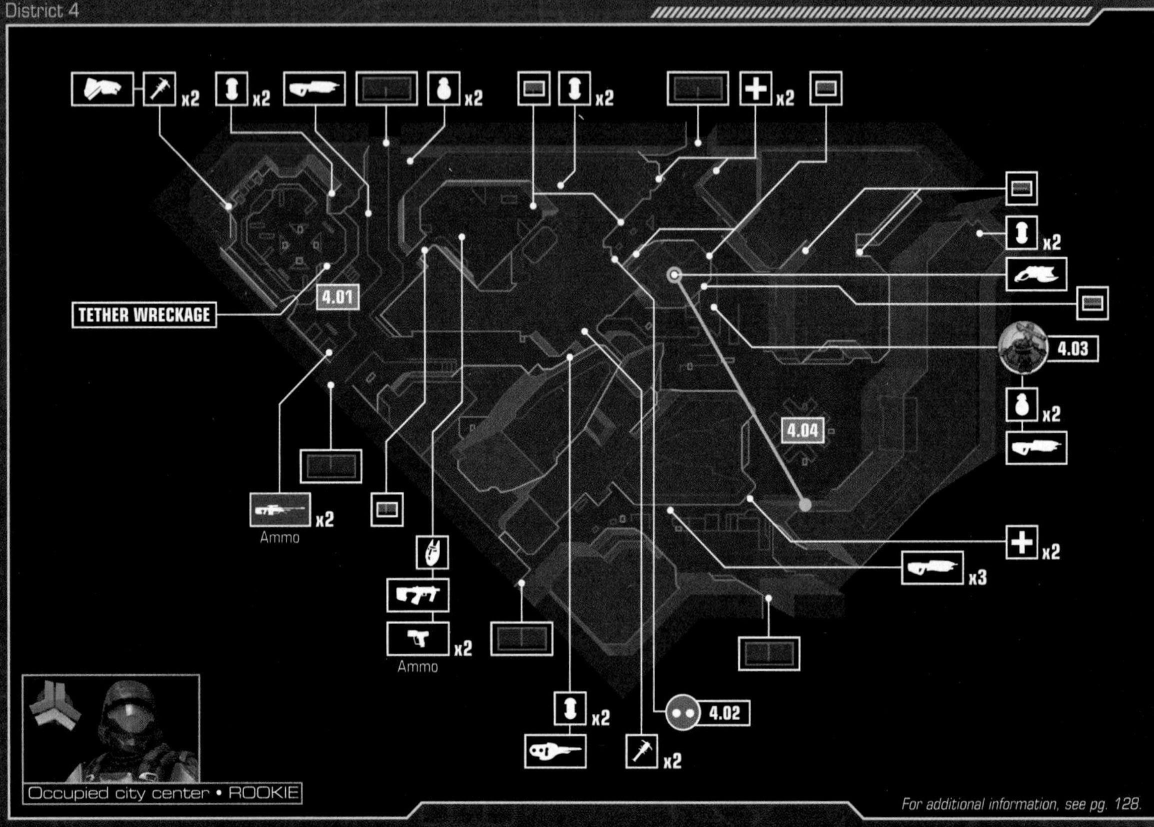

For additional information, see pg. 128.

District 5

Number of COMM Terminals: 1 **Mirror Image of:** None

District 5

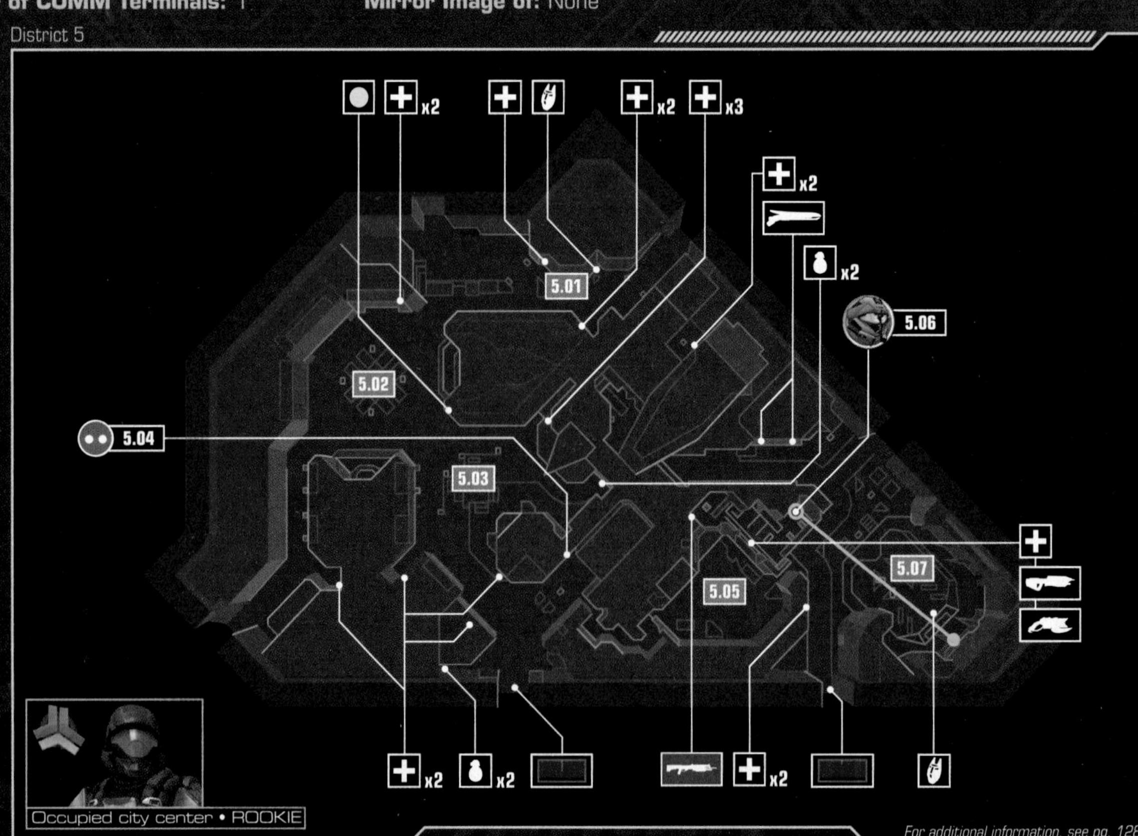

For additional information, see pg. 128.

CAMPAIGN

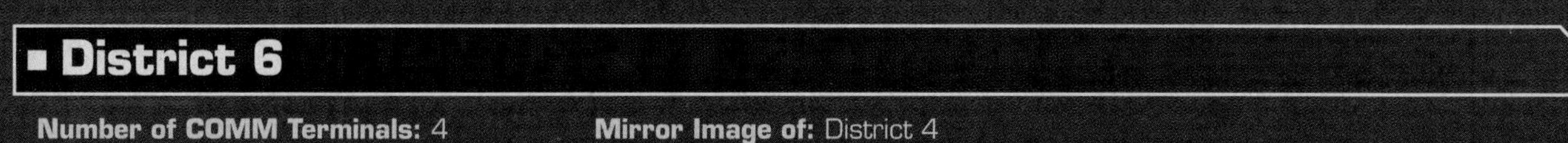

District 6

Number of COMM Terminals: 4 **Mirror Image of:** District 4

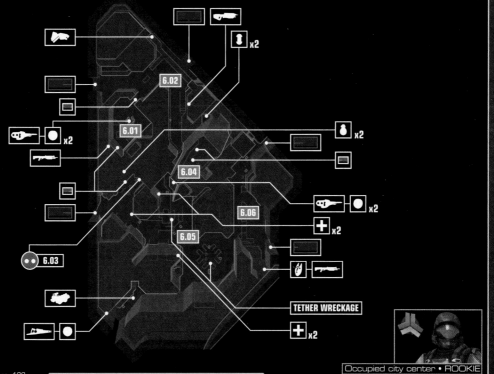

For additional information, see pg. 129.

District 8

Number of COMM Terminals: 7 **Mirror Image of:** District 3

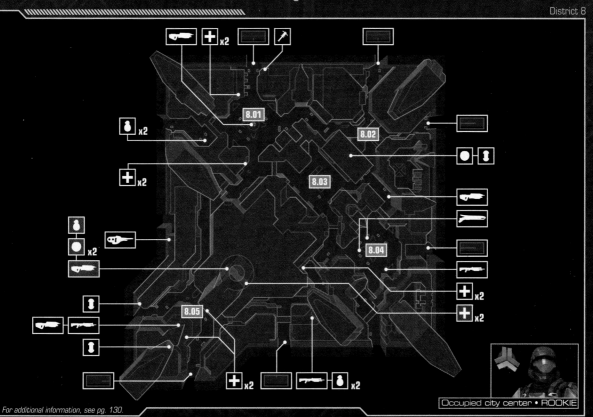

For additional information, see pg. 130.

District 9

Number of COMM Terminals: 2 **Mirror Image of:** District 0

District 9

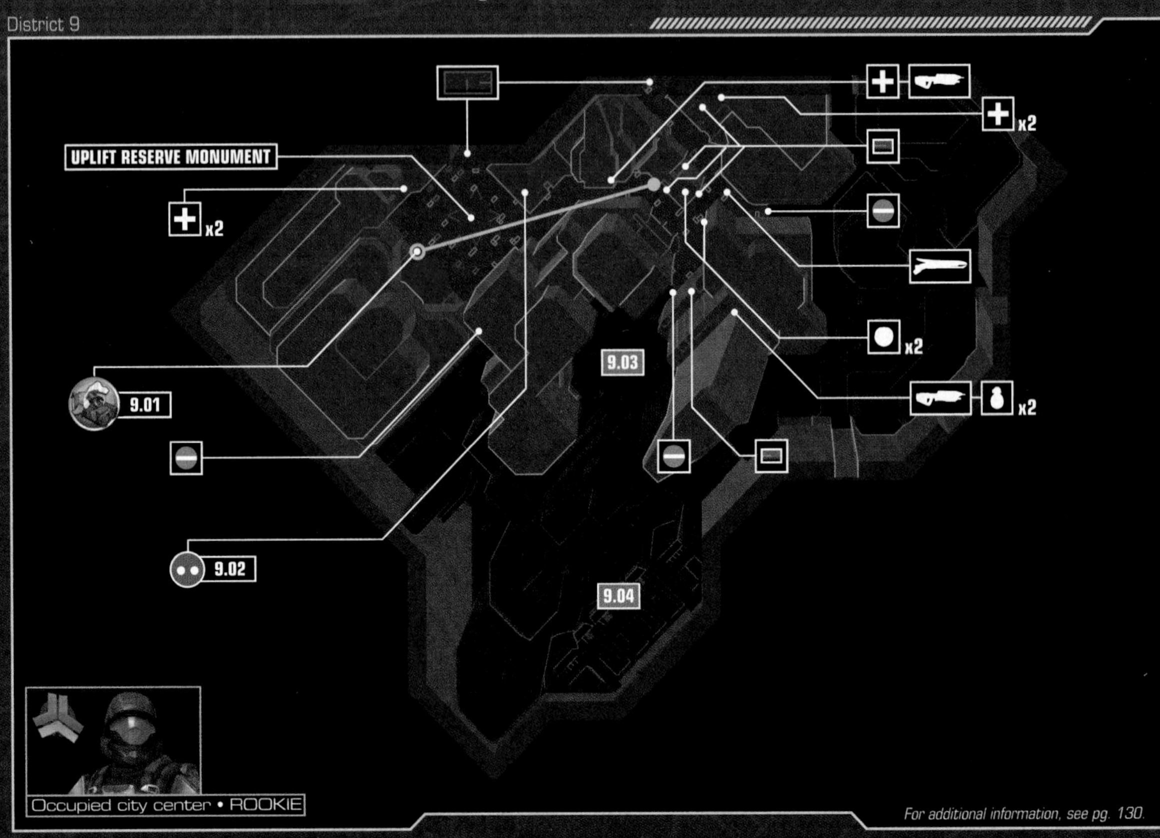

For additional information, see pg. 130.

District 10

Number of COMM Terminals: 2 **Mirror Image of:** None

District 10

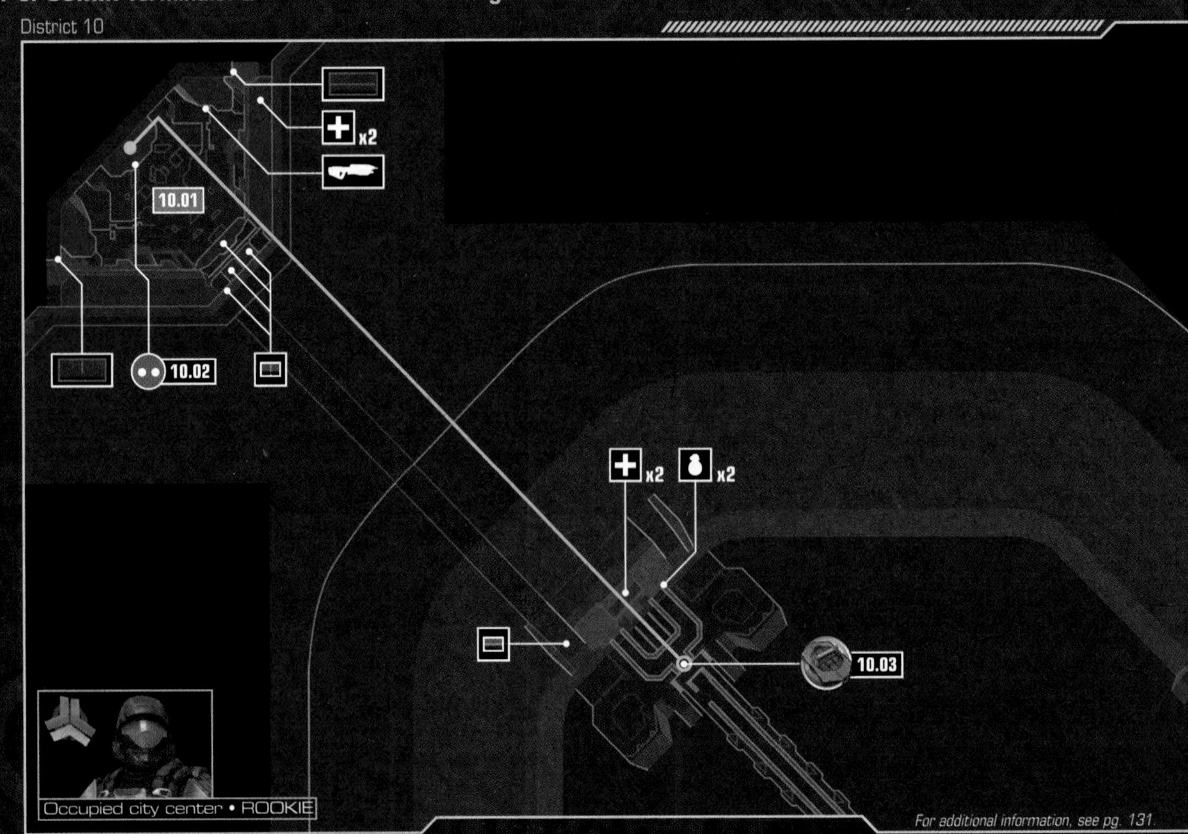

For additional information, see pg. 131.

CAMPAIGN

District 0

0.01 Kikowani Station: Bus Terminal Clue

The northern tip of Mombasa Streets is comprised of a small bus terminal zone with two roads linked to it. The clue is under the metal awning: the Bio-Foam Canister.

0.02 Brutal Plaza

Named after the concentration of Brutes that sometimes roam this area later in your expedition, this links you to other plazas in the district and offers access to the station area, too.

0.03 Kikowani Plaza

A stepped central area of planters with a road surrounding it is the most direct route to the bus terminal. There's an internal set of steps to a balcony overlooking this plaza for the sniper professional.

0.04 Optican Roundabout

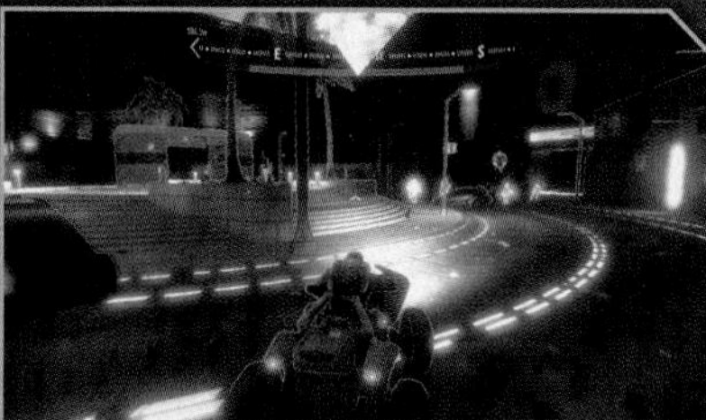

Named after the Optican Kiosk in the middle of this circular open area, this offers access to this district's only weapons cache and to the rest of the district, including the northeastern section, which is half covered on your in-game NAV map.

0.05 Weapon Cache (Set 3)

This opens up once you find 16 COMM Terminals. It contains Rocket Launchers (2), Rocket Launcher Ammo (2), Magnums (4), Silenced SMGs (4), and Frag Grenades (4).

District 3

3.01 NMPD Headquarters Clue

Offering several dead-end and linking roads, this plaza is easily remembered because of its unique, curved sculpture in the middle and numerous cable wires, with the clue hanging from one of them: Romeo's Bent Sniper Rifle.

3.02 Scorpion Protruding Roof Plaza

Although no Scorpion Tanks are available in Campaign Mission 10, this is where you boarded a tank during Campaign Mission 04. A stepped and partially covered plaza, complete with access to an underground circular road to the southwest, this offers access to District 0 and a weapons cache. It is a mirror image of location 8.05.

3.03 Weapon Cache (Set 2)

This opens up once you find eight COMM Terminals. It contains Magnums (4), Silenced SMGs (4), Frag Grenades (4), and Mongooses (2).

3.04 Stepped Plaza

Close to the center of this district, this is a heavily traveled thoroughfare and is the scene of a vicious tank fight during Campaign Mission 04. The building to the southwest has sections of the space elevator on it and may still be burning.

3.05 Roundabout Plaza

Except when accessing District 4, this area isn't heavily trafficked, although it features building interiors and a main walkway, just like location 8.02. Beware of Snipers here, and don't confuse the two landmark areas.

3.06 Sniper's Walkway II

Offering access around and north to the protruding roof plaza and weapons cache, this also allows you to head west into a small maze of side streets, on your hunt for a hidden COMM Terminal. There are multiple exits here.

■ District 4

4.01 Sunken Plaza

Aside from the hidden COMM Terminals, there's little to attract you to this area, which is on the route to District 0 but isn't as well traversed as the eastern part of this area.

4.02 Weapon Cache (Set 3)

This opens up once you find 16 COMM Terminals. It contains Rocket Launchers (2), Rocket Launcher Ammo (2), Magnums (4), Silenced SMGs (4), and Frag Grenades (4).

4.03 Kizingo Boulevard Clue

There are two main plazas here, with side streets to the southwest that allow alternate access from the south to the northwest areas of this district. The main area is this multistepped concrete plaza with a Gauss Turret guarding the lower roundabout. Enter the building to the northwest, and move through it to reach an upper balcony, where the clue—another Gauss Turret—is located.

4.04 Kizingo Boulevard Lower Roundabout

You'll fight Wraiths here during Mission 04, but during the night, there are fewer enemies to worry about. Note the building you can enter just north of here, and there is access to District 10's Rally Point and a gate into District 6. There is also a side street access toward the Sunken Plaza.

■ District 5

5.01 Rookie Landing Pod

You investigate the first six of these locations throughout Mission 01. This landing spot, when viewed as part of Mombasa Streets as a whole, allows you to spatially understand how this district relates to all the others. Near here, you interact with your first Optican Kiosk, and you can check the pedestrian dead-end side street that's southeast of here.

5.02 Roundabout Plaza

Between the Rookie Landing Pod and here, you encounter your first foes. There are more in this roundabout plaza, which features numerous locations to use as cover.

5.03 Superintendent Plaza

Between the Roundabout Plaza and this stepped location, you'll find and access the Superintendent's first COMM Terminal, although this one isn't counted toward the 30 you're attempting to find. Don't forget the nearby weapons cache, which doesn't open until well into your missions.

5.04 Weapon Cache (Set 2)

This opens up once you find eight COMM Terminals. It contains Magnums (4), Silenced SMGs (4), Frag Grenades (4), and Mongooses (2).

5.05 Grunts' Dozing Courtyard

After accessing a building interior near the weapons cache, you can enter this enclosed courtyard, which has sleeping Grunts. Wake them up with violence, or tiptoe toward the Tayari Plaza clue.

5.06 Tayari Plaza Clue

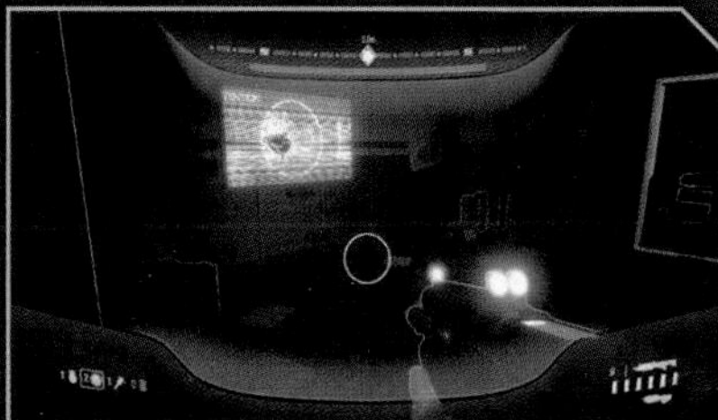

Located inside the building accessed via location 5.05, there are numerous weapons to scavenge on your way to this room, which overlooks the Tayari Plaza. The clue is Dare's Combat Helmet, embedded in the wall-mounted TV screen. Locate this clue last during Mission 10 (only), and the entrance to "Mission 08: Data Hive" appears on the perimeter of Tayari Plaza.

5.07 Tayari Plaza

Lightly guarded by Grunts on your first visit, this features a lower "crater" area with Dare's Pod and a covered area to the northwest. This is the location of "Mission 01: Crater" and "Mission 09: Crater (Night)" in Firefight mode. This is also the final objective for Buck in Campaign Mission 02.

District 6

6.01 Engineers' Courtyard

Usually accessed from the south via an internal building entrance, this area sometimes features two nonaggressive Engineers floating about above you. Attack with charged Plasma Pistols or leave them be.

6.02 Walkway and Thoroughfare

Allowing you to easily head from or to District 8 or 4, this is where you attacked the Jackal Watchtower during Campaign Mission 02. The pedestrian walkway spans the area above the District 4 gate.

6.03 Weapon Cache (Set 1)

This opens up once you find four COMM Terminals. It contains Sniper Rifles (2), Sniper Ammo (2), Magnums (4), Silenced SMGs (4), and Frag Grenades (4).

6.04 Narrow Road Blockade

This is a side street where Buck meets the two Marines and Brute squad during Campaign Mission 02. This area offers narrow access north, toward the pedestrian walkway bridge.

6.05 Wrecked and Lower Plaza

Feeling the brunt of the falling space elevator, much of these two connected plazas have giant pieces of wreckage everywhere and are in complete darkness. Navigate around here for quick access to Districts 4 and 10.

6.06 Stepped Roadway

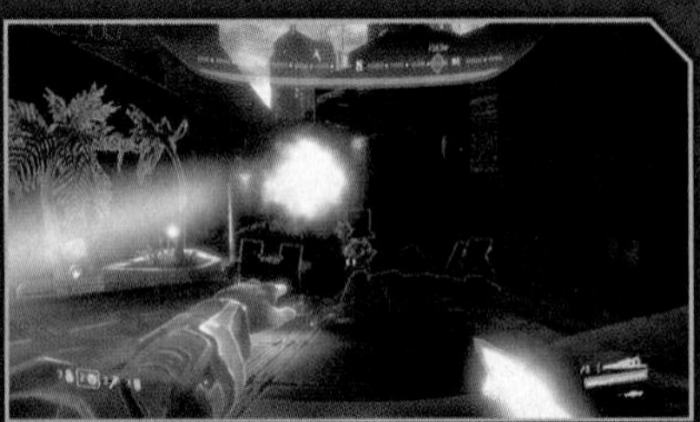

A series of stepped concrete walls and planters that drops down to a road and a gate into District 4, this is where Buck begins his search for Dare's Pod in Campaign Mission 02. Head north from here to access the side street (6.04).

District 8

8.01 Circular Plaza

Not usually part of the pathways you traverse until you begin Campaign Mission 10, this circular plaza offers some perimeter sections to search through and quick access to District 5.

8.02 Sniper's Walkway

A crossroads that allows easy access to both Districts 5 and 6, you fight through this location twice—on your way to locating Dare's crashed Pod in Campaign Mission 02 and later in Mission 02 when playing as Rookie, en route to the Uplift Reserve in District 9. You'll face Hunters, Engineers, and Brutes, but the biggest problems when you return here are likely to be Jackal Snipers.

8.03 Stepped Plaza

Located in the middle of this district, this plaza offers accessible roads to all other landmarks close by. Don't confuse this stepped plaza with the identical one in District 3, where you drove the Scorpion Tank during Campaign Mission 04.

8.04 Stone Pergola Plaza

There is an easily visualized hexagonal pergola in the middle of a plaza, so you know where you are when you return here from District 6 to the east. There's access to some dead-end streets and to the two gates to District 9.

8.05 Protruding Roof Plaza

This is a large area with a number of covered stepped planters and steps up along the southwestern side. There is also an entrance to an underground, circular road (to the northeast), where additional supplies are likely.

District 9

9.01 Uplift Reserve Clue

This large, circular plaza is one of the entrances to the Uplift Reserve and has a weapons cache on the northeastern side. Easily distinguishable thanks to a central monument with a crashed Pelican embedded in it, the entrance steps hold the Uplift Reserve Clue: Drone Fighter Optics.

9.02 Weapon Cache (Set 1)

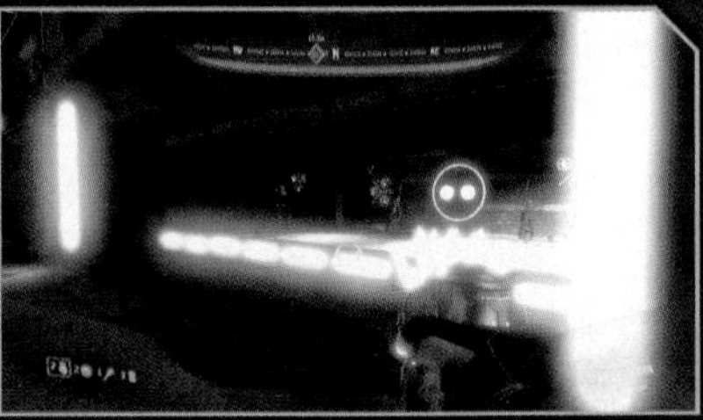

This opens up once you find four COMM Terminals. It contains Sniper Rifles (2), Sniper Ammo (2), Magnums (4), Silenced SMGs (4), and Frag Grenades (4).

9.03 Southern Plaza

This area is never visited due to energy wall barriers blocking your path. To the northeast is a small pedestrian area at the junction of the road, but this zone is mainly linking roads. Seek other means of accessing roads to the north when you wish to leave District 9.

9.04 Southern Terminal

This dead-end is the southern tip of the streets in New Mombasa, and energy wall barriers to the north prevent you from accessing this locale.

District 10

10.01 Rally Point

This is a large, stepped plaza with a road running around it. The lower central area houses a weapons cache, and there are balconies and walkway bridges around the perimeter, with covered upper balconies leading to a building interior (complete with items) to the southeast. This is the location of "Mission 03: Rally Point," and "Mission 10: Rally (Night)" in Firefight mode. Locate this clue last during the Campaign, and the entrance to "Mission 08: Data Hive" appears above the weapon cache.

10.02 Weapon Cache (Set 2)

This opens up once you find eight COMM Terminals. It contains Magnums (4), Silenced SMGs (4), Frag Grenades (4), and Mongooses (2).

10.03 ONI Alpha Site Clue

This platform overlooks the smoking remains of a bridge that led to the ONI Building. The clue is a Remote Detonator.

FIREFIGHT

Firefight Guide Lobby

The Basics of Firefight Missions

Setting up Firefight games from the appropriate menu is easy and is covered in your instruction manual, but we will cover the fundamentals of this epic (and ultimately hopeless) struggle against the forces of the Covenant. For this, we'll study the following labeled screenshot and will reveal the basic tenets of Firefight mode in the process.

Basic Tenets

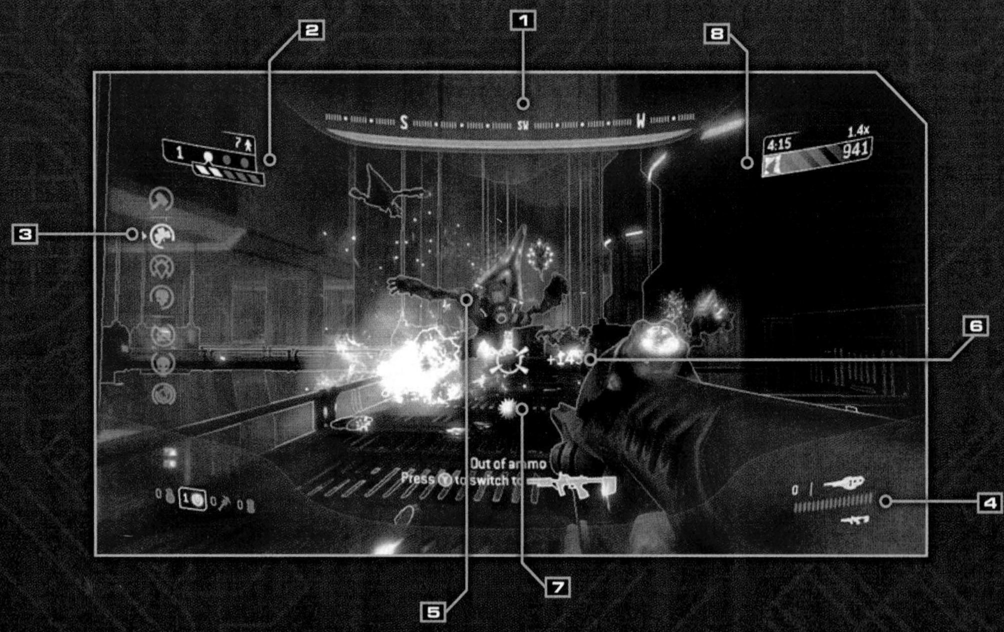

This example snapshot was taken during the **Firefight Mission: Chasm Ten**. Only information pertinent to Firefight has been labeled. Here's how all the information breaks down:

1 **Compass and VISR Readout:** This stores pertinent directional information and allows you to yell to your teammates when, for example, a new influx of foes appears and you need to give compass directions your team can easily follow. The periodic readouts (not shown) under your Health bar indicate when a wave has only a few enemies left or how many total points you get during a bonus round.

2 **Match Data:** This provides extremely helpful knowledge on how the match is progressing. The top section shows the number of lives your team has (in this case, seven). The middle section, comprised of a number and three dots that gradually fill up, indicates how far through a set you are. The bottom section, comprised of five yellow bars that gradually fill up, indicates how far through a round you are. Each of the yellow bars comprises a single wave. In this example, the player is three waves through his first round of his first set.

3 **Skulls:** In every Firefight, the same seven skulls become active at different times during a match, and the number and type of skulls varies from round to round. However, the same skulls are always active during the same rounds and sets. In this example, only Tough Luck is active. The more skulls that are active, the more difficult the round becomes, and this can lead to a change in tactics. The first three skulls (Tough Luck, Catch, and Black Eye) are activated during consecutive rounds. The second three (Tilt, Famine, Mythic) are activated during consecutive sets. The last skull (Iron) is activated only during bonus rounds.

NOTE There are other, secondary skulls that you can set as active from the Firefight menu. These don't affect the gameplay and are purely optional, with two exceptions:

Blind: This removes your player HUD, so you must rely on the announcer's voice to tell you when you've cleared a set, round, and wave.

Cowbell: This increases the effects of physics, making detonations much bigger. Couple this with Catch for a pretty explosive combination!

No secondary skull impacts the points you earn, though.

4 Primary and Reserve Weapon ("Weapon Combo"): The two weapons you can constantly pick up, use, reload, or swap for new weapons are shown here. However, throughout this chapter, we refer to "weapon combinations." These are preferred pairs of weapons you should carry under particular circumstances—tactical occasions designed for you to perform a particular task more effectively than simply rushing about without a plan.

5 Enemy (RIP): A number of Grunts have been blown off a high catwalk thanks to a well-placed Plasma Grenade. This foe has been labeled because it's the ugliest and is heading toward the player. Enemies leave weapons and Grenades behind, and scavenging certain ordnance can be the key to surviving longer.

6 Kill Points: This shows how many points the player received for this kill (+143). As the object of Firefight is to accrue as many points as possible, the key to scoring a massive amount stems from killing everything in sight and doing so proficiently enough to be awarded additional points in the form of multipliers and other statistical elements. The different ways to augment your score are listed below, in the "Accrue More Points" section.

7 Medal: During your Firefight battles, you are awarded medals for particularly satisfying or amusing takedowns. These range from sprees (culling multiple foes in quick succession) to enemy deaths with a specific weapon, and they are an easy way to instantly see that you're doing well. In this case, we won the Grenade Stick Medal for killing the Grunts with a thrown Plasma Grenade.

8 Match Data (Additional): The time spent on this Firefight match is shown (in this case, four minutes and 15 seconds), as are the current points or score multiplier (in this case, 1.4x), which varies depending on several factors, listed in the "Accrue More Points" section. Finally, there's your score (along with the insignia and base color you chose when you outfitted your character). As this ODST trooper was playing a Solo Firefight, the team score isn't shown but appears here during two-, three-, or four-player matches.

What to Do

After emerging from your spawning corridor (which can be one of two adjacent locations and is the place where you respawn after dying), your task is to get into a tactically advantageous position in readiness for a Covenant incursion. These take place from one of two locations:

Phantom drop 1: At least one Phantom dropship comes into view and descends to a drop-point location. Covenant spill out, either via side hatchways or a hole in the base of the Phantom's superstructure. As this is going on, the Phantom's Plasma Turrets provide a constant barrage. You can knock these turrets out of commission with explosive ordnance, and your team can then use them.

Monster closets 2: Nicknamed by the ODSTs, "monster closets" are sealed doorways you cannot enter; however, they periodically open to reveal an energy wall, through which you cannot pass but the Covenant can. Expect one or more doorways (or "closets") to open at a time.

NOTE **Some screenshots in this section appear in third-person perspective. You cannot access this view during matches, but it is available using the "Save Film" playback feature. With this innovative and highly entertaining mode, you can save film playback, creating your own videos, and you can take your own screenshots. All of this content can be shared on Bungie.net. Consult your instruction manual for further information.**

Attack!

Once enemies are present, your team takes down the threat until no more foes are present and the wave is complete. Then the next wave randomly appears from either type of location detailed previously.

Weapons Detail

Attack foes with the weapons you were given at the beginning of the round, which have easily obtainable ammunition at your spawning point; with weapons you pick up from fallen foes, which can be very potent, although scavenging for ammunition can be problematic; with weapons positioned on the map, like the Rocket Launcher or Sniper Rifle (only one team member should attempt to use this due to the lack of weapons and ammo); or with Turrets, which are stationary and offer impressive and infinite ammunition as long as the Turret is still attached to its base (if you take the Turret off the base, the ammo can be depleted).

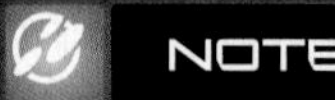

All non-Covenant weaponry and health is restored at the beginning of each subsequent round thanks to an instant and automatic weapons drop. All Covenant weaponry and vehicles disappear at the beginning of each round, unless a player is using it.

How to Do It

▲ An example of combat during a four-player match. With everyone knowing their role, weapon locations, and enemy incursion points, expect to pile on the points. With everyone milling around like Grunts without a Brute leader, expect an embarrassment of deaths.

Accrue Points

The one overriding goal in Firefight is to score as many points as possible for your team. You and your team's specific points are shown, and once the match is over (i.e., you've all been killed, or you stopped the match), inspect the Postgame Carnage Report to see how you did. Remember that the goal here is to score as many points possible as a team, not as an individual. There are some tactics that help your team's score and not your own.

Accrue More Points

Simply killing everything in sight is an excellent plan, but you should be figuring out how to make every shot count for more than just basic points. To this end, you need to consider how to maximize your score potential. Naturally, the bigger and more ferocious a foe you slay, the more points you gain. But there are other ways to pile on the points, too:

Skulls: When certain Skulls are active, your points multiplier fluctuates. For example, when Black Eye is turned on, your multiplier value is 1.5x. When Mythic is on, the value is 2x.

Difficulty: Choose a difficulty, and the harder the match, the more points you obtain. While Easy reduces your points by .25x, Legendary increases it by 4x. However, actually surviving on Legendary is insanely improbable, so Normal or Heroic are the better bets for an overall higher score.

Quick kills: Tagging foes in quick succession (by constant headshots, massive wallops with a Gravity Hammer, or well-aimed ordnance into clusters of foes that are disembarking from their release locations) results in multikills. The more you do, the higher the multiplier.

Sets: Expect your score multiplier to increase on each subsequent set you reach. Complete three rounds and the bonus, and your next set rewards you with a +0.5x overall multiplier increase.

Stylish kills: Many of the more esoteric weapons have their own points multiplier if you choose to destroy the Covenant using them.

Multiple kills (sprees): Killing sprees or kill chains entail defeating a large number of foes without pause (which is different from quick kills, as you can keep your spree going over time) and result in a large points boost. Try different weapons or vehicles, too.

Enemy threat: Take down a Grunt, and your basic points reward is only 10. Take down a Brute Captain in armor and your basic points reward is 150. It seems like the Brute Captain is your takedown choice (especially if he's carrying a Fuel Rod Cannon!), but can you kill 15 Grunts in the same time as facing a Brute Captain in dangerous combat?

Achievements: There are nine Achievements specific to this mode, although eight of them simply expect you to score 200,000 points during a match on a specific map. A tenth, Vidmaster: Endure Achievement (passing the fourth set of a Firefight match on LIVE Co-op), is also available.

Friendly fire: The one way to ruin friendships and your team score is to kill one of your teammates (accidentally or otherwise), as this reduces your points total. Reduce the opportunities for friendly fire by being proactive; talking to your team; and, if worse comes to worst, taking down a teammate who's being reckless and trying to increase their own score at the expense of others.

NOTE **The Appendices at the back of this guide provide copious details on the bonuses and multipliers you receive for specific ways of taking down enemies. They also cover all the Firefight medals you can obtain and how best to complete the specific Achievements. Make sure you check the Appendices to improve your matches.**

■ Team Etiquette

Once a match begins, there are many ways to help both your score and your team without being labeled a troublemaker:

Getting into the zone: Prior to the match, designate team members to patrol each area of the map. If your squad can handle enemy types in a specific part of a map, and the rest of the team are flexible enough to provide support when needed, you'll go far.

Nomenclature: Develop a series of nicknames for the scenery, buildings, and other structures that exist on the map, and provide periodic safety updates. Be careful using numbers that appear on barricades, though; some of those numbers are repeated. Yelling "Covenant Wraith, north courtyard! I got it!" should provide all the information the rest of your team needs to know (i.e., what the enemy is, where it is, and whether it is a threat). Compare this to "Oh crap, there's a big purple thing, and I'm scared!" which is far less informational, except to showcase your ineptitude.

Flanking fire: Enemies love being able to shoot or lob Grenades at a group of ODSTs bunched together; therefore, spread out across the map so you can cut down enemy incursions from two or more angles.

Flexibility: Working in unison and learning the map layouts allows you to develop a kind of sixth sense so you know when a friend is in trouble (or when they are likely to be in trouble) and when the more horrific Covenant entities are going to show up during a round.

Prediction: Although Covenant forces and entity types appear semirandomly, there's some degree of prediction involved. For example, if you've just tackled foes from a Phantom to the north, it isn't likely to appear there again. Being aware of enemies by sight or sound (e.g., seeing Phantoms on the horizon and energy walls activating in preparation for Covenant release and hearing the noise Phantoms and energy walls make) and waiting to strike is better than spotting a mass of foes spreading out before acting.

Preparation: There's just enough time between waves and rounds to tool up with your preferred killing ordnance; always stay on the move, and with a purpose.

Fighting style: Some team members love camping out and sniping. Others enjoy tearing through masses of foes with a Gravity Hammer. Play to your particular strengths, although you'll get further (especially on higher difficulties) if the majority of your team tackles foes from range.

Weapon specialists: With the optimal weapon combinations available, you should choose the exact weapon types to wield ahead of a match, and ensure your team members do the same. Due to the lack of ammunition for some weapons (such as the Rocket Launcher, and Plasma Pistol in later Sets), having everyone use the same weapon is a terrible idea; you'll all end up with limited ammunition and being overrun. Instead, pick squadmates with a particular weapon and have them choose a role related to that weapon. For example, the squadmate with the Plasma Pistol should take down Engineers and reduce Brute shields.

Pairing up: Taking a friend with you can prevent you from patrolling a zone effectively, as you're concentrating on each other as well as the enemy, but it has other benefits instead; you have double the firepower, you're able to shoot from two directions, and you're less likely to be outflanked or overrun.

A healthy outlook: Each map has only four Health Packs available, which are replenished after every round. Use only one per round so your friends have a chance to heal, too. Also, it is always better to wait for your Stamina to recharge than grabbing a Health Pack; use them only when you're about to die and have a pitiful amount of health left.

Stockpiling: Each map's weapon caches (featuring Silenced SMGs, Magnums, and Grenades), harder-hitting weapons (such as the Rocket Launcher), and Turrets that have been removed from their stands are replenished after every round. Increase your available offense by grabbing these items (especially the Turret) and carrying them. Once the next round starts, place them in a designated area so your teammates can utilize them, effectively doubling your ordnance. This works with vehicles, too—although, you must be holding a weapon or riding an enemy vehicle at the end of the round or it disappears.

The Postgame Carnage Report

After every match is over (whether you died or quit), you can review all your kills, medals, favored weapons, number of slain enemies, preferred weapons, and a host of other information in the Postgame Carnage Report. This shows you how each team member played, and you can hone their combat effectiveness in the future by playing on the strengths they display in this report. For example, if one of your team had a massive Headshot Medal count, you know they're the best choice for sniping and using their preferred ranged weapon.

Legendary Difficulty

Playing Firefight on Legendary tests the mettle of the very best players, and simply ramping up the difficulty and expecting to last more than ten minutes is naive and reckless. Legendary Firefights require you to stay hidden much more frequently and usually result in your team staying close to their spawning positions and holding them. Unless your squad is comprised of truly unstoppable players, consider Normal or Heroic difficulty to garner the most enjoyment from Firefight. However, there is one map (Windward) on which surviving on Legendary for an obscenely long time is possible.

Patterns in Randomness

Now that you have a broad knowledge of the basics, it is worth remembering the following information:

No end in sight: There is no upper limit to Firefight. You can keep going as long as you have lives left and your hands haven't cramped up.

Enemy waves: There isn't really a pattern to how enemy waves appear, but there are some elements that are a constant: The first wave of any round always has Grunts and/or Jackals in it. The three middle waves always consist of different enemy types that randomly rush you. The final wave of a round always has a Chieftain in it—sometimes more than one!

Middle three waves: Between the first and last waves of a round, there are three "middle" waves. These escalate in difficulty and enemy type as you progress further into a set or during subsequent sets. For example, the middle three waves of the first round are relatively easy. But by the third round, the enemies and weapons they carry become much more problematic. For example, take Jackals: In the first round of any set, they wouldn't ever carry a Beam Rifle. However, by Round 3, they will probably be using this powerful sniping tool. You can apply this rule to all the different enemy waves, with one exception: Hunters' weapons never change; they're always crazy enough!

Back from the dead: Look for certain milestones during a match for which you are awarded after the completion of a wave: If you are out of lives and everyone is dead except one player and that person remains alive long enough to see the "Reinforcements" sign appear on their HUD, they bring the others to life. Once this resurrection happens, the player is awarded with a special Hero medal for their bravery.

Ready for the next round: You gain lives for your team each time a round is passed. Between rounds, listen for the announcer to acknowledge the replenishment of your health and the respawning of all your weapons (including Turrets). Take advantage of this restock by "stockpiling" at the correct time.

General Tactical Advice

Use the following information to gain an advantage over the Covenant in this combat zone:

Pinging: This is the art of shooting a single bullet into a troublesome foe (who is almost always far away, partially hidden, or invisible), such as firing on a Brute Stalker so you can ascertain their location, to let your team know where a foe is. Refer to each specific mission tactic for more information.

Know your enemy: For every enemy type, there is a weapon proficient in killing them. For general strategies on taking out the various Covenant scum, consult the chapter "Know Your Enemy."

Plasma plans: Weapons using this type of energy (such as the Pistol or Rifle) are excellent at deteriorating enemy shields and should be saved for Brutes, certain Drones, and Engineers.

Problem Skulls I: Be wary when certain skulls are active. In category one, Black Eye (which prevents your stamina from regenerating unless you melee enemies or use a Health Pack) is a real problem, so make sure you know when it is active and why your screen is tinged red and you haven't recovered; then pistol-whip a foe as soon as it is safe.

Problem Skulls II: In Category 2, Tilt and Mythic are troublesome. Tilt reduces the effectiveness bullet-based weapons have on enemies with shields (Brutes, Shielded Drones, Engineers), making them more difficult to hit; use Plasma rounds instead or sidestep a Brute and do a melee attack from behind. Mythic doubles the health of all enemies; this makes headshots a necessity. With Tilt and Mythic both active, expect trouble!

Random predictions: Although waves appear randomly, the first wave of a round usually has Jackals to defeat. The last wave in each round always contains Brute Chieftains. Chieftains are always dropped off via Phantoms, except in Chasm Ten.

Turret plan: Generally, you should keep any Turrets on their bases, as the ammunition they use is infinite. However, this isn't the case when you wrench the Turret off its stand. Stockpiling at the end of each round (not wave!) is recommended.

General Weapon Combinations

...he Optimal or Preferred weapon combinations are not available due to team members already accessing such ordnance, ...ow this general list of weapon combinations, which can help you survive a set or two:

ALL MISSIONS

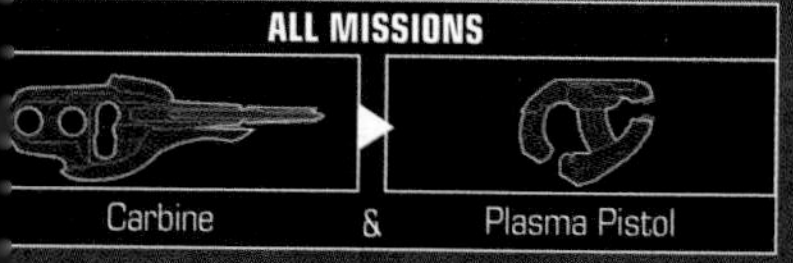

Carbine & Plasma Pistol

ALL MISSIONS

Magnum & Plasma Pistol

ALL MISSIONS

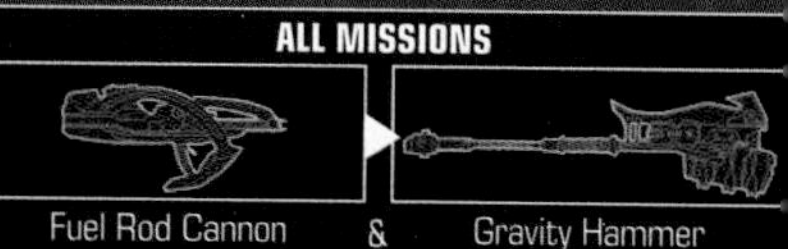

Fuel Rod Cannon & Gravity Hammer

LOST PLATOON

Brute Chopper

CRATER (NIGHT)

Plasma Pistol (Engineer takedowns)

RALLY (NIGHT)

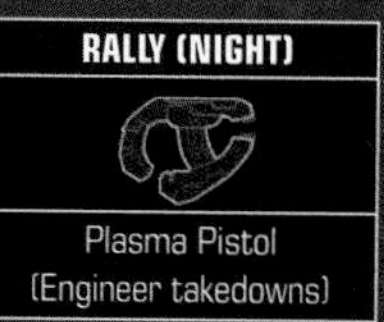

Plasma Pistol (Engineer takedowns)

User Preview and Preamble

...eleased with *Halo: ODST* are ten Firefight missions; eight separate maps; two nighttime versions of Crater and Rally Point, ...hich involve more judicious use of your VISR Enhanced Vision; and Engineer enemies. We have thoroughly play-tested all ...ssions and have recorded the optimal tactics in the remainder of this chapter. Here's how the information breaks down:

1 Overview: The mission name (and Night variant if applicable), the mission's motto, and a quick overview explaining the general layout of the map.

2 Expected enemies: This lists the general entities you should expect to repel throughout a Firefight match. Specific colors of Hunters or Drones are not mentioned, as they don't tend to affect your combat. Enemies are not listed in a particular order, because they arrive somewhat randomly.

3 Special enemies: Almost every Firefight mission has one or more specific enemy types that are particular to this map, such as the Jackal Snipers in Crater, or the Brute Chopper Riders in Lost Platoon. This tells you what to expect.

4 Expected vehicles: All expected vehicular activity is noted here, including whether Covenant Phantoms drop in to deliver infantry payloads or whether other Covenant (or UNSC) vehicles are available, some of which your team can appropriate and utilize.

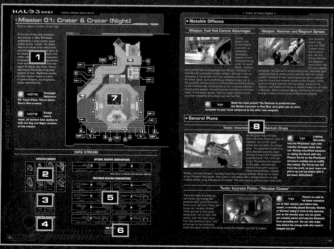

8 Tactical notation: The remainder of the mission information is broken down into helpful tactical advice. There's a section on notable offense, including what weapons or other equipment work well against the Covenant on a particular map; general plans, including the overall techniques to try during a Firefight on this mission; cooperative plans, which are specific tactics designed for solid team play; and bonus round plans, which help you maximize your score during the Grunt invasion between sets.

5 Weapon combinations: Although your personal preferences may vary, we have developed (through

6 Par score: The expected "par" (or average) score for

7 Map: Always handy, maps detail the entire area, showing multiple floors, your spawning

Mission 01: Crater & Crater (Night)

Fight in Dare's Sunken Crash Site

From one of two side corridors, you emerge in New Mombasa, overlooking a large sunken plaza known as the "crater." On either side is an alcove from which foes periodically stream in, and there is an alcove on the lower level to the north, where the Rocket Launcher is housed. Expect incoming attacks from doorways here and from the upper street to the north. This is also where Phantoms drop their payload of foes. Nighttime sorties on this mission result in a lack of Jackal Snipers, but Engineers arrive intermittently.

NOTE Campaign Reference 02: Tayari Plaza. This is where Dare's Pod crashed.

NOTE Except where noted, all tactical data applies to both the Day and Night versions of this mission.

Firefight: Crater

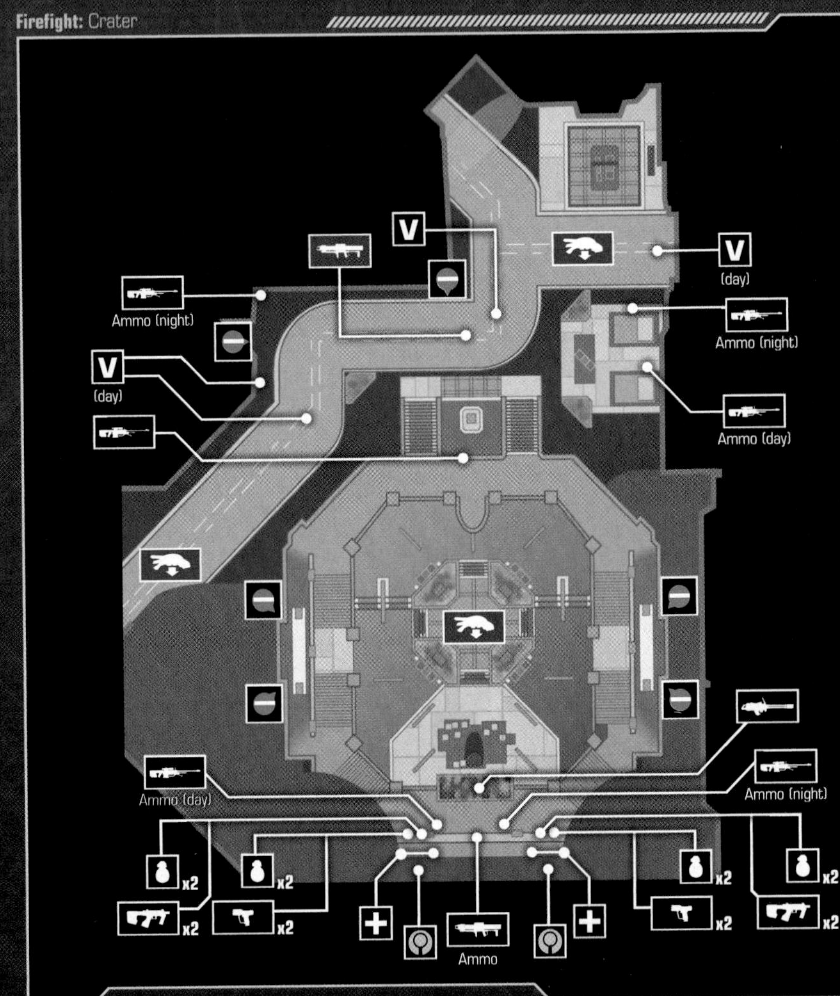

DATA STREAM

EXPECTED ENEMIES

Grunts

Jackals

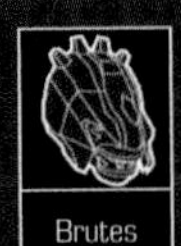
Brutes

Brute Chieftains

Jump-Pack Brutes

Brute Stalkers

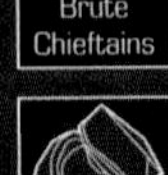
Drones

Hunters

SPECIAL ENEMIES

Jackal Snipers (Crater only)

Engineers (Crater Night only)

EXPECTED VEHICLES

OPTIMAL WEAPON COMBINATIONS

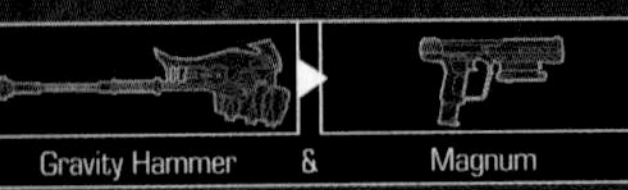
Gravity Hammer & Magnum

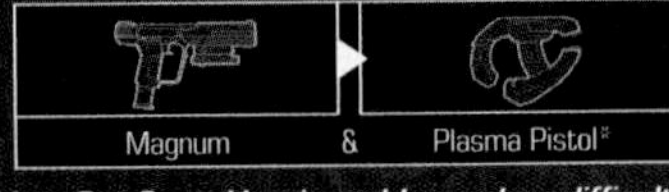
Magnum & Plasma Pistol*

**After Set 3, on Heroic and Legendary difficulty*

PREFERRED WEAPON COMBINATIONS

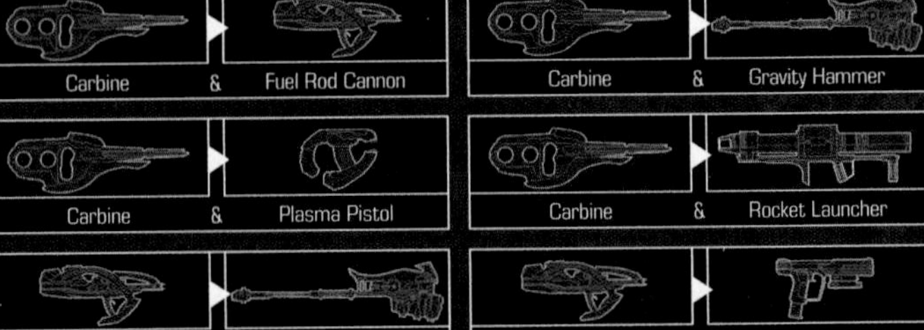
Carbine & Fuel Rod Cannon

Carbine & Gravity Hammer

Carbine & Plasma Pistol

Carbine & Rocket Launcher

Fuel Rod Cannon & Gravity Hammer

Fuel Rod Cannon & Magnum

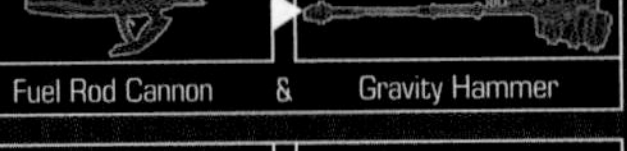

Notable Offense

Weapon: Fuel Rod Cannon Advantages

Usually, players race for the Rocket Launcher—an undeniably devastating weapon—in the northwest alcove under the upper street. However, the Fuel Rod Cannon (scavenged from Brutes, Chieftains, or even Grunts) is arguably a better weapon. Although it isn't as damaging, it has greater and more accessible ammunition. For every round, you're given only six rockets to use: four in the Launcher and two more in a Rocket Pack behind the Turret on the entrance wall. Compare this to the numerous enemies dropping this weapon, and you'll see the Fuel Rod is a fine alternative. In four-player games, have one player use the Rocket Launcher constantly while others use the Fuel Rod.

Weapon: Hammer and Magnum Sprees

Your personal choice may vary, but ODST Troopers have had excellent luck with the Gravity Hammer and Magnum combination due to a very specific advantage: the accrual of all-important points. Maximize your points potential by dashing about with the Hammer, culling multiple Covenant at their spawning points; you're awarded large kill chains and Hammer sprees in the process. While you're running to Hammer the next group, bring out the Magnum and headshot a Grunt or Jackal to keep the kill chain continuous. When executed adeptly, performing kill chains through multiple enemy waves is difficult but possible.

TIP

Need the most points? The Hammer is preferred over the Rocket Launcher or Fuel Rod, as it gives you an extra multiplier to your score compared to the other two weapons.

General Plans

Tactic: Incursion Points—Phantom Drops

As the guide map indicates, there are three Phantom drop-off locations: two on the upper street and one within the Crater plaza. The upper-left (south) drop point deposits Covenant down through a hole in the Phantom's superstructure. The north and Crater Phantoms have hatches on the sides, and enemies descend from both locations; these include Grunts, Jackals, Brutes, and even Hunters. Learning these two dropping methods allows you to camp at the Phantom drop points, then wade in and wallop with a Gravity Hammer or with multiple strikes using a Rocket or Grenades. This adds serious points to your team total.

TIP

Lobbing Grenades into the Phantoms' open side hatches damages many foes, too. Aiming area-effect weapons or raking the Grunt with the Plasma Turret on the Phantoms' structure enables you to nullify this attack. The Turret can fall from the craft, so your team can pick it up and lay waste with it (on lower difficulties)!

Tactic: Incursion Points—"Monster Closets"

There are eight doorways you can't enter (an energy wall prevents you), where Covenant forces pour out from. These are known as "monster closets." There are two on the upper street level; two on each side alcove, near the steps down from the starting location; and a final two to the northwest, under the upper street in the alcove where the Rocket Launcher is located.

TIP

There's no need to let these monsters out of their closets; just before they spawn, a carefully placed Grenade, Rocket, or Hammer swing in front of the doorway just as the enemies pour out can grant you massive points and keep the Covenant from spreading out. You can also snipe foes behind the energy walls who haven't stepped out yet!

Tactic: Near and Far

If you're attempting to keep your team's deaths down, it is imperative you equip yourself with one of the recommended weapon pairings listed previously. However, it is preferable to keep one weapon for "heavy-hitting," such as a Gravity Hammer or Rocket Launcher, while the other is scoped and excellent for headshots. The Covenant congregate in the lower plaza, as they stream out of doors, or as they drop down from Phantoms; this means a weapon with a large splash-damage radius is handy **[1]**. When playing Crater during daylight hours, at least two of your group should keep a lookout for Jackal Snipers appearing along the tops of the buildings **[2]**, along the left (southwest) and far (northwest) sides of this map. They can wreak real havoc if they aren't decapitated quickly, especially on Legendary, when one or two sniper shots is enough to kill a squadmate. For Crater (Night), make sure one or two of your team respond early and promptly to the periodic entrance of an Engineer or two.

Tactic: Turret's Syndrome

The Turret on the fern planter outside your spawn point is exceptionally useful. During initial waves, you can simply operate the Turret and rake fire on the squads of Grunts and Jackals staggering out or dropping down from their entrance points. But it is wise to learn when and when not to operate the Turret:

- The best time to use a Turret is during a wave of Drones; the Turret's infinite ammo and quick kills (only two or three shots per Drone) allow good kill-chain possibilities.
- The more dangerous time is when the Catch Skull is enabled; you won't have time to dodge any incoming Grenades, especially if multiple ones are incoming at once.
- The Turret's turning radius is about 180 degrees left and right and 160 degrees up and down. This means you can't hit foes directly below you in the plaza or those advancing from the tops of the stairs to the left and right.
- Couple a Turret with another player's attacks on the same toughened target to take out troublesome targets, such as Phantom Turret Gunners, Snipers (Day only), Engineers (Night only), and Brute Chieftains.
- Hunters cannot melee attack you when you're operating a Turret attached to its base. This allows you to pepper the Hunter with bullets while a friend occupies the beast.

Tactic: Staying Put

The initial balcony near the starting chambers is an excellent place to hang out (at least one of you should remain here during four-player matches), as it gives you tactical advantages: You have easy access to the available Health Packs (there are four, two on either side of each starting door); additional ammunition, which is handy for those wanting continuous Magnum headshots; and the Turret for rapid-fire multikills. There are also plenty of crates and pillars to use as cover when you come under fire, and the Covenant can only physically reach you by ascending the steps at either side, meaning you aren't likely to be overrun. The only exception are Drones or Jump-Pack Brutes who ignore the stairs, so kill them early to avoid being swarmed.

TIP **If you're having a horrendous time or need to make it through a final round to start a new set, retreat inside the spawning corridors; the enemies do not follow you in here, and you have time to rest and increase your Stamina.**

Tactic: From Pillar to Post

The alcoves, central crater plaza, and Rocket Launcher alcoves all have numerous pillars, planters, and posts to use as cover. This is highly recommended, ideally when Phantoms are descending to deposit foes and you don't have multiple players firing on the nose Turret, which can peel through your armor and Stamina in seconds. Most enemy projectiles will hit pillars you're lurking behind, so you'll need to tactically move from pillar to pillar. The abundance of cover makes tactically moving from pillar to pillar an excellent plan.

Tactic: Exit the Engineer (Night Only)

Instead of Jackal Snipers, the Crater (Night) variant of this mission has two Engineers that periodically fly over the map, coming in from the far upper left and right sides. Engineers are troublesome, as they grant all enemies in a moderate radius below them an overshield, including other Engineers if they are close enough. Overshields give enemies much more resilience, and Engineers have one small advantage: Their power reveals any Brute Stalkers in the vicinity. Resilient against many Covenant and UNSC weaponry, they can be difficult to take down and should be a priority; otherwise, all other combat is harder. By far the best way to take down an Engineer is with a fully charged Plasma Pistol blast; the Engineer panics and explodes after a few seconds, after which the Covenants' overshields are depleted. If you don't have a Plasma Pistol, tag it with your Turret, Sniper Rifle, or a weapon without a "projectile arc," as these foes float quite a distance away from you.

■ Cooperative Plans

Tactic: Four-Player Foresight

Competent team tactics should include variations on the following: One team member should stay at the Turret and be responsible for raking multiple foes, dealing with Drones, and tagging Snipers (Day) or Engineers (Night). Players two and three should choose a side and patrol the stairs down from the start, to the alcove where the two enemy doors are located. They can easily move to back up other teammates when their side is "quiet." The fourth player, who is likely the most experienced, should be responsible for patrolling the upper street and the Rocket Launcher alcove underneath, calling on players two and three when a deluge of foes threaten to overwhelm.

Tactic: Other Plans

Typically, another good plan is to execute a roving patrol with two players responsible for each other and for the enemies they encounter along the way. However, in Crater, if you have less than four players or if you're working in two teams of two, have one player tackle the right staircase side and stay there until called on for assistance. This usually prevents the Covenant from outflanking you.

Health is a precious commodity, cherished almost as much as Rocket ammunition. Be mindful of Health Packs and how many are left. If you're taking a pack, tell your team which one and how many are left; they are only replenished at the start of each round, so unless instructed otherwise, take only one pack per round so your team can access health as well. And don't take the Rocket ammunition if you're not using the weapon in question!

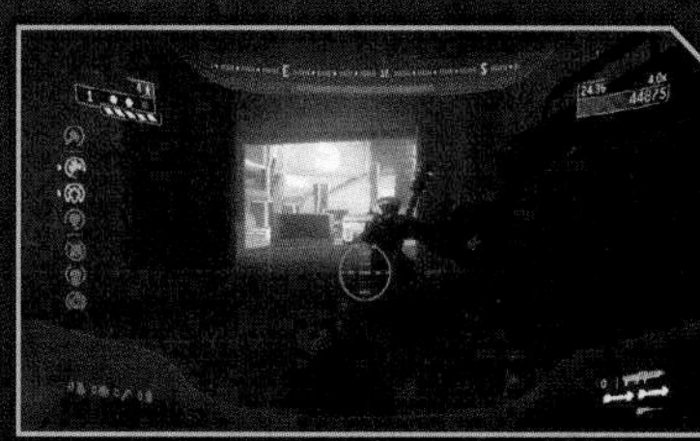

Tactic: Cooperative Engineer Culling (Night Only)

During nighttime excursions into Crater, it is wise to designate one member of your team as the Engineer dispatcher, armed with the Plasma Pistol. This is preferable to having multiple teammates using this weapon and not being properly equipped—and therefore being susceptible to getting overrun or dying quickly. Pairing your Plasma Pistol with a Carbine or Magnum still allows this teammate to tackle Grunts, Shield Jackals, Brutes, and Drones without taking themselves out of the action between Engineer takedowns. Naturally, they won't be adding much to the team score, but this isn't an individual tournament. Picking a single team member to wield the Plasma Pistol becomes even more prevalent once the Famine Skull is permanently on, as ammunition for it can really sustain only one team member by that time. You can also dispatch Engineers by using the Turret.

TIP

You can annoy the Plasma Pistol wielder by waiting for them to send the Engineer into its death-cycle spasm, then shoot it before it explodes and claim the Kill Points!

■ Bonus Round Plans

Tactic: Headshot Kill Chains

Assuming you make it to the first and subsequent bonus rounds, your weapons of choice are the Magnum or Carbine (or both), plus enough ammunition for plenty of headshot kill chains. All foes are Grunts, but because all Skulls are active, expect a large number of enemy Plasma Grenades and Suicide Grunts. Keep moving so the enemies' Grenades are less likely to hit. Run around the map and attempt as many headshots as possible, but don't enter the central plaza area, as Grunts converge on this location from all directions. Instead, most of your team should stay near the Turret (but don't operate it or you'll be showered with Grenades; pick it up if you must); the height and cover allows for the largest score and survival time.

Mission 02: Lost Platoon

Fight in the Dead Center of the Park

A lone building in the middle of the Uplift Reserve is the setting for an all-out, and mainly vehicular battle, against the Covenant, who are always dropped in by Phantoms. To the north and west, there's an area of flat ground; beware Phantoms carrying Wraiths here. To the south is a shallow ravine with a path curving around to the eastern hill, where Phantoms drop Wraiths periodically. Use the cover of the central building and the Covenant's Choppers to your advantage here.

Firefight: Lost Platoon

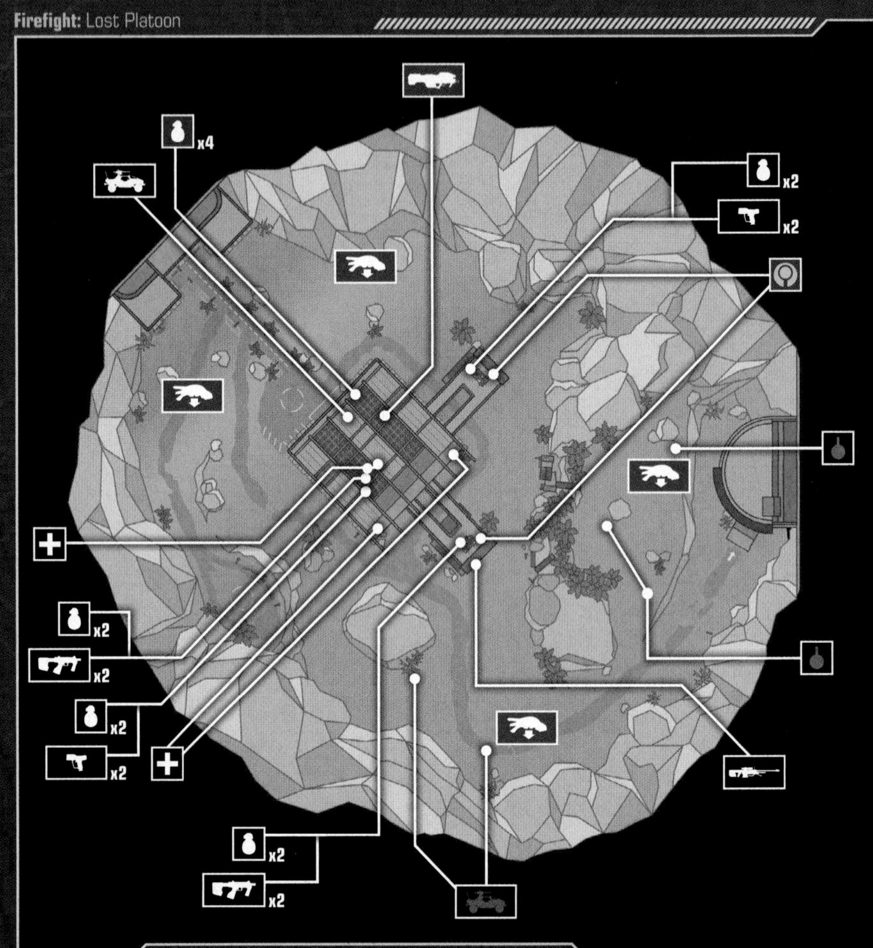

 NOTE

Campaign Reference 03: Uplift Reserve. UNSC rendezvous point prior to locating the colonel on the bridge.

DATA STREAM

EXPECTED ENEMIES

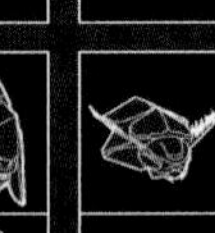

Grunts | Jackals | Brutes | Brute Chieftains

Jump-Pack Brutes | Brute Stalkers | Drones | Hunters

SPECIAL ENEMIES

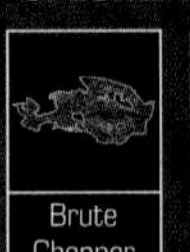

Brute Chopper Riders | Covenant Wraith Brutes

OPTIMAL WEAPON COMBINATIONS

Magnum & Spartan Laser riding Brute Chopper

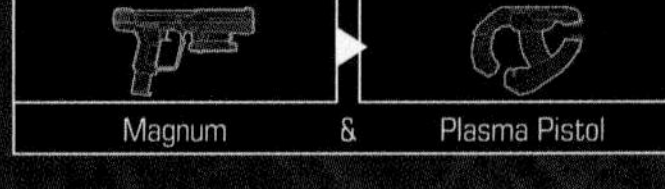

Magnum & Plasma Pistol

PREFERRED WEAPON COMBINATIONS

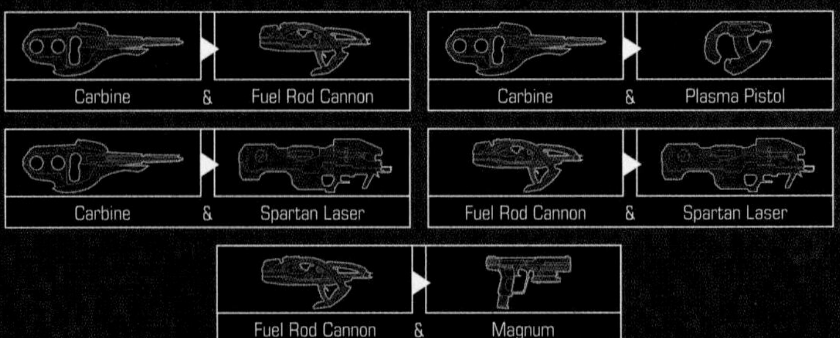

Carbine & Fuel Rod Cannon

Carbine & Plasma Pistol

Carbine & Spartan Laser

Fuel Rod Cannon & Spartan Laser

Fuel Rod Cannon & Magnum

EXPECTED VEHICLES

Covenant Phantoms

Covenant Choppers

Covenant Wraiths

UNSC Warthog

PAR SCORE

200,000 Points

■ Notable Offense

Weapons: Spartan Laser and Magnum

Unfortunately, not all of your team can utilize this weapon combo, but for one or two team members, this combination (when you aren't utilizing the Brute Chopper) is incredibly effective at disposing of foes and, more importantly, accumulating points. Use the Spartan Laser, which you find at the central building, to deliver a single, devastating shot at a Wraith. Each Wraith kill gives you three kills for an instant kill chain and large points. You also gain the Spartan Laser medal for further points. Switch to your Magnum between Wraith drops and during the bonus round. A single Phantom deposits numerous Grunts in a single spot, allowing for easy headshot chaining. Place yourself on the upper, open-air floor of the central UNSC building during the Wraith-defeating and bonus periods; from here, you have easy access to ammunition for these weapons.

 TIP

Over-relying on the Spartan Laser for Wraith takedowns? This is normal, and if your Spartan Laser wielder is less than competent, remember you can take down a Wraith the old-fashioned way: by destroying the exhaust port to the rear of the vehicle.

Weapon: Brute Chopper

When you aren't attacking Wraiths or Bonus Grunts, ride the Brute Chopper for the rest of the battle (make sure to tell your teammates the parked Chopper is yours). Using the Chopper, mop up the Covenant infantry after a Wraith explosion. This weapon easily runs enemies over, allowing for additional points for Splatter Medals. Even better, the powerful, front-mounted guns have infinite ammunition. Tear into groups of foes, and don't worry about being struck on the front of the vehicle; it is specially reinforced, reducing damage you take when enemies fire at the front of the Chopper. This extra protection isn't afforded at the back of the vehicle, so always charge your foes head-on, hoping for a ramming death or for the Chopper's dual cannons to do their job. Then hop off and bring out the Laser when you spot Phantoms.

 CAUTION

Don't bother searching for a Rocket Launcher; this is the only Firefight mission in which the UNSC have removed the weapon from your available arsenal.

■ General Plans

Tactic: Incursion Points—Breaking NEWS

There are no monster closets in this mission; the Covenant arrive from one of four locations: north, east, west, or south of the central building. It helps to have a teammate on the building's upper level, acting as a spotter. As a Phantom descends onto each of these "corner" locations, you should be able to thoroughly prepare for the incursions, which usually happen two Phantoms at a time. Phantom drops to the north and south may deposit a Covenant Brute Chopper, which you should hijack and use as the optimal killing machine for this mission. Phantom drops to the east and west may deposit a Covenant Wraith; you cannot drive this, but you can destroy it with ordnance or with a Grenade deposited into the vehicle after a teammate clambers onto the craft at melee range.

 TIP

With a spotter and quick-moving squadmates on Choppers, you can easily spot an incoming Phantom from a distance, then move into flanking camping spots to easily cull enemies that are being dropped off, blasting them from multiple directions.

Tactic: Vehicular Gruntslaughter

A critical advantage for your team, vehicles are incredibly helpful in this mission and should be utilized, especially considering the distances you must travel to reach the perimeters of this location. The key to a sustained Firefight is multiple squadmates on separate vehicles, constantly maneuvering around the map and defeating Covenant waves **[1]**; this makes kill chains a lot easier to obtain and players much more difficult to defeat, as you are all in constant movement. As an added technique, if two or more of your team are on a vehicle, have everyone patrol the map in the same direction so you don't run into each other **[2]**.

TIP **Although the UNSC Warthog is an adept fighting vehicle that you should use initially, once you slay Brute Choppers, switch to these. The reason is simple: It takes two of your squadmates to effectively man the Warthog, and they are both better employed each riding a Chopper. This effectively doubles your firepower and ramming potential.**

TIP **Trying to last as long as possible? Then make sure one squadmate is in charge of building up a "parking lot" of Choppers, parking them in or around the central building so that players who die can instantly get back on the vehicle and into the fray.**

Tactic: Holding the UNSC Hub

The central building with its multiple staircases and small chambers is where you spawn and where your team's ammunition caches, Health Packs, and weapons are stored. It offers excellent defensive and vantage points for sniping or firing the Spartan Laser) at foes dropping in from the Phantoms **[1]**. However, this structure is easily overrun if you aren't proficient in holding it. It is also susceptible to devastating Wraith fire, meaning you need to constantly watch for incoming plasma mortar. Be sure you study the guide map closely, noting the locations of the Health Packs and the specific weapons (including the Spartan Laser) held in racks in and atop the structure.

A UNSC Warthog is parked at the northwest ground entrance, near the stairs and a chamber with a Spartan Laser on a wall hook. Also remember the Health Packs behind the tree, to the right of the stairs; these are usually the ones that are grabbed first, so inform your team of this if you take one. Head up the stairs for an ammo cache (Submachine Guns, Magnums, and Frag Grenades) to the right and two more Health Packs against the walls on the east and western corners of the upper deck. To the southeast is a balcony with a second ammo cache (Submachine Guns and Frag Grenades) and some metal barriers to use as cover. To the northeast is a bridge; a third cache (Magnums and Grenades), located on the roof of another structure; and a single barrier. The last cache (Sniper Rifle attached to the low wall) is to the southeast, overlooking the south and east Phantom drop points; this area also features more barriers **[2]**. Watch for foes ascending the adjacent outer steps here and around the building itself.

TIP **Keep a Spartan Laser and Sniper teammate patrolling the building's top floor, and make sure they know if any foes have broken through from the rest of the team's vehicular slaughtering. You benefit from enemies not being able to reach you if you're on the roof; only worry about flying foes like Drones, Jump-Pack Brutes, and Wraith ordnance.**

Cooperative Plans

Tactic: Four-Player Foresight

Optimally, and with room for constant flexibility, one squadmate should deem themselves the "caller" and man themselves on the central building's roof. They shout the compass directions for incoming Phantoms, then deliver a quick and certain Spartan Laser shot into each Wraith that appears, swapping to a Sniper Rifle or Magnum to tag Jackals and Grunts. The remaining teammates use preferred weapon combos to drop all other ground troops. However, ensure Chopper Brutes are taken out without the Chopper exploding, after which all other teammates should attack constantly with the Choppers and leave the Wraith to the Spartan Laser user.

CAUTION

The Warthog is initially an amusing method of Covenant destruction but becomes increasingly ineffective as combat progresses; in addition to it needing at least two teammates to operate, the more Skulls that are active, the more problematic the Warthog becomes. Ditch it after Set 2, when the Tilt Skull becomes permanently active.

Tactic: Shields Down

Another option is to split into two teams of two. One squadmate focuses on Plasma-powered weaponry, while the other collects bullet-based ordnance. The synergy can result in quick, easy wave progression as the Plasma-weapon soldier removes enemy shields, and the other finishes off the foes. Although the Plasma-weapon wielder sacrifices their score (as they remove only shields and don't receive points for kills or assists), the score you're aiming for is accumulated. If your pride can handle that, try this tactic. This becomes even more important once the Famine Skull activates, which limits the ammo you can gather. If everyone shares the same weapon type, you're asking for trouble. Instead, for example, have one squadmate collect only Plasma-powered guns from fallen foes, rather than having two or three of your team doing this.

TIP

Health Packs are a luxury; be mindful of how many are remaining, and remember they are replenished only at the start of every round. Use only one per round so your friends have access to one, too. Also, let your team know where remaining Health Packs are located.

Bonus Round Plans

Tactic: On the Nose

This tactic calls for multiple team members to work in unison. When the Phantom carrying the Grunts descends, you must destroy as many of the ship's Plasma Turrets as possible; the priority turret is the one on the Phantom's nose. Attack the turrets from different directions so it can't hit all of you. Then stay at a distance, using a Magnum or Carbine to kill-chain multiple Grunts with headshots until you reach the bonus round Par Score. The farther away you are from the Phantom drop point, the better; you have more time to react to incoming fire and Grenades and to line up headshots.

Tactic: Get to the Chopper!

The more reckless squadmate should try continuing their Brute Chopper prowess to achieve multiple splatter kills and equally massive kill-chain scores. While snipers tag Grunt heads from hiding spots, the Chopper rider rapidly fires the Chopper cannons to keep the Grunts from throwing Grenades onto the vehicle; watch for dropped Grenades on the ground in front of them and swerve to avoid them. Charge in, disrupting the Grunts' movement and attacks so your snipers get more kills, and try ramming foes. Count yourself lucky if you aren't struck by a Grenade; that requires perfect driving and dodging.

Mission 03: Rally Point & Rally (Night)

Fight with Your Back Against the Wall

You begin inside a two-level building that the Covenant can easily overrun, so head outside to the top of a ramped road, where Covenant defenses are positioned. From here, you can survey a catwalk and bridges along each side, where Phantoms drop their Covenant cargo; a series of steps and planters in the middle of the map; and a road that travels in a long semicircle from one side to the other, behind which monsters emerge. Beware of a Wraith being dropped onto the street, too. During nighttime battles, be on your guard for the arrival of Engineers.

Campaign Reference 04: Kizingo Blvd. The rally point in New Mombasa.

Except where noted, all tactical data applies to both the Day and Night versions of this mission.

Firefight: Rally Point

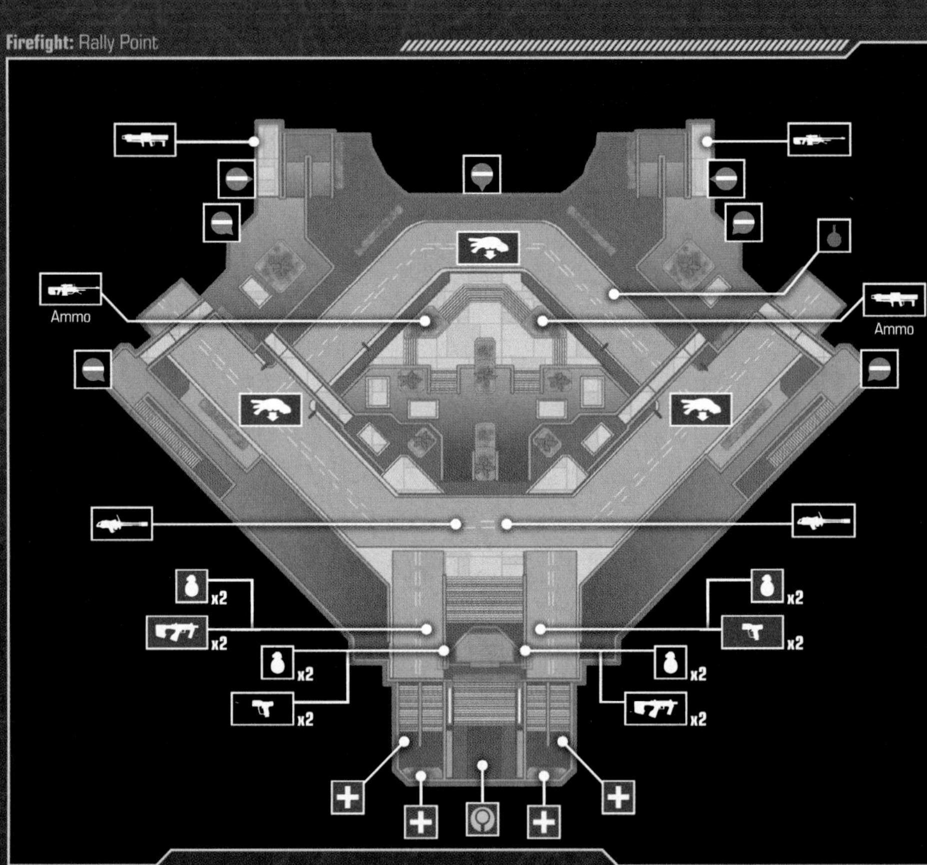

DATA STREAM

EXPECTED ENEMIES

Grunts

Jackals

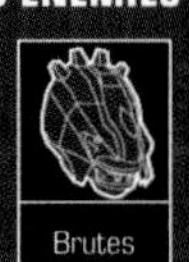
Brutes

Brute Chieftains

Jump-Pack Brutes

Brute Stalkers

Drones

Hunters

SPECIAL ENEMIES

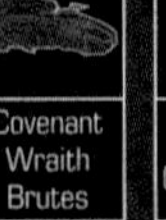
Covenant Wraith Brutes

Engineers (Night only)

EXPECTED VEHICLES

Covenant Phantoms

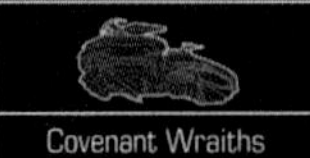
Covenant Wraiths

OPTIMAL WEAPON COMBINATIONS

Fuel Rod Cannon & Magnum

Magnum & Plasma Pistol*

***After Set 3.*

PREFERRED WEAPON COMBINATIONS

Carbine & Fuel Rod Cannon

Carbine & Plasma Pistol

Carbine & Rocket Launcher

Fuel Rod Cannon & Rocket Launcher

Gravity Hammer & Magnum

PAR SCORE

200,000 Points

Notable Offense

Weapons: Fuel Rod Cannon and Magnum

The Fuel Rod Cannon is dropped by an enemy Brute, Chieftain, or Grunt. When you get it, use it with your trusty Magnum if you want to obtain the largest score in the fastest time with the least amount of danger. During battles with clusters of enemies, the Fuel Rod Cannon delivers pleasing—and devastating—damage, with the potential of killing large groups of foes, after which you can extend your killing sprees by popping the heads of any remaining stragglers. Both weapons are effective at longer ranges, too, meaning you can remain active but away from the focus of the Covenant's attacks.

 TIP

A fast time isn't a relevant factor when determining your scores, so take your time, using cover and letting enemies come to you.

Weapon: The Two Turrets

There are two Turrets available on this map, and both are easily reached from the ODST spawning building. However, unlike the Turret in Crater, they offer only limited help; use them only under certain circumstances, such as when you're low on other ammunition or you're detaching the Turret before the next round begins and want a more mobile method of strafing foes coming up the road. The Turrets' main drawback is their limited fire radius; the ODST defenses prevent you from shooting in more than a 90-degree arc. Enemies can easily break in behind you, too, so employ Turrets to take down Phantom Plasma Turrets and groups of foes during initial confrontations.

 TIP

Turrets have their uses: those that are fastened to their mountings give you infinite ammunition and allow you to decimate the Drone waves and, to a lesser extent, Jump-Pack Brutes.

General Plans

Tactic: Incursion Points—Phantom Drops

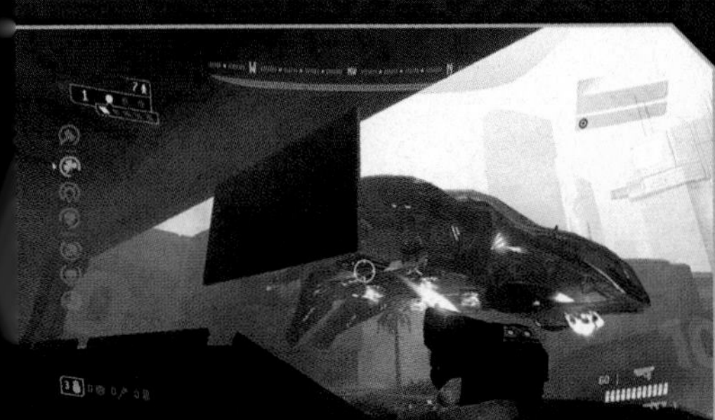

As shown on this guide's map, there are three drop points at which Phantoms can descend before dropping off enemy troops. Phantoms tend to descend one at a time, but reinforcements arrive from additional Phantoms at a quicker rate than Crater, for example. Of the three positions, two involve the Phantom hovering above the narrow bridges at the map's far north and western corners, opening side bay doors, and letting Covenant pour out from either side. A Phantom that descends to the middle (northwest) of the main street opposite the UNSC spawn point and defenses always drops a Wraith; if you see such a Phantom, you know you have a grav-tank to deal with.

TIP

Team spawn-camping diminishes the problems Phantom drops pose: Make sure your team seeks cover, attacks from multiple angles, devastates enemies with headshots and Grenades, and destroys Plasma Turrets (allowing

Tactic: Incursion Points—Closets Large and Small

In addition to Phantom drop points, there are seven monster closets along the opposite (northwest) wall. Some of these entrances are a lot wider than others. Due to the large number of openings, it is often difficult to stop the Covenant from spreading out, although training your team to guard certain areas (see "Tactic: Four-Player Foresight" below) helps you raise the alarm. There are three narrow doorways on the ground and upper levels near the two bridges on each side of the map **[1]**, as well as a large central "cache" garage door that opens periodically **[2]**, behind where the Wraith is deposited. As expected, preventing the Covenant from exiting these locations is almost impossible.

TIP

Although almost impossible, containment is still an excellent way to diminish continuous attacks from multiple angles. Lob in Grenades as foes are about to exit, or snipe them while they are bunched together, or behind the energy wall.

Tactic: Wraith Killing

Your number-one goal for surviving this mission is to appoint a "Wraith killer," an adept player whose primary job is to destroy the Wraith tank that periodically drops from a Phantom into the middle of the map's northwest area. Failure to eliminate the Wraith means you will be continuously overrun by other Covenant forces, as other team members become more concerned with tackling other incursions and don't see an incoming Plasma mortar until it is too late. There are two main ways to take care of a Wraith. The first is to circle-strafe behind the vehicle, then unleash a Fuel Rod or Rocket ordnance into its lightly protected exhaust port **[1]**. The second is to risk being run over and leap onto the vehicle, wrestling with the driver and dropping in a Grenade to deliver the killing blow **[2]**. Both these plans take skill, so you might want to appoint a backup Wraith killer among your team!

TIP

Wait under the central Phantom drop point and board the Wraith immediately for an easier kill.

Tactic: Spawning Grounds

The sloping roadway and ODST spawning building entrance is arguably the safest and optimal position to stay at. You are close to the additional ammunition and health inside the spawning building and to the ODST wall defenses and both Turrets. Head up and around to the rear perimeter, near the hub gates (which don't open): From here, your foes can only approach from the road ahead (northwest) or via the catwalks to the left and right, which are easily defended. You also have excellent views of the steps and concrete planters down to the

CAUTION

Unlike some other Firefight missions, enemies enter your spawning building, which is problematic when you're retreating to find health. Learn to retreat backward, training your weapon on the

Tactic: Cornering Your Foes

Another great tactical position is in front of the door in the left (southwest) or right (northeast) corners of the map, with the back wall behind you. From this location, every enemy attacks you from the front, so you don't need to worry about being ambushed from behind or the sides. You're above the road and can see across the bridges toward the map's center; this extra height lets you easily spot and snipe foes. In addition, enemies are usually funneled along the streets below, making for an easy shooting gallery (when the enemies aren't heading out of the doors near your location, of course). The only shortcoming of this location is the lack of additional ammo and Health Packs. You'll be tagging foes in the street below and will have to dash down to grab any ammo, and you must return to your spawning area to get Health Packs. For these reasons, it's a good idea to warn your friends when you're retreating to locate health or ammo.

There are places that are tactically disadvantageous, such as the inner bridges spanning the road, which are narrow and are a favorite place for Grunts to throw Grenades at. You can strafe, but not freely, which hinders your progress, so stay only on this bridge if you're under a Phantom, tagging foes before they have chance to group together. Other dangerous locations include the steps and concrete planters in the middle of the map and the lower road. The lack of height puts you at a disadvantage, and foes can converge on you from all directions. Mill around at the defenses near the Turrets, unless you're on a kill-crazy rampage with a Gravity Hammer.

Cooperative Plans

Tactic: Four-Player Foresight

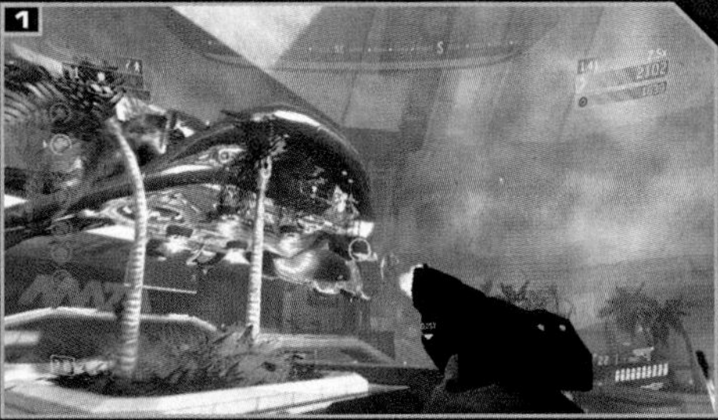

Team positions obviously vary from round to round, but general patrol patterns can help you finish the fight: Have one of your team take each corner on the far southwest and northeast corners of the map **[1]**. Here, they can cover Phantom drops by the bridge, can tear through foes appearing from any monster closet, and can tackle any flying foes landing on the catwalks above your entrance. They can venture to the map's center to provide supporting fire. The third and fourth teammates should stay at the ODST entrance **[2]** to do the following: quickly react to incoming Wraiths by sprinting down to the road, to face Drone attacks by manning the Turrets, or to confront Brutes by outflanking these foes and blasting them from each side. This also allows flexibility; you can move to the corners or back to the base along the upper catwalks and maintain the height advantage.

TIP

Stay healthy and well equipped: Remember how many Health Packs are remaining. Shout to your team if you're taking one, and tell them where the Pack is. Use only one Pack per round so everyone has access. Also, if you love the Fuel Rod Cannon, but your friend is exceptional with it, give it up for the sake of the team. Weapons with limited ammunition (the Rocket Launcher) should be accessed by a single player only.

Tactic: Ending the Engineer (Night Only)

Designate one of your team as the Engineer killer and arm them with a Plasma Pistol. Although other weapons, such as Turrets, do a reasonable job of taking out Engineers, a charged Plasma Pistol can make an Engineer fall from the sky in a death spasm. If all your team carries this weapon, you're ill-equipped as a unit to deal with the other foes, especially once the Famine Skull has activated. The Engineer killer should pair the Plasma Pistol with a Carbine or Magnum so they can still take down Grunts, Shield Jackals, Brutes, and Drones. Another way to dispatch Engineers involves using the Turret. As Engineers provide overshield protection to your enemies, this can reveal the location of Brute Stalkers. You can also annoy the Plasma Pistol wielder by waiting for them to send the Engineer into its death cycle spasm, then shoot it before it explodes and claim the Kill Points!

Bonus Round Plans

Tactic: Perpetual Motion

The tried and true method of killing everything in sight involves the Gravity Hammer, which you can use to swing at Grunts just as they start swarming onto the map; the Rocket Launcher, which can inflict horrendous carnage on the Grunts before they disperse; and the Magnum for kill-chain headshots after the initial carnage. It is imperative you keep moving or you'll be deluged with Grenades.

Mission 04: Security Zone

Fight in the Wide-Open ONI Exterior

A long and sprawling downhill series of steps, concrete walls, planters, and scenic viewpoints is the stage for this Covenant invasion. After emerging from one of two spawning corridors, climb the steps to the top of the hill, peering down toward the base of the map, where the majority of the enemies come from and where Phantoms drop dozens of infantry. In addition, Wraith tanks mean that taking cover is a must. A rarely grabbed Sniper Rifle is located on the map's northwest edge.

NOTE

Campaign Reference 05: ONI Alpha Site. The exterior steps to the ONI building.

Firefight: Security Zone

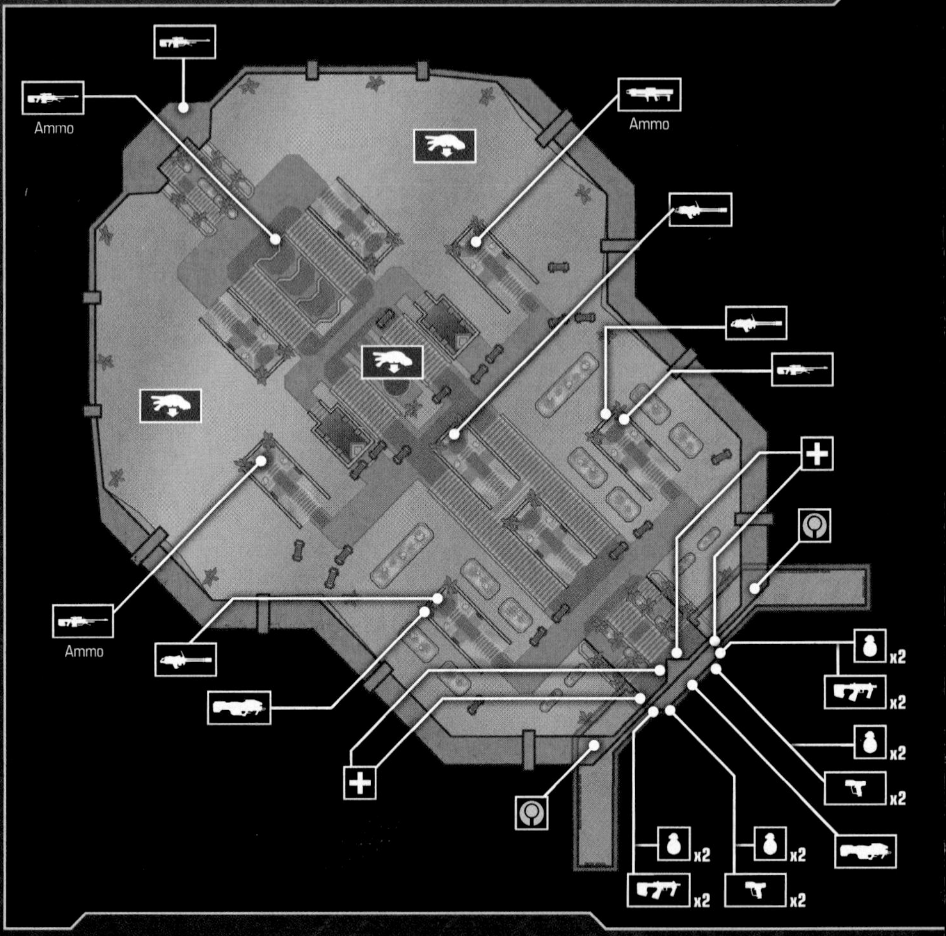

Ammo
Ammo
Ammo
x2
x2
x2
x2
x2
x2
x2
x2

DATA STREAM

EXPECTED ENEMIES

Grunts | Jackals | Brutes | Brute Chieftains

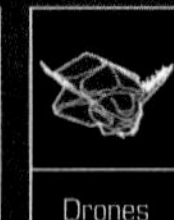

Jump-Pack Brutes | Brute Stalkers | Drones | Hunters

SPECIAL ENEMIES

Covenant Wraith Brutes

EXPECTED VEHICLES

Covenant Phantoms

Covenant Wraiths

OPTIMAL WEAPON COMBINATIONS

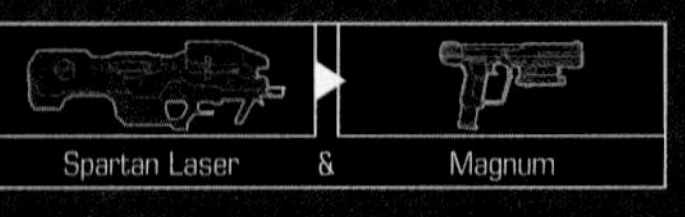
Spartan Laser & Magnum

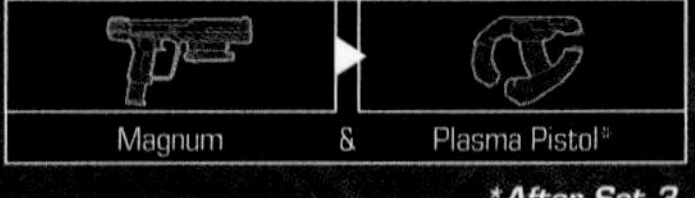
Magnum & Plasma Pistol*

*After Set 3.

PREFERRED WEAPON COMBINATIONS

Carbine & Plasma Pistol

Carbine & Rocket Launcher

Carbine & Spartan Laser

Magnum & Rocket Launcher

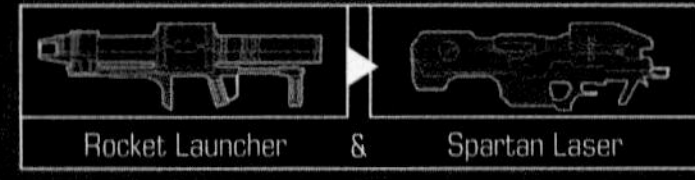
Rocket Launcher & Spartan Laser

PAR SCORE

200,000 Points

■ Notable Offense

Weapons: Spartan Laser and Magnum

Although not every team member can use this weapon combination, the Spartan Laser (located on the west-side upper planter platform) and the Magnum (available from the start) are excellent to employ throughout Firefights in this mission. A steady aim from long distance allows you to completely nullify the Wraiths that are dropped in at the bottom (northwest) end of the hill, and the Magnum is an adept backup weapon that allows you to tag Grunts and Jackals that move too close to you. This single-shot Magnum tagging is less effective on all varieties of Brutes, it is wise to provide Grenade support to a fellow teammate who is paired with you and tasked to help you eliminate Brutes overrunning your area. Or, simply drop the Laser temporarily and pick up a Carbine or the Plasma Pistol.

CAUTION **There is a Sniper Rifle at the far end of this map, down the steps behind where the Wraiths are dropped, but getting there takes too long, keeps you from taking a defensive position and shooting incoming foes, and risks your team being overrun. You would then have to sprint back again; getting this weapon is not wise when Carbines and Magnums do the job just as well.**

Weapons: Plasma Pistol and Carbine

This combination or ordnance, or variants thereof (which include the Plasma Pistol), is incredibly useful for dealing with enemies that the Spartan Laser and Magnum combination have trouble with, especially Brutes. A charged and well-timed strike from the Plasma Pistol can nullify any Brute armor; follow this up with Carbine headshots until the Brute falls. For best results, employ this on Captains and Chieftains as they close, and make sure you're continuously moving.

CAUTION **You may be tempted to employ the Gravity Hammer against foes, especially after the first set of Chieftains storm your defenses. Although this is a great weapon to use, tagging swarms of foes at a distance from the top of the map prevents you from being overrun, and a maniac with a hammer stops you from lobbing in Grenades or launching Rockets.**

■ General Plans

Tactic: Incursion Points—Phantom Drops

1

2

There are five Phantom drop points in this mission and no monster closets; this means death from above is an ever-present danger. However, this also means that spotters on high ground can inform teammates about the type of enemy about to scale the hill. For all rounds except the bonus, two Phantoms drop in to the far left or right and toward the middle of the map. The bonus-round Phantom descends above a central platform. A Covenant Wraith and enemy troops always appear at the drop points at the far left and right **[1]**. The middle-level drop points are closer to the hill's bottom or farther up the hill, near the Turrets **[2]**.

TIP **Learning these locations enables you to predict where the Phantoms will arrive, allowing you to attack the ships and troops from various angles and kill Covenant before they hit the ground.**

Tactic: Wraith Takedowns

With the Spartan Laser, the Wraiths pose little threat to your team, although you should destroy them with an accurate strike as early as possible **[1]**; you don't need plasma mortar shots raining down as you're trying to snipe Grunts! If the Spartan Laser has not respawned yet or is being kept by an incompetent player, you'll need to send two players from your team down toward the Wraith. Although highly dangerous, it is possible for one player to blast it with a charged Plasma Pistol to disable the Wraith, while the other circles behind it to board and destroy it **[2]**. Three Rockets can also do the trick, but the Wraith can easily maneuver away from the incoming missiles.

Tactic: Playing Defense

With a map that becomes much more dangerous the farther down the steps you descend, using the scenery to your advantage becomes critical to your survival. The concrete planters, walls, UNSC panel defenses, and other barriers are key to your defensive (and therefore longer-lasting) plans. While one of your team makes full use of the Spartan Laser against Wraiths, another should prep Turrets **[1]** by taking them off their base (this is not the usual tactic but is better than being struck by a Wraith's plasma mortar) and stockpiling them at the top of the hill, ready to tackle Drones with an abundance of cover that works in your favor. Also, stay on one side of the map; don't venture into the middle **[2]** or you'll be struck by incoming fire from all directions instead of from certain angles, which you can more easily react to.

TIP

For the ultimate in defensive posturing, retreat back into the spawning corridor, which is close to the Rocket Launcher, weapon caches, and your Health Packs. Standing in the corridor allows you to step in and out, tagging foes on the steps with ease, as the Covenant doesn't enter these areas.

Cooperative Plans

Tactic: Two-Player Plans

Pairing up for a Covenant showdown is even more advantageous in this mission, due to the lack of space you can use completely as cover (as you're usually overrun or outflanked if you remain in one place). Watching each other's backs becomes critical. Stay in the "safe" zone at the top of the hill; being coaxed down to a group of foes usually results in you being surrounded and dying as you scramble back for a Health Pack. Step behind the UNSC barriers as the Phantoms fire on you; then, using a ranged weapon, snipe Grunts and Jackals as they trot up the hill toward you.

For Brutes, have one of your pair shoot them with a charged Plasma Pistol so the Brutes go berserk (which makes them easy to tag) or are weakened. If no one is taking out the Wraith, both of you should emerge from the top of the hill, with one grabbing the Spartan Laser and firing on the Wraith from a distance before returning to your previous position. Meanwhile, the other player should cover the first player. When dealing with Drones and, to a lesser extent, Jump-Pack Brutes, both of you should equip the Silenced SMG or use detached Turrets to tackle these foes. For Drone

TIP The Turrets atop the protruding vantage points aren't as devastating as those at Crater, simply because you can't easily dodge an incoming plasma mortar from a Wraith, and you're easily swarmed from behind. You can, and should, detach and stockpile Turrets for Drone and any other attacks, though.

Tactic: Four-Player Foresight

1

2

As you're under constant threat of being outflanked, and defensive cover is difficult to maintain, the best four-player tactic is to break off into two teams of two **[1]**. Aside from the previously mentioned tactics, there are additional measures you can take. Each pair should be responsible for one side of the hill (left and right). Stay close to the "safe" zone for as long as possible, and always retreat to the hilltop after you venture downhill, or you're likely to be overrun. There's no need to encroach on the Phantom drops unless you're having trouble tackling a Wraith and don't have access to the Spartan Laser; then employ the Wraith takedown tactic mentioned previously. As with two-player plans, during Drone fights, slay them with SMGs or detached Turrets as quickly as possible **[2]**.

If one member of your two-man or four-man squad succumbs to Covenant fire, all members should retreat to the entrance steps and link back after the respawn occurs. Lone wolves are usually cut down in seconds.

Bonus Round Plans

Tactic: Snipe or Slaughter

A single Phantom drops off a huge number of Grunts at the central platform. Your first priority is to have your team train multiple weapons on the Plasma Turret located on the Phantom's nose to prevent it from ripping through your health and stamina. Then situate yourselves on the high ground and begin sniping at Grunts with the Magnum or Carbine. If you're some distance away, you can remain in partial cover until the Grunts close in before constantly moving and attempting headshots to maximize your longevity. Another, usually fatal but point-accruing, plan is to stand on the central platform, just above the Phantom drop point. Arm yourself with a Rocket Launcher and a Fuel Rod Cannon, and lay waste to the Grunts as they disembark. Of course, you're usually tagged with a Sticky Grenade, so make this suicide maneuver count! For even more danger but similar points, employ the Gravity Hammer until you're inevitably struck by a Plasma Grenade.

Mission 05: Alpha Site

Fight in the Close-Quarters ONI Interior

After emerging from one of two spawning corridors, you have moments to race northeast toward a central elevator lobby, passing a Sniper Rifle and a dark alcove near either set of stairs; these house your health and caches. From the elevator shafts, there are two narrow sets of steps leading to an open-air balcony with dotted pillars, and there are exterior steps leading to two different platforms. Except during bonus rounds, all foes are dropped onto either platform by Phantoms.

NOTE

Campaign Reference 05: ONI Alpha Site. ONI building interior (prior to exit).

Firefight: Alpha Site

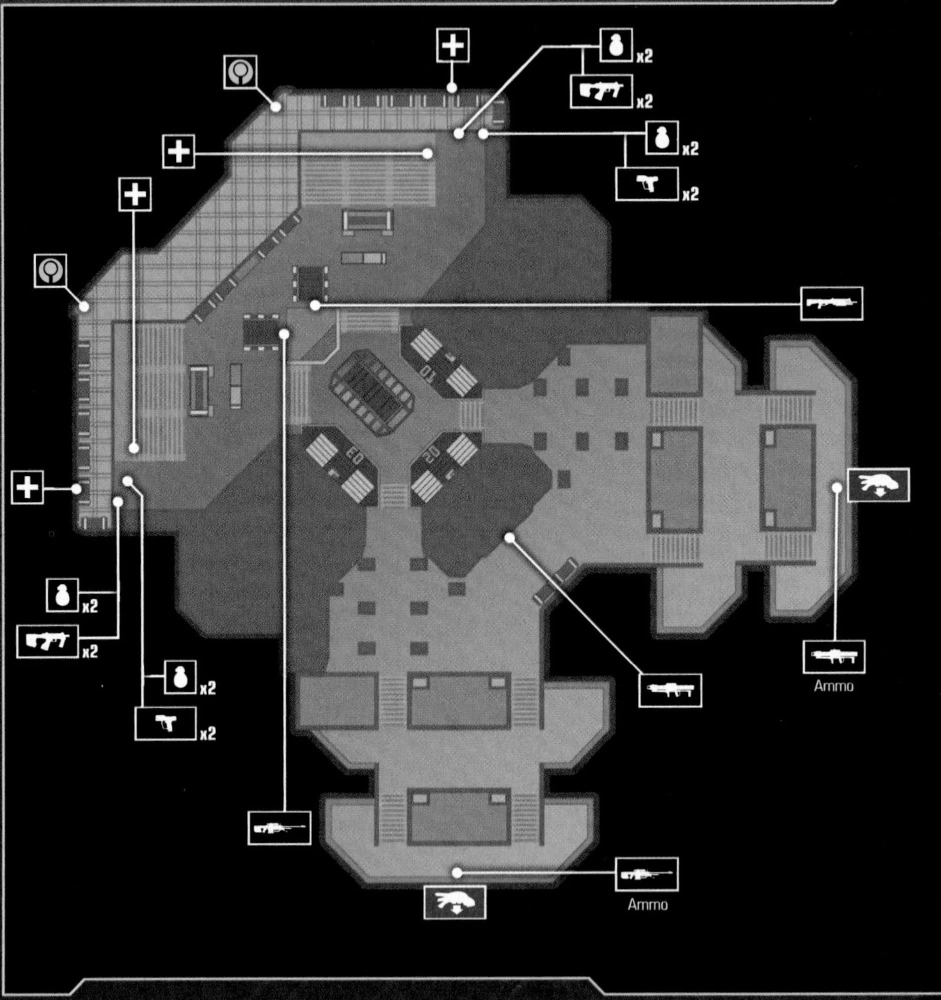

DATA STREAM

EXPECTED ENEMIES

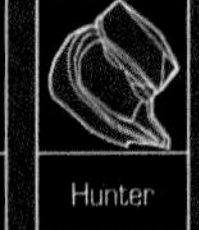

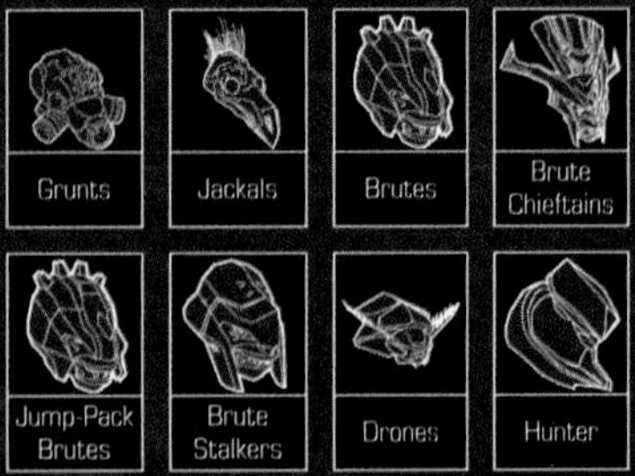

Grunts | Jackals | Brutes | Brute Chieftains

Jump-Pack Brutes | Brute Stalkers | Drones | Hunter

SPECIAL ENEMIES

None

EXPECTED VEHICLES

Covenant Phantoms

OPTIMAL WEAPON COMBINATIONS

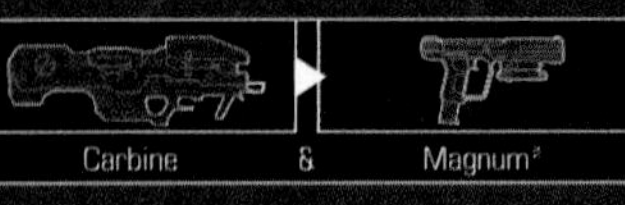

Carbine & Magnum*

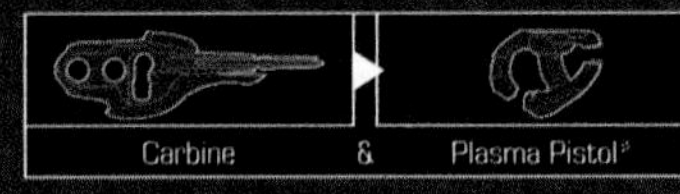

Carbine & Plasma Pistol*

**For all sets, including after Set 3.*

PREFERRED WEAPON COMBINATIONS

Carbine & Fuel Rod Cannon

Carbine & Rocket Launcher

Fuel Rod Cannon & Magnum

Rocket Launcher & Magnum

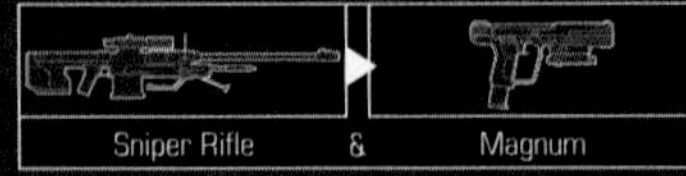

Sniper Rifle & Magnum

Notable Offense

Weapons: Plasma Pistol and Carbine (or Magnum)

For seasoned ODST soldiers who wish to last the longest, and with the high possibility for kill chains and other bonuses, there are only two weapon combinations that make sense: the Plasma Pistol and Carbine, or the Plasma Pistol and Magnum. These weapons are preferred because of the enemies you face in this mission. There are no vehicles to worry about, and the infantry-only foes allow you to charge a Plasma Pistol shot to remove any armor if applicable (e.g., for Jackals and Brutes) before following that up with the old favorite: the headshot. Although you may favor other weapon combos, including ones never listed in this guide, many hours of play-testing have proved that headshot sniping is the safest and easiest way to accrue a large number of points in most circumstances. Read through the Tactic sections below for advice on where to stand.

NOTE

Unlike other Firefight missions, there are no special enemies to worry about—there is just the usual deluge of Grunts, Jackals, Brutes, and Drones!

Weapon: Grabbing the Gravity Hammer

When Brute Chieftains drop their powerful weapons, especially the Fuel Rod Cannon and Gravity Hammer, some of your team may develop a reckless streak, abandoning good, tactical planning for adrenaline-fueled rampages. This area is much narrower than Crater, and the risks of standing on a Grenade while bludgeoning a foe with your Hammer outweigh the fun you'll have. Storming up to the Phantoms with a Hammer and laying waste to foes as they fall to the balconies can gain you points, but your sniper squadmates are limited in their aiming while you're leaping about like a madman. A way around this is to have your snipers train on the other Phantom drop point to avoid friendly fire. Although the Gravity Hammer has its place, "funneling" foes gains more score and less team deaths.

There are four Health Packs: two are shrouded in darkness on either side of the entrance stairs (near the weapon caches), and two are at the end of each spawning corridor.

General Plans

Tactic: Incursion Point—Phantom Drops

The locations of your incoming foes are much easier to learn on this map, as there are only two exterior balconies **[1 and 2]** along the southeast side of the map, accessed via one of two short sets of steps. These platforms usually receive a Phantom drop one side at a time, allowing you time to relay the location of the next Phantom to your teammates and to prepare a suitable attack. When the Phantoms release their payload of foes, they drop straight down from an exit hole, rather than from the side doors. The only time foes appear inside the Alpha Site building is during the bonus round.

TIP If you're not planning on funneling foes, the best way to continuously slaughter the Covenant is to camp the Phantom drop points with heavy weapons, such as the Rocket Launcher, Fuel Rod Cannon, and Grenades. Then lob a Grenade at the ground the foes are landing on, or launch Rockets or other ordnance at the holes on the Phantom's underside chassis. The more manic teammate can try Gravity Hammer strikes here, too.

Tactic: Funneling Foes

Learning the two mirrored choke points and using them to your advantage is the key to a long-lasting, high-point Firefight. The two choke points are the staircases on either side of the elevators in the center of the lobby area **[1]**. The tall walls and narrow thoroughfares allow you to try an exceptionally useful "funneling" tactic. Basically, enemies landing outside are forced to head down these steps, allowing well-positioned ODST squads to launch all manner of attacks at them, such as sniped headshots and Grenades. The latter are especially lethal, as your foes can't dodge in the narrow confines of the stairs and corridor. Stay near the spawning location staircase and tag foes from medium range. Even when the Drones arrive **[2]** and can fly into the lobby, they still must navigate the narrow opening above the stairs; if you have one or more adept snipers, this tactic demolishes wave after wave of foes incredibly easily.

TIP **If you're a fan of the hard-hitting Sniper Rifle, you'll be pleased to find one on this map, at the bottom of the first set of stairs attached to the large central pillar marked "administration." Apply any of the sniping and headshot tactics while using this armament; lining up multiple funneled foes for a single takedown is always a joy!**

Cooperative Plans

Tactic: Crate Camping

The central lobby and elevator shaft area has two large crates in the center. These are excellent obstacles to use in a couple of ways: First, two of your team should leap atop these crates, gaining a height and view advantage in the process. You can now shoot over the glass walls that surround the elevator corridors, allowing you to snipe foes from the moment they descend from the Phantoms' drop points. If the enemies close, simply fall from the crate and use it as cover, especially during the funneling tactic.

Second, if you have four players, keep two on the crates, while the other two tool up with close-assault weaponry, such as the Mauler or Gravity Hammer. These teammates are responsible for listening and watching the crate guards and for attacking any foes that manage to break through the crate duo's sniper fire, keeping all of your team safe.

Tactic: Shields Down

Split into two teams of two. One squadmate focuses on Plasma-powered weaponry, while the other collects bullet armaments. Now lay waste to foes in double time as the Plasma-weapon teammate removes enemy shields, and the other finishes off the foes. Although the Plasma-weapon wielder sacrifices their score (as they only remove shields and don't receive points for kills or assists), the total you're aiming for is accumulated. If your pride can handle that, try this tactic. This becomes even more important once the Famine Skull activates, limiting the ammo you can gather. At this point, specify a squadmate to, say, collect only Plasma-powered guns from fallen foes, instead of devoting two or three of your team to the task so you don't collectively run out of ammunition.

Whether there are two or four players holding back the Covenant waves, the biggest threat is being outflanked by foes heading down through an unguarded funnel-stair corridor. Have half your team responsible for the left side of the map and half for the right.

Tactic: Four-Player Foresight

The optimal way to spread out your four-player team is to position two squadmates in the lobby, one on each crate and each aiming at a different funnel-corridor stair **[1]**. Behind them should lurk your other two friends, each with long-range sniping armaments, so you're all ready to start the funnel tactic **[2]**. When different weapons are accessed or when teammates request closer assaults, you should move the two "crate" squadmates behind pillars that have excellent visibility to incoming Phantoms; this allows them to lob Grenades, launch Rockets, or fire Fuel Rod Cannons. The remaining two friends move up to the funnel stairs, ready to continue sniping; they can also retreat to the previous position if a friendly death or a large influx of enemies can't be contained outside.

TIP

The Sniper Rifle and the Magnum caches by the spawning stairs allow your rear guards a good amount of ordnance to use for long-range tagging.

■ Bonus Round Plans

Tactic: Exterior Grunt Hunt

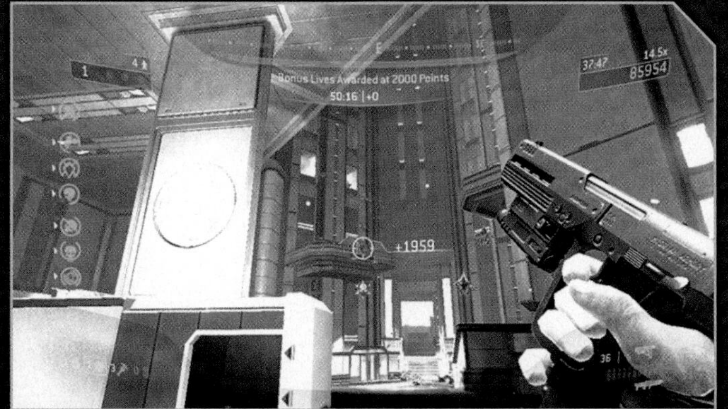

The only time enemies don't appear from one of two Phantoms dropping in on the exterior balconies is during the bonus round. In the bonus round, masses of Grunts leap down from the upper elevator doors in the middle of this map, landing in the central lobby. Although the usual back-off-and-get-a-headshot tactic is worth trying for the additional points you accrue, you'll find yourself and your team quickly overwhelmed. Wading in with a close-assault weapon like the Gravity Hammer is another tactic, but one that usually results in a Grenade-based death. Instead, in the moments prior to the bonus round starting, split up and dash east or south, up the stairs and onto the outside balconies to where the Phantoms arrived. Switch to a Carbine or Magnum, and headshot every Grunt that falls into the lobby. Continue the carnage as the Grunts waddle up through the steps to reach you; clusters of these foes are easily tagged in the head. Be sure you use both balcony exits, though, as the Grunts throw a deluge of Grenades at you.

Mission 06: Windward

Fight High Above the City Streets

In this mission, you fight in a two-sided structure with an interior, two-level spawning building in the middle with three exits outside. The northern edge of the map exterior is a sheer drop to your death, so concentrate on remaining on the ground. There are two Pelican platforms, and a tiered open-air area on each side of the map. A winding corridor links the platform to the tiered areas. A sky bridge links from east to west but is inaccessible. Use the unique Missile Pod Turrets, as Banshee attacks and Covenant infantry squads are expected.

Firefight: Windward

Ammo

Ammo

Ammo

Ammo

Ammo

NOTE

Campaign Reference 06: NMPD HQ. Police HQ Building (Pelican drop platforms).

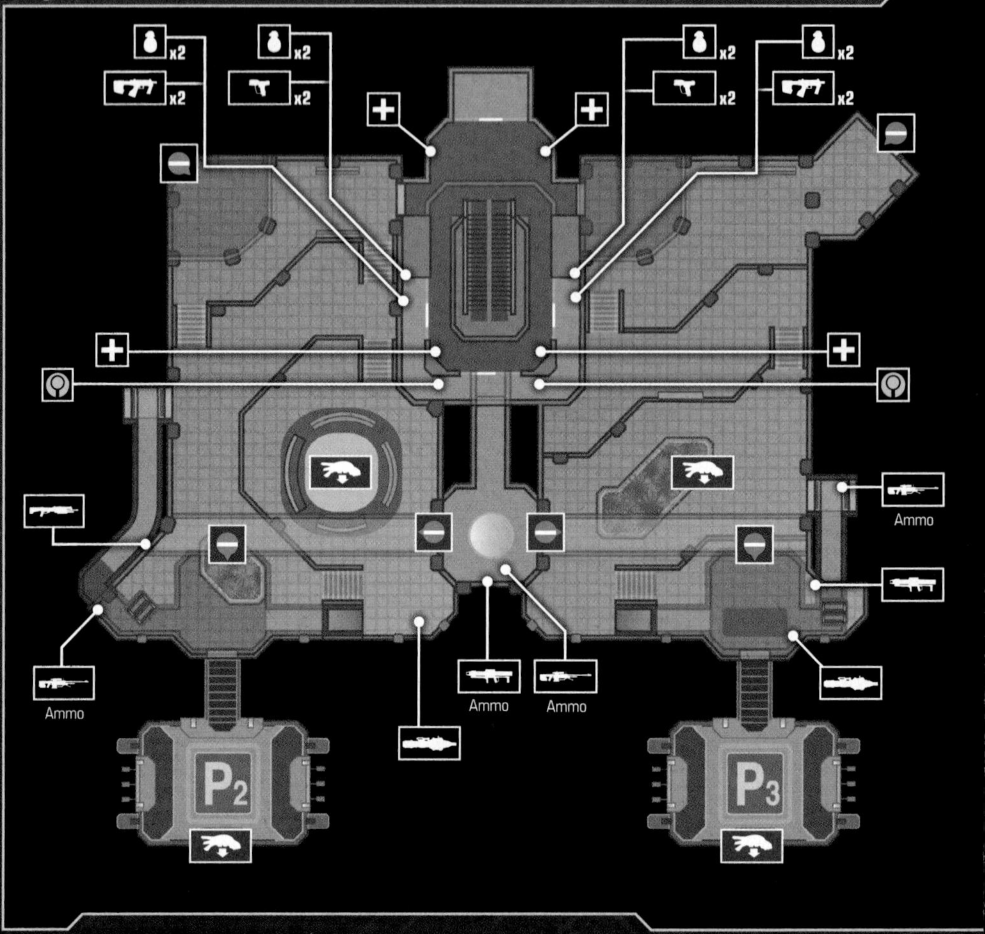

DATA STREAM

EXPECTED ENEMIES

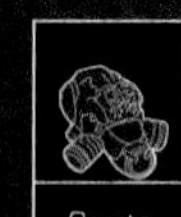
Grunts

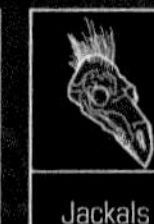
Jackals

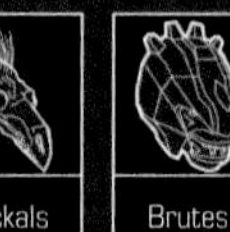
Brutes

Brute Chieftains

Jump-Pack Brutes

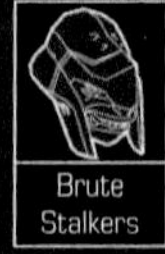
Brute Stalkers

Drones

Hunters

SPECIAL ENEMIES

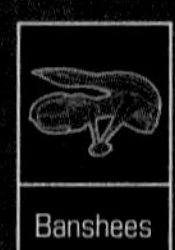
Banshees

EXPECTED VEHICLES

Covenant Phantoms

Covenant Banshees

OPTIMAL WEAPON COMBINATIONS

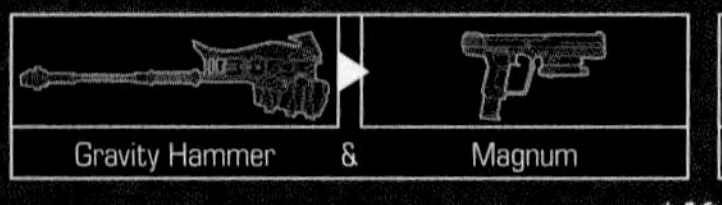
Gravity Hammer & Magnum

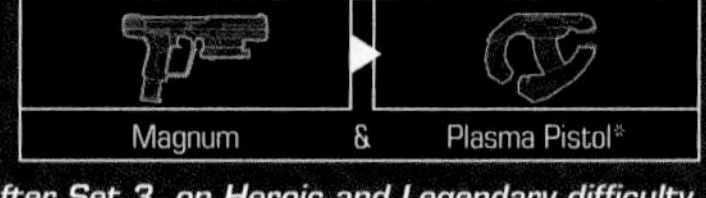
Magnum & Plasma Pistol*

**After Set 3, on Heroic and Legendary difficulty.*

PREFERRED WEAPON COMBINATIONS

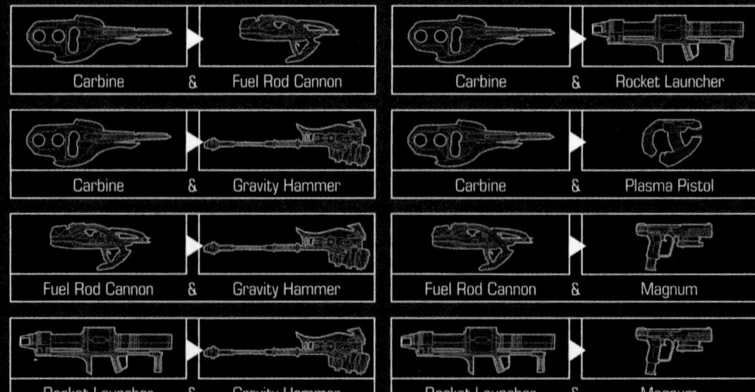

PAR SCORE

200,000 Points

■ Notable Offense

Weapon: Fuel Rod Cannon or Rocket Launcher?

Although the Fuel Rod Cannon and the Rocket Launcher are excellent and highly damaging, the Fuel Rod Cannon is slightly more proficient at getting the job done. It may not be as powerful, but it has much more available ammunition; foes drop this weapon somewhat frequently, so you can pick it up from the ground after combat with them. Fuel Rod ammunition is abundant compared to the Rocket Launcher's missiles; you are only given six in total to fire (four from the Launcher and two from a Rocket Pack close to your spawning location). The Rocket Launcher is on the wall on the map's southeastern edge, overlooking a Pelican platform, and the Fuel Rod Cannon is dropped by some Brutes, Chieftains, and Grunts.

Weapons: Gravity Hammer and Magnum Mayhem

Highly entertaining and thoroughly recommended, the Gravity Hammer and Magnum perform a very specific function: accumulating masses of points in the easiest possible way. Dash about with the Gravity Hammer, killing large groups of enemies for lengthy kill chains and hammer sprees before swapping to the Magnum and running to the next group of foes, plugging Grunts and Jackals in the head to keep the kill chain going. With practice, you can continue this kill chain through multiple waves of foes. Choose the Hammer over the Rocket Launcher or Fuel Rod Cannon, as it gives you an additional multiplier to your score.

Weapon: Pistol Packing in the Later Rounds

As the Firefight wears on, especially on higher difficulty levels, the Plasma Pistol, coupled with a quick-firing and accurate weapon such as the Carbine or Magnum, is the optimal combination with which to kill the Covenant. For enemies without shields, employ the Magnum or Carbine. For Jackals, "ping" their shield with a single Carbine or Magnum shot, then immediately follow up with a headshot execution. For foes with shields, such as Brutes, charge your Plasma Pistol and fire it to deplete their shields, then quickly swap weapons for a headshot to finish them off.

TIP **Quick bursts of SMG fire can easily drop countless Drones from the skies, while a charged Plasma Pistol can circumvent Drones' shields before SMG fire finishes them off. Brute Stalkers are even more troublesome because of the narrow environment, the chokepoints and because they are so difficult to see. As they use Active Camo, Firebomb Grenades, and Maulers to take you down, flick on your VISR Enhanced Vision so you can make them out. Also try pinging them with a Magnum shot so their shields flicker, giving you or your team a position to launch ordnance into.**

■ General Plans

Tactic: Incursion Points—Phantom Drops

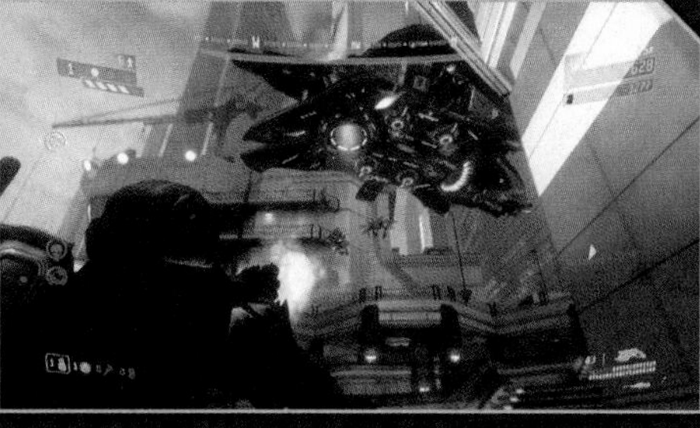

Brace yourself for four possible disembarking spots where Covenant Phantoms hover before depositing their brood: both Pelican landing platforms at the front of the map and above the stepped exterior tiers to the sides of your team's spawning interior building. Using Rockets or the Missile Pod Turrets, deal with the incoming Phantoms at the Pelican landing platforms by wiping out as many foes as possible prior to them spilling out of the craft. When foes drop onto the platform, have a Gravity Hammer–wielding ODST lunatic waiting for them or a well-placed Rocket or Grenade that kills multiple foes. Have snipers on the platform above near the Missile Turrets backing up these attacks. When Phantoms encroach the exterior tiered area, retreat to higher ground, using the doors to the middle spawning building as partial cover and culling as many foes as you can as they drop from the craft. Then, mop up remaining foes (usually Brutes) with your favored weapon combinations.

TIP **Camp at the four Phantom drop points with a Gravity Hammer. As foes drop in, swing wildly; hammer sprees and kill chains are commonplace. Or, cause impressive hurting with Grenades, Fuel Rod Cannons, or Rockets. Removing a Phantom's Plasma Turret also yields dividends: Launch Rockets, Missiles from the Turret Pods, Fuel Cannon shots, or Grenades, and try to knock the Plasma Turrets off the Phantoms. Then quickly grab the Turret and mow down enemies, especially Drones.**

Tactic: Incursion Points—Monster Closets

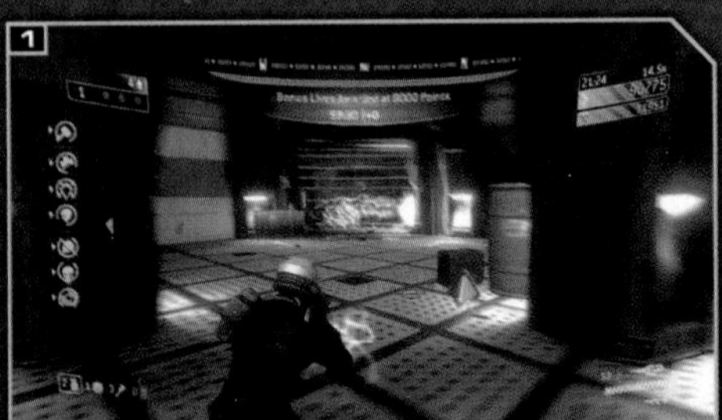

There are eight monster closets for Covenant foes to stream out of, making the location of each wave much more harrowing than on other missions. There are two doorways in the chamber leading to the landing platforms **[1]**, two outside on the upper tiered area on the same level as the upper doors leading to your spawning building, two inside the room atop the landing platform walkway, and two on the rooftops that lead to the sky bridges **[2]**. Reacting early to enemies exiting these doorways is the key here; after you've defeated each round of foes, post two teammates to scan the sky for Phantoms or intrusions on the tiered areas, while the other two check the chambers linking the landing platforms and the sky bridge.

TIP **If you spot the crackling energy wall of a doorway that's about to spill out enemies, launch a Grenade or Rocket just as the enemies appear. The Firebomb Grenade sets multiple foes ablaze for extra damage.**

Tactic: Inside or Out?

There are numerous defensive sections of environment to use to your advantage, such as the inside of buildings, especially the interior with the three doors in the map's center, allowing a quick retreat to the spawning building or to the map's other side; on top of walkways; and behind support pillars. If you aren't interested in taking out the Phantom's Turret, then dive behind cover when Phantoms head in to drop their enemies. With multiple cover opportunities, you can avoid most projectiles if you keep your distance and try staying at a higher vantage point than your foes.

Tactic: Correct Weapon Pairing

The biggest threat during the waves of foes that swarm you in this mission is not having the flexibility to deal with any offensive situation. Mitigate this problem by complementing a heavy-hitting weapon with a quick-firing, accurate piece of ordnance. The Pelican platforms, the corridors from the platforms, and the stepped exterior platforms are locations where the enemy tends to congregate. In these highly populated areas, employ the Rocket Launcher, the Fuel Rod Cannon, or Grenades to blow multiple foes to smithereens in a single shot before finishing stragglers with a slightly more focused weapon.

TIP **Don't forget the two Missile Pod Turrets located on either side of the map's front edge. Remove these Turrets just before a round ends so you can "stockpile" them (along with any weapons left inside the spawning building). Use them to destroy incoming Banshees, Turrets, or Phantoms. You can also destroy Banshees with a charged Plasma Pistol shot. Hunters cannot attack you using melee weapons if you are operating a Missile Pod Turret still attached to its base. This is useful, as you can have a friend coax the Hunter into attacking while you rake them with Missiles.**

■ Cooperative Plans

Tactic: Two-Player Takedowns

If you have only two players against the Covenant, it is usually better to have each person stay on one side of the map (one on the left, one on the right). Stay there unless called upon to help; this helps prevent you both being outflanked. Or you can try the following tactic, which is usually utilized when playing on a four-person team; however, you should each partner into two pairs of two and stay together while patrolling one side of the map while the other takes the opposite side. This reduces the number of foes that you'll face in a single encounter. If you experience heavy enemy fire, an often under-used area is the corridor from the outer side building that winds around to the lower Pelican platform door and back up to the central structure's entrance. These places come in handy during Drone takedown battles or to flee from dropped Grenades or lunatic Brute Chieftains.

Tactic: Four-Player Foresight

Aside from having adept communication, warning teammates early of foes, and having the flexibility to aid teammates, four-player tactics involve positioning yourselves to quickly sort out any potential threats. First, split the team into two pairs, each responsible for one side of the map. Second, launch shots from Missile Pods or Rockets at incoming Banshees and Phantoms. If Phantoms arrive, have one or both members lob ordnance at foes before they depart, with one teammate optionally mopping up with sniper fire. For doorway incursions, quickly ascertain the location of the threat, lob in Grenades or Rockets, and seek higher ground and begin methodical sniping takedowns of the survivors.

Legendary Tactics

Obtain the highest possible Firefight score by staying within the spawning building interior. Keep two team members on the upper balcony watching each door and keep two on the lower floor watching the large door. Lure enemies toward while one teammate triggers the door opening, allowing visible enemies to be tagged with sniper or Grenade attacks. Expect more enemies to charge you from the lower door. During Brute Chieftain battles, be sure to have a squadmate fire on the foe with a Fuel Rod Cannon, especially if they enter the spawning building. This prevents the Brute from firing its weapon, which usually kills you with one shot (on Legendary difficulty).

■ Bonus Round Plans

Tactic: Heads-up

Prepare for the bonus round by obtaining a Carbine or Magnum (or both) with large ammunition reserves, and begin the infamous headshot kill chain tactic. The Plasma Grenades that you must avoid come thick and fast, so stay farther away than normal while tagging your Grunts, ideally near the spawning building's doors, and keep moving so you aren't struck by a Sticky Grenade. Try to cause chain reactions by lobbing in Plasma Grenades at Grunts.

Mission 07: Chasm Ten

Fight in the Infested Underground

The ODST "safe zone" is along the map's south side; this area consists of a long east-west corridor with two air lifts that allow access to an identical upper corridor and to the chasm area itself. The "danger zone" is a series of interlocking catwalks with a deadly chasm below and a line of additional air lifts that allow access to an upper floor; there, more catwalks and an impenetrable energy wall to a Drone hive are available. Expect incursions from both floors, along the north and east or west walls.

NOTE

Campaign Reference 08: Data Hive. Hive Chasm prior to Vergil extraction.

Firefight: Chasm Ten

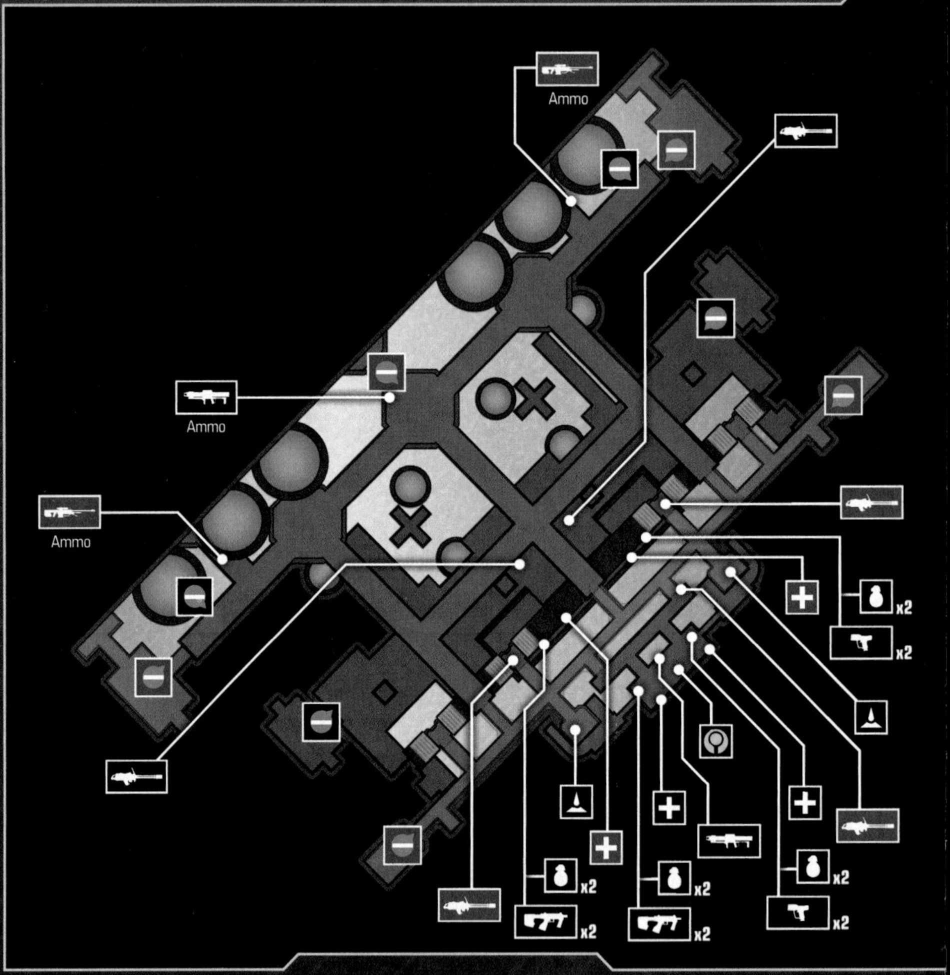

DATA STREAM

EXPECTED ENEMIES

Grunts

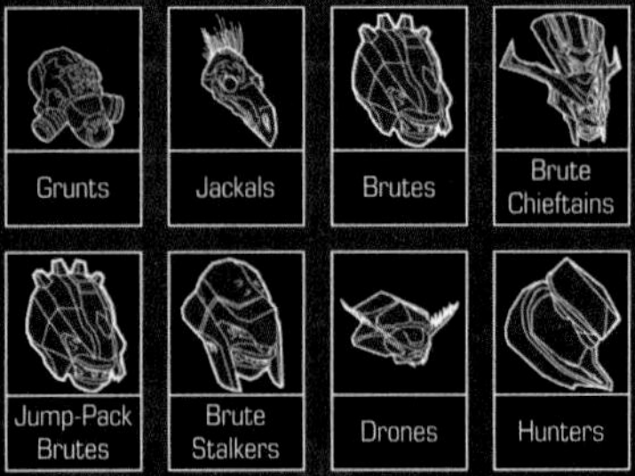

Jackals

Brutes

Brute Chieftains

Jump-Pack Brutes

Brute Stalkers

Drones

Hunters

SPECIAL ENEMIES

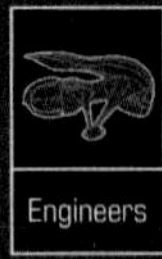
Engineers

OPTIMAL WEAPON COMBINATIONS

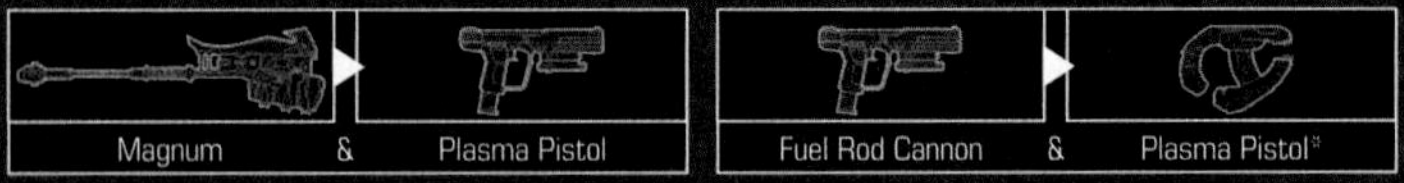

Magnum & Plasma Pistol

Fuel Rod Cannon & Plasma Pistol*

**After Set 3.*

PREFERRED WEAPON COMBINATIONS

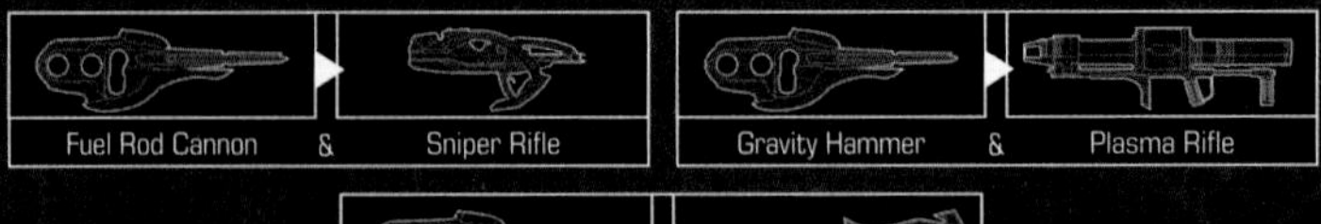
Fuel Rod Cannon & Sniper Rifle

Gravity Hammer & Plasma Rifle

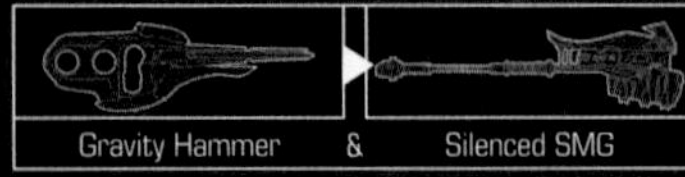
Gravity Hammer & Silenced SMG

PAR SCORE

200,000 Points

■ Notable Offense

Weapon: Plasma Pistol Packing

Periodically, Engineers float into the fray and are a perfect target for a Turret, or using a high-strength ranged weapon (such as the Beam Rifle shown) on the upper level. Otherwise, Engineers should be tackled by a specific team member (and optionally a second in four-player matches) whose job is to secure a Plasma Pistol and ammunition while the others stay away from this weapon or give up that ammo. The Plasma Pistol–wielding teammate should take down the Engineers as rapidly as possible, using the charged Plasma Pistol blast, which is vital if you're playing solo and thoroughly recommended when there is only one or two players. As Engineers enhance the strength of nearby Covenant overshields, their deaths are of primary importance.

 TIP

Steal points from your teammate—which isn't really necessary unless you're engaged in a good-natured rivalry—by pinging an Engineer once it enters its death cycle but before it explodes; you then receive the Kill Points.

Weapon: Top Floor Turrets

The "safe zone" is much safer on the upper ledge running the length of the southern wall outside the main corridor, as there are two Turrets you can man. These are much preferred over the Turrets on the lower level; those are dangerous to man, as they are too far north of the safe zone, and you can be outflanked easily. Grab those Turrets and stockpile them instead. However, the upper Turrets are excellent and defensible, as you have your back to the southern wall and can't be easily outflanked (although it is possible, as your turning circle can't reach to the extreme sides). Keep the Turret locked onto its tripod, and strafe Drones, Jackals, and Grunts from any distance, racking up sizable points in the process. The infinite ammo is the main advantage here (remember, the ammo is infinite only if the Turret is on its base). Execute enemies closest to you first so you aren't the victim of a Grenade attack. Leave the Turret only when facing Brutes and if the Tilt Skull is active; this dramatically reduces the effectiveness of Turrets against this foe.

 TIP

Detach the Turret or bring a Turret up from the lower level; just before the Drones arrive, carry the Turret to the long catwalk near to where the Drones fly out from, then lay waste to them with a perfectly straight line of sight. Rack up the points and cut down a wave of otherwise-troublesome foes in seconds.

Weapon: The Shortfalls (and Long Falls) of Using a Hammer

During later sets, enemies drop enough Fuel Rod Cannons for at least a four-person team to use as part of an effective weapon combo. The tactical advice is straightforward but really effective: Keep your distance at all times, and use the Fuel Rod to destroy groups of enemies efficiently, ideally as they emerge from their doorways. Conversely, the Gravity Hammer is a highly effective, but highly dangerous, weapon to wield in this mission. A mixture of bravery and madness is needed to sprint into the middle of the Covenant forces and try to begin large-scale kill chains to increase your team's score substantially. The drawback of the Hammer is the safety aspect; you can strike a foe and be knocked backward, into the chasm below, and there's almost no room to dodge Grenades. For this reason, ranged combat is favored more than normal.

 CAUTION

The Rocket Launcher can also be a devastating weapon, and one of your team is likely to utilize it (as the Rocket Launcher is accessed in the lower spawning corridor), but it is more dangerous to use in the narrow corridors and catwalks, and user error is an all-too-common occurrence.

General Plans

Tactic: Incursion Points—Monster Closets

There are no Phantom drops inside Chasm Ten; expect enemy encroachment from one of seven different locations. There are four side doors (two on the east wall (with one on the lower level, one on the upper level), and two more on the west wall in identical locations). There are also two larger doors that open beneath the massive horizontal red pipe embedded in the north wall, on the lower level. Finally, there's a central opening on the upper floor that leads to a Drone hive, which you cannot access. Expect all Covenant enemy types to appear from any of these locations. When you've learned the locations of these monster closet doorways, you'll migrate to the upper-level catwalks for the majority of this mission, as you have the height—and therefore the aiming—advantage no matter where foes appear from. Survey the entire area as you formulate the best way to tackle a particular incursion. The only problem is watching your footing on the catwalks; there are no guardrails, and you risk falling into the chasm if you're overzealous, foolish, or unwary.

TIP **The side doors positioned at the end of the catwalks are particularly easy to defend against. Your foes have limited maneuverable space as they exit the closet, so exploit this by lobbing in Grenades to nullify an attack wave before it even begins. Bring out a long-range sniping weapon of choice, and camp across from the airlifts throughout the central part of this map. When enemies utilize the airlifts, they do not engage your team with their weapons, allowing you to tag weaker foes as they rise through the air or to diminish Brute shields with charged Plasma Pistol strikes.**

Tactic: The Melee Flee

When the more terrifying of the Covenant's forces begin to cut a swath through your defenses, you need to secure a safe location from which you can face them without being smacked into the chasm. As Hunters **[1]** or Brute Chieftains **[2]** armed with Hammers arrive, and melee combat becomes a possibility, retreat to the safe zone's lower level. While your fellow teammates weaken them with ranged fire from Turrets or sniper weaponry, coax these behemoths to the exit forecourt outside the spawning corridor, where the Turrets are. The extra ground space allows you enough room to circle-strafe behind and tag their backs with ordnance, and if you're struck, you're less likely to fall screaming into the chasm—and you should expect to be knocked about when facing these foes at close quarters.

Cooperative Plans

Tactic: Four-Player Foresight

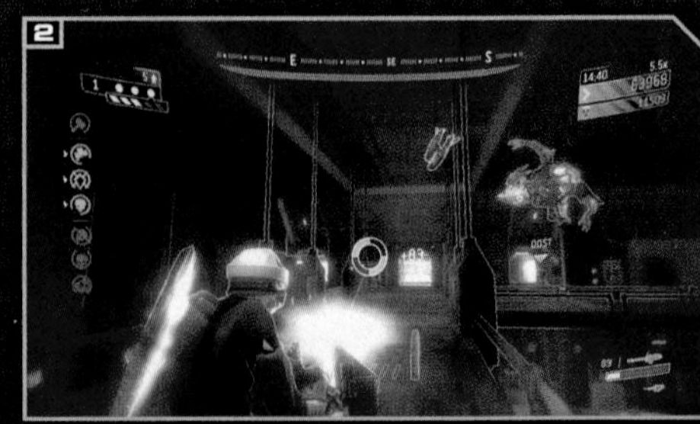

Four-player teams should follow most of these tactics: It is wise to reach the upper catwalks as soon as possible; you should be raining death on the Covenant from above, not blindly looking for foes encroaching on you from above! With all four friends on the upper level, which you can access via the airlifts within or outside the "safe zone," appoint two players to stay on the Turrets and rake all the smaller enemies. They should stop only to wrench their Turret off its stand before the next round so others can use this stockpiled weapon. Meanwhile, the other two players should be armed with Plasma Pistols to drop Engineers out of the air but are usually in position to lob Grenades at the opening monster closets before any foes can appear and swarm the catwalks. When enemies break through this mesh of ODST ordnance, have the mobile teammates fall back to snipe foes on airlifts, and protect the Turret gunners from becoming surrounded.

Tactic: Two-player Turrets

If your team consists of only two members, your tactics are somewhat different, although you can try this plan during four-player matches if you've each paired with a friend. During waves where the majority of foes are Grunts, Jackals, or Drones, each of you should man an upper Turret. One should switch and take down both Engineers with charged Plasma Pistol shots when these foes intermittently appear. When Brutes or Hunters arrive, leave the Turrets and choose any Brute-takedown plan you've previously had success with (such as the Plasma Pistol tactic below). At all other times, use the Turret: If your partner needs to descend for health, make sure they tell you, as the Covenant can use the flank with the now-unmanned Turret to reach and attack you unexpectedly.

TIP

Health Packs are a key commodity, and the four available Packs are split between the lower spawning room and the ledge near each upper Turret. Aim to use only one Health Pack per round, unless your team is fine with your health-hogging!

Tactic: Your Plasma Pistol Pal

This is another mission in which pairing into one team of two (with two players) or two teams of two (with four players) is advantageous, as long as each member of the pair focuses on a specific task. The first team member should be armed with a Plasma weapon, such as the Plasma Rifle or Pistol, while the other should employ regular bullets. The Plasma-weapon wielder whittles down an opponent's shields, while the other finishes them off with a headshot or two. The Plasma specialist won't accumulate many points, but their assists are just as important. Remember to specify a team member to grab all Plasma-based ammunition so you don't run out when the Famine Skull is active.

TIP

The Plasma Pistol is the go-to weapon for taking down enemy shields, but the Plasma Rifle is also great at cutting down a Brute's shields; use the Rifle if the Pistol isn't accessible.

■ Bonus Round Plans

Tactic: Range, not Rampage

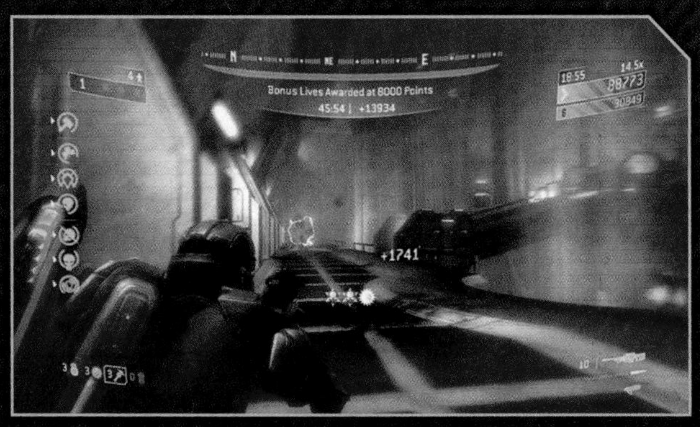

The swarm of Grunts that greet your team during the bonus round are much more of a threat on this mission, as their constant stream of thrown Grenades is difficult to dodge on the upper catwalks. Those armed with Gravity Hammers are faced with similar problems; you're more likely to be stuck with a deadly Plasma Grenade on your arm than reach a cluster of Grunts to use your Hammer effectively. Grenades are deadly because of their stickiness and explosion and because their force can knock you into the chasm. Lob a few Grenades at the two side doorways adjacent to the catwalks to destroy the initial waves and to gain some early points. Then stay at a distance, bringing out a Magnum or a scoped weapon of choice, and start kill chains. The Fuel Rod Cannon or the Sniper Rifle is great for dropping multiple Grunts with a single shot, if you have the line of sight. Some Grunts carry the Fuel Rod Cannon, so ammunition should be available.

Mission 08: Last Exit

Fight at the End of the Road

The entrance to the Uplift Reserve national park is closed. The ticket office building is now a place where you can grab weapons and health before venturing outside to the main steps. On either side of the main steps, there is access to an upper parking lot and an upper stone balcony above the ground entrance. A central lower courtyard allows access down to the coastal highway entrance (now sealed by an energy wall), while the upper parking lot provides helpful views and low wall cover.

NOTE

Campaign Reference 09: Coastal Highway. ODST team rendezvous point prior to escape..

Firefight: Last Exit

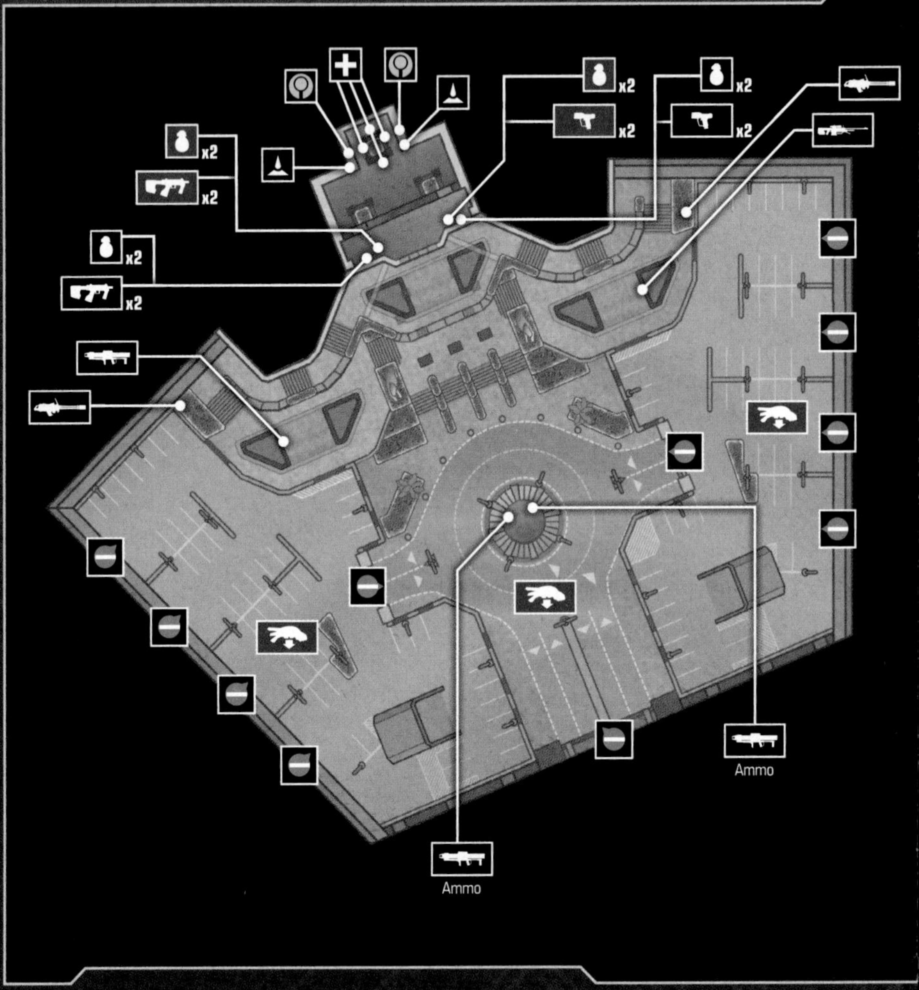

x2

x2

x2

x2

x2

x2

x2

x2

Ammo

Ammo

DATA STREAM

EXPECTED ENEMIES

Grunts

Jackals

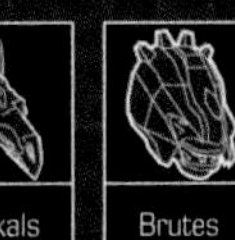
Brutes

Brute Chieftains

Jump-Pack Brutes

Brute Stalkers

Drones

Hunters

SPECIAL ENEMIES

Ghosts

EXPECTED VEHICLES

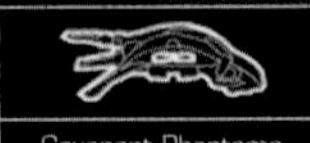
Covenant Phantoms

Covenant Ghosts

OPTIMAL WEAPON COMBINATIONS

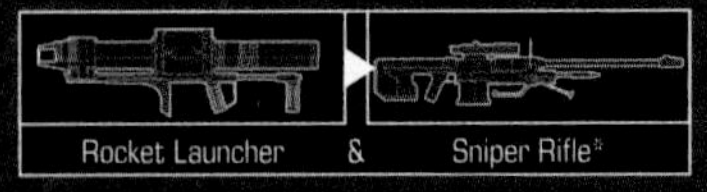
Rocket Launcher & Sniper Rifle*

Magnum & Plasma Pistol*

**For early sets; † for later sets.*

PREFERRED WEAPON COMBINATIONS

Carbine & Magnum

Carbine & Mauler

Gravity Hammer & Plasma Rifle

Magnum & Rocket Launcher

Rocket Launcher & Silenced SMG

PAR SCORE

200,000 Points

Notable Offense

Weapons: Rockets and Sniper Slugs

The Rocket Launcher and the Sniper Rifle are usually recommended but this combination pays dividends incredibly successfully during the early sets. The Rocket Launcher is located on the concrete hut to the right of the spawning room, at the parking lot entrance; extra ammunition is in the middle gazebo. The Sniper Rifle is located on an identical-looking hut to the left of the spawning room. They make quick work of the initial waves of enemies and allow you to stay on the parking lot balconies at a distance from your foes, keeping your height advantage. You also have the protection of the low walls, and foes can't easily reach you. The only time you're ineffective with this weapon combo is during Drone swarms, so move to either of the Turrets or wrench a Turret off its base and place it where you're camping, and use this weapon. During later sets, when more skulls are active and there are foes with harder overshields to shoot through, try replacing either the Rocket Launcher or the Sniper Rifle with a Plasma weapon to remove the shields first, then follow up with either original weapon to finish the foe. This allows you to focus on collecting only the specific ammunition you need.

Weapon: A Ghost of a Chance

This mission offers a unique piece of equipment to those ready to defeat the Covenant riders manning Ghosts. The most adept way to part a Brute from his vehicle is to charge your Plasma Pistol and fire it at the Ghost's rider. Then hop on, easily hijacking the craft. Once you're driving the Ghost, your top priority is running over foes; this leads to fast round completion. However, careful driving is necessary, as you have confined spaces, such as stairs up to the parking lots, to navigate; failure to smoothly scrape through here leaves you a sitting target. Ghosts become very useful just after a Phantom drop; as soon as a group of foes lands on the ground, Boost straight through them, punishing them all in a single burst of acceleration. This tactic depends on you having good cover, such as low walls, concrete planters, or the opposite side of the middle gazebo, while you wait for the perfect ramming opportunity. Afterward, you must retreat quickly, relying on other teammates to mop up after your charge.

TIP

The Ghost is more than just a pair of cannons with unlimited ammo and a great charging vehicle; it can be an annoying obstacle for the Covenant, too! At the choke points, such as the entrance to the spawn building or the steps up to the parking lot, you can park a Ghost in a narrow thoroughfare, impeding your foes' progress, forcing them around, and slowing them down, allowing easy slaughtering! Make sure you mount the Ghost at the end of each round so it doesn't disappear at the start of the next round.

CAUTION

The only time you shouldn't Boost a Ghost is against the energy wall of a monster closet. This ends in violent damage and instant enemy retaliation.

Weapon: Turret Techniques

There are two Turrets on this map, and both are half-hidden on a grassy concrete planter near stairs up to the main spawning building, overlooking each parking lot. The Turrets are easily overlooked but extremely important, and it is wise to man them when you have numerous smaller enemies (Grunts, Jackals, and Drones) to deal with, especially as it's very difficult to outflank you on this planter. The only problem is you can't see much of the lower courtyard area, which nullifies the Turrets' use during certain waves. Negate this shortfall by making every weapon drop count; before the end of each round, wrench each Turret off its base, and drop them near cover points that your team uses, such as low walls overlooking the central courtyard or behind the spawning building's entrance doors. When the next round starts, the two Turrets respawn, effectively doubling your Turret total. Now all four of you can assist during Drone takedowns, which can be extremely difficult the longer your Firefight lasts.

CAUTION

Drones are a real pain in this mission due to their maneuverability, especially if you have to move from lower ground up to encounter them; in a pinch, use the Turrets, the Silenced SMG, or any bullet-spraying rapid-fire weapon.

General Plans

Tactic: Incursion Points—Phantom Drops

1

2

There are three Phantom drop points in this mission; one is on the lower-level courtyard near the central gazebo bus-stop structure **[1]**, and there are two above the parking lot **[2]**, one on each side of the map. Pay particular attention to the incoming flight paths of the Phantoms, as those that deposit their troops on the parking lots fly in at a low level, passing you at slow speeds and delivering heavy damage to anyone standing in the open, thanks to the ships' Plasma Turrets. Stay in cover for best results, or face extreme stamina damage and possible death. If you're in cover (either full or partial), you can race close to the Phantom's drop point and lob in a Grenade at the Plasma Turret, the bay doors, or the ground where the enemies fall to; as always, taking care of as many foes as early as possible during a round helps your entire team.

Tactic: Incursion Points—Monster Closets

1

2

There are nine monster closets from which entities appear on this map. On the lower level, the energy wall leading to the inaccessible coastal highway is one such location, as are the garage doorways on either side of the gazebo, under the parking lot wall **[1]**. The remaining six are two garage doors on each perimeter side of either parking lot, and a ramped, covered area leading into the parking lot interior **[2]**, which is inaccessible. Both the Phantoms and the energy walls that prevent you entering the closets have an associated "hum" to them. Listen for this hum to predict where your attackers will be coming from. Then get in position to view the closets and strike immediately as the foes emerge; a Rocket, Fuel Rod shot, sniper fire, or Grenades are all excellent for hitting bunches of foes as they emerge.

TIP

The central Phantom drop point is a good location for camping with a power weapon like the Rocket Launcher or Ghost, as you can blast (or Boost) into enemies as they contact the ground or exit the lower garages. The compromise is being out in the open, so pay close attention where the rest of the wave is so you aren't attacked from the sides or from behind.

Tactic: Multitiered Strategy

To survive and thrive, utilize the high ground around the edge of the parking lot and the multilevel platforms of concrete planters surrounding the golden zebra statues near and above the spawning building. Positioning yourselves on the platforms forces your foes to cover a large amount of ground from any of their entry points in order to reach you, thus giving you more opportunities to cut down their numbers or their shields. As the interior of the spawning building is useful only for racing back for health or caches, there's limited interior cover; for instance, the two-floored building has an airlift that prevents you from being cornered and allows quick access between floors. The airlift is easily missed, so watch for it. As for cover, try the ticket counters, concrete huts, planters, zebra statues, and pillars as you navigate this open space, especially when Phantoms are dropping in new waves.

especially if other explosions are occurring nearby.

Cooperative Plans

Tactic: Your Plasma Pal Is Back!

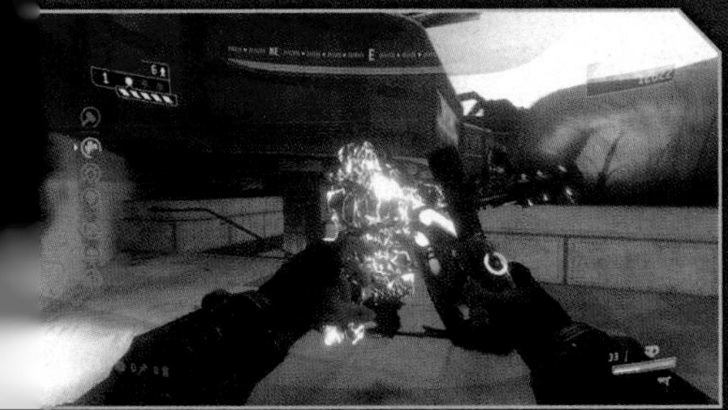

This is another mission in which pairing off into one team of two (with two players) or two teams of two (with four players) is advantageous: The first team member needs to be armed with a Plasma weapon (such as the Plasma Rifle or Pistol), while the other should employ regular bullets. The Plasma-weapon wielder whittles down an opponent's shields, while the other finishes them off with a headshot or two. The Plasma specialist won't accumulate many points, but their assists are just as important. Remember to specify a team member to grab all Plasma-based ammunition so you don't run out once the Famine Skull is active.

 TIP

The Plasma Pistol is the go-to weapon for taking down enemy shields, but the Plasma Rifle is also great at cutting down a Brute's shields; use the Rifle if the Pistol isn't accessible.

Tactic: Four-Player Foresight

When working well with others, a major part of your tactics involve figuring out a great place to stand. As with many other maps, it helps to give each team member a separate zone to "guard," but with the flexibility of leaving that zone to help another squadmate who is being overrun, which, alas, happens almost all the time on higher settings. For this mission, the left upper parking lot is one zone, and the right upper parking lot is the second **[1]**. The lower, circular gazebo and courtyard is a third zone **[2]**, where two teammates should guard. This zone has two fallback positions—both toward the stairs up to the spawning building—with one player covering each of them. Now the players covering the parking lots can quickly snipe from height or jump down to assist the courtyard zone. Unfortunately, it's more of a slog for the lower-zone players to reach the parking lot, which is why the fallback positions on either side of this courtyard allow the closer two players to head up to help a friend on the parking lot.

TIP

Make sure the weapons at each of these zones is utilized by the player in that zone, although flexibility is the key here; the Rocket Launcher ammo is in the gazebo, so one of the lower-level players may opt for this, as well as riding a Ghost. Meanwhile, the upper parking lot players should race to the Turrets, which are in their zones, in time to confront a Drone wave, for example.

Bonus Round Plans

Tactic: Preventing a Sticky Situation

Expect Grunts to pour out of numerous monster closets during this round. The chosen openings are random, so spread your team out to gain as much coverage as possible, then move your team in to focus on the openings that actually spawn Grunts. Due to the endless supply of Plasma Grenades the Grunts lob, and the Fuel Rod Cannons some are carrying, you'd be wise not to get pinned into a corner, as you'll be facing multiple Grenades lobbed from different angles. Although Boosting through a Grunt cluster in a Ghost seems like a fine plan, it only pays off (and does big-time) if you can avoid the Grenades, sticky or otherwise. For the safest way to rack up bonus points, choose your faithful Magnum and continuously attempt headshots. Before

HALO 3 MULTIPLAYER MAPS

Welcome to the *Halo 3* multiplayer maps section of this guide, showcasing all 24 *Halo 3* multiplayer maps; three maps (Citadel, Heretic, and Longshore) are brand-new with the release of *Halo 3: ODST*. All the multiplayer strategies in this section were provided by tournament-level players from the PMS clan. For each level, there are labeled maps, location information and tactics, ideal sniping spots, and more.

ASSEMBLY

PMS Solincia

The Covenant war machine continues its march to conquest; even with its head severed, it is still dangerous.

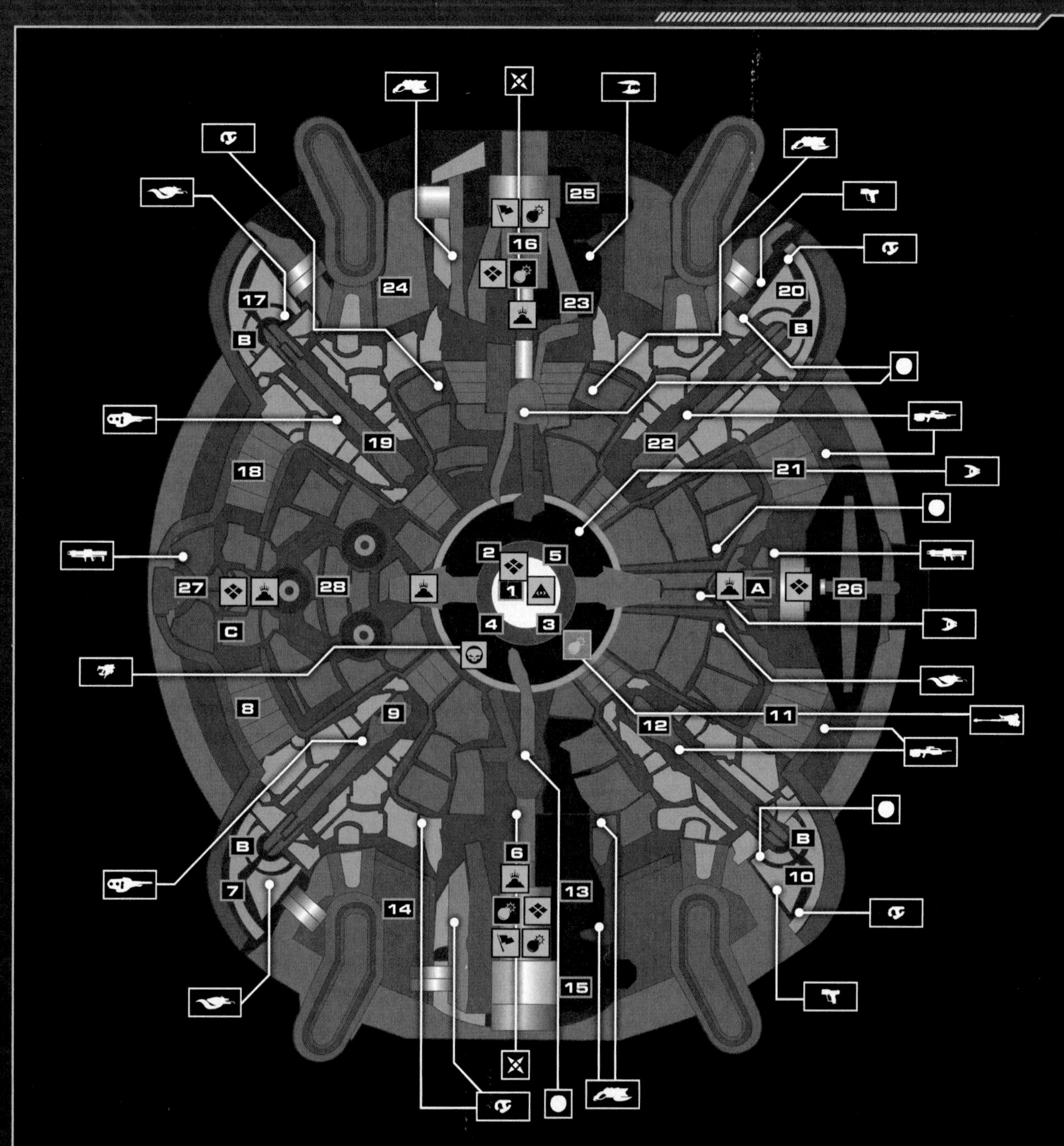

DATA STREAM

Recommended Game Variants: Slayer, Team Slayer, Capture the Flag (CTF)

Recommended/Maximum Number of Players: 2–8/8

Advantageous Equipment: Rockets, Mauler, Active Camouflage, Gravity Hammer

AVAILABLE EQUIPMENT AND GEAR RESPAWN TIMES

1 skull = Slow 5 skulls = Fast

Weapons	Respawn (skulls of 5)
Battle Rifle	5
Brute Shot	3
Carbine	5
Gravity Hammer	1
Grenade, Frag	5
Grenade, Plasma	5

Weapons	Respawn (skulls of 5)
Magnum	4
Mauler	3
Needler	3
Plasma Pistol	4
Plasma Rifle	4
Rocket Launcher	2

Weapons	Respawn (skulls of 5)
Spiker	4
Equipment	
Active Camo	4
Bubble Shield	3
Power Drain	3
Regenerator	3

Topographical Overview

- The setting is that of an assembly line, contained within a Covenant Scarab factory. Assembly's tunnels and corridors make it easy to hide from your enemy and take cover.
- Weapons within the maps containment area are of Human, Covenant, and Brute origin—a broad range of weapons to suit anyone's fancy.
- This map is great for Slayer and Team Slayer play.
- Assembly is two-way symmetrical (from base to base), rather than four-way (all four corners being the same).
- The map can be split into four quadrants. From each section, a road leads to the center of the map, where you'll find a brilliant stream rising into the sky. This powers the Scarab machines and houses the Active Camo. This area is known as "Camouflage (Camo) Tower."

Call-out Locations

Camo Tower

Other names: N/A

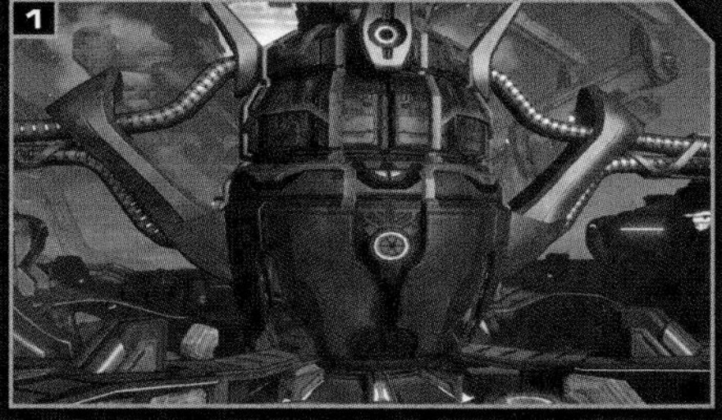

Placed within the center of the map, Camouflage Tower is a pivotal structure of Assembly. The structure possesses two levels and multiple access points and is not easily captured.

Bottom Camo

Other names: N/A

Bottom Camo is located on the lower, ground level of Camouflage Tower and has two entry points. Each doorway faces the Orange Base and the Yellow Base. You will also find the Gravity Hammer in this area.

Middle Camo

Other names: N/A

Middle Camo Tower is on the main level of the playing field. There are four entry points—off the light and dark runways—to Middle Camo. A center energy stream rises into the air to the Scarab Assembly line. Middle Camo houses the Active Camo within its central beam, rendering you invisible for a brief period of time.

Light Side Camo Shelf

Other names: N/A

Mounted to the interior walls of the Camouflage Tower, Light Side Camo Shelf often goes unnoticed. However, pay close attention and you'll find the Mauler—a sharp, quick weapon that packs a nasty punch. Crouch on the shelf, ready to pounce on your opponent with the Mauler. This is always sure to bring about a quick kill.

Dark Side Camo Shelf

Other names: N/A

5

Just as the Light Side Shelf contains the Mauler, the Dark Side Shelf contains a weapon just as deadly—the Needler. While not meant for close-range fighting, the Needler is a deadly object meant for cross-map game warfare.

Orange Base

Other names: Blue or Red Base (depending on the spawn points)

6

Like most of Bungie's maps, Assembly contains two bases: Yellow Base and Orange Base. While most bases usually are restricted to their internal areas, Assembly's bases extend beyond their exterior walls to the surrounding areas. These locations are designated by name and the weapons they keep and by another one of Bungie's usual features—a light side and dark side. The light side of Assembly is illuminated by the outer walls of the Scarab Factory, while the dark side is shrouded by the assembly line above.

Orange Base Light Court

Other names: N/A

7

Located on the light side of the map, directly next to Orange Base, Light Court is an obvious place for taking cover and ambushing your enemies as they attempt to invade your territory. Within the Light Court, directly behind the court Mohawk, you will find the Brute Shot.

Orange Base Light Ramp

Other names: N/A

8

Allowing access from the base doorway to the Regenerator Platform, the Orange Base Light Ramp extends the length of Assembly's light side. It is designated by the base side that it's located on.

Orange Base Light Runway

Other names: N/A

9

As you exit either doorway of the team base, you are met with runways leading to the Camouflage Tower. These runways provide access to the Active Camo, and Light Runways contain a Mohawk protruding from their bases. You will find a Covenant Carbine alongside here.

Orange Base Dark Court

Other names: N/A

10

Beyond the side of the dark side of Orange Base is the perfect ambush point. This area is known as the Orange Base Dark Court. This area contains only three weapon types: two Plasma Grenades, one Magnum Pistol, and one Plasma Pistol.

Orange Base Cut

Other names: N/A

11

One of the most important yet sometimes overlooked areas on the map is the Base Cut. This area is located on the dark side of the map. It contains a Battle Rifle and leads you to the coveted Rocket Launcher tower. While you can scoop up the BR and be on the move, from this location, you can see the majority of the map, allowing you to shoot across it and take out your opponents. Also from this location, you can throw a Grenade into the pit below and then finish off your foe with one BR shot.

Orange Base Dark Runway

Other names: N/A

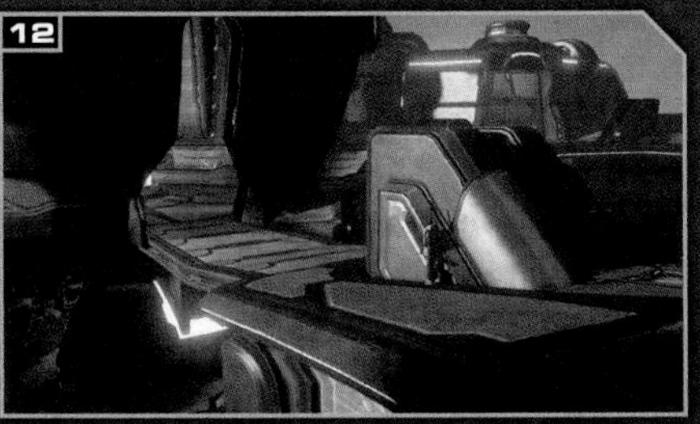
12

As with the light side, the dark side of the map also contains a runway from the base to Camouflage Tower. As you head across, pick up the Battle Rifle resting alongside the Dark Runway Mohawk.

Bottom Orange Base

Other names: N/A

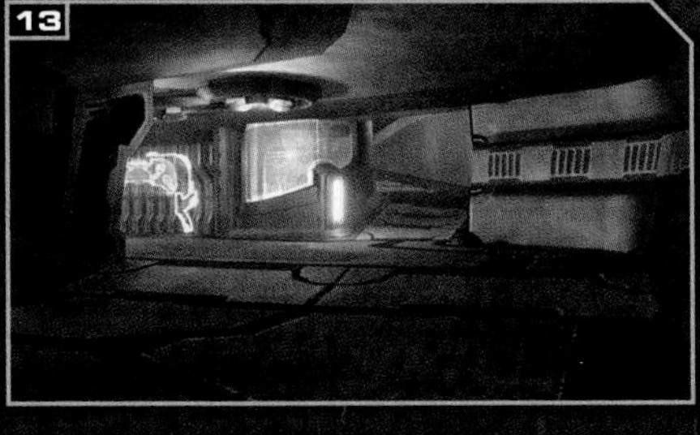
13

The bottom of the bases are just as important to control as the top. Bottom Orange Base has two hallway entry points, with a Grav Lift hallway streaming through the middle that takes you to Top Base. This Grav Lift has a front side and a back side. On the lift's back side, you can snatch up the Power Drain to weaken your opponent. The two entry points to the front side house one Plasma Pistol and one Brute Spiker. Holding down this area will prevent your opponent from entering your base unchecked from the basement!

Top Base

Other names: N/A

14

Entering the base from either doorway, you are now in Top Base. This is the landing point for the Grav Lift from Bottom Base; you will find two weapons here—the Brute Spiker and the Plasma Rifle.

Back Base

Other names: N/A

15

Located in the rear of Orange Base is the Back Base. Here you'll find the entrance to the ramp leading down to Bottom Base. Watch this area closely, as Top Base and Back Base are divided by solid walls that can provide cover for your enemy.

Yellow Base

Other names: Blue or Red Base (depending on the spawn points)

16

Like most of Bungie's maps, Assembly contains two bases: Yellow Base and Orange Base. Most bases are restricted to their internal areas, but Assembly's bases extend beyond their exterior walls to the surrounding areas. These locations are designated by name and the weapons they keep and by another one of Bungie's usual features—a light side and a dark side. The light side of Assembly is illuminated by the outer walls of the Scarab Factory, while the dark side is shrouded by the assembly line above.

Yellow Base Light Court

Other names: N/A

Located on the light side of the map, directly next to the Yellow Base, Light Court is an obvious place for taking cover and ambushing your enemies as they attempt to invade your territory. Within Light Court, directly behind the court Mohawk, you will find the Brute Shot.

Yellow Base Light Ramp

Other names: N/A

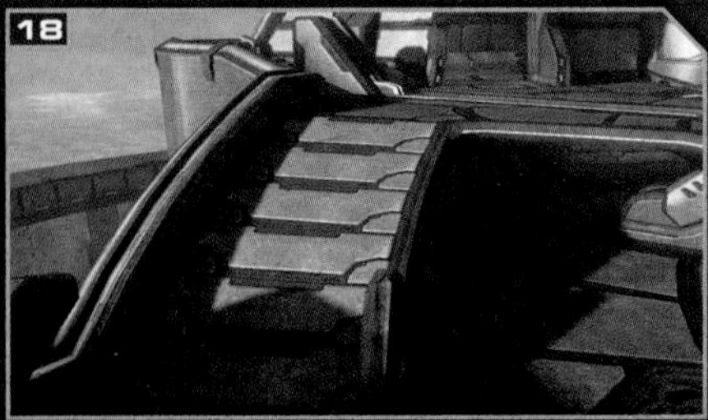

Allowing access from the base doorway to the Regenerator Platform, the Yellow Base Light Ramp extends the length of Assembly's light side. It is designated by the base side that it's located on.

Yellow Base Light Runway

Other names: N/A

As you exit either doorway of the team base, you encounter runways leading to the Camouflage Tower. These runways provide access to the Active Camo and contain a Mohawk protruding from their base. You will find the Covenant Carbine alongside here.

Yellow Base Dark Court

Other names: N/A

Extending beyond the side of Yellow Base's dark side, you will find the perfect ambush point. This area is known as Yellow Base Dark Court. This area contains only three weapon types: two Plasma Grenades, one Magnum Pistol, and one Plasma Pistol.

[21] Yellow Base Cut

Other names: N/A

One of the most important yet sometimes overlooked areas on the map is Base Cut. This area is located on the dark side of the map. It contains a Battle Rifle and leads to the coveted Rocket Launcher tower. While you can scoop up the BR and be on the move, from this location, you can see the majority of the map, allowing you to shoot across it and take out your opponents. Also from this location, you can throw a Grenade into the pit below and finish off your foe with one BR shot.

Yellow Base Dark Runway

Other names: N/A

As with the map's light side, the dark side also contains a runway from the base to Camouflage Tower. As you head across, notice the Battle Rifle resting alongside the Dark Runway Mohawk.

Bottom Yellow Base

Other names: N/A

The bottom of the bases are just as important to control as the top. Bottom Yellow Base has two hallway entry points, with a Grav Lift hallway streaming through the middle that takes you to Top Base. This Grav Lift has a front side and a back side. On the lift's back side, you can snatch up the Power Drain to weaken your opponent. The two entry points to the front side house one Plasma Pistol and one Brute Spiker. Holding down this area will prevent your opponent from entering your base unchecked from the basement!

Top Base

Other names: N/A

Entering the base from either doorway, you are now in Top Base. Here is the landing point for the Grav Lift from Bottom Base. You will find two weapons here—the Brute Spiker and the Plasma Rifle.

Back Base

Other names: N/A

Located in the rear of Yellow Base is Back Base. Here you'll find the entrance to the ramp leading down to Bottom Base. Watch this area closely, as Top Base and Back Base are divided by solid walls that can provide easy cover for your enemy.

Rocket Launcher Tower

Other names: N/A

Located on the dark side of the map, Rocket Launcher Tower is a place of power in any game type. There are three levels to this tower:

Bottom Rockets Lift: Located on Assembly's ground level, the Bottom Rockets Lift takes you to the third level of Rockets. On the ground directly in front of the lift are two Plasma Grenades and one Needler. Throw the Plasma Grenades up the Grav Lift while your opponent is on the Rockets Platform to weaken their defenses.

Mid-Rockets: Between the dark cuts of either base, with a ramp leading to the lower ground level, you will find the pass-through of Mid-Rockets. The Bubble Shield is on the platform.

Top Rockets: Access this location either by jumping from the dark cuts of either base to the back of Rocket Launcher Tower or by using the Rockets Lift. Top Rockets contains a platform where the Rockets spawn. This area gives an advantageous viewpoint, as you are perched high above the rest of the playable areas on the map.

Regenerator Platform

Other names: N/A

Standing alone on the light side of Assembly, in the center of two bases, you will experience the Regenerator Platform. Also called "Regen Plat," this area has two levels. The lower level contains no weapons, but resting atop the upper level is the Regenerator, which brings health and shields to the player who utilizes it.

Batteries

Other names: N/A

Powering the Scarab assembly line with its energy, the Batteries are located directly between the Regen Plat

Tactical Knowledge

Utilizing the Four Quadrants and Camo Tower

Rockets Tower

- To gain advantage in any game variant, utilizing the Rocket Launcher Tower is essential. Rushing for the Rocket Launcher will come at a price, as you'll have to fight your way to it. Pick up a Battle Rifle on the "Cut" on your way. Take down your opponent, then hold down the Tower with your teammates.
- Once at the tower, you have an advantage because you can see the entire map. Save the Rockets for when you need them; instead, use your Battle Rifle and "team BR" your opponents from above.
- Having top-map advantage will always give you kills, as it's easier to shoot below you than shooting above.

Regenerator Platform

- Grabbing the Regenerator and holding down the platform will put you in the open. This area of the map is easily exposed to both bases. Watch for the team controlling Rocket Launcher Tower, as you can easily be taken out if you move off the Regen Platform.
- Taking the Regenerator back to your base to continue shooting long range across the map will benefit you and your team.

Active Camouflage Tower

- You'll have to fight your way across the runways to the Camo Tower. The opposing team will be looking to do the same thing.
- Grab some Sticky Grenades on your way. Pick up either the Battle Rifle or the Carbine, and head through enemy fire to the tower.
- Once you attain the Camo Shield, you can pick up the Mauler in Camo Tower and make your way to the Back Base of the other team. This will allow you to spawn-trap, Mauler, and melee the opposing team.

Base Control

- Hold down your own base.
- Don't let the other team sneak into your base, as you'll be at their mercy as they attempt to spawn-kill you.
- As the opposing team tries to shoot you down from across the map, use the Mohawks in the base's Courts as cover.

Professional Planning

- Assembly has some symmetrical elements, making it easy for a team to control their side of the base. By positioning your team in strategic places on Base Side, Light Side, and Dark Side, you can have easy map control.
- Watching Lower Base and Upper Base is an important strategy when controlling your base's side. The opposing team can steal Active Camo and make their way to your lower base ramps to sneak up behind you. Make sure you have a teammate watching this area of the map.
- Controlling Rocket Launcher Tower will give any team the upper advantage; however, to ensure success, have a teammate below covering the Cut and the Court areas to prevent sneak attacks. The teammate who is covering the lower base area should ensure that no one is heading up Rockets Lift to come after you and should call out if they see someone doing so.
- Positioning a team member on the Light Side Court will give you the advantage of seeing the entire light side of the map.
- Controlling these four areas—Light Side, Rocket Launcher Tower, Cut/Dark Court, and Bottom Base—will keep the opposing team at bay.
- Once everyone is in their respective positions, utilize this positioning to team-shoot across the map; this makes it difficult for your adversaries to pinpoint where the fire is coming from.

Weapon Tactics

Priority 1 Weapons

As with any map within the *Halo 3* Matchmaking realm, it's best to know where to find power weapons. These weapons will provide the player with the best offensive and defensive in any match type. By using and controlling the power weapons, you can dominate your opponent from almost anywhere on the map. Assembly contains these power weapons:

Rockets: These are placed strategically in a tower, allowing you to look down upon your adversary and blast them out of gameplay and pick up kills.

Active Camo: This allows you to sneak up on your opponent and use stealth to gain entry to the opponent's base, and it gives you the opportunity to attain additional power weapons while going unnoticed.

Gravity Hammer: This weapon is definitely a force to be reckoned with. With one swipe of the Gravity Hammer, you can take out multiple opponents. One trick, however, is doing this in a sneak attack. The Gravity Hammer is a short-range weapon, so wielding it outside of close-quarter combat means your death is sure.

Mauler: This is another short-range weapon that packs a punch. While a Battle Rifle or Carbine is great for long-range gameplay, the Mauler will take out your opponent at close range. A Mauler shot combined with a beatdown will always give you a quick kill.

Enhanced Knowledge

- In Capture the Flag (CTF), the importance of staying and capturing the power weapons to attain map control is paramount.
- As with any Objective game, Team Slayer tactics should always be used. After "setting up" in the Slayer areas, taking down the opposing team should be the priority before rushing in and taking the other team's flag.
- Always kill at least two or three opponents while pushing forward; this ensures that during your enemy's respawn, one of your team members can grab the flag.
- After capturing the opposing team's flag, never underestimate their ability to kill you and your inability to get that flag back to your base. While your teammates will be firing from across the map, trying to keep the opponent at bay, the best idea is to "juggle" the flag by dropping it and picking it back up; this allows you to shoot at those attempting to chase you down.

Advanced Tactics

General

- Whether you spawn with a Battle Rifle or an Assault Rifle, depending on the game variant, it's best to have a secondary weapon. Having a long-range weapon in combination with a short-range weapon will provide you the opportunity to switch between the two, depending on your situation.
- Assembly offers shield walls that provide cover while you wait for your opponent to draw near, giving you the time to switch between your primary and secondary weapons. If a foe is coming your way, instead of driving toward him, take a step back, switch weapons, and go for the quick kill as he approaches.
- Assembly has a variety of weapons, offering both short- and long-range weapons to accomplish any player's goals.

Sniping

Top Rockets

This area provides an advantageous view over the entire map, except for the Regen Platform.

Base Courts

Hidden within the shadows of the bases, the Dark Court sides will allow you to take out your opponents with a Sniper Rifle or to rush nearby foes with a Mauler while going undetected. Also, use the Mohawks as a shield against their bullets; you won't be an easy target.

Bottom Regen

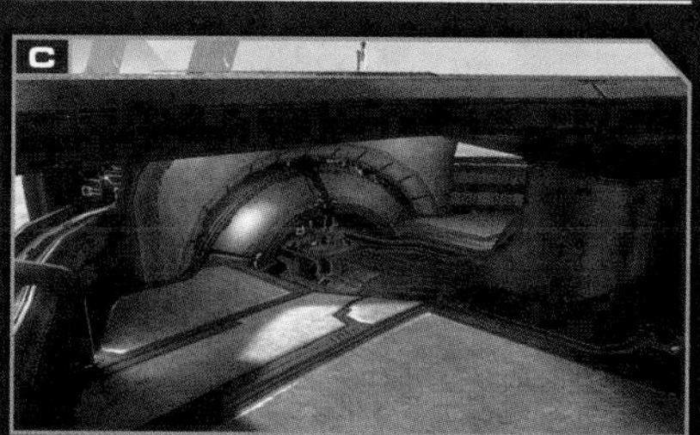

With cover from the Batteries and in the shadow of the Regenerator Platform (using the Regenerator as additional protection), you can easily snipe or shoot out your opponent as they are on the bottom level of the map. By strafing side to side (Yellow Base side to Orange Base side), you can avoid your foe's bullets as they come at you.

AVALANCHE

PMS Ovaryacting, Athena AzMA

reezing winds scour blasted terrain, and ancient battle scars are a grim reminder that this is a precious prize.

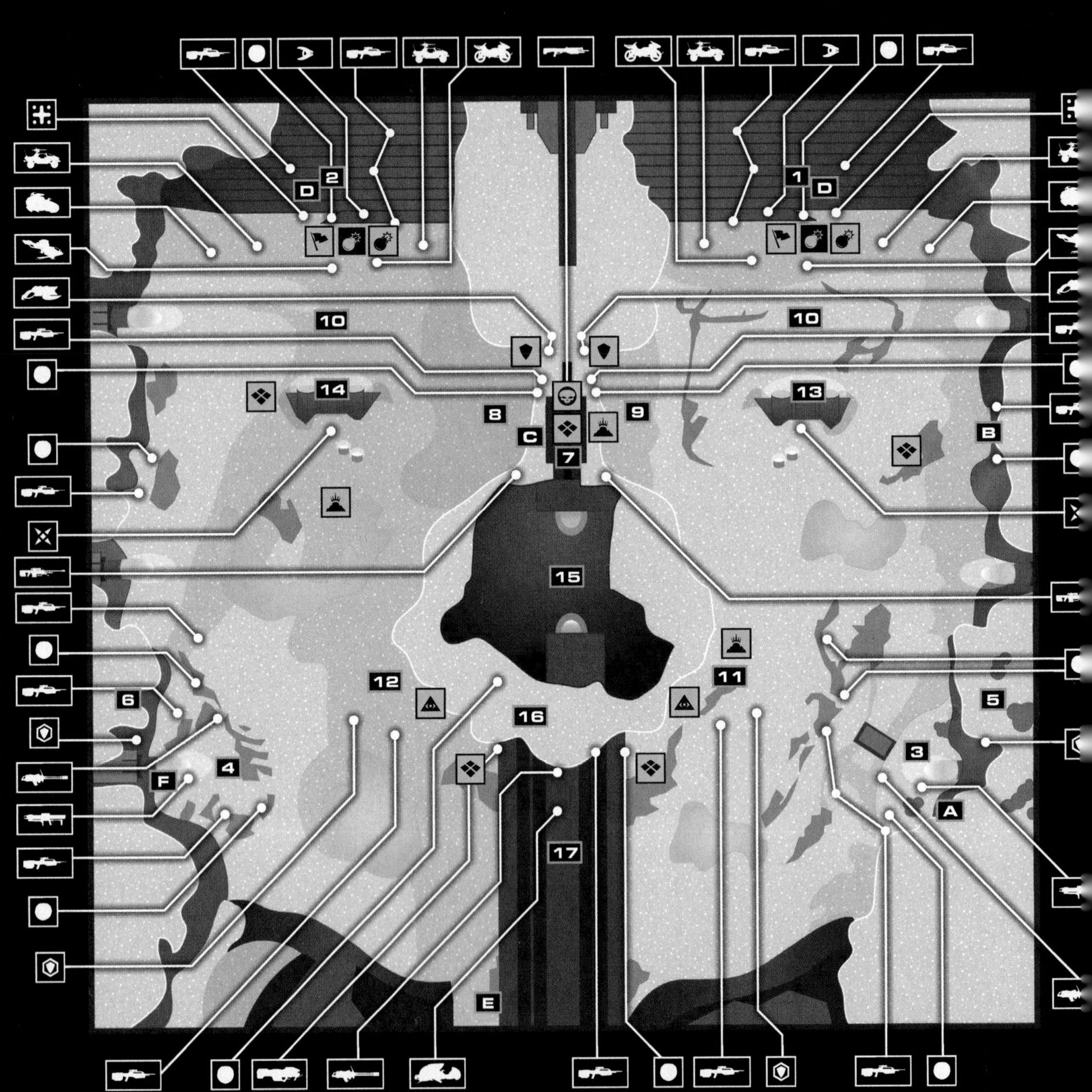

1 of 5 skulls = Slow 5 of 5 skulls = Fast

Weapons	
Battle Rifle	5 of 5 skulls
Brute Shot	4 of 5 skulls
Grenade, Frag	5 of 5 skulls
Grenade, Plasma	1 of 5 skulls
Machinegun Turret	1 of 5 skulls
Needler	3 of 5 skulls
Plasma Pistol	4 of 5 skulls
Rocket Launcher	3 of 5 skulls
Shotgun	3 of 5 skulls
Sniper Rifle	2 of 5 skulls

Weapons	
Spartan Laser	1 of 5 skulls
Spiker	4 of 5 skulls
Vehicles	
Ghost	3 of 5 skulls
Hornet	1 of 5 skulls
Mongoose	4 of 5 skulls
Warthog	4 of 5 skulls
Wraith	3 of 5 skulls
Banshee	3 of 5 skulls
Choppers	4 of 5 skulls

Vehicles	
Scorpion Tank*	2 of 5 skulls
Equipment	
Bubble Shield	3 of 5 skulls
Active Camo	1 of 5 skulls
Overshield	1 of 5 skulls
Power Drain	3 of 5 skulls
Regenerator	3 of 5 skulls
Trip Mine	3 of 5 skulls

** Available only in one-sided matches*

NOTE **The Scorpion Tank is available only to the assaulting team in one-sided Objective-based games; during Team Slayer, Neutral, and Multi-objective games, both sides will have the Wraith Tank.**

Topographical Overview

Avalanche is a symmetrical map featuring two bases separated by a middle forerunner cave. This creates a U-shaped battlefield. If the Matchmaking is one-sided (One Bomb, One CTF), the attacking team has UNSC vehicles, and the defending team has Covenant vehicles and Warthogs. See the "Zone Knowledge" section for locations of primary weapons and vehicles.

In addition, call-outs consist of "their side" and "our side"; for example, "Their Teleport," or "Our Sniper."

Call-out Locations

Light Base

Other names: Blue Base

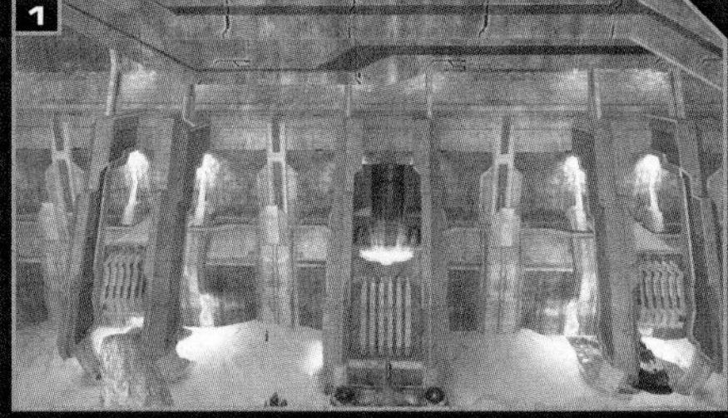

1

There are three levels in the base. The first, upper level has a flag spawn and a Man Cannon. The second level has the teleporter and a ramp that takes you to the base's lower level. This level also contains two Battle Rifles, up against the walls, one on each side. In addition, you will capture the flag on the second level. The third, lower level of the base is where you'll find a Needler, Frag Grenades, and a Regenerator. The outside part of the base has an upper ledge, which will take you to either cliff side or Keyhole.

Dark Base

Other names: Red Base

2

There are three levels in the base. The first, upper level has a flag spawn and a Man Cannon. The second level has the teleporter and a ramp that takes you to the base's lower level. This level also contains two Battle Rifles, up against the walls, one on each side. In addition, you will capture the flag on the second level. The third, lower level of the base is where you'll find a Needler, Frag Grenades, and a Regenerator. The outside part of the base has an upper ledge, which will take you to either cliff side or Keyhole.

Blue Base 2

Other names: Blue Turret, Light Base Turret, Blue Rockets, Light Base Rockets, Rocket Spawn

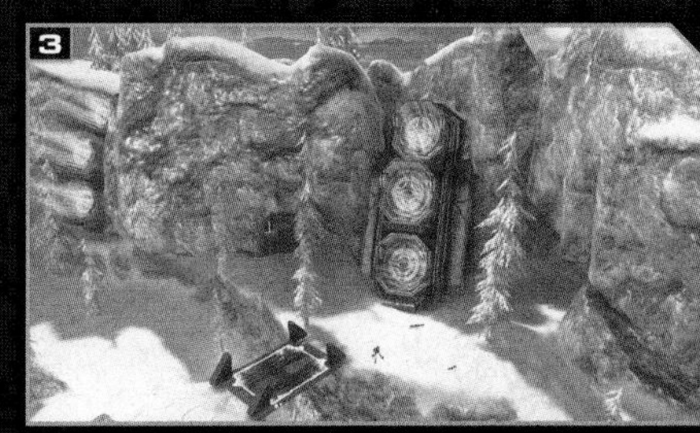

3

On this side, there is a bridge connecting two rocks. The Turret is located on the ledge, allowing you to see vehicles/players who will come around the "U" to your side. You can also watch people going into Laser spawn. Located here is a Rocket Launcher, a Battle Rifle, and a Bubble Shield, right outside the teleporter door. There is also a Man Cannon that will launch you toward Ghost spawn; this vehicle allows you to quickly travel across the map.

Red Base 2

Other names: Red Turret, Dark Turret, Red Rockets, Dark Base Rockets, Rocket Spawn

4

The Turret is located on the ledge, allowing you to see vehicles/players who will come around the "U" to your side. You can also watch people going into Laser spawn. Located here is a Rocket Launcher, a Battle Rifle, and a Bubble Shield, right outside the teleporter door. There is also a Man Cannon that will launch you toward Ghost spawn; this vehicle allows you to quickly travel across the map.

Blue Teleporter

Other names: N/A

5

The Teleporter links you between your base and Turret.

Red Teleporter

Other names: N/A

6

Using the Teleporter allows you to advance on your foes unseen.

Keyhole

Other names: Shotgun Spawn, Shotty, Top Mid

7

Keyhole is located at the map's center. It is a heated spot for battles. The Shotgun is located here, as is the Man Cannon, which will take you over the Center Pit to Laser spawn. The Middle Corridor between the two sides separates the base.

Dark Sniper

Other names: Red Sniper

8

Dark Sniper is located outside Keyhole. Here you'll find the Overshield, a Battle Rifle, two Plasma Grenades, and a pair of Spikers.

Light Sniper

Other names: Blue Sniper

9

Dark Sniper is located outside Keyhole. Here you'll find the Overshield, a Battle Rifle, two Plasma Grenades, and a pair of Spikers.

Vehicle Pit

Other names: N/A

10

Each base has a Vehicle Pit, where the vehicles spawn. The pit is located between the base's two Man Cannons.

Blue Camo

Other names: N/A

11

This is located next to the tree on Light Side. Here you'll find Brute Shot and a Bubble Shield.

Red Camo

Other names: N/A

This is located next to the rock on Dark Side. Here you'll find Brute Shot and a Bubble Shield.

Blue Man Cannon

Other names: N/A

This is the big Man Cannon on the ground that will lead you into the base. A Power Drain is also located here.

Red Man Cannon

Other names: N/A

This is the big Man Cannon on the ground that will lead you into the base. A Power Drain is also located here.

Center Pit

Other names: N/A

Center Pit is located in the middle of the map and connects Keyhole to Laser spawn. It allows quick travel from one end of the map to the other.

Laser Spawn

Other names: Laser

This is located in the middle of the map, on the back side near Ghost spawn. Located on each side of the Laser are Plasma Grenades.

Ghost Spawn

Other names: Back Mid, Back U

This is where both Turret Man Cannons land players. It is also a heated spot for battles. Next to the door leading you to the Laser is a Battle Rifle and a Trip Mine.

Tactical Knowledge

- At the start of the game, depending on which side of the map you are on, you should look either left or right to see which side of the landing has the upward ramp. Go that way to find a portal that leads directly to the Rocket spawn and Turret emplacement. From there, you can jump into the large Man Cannon and fly to the Spartan Laser spawn point. You are likely to meet heavy resistance here, so going in alone will pretty much guarantee that you will not secure it, unless you get very lucky or are very good in close combat.
- After acquiring the Laser, you should secure the Sniper Rifle early in the match to act as first alert if enemies are rushing the base. It can also serve as an anti–Spartan Laser/Turret weapon.
- Next is the Brute Shot. Since this level is heavy on vehicular attacks, you should secure the Brute Shot to assist in stopping the inevitable Warthog, Wraith, Ghost, and Hornet rush that will attack your troops.
- Last is the Shotgun. There is only one of these on the map, and it is positioned where most of the close-quarter fighting takes place—Keyhole.
- Sniper Rifles are located next to the main cave in the middle of the map, on both sides. The easiest way to reach them is to go out of your lower base, hop on a Mongoose, and drive there. This is also a way to reach the Spartan Laser if you need to, as the cannons in the cave will transport you from the upper part of the cave to the lower part.
- The Brute Shot is right next to the Active Camo. The easiest way to get there is by taking the front Man Cannon out of the top of your base and running to it.
- Warthogs are located to the left and right of the base's front door if you spawn on the UNSC side of the map. The Wraith is positioned to either the left or the right, farthest away from the map's center, depending on which side of the map you're on. Hornets are directly in front of the front door. Choppers will occupy the Warthog locations if you are on the Covenant side.

Enhanced Knowledge

Due to the abundance of vehicles on the map, every team's primary goal is acquiring the Spartan Laser and the Rocket Launchers. Holding these items will greatly increase your chances of keeping the enemy team immobile while keeping your team highly mobile. Significant effort should be made to secure the Spartan Laser, as it is the most effective way to knock the enemy Hornets out of the sky and destroy enemy Wraiths and other vehicles. Try to limit yourself on single-player shots. Controlling the Laser will determine if you will have vehicle control over the map.

One Bomb, One Flag, and Capture-the-Flag Tactics

- Turret spawn provides a great vantage point for a sniper to scan the map for enemies. Pair the sniper with another player (preferably a strong BR shooter) who can provide backup and protection. Also, this player has quick access to the base via teleporter if the opposing team enters the base and teammates need help.
- Have two players watching Keyhole and grabbing Custom Power-ups during a heated battle, because this makes you invincible for three seconds.
- Try not to abandon all positions unless necessary.
- Don't go alone into the opponent's base.
- Have more than one person protecting your flag and watching for the opposing team approaching the base to plant the bomb.
- When planting the bomb, have a Warthog, Hornet, or Wraith distract the players while your team sneaks in with the bomb via teleporter.
- Have a person at Turret spawn watching for incoming vehicles to notify your team so that they are prepared with a Power Drain and/or Rockets.
- Crouch-walking on the base's outer ledge can give you a sneaky entry to grab the opponent's flag or plant your bomb.
- Don't send all vehicles to the opposing side; try to leave a Warthog and the Wraith to protect your base from incoming enemies.
- Using Camo allows you to remain unseen (except by radar); if you use this wisely, you can sneak into the opposing base via teleporter. You can also flank the opposing team on their side of Keyhole.
- If someone is exiting or entering your base via front Man Cannon, throw Plasma or Frag Grenades and simply use you BR to finish them off. This tactic will also work with the Center Pit cannons.
- If the opposing team is going to grab the flag, throw a Plasma Grenade at the flag so it weakens the foe as they try picking it up.
- When in Keyhole, have a Shotgun and stand up on the slanted ledge near the opposing team's entrance. This allows for surprise kills.
- If your sniper is in Keyhole, look down at the Laser spawn for approaching attackers.
- The Ghost is a great tool for splattering anyone who dares walk on the ground alone and in the open.
- Good Laser spots include the down side of Sniper spawn, Turret spawn, Base Platform, and Keyhole. Use the Laser more for vehicles than for a single opponent.
- Trip Mines are tricky. Place them safely away from your team; however, you can place the Trip Mine over Flag spawn or where the opponent will plant the bomb. Also place the Trip Mine around corners that vehicles would turn from. Sometimes throwing the Trip Mine into the Keyhole during a heated battle will lower opponents' shields, whereupon you can take them out with one shot.
- Blocking teleporters with a Mongoose inside your base will keep opponents from entering. Also, placing a Mongoose over the flag will keep your foes from grabbing the flag (they will get on the Mongoose instead), or you can place it over the area where they will plant the bomb, hindering them from planting the bomb quickly.

Offense

- Never try to take the flag or plant the bomb by yourself. Coordinate an attack with your teammates. Have a team member or two attempt to take control of the defending team and use the Spartan Laser effectively. Make sure to take down your foe's air support and tanks.
- Using the teleporter is great for stealing the flag and escaping the base quickly; however, when you first go through the teleporter, turn and wait to see if anyone is following you. As your opponent comes out of the teleporter, you can get easy flag-carrier kills.
- The Hornet is good for air support and for dropping and picking up players at the bases or teleporters. Try not to hover with the Hornet; continuously move so that you are not a sitting duck for a Wraith or Rocket Launcher. Sometimes if you are low enough, and with the Man Cannons allowing people to be high in the air, the Hornet becomes an easy target for Plasma Grenades.
- Driving the Warthog or Mongoose with the Flag or Bomb in the passenger seat is the best strategy. If done right, the Warthog and Mongoose can get your team into the base, capture or plant the flag or bomb, and get out within minutes. All three seats in the Warthog should be full—a driver, a Turret operator, and a footman to plant or capture the bomb or flag.
- After you pick up Active Camo, check to see if the enemy's Active Camo has been taken; if it hasn't, pick it up and just run or hop through their Mid Pit to the middle Man Cannon, which can launch you into your opponent's base unnoticed.

Defense

- Place your players wisely on the map. Do not completely desert the base to capture the power weapons, but do not have everybody hide in the base waiting for the eventual attack from the bomb carrier or flag bandit. Get the Spartan Laser to take out incoming vehicles, and use the Machinegun Turret to take out footmen before they get into your base. Leave a few teammates inside the base to protect the exits.
- Taking the Machinegun Turret to your base, along with someone with Rockets, is a great ploy for defense. But remember: one man alone cannot defend the base.
- If your opponent steals your flag, consider taking a Mongoose to cut off the other team before they make with the flag.
- Remember, you will not be able to see the enemy's bomb or your stolen flag when the other team has possession of them.
- In One Flag CTF, the Scorpion is on your side and can dominate a team by itself with minimal cover from the rest of your team. It will take out the Wraith and the Ghosts with ease. But if it falls into enemy hands, it must become your primary target.
- Crouching inside Keyhole with the Shotgun or outside the door on your side will stop ambushes through the middle. Also having the Turret here could do some damage.
- Sniping from the base will also give you an advantage. There is a ledge outside the bases that offers different areas for cover and different vantage points. You will be able to watch Keyhole and your teleporter from here.

■ Sniping

There is a lot of landscape on this map for sniping positions. The following are a few popular snipe positions.

Turret

From the Turret ledge, you have a great view of approaching enemies and vehicles.

Base

The base area provides cover and weapons for sniping.

Keyhole

This spot is in the center of the map, with lots of available weapons.

Underpass

This sniping spot is in the back of the map, near the edge in the shadows under the underpass.

Cliff Side

Snipe from Cliff Side by the Man Cannon facing Keyhole.

Ambush Points

- Ambush teleporters, bases, and front Man Cannons. Doing all three at once can give you a great advantage during CTF and Assault.
- During heated battles at Keyhole, take the Man Cannon from the Turret/Rocket Launcher spawn, go through the Laser with other team members, and take the Man Cannon from the Center Pit. Attack from there, helping your team. You can also go through Keyhole, take the cannon over to the Laser, and help out.

BLACKOUT

PMS Doom, PMS Pip Sq3ak, PMS Ovaryacting, PMS Disco

Bathed in frozen moonlight, this abandoned drilling platform is now a monument to human frailty.

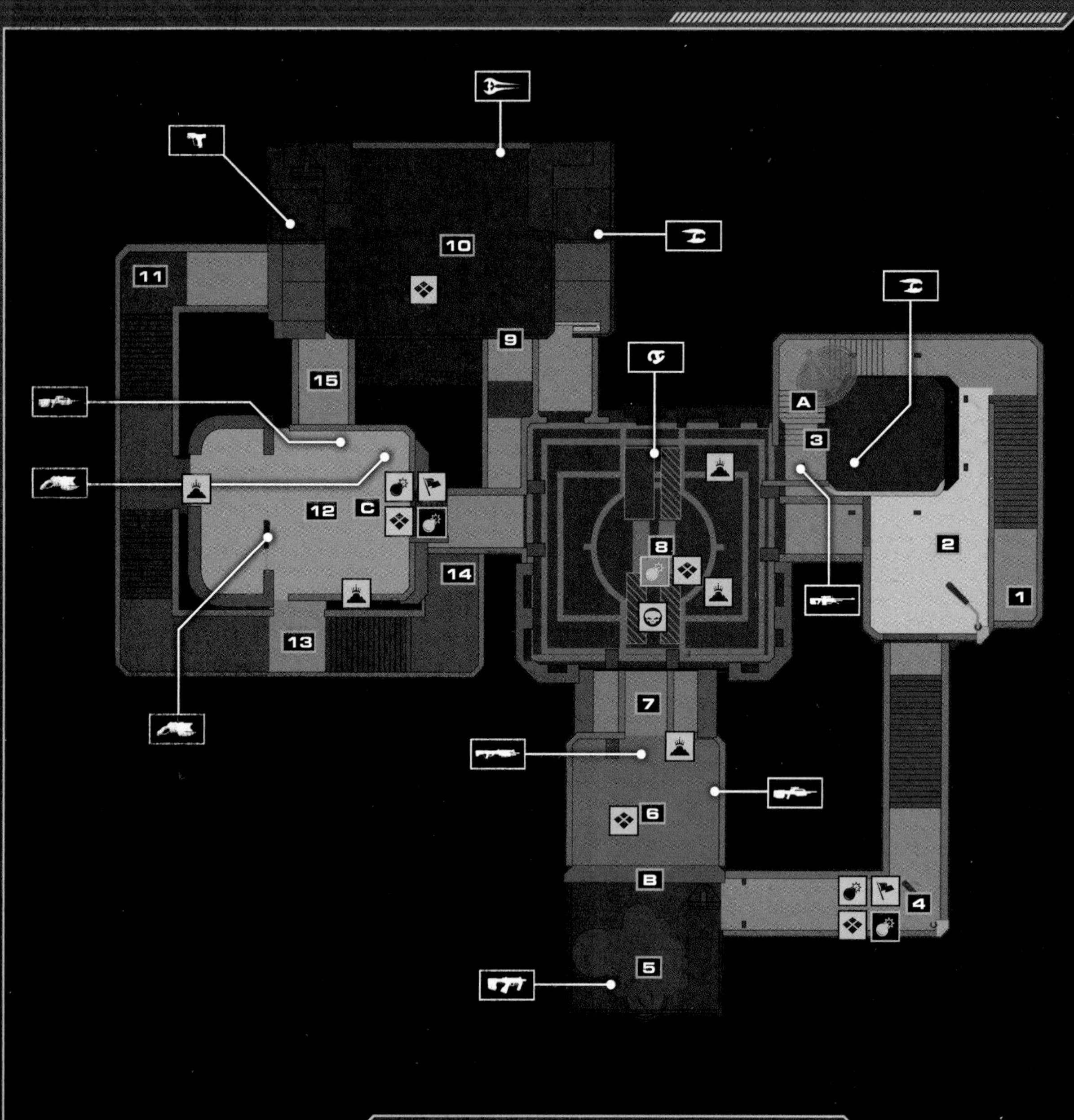

DATA STREAM

Recommended Game Variants: Team Slayer, CTF, Krazy King, Slayer, Oddball, One Bomb

Recommended/Maximum Number of Players: 2–8

Advantageous Equipment: Sniper, Sword, Shotgun

AVAILABLE EQUIPMENT AND GEAR RESPAWN TIMES

●○○○○ = Slow ●●●●● = Fast

Weapons	Respawn
Battle Rifle	●●●●○
Energy Sword	●●○○○
Grenade, Frag	●●●●●
Grenade, Plasma	●●●●●
Magnum	●●●●○

Weapons	Respawn
Plasma Pistol	●●●●○
Plasma Rifle	●●●●○
Shotgun	●○○○○
SMG	●●●●○
Sniper Rifle	●○○○○

Weapons	Respawn
Spiker	●●●●○
Equipment	
Bubble Shield	●●●○○
Power Drain	●●●○○
Regenerator	●●●○○

Topographical Overview

Call-out Locations

Snipe Tower

Other names: Sniper, S1, S2, S3

This tower is marked with blue painted lines on the outside. The sniper spawns at the top level, S2, which connects to Elbow and Bottom Mid.

Elbow

Other names: N/A

This is the L-shaped walkway that connects Bottom Red and S1.

Red Lift

Other names: Top Red, Bottom Red

Located across the map from Library, this building has a Red Lift (marked by red painted lines) that carries you to the second level and serves as a primary spawn point at the start of the map. On Top Red, the gray area outside the lift near Top Mid is referred to as Red Platform (Red Plat).

Red Platform/Shotty Underneath

Other names: Red Plat, Front Red

This is the gray area with one Battle Rifle in front of Top Red, located directly above Shotgun Spawn. The Shotgun Spawn is accessible only from Bottom Mid or Bottom Red. This small hallway is a death trap if you camp.

Middle

Other names: Top Mid, Bottom Mid

In the middle of the map, the square figure that connects BR Tower, Library, Snipe Tower, and Red Lift is known as Mid. The second level of Mid is known as Top Mid, and the lower level is Bottom Mid. Bottom Mid has a hole in the ground that drops you on top of Shotgun Spawn and leads to Bottom Red.

Sword

Other names: N/A

Located directly below Library, this confined area houses the Sword and connects to BR 1 and Lower Mid.

Library

Other names: N/A

Library is a primary spawn point at the start of the game. It is located across from Red Lift and contains two Plasma Grenades and a hole in the room's center that leads to Sword Spawn.

Battle Rifle Tower

Other names: BR Tower, BR 1 (first level), BR 2 (second level), BR 3 (third level), Back BR

▲ Back BR

▲ Third level

▲ Second level

▲ First level

Battle Rifle Tower is the tallest tower on the map and is made of three levels with yellow painted lines on the outside. Access this tower via the connector (Back BR) from Library, BR Ramp that runs along the entire building, Top Mid/Lower Mid, and Sword Room.

▲ BR Ramp

Zone Knowledge

There are three main towers within Blackout: Snipe Tower, BR Tower, and Red Lift. BR Tower and Snipe Tower consist of three levels. The BR Tower's bottom level, commonly referred to as BR 1, connects to Bottom Middle and to the small section housing the Sword. The second level of BR Tower, BR 2, connects to the Library (where you can drop down and pick up the Sword). It also has a ramp leading up to BR 3, the top and final level of the BR Tower. Positioning your team at the BR Tower allows the players to have a wide view of the entire map.

The Snipe Tower is also a very versatile spot on the map, as it houses three levels, similar to the BR Tower. The bottom level is Snipe One and connects to Bottom Mid, where you can drop down and pick up the Shotgun. You can also easily reach Red Lift by going through Elbow. The second level of the Snipe Tower is called Snipe Two and has a Bubble Shield, which is always useful. You can also see Top Middle, top of Red Lift, BR 2 and 3, and some of Library. Snipe Three, the uppermost level of the Snipe Tower, houses the Sniper Rifle. Be careful in Snipe Three, as there is an exploding crate directly next to the Sniper Rifle.

Red Lift consists of two levels, connected by a lift. On both sides of the lift, there are two platforms that you can reach by dropping down from the top of the lift. In the beginning of a Team Slayer match, one team usually spawns at the bottom of Red Lift, but it is not an advisable spot to set up in. Red Lift has a wide view of the open top middle, Snipe Tower, and BR Tower; however, you are very vulnerable here, as it is in perfect view of both main towers. But having one player at this spot can be very advantageous to a team, because they can kill or weaken any enemies who do not see Red Lift as a true threat.

Weapon Tactics

Sniper Rifle: Use a Sniper Rifle at BR 3 to help support your teammates throughout the map. There are not many power weapons on this map, so even if your team does not use a Sniper Rifle, it is wise to at least toss it over the ledge. This prevents your foes from using it.

Sword: Because Blackout has many small areas and levels stacked on top of one another, the Sword is great for dropping down on opponents or hiding in corners to surprise your enemy. Keep in mind that you must be very close to your teammate in order to attack with the Sword, so do not run across the map with your Sword out.

Shotgun: If you have to choose between the Shotgun and the Sword, take the Shotgun. Like the Sword, the Shotgun is most effective when used at close range. For a quick kill, add a beatdown after you take your shot—that is, use the Shotgun to shoot your enemy, then hit them with it to finish them off.

Enhanced Knowledge

In Blackout, whether you are on offense or defense, make sure your team has control over a crucial spot on the map. The most crucial spots are the Snipe Tower and the BR Tower.

Offense

- Power weapons like the Shotgun, Sword, and Sniper Rifle are your best offensive tools.
- After spawning, have one player go straight for the Shotgun and one player go for the Sniper Rifle. After obtaining both weapons, regroup with your team at Snipe Tower. Then, have the player with the Shotgun rush with another player to grab the Sword, while the other two players remain at Snipe Tower to clean up any enemies wandering in the open.
- When all power weapons are obtained, have the entire team "push" to wherever the enemies have set up camp. With all power weapons in your team's possession, the push should go smoothly and you should eliminate all opponents.
- Always have a sniper on the uppermost parts of the level (BR 3, S3) while the sneaky players who possess the close-range power weapons (Sword, Shotgun) ambush the enemies who are focused on your team's sniper.

Defense

- Power weapons are very important in a defensive setup. Rather than grabbing the power weapons and pushing the enemy's base, a defensive team should gain control of the weapons and hold a secure lockdown on whatever tower they set up on.
- Have two players go for the Shotgun and two players go for the Sniper Rifle. If you are successful in grabbing the Sniper Rifle, have your team set up at Snipe Tower; if you are unsuccessful in obtaining the Sniper Rifle, move your team back toward BR Tower.
- Be patient. If one of your teammates runs out and tries to kill four enemies on his own, your setup becomes vulnerable. Remember to wait for the other team to make a push and ambush them with your close-ranged power weapons.
- The Bubble Shield (located at the BR Ramp leading up to BR 3) and the Regenerator (located at the Snipe Ramp leading up to S3) are very useful in a defensive setup. If the enemy team attempts to rush your team, throwing down a Bubble Shield to regain your health can be lifesaving.

Professional Planning

- Blackout does not have any power-ups on the map, so the sniper and height advantage are key. Have one teammate with a Sniper Rifle on BR 3 while another teammate watches their back.
- Support your teammates on BR 3 by spacing out and creating a cross fire with a teammate at Red Lift and another at Library/BR 2.
- There is a set of spawn points located in each building on the map. By having teammates at Snipe and BR Towers, you force your opponent to spawn at Red Lift or Library. Use your knowledge of spawn locations to continue the "blanket of chaos," while the enemy spawns.

Objective Plotting

- In Capture the Flag (CTF), the flag spawns on Elbow. Although Red Lift is easily accessible, do *not* use it, even if you just killed your opponent. Your foe will probably spawn at Library or BR Tower, and once you go into Red Lift, there is only one exit, which makes you highly susceptible to Grenades. Instead, go from Snipe Tower to Top Mid and jump on the High Rails to BR 3 from Top Mid. Another option is to take Bottom Mid and then run the flag once you hit the BR Ramp.
- Even though running the flag is more efficient than just holding it, sometimes it's wise to take your time and ninja through the map and then start flag running when you are on the BR Ramp. If your teammate tries to distract the opponent, this strategy will most always allow you to cap.
- BR 1 is a great area to hold the oddball while another teammate with a Shotgun or Sword camps on the shelves lining the room. Take note: The Shotgun will almost always beat a player with the Sword.
- On defense during CTF, take advantage of the high ground around the flag like Top Red and Snipe Tower; even BR 3 has a decent view of Elbow. Once the opponent pulls the flag, you can easily close in on them and return the flag.

Sniping

Sniper Three

A

The sniper spawns at this level of Snipe Tower. You can see Elbow, Top Lift, all of Top Mid, BR 2 and 3, and Library Entrance. If enemies come up the lift, you can snipe them as they rise. BR 3 is open and makes it easy to kill enemies. Before you set up, blow up the fusion coils on S3.

Top Lift

B

Top Lift is pretty open, allowing you to see most of the map. Anyone rushing Top Mid or running on Elbow is an easy target. You can also see Snipe Three, Snipe Two, BR 3, the ramps leading to BR 3, and the inside of the Library.

BR 3

C

You can almost see the whole map from here. This position is good for killing opponents on Sniper Two, Sniper Three, and Top Lift and for killing anyone who is rushing Top Mid. Watch for the opposing team coming up behind you and trying to kill you. Also, don't stand directly next to the fusion coils on BR 3.

CITADEL

David S.J. Hodgson

In the heart of this Forerunner structure, far above the troubled surface of the Ark, another battle rages.

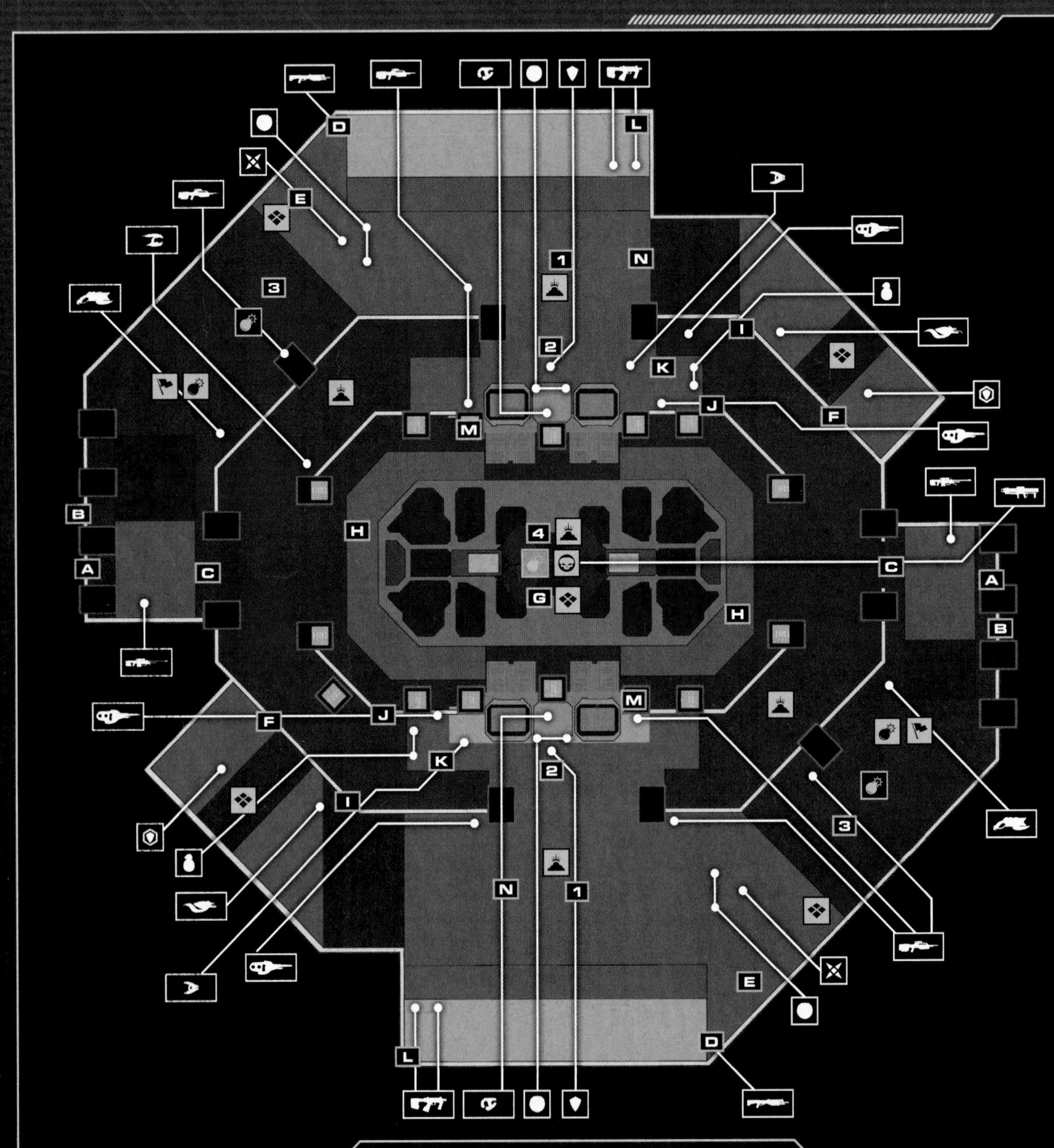

DATA STREAM

Recommended Game Variants: Infection, Juggernaut, King of the Hill, Slayer, Team Slayer, VIP

Recommended Number of Players: 2–6

Advantageous Equipment: Battle Rifle, Sniper Rifle, Rocket Launcher, Power Drain, Overshield, Bubble Shield

AVAILABLE EQUIPMENT AND GEAR RESPAWN TIMES

1 of 5 skulls = Slow 5 of 5 skulls = Fast

Weapons	Respawn
Battle Rifle	4/5
Brute Shot	1/5
Carbine	2/5
Grenade, Frag	1/5
Grenade, Plasma	5/5
Needler	2/5

Weapons	Respawn
Plasma Pistol	2/5
Plasma Rifle	5/5
Rocket Launcher	1/5
Shotgun	1/5
SMG	5/5
Spiker	5/5

Weapons	Respawn
Sniper Rifle	1/5
Equipment	
Bubble Shield	2/5
Overshield	1/5
Power Drain	3/5

Topographical Overview

Call-Out Locations

Base

Other names: loft, deck, upper base, yellow/red base, blue base

The red and blue bases are mirror images of each other and are set apart on opposite sides of the map. The "base" in question is comprised of an upper platform with a slightly raised rear section. To the rear are SMGs and a ramp down to the raised area **3** that allows for quick ambushes from behind. Otherwise, there's a second ramp to the raised area, open areas from the platform down to ground level and the Overshield corridor **2**, and the Rocket Launcher area **4**. Note that you can see all the way across to the opposite base, making this map somewhat hectic.

Ramp Archway and Raised Area

Other names: arch, ramp, (with "yellow/red" or "blue" prefix)

At the narrower edges at each end of the map is a raised area with a total of three ramps. There is also an open area where you can easily drop down to access either Overshield corridor **2** or the Rocket Launcher area **4**. Locating yourself here usually means you wish to lurk in the shadows or crouch on the sloping roof supports or the light above the archway so you can ambush or snipe foes; from here, you have extremely good line of sight to one of the bases, both Overshield corridors, and the Rocket Launcher area. You can easily escape, too. There are two ramps, both leading to the same base.

Overshield Corridors

Other names: OS, shield spawn, shield corridor, corridor (with "yellow/red" or "blue" prefix)

Running parallel on either side of the Rocket Launcher area **4** are two identical Overshield corridors, which provide the other main hot spot of activity and are a choke point for such a small map. With weaponry at one end and an Overshield toward the middle, this is one of the first locations where players normally head but one that is likely to be heavily sniped, too. At either end of the corridor is a raised area **3** and a side ramp leading up to one of the bases. You can drop down from (or Grenade-jump up to) the base area from here, too. The sloped pillars and columns also make excellent ambush points. The corridor is open along the inside wall, allowing access into the Rocket Launcher area **4**.

Rocket Launcher Area

Other names: middle, platform, platty

The location where the most deaths usually take place is in the middle of the map and is the only location without a mirror image (as it is centrally located). A platform with ramps on either side and with a Rocket Launcher resting on it can be accessed from the entrance at either end of this open corridor (which offers great sniping opportunities from the raised area **3**), from either Overshield corridor **2**, or from the platform at either base **1**. Basically, this is a heavily trafficked and highly dangerous area, complete with an equally dangerous prize.

Zone Knowledge

Base and Raised Platform Vicinity

▲ The base and raised platform vicinity, where professional players tend to hide and snipe from.

▲ The Overshield corridor and rocket launcher vicinity, where the foolhardy player attempts to grab powerful items and fails.

This is a symmetrical map with even weapon distribution. There are balconies on each base that overlook the central chamber. These balconies are often used to snipe opposing bases, which is encouraged. As there are two ramps accessing each base, players can also jump from the central chamber to enter either base. The Overshield corridor simply has too many exits to make it safe for longer than a second or two, but rush for either shield if you really need it. More savvy players are likely to cut you down from an ambush point before you reach it. The central platform with the Rocket Launcher on it is even more dangerous, although you can flee into either base or Overshield corridor from this position. An early rush to the Rocket Launcher is better than a late one, as opponents have less time to set up ambush points.

In an elongated L-shape that only reaches ground level at the archway door, the raised platform and base area run around this map's perimeter. This area is perfect for two teams of two to secure and patrol, cutting down enemies as they try to locate the Power Drain, Overshield, or Rocket Launcher. If you have one of your team roaming the area—don't get close to the Overshields, which are a great lure to leave available for a hapless foe, before cutting them down prior to them reaching the power-up—the other can locate a favorite sniping or ambush point and provide covering fire for the other. There are many ambush points; we've shown all the best ones, which you should use to cut down enemies, firing on them while they're still trying to figure out where the damage is coming from.

Enhanced Knowledge

Offensive and Defensive Posturing

- During single-player matches, the bases are the preferred places to be. Your battle plan should involve grabbing the Rocket Launcher immediately so you can achieve some multikills at the beginning of the match. When you're inside either base, use a Battle Rifle or Carbine to snipe foes, but also make good use of Grenades to weaken players as they attempt to usurp you from this powerful position by rushing the ramps on either side. Also be aware of the explosive Power Cores (aka blue fusion coils); these can be used against you if you're standing too close to them. However, you shouldn't simply detonate them; instead, keep away from the Cores, and blast them as foes enter the base, turning them into traps.
- The Overshields beneath both bases are extremely useful; grab them to prevent others picking them up and when you're low on shields. Naturally, you're likely to be walking into an ambush, so prepare yourself!
- You can snipe from base to base using Battle Rifles or Carbines that are available without you needing to find them; they are available at the beginning of the match. There are also multiple alcoves on either side of each base (many of which are detailed in the "Sniping/Ambush Positions" section) that should be utilized and jumped on, so you have firing opportunities on base entrances.
- Although scattered about, the compact nature of this map means that every weapon is useful. Consult the "Arms and Equipment" chapter for specific advice on using each armament. Aside from sniping down an entire corridor, there's not many long-range takedown opportunities, meaning usually overlooked weapons work well, too.
- There's no Active Camo on this map, but the dark shadows work almost as well; holing up in an alcove with a sniper with a great view and no blind spots can really help your cause.
- Are enemies consistently staying in bases and annoying you? Utilize the Power Drain to weaken these foes, and eventually take the base's advantageous positions yourself.
- You don't need to dash up ramps to reach a base; you can jump from your base to the Rocket Launcher platform, and across to the opposite base with a swift series of leaps. This may be dangerous, so check for foes, first!

Professional Planning

- In team games, the most important strategy is to keep together and avoid heading into the central chamber with the Rocket Launcher, unless you are grabbing the weapon or an Overshield; then retreat back to the base or raised platform area. Staying in the center leaves you or your team extremely vulnerable to multiple incoming Grenades, Carbine sniping from foes, or Battle Rifle takedowns from your enemies.
- In all game types, it helps to learn the respawn times of the power-ups and power weapons on the map. Learn when you should run for that Rocket Launcher and when to drop from your base to grab an Overshield—on your side or your enemies'.
- The Overshield makes an electronic sound when it respawns. Listen for this to help time visits to the Overshield hall.

Objective Planning

- This map is best suited for King of the Hill, Slayer or Team Slayer, Juggernaut, Oddball, VIP, and Infection; due to the Overshield placements, players can easily exploit the power-ups in games like Capture the Flag and Assault.
- Employ the Bubble Shield in various game types, such as Oddball, Juggernaut, and VIP.
- Infection: You can use some of the alcoves on either side of each base to make it much more difficult for zombies to reach them. On the upper platform of either base, move past the power cores (fusion coils) to the two side windows. Carefully crouch-jump on top of the nearest center wall support (see location **J**).
- Forge: Variant 1—Block off the central portion of the map with walls and energy blockers, creating a multitiered set of "racing tracks." Then use spawned Mongoose vehicles on this map during VIP games to reach Rally Points.
- Forge: Variant 2—For a more challenging game of Capture the Flag or Assault, block off the upper platform base openings that are accessed from the Rocket Launcher platform. Move the Flag and Bomb destination point into the center of each base, allowing for easier defense.
- Forge: Variant 3—Try using "man cannons" to link certain sections of the map for quicker access. From the Sniper Rifle spawn points, place man cannons so they are facing the opposite Sniper Rifle spawn. This sends players flying over the central Rocket Launcher. You can also use man cannons to link the upper levels of the two bases.

Sniping/Ambush Positions

Archway Perimeter Wall

Easily accessed via a jump from the ramp, this offers particularly good coverage of the Rocket Launcher platform, although you can't see the right side of the level. Periodically look left for enemies accessing this area from the perimeter ramps or jumping from the Overshield corridor to the raised floor you're close to.

Perimeter Sloped Roof Edge

Accessed via a Grenade Jump or Brute Shot, this offers many of the advantages of sniping location **A** but with the added benefit that your opponents may not be expecting you to be crouched above any of the windows in the raised area. With horizontal pivoting, you can cover both ramps and the ground level below, but views across the interior of the Rocket Launcher area are limited.

Archway Light

A difficult Brute Shot Jump, using a teammate, is the better way of reaching this cunning hiding spot. Although there's not much room to move, there's a whole lot of time to catch a foe running through the archway and ambush them from behind. You can turn right and take down foes on the raised area as well, since they won't initially know where you're hidden.

In the Shadows

This is one example of taking up a defensive position in some of the more shadowy locations of this map. Place yourself by the ramp leading up to the rear of the base, and you have a great view across one entire end of the map. You can tag anyone leaping up to the raised area without them spotting you, or even those taking either ramp down from the base.

Power Drain Ramp

Edging forward from sniping point **D**, you can guard the Power Drain and ambush enemies who are drawn to this item. You need to watch your back and the enemies heading down the ramp from the rear of the base, but otherwise, this raised area and the nearby columns allow you to prowl and quickly reach cover while your foe flounders attempting to reach the raised area.

Perimeter Ramp Overlooking Overshield

At the edge of the perimeter ramp that leads up to the base and the Overshield corridor, this offers great views of the Overshield and provides access and views of the ramp to your right, so you can swiftly deal with foes in either location. However, watch for attacks from the left.

Rocket Launcher Platform

G

Standing here results in a short and frantic life, but if you're armed with the Rocket Launcher, you can quickly take down any foe with a single, well-placed shot. The trick is to grab the Rocket Launcher and leave the area immediately, as there are too many locations from which you can be struck.

Sloped Pillar (Main Entrance)

H

Using the Brute Shot or Grenades, blast yourself up to the top of this sloping pillar or any identical pillar that surrounds the main central chamber. This pillar is a good choice, as you can snipe the raised area, the ground, and the Rocket Launcher area from this spot, or the pillar to the right on the other side of the main entrance.

Overshield Side Column

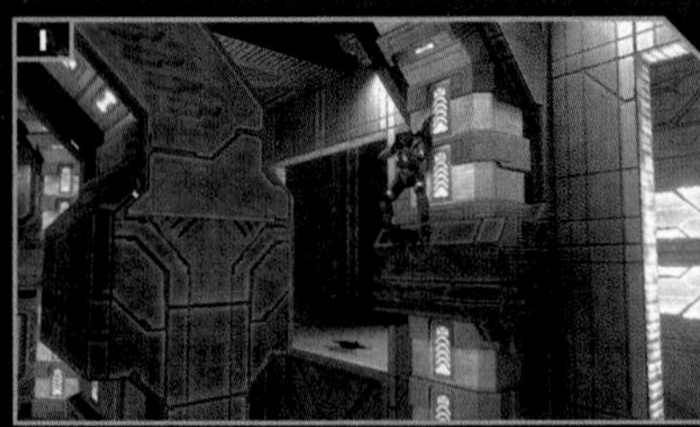
I

Above the Overshield corridor is the column and others like it. If you're spotted, you can quickly escape to the side ramp leading to the base, but this position, high in the eaves, allows you to ambush foes below you.

Overshield Sloped Pillar (Window)

J

Squeezing in just under the ceiling, access this sloping area (there is an identical point on each side of the base) above the Overshield corridor by carefully jumping from the gap by the window. You can maneuver around this entire sloped area, from the windows to the pillars. From here, watch foes dropping down from the base or heading along the corridor below before you ambush or snipe them.

Base: Platform Upper Deck

K

Expect heavy combat on this upper deck, which is the main part of your and your foe's base. It is always under contention no matter what mode of play you choose. When holding this prized location in team games, your height advantage plays an important role in both offensive and defensive activities. Players generally pass through the base's upper deck before combat begins over the Rocket Launcher. This location then becomes a critical defensive or ambush point: Watch for attacks from the ramps to the side and behind you by standing atop the ramps; you have the advantage over adversaries running up the side ramps, jumping from the Rocket Launcher platform, or running under the Overshield corridor. The importance of this location cannot be overstated!

Base: Back Wall and Corner

L

The back wall is a decent sniping position, with rear access to the sniper ramp and a Shotgun waiting nearby. A sniper can fire shots across the map into the other base from here, using both the crates in the middle of the base and the nearby pillars for cover. Grabbing the nearby Shotgun offers some protection from an ambush coming from the ramps on the sides.

If you move to the corners and sneak back here, you can also tag foes heading up from the side ramps and those milling about in the middle Rocket Launcher area or opposite base. Watch for foes moving toward you from the right side, heading up from the raised area.

Base: Sloped Pillar

M

This is a strong position for midranged combat, but mind the ledges: Standing on the glass floors exposes you to several lines of sight. Stand back from the ledge and control the center of the map with a Battle Rifle or a Carbine. Climb up the inside of the sloped pillar to protect yourself if you're getting overwhelmed by opposing fire and Grenades. Approach the ledge only if you plan to jump down for the Overshield or Rocket Launcher or plan to escape from opponents inside the base. The window to the left offers a strong sight line and another opportunity to escape if necessary.

Base: Crates

N

These moveable objects can quickly be positioned as cover if you're ambushed from the ramps leading to the upper deck. If you have snipers hanging out against the back wall, they can briefly crouch behind the crates and use them as cover. Similarly, a player can throw a Grenade at one side of a crate before ducking around the other side, creating a trap for would-be ambushers. Plan these types of tactics around the base crates, as a lot of combat occurs around them.

COLD STORAGE

PMS Ruin, PMS Dark Ivory, PMS Jezabelle

Deep in the bowels of Installation 05, things have gotten a little out of hand. I hope you packed extra underwear.

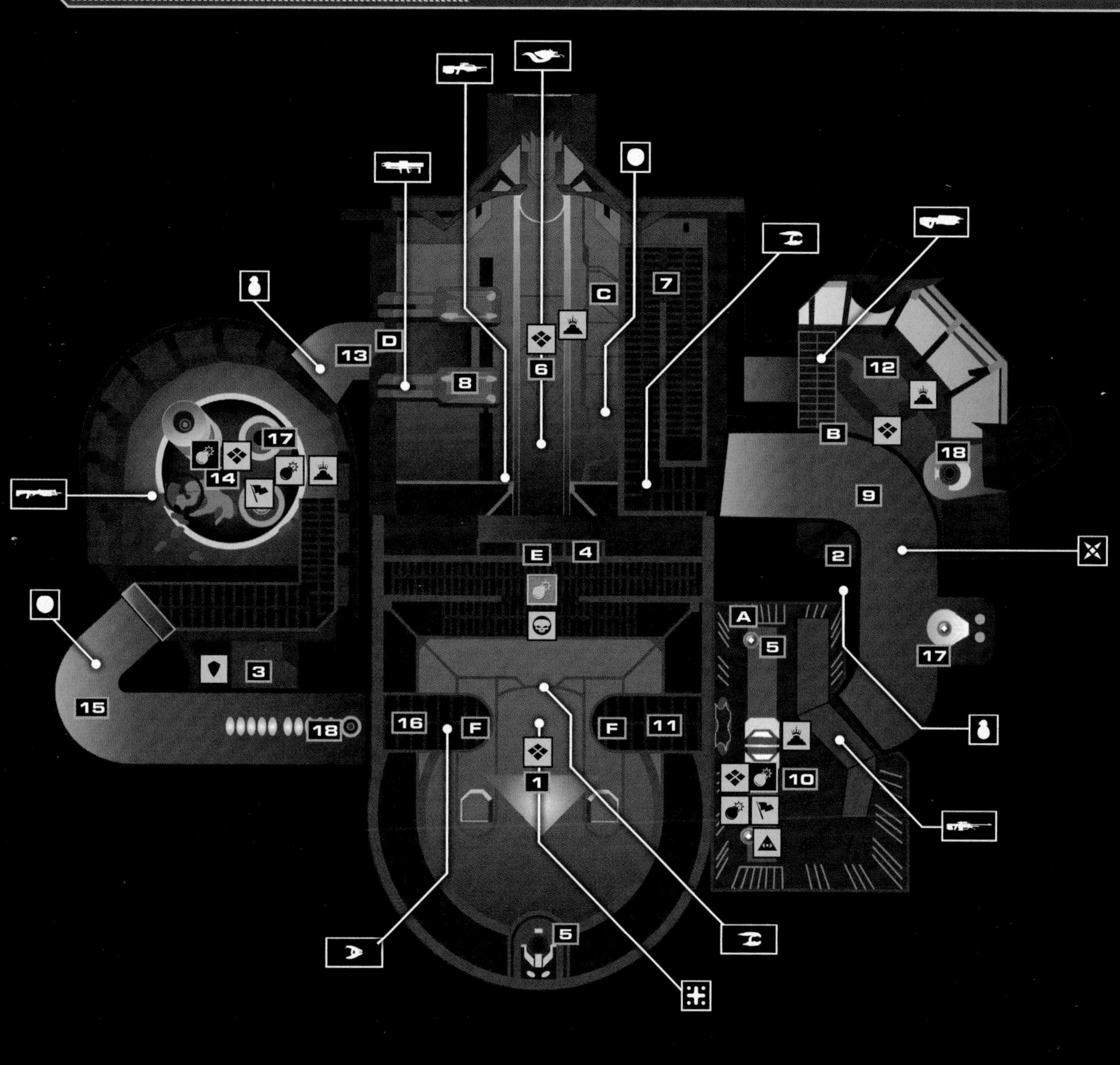

DATA STREAM

Recommended Game Variants: Team Slayer, Team Swat, King of the Hill

Recommended/Maximum Number of Players: 4/10

Advantageous Equipment: Rocket Launcher, Sniper Rifle, Shotgun, Power Drain

AVAILABLE EQUIPMENT AND GEAR RESPAWN TIMES

●○○○○ = Slow ●●●●● = Fast

Weapons		
	Assault Rifle	●●●●●
	Battle Rifle	●●●●●
	Grenade, Frag	●●●●●
	Grenade, Plasma	●●●●●
	Needler	●●●○○

Weapons		
	Plasma Rifle	●●●●●
	Rocket Launcher	●●○○○
	Shotgun	●●○○○
	Sniper Rifle	●●○○○

Equipment		
	Active Camo	●○○○○
	Bubble Shield	●●●○○
	Overshield	●○○○○
	Power Drain	●●●○○
	Regenerator	●●●○○

Topographical Overview

Cold Storage is a large building of interlocking rooms connected by ramps, corridors, and teleporters.

Call-out Locations

Main Room

Other names: N/A

1

This is the biggest room, with two protruding ledges, two standing pillars, and a teleporter.

High Ledge

Other names: N/A

4

You can walk on this wall, which separates Main Room and Rocket Room.

Yellow Hallway

Other names: N/A

2

The walkway on the floor from Main Room to Yellow Room.

Camo Teleporter

Other names: N/A

5

This teleporter is located in Main Room and takes you to Camo Room.

OS Hallway

Other names: N/A

3

Walkway from the Main Room to OS.

Rocket Room

Other names: N/A

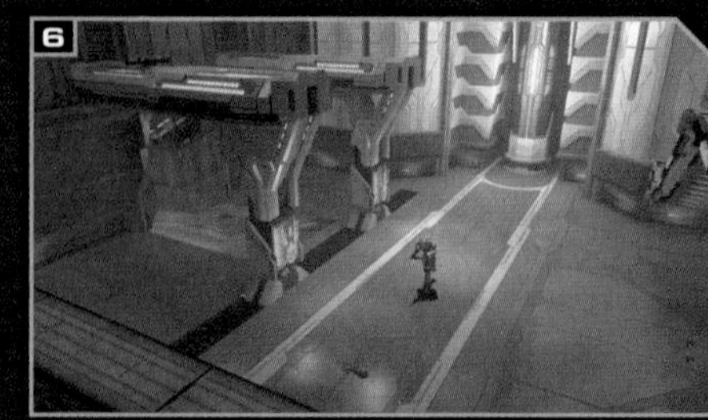
6

This is across from Main Room, separated by High Ledge. Contains one elevating ramp and two pillars holding up a ledge.

Rocket Ramp

Other names: N/A

The only ramp in Rocket Room that leads to Pink Hallway.

Rocket Ledge

Other names: Rockets

This ledge is being held up by two pillars. Rockets are located here.

Pink Hallway

Other names: Window

This is the walkway leading from Rocket Ramp to Camo Room. Also called the Window due to the opening that drops to Yellow Room.

Camo Room

Other names: Sniper

This is a small upper-level room that you can access by Camo Teleporter or Pink Hall.

Camo Ledge

Other names: N/A

This is the protruding balcony-like structure connected to Camo Room. It hangs into the Main Room.

Yellow Room

Other names: Pink Room

This is a small lower-level room that is gold in color and houses a teleporter to Needler Hallway. Accessible through Yellow Hall, Pink Hall Drop, and Rocket Hall.

Rocket Hall

Other names: N/A

This is a lower-level walkway leading to Yellow Room from Rocket Room.

Shotgun Room

Other names: Shotty, Shotty Room

This is a lower-level room located on the opposite side of Yellow Room. Contains a glass flood pod, remnants of another

Needler Hallway

Other names: N/A

This is the wrapping walkway from Shotty Room to Needle Ledge.

Needle Ledge

Other names: N/A

This balcony-like structure is directly connected to Needle Hall and hangs over the Main Room.

Shotty Teleporter

Other names: N/A

This teleporter is located in Pink Hall which takes you to Shotty Room.

Needler Teleporter

Other names: N/A

This teleporter is located in Yellow Room and takes you to Needle Hall.

TIP **As with any *Halo 3* map, controlling the power weapons will assist you in clearing any groups of players coming to attack. Rockets can damage larger groups of opponents in one round. Try to acquire the Shotgun for use when running through the corridors and hallways.**

Enhanced Knowledge

Team Slayer

Staying in the top rooms makes it harder for enemies to attack. With your team controlling the upper levels, your focus of attack is narrowed to corridors and teleporters. A group favorite is the Camo Room. The Camo Room contains a Sniper Rifle, and you can easily control the only two entry points: through the Pink Hall or via the teleporter from Main Room. Someone can situate themselves against the wall of the teleporter and clean up any foe with a single melee. The Pink Hall's drop into Yellow Room can assist in any heavy attacks and pushes by the opposing team.

If the other team is already camped in Camo Room, equip one player with the Power Drain and jump from Needle Ledge to Camo Ledge, deploying the Power Drain before they fall. You can also do this with any Grenades to dish out damage to the camping team. Once you've dealt some damage remotely, send two people through the teleporter and one through the hall to attack. Coordination is key.

Professional Planning

- Keep an eye on all teleporters, as players can be blindsided coming through them. Quick shots can easily confuse anyone pushing through.
- You can easily launch Power Drains from above into almost every room. Then your team can just move in for cleanup kills.

Objective Plotting

King of the Hill

Camp the ledges around the hill for teammate support. Keep only one person on the hill at all times, ideally equipped with a Bubble Shield and a Shotgun.

Advanced Tactics

Post your team in Camo Room. With easy access to major power weapons and few entry points, you can easily rush down to grab Rockets and head back to support your team. Have one person set up with a Sniper Rifle and focus on the Needle Ledge, as this is a popular jump site due to the teleporter access.

Sniping

Camo Camp

Stand behind the teleporter exit in the Camo Room to easily melee and assassinate any players traveling through.

Pink Hall

There's a small crack in the wall of Pink Hallway through which you can drop down into Yellow Room. Squeeze through and jump down onto unaware players.

Ramp Camp

You can hide under any of the ramps that lead into a room. This is another easy way to score quick assassinations.

Rocket Camp

In between the two pillars making up the Rocket Ledge is a doorway leading to Camo Hall. The doorway's entrance protrudes just enough for you to stand on. Just look down and wait for players to walk through, or stay put for surprise attacks on players entering the Rocket Room.

High Ledge Camp

High Ledge is located in the middle of the map and high above any possible attacks by foes with Frag Grenades. This location makes for a unique ambush point when equipped with any mid- to long-range weapons, such as the Battle Rifle, Sniper, Rockets.

Ledge Jumping

There are many ledges that you can use for a high attack or a melee ambush. These include the Rocket Ledge , Needle Ledge, Camo Ledge, and High Ledge.

CONSTRUCT

PMS Ruin, PMS Dark Ivory, PMS Jezabelle

Vast quantities of water and other raw materials are consumed in creating even the smallest orbital installations.

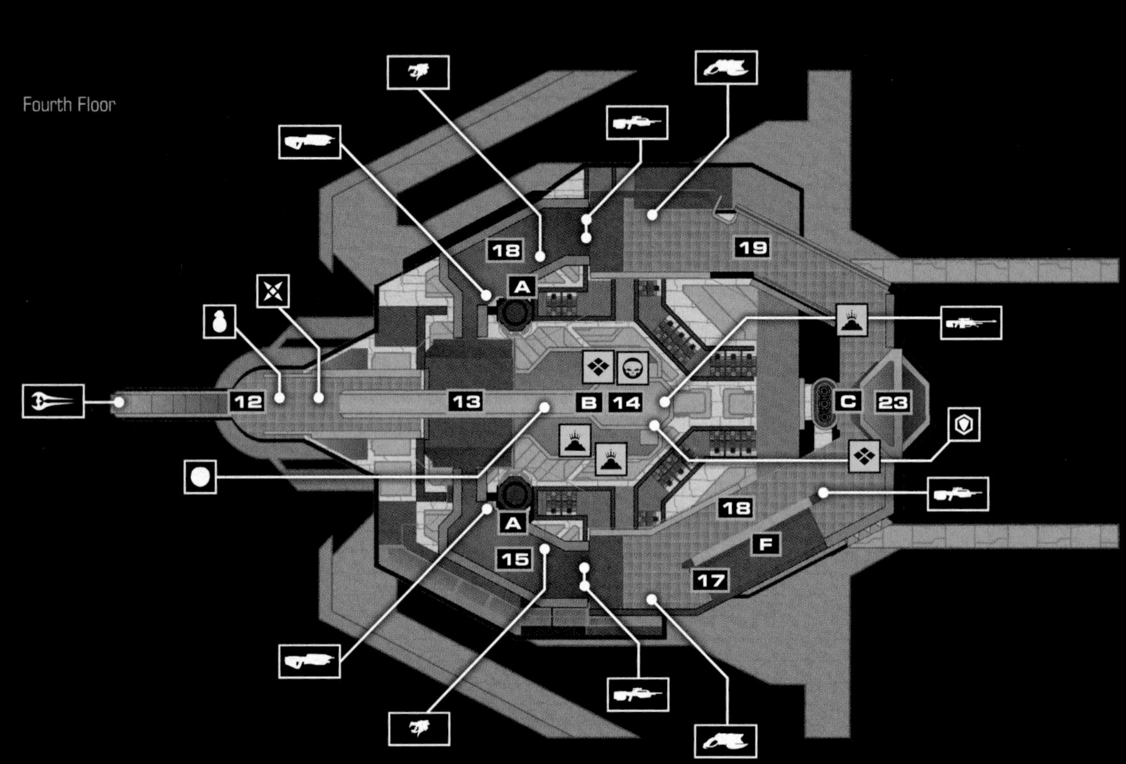

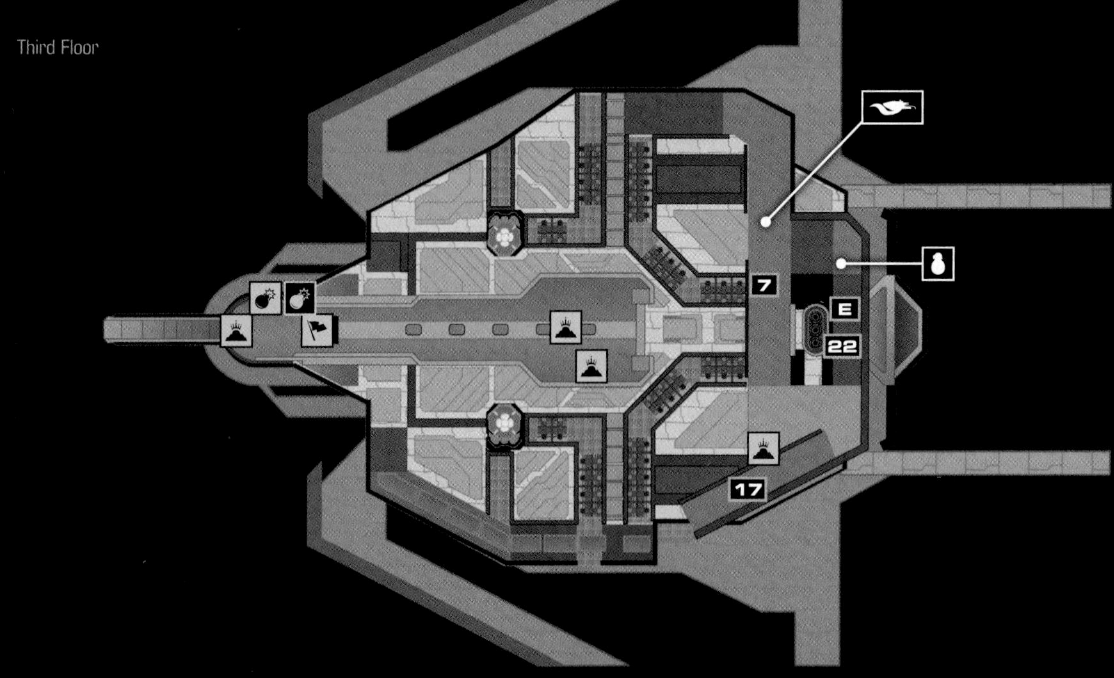

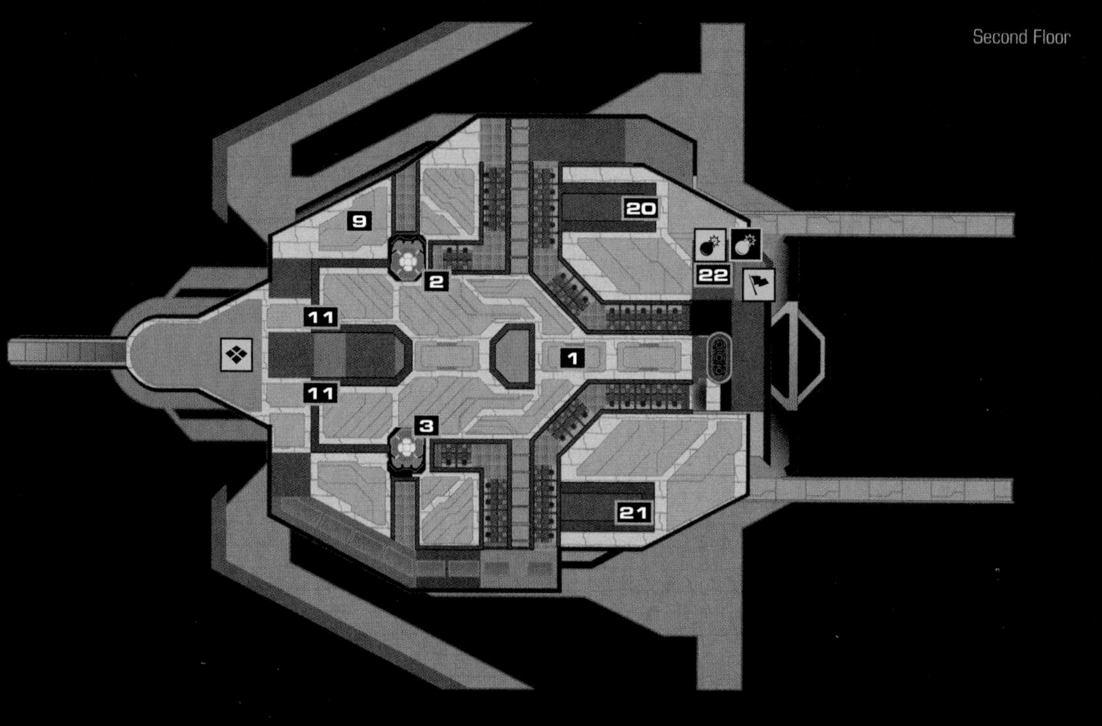

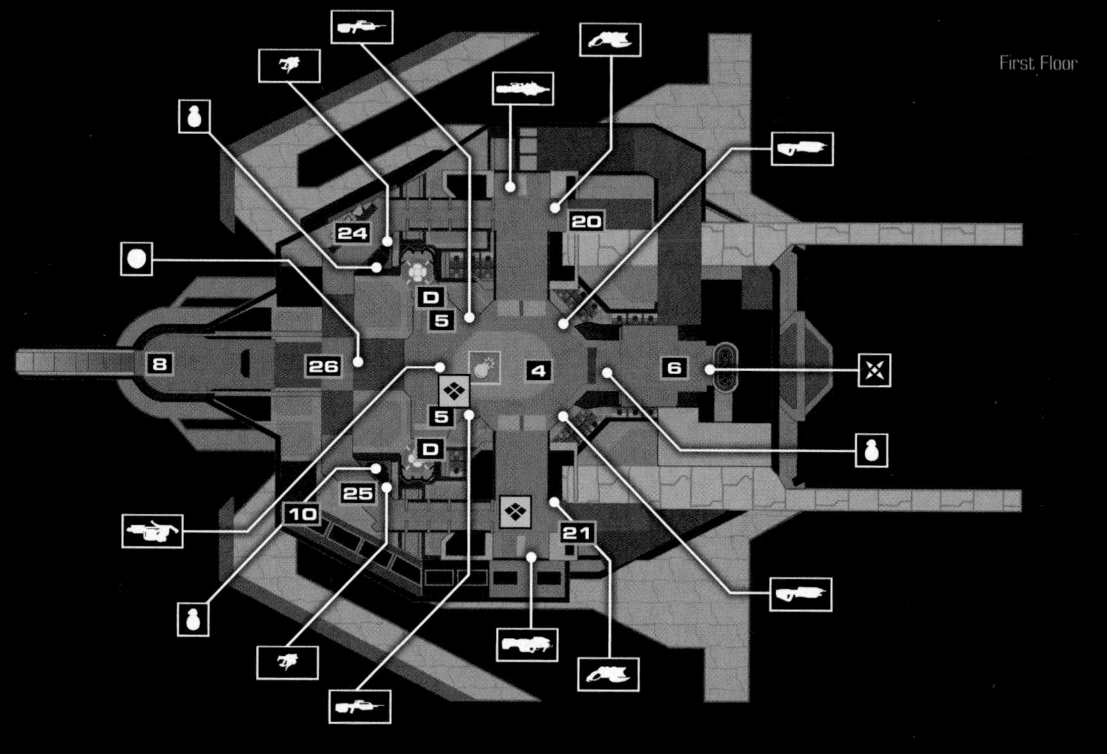

DATA STREAM

Recommended Game Variants: Team Slayer, King of the Hill, Team Snipers

Recommended/Maximum Number of Players: 4/10

Advantageous Equipment: Sniper Rifle, Mauler, Laser, Sword

AVAILABLE EQUIPMENT AND GEAR RESPAWN TIMES

●○○○○ = Slow ●●●●● = Fast

Weapons	Respawn
Assault Rifle	●●●●○
Battle Rifle	●●●●○
Brute Shot	●●●●○
Energy Sword	●○○○○
Flamethrower	●●○○○
Grenade, Frag	●●●●●

Weapons	Respawn
Grenade, Plasma	●●●●●
Mauler	●●●●○
Missile Pod	●●○○○
Plasma Pistol	●●●●○
Sniper Rifle	●○○○○
Spartan Laser	●●○○○

Weapons	Respawn
Spiker	●●●●○
Equipment	
Bubble Shield	●●●○○
Power Drain	●●●○○

Topographical Overview

Construct is a large trilevel circular map with lifts, ramps, and long walkways.

Call-out Locations

Open Mid

Other names: Mid Map, Open Floor, Floor

Starting spawn point for all Slayer games. This is the largest open area in Construct and makes up the entire second floor. This area contains a hole that drops to the lower level.

C2

Other names: Closed Floor

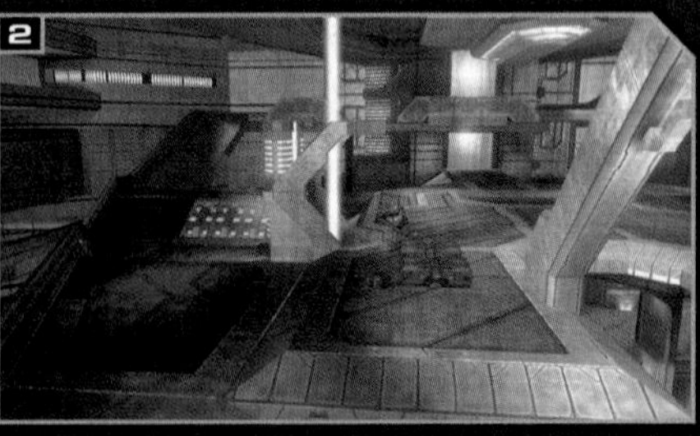

Located on Open Mid, C2 is the area surrounding the lift to Closed Side.

O2

Other names: Open Floor

Located at Open Mid, opposite of C2. This location consists of the area around the lift to Open Side.

Basement

Other names: Bottom

This is accessible from the drop at Open Mid. Basement is the bottom of the map, with entrances to the third floor via Gold Lift and Open and Closed Lifts. There is a single entrance to the second floor via Main Ramp.

C1/01

Other names: N/A

This is the bottom area surrounding each of the lifts. C1 is the closed side, and 01 is the open side.

Gold 1

Other names: Bottom Gold, Bottom Yellow, Yellow 1

This is the area surrounding the Gold Lift in the Basement.

Gold 2

Other names: Mid Gold, Mid Yellow, Yellow 2

This is the walkway and entrance to Gold from Open Mid. It is an elevated ramp.

Patio

Other names: Back Porch, Sniper

The Patio is a large flattened structure directly connecting the River and Upstream as well as the Ramp to the Basement.

Upstream

Other names: N/A

This is the walkway that curves around C2 from the Patio up to Back Gold.

River

Other names: N/A

This is the walkway that curves under O2 from the Patio.

Legs

Other names: Shortcut to Sword

These are the two large pillarlike beams that begin on Open Mid near the lifts that stretch into the third floor in Sword Room.

Sword Room

Other names: N/A

Sword Room is located on the third level and hangs directly above the Patio. You can access the Sword here, which has an entrance from the Legs or Lobby.

Lobby

Other names: Glass Room

The Lobby is the small glass lines structure directly across from the Gold Lift. The Lobby has entrances to C3, O3, and Sniper.

Sniper

Other names: N/A

This is a hanging elongated structure from Lobby. It contains an upper and lower level—S1 is the bottom, and S2 is the top, where you actually cover Sniper.

O3

Other names: Open Purple

This is the topmost level, which you can reach from Open Lift. O3 has entrances to the Lobby and Open Street.

Open Street

Other names: N/A

Open Street is the large walkway extending to the Gold Lift from O3.

Open Ramp

Other names: N/A

This ramp connects Back Gold to Open Street.

C3

Other names: Closed Purple

C3 is a small upper-level room you can reach from the Closed Side Lift. Accessible from Lobby and Closed Street.

Closed Street

Other names: N/A

This is a large walkway wrapping from C3 to Gold Lift. Closed Street contains one small drop hole that you can use to escape fire.

Missile Ramp

Other names: "Down" to Missile

This ramp leads from Open Mid to Basement. Located on Closed Side with a missile pod at the bottom/Basement side.

Laser Ramp

Other names: "Down" to Laser

This ramp leads to Basement from Open Mid. Located on the Open Side of the map, it has a laser at the bottom/Basement side.

Back Gold

Other names: Gold Ramp

The territory for this ramp begins at Open Mid and wraps around the back of Gold Lift.

Gold 3

Other names: Top Gold, Top Yellow, Yellow 3, Y3, G3

The topmost area of Gold Lift. Top Gold is accessible from Closed and Open Street and from Gold Lift.

Missile Hall

Other names: Closed Hall

This corridor begins at the missile pod that stretches to the bottom of Main Ramp.

Laser Hall

Other names: Open Hall

This corridor begins at the base of Laser Ramp and stretches to the bottom of Main Ramp.

Main Ramp

Other names: Ramp

This centrally located ramp in the Basement takes you directly to the Patio.

Tactical I

Try to quickly move your team to the map's top level to gain and keep control. In any map, hanging around below gives your opponent easy attacks. In some locations, the opponent doesn't even have to drop down to begin attacking you. There are plenty of Battle Rifles scattered around, which make it easy to attack from across the map; for example, you can fire from Open to Closed Side, down each street, and from Open or Closed Street to Open Mid.

Enhanced Knowledge

Professional Planning

- Always team-shoot opponents, whether they're doubled up in streets or in C3/O3.
- Throw Grenades at the back edges of the streets to bounce into C3/O3 and Back Gold.
- From Closed/Open Street, frequently look down the lifts at Open Mid. Lifts leave players vulnerable, because they are translucent. Be aware and you'll be able to call out every opponent riding lifts.

Objective Plotting

King of the Hill

Keep an eye on the game clock. During Krazy King, the hill will move every 30 seconds, and it will do so randomly. The same goes for Team King, except the hill will move every minute.

Advanced Tactics

Keep a teammate in every lift, with one rotating the street from Top Gold to C3/O3 (whichever side you choose to post up on).

By camping the lifts, you give your team the advantage in applying quick combat. Riding lifts leaves you slightly blinded until you get firmly situated back on the ground. Since every lift has the same drop zone, a planted Grenade or Power Drain (on Top Gold) can damage larger groups of players rushing the lifts.

Sniping

Lift Camper

Squat down in each of the top lifts to easily kill any approaching players from the lift.

Sniper Spawn

Since the sniper is centrally located on the map, it makes shooting into Open and Closed Street easy, with plenty of room to drop down and avoid fire.

Gold Camping

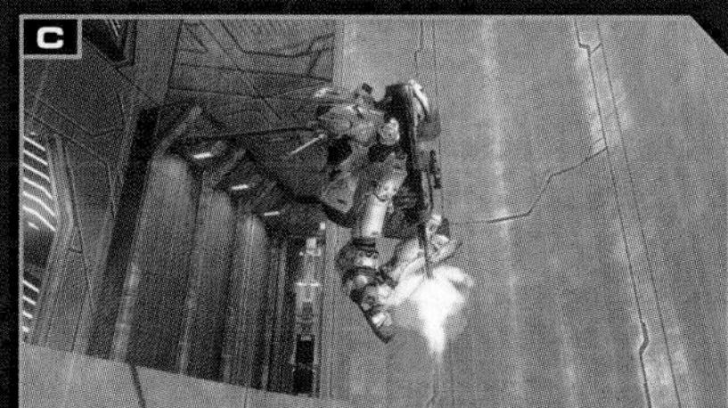

Jump into the Gold Lift on Top Gold. Anyone who attempts to take the lift can be shot at approximately two times. Try a melee to make an easy kill afterward.

Battery Lift

From C1/O1, you can push the batteries up the lift into the third level. When followed by a Frag Grenade, the

Nade Toss

From Back Gold, you can bounce a Frag Grenade off the wall up to Gold 3 to cause damage and clean up kills.

Window Walk

There's a small ledge on the windowpanes of Open Ramp. You can perch up here and attack players coming up and down the ramp and

EPITAPH

PMS Solincia, PMS Serenity yo

Some believe the Forerunners preferred desolate places. Others suggest that few other sites survived the Flood.

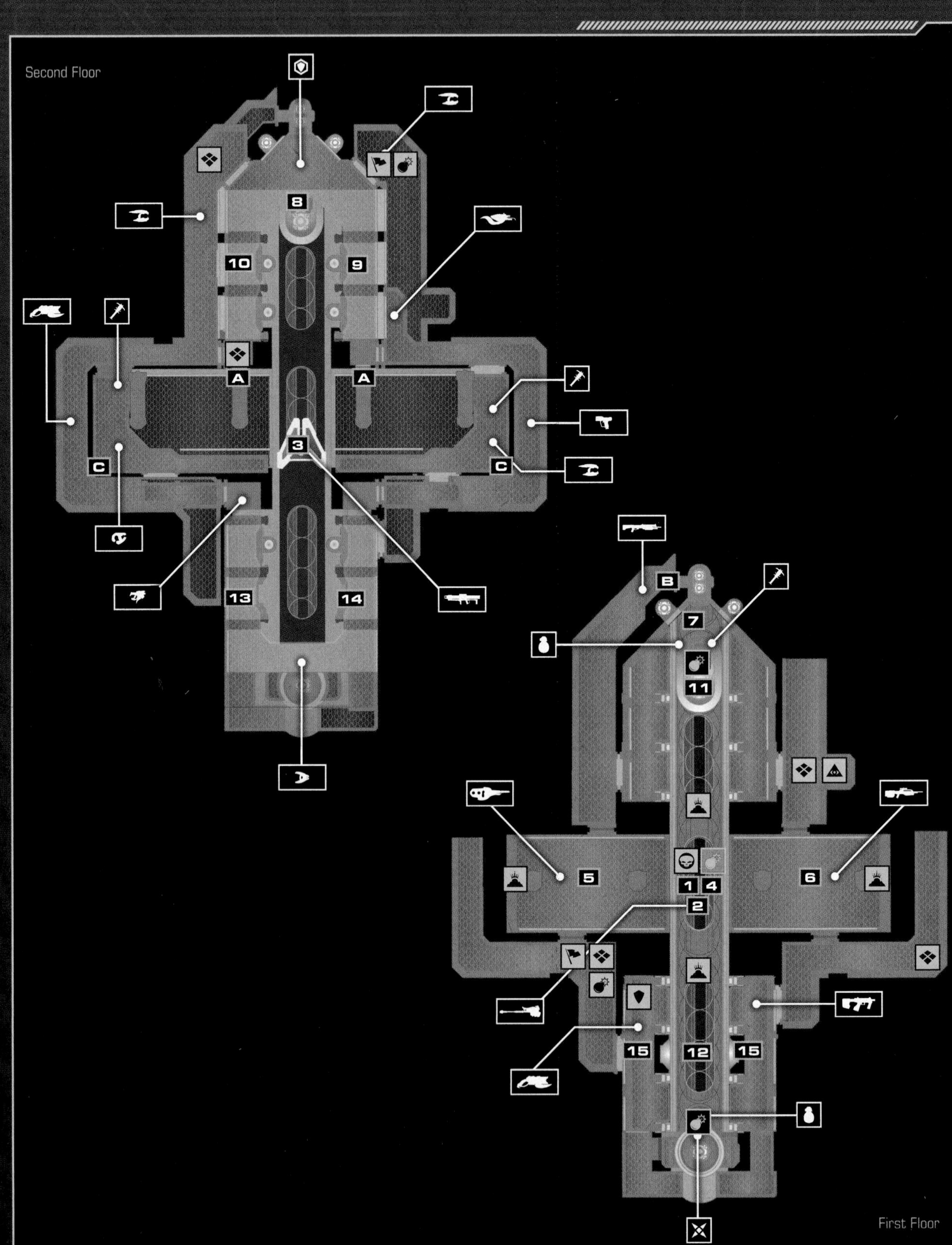

DATA STREAM

Recommended Game Variants: Slayer, Team Slayer, Oddball, King of the Hill

Recommended/Maximum Number of Players: 2–8

Advantageous Equipment: Rocket Launcher, Gravity Hammer, Shotgun

AVAILABLE EQUIPMENT AND GEAR RESPAWN TIMES

1 of 5 skulls = Slow 5 of 5 skulls = Fast

Weapons	Respawn (skulls of 5)
Battle Rifle	3
Brute Shot	2
Carbine	3
Gravity Hammer	1
Grenade, Frag	5
Grenade, Spike	5
Magnum	4

Weapons	Respawn (skulls of 5)
Mauler	3
Needler	2
Plasma Pistol	2
Plasma Rifle	5
Rocket Launcher	1
Shotgun	1
SMG	5

Weapons	Respawn (skulls of 5)
Spiker	3
Equipment	
Active Camo	1
Bubble Shield	2
Overshield	1
Power Drain	2

Topographical Overview

- Set in the middle of a vast sand dune, Epitaph is a massive cathedral-like structure rising high to the sky, reaching to the Halo Heavens.
- With its interior structure similar to that of great European cathedrals, it's thought to be a former Forerunner structure from ages ago, possibly a tomb or a cathedral.
- While at first glance the structure appears symmetrical, it is anything but. Looking at the overhead and outside views of Epitaph, one can see that with its exterior ramps and internal hiding places, Epitaph is a complex and challenging map.
- This map is great for Slayer, Team Slayer, Swat, and Oddball games. If you want to play in Matchmaking mode, you're more likely to see the Epilogue variant of the Epitaph map.. The Epilogue variant of the map has no shield doors, and there are some differences in weapon availability and placement.
- On this map, there is great opportunity to surprise your opponent. You can perform a variety of jumps off Epitaph's many halls and corridors; these will throw off any adversary trying to chase you down.
- Epitaph is laid out in the shape of a cross. Two wings extend off the main corridor and meet at the crossing, or "the court."
- Epitaph, like many of Bungie's maps, has a light side and a dark side.
- Like a cathedral, there is a Choir, a Court, and a Nave. The area with the Forerunner Structure is the Choir and contains a Gold Gravity Lift that will take you to the second-level platform. The Choir contains two levels: Top Choir and Bottom Choir. The area opposite this has a similar Gold Gravity Lift; however, this lift takes you to the center of the crossing, on a platform containing the Rocket Launcher. The Transepts cross the Nave and Choir in the middle and contain elevated structures that are akin to flying buttresses; we call these "ribs."

Call-out Locations

Court

Other names: N/A

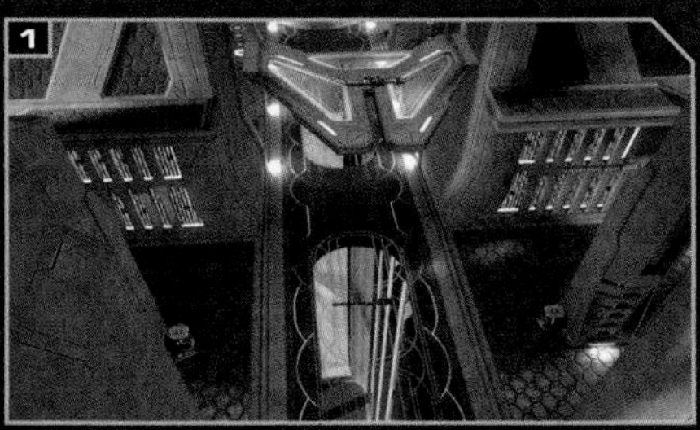

1

The Court is the center of the Nave and Choir, and the two halls that extend out from it in either direction are Light Side Court and Dark Side Court. . This is the meeting place, the central heart of the map. During games such as King of the Hill or Slayer, you'll often find many players passing through.

Center Court

Other names: N/A

2

Center Court consists of two areas—Top Court and Bottom Court.

Top Court

Other names: N/A

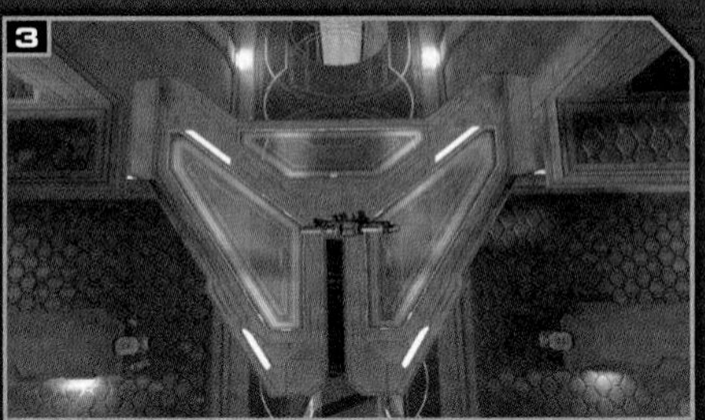

Top Court is a floating platform on which rests the Rocket Launcher. When standing on the platform, make sure you or a teammate possess the Rocket Launcher, as the platform will sway if shot with a Rocket, knocking you off to your opponents below. Access Top Court via the Gold Nave Lift or via the runways on either side of Light Court and Dark Court.

Bottom Court

Other names: N/A

Bottom Court is the very heart of Epitaph. Located at ground level below the Rocket Platform, Bottom Court houses a fierce weapon—the Gravity Hammer. This area is very dangerous, as it can be seen from anywhere on the map's interior, and any player standing within it can easily be picked off with a Grenade or long-range weapon.

Dark Side Court

Other names: N/A

The Dark Side Court has two ribs—great columns that attach to the building and extend to the exterior—and two doorways. Against the first rib, on the bottom back side, you'll find the Covenant Carbine. There is one Runway in Dark Side Court; this leads to the only doorway on Dark Side Nave and to Dark Side Choir walkway.

Light Side Court

Other names: N/A

The Light Side Court has two ribs—great columns that attach to the building and extend to the exterior—and two doorways. Against the first rib, on the bottom back side, you'll find the Battle Rifle. There is one runway in Light Side Court, which leads to the only doorway on Light Side Nave and Light Side Choir walkway. This runway connects the various sides of the map without making the player walk on Bottom Court, and it allows the player access to the Rocket Platform. This runway in the Court is the connection between both the Choir and Nave.

Choir

Other names: N/A

The Choir is easily recognized by the relic Forerunner statue looming above it. This area of the map contains several halls and doorways and a center battle arena. These areas are named as to where they are located; for example, Top Choir is the second level of the Choir, and Bottom Choir is the first level of the Choir.

Top Choir Platform

Other names: N/A

Choir Platform is located directly in front of the Choir Top Gold Lift, on Top Choir. When you take the Choir Gold Lift to the Platform, you'll immediately see the Bubble Shield on the floor in front of you. On either side of Choir Gold Lift are two alcoves. You can drop down these to Bottom Choir if an enemy is coming your way.

Light Choir Runway

Other names: N/A

If you're facing the Center Court on Top Choir Platform, to your left is Light Side. Here you'll find three doorways, all without shield doors, as the map's Light Side does not contain these. Door 1 of Light Choir Runway is closest to Gold Lift and houses one weapon, the Plasma Rifle. Continuing on, you'll follow this runway down to the Light Choir Ramp and then to the Lower Light Court, passing the Active Camo along the way. Door 2 of Light Choir Runway leads to the Light Side Walkway; then you can head to the Light Side Court Platform. As you enter Door 2, you'll see the Brute Shot. Door 3 of Light Choir Runway is another avenue you can take to escape your enemies; it leads to the same area as Door 2 and is the farthest door available on this runway.

Dark Choir Runway

Other names: N/A

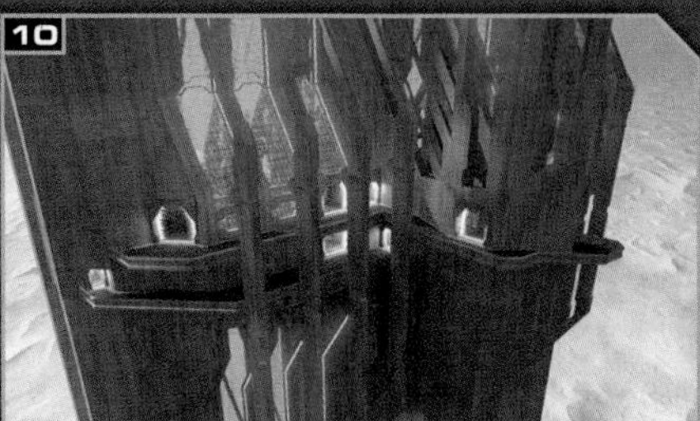

Dark Choir Runway is located on the Choir's second level and is on the right side of Gold Choir Lift Platform if you are facing the Center Court. This area contains three doorways, all with shield doors. Door 1 is the closest to Choir Lift and contains one weapon, the Plasma Rifle. Door 2 leads to the Dark Side Top Walkway. Door 3 also leads to the Dark Side Top Walkway; there is an exploding barrel as you pass by this door—so don't let your opponent easily kill you with one shot to the barrel!

Bottom Choir

Other names: N/A

Bottom Choir contains an open area for gameplay; multiple columns, doorways, and aisles; and the base of Gold Lift, where you'll find two Spike Grenades and two Frag Grenades. On either side of the bottom area of the Choir are aisles, under the Top Choir Runways. These are great locations to fool your opponent as you pass back and forth between them, shielding yourself from gunfire. There are two sides to this area: the Bottom Choir Light Side Aisle, which contains one doorway (no shield) and leads to the Bottom Choir Ramp. Here you'll find one power-up, the Active Camo, and the Bottom Choir Dark Side Aisle, which contains one doorway (with shield) and leads to the Dark Side Bottom Court. This aisle also leads to the back of Choir Lift.

Nave

Other names: N/A

The Nave is located on the opposite side of the map from Choir; it is the bottom of Epitaph's "cross." Here you have Top Nave and Bottom Nave, with weapons, runways, and aisles similar to that of Choir. In front of Gold Lift is the top nave platform, where you'll find one weapon, the Needler. This area is usually a pass-through from Light Side doorways to Dark Side doorways. The Gold Lift here will also elevate a player to the Rocket Platform. On either side of the Nave are runways that lead to the outside walkways on both Light Side and Dark Side.

Bottom Nave Gold Lift will catapult you to the Central Court, where you'll land on the Rocket Platform. In front of the Gold Lift, at its base, you'll find two Frag Grenades. Hidden from view and unknown to amateur players, Back Gold Lift is a great place to hide from your opponents, whether you're attempting a sneak attack or allowing your shields to recharge. Here you'll find one piece of equipment, the Power Drain. You can also jump from Back Gold Lift to the Top Nave Platform if you carefully jump at its sides. This area also leads to the Dark Side Nave Runway and the Light Side Nave Aisles.

Top Nave Light Side Runway

Other names: N/A

On the Light Side, the inside runway leads through the unshielded Light Side door to the outside walkways of Epitaph. There is only one doorway on this side of the upper runway.

Top Nave Dark Side Runway

Other names: N/A

Taking the inside runway to the outside walkway leads you through a shield door. There is only one door on this upper runway. Here you'll find a Mauler as well.

Nave Aisles

Other names: N/A

If you're standing in front of the Nave Gold Lift, you'll see the aisles on either side of the playing arena. There are also hidden areas behind columns, as well as a light side and a dark side. These are differentiated by unshielded and shielded doors, respectively. Passing through Light Side Nave Aisle, you'll find the SMG. Passing through the Dark Side Nave Aisle, you will find the Spiker and the Overshield, a valuable tool in anyone's arsenal.

Tactical Knowledge

Offense

On Epitaph, the key is staying out of the Center Court and finding a place to perch and take out the enemy below. If you're in a battle during Team Slayer, placement is key. Have teammates in all four major areas of the map so you can shoot "team BR" style across the playing field. Also, if your teammates are within view of one another, you can let each other know if someone is trying to sneak up behind you.

Enhanced Knowledge

Advanced Tactics

Jumping

Window-Ledge Jumping

You can jump from the Nave Ramps to the ribs and then to the window ledges. This gives you an overhead advantage against your opponent. Also, you can use a Brute Shot to catapult to the window's upper ledge. Having a sniper at this location? is ideal, as you can pick off your opponents down below without them knowing where you are!

Slide Jumping

In the transept area, just below the walkway, you can jump onto the wall grates and slide-jump to the upper walkway. This enables you to quickly jump out of harm's way as the fight gets lethal on the ground. Quickly jump against the wall grate, slide your analog stick over, and jump again. You now have the advantage of using your Battle Rifle or other weapon of choice to take out your adversary below.

Walkway Jumps

▲ First jump

▲ Second jump

There are several locations on Epitaph's outside walkways where you can jump up or down to another walkway. Use this technique to quickly attack your opponent from above or below. Epitaph is open to your imagination, as the entire map is full of walkways and runways, perfect for quickly ducking in and out of sight.

Sniping

Light Side and Dark Side Court Hidden Doorways

On the Light Side of the Court, find your way up to the Rocket Platform and jump to the first rib on either Light Side or Dark Side Court. Here you'll find a doorway. You can tuck yourself back into the shadows of the doorway, making this an excellent spot from which to snipe. If you're being shot at from this position, quickly duck back, drop to the floor, and go through the door and out of harm's way. The unknowing opponent won't know where you went. Also, you can balance yourself on the edge of the doorway and look down below; your unsuspecting prey will come along as you drop down to take them out!

Shotgun Ledge

Just on the other side of the outside walkway railing, by the Shotgun, there is a ledge known as the Shotgun Ledge. You can crouch and take cover here, then pounce on your opponent as they unknowingly pass by on their way to Back Gold Lift. Then, after you take out your opponent, you can quickly escape from anyone who heard the shot—just rush up the back door of Choir Gold Lift!

Court Corner Ledges

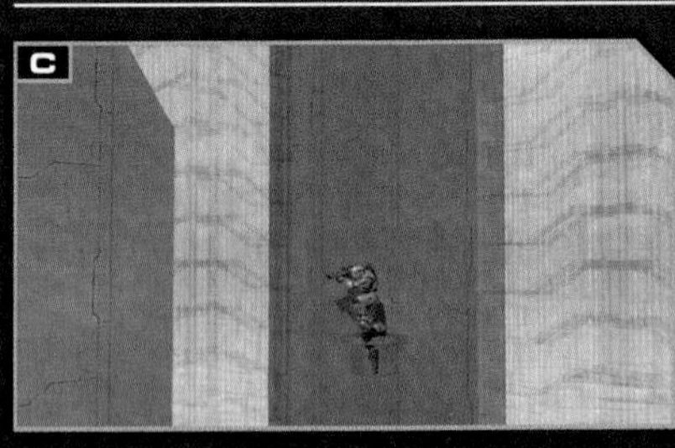

In the Court's upper corners are ledges that you can use to keep yourself out of sight. While your opponents are looking in the obvious places on the map, you'll be lurking above them, poised and ready to take them out.

FOUNDRY

PMS Meow, PMS Padme, PMS Elektra Fox

After the orbital elevator fell, supply warehouses sending munitions to space were soon abandoned.

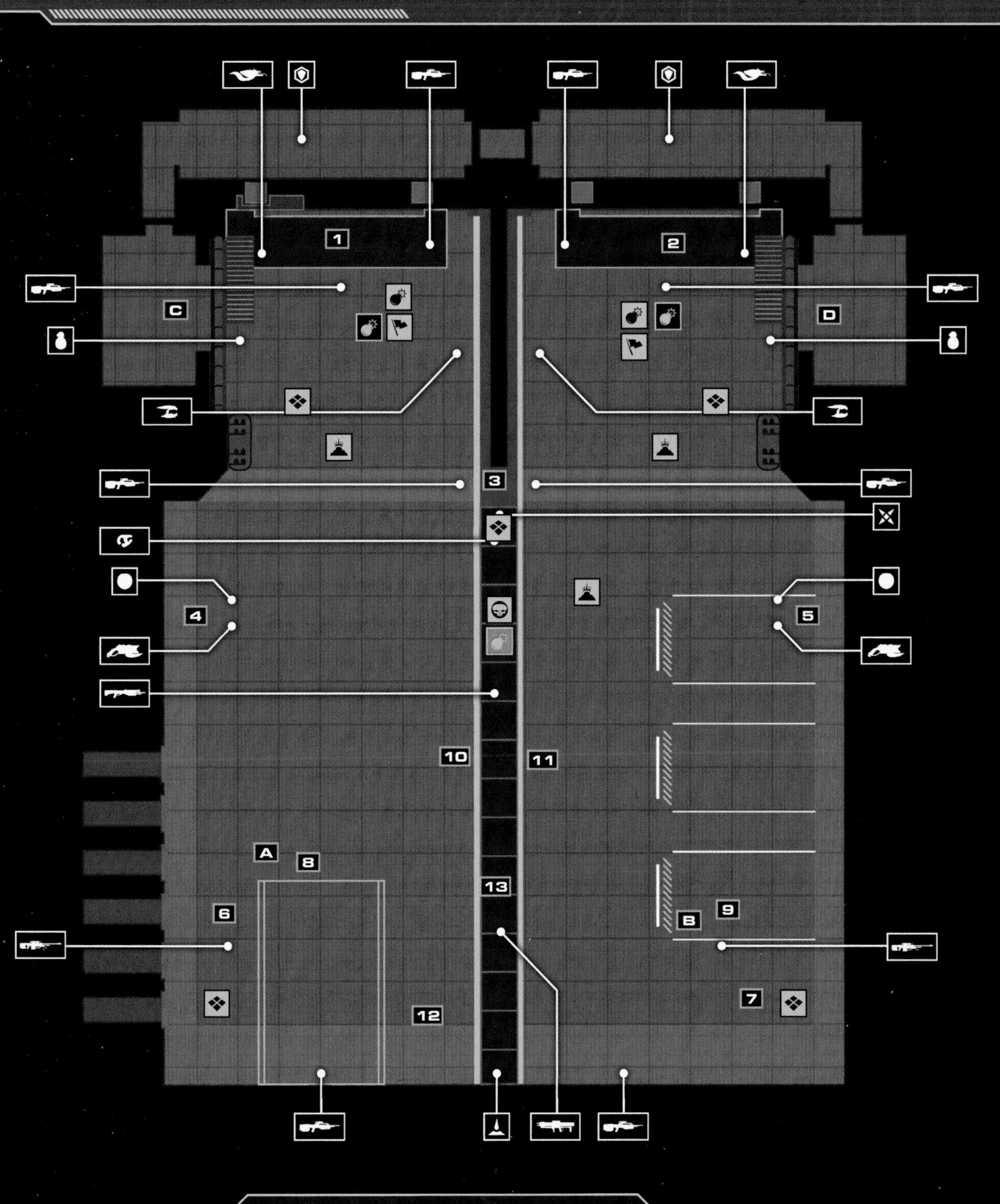

DATA STREAM

Recommended Game Variants: Forge, Team Slayer, Multiflag, King of the Hill, VIP

Recommended/Maximum Number of Players: 4–8/16

Advantageous Equipment: Rocket Launcher, Sniper Rifle, Bubble Shield, Power Drain, Portable Grav Lift

AVAILABLE EQUIPMENT AND GEAR RESPAWN TIMES

●○○○○ = Slow ●●●●● = Fast

	Weapons	
	Battle Rifle	●●●●○
	Brute Shot	●●●●○
	Grenade, Frag	●●●●●
	Grenade, Plasma	●●●●●
	Plasma Pistol	●●●●○

	Weapons	
	Plasma Rifle	●●●●○
	Rocket Launcher	●●○○○
	Shotgun	●○○○○
	Sniper Rifle	●●○○○
	Spiker	●●●●○

	Equipment	
	Bubble Shield	●●●○○
	Grav Lift	●●●○○
	Power Drain	●●●○○

Topographical Overview

Call-out Locations

A-Base

Other names: A-Side Spawn, Yellow Base

This is the starting spawn point for one of the two teams. It is sometimes called "Yellow Base" because of the yellow signs indicating the A side of the map. Although each team spawns at their own base, it is a bad idea to stay back and camp in these areas, because there is only one way out and you can be cornered very easily.

B-Base

Other names: B-Side Spawn, Red Base

This is the starting spawn point for one of the two teams. It is sometimes called "Red Base" because of the red signs indicating the B side of the map. Although each team spawns at their own base, it is a bad idea to stay back and camp in these areas, because there is only one way out and you can be cornered very easily.

Power Drain

Other names: Mid Stage

This platform is in the middle of the map and is the first point where the two teams can meet after the initial spawn. On this platform is a Power Drain, the first available advantageous item on the map after spawning in either base.

A-Sign

Other names: A-Side Stickies, A-Stairs, A-Ramp

The A-Sign is the easiest way to tell that you're on the map's A-Side. In front of this indicator sign are two Plasma Grenades and a Spiker. This is the fastest route to take when going from A-Base to either A-Side Sniper Rifle or the back of the map.

B-Sign

Other names: B-Side Stickies, B-Stairs, B-Ramp

The B-Sign is the easiest way to tell that you're on the map's B-Side. In front of this indicator sign are two Plasma Grenades and a Spiker. This is the fastest route to take when going from B-Base to either B-Side Sniper Rifle or the back of the map.

A-Snipe

Other names: Back A Corner

This is where one of the two Sniper Rifles on the map spawns. It is called "A-Snipe" because it is located on the A-Side of the map and is the primary Sniper Rifle for the team that spawns on A-Side. This is a very important area of the map to control, because one of the most powerful weapons spawns here.

B-Snipe

Other names: Back B Corner

This is where one of the two Sniper Rifles on the map spawns. It is called "B-Snipe" because it is located on the B-Side of the map and is the primary Sniper Rifle for the team that spawns on B-Side. This is a very important area of the map to control, because one of the most powerful weapons spawns here.

Top A-Snipe

Other names: n/a

This is the area above where the A-Side sniper spawns. This is a great location to sit with the Sniper Rifle, because you are high on the map and can see most of B-Base. This is vital, because you can see if the other team is spawning in B-Base; you can then call out this information to your team.

Top B-Snipe

Other names: N/A

This is the area above where the B-Side Snipe spawns. This is a great area to sit with the Sniper Rifle because you are high on the map which gives you the advantage over other players.

A-Side Pit

Other names: A-Side Fence, A-Fence

This is a good place to sit if you are watching for people spawning in A-Base. When standing here, you can also look through the fence in the middle of the map to see if anyone is sitting in B-Side Pit.

B-Side Pit

Other names: B-Side Fence, B-Fence

This is a good place to sit if you are watching for people spawning in B-Base. When standing here, you can also look through the fence in the middle of the map to see if anyone is sitting in A-Side Pit. However, be careful, as there are fusion coils in the middle of B-Side Pit that will explode if shot.

Truck

Other names: Car, Semi

This truck is between A-Snipe and A-Pit. Use it to jump up to Top A-Snipe, which also has a path to Rocket Tunnel. You can also use this truck as cover if you are being rushed from A-Pit or from B-Side Snipe.

Rockets

Other names: Rocket Tunnel, Rocket Hall

This is the home to what is possibly the most powerful weapon on the map, the Rocket Launcher. This weapon is located at the back of the base right in the middle of both sniper spawn points. There is a Portable Grav Lift below the Rockets that you can use to launch yourself to Rocket Tunnel, or there are two bridges coming from both Top A-Snipe and Top B-Snipe. Many players like to sit on top of Rocket Tunnel with a Sniper Rifle, since it is the highest point on the map.

Tactical Knowledge

A/B Base Vicinity: The bases are closed off and provide good cover; however, you don't want to be there longer than needed or else your team will get spawn-killed.

Sniper Vicinity: Immediately after spawning, your team must gain control of the Sniper Rifle and take out the other team's sniper. This will make it easier to get the Rockets. The two platforms above where each sniper spawns provide an excellent view of the opposing team's half of the map.

Rocket Vicinity: In addition to immediately going for the Sniper Rifle after spawning, your team needs to make a push for Rockets. Obtaining this weapon is a team effort. After picking up the Rockets, head for the back of the map. The bases provide a good view of Rocket Spawn, and if you linger too long there, you will be killed quickly.

Enhanced Knowledge

Offensive and Defensive Posturing

Right from the start, have your best sniper head straight for the Sniper Rifle. The other teammates will follow, battling for Rocket control. After you gain control of the half of the map that contains Rockets and Sniper Rifles, simply wait for the other team to come to you.

Professional Planning

If the other team has map control, try to send two teammates to the map's left side while the other two flank the opposite side. Your goal is to try surprising the opposing team before the new Rockets come up; this gives you a chance to claim the better half of the map just in time for Rockets.

Objective Plotting

Few objective game types are played on Foundry; the main one is Oddball. With Oddball, your team will want to get control of the Sniper Rifle and Rockets. Having these weapons will make it easy for your team to dominate the opposing team, while the ball carrier gathers time sitting in the safety of your team's base.

Sniping

A Snipe

After picking up the Sniper Rifle, position yourself on the platform in front of you. From there, you have a good view of the other team's side of the map, where you can easily pick off opponents your teammates have weakened, or weaken opponents for your teammates to pick off.

B Snipe

Similar to if you were picking up the A-Side Sniper Rifle, position yourself on the platform above you. From here, you have a good view of the opposing team's side of the map. You can easily pick people off or weaken them for your teammates to kill.

A Side Back Room

This back room has only one entrance, which is the hall where you find the Bubble Shield. This room has open windows that allow you to view the Back B Side of the map, which is essential for taking down the B sniper. This room is also very safe, because it has only one entrance, and you can see when people try and rush in to kill you.

B Side Back Room

This room is the mirror image of A Side Back Room but instead has a window view of Back A Side Snipe. Similar to A Side Back Room, this room has only one entrance, which is accessed from the Bubble Shield hall. This makes it very easy to see if an opponent is trying to rush in and ambush you.

GHOST TOWN

PMS Arkathia, PMS Nitemare, Athena AzMADEUS

These fractured remains near Voi remind us that brave souls died here to buy our salvation.

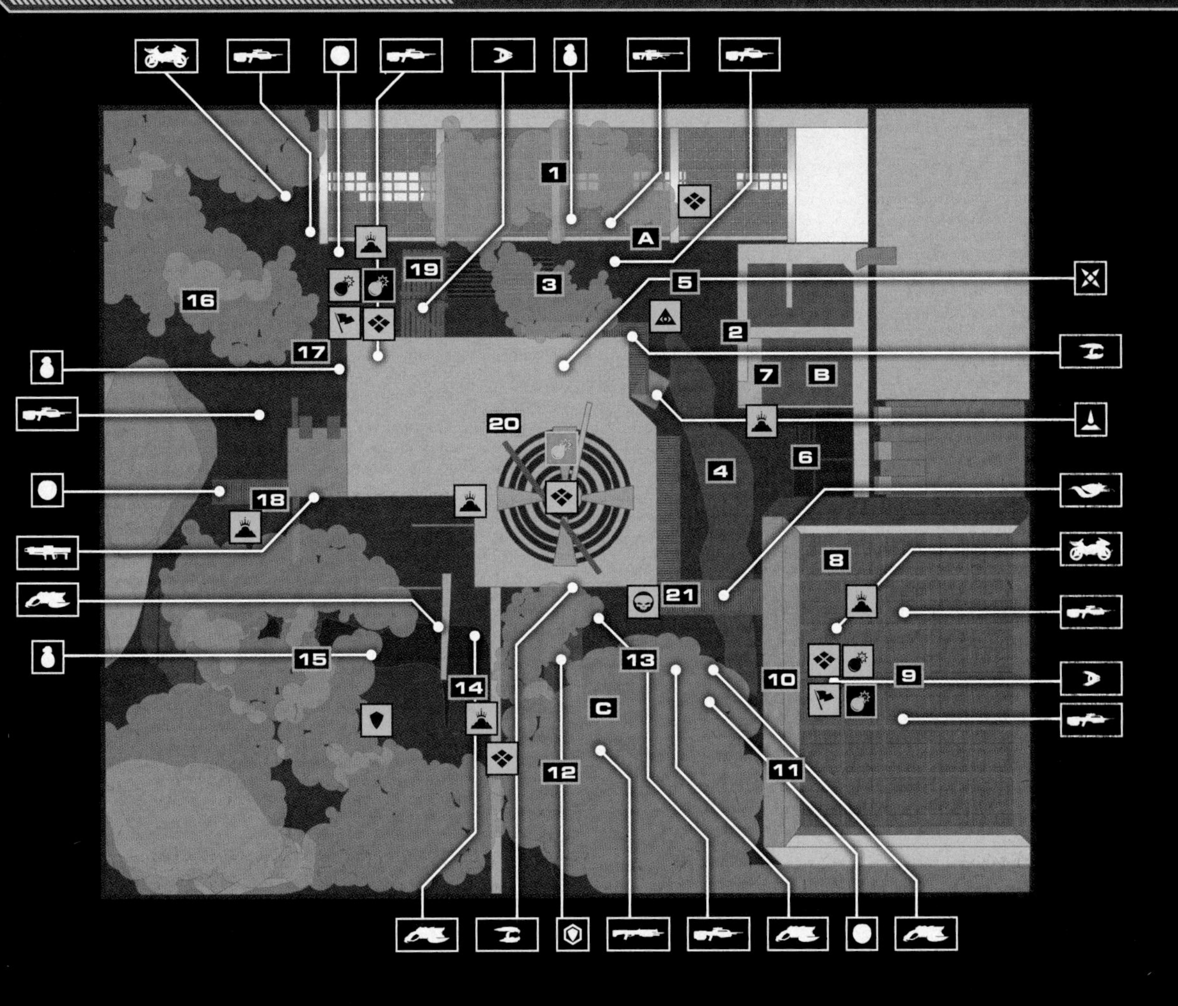

DATA STREAM

Recommended Game Variants: Team Slayer, Oddball, Assault, Capture the Flag/Forge

Recommended/Maximum Number of Players: 4–12/16

Advantageous Equipment: Rocket Launcher, Sniper Rifle, Active Camo, Overshield

AVAILABLE EQUIPMENT AND GEAR RESPAWN TIMES

💀 = Slow 💀💀💀💀💀 = Fast

Weapons	
Battle Rifle	💀💀💀💀💀
Brute Shot	💀💀
Grenade, Frag	💀💀💀💀💀
Grenade, Plasma	💀💀💀💀💀
Needler	💀💀
Plasma Pistol	💀💀💀💀
Plasma Rifle	💀💀💀💀

Weapons	
Rocket Launcher	💀
Shotgun	💀
Sniper Rifle	💀
Spiker	💀💀💀💀
Vehicles	
Mongoose	💀💀💀💀

Equipment	
Active Camo	💀
Bubble Shield	💀💀💀
Grav Lift	💀💀💀
Overshield	💀
Power Drain	💀💀💀

Topographical Overview

Call-out Locations

Snipe Green

Other names: Snipe Tower, Snipe, Green House, Green

This is where you'll find the Sniper Rifle. It's right across from the tunnels/Red Base. Have a teammate with you while in Snipe Green to ensure that you don't get assassinated; there are many doorways and holes blown into the walls that your opponent can hide in and take you out.

Top Snipe Green

Other names: Top Snipe

The top level contains the Sniper Rifle, which is located next to a window commonly called Sniper Window. The ramp and door directly below Sniper Window are referred to as Sniper Ramp and Sniper Door.

Bottom Snipe Green

Other names: Bottom Snipe

This area is directly below Top Snipe. Closely watch the two large holes blown into the wall; intruders could be lurking here.

Hideout

Other names: Snipe Hideout

The tunnel leading out of Snipe Green is called Hideout and is another great area from which to snipe. You can also see the Camo and

Red Street

Other names: N/A

Red Street extends from Red Base to Snipe Green.

Blue Street

Other names: n/a

Blue Street leads from Snipe Green to the Warehouse.

Corner

Other names: N/A

The area where Red Street and Blue Street connect is simply know as Corner. You'll find two pipes that house the Camo and the Grav Lift.

Scaffold and Scaffold Cubby

Other names: N/A

This is the multilevel scaffolding that allows to you reach the Attic. In the back of the scaffolding is a little hidden hallway, called Scaffold Cubby, that leads to the Warehouse's Stairwell.

Attic

Other names: N/A

This is the platform directly above Hideout (the area where two of the four walls are blown off).

Stairwell

Other names: N/A

There are three levels to the Stairwell (Bottom Stairwell, Mid Stairwell, Top Stairwell) that will lead you to the Warehouse.

Warehouse

Other names: the Plant, Blue Base

This is where the blue team spawns. In this area you can find a Mongoose, two Battle Rifles, and a Needler.

Needler, Above Needler

Other names: Needler Level, Needler Hallway, Above Needler Level, Above Needler Hallway

There are two levels or hallways above the Warehouse's large doorway that lead to scaffolds. The Needler is located on the bottom level; thus, this area is called Needler. The top level is called Above Needler.

The Hole

Other names: N/A

Located in the Warehouse next to the large doorway.

Shotgun, Shotgun Bridge

Other names: Bubble Bridge

In this green, junglelike area, you'll find the Shotgun and the Shotgun Bridge with a Bubble Shield resting on it.

Hallway

Other names: Hallway Street

Hallway Street will lead you to the Warehouse, Hideout, Camo, and Overshield. Hallway is a high-traffic area in which you'll find a Battle Rifle.

Archway and Above Archway

Other names: N/A

This archway connects Hallway to the Jungle. The area above the archway is simply known as Above Archway.

Jungle

Other names: Overshield Spawn, Overshield

This area is so named because of its junglelike appearance. In the Jungle is the Overshield. In addition, the Rocket Spawn is across from the Jungle.

Tunnels

Other names: N/A

Red team spawns outside of the Tunnels. Inside the Tunnels is a good spot to hide, and they lead to the Overshield. If blue team takes control of Snipe Tower, be careful when you exit the Tunnels. Also, the Mongoose and two Battle Rifles are outside of the Tunnels, lying next to the large holes blown into Snipe Green.

Brute Shot Ramp

Other names: N/A

This ramp leads from the Tunnels up to the House, where the Brute Shot lies at the top of the ramp. .

Rocket Spawn

Other names: Rockets

The door (Rocket Door) to the ramp's right will lead you to Rocket Spawn and to two Plasma Grenades.

Needler Bridge and Needler Ramp

Other names: N/A

The door to the ramp's left will lead you to the Needler Bridge and Needler Ramp.

House, H1/H2

Other names: N/A

The hallway in front of Brute Shot Ramp takes you deeper inside the House. A Brute Shot and the Power Drain are in the hallways. House is a high-traffic area and has multiple entry points and two levels, H1 and H2. H1 is the little room with a ramp leading up to H2. H2 leads outside to the Catwalk or to the door (Jungle Door) leading to the Jungle.

Catwalk

Other names: Bridge

The Catwalk connects the Warehouse and the House. You can find a Plasma Rifle and a Brute Shot in this area.

Tactical Knowledge

- Ghost Town consists of both an indoor and outdoor environment. You are placed in the ruins of an old water plant, so your cover isn't always within a closed area. The blue team will spawn in the plant/Warehouse, while the red team will spawn outside behind the greenhouse. The map is separated by a two-story structure.
- There are many places for both defensive and offensive placement, and the water pipes can come in handy if you need a place to hide. Each spawn point for the team is equipped with Battle Rifles.
- The Warehouse/plant is one of the major spawn points for Team Slayer. Blue team usually spawns here, and if playing Capture the Flag (CTF), your flag will also spawn here.
- There are two main floors. If you head up the stairs, the connecting bridge will lead you to the middle structure. To the opposite side of the stairs is the Shotgun location.
- The House has multiple entry points and is connected to each location via bridge or openings. From the heat map, you can see it is a high-traffic area.
- Snipe Green is where the Sniper Rifle will spawn. There are three main entry/exit points. One entry point leads you from Hideout to the second floor of Snipe Green; there is a second entry point off the bridge that connects to the second floor of the House, and the final entry point is through the window next to the Sniper Rifle spawn point.

Offense

- You want to have control and not let the opposing team spread out where they can pick you off. The power weapons are key, especially the Rockets; if you can get the opposing team together inside the house, you can easily take them out with one or two Rocket launches or with the Sniper Rifle.
- Stay up top to ambush below and keep an eye on player movements.
- At the match's start, head for the power weapons and special equipment to take control of the map.
- Try and drive you enemies into the confines of the house.
- Most teams try to apply pressure from the outside surrounding area to force the opposing team together.

Defense

Getting control of the middle structure can be valuable, as you will have access to all points of the map and can view other player movements; however, it can also be your downfall if you do not keep track of your enemies.

Enhanced Knowledge

- In Oddball games, the Hole just below the plant is a good place to hide. You can easily tuck yourself into the corner and fight off attacks from enemies.
- The Tunnels are also a great place to hide in Oddball. With the facility in ruins, there is always a place to hide from enemies.
- In Oddball and Assault, avoiding the House helps you accumulate points. Maneuvering around the plant can give you valuable time, and taking the Shotgun path when making you way outside can provide cover.
- The Attic is an excellent area to sit while holding the ball; it is difficult to reach and difficult to fire upon. You must use the scaffolds to reach the Attic.
- Have your teammates hold the Scaffolds at all times to prevent the other team from reaching the ball carrier. If all of your teammates are in place, the only other way to reach and kill the ball carrier is by way of the Catwalk, Needler Level, Above Needler Level, and Scaffold Cubby. Make sure your teams hold those areas or destroy anybody that comes out of them. If your ball carrier dies, the ball will remain in the Attic, safely away from the other team. Just destroy any nearby enemies and replace the ball carrier with one of the men holding the scaffolds. Always make sure to replace the man at the scaffolds.

Sniping and Ambush Locations

Sniper Window

In the greenhouse, where the sniper spawns, is a good place to pick off opposing enemies as they leave the plant or enter the middle structure from the ramp. There are also two other access points to your location: behind you and to the side. You can be ambushed here, so always be on the lookout.

Ambush Corner

Tucking yourself away in this corner gives you a sight line to both the bridge that connects the greenhouse to the middle structure and the bridge that connects the Warehouse to the middle structure.

Ambush Tree

Tucking yourself away in this tree trunk can give you a couple seconds' advantage over any unsuspecting enemies entering the area.

Rocket Launch

Picking up Rockets and heading to the hallway between Overshield and Rocket Spawn is a great way to pick off the opposition as they leave the Warehouse. The hallway gives you a direct view of the Warehouse.

GUARDIAN

PMS Doom, PMS Pip Sq3ak, PMS Ovaryacting

Millennia of tending has produced trees as ancient as the Forerunner structures they have grown around.

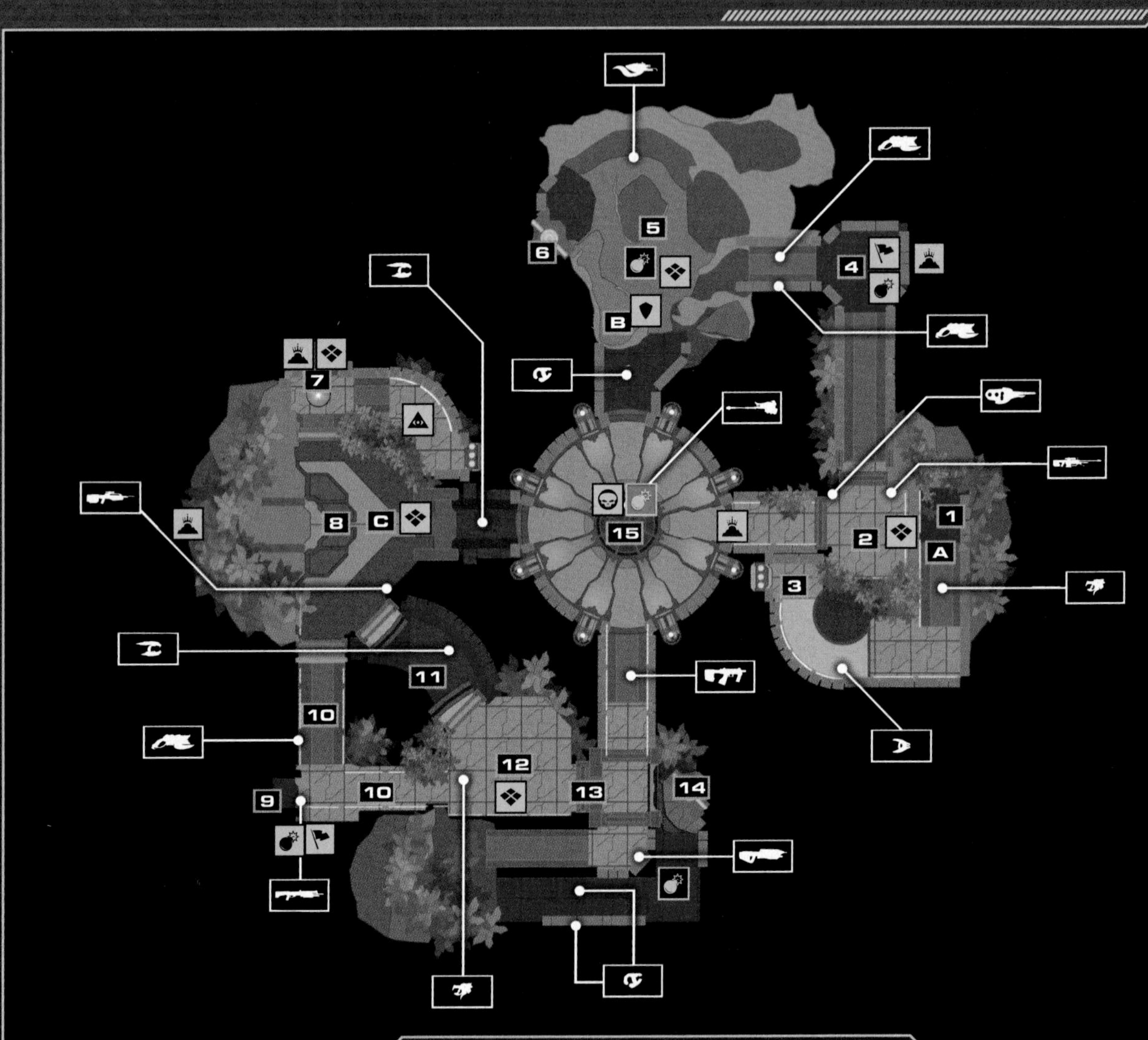

DATA STREAM

Recommended Game Variants: Free for All, Team Slayer, Oddball, Crazy King

Recommended/Maximum Number of Players: 2–8/8

Advantageous Equipment: Sniper, Shotgun, Active Camo, Overshield

AVAILABLE EQUIPMENT AND GEAR RESPAWN TIMES

●○○○○ = Slow ●●●●● = Fast

Weapons	
Assault Rifle	●●●●●
Battle Rifle	●●●●○
Brute Shot	●○○○○
Carbine	●●●●○
Grenade, Frag	●●●●●
Grenade, Plasma	●●●●●
Gravity Hammer	●○○○○

Weapons	
Magnum	●●●●○
Mauler	●●●●○
Needler	●○○○○
Plasma Pistol	●●○○○
Plasma Rifle	●●●●●
Shotgun	●○○○○
SMG	●●●●●

Weapons	
Sniper Rifle	●○○○○
Spiker	●●●●●
Equipment	
Active Camo	●○○○○
Bubble Shield	●●●○○
Flare	●●○○○
Overshield	●○○○○

Call-out Locations

Sniper Tower

Other names: S1 (Snipe 1st Floor), S2 (Snipe 2nd Floor), S3 (Snipe 3rd Floor)

This area is home to the Sniper Rifle and connects to Elbow, Top Mid, and Bottom Mid. It is accessible from the lift in Bottom Blue. Sniper Tower also serves as a primary spawn point. In Social Slayer, the Sniper Rifle spawns on S1 (Snipe 1, the tower's first level) and the Overshield spawns on S2. In MLG, the Sniper Rifle spawns on S3.

Elbow

Other names: N/A

This L-shaped walkway connects Sniper Tower and Forest.

Forest

Other names: Bottom Green, Top Green, Stump

Forest is a secondary spawn location and connects to Elbow and Bottom Mid. It also contains a tree stump for access to Top Mid, along with a lift to Active Camo at Top Gold.

Camo Lift

Other names: N/A

Located in Forest, this lift ends at the Active Camo.

Active Camo

Other names: Camo

Home of the Camouflage and two Plasma Grenades near the blue lift to Top Mid.

Gold Lift

Other names: Bottom Gold, Top Gold

Gold Lift is opposite Sniper Tower and is split into two levels: Top Gold and Bottom Gold. Top Gold connects to Blue Hall and the Active Camo spawn and serves as a primary spawn.

Shotgun

Other names: Shotty

Located beneath Blue Hall, this area is home to the Shotgun in Social Slayer or to two Plasma Grenades in MLG.

Blue Hall

Other names: Blue Barrels

This section serves as the connector for Top Gold and Blue Room.

Shortcut

Other names: N/A

This area serves as a quick escape from Gold Room to Blue Room or vice versa; just jump and crouch.

Blue Room

Other names: N/A

Blue Room is considered a secondary spawn and is located across the map from Forest. Gold Room lies on the left of Blue Room and Sniper Tower is on the right.

Blue Window

Other names: Blue Glass

Covered by glass from Sniper Tower, this area offers some protection and allows easy access to Blue Room, Sniper Lift, Gold Room, and Top Mid.

Sniper Lift

Other names: Snipe Lift

Located directly below Blue Window, this lift will take you to S3.

Top Middle

Other names: Top Mid

Located in the dead center of the map, this circular area offers no protection but allows you to connect to any section of the map through its outlets.

Bottom Middle

Other names: Hammer Spawn, Mauler Spawn

This area is home to the Gravity Hammer in Social games or to the Mauler in MLG games. Bottom Mid connects to Bottom Green, S1, and Bottom Gold.

Tactical Knowledge

- The three most essential spots in Guardian are Green, Sniper Tower, and Gold. These spots are very open and allow unique views of the map.
- Green, or Forest, can be reached by Elbow, Top Middle, and Bottom Middle. It has a lift that takes you over to Top Gold and lets you see any enemies approaching from Top Middle. Although Green offers a view of the entire Top Middle, it is a vulnerable spot to be in, as you are in view of almost all the most important zones. Green is also dangerous, as it has an exploding crate in the back of it. Shoot this crate as soon as you see it to avoid being killed. Directly in front of the barrel are Brute Shots. These weapons can be very powerful if used correctly. On the top level of Forest (Top Green), there is a Bubble Shield. Pick this up as soon as you see it, as it can be very beneficial to your survival.
- Sniper Tower has three levels: Snipe 1 (S1), which is the lowest level; Snipe 2 (S2), which is the middle level; and Snipe 3 (S3), which is the top level. The Sniper Rifle is located on S1, the Overshield is on S2, and the Needler is on the ramp leading up from S1 and S2 to S3. On S3, there is another exploding barrel. With a large view of the map, Sniper Tower is a very useful place at which to camp.
- Gold Room has two levels and various routes to crucial locations on Guardian. The two levels of Gold are known as Bottom Gold and Top Gold, and both are connected by a lift. To the left of Gold (if you're looking at Sniper Tower), Camouflage and two Plasma Grenades spawn. To the right of Gold is the Blue Room. Also, on the way to Blue Room, there are more exploding crates inside the halls, which are known as Blue Halls. Shoot these crates (from a safe distance) to avoid being killed by an enemy behind them. In the Blue Room, there is a flare that you can use to blind enemies. Below the Blue Room, there is the Green Hall, which houses the Shotgun.

Offense

- Because there are so many different weapons on Guardian, an offensive setup is always fun.
- Always keep control of the main power weapons—the Shotgun and the Sniper Rifle. Your team can easily win the game if these weapons

- Take advantage of the strong power-ups on this map—Camo and Overshield. The Shotgun and Camo or the Shotgun and Overshield can be deadly to any unsuspecting enemies.
- After your team has control of the power weapons, push to wherever the opposing team is setting up. Have your team's sniper stay at Sniper Tower, always checking behind him to make sure that he is in the clear to snipe.
- Make sure the player with the Shotgun can sneak around the map—either by crouch-walking or hiding in ambush spots—and kill unsuspecting enemies.
- Another important power weapon is the Gravity Hammer, located at Bottom Middle. Have a player who is skilled with this weapon (as it is sometimes tricky to use) mimic the player with the Shotgun by sneaking around the enemy's setup and taking them by surprise.
- No matter where your enemies spawn, always rush them in an organized fashion. Make sure your entire team is with you while you rush your enemies, but do not stand directly next to each other, as this is an easy triple kill for the opposing team.

Defense

- Even though there are a variety of weapons on Guardian that make it tougher to set up a defense, gaining control of these weapons and taking advantage of the power-ups can make for a healthy defensive setup.
- Have two teammates go for the Sniper Rifle and two teammates sneak for the Shotgun; these are the power weapons, and an enemy with a Shotgun can absolutely destroy a defensive setup.
- It is important to make sure that your team has the power-ups on the map, as an enemy with an Overshield is twice as hard to kill.
- Pick the Gold Room, the Blue Room, or the Sniper Tower to be the home for your team. You want your team to control all possible entrances to your base so that whenever an enemy approaches, your team knows where they are coming from.
- When Camo spawns, have one player (preferably the one with the Shotgun) grab it, wait until he is fully invisible, and then crouch-walk or sneak around and assassinate foes. Do not have your team push with the invisible player, as it will give away his position. The invisible player should always try to assassinate an enemy, as this is the easiest and most effective way to use the Camo to your advantage.
- If an enemy with the Overshield approaches your team, have a majority of your teammates attempt to kill him. The more shots this enemy takes, the quicker his Overshield will go down and the quicker he will be eliminated.
- Wait for the opposing team to push/rush your team; do not rush out on your own, and make sure that your team knows they will be holding a defensive position.

Enhanced Knowledge

- In Oddball, your main objective is to score as many points as possible; however, you should "bait the ball" at the start of the game. This means that you allow your opponent to run after the ball, then your team opens fire on them. After you kill three or four of them, try to get the ball and return to your team.
- Blue Room and Sniper Tower are two great areas at which to hold the ball. Blue Room provides a little bit more cover if your team is uncomfortable at Sniper Tower. If you hold the ball at Blue Room, have a teammate across at Forest and another at Sniper Tower or Gold Room. This allows your team to have eyes on all of the map and hopefully kill the opponent before they reach your other two teammates with the ball in Blue Room.
- If you have the oddball and are about to die, try and "play ball"—throw the ball over the edge so it respawns on Top Mid. This allows your team to set up and respawn if necessary while the opponent gains little to no time with the ball.
- Crazy King is a free-for-all variant of King of the Hill. Familiarize yourself with the rotation of the hill in order to succeed. When playing, leave the hill a few seconds early as you run to the next location for the new hill. You will be surprised at how much extra time this gives you for each game!

Sniping

Snipe 1

The Sniper Rifle spawns at this level of Sniper Tower. You can see all of Bottom Middle and Top Gold. This position is great for killing approaching enemies. Opponents who drop down to Bottom Gold or rush Bottom Middle from Green or Top Middle make easy targets to kill.

Green

This is a great spot for sniping. You can see the entrance to Blue Room, all of Top Middle, the entrance to Top Gold, Camo Spawn, Bottom Middle, Elbow, and Sniper Tower. Being able to see all of these areas allows you to call out enemy locations to your teammates and even get a few kills in the

Top Gold

Sniping from Top Gold is always a good choice. From Top Gold, you can see all of Top Middle, Top Green, Bottom Middle, Blue Room, Sniper Tower, and Barrels Hallway. Have the sniper on Top Gold, where it's easy to kill opponents on Snipe 2 and Snipe 3.

HERETIC

David S.J. Hodgson

Because of its speed and luxury, the Pious Inquisitor has become an irresistible prize during these dark times.

DATA STREAM

Recommended Game Variants: Assault, Capture the Flag, Infection, Juggernaut, Oddball, Slayer, Team Slayer

Recommended Number of Players: 2–8

Advantageous Equipment: Battle Rifle, Carbine, Bubble Shield, Energy

NOTE

Those of you with previous *Halo 2* multiplayer experience may recognize this as a remake of the map Midship. Aside from the addition of a Bubble Shield on the lower ground of the tower

AVAILABLE EQUIPMENT AND GEAR RESPAWN TIMES

●○○○○ = Slow ●●●●● = Fast

	Weapons	
	Battle Rifle	●●●●●
	Carbine	●●●●○
	Energy Sword	●○○○○
	Grenade, Frag	●○○○○
	Grenade, Plasma	●●●●●

	Weapons	
	Needler	●●○○○
	Plasma Pistol	●●●○○
	Plasma Rifle	●●●●●
	Shotgun	●○○○○
	SMG	●●●●○

	Weapons	
	Spiker	●●●●●
	Equipment	
	Bubble Shield	●●○○○

Topographical Overview

Call-Out Locations

Base

Other names: flag, flag spawn, deck

Perfectly symmetrical, this area features a base at either side of a long, central bridge platform **2**. The bases are simple two-story structures with a Grav Lift linking the lower and upper areas. Access the lower level via two entrances, while the top floor has three. The top entrance faces the bridge and offers wide views of the entire map.

Bridge and Lower Grav Lifts

Other names: sword, plateau, middle

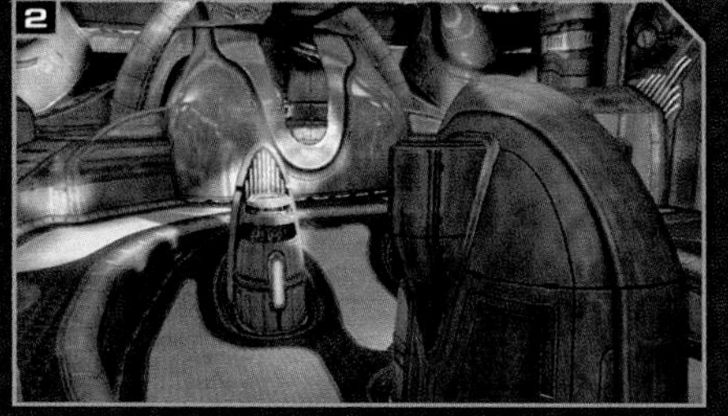

While the rest of the map is comprised of narrow balcony pathways that link the bases **1**, Carbine Pod **3**, and tower **4**, the central bridge area is wide open and features a lower, concave zone with three smaller Grav Lifts and a Shotgun, and there's a platform holding a prized Energy Sword. Weigh up the strength of these weapons with your ability to reach them before being gunned down in the open.

Carbine and Needler Pod

Other names: carbine, carb, pink, purple

With the two bases facing each other on opposite walls, the Carbine Pod (aka "purple") and tower ("pink") face each other on the other opposing walls and are linked by the bridge **2**. The Carbine Pod, named after the weapon you find inside the structure, offers quick access to either base and to ambush opportunities. There are curved walkways linking the two floors of this structure.

Tower

Other names: Pink, Bubble Shield

The pink and purple-hued structure at the map's opposite end to the Carbine Pod **3** is known as the tower (aka "pink") and features a small chamber containing a Plasma Pistol and Bubble Shield. It also has a covered upper chamber that affords protection and easy access onto the bridge. Snipers enjoy the shadows on the curved roof of this building, too.

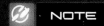

NOTE **The color-coded names of Locations 3 and 4 (purple and pink) were used by professional players after the release of Halo 2, when it was known as Midship. The color differences of the walls were the reasons for the names, because it was easier to shout "Purple Two!" than "above the Carbine!" Try this out during your matches, too.**

Zone Knowledge

The compact nature of this map allows you to see the bridge, tower, and Red Base in a single panorama.

The lower level features three Grav Lifts that are more for show than help; but there's a powerful Shotgun down here, too.

Heretic is a small, symmetrical map with impressive weapon diversity and distribution. Upon inspecting either base, you'll find several openings that overlook the map's central bridge area. Ramps connect the area under the bridge, the corridors that run around the map perimeter, and the two main floors of the structure, including both floors of the bases, with openings on both levels facing the center and sides of the map. Gravity Lifts allow players in the lower part of the base to quickly ascend to the upper part. Players can also jump from the upper-central bridge, with its Energy Sword platform above, and enter either base. Regardless of game type, this map rewards those who are fast, aggressive, and are accurate with Grenades.

Enhanced Knowledge

Offensive and Defensive Posturing

- In single-player matches, the upper areas on either side of the central platform are the best places to be; try to obtain the Shotgun or Energy Sword first, so you can get multikills early on. This weapon combo is particularly deadly.
- Use the Battle Rifle or Carbine to strike enemies from a distance.
- The explosive Power Cores (or "fusion coils") have good offensive potential, but they can also be dangerous; use them to damage foes that run near them, but don't get caught near an exploding one yourself.
- Don't overlook the Needler; on this small map, it's easy to target players not seeking cover, which is where the Needler's strengths come into play.
- Low on shields? Then use the Bubble Shield, or flee to cover (or any room) and allow your shields to recharge.
- There are ample supplies of Grenades, and lobbing them at expected enemy locations can yield unexpected—but required—kills. "Grenadespamming" is a fine plan that infuriates your foes.
- The lack of Sniper Rifles on this map shouldn't dissuade a camper; the Carbine or Battle Rifle can be just as effective at long-distance kills.
- The central bridge and lower Grav Lifts are dangerous; unless you are sprinting for the Energy Sword or Shotgun, you are vulnerable to Grenade-spamming and enemy fire.
- Don't forget the Plasma Pistol located near the Bubble Shield at the base of the tower. Use it to remove your opponent's shields, then quickly switch to any preferred sidearm to finish them off.
- The advantage of height is key on this map: you can easily see foes below you, and they'll have trouble moving and firing up at you. Finish the job by using upper levels to drop down on foes and assassinate them.
- The best camping spots are atop the structure: hide in the dark shadows there. The corners of balconies, corridors, or covered areas are also great places for ambushing adversaries.
- Aside from the ambush points, the base columns and base archway (accessed via grenade-jumping or player stacking) are the main favorite camping locations where you can fire down on foes, confusing them.
- Prior to a professional match, learn how Frag Grenades bounce; they're propelled varying distances depending on the type of ground or structure they first hit.

Professional Planning

- In team games, keep close together and cover each other's backs. Don't move too near your teammates, though, as there's the danger of being struck by a Grenade that hits or sticks to a colleague.
- Weapon dispersal is key to victory here; one of you should sprint for the Energy Sword, another should take either the Carbine or Battle Rifle for sniping, while a third heads for the Plasma Pistol to use in a combo with another weapon. A fourth player can snag the Shotgun.
- Learn this map's numerous levels and cover points, so you're constantly aware of what is above, below, and surrounding you.
- You'll often be struck by a foe you can't immediately see, from an odd angle, so check all locations—there are many ledges or cover points foes could be shooting from.
- Use this "odd angle" plan when ascending onto the upper base floor; step on the corner of the lift so you spend less time hovering and can avoid any incoming fire when you reach the floor above.
- Keep moving, stopping only to hide as your shields recharge. There is a lot of motion in this map, and lots of explosions. Keeping on the move will help you avoid Plasma Grenades or getting pinned by enemy fire.
- This map has several less-than-obvious shortcuts. For example, you can use the crates in the map's center to jump to the second level of a base. Keep an eye out for other such alternate paths.

Objective Plotting

- When playing in a four-player team game that involves base security, defense is the best offense: Make sure two of your team stay in the upper part of the base to repel invaders with tactical use of Grenades.
- One of your team should immediately grab the Shotgun from the lower-middle section of this map, to aid in defending your base, to fend off attackers, or to grab it before your foes can get to it.
- The addition of the Bubble Shield in Oddball games gives the player with the oddball an excellent defensive advantage: simply deploy the shield and strike anyone entering or nearing the bubble.
- There are no places to camp or hide where you cannot be shot or tracked down by Zombies when playing Infection mode.

Sniping/Ambush Positions

Corridor Archway

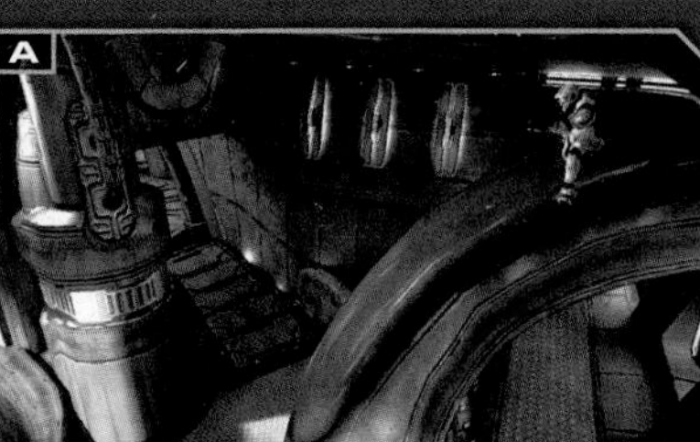

Many of the perimeter balcony corridors have curved supporting structures above them. A sniper can utilize these, as they offer excellent views across most of the map and provide drop-down opportunities to the two lower levels. In this example, you have access to cover and a base and can watch items respawn before dropping to collect them.

Top of Base Conduit

Access this area via a tricky Grenade-jump from the two-level corner behind, which has a Power Core on the top balcony. This offers cunning sniping fun when you're armed with the Carbine or Battle Rifle. Your foes won't immediately know where you are, and you can even continue vertically upward. Remember to check this location if you're being fired on!

Top of Tower (First Location)

The pink-hued tower has a swooping roofline that descends to the bridge, which is where you can access the roof and charge up the slope to a darkened crouch spot where the tower and ceiling meet. From here, you have reasonable protection from one side and good sniping opportunities across the other. You can easily escape, too.

Top of Tower (Second Location)

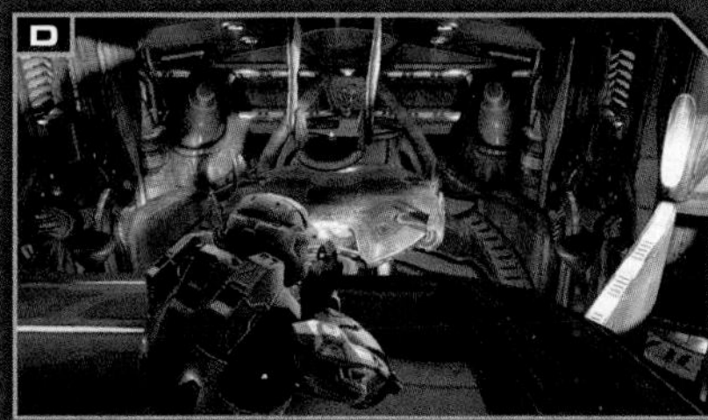

Moving to the middle of the tower roof allows you commanding views of the entire map, at the expense of being prone. However, you can quickly return to the first location if you want side cover; this is particularly useful if your team commands one side of the map, and your job is to cut down aggressors.

Energy Sword Platform Support

With a mixture of determination and dashing, you can ascend the narrow support structure that holds either side of the Energy Sword platform in place. It is difficult to spot a player when you're dashing toward the Energy Sword from the opposite direction. Then you can rain down Grenades or drop down to ambush foes.

Base Archway

With a friend to stand on or a Grenade-jump, you can leap and remain on the lip of the archway above the central exit to either base. This allows you to remain safe from Grav-Lift Grenade throws (see below) or from enemies tagging you from openings all across the level. When foes infiltrate your base, you'll be waiting for them. You sacrifice mobility for cover here.

Base Grav Lift

The lower chamber of either base is a great place to try the ascending Grenade trick! This is an ambush for which you don't need to see to be effective; simply lob a Grenade at the Grav Lift, then watch it disappear upward. A second later, there's an explosion. Then follow the Grenade up and finish any wounded foes caught in that explosion. Remember to use your radar to spot a foe.

Top of Carbine Pod

Ambush points don't have to be in hidden, dark corners. The numerous balcony corridors allow great overviews of this map, and guarding certain weapons (in this case, the Needler and Carbine down below) allows you to tag foes coming in from any direction with the intention of grabbing a high-power weapon.

At the Bubble Shield

The same plan is true on the opposite side of the map, where you can keep an eye on the Bubble Shield from the chamber or from an area where you have full view of a foe attempting to rush for the power-up. Make sure they never reach it or the Plasma Pistol. Sometimes, it is better to leave these weapons as bait.

HIGH GROUND

PMS Unforgiven

A relic of older conflicts, this base was reactivated after the New Mombasa Slipspace Event.

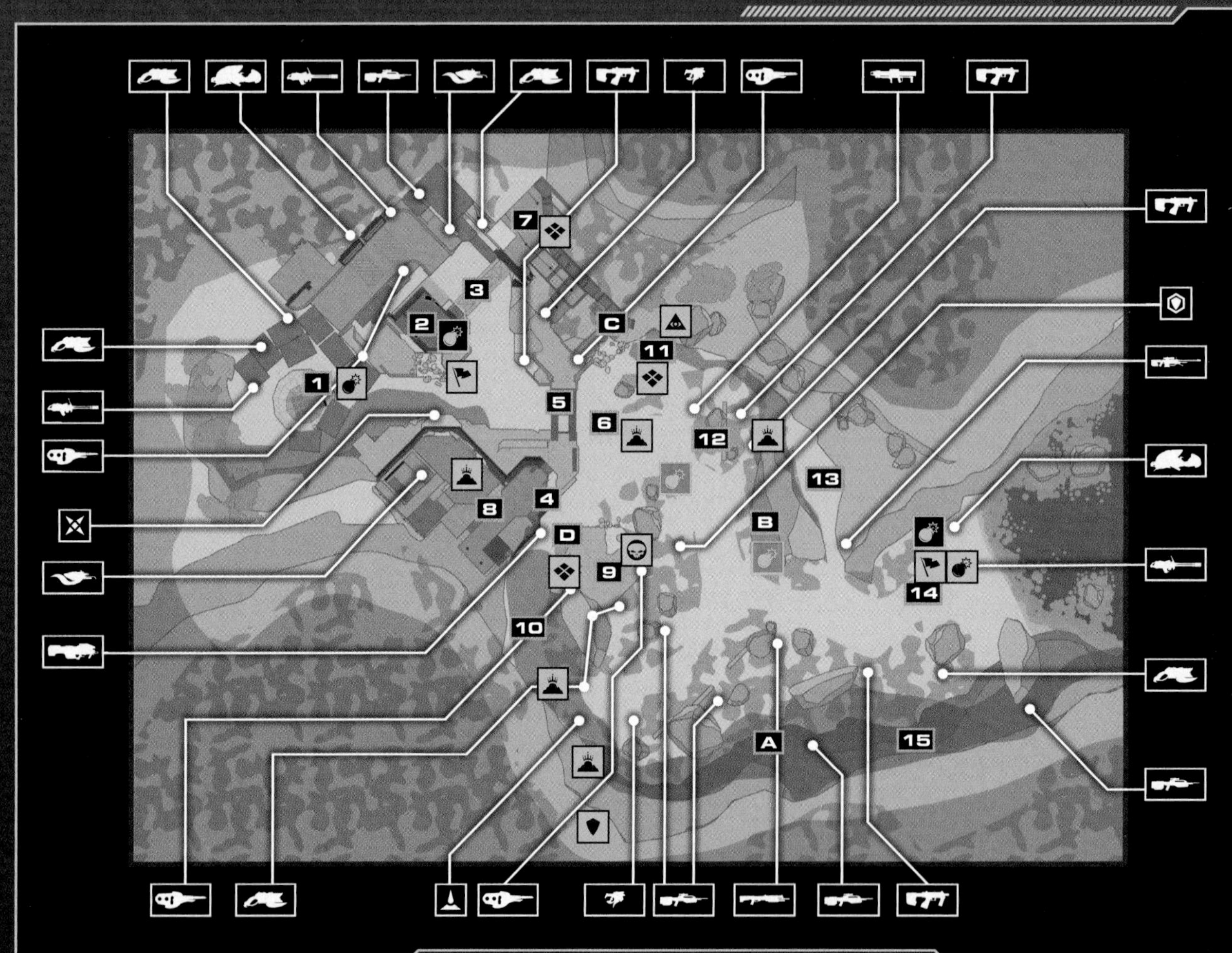

DATA STREAM

Recommended Game Variants: Slayer, One Flag, One Bomb, Territories, Team BRs

Recommended/Maximum Number of Players: 4–12

Advantageous Equipment: Spartan Laser, Sniper Rifle, Rocket Launcher, Machinegun Turret, Ghost

AVAILABLE EQUIPMENT AND GEAR RESPAWN TIMES

●○○○○ = Slow ●●●●● = Fast

Weapons	
Battle Rifle	●●●●○
Brute Shot	●○○○○
Carbine	●●●●○
Grenade, Spike	●●●●●
Mauler	●●●●○
Machinegun Turret	●○○○○
Needler	●●●○○
Plasma Pistol	●●●○○

Weapons	
Rocket Launcher	●○○○○
Shotgun	●●○○○
Sniper Rifle	●●○○○
Spartan Laser	●○○○○
Spiker	●●●●○
Vehicles	
Ghost	●○○○○

Vehicles	
Mongoose	●●●●●
Equipment	
Active Camo	●○○○○
Bubble Shield	●●○○○
Grav Lift	●●○○○
Overshield	●○○○○
Power Drain	●○○○○

Topographical Overview

Call-out Locations

Garage

Other names: Hangar

The Mongoose and Ghost spawn in this open area. This is one of the primary spawns when you first start the game.

Computer Room

Other names: Flag Room

This room has three openings, where the flag spawns and where you arm the bomb. You are vulnerable in this spot, as there is nowhere to take cover.

Back Bridge

Other names: Small Bridge

This very short bridge is one way to get from the Computer Room to the Pipe Room.

Laser Tower

Other names: Laser Spawn, Crow's Nest

This is where the Laser spawns. You are vulnerable here, but this position is the highest area on the map, giving you a great view of the entire map.

Turret Bridge

Other names: Base Bridge

This is where the Turret is located, right above the gate. A walkway connects Laser Tower to Camo Cave.

Gate

Other names: Main Gate, Main Door

This gate is located right below the Turret. Depending on the game type you choose, the gate may be closed or open. If the gate is closed, open it with the lever or switch located on your right at the top of a small flight of stairs. You cannot close the gate once it is open.

Pipe Room

Other names: Tunnel Room

A small room with a pipe inside that gives you easy but slow access to outside the base.

Bottom Base

Other names: Under Laser

Located right below the Laser Tower, the Bottom Base has many entrances. There are fusion coils placed inside the base, so beware.

Bunker

Other names: N/A

The Bunker has windows and multiple entrances. Usually the majority of fighting takes place here. The Bunker has a flat surface above it known as Top Bunker; there's a small hatch up here that allows stealthy entry to the Bunker.

Grav Lift Cave

Other names: N/A

This cave is where the Grav Lift is located. It is open and has no cover.

Camo Cave

Other names: Invis Cave

Camo, or "invis," spawns in this cave.

Rocket Spawn

Other names: N/A

Rockets spawn in this broken wall located out in the open. Everyone rushes this area in the beginning of the game, because Rockets are one of the primary power weapons.

Sniper Cave

Other names: N/A

Sniper Cave is usually the most popular cave, as it is on high ground and the Sniper Rifle—which is one of the power weapons—spawns here.

Beach

Other names: N/A

The Beach is an open area that is one of the primary spawning locations in the beginning of the game. The Ghost and Mongoose spawn in this area as well.

OS Spawn

Other names: Cliff Side, Mountain Path

OS Spawn is one of the most elevated areas. The Overshield—one of the power weapons—spawns in this area. Also, this location is one of the primary spawn points in the beginning of the game.

Tactical Knowledge

- Be careful on the Laser Tower, as it is somewhat vulnerable. There are also some fusion coils stacked on one side of it.
- Once you take control of the Laser Tower, you have a great advantage: There are two Ghosts on the map that you can easily laser from this location, and you have a great view of the entire map.

- In team play, spawning at the beach gives your team the advantage of the Sniper Rifle. Have one person acquire the Sniper Rifle and move up through Sniper Cave, attempting to take out your enemy in the crow's nest. No doubt they'll be trying to counter your attack with the Laser.
- Have another team member follow the sniper and acquire the Rockets, then push toward the Active Camo. Take out the opposition positioned on the bridge—Rockets allow you to kill multiple opponents and destroy the Bridge Turret. Other teammates can then use this distraction to enter through the Bunker and get behind enemy lines and eliminate the other team.
- If spawning in the base, two teammates should head to the crow's nest and acquire the Spartan Laser to take out any enemy vehicles that might attempt to rush for Active Camo and Rockets.
- The other team should hold down the base at Mauler and Bottom Bunker, with another guarding the bridge.

Enhanced Knowledge

One Bomb/One Flag

- When playing One Bomb or One Flag, you must try to kill your opponents before arming the bomb or taking the flag; there are so many available weapons and sniper points that you'll always be vulnerable if you leave enemies alive.
- If you can get access to the Turret Bridge, there is a device that allows you to open the gate. From there, you have a faster route to arm the bomb or steal the flag.

Advanced Tactics

- Whether you spawn with a Battle Rifle or the Assault Rifle, depending on the game, it's best to have a secondary weapon. High Ground is an open map, so it is wise to have a long-range weapon at all times.
- The Ghost can play a major role on High Ground. There are two located on opposite ends of the map. You can easily use this to help your teammates gain control of the power weapons or you can go for the quick kill.

Sniping & Ambush Locations

Sniper Position 1

Facing the base from the beach, this darkened ledge is on your immediate left. You have a great view of the map from here. Snipers love to grab the nearby Overshield and pick off players throughout the map.

Sniper Position 2

This is another easy-to-miss ledge on the right. You can jump on the ledge once you grab the Sniper Rifle, which is located right in front of Sniper Cave. Also, look for snipers behind the small wall and in the tree.

Sniper Position 3

The pipe is a good position for the sniper. It is easy to hide here, where players cannot spot you, and you have an open view of the map. Be careful, though, as someone can easily Grenade you out or come from behind and melee you.

Ambush Position 1: Laser Tower

When the opposing team has control over Laser Tower, it is very important to work as a team to gain control of this location. Coming from the beach side, two teammates can head directly to Bunker side and come up from under the opponent, while the others get the Grav Lift and Camo. Once all players are in position, they should attack to break this setup. Killing two or more enemies is a success, because this makes them lose control of Laser Tower.

Ambush Position 2

While playing One Bomb or One Flag, it is key to get the Camo and Rockets before pushing in for the objective. Once gaining control of these items, send the team (in twos) through Bunker side and Pipe Room. Sending one player through the Pipe Tunnel can give you a sneaky attack. Once the player has successfully made it through the Pipe Room, all other teammates can then push together. You must eliminate the other team before planting the bomb or grabbing the flag.

ISOLATION

PMS Deception, PMS Ruin, Athena AzMADEUS, PMS Eclipse

Containment protocols are almost impervious to pre-Gravemind infestations. What could possibly go wrong?

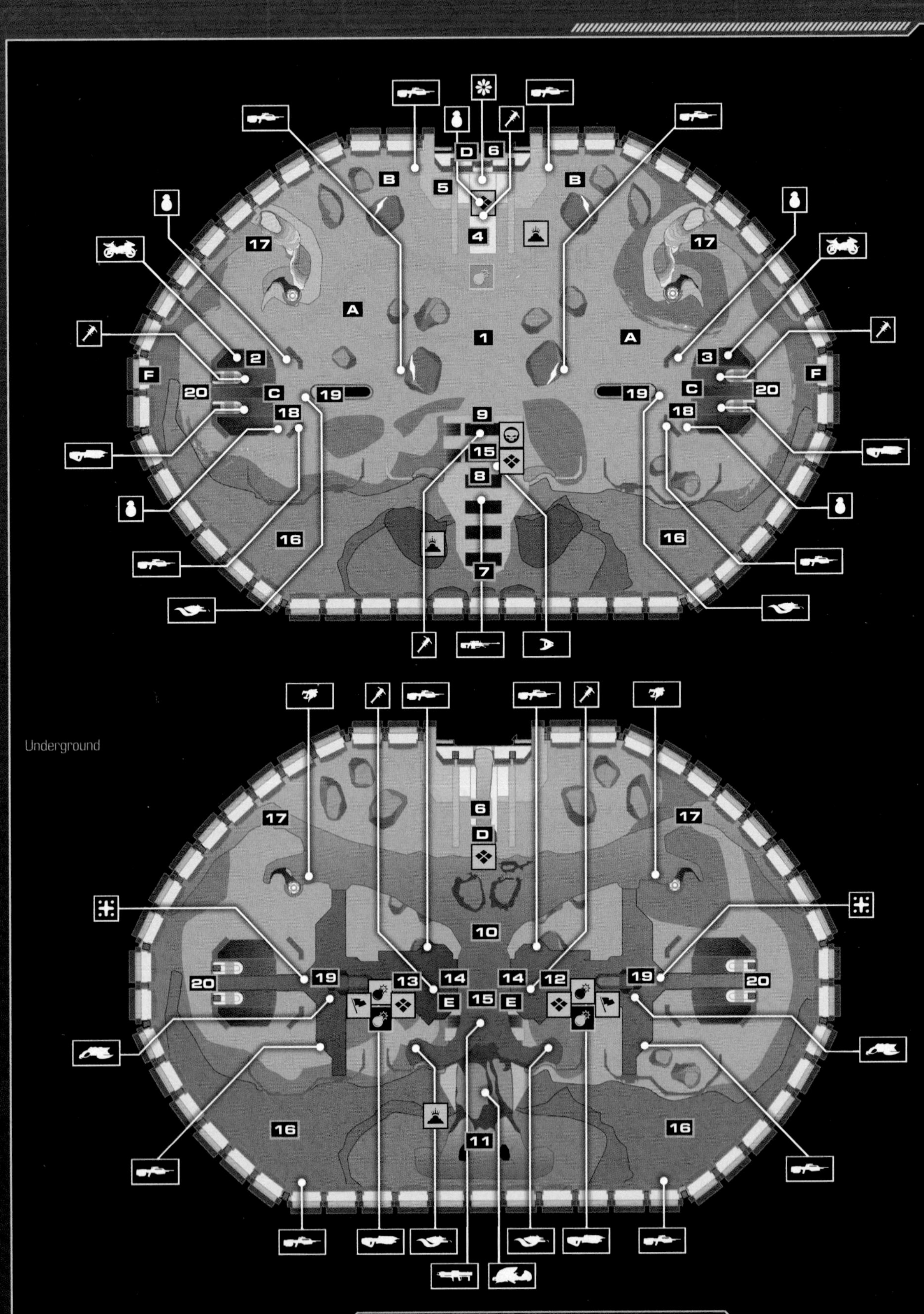

DATA STREAM

Recommended Game Variants: Slayer, Team Slayer, Team Swat, and Symmetrical Objective game types (Capture the Flag, One Bomb)

Recommended/Maximum Number of Players: 4/10

Advantageous Equipment: Sniper, Rocket Launcher, Shotgun, Ghost, Regenerator

AVAILABLE EQUIPMENT AND GEAR RESPAWN TIMES

●○○○○ = Slow ●●●●● = Fast

Weapons	
Assault Rifle	●●●●○
Battle Rifle	●●●●●
Brute Shot	●●●●○
Grenade, Frag	●●●●●
Grenade, Spike	●●●●●

Weapons	
Mauler	●●●●○
Needler	●●●●○
Rocket Launcher	●○○○○
Sniper Rifle	●○○○○
Spiker	●●●●●

Vehicles	
Ghost	●○○○○
Mongoose	●●●●○
Equipment	
Flare	●●●○○
Regenerator	●●●○○

Topographical Overview

Call-out Locations

Top Mid

Other names: Hill

Centrally positioned between the Blue and Red Bases.

Shotgun

Other names: Shotty, Bottom Concrete

Shotgun is located in the concrete standing structure against the back wall of Top Mid.

Blue Base

Other names: Blue

If standing on Sniper Bridge and facing Shotgun, Blue Base is located on the left side of the map.

Top Shotgun

Other names: Top Shotty, Top Concrete

This is the top level of Shotgun.

Red Base

Other names: Red

If standing on Sniper Bridge and facing

Wormhole

Other names: Chute, Tunnel

On Top Shotgun, there is an opening in the

Sniper Bridge

Other names: Bridge

Splitting the map in two, there is a large muddy bridge that stretches from the middle area of the map and hangs over, with views of the map's bottom level.

Dugout

Other names: Needles, Snipe Bunker

The Dugout is a small concrete structure shaped like an octagon cut in half. It marks the beginning of Sniper Bridge and is where you can find the Sniper Rifle and Needler. Like Top Shotgun, there is an opening in the back of the Dugout that drops you to Bottom Mid.

Top Dugout

Other names: Top Snipe, Top Needler

This is the topside of the Dugout.

Bottom Mid

Other names: Rockets

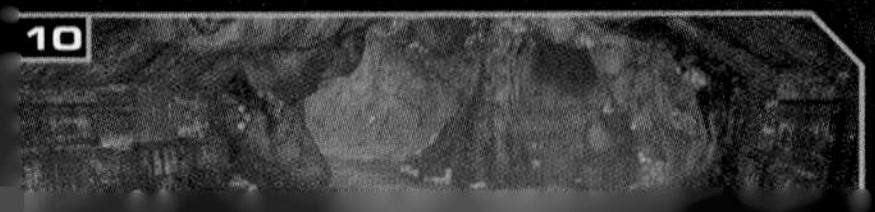

This location consists of the open area

Bottom Bridge

Other names: Ghost, Bottom Snipe, Bot

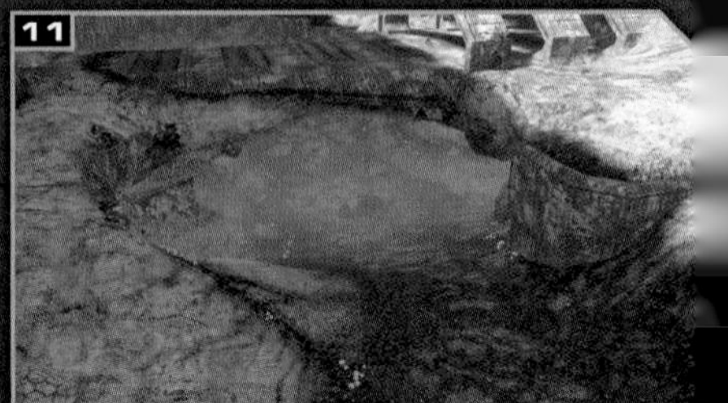

Red Bunker

Other names: Red Flag, Red Objective

Blue Bunker

Other names: Blue Flag, Blue Objective

Blue/Red Window

Other names: N/A

Rocket Drop

Other names: Rocket Hole

This opening in the back of the Dugout drops you to Bottom Mid, right on top of Rockets.

Blue/Red Pit

Other names: (not advised call-outs) Bottom Red, Bottom Blue

Each base has an area located between the topside and Sniper Bridge. It gradually declines toward Bottom Bridge and Bottom Mid. You can access it by jumping from Top Mid or the Dugout on down or by using the path behind each base and walking down.

Blue/Red Tunnel

Other names: N/A

This is used as a back entrance to the bases located on each side of Shotgun/Top Mid, toward the rear of the map.

Blue/Red Top Base

Other names: Top Red, Top Blue

This is the topside level of each base.

Blue/Red Drop-in

Other names: N/A

This oval-shaped structure is located on each Top Base. Use it to jump down into the bottom levels of the base.

Blue/Red Base Ramp

Other names: Ramp

This ramp is located on each Top Base and descends into the bottom level toward the Bunker.

General Tactics

Weapon and Vehicle Tactics

- A good combo for weapons is a Battle Rifle, a Shotgun, and a Regenerator.
- Going to the basement through the "chute" is a good escape route. If your foe is pursuing you, throw Grenades at an exit of the chute to either kill or wound your opponent.
- You can use to your advantage many of the "spore pods" that explode. They are located in the underground part of the map.
- Securing the Ghost and attacking opponents in the lower levels is a good strategy. The underground is a tiny area that is hard to escape, so players are trapped, giving you a good chance of splattering them.

Offense and Defense

- You can rush for the Sniper Rifle or the Rockets at the beginning of the game; however, you can also camp beside the two weapons and wait to ambush your opponent as they attempt to pick them up. This way you know they are down a teammate or two, and you can acquire the weapons without having to immediately defend an attack.
- If sniping is your best or preferred tactic, grab the Sniper Rifle and stay on the outermost edges of this map. This will help prevent your enemy teaming up on you. A good backup tactic is having a teammate with the Assault Rifle get the Regenerator. But if you're going to work with the Sniper Rifle, try keeping your kills to a minimum unless you prefer to be hunted down.

- A teammate who holds position atop a structure can easily spot enemies and call out their position so the whole team can find them quickly and score easily.
- You can also join a teammate and get on a Mongoose with a Brute Shot. This can be very useful in getting quick kills and damaging the opposing team. Watch out, though—you are an easy target for the Battle Rifle and can be flipped easy with a well-planted Grenade.

Enhanced Knowledge

Game Variant Tactics

- For Free for Alls and Multiteam, stay on the map's edges to prevent the enemy from ganging up on you. You can gang up on others, but it can be easy for your foes to steal your kills or kill you.
- In Infection Spree games such as Mmmm Brains, if you start out as a human, communicate with your team as much as possible. Get your team to go down into the Bunker. The Red Bunker is the best one to be in, because the zombies spawn in the Blue Bunker. Once you're in the Bunker, give each teammate a job. Have some guard the doors, some guard the windows, and the others guard the hole in the ceiling. Enemies will usually have a hard time killing you, but if they get one of your teammates, you'll have less help against the zombies, which multiply fast. The people guarding the doors are most likely to get killed first.

Advanced Tactics

- When getting shot by a pesky Ghost and you don't have Rockets, use a Brute Shot to easily flip this vehicle. Or you can use a Spike Grenade to kill them.
- Holding Top Mid with your team can be a good tactic, because you can watch where the enemy is spawning and get a good target on them. Have one by Shotgun, one by Sniper Bridge, and two holding out the hill.
- If your teammates can control the map with all Battle Rifles, Regenerators, power weapons, and the Ghost, you've pretty much won the game.
- If you go slightly down the ramp into your base, you can jump onto the ledge above. It proves to be easier to reach other major spots at the beginning of the game.
- Have all team members throw Grenades at the Sniper Rifle spawn while your opponents run to get this weapon. It can be quite easy to snag a few kills while securing the sniper area.

Sniping & Ambush Locations

Tree Camper

Climbing trees in this map gives you good ambush spots. If you go to the end branches and crouch with your preferred weapon, you can sometimes score easy kills, because inattentive opponents who don't survey their surroundings will become easy targets for you to score on.

Cover Sniping

The best environment for a sniper is behind rocks, on trees, or in a heavily sheltered place that has a "chute."

Goose Jump

You can use a Mongoose that is located near the base to jump onto a ledge on top of the bases. Use it to snipe or ambush unsuspecting foes trying to sneak into your base.

Ledge Camping

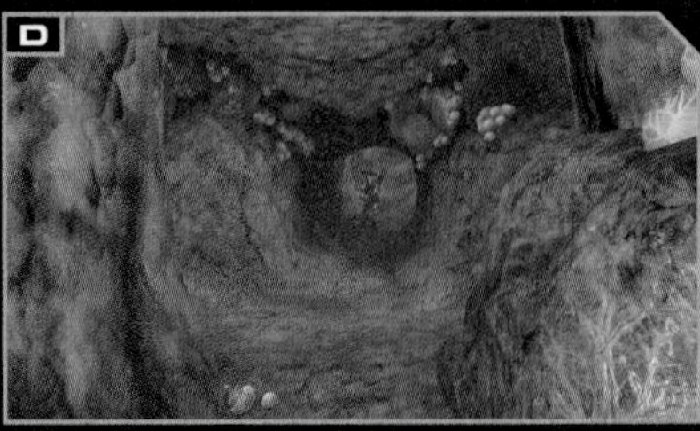

Another great spot to hide is in the Wormhole located atop the Shotgun Base. If you walk off there slowly, you can land on a small ledge, where you will be well hidden. It provides enough room for two players to hide and ambush.

Window-Shopping

Another good way to surprise the enemy is going down into your base to the window. You can see the other base and the Rockets on the floor there. A good tactic is to pick up Spike Grenades (in front of the window) and throw them at the floor or the enemy to score an easy kill.

Cubbyhole

In the back of each base, there is a small cubby that you can jump into. Use this for camouflaged sniping.

LAST RESORT

PMS Heartbreakr, Athena AzMADEUS

Remote industrial sites like this one are routinely requisitioned and razed as part of Spartan training exercises.

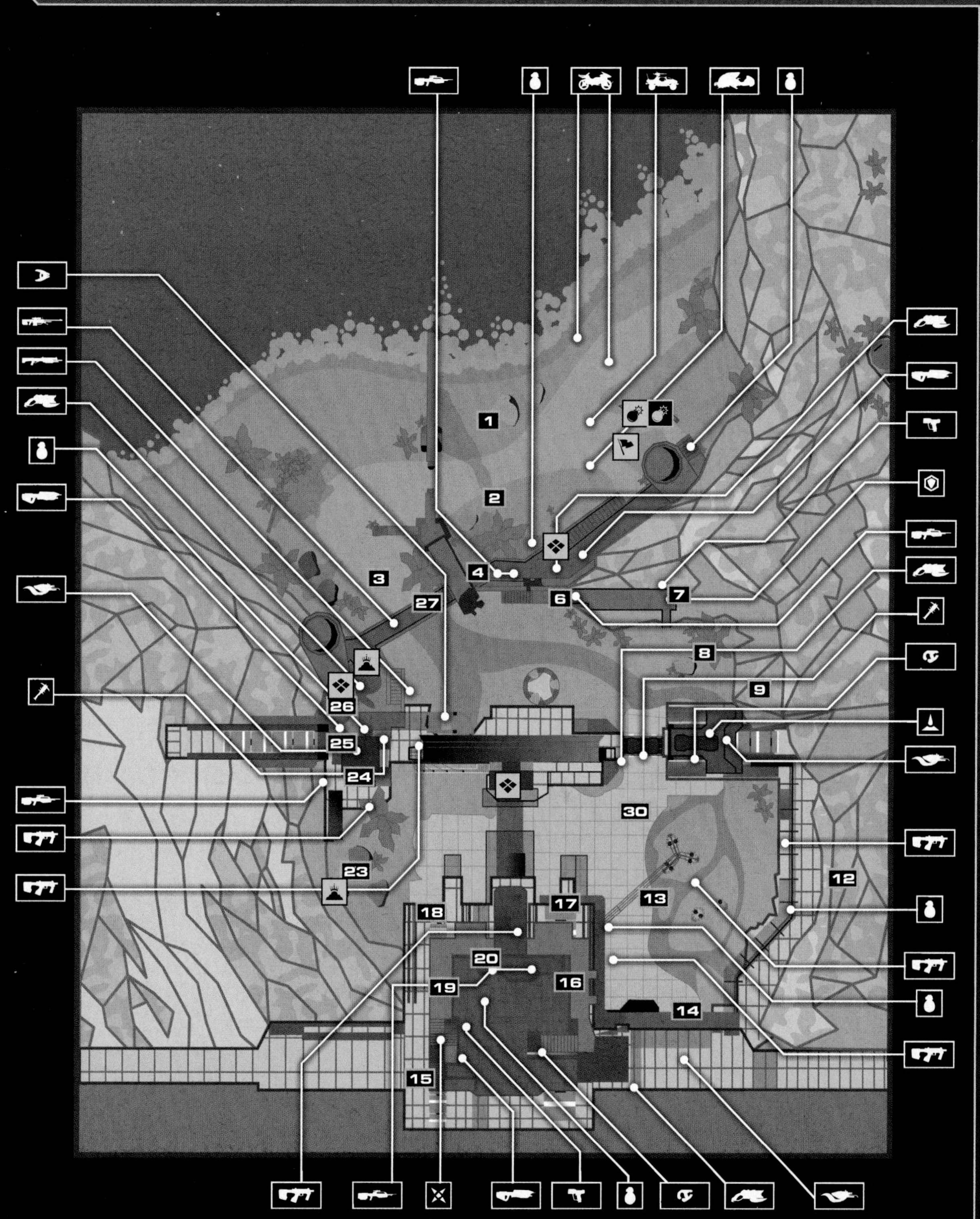

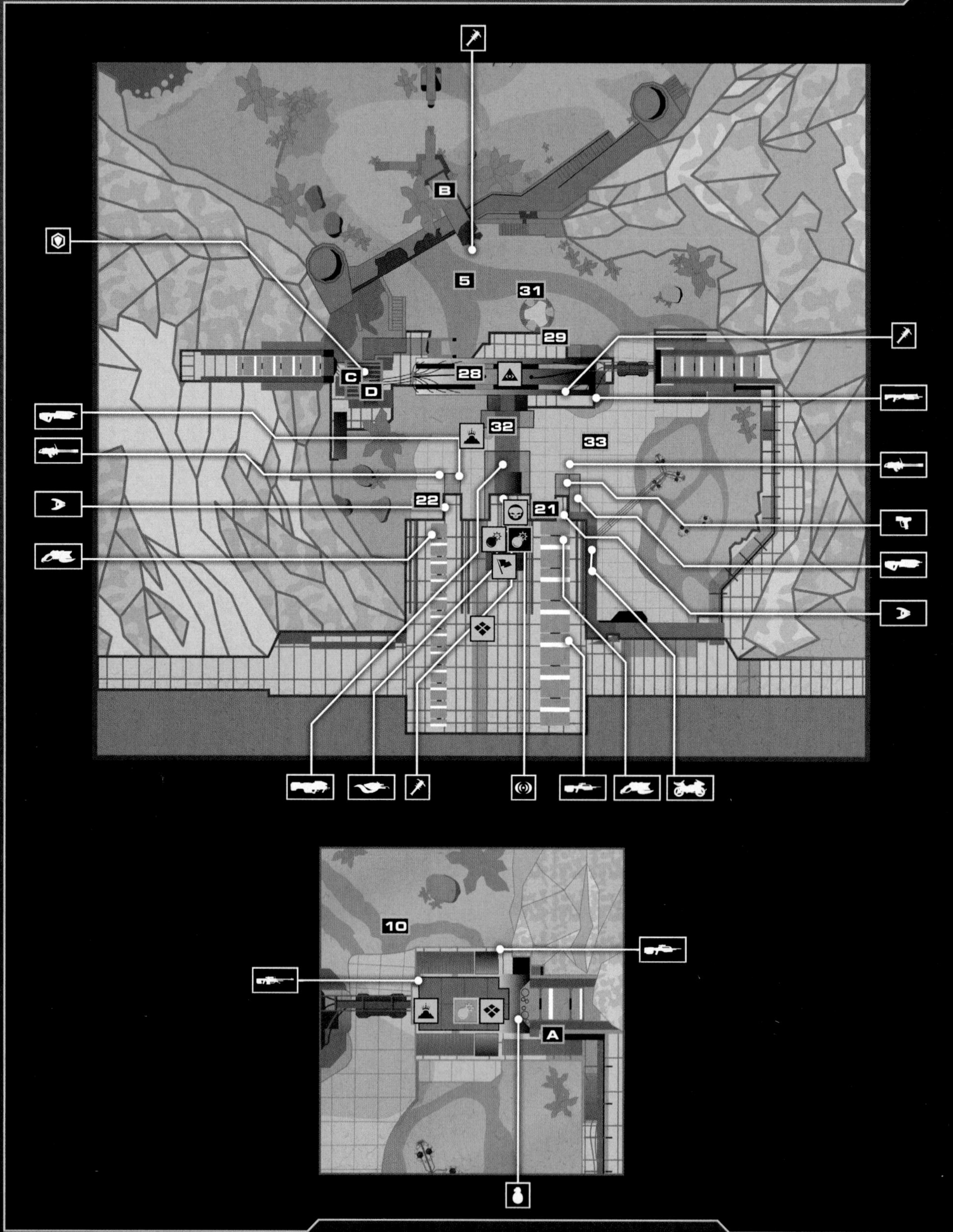

DATA STREAM

Recommended Game Variants: Team Slayer, One Flag, One Bomb, Territories

Recommended/Maximum Number of Players: 4–12/12

Advantageous Equipment: Spartan Laser, Sniper Rifle, Machinegun Turret (Objective), Warthog (Slayer and Objective), Active Camo (Slayer and Objective)

●○○○○ = Slow ●●●●● = Fast

Weapons	
Assault Rifle	●●●●○
Battle Rifle	●●●●●
Brute Shot	●●●○○
Grenade, Frag	●●●●●
Grenade, Spike	●●●●●
Machinegun Turret	●○○○○
Magnum	●●●●○
Plasma Pistol	●●●○○

Weapons	
Needler	●●●●○
Shotgun	●●○○○
SMG	●●●●○
Sniper Rifle	●○○○○
Spartan Laser	●○○○○
Spiker	●●●●○
Vehicles	
Ghost	●○○○○

Vehicles	
Mongoose	●●●●●
Warthog	●○○○○
Equipment	
Active Camo	●●●○○
Bubble Shield	●●●○○
Grav Lift	●●●○○
Power Drain	●●●○○
Radar Jammer	●●●○○

Topographical Overview

Call-Out Locations

Beach

Other names: N/A

The Beach is the offensive spawn for Capture the Flag and Bomb games. One end of the beach contains a Warthog, two Mongooses, a Ghost, and the Bomb spawn for One Bomb. Near these vehicles are two staircases leading up to the seawall (the large wall separating the beach from the interior of the map). You can take the vehicles to the other side of the beach through the archway, which leads you into the map's interior. You can also scale the bottom of the seawall to find a little walkway or tunnel leading to the archway.

Seawall

Other names: Territory 1

The seawall divides the beach from the interior of the map. Atop the staircases on the seawall are two pathways. One leads to your left and the other to your right. Near these pathways lie two Battle Rifles, an Assault Rifle, a Spiker, and two Frag Grenades.

Seawall Windows

Other names: N/A

Just above the Battle Rifles, you will see a rocky path leading to the seawall windows. The windows provide a good sniping position into the interior of the map. There are also two Spike Grenades lying at the foot of the window.

Seawall Cubby and BR Window

Other names: N/A

Taking the left pathway from the seawall, you will find the pathway splits in two. The left side leads to the seawall cubby, which spawns a Bubble Shield and a Magnum. The right path leads to BR Window and BR staircase. BR Window has a little window with a Battle Rifle resting below it and a staircase. Looking through the window, you can see a large open expanse with a huge rotating wheel. The stairway leads out to this open expanse.

Jumping out of the seawall cubby, you will land in Froman Rocks and a small structure called Camp Froman.

Camp Froman

Other names: Froman, Top Froman, Bottom Froman, Territory 3

5

Camp Froman is a small, two-level platform with stairs running up both sides. There is a hole in the rear of the top level; this allows you to drop into the bottom level. This platform is called Camp Froman because of the small plaque with the words "Froman" mounted on the wall on the top level. The top and bottom levels are called Top Froman and Bottom Froman.

Top Froman

Other names: Froman 2, Territory 3

6

At the top of the staircases on the seawall side lies a Battle Rifle. Inside Top Froman you will find a Sniper Rifle, four fusion coils, and two Frag Grenades.

Bottom Froman

Other names: Froman 1

7

If you fall down the hole in the rear of Top Froman, you will land inside Bottom Froman, where you will find three doors. One to your left, which leads to the generators; one to your right, which leads to Froman Rock; and one straight in front of you, which leads to the wheel. Below your feet lie Brute Shot and the Gravity Lift (which you can use to return to Top Froman by placing it beneath the hole). To the right you will find a Spiker and two Spike Grenades. To the left lies a Plasma Pistol. The door directly in front of you has another fusion coil, which you can use to destroy approaching enemies (but do not stand too close because it can be used against you).

Froman Rocks

Other names: N/A

8

This is the small group of rocks outside Camp Froman. Two Frag Grenades spawn next to the door leading into Bottom Froman.

Catwalk

Other names: Catwalk Stairs

9

The set of stairs on the base side (catwalk stairs) on Top Froman leads to a catwalk that traverses the side of the map. The catwalk contains seven fusion coils and an SMG. From the catwalk, you can see down into the generators and can view a large part of the map. This is a good spot from which to snipe, but it has little to no cover. At the end of the catwalk, there is a hole in the grating that leads down to the generators.

Generators

Other names: Pillars

10

The generators are the large pillarlike structures in the open area between the Garage and Camp Froman. There are two sets: a set of three and a set of two. Behind the generators below the catwalk on the small cemented area lie two Frag Grenades. Only pass through this area to reach the base or escape with a flag; the low ground here makes it very easy for enemies to pick you off.

Garage

Other names: N/A

If you are standing in the generators, there are two large openings into the base area. The one to your left leads to the garage. Just at the opening are several barriers or gates that you can open by using the gate control in the base. This room is referred to as the "garage," which contains one Brute Shot and leads into a large room called the "base."

Above Garage

Other names: N/A

If you are on the catwalk and pass the hole that drops down into the generators, you are in the area called "Above Garage." This area will lead you into the top level of the base.

Base

Other names: Base, Bottom Side Froman, Bottom Side Bubble, gate control, loading bay, Froman Side Turret, Bubble Side Turret, Territory 5

The base is the defensive spawn for Capture the Flag and One Bomb games. The base is a multilevel area with multiple stairways and entrances leading in and out. It is your defensive stronghold to protect your flag from thieves or to protect your base from enemy bombs. The bottom level of the base is heavily equipped for defense with two Assault Rifles, two Battle Rifles, two Frag Grenades, an SMG, a Spiker, a Plasma Pistol, a Magnum, and three fusion coils. There are two small doorways leading outside the base and one very large gated opening called Loading Bay. The two bottom doors lead to Bottom Side Froman and Bottom Side Bubble. There are three staircases leading to the top level. The top of the staircase nearest to the garage has a Battle Rifle and an entryway to Above Garage and the base's top level. The staircase directly opposite the garage has a Power Drain and breaks off to the second level of the base and a miniature catwalk above your head.

Bottom Side Froman and Bottom Side Bubble

Other names: N/A

The two doorways from the base's bottom level lead to these two small rooms. The side nearest Camp Froman is Bottom Side Froman, and the side nearest Bubble Tower is Bottom Side Bubble. Offensive teams will use these doorways a lot; oftentimes, in Objective games, enemies will camp in there while waiting for their team. So check them periodically to make sure there aren't any lurkers!

Base 2

Other names: N/A

The third staircase between the doors leading to Bottom Side Froman and Bottom Side Bubble will lead you to the base's second floor. This staircase has two Spike Grenades and a Brute Shot and will lead you to Base 2. At the top of the staircase, you can take one of the two doorways to your right or left; both go to the gate controls. Holding the right bumper at the gate controls opens the gates sitting at the bottom of the loading bay and garage. The two doors behind you to your right and left, which contain a Spiker on both sides, lead to Froman Side Turret and Bubble Side Turret. The hole blown into the wall at the far side of Base 2 leads outside to the Bubble Tower. Directly behind you, you can continue to follow the stairs out to Spartan Laser Spawn.

Froman Turret and Bubble Turret

Other names: Froman Side Turret, Bubble Side Turret

These are the two platforms from the doorways in Base 2. One leads to Camp Froman and the other to Bubble Tower. In the covered entrances on each side, there is a Needler and two Assault Rifles (one on each side of the platforms). Use these Turrets for defense in an Objective game and as backup to take out vehicles. However, if the other team has a sniper, you are an easy target sitting still on a Turret.

Bubble Tower

Other names: N/A

The Bubble Tower is the structure between the seawall and the base. It has two levels—Top Bubble and Bottom Bubble—and a small group of rocks next to it.

Top Bubble

Other names: Bubble 2

This is the upper level of the Bubble Tower. It contains the Bubble Shield and leads to the Wheel Bridge. On the way up to Top Bubble from Shotgun Spawn, you will find a Battle Rifle lying against the wall. This is a good vantage point to watch for people trying to rush your base. Grab the Shotgun from the wheel end and take it to Top Bubble; easily kill people walking through to the base.

Bottom Bubble

Other names: Bubble 1

The lower level of Bubble Tower contains a Brute Shot and leads to Bottom Wheel. Directly outside the door leading to the wheel are two Spike Grenades and a fusion coil.

Bubble Rocks

Other names: N/A

The small group of rocks next to Bubble Tower leading to the base is Bubble Rocks. People may crouch behind these rocks, so always make sure the area is clear if you're defending.

Shotgun Spawn

Other names: Territory 2

The small landing between Sniper Spawn and Bubble Tower is called Shotgun Spawn, which over looks the Wheel Courtyard. This is the spawn point for Red Team. The Shotgun is at the top of the stairs, coming from the archway. Near the bottom of the stairs, close to the rotating wheel, lies a Needler. A Spiker rests against the column in the middle of Shotgun Spawn. Leaning up against Bottom Bubble is an Assault Rifle and two Frag Grenades.

Sniper Spawn

Other names: N/A

This pathway is between Shotgun Spawn and the seawall and is directly above the archway. Sniper Spawn contains one of the two Sniper Rifles and has a good vantage point of Camp Froman and Bubble Turret. The sniper stairs take you back to the seawall.

Wheel

Other names: N/A

The wheel is the large rotating fan set in the center of the map. It has two levels and contains Wheel Bridge and allows you to see down into the Wheel Courtyard.

Top Wheel

Other names: Wheel 2, Territory 4

24

You can reach the Top Wheel (the smaller wheel in the center of the large wheel) from Top Bubble. To get to Top Wheel from Top Bubble, you must release the bridge by performing a melee attack on the small box on the gate. This will lower the gate leading to Top Wheel. You can also reach Top Bubble from Laser Spawn and can drop in one of the holes in the axis of the wheel to reach the Active Camo. You also have a vantage point on enemies in the Wheel Courtyard trying to make their way into the base.

Bottom Wheel

Other names: N/A

25

A Shotgun spawns at the wheel's bottom section, near the far end (the end nearest Camp Froman, referred to as Wheel End).. An SMG spawns on the side opposite Wheel End. It is a good idea not to stay here, as it is the lowest point of the map, making you vulnerable to attack.

Wheel Courtyard

Other names: N/A

26

A Needler is in the open expanse between the wheel and the seawall, lying up against the wall of Bottom Wheel nearest Bubble Tower. It is recommended that you only drive through here; if you walk, you will probably get sniped or taken out by people on higher ground. You can take BR Staircase toward the seawall or the staircase up to Shotgun Spawn if you need cover.

Wheel Bridge

Other names: N/A

27

You can let down the bridge to reach Top Wheel; to release it, melee it or shoot it. Releasing the bridge will make a lot of noise, so it's not the stealthiest approach.

Laser Spawn

Other names: N/A

28

The Laser platform is between Top Wheel and the base. The Spartan Laser spawns here, and you can take out vehicles and people running into the base. There isn't very much cover, so be careful and retreat into the base if necessary.

Under Laser

Other names: N/A

29

The area underneath Laser Spawn contains two fusion coils. People will walk through here to get into Bottom Side Bubble and Bottom Side Froman. You can easily snipe people walking through here from Top Froman or the catwalk. There are two Frag Grenades lying against the wall in between Bottom Side Froman and Bottom Side Bubble. Next to the entryway to Bottom Side Bubble are two fusion coils.

Tactical Knowledge

- Good advice for most Team Slayer or Objective games is to *stay with your team*. Do not run off by yourself and attack. Beware of your surroundings; do not rush into groups of enemies in which you are outnumbered. This is a sure way of ending up with multiple members of the other team firing on you. Always keep with your teammates to watch each other's back.
- Use "team killing" tactics. If one of your teammates is being fired upon, fire at the assailant. They will appreciate it when you have saved their lives, and you will appreciate it when they have saved yours.
- Prioritize the weapons you pick up. Since this map is mostly a large open area, we recommend going for mid- and long-range weapons such as the Sniper Rifle, Spartan Laser, and Battle Rifle.
- Usually controlling the base, using the Spartan Laser at Laser Spawn, and taking cover in the base while shields are low will be a great advantage for your game.

Enhanced Knowledge

Team Slayer Tactics

- Work with your team to hold a base or position wherever you spawn. For example, if your team spawns near Camp Froman, stay there and hold that area once you have control. Take out the enemy team by communicating to your team which position you want to move to and move together.
- Stay out of the courtyards or anywhere on the ground. There are many high points on this map, and if you are running around on the ground, it won't be long before you die. If you spawn on the ground, your first priority is getting to higher ground.
- Always use call-outs. Even if you die, you can alert your team to where the enemy is , and your team can take advantage before the foe's shields recharge.

One Flag/One Bomb Tactics

Defense

- Place your players wisely on the map. Do not completely desert the base to capture the power weapons, but also do not have everybody hide in the base waiting for the eventual attack from the bomb carrier or flag bandit. Send a few to patrol the area, and get the Laser to take out incoming vehicles and the Sniper Rifle to take out footmen before they get into your base.
- The Turret can also help quickly destroy a group of footmen or a Warthog. Leave a few teammates inside the base to protect the many entryways. Preferably, use short-range power weapons such as the Shotgun or dual-wielding SMGs or Spikers.
- Watch out for Mongooses and Warthogs coming from the beach. Use the Spartan Laser and Turrets to take them out. Also protect the gate controls to prevent vehicles from driving into your base.
- If your flag is taken, consider taking a Mongoose to the beach to cut off the other team before they score the flag.
- Remember, you will not be able to see the enemy's bomb or your stolen flag when the other team picks them up. So communicate with your team the direction the flag carrier is going.
- If you are planting the bomb or capturing the flag, use the Active Camo.

Offense

- Never try taking the flag or planting the bomb by yourself. Coordinate an attack with your teammates. Have a sniper attempt to take out the opposing sniper and laser.
- Driving the Warthog or Mongoose with your bomb carrier or flag stealer in the passenger seat is the recommended strategy. The Warthog and Mongoose can get your team into the other base, capture the flag or plant the bomb, and get out within minutes. All three seats in the Warthog should be full (a driver, a Turret shooter, and a footman to plant the bomb or capture the flag).
- Taking the Warthog requires teamwork and communication. You need to have your sniper or other teammates communicate if the Laser has been taken by the other team.
- If you take the Warthog, do not drive through the wheel. Instead, go around the wheel in front of Camp Froman, into the generator area. This way the Laser won't have time to tag you. Exit the vehicle quickly so the Laser doesn't jump down from Laser Spawn and destroy your vehicle.
- Crouch-walking makes you invisible to enemy radar. When you are storming the base, this can be an excellent method for sneaking in undetected with the bomb or grabbing the flag when the other team is not looking.
- If you are the bomb carrier or have just stolen the flag, try not to hang on to the bomb/flag for dear life when someone is trying to kill you. You can get an instant kill with a bomb/flag melee, but if enemies aren't in close quarters, it's best to drop your load and fight off the other team with your weapons on hand.
- Once you obtain the flag, you need to know whether the opposing team is using the Laser. If it isn't, then take a vehicle back to the beach. If they are using the Laser, then you should walk to the flag. Communicate with your team on the enemy team's location to determine which way is best to walk the flag.
- When planting the bomb, do not desert the area. Stay around and protect the bomb so the other team does not disarm it. Throw Grenades or Power Drains on the bomb when the other team attempts to disarm it. You may leave the base or take cover when the time reaches five seconds—that is the time it will take the enemy to disarm the bomb. If they have less than five seconds, it's not possible for the opposing team to disarm it.

Territory Tactics

Defense

- Defend your five territories within the rounds, trying to keep the other team's score as low as possible. Work with your team and concentrate on the territories that are being taken.
- Note how the other team is playing (for example, are they sending all of their team to one territory, or are they spreading out to many territories?). Also, watch for people on vehicles trying to sneak into the base while you're distracted with the farther territories.

- Try rushing to Territory 1 on the seawall (take a Mongoose, as they are faster and more discreet). Players often capture Territory 1 and become complacent, because they don't think anyone is going to stop them. If you can fight them off for the first minute or two of the game, it can be quite discouraging for them and gives them less time to capture the other territories before the round ends.
- As always, communication is key. If you see a territory flashing, immediately announce it to the entire team; the more people that storm that territory with Grenades and shots, the less chance the other team has of capturing it.
- Territory 1 will probably be taken eventually. After this, you can have easy visibility of most territories from Territory 4. Someone else should be protecting Territory 2. If you see an X (indicating a teammate's death) and have positioned yourself with a midrange weapon, you should be able to run over to Wheel Bridge to take out the foe. Having the higher ground will give you the advantage, and your foe's shields should be down from the battle with your teammate.
- If you are seizing a territory and it's almost captured but you see a group of opponents rushing you, throw down a Bubble Shield (if you have one) to get the last few seconds to capture the territory.

Offense

- Try to capture the most amount of territories in the given amount of time. You will spawn closest to Territory 1; always go for this territory first but watch for people possibly rushing from the other team. Listen up and watch your radar for people entering from BR Stairs.
- Once you have Territory 1, you can either split up to Territory 2 and 3 or try to send all your team to capture one territory at a time. Keep in mind the more players on a territory, the faster it is captured. Don't put more than two players in at a time or you are just giving the other team a triple kill.
- Try to reach the base on a small fast vehicle. Before you go for the territory, open the gate. If you're lucky, the other team has left for weapons and farther territories and you can capture it without dying. If you're not that lucky, take another small vehicle when you respawn and drive it into the garage this time. If you can, take someone on the backseat of the Mongoose; you will be more likely to succeed. Make sure to get off the vehicle in the garage. You don't want to be so obvious driving right in. The garage entrance gives you a good view of people who you need to take out in the base before capturing the territory.

■ Sniping

Above Camp Froman

Summon the Grav Lift at the top of the catwalk stairs. Step on the Grav Lift and land on the steel bracket sticking out of the wall. Walk up it and step on the copper pipe. Follow the pipe against the wall until you reach the little nook above Camp Froman. This area is almost directly underneath the area that says "Section K2433." This spot has an excellent view and is great to snipe from. However, there is not a lot of cover, so you may have to leave if you are discovered.

Top Seawall

The walkway in between the seawall and Sniper Spawn has an access you can use to reach the roof of the sniper stairs section. The wall next to the Sniper Rifle is crumbled away. You can step on this wall and follow it up to the roof. This is a common sniping position and gives you a good view of the map. Players commonly call this place "top of seawall." You can also jump onto the right palm tree (nearest Sniper Spawn) and snipe from there and can get atop the seawall from Seawall Side. There is another crumbled wall to the left of the Battle Rifles. Get on this wall and scale the top of Sniper Windows, then jump onto the top of the seawall. If you need to recharge your shields while sniping, you can run to the back of the roof.

Top Bubble Tower

Ride the wheel spoke to the top of Bubble Tower. Stand inside the bottom of the wheel and ride the spoke or fan upward. Once the wheel spoke is horizontal to the ground, back up to get some running room. Run forward and jump into the little nook sliced into the wheel. From there, jump from the square metal railing to the wires on top of Bubble Tower. Do not move off the wires or you will slide off the roof.

Another way to get atop Bubble Tower that is easier and requires less time than the previous method is to throw a Grav Lift on the cement handrail on the stairs that go from Bottom Bubble to Top Bubble. Jump on the Grav Lift and let it lift you up once. At the top of the lift, move a little to the right or left to get a slightly larger lift. Allow yourself to lower back down. Let yourself be lifted up a second time. At the height of the second lift, jump again and move yourself over onto the wires.

ONGSHORE

David S.J. Hodg

andoned during the invasion of Earth, the Mombasa Quays are now bereft of commerce, but rife with danger.

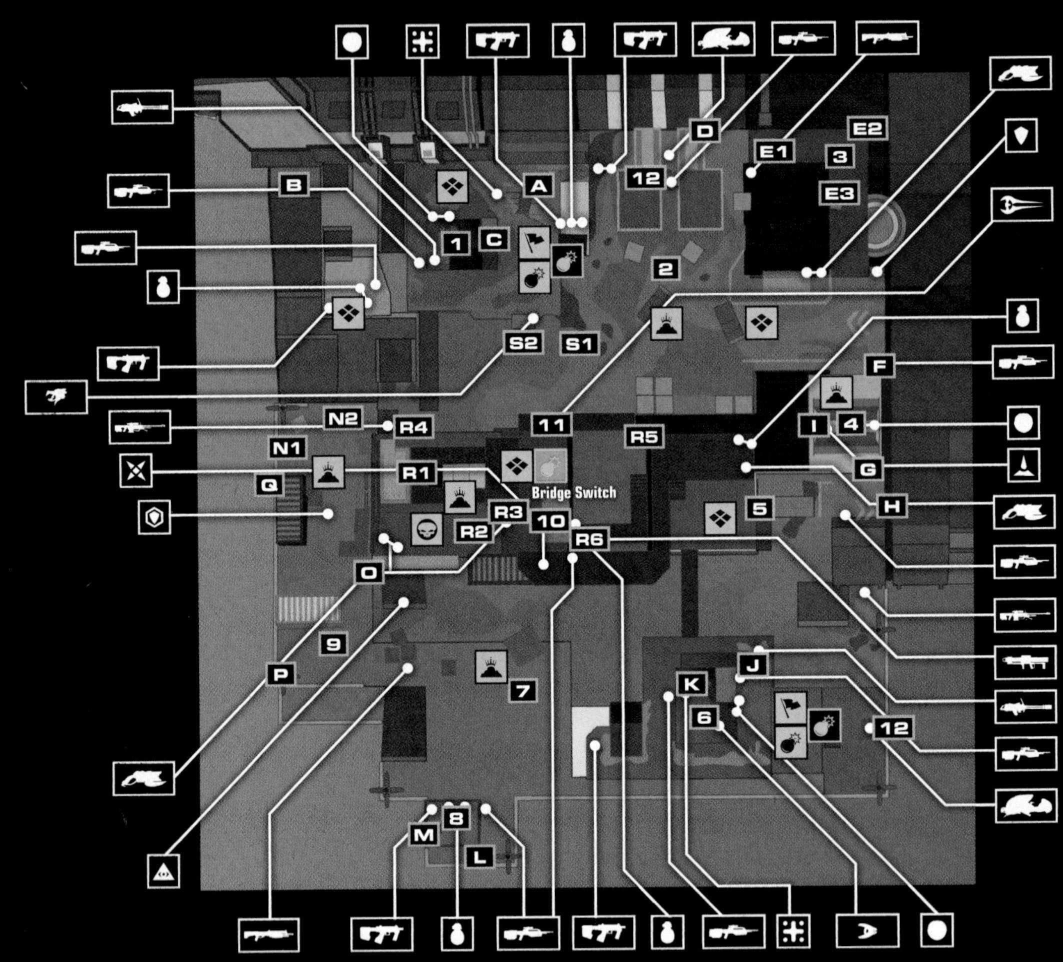

DATA STREAM

Recommended Game Variants: Assault, Capture the Flag, Infection, King of the Hill, Oddball, Slayer (Free-for-All), Team Slaye

Recommended Number of Players: 4–12

Advantageous Equipment: Battle Rifle, Cloaking, Energy Sword, Ghost, Grav Lift, Overshield, Rocket Launcher, Shotgun

AVAILABLE EQUIPMENT AND GEAR RESPAWN TIMES

●○○○○ = Slow ●●●●● = Fast

Weapons	
Battle Rifle	●●○○○
Energy Sword	●○○○○
Grenade, Frag	●●●●●
Grenade, Plasma	
Machinegun Turret	●○○○○
Needler	●●○○○

Weapons	
Plasma Pistol	●●●●●
Rocket Launcher	●●○○○
Shotgun	●○○○○
SMG	●●●●●
Spiker	●●●●●
Sniper Rifle	●○○○○

Equipment	
Active Camo	●○○○
Bubble Shield	●●●○
Grav Lift	●●●●
Overshield	●○○○
Power Drain	●●●○
Regenerator	●●●○

Call-Out Locations

Building K

Other names: Base, Controls, Sword, Turret, K

The defenders' base, this multilevel location has an interior you can enter from numerous openings, and a rusting ramp offers excellent views of the container yard. Atop the building is a Turret, and the building offers excellent views into the hopper and across the inlet courtyard, too. The control room in the building also activates the hopper bridge.

Inlet Plant Courtyard

Other names: Courtyard, cargo bay, cargo, forklift, Sword

This is a very large area with several crates and an accessible balcony leading to the hopper room. There's an Energy Sword on this balcony and a forklift truck underneath. There's free access around to the container yard and broiler areas, and the rear of the chamber offers access to the L-shaped room. There's an Overshield near here and a parked Ghost.

L-Corridor

Other names: L, corner, Overshield

Hidden in the far corner of the inlet plant courtyard is an L-shaped corridor, offering both defensive cover and sniping opportunities across the previous two locations and through the broiler itself. Just outside the L-corridor is the Overshield.

Broiler

Other names: orange, cones

The most direct access to and from the adjacent areas of the two bases is through this cube-shaped chamber. Open garage doors at either end allow for excellent access and a variety of ambush or sniping points. The inside corners of this room provide cover; there's even a Grav Lift surprise or two, as well as the power-up to take in here.

Broiler/Freezer Exterior

Other names: metal bridge, two-tier zone, freezer entrance, docks

On the quayside area of the map, located next to the main quayside thoroughfare, are two raised areas, both of which can be easily accessed. The top one leads directly into the hopper room and to a balcony that leads to the area above the freezer entrance. It also leads to Building M via a narrow metal bridge. The lower area leads down to the quayside exterior, the broiler, or up to the other area. This is a dangerous zone to remain in.

Building M

Other names: base, dock base, M, Ghost, Turret

Although it doesn't have as many floors and is lower to the ground than Building K, the other (offensive) base is located on the docks themselves and features a roof access to and from the metal bridge **5,** a Turret on the roof, and entrances into the building. To the side is parked a Ghost. You can run completely around this building.

Quayside Exterior

Other names: docks, pier

7

The main, lower thoroughfare stretches along the exterior side of this map from the container yard, all the way to the Ghost in the corner near Building M. From here, you can access the covered quay, yard, hopper, freezer, and broiler exterior areas, plus the taco hut, and is where this side's team races in from.

Taco Hut

Other names: Fish Taco Hut

8

Offering some of the best cover and sniping opportunities, the Fish Taco Hut is a cube-shaped building on the corner of the map, offering views across the container yard and covered quay. Step around the back of the building for protection, dashing in for the Energy Sword, Active Camo, or Rocket Launcher when the coast is clear. You can even snipe from the roof, too, if you use the Grav Lift.

Container Yard and Covered Quay

Other names: boxes, lamppost, dinghies, lower dock, Fronks sign

9

Expect a crush of foes milling about this area due to the numerous cover opportunities. This links the exterior area from the dock side of the map to Building K. It also offers access into the hopper and a covered quay that houses a Shotgun and Active Camo. There's a ramp up to Building K, too. Use the containers for cover and as stepping stones up to some amazing camping spots!

Freezer and Hopper

Other names: bridge entrance, hopper, freezer, barrels, Rocket, Sword

10

The two separate rooms inside the middle building offer views straight through from Building K to the exterior docks. They also house two of the most important and powerful weapons: the Energy Sword and Rocket Launcher. A key choke point, the Hopper is multifloored and allows access up toward a gate and the hopper bridge. There are several ambush points in here, which you can access from the inlet courtyard, the quayside, or the hopper exterior.

Hopper Bridge Extension

Other names: nest, sniper, overlook

11

This is the most cunning of locations. Once you unlock the gate and extend the bridge (which is done at the top of the hopper room or inside Building K, depending on the game mode), this offers some of the best sniping or ambushing points of all. With two teammates up here, you can rain death down onto Building K. You can even access the extended bridge from Building K using a Grav Lift.

Ghost Riders

12

12

There are two Ghosts on this map, one parked in the inlet plant courtyard near Building K and the other adjacent to Building M. Once you're driving a Ghost, it is relatively easy to maneuver the map perimeter, driving the quayside around the container yard, into the inlet courtyard, and around to the broiler. You rack up a good number of kills by using the infinite ammunition of the Ghost's cannons or by Boosting into foes. Or, you can stop the other team from making a capture.

· Zone Knowledge

▲ Building K, freezer access, and inlet plant: the "interior" side of this map and slightly easier to defend

Building K, the freezer and hopper access chambers, and the inlet plant courtyard that leads to the L-corridor and broiler are slightly easier to defend. They are darker, making sniping more advantageous, the area is wider from the perimeter to the Energy Sword location, the courtyard and Building K floor is larger, and there's no water to accidentally fall into. The forklift truck (which can be destroyed) and balcony allow you to quickly take the Energy Sword before wading in to slay those trying to take the Rocket Launcher or backing up to the Overshield and heading around to attempt your own type of rampage. Building K is a multilevel hideout; with a couple of friends, it can be easily defended from all sides. Drop into the courtyard, and you have quick access to the Ghost and numerous crates to hide behind. The L-corridor is built for sniping and can stop almost all rushes from the outside.

▲ Building M, freezer access, and broiler: the "exterior" side of this map, offering easier access to the freezer

Built lower to the ground, the exterior base may have a smaller maneuvering quayside to run about in, but there are still numerous places to stop foes from entering. The broiler room can be targeted from the base, and the cover the base provides can easily stop an attack from the right. The Turret can doubly make sure of this, but always be on the lookout for foes heading out of the upper hopper chamber—an alternative route to the Energy Sword and Rocket Launcher your team should try to use. The usual route into this cluster of buildings is up the ramp on the ground or the other ramp under the "Fronks" sign, which is dangerous, but with backup or distractions in other areas, you should be able to claim one of these mighty weapons.

▲ Container yard, hopper access, and taco hut: The "exterior" thoroughfare between bases, with two levels of access

The exterior corner of the map has several rusty containers that offer protection both inside and out. There are also a couple of worthy sniping spots accessible only via a Grav Lift, and there's the taco hut, which is an excellent place to prowl and snipe from, as it offers views of many entrances across the exterior side of the map. Be aware of flank attacks from the opposite side, especially as Ghosts are available. There's also a lower quay to navigate, so make sure your team has already claimed the Active Camo and Shotgun down here, which can help repel attackers immeasurably. Access into the hopper via the "Fronks" sign usually results in a battle, so you might wish to sneak around toward the rusting ramp left of Building K if you're assaulting the base.

▲ Freezer interior and bridge extension access: the interior, offering access outside and in, and the bridge where you can rain down death from above

Inside the hopper and freezer chambers, expect fights every few seconds, due to the two most powerful weapons being in close proximity to each other. As described at the end of this section, there are several excellent ambush points all the way up the multifloored hopper interior. The freezer is a simple affair with only two entrances. Bring the Grav Lift if you want to hide yourself in the more shadowy locations! The hopper is very difficult to hold, as there are entrances everywhere, so you may wish to retreat to the top of the chamber, or at least the upper level, and rain death on those down below who think the coast is clear. Finally, there's a bridge you can half extend, which allows you to leap onto Building K—a real problem if you're trying to defend it! The bridge, which is accessed only via the top of the hopper room, offers great protection and views of the interior side of the map. Remember to check where that wayward fire is coming from; it might be a foe on this bridge.

· Tactical Knowledge

Longshore is an asymmetrical map that is built for objective game styles. There are two bases, Building K and Building M, located on either side of the map, and there are three ways to reach each of them: via the container yard, the freezer (with multiple exits), or through the broiler. Between the two bases segmenting the two bases are the upper and lower quayside docks, the freezer and hopper (the room adjacent to the freezer), the bridge (which is accessed from the top of the hopper or via Grav Lift from Building K), and the broiler. The defending team's map is Building K, while the attackers use Building M as their base of operations. Each base has a Ghost parked next to it and a Turret to utilize. The majority of combat occurs inside the hopper, the lower quayside, the top of Building K, and inside the broiler.

Enhanced Knowledge

Offensive and Defensive Posturing

- Generally, the first few moments of a match on this map involve a race to the Rocket Launcher in the freezer. This is especially true, as there's a nearby Energy Sword to grab as well. Of course, entering this high-traffic area is risky, and there are four exits you can expect enemies to attack from when you're in the freezer and adjacent hopper.
- Battle Rifles are both numerous and devastating on this map; use them to dominate your foes thanks to the countless sniping possibilities and the closer-combat prowess they exhibit.
- When using the Battle Rifle or another powerful weapon, try extending the hopper bridge and then sit in the middle, using your weapon to rain fire down on foes milling around Building K. You can also pick off players coming up the ramp behind you; this is an easily defended location. Be sure to keep your back covered, either with a teammate or by looking behind you periodically. To remove a foe from this spot, use Grenades.
- In general, you should be sniping from hallways with a long line of sight (such as the L-corridor) or from high points like the top of the taco hut.
- The Shotgun and Cloaking are adjacent to each other on the lower quayside by Building M. This combination is much sought after and is deadly to most foes. Alternatively, you can grab the Shotgun or Energy Sword and run along inside the interior of Building K; this is a great area to attempt multiple kills. In general, the more powerful the weapon, the more advantageous it is to use it on this map.
- Although the Chaingun Turret is heavier and you turn more slowly when you detach it, there is still great potential to use this devastating weapon, due to the long line-of-sight opportunities this map has. Turrets are also useful when attached, because their ammunition is limitless while mounted, but you're an easy target for being picked off from long range with a Sniper or Battle Rifle.

Professional Planning

- This map is suitable for objective games like Capture the Flag, Oddball, King of the Hill, Infect, Assault, and Team Slayer. Due to the powerful weapons such as the Battle Rifles, Rocket Launcher, and Sniper Rifles, Slayer games are recommended, too.
- Because Longshore is asymmetrical, it is extremely well suited to One-Flag Capture-the-Flag (CTF) or One-Bomb Assault matches (where one team's location is much easier to defend than the others, with teams taking turns defending and attacking). Use this type of match instead of normal CTF matches, for example.
- In these types of objective games (such as Capture the Flag or Assault), the attacking team should always try to extend the hopper bridge that is accessed by and located above the hopper. You can easily reach Building K from this point. The switch extending the bridge is normally located atop the hopper room, but it changes to the middle floor of Building K in team games.

Objective Plotting

- King of the Hill (KOTH): There are several advantageous King-of-the-Hill tactics to try on Longshore. The first is the hopper room; grab the Rocket Launcher and move to freezer and hopper interior S1, S2. Blast the barrels with the Rocket Launcher to push them slightly away from the wall so you're only visible from one angle approaching the Hill. Remember, in King of the Hill, out of sight means out of mind!
- King of the Hill: In the inlet courtyard **2**, maintain a position close to the forklift truck, under the hopper bridge. You won't need to worry about attacks from behind, and the position can be enhanced by obtaining the adjacent Overshield and Energy Sword.
- King of the Hill: Become King of the Container Hill by obtaining the position inside the small Traxus crate; it allows for cover, gives you a shaded position, and allows you to rack up the points during the time you're out of sight.
- King of the Hill: The lower quayside under the container yard with the dinghies is another spot to try. Grab the Active Camo and Shotgun nearby if you can, and defend the position between the roof beam that bisects the corner next to the Camo. Use the corner and nearby column as cover.
- Broiler: Set up shop completely within the broiler, deploying the Grav Lift (as shown under "I Broiler: Surprise" in the "Sniping/Ambush Positions" section) in one corner and riding it up against the ceiling. You avoid immediate notice by the enemy and have the upper hand when attacking, obtaining extra and precious KOTH points in the process.
- Oddball: Using Active Camo is encouraged. This power-up is found on the lower quayside under the container yard. You can also use the Active Camo to sneak into bases with less attempts on your life.
- Forge: Longshore already has an excellent default layout and offers entertaining match possibilities of any type. Although it is difficult to build upon this fantastic layout, you can try to make the map more "sniper" friendly. Add more long-range weaponry, as there are many long lines of sight and a large amount of cover, making this map more adaptable than most to sniper weaponry.
- Forge: Because of this map's relatively large size and being easily navigated by vehicles, a "rocket race" or "Mongoose VIP race" has been tested and found to be most entertaining.
- There are a large number of sniper positions to try, but the best are on the tops and sides of either base, near the Fish Taco Hut, on top of the stand (accessed via Grav Lift and either entrance to the broiler).
- The following sniping or ambush positions have been play-tested and chosen as the best places to camp or launch a surprise attack from. Many of these positions keep you unharmed during Infection games, and most offer fantastic vantage points you can exploit during team matches.

Sniping/Ambush Positions

Building K and Inlet Plant

Building K: Overlooking the Inlet Plant

Moving to the rear of Building K's roof is a better strategy than staying at the front, where you are easily spotted and cut down from the Energy Sword balcony or rusting ramp. Move about at the back of this area, training your weapon on the broiler and periodically checking the L-corridor, balcony, or rusting ramp.

Building K: Rusting Ramp

You can quickly sidestep left, into the cover afforded by the height and the concrete points of Building K, while using this to snipe at foes all the way to the taco hut. You can easily fall back, and (in team games) assume you have friends guarding your left side, which is the only area you can't scan effectively. Check for foes heading up from the Energy Sword hopper balcony, container yard, or lower quayside.

Building K: Interior

It is well worth keeping a presence inside Building K, especially if you're guarding the controls to the bridge. You also have two doorways to fire from, and the walls offer the extra protection you need. There's little room to maneuver from a thrown Grenade, but you should have tagged foes coming in from the broiler or hopper before this occurs.

Inlet Plant Lighting

This is not a particularly easy place to stand, as you're likely to slide off, and it requires you to jump on a parked Ghost to a crate (which is another good place to stand, close to the L-corridor); you then take a Grav Lift and jump up to the spiked light. This offers a commanding view of the inlet plant courtyard, but you'll drop down if you're not careful.

L-Corridor Ambush

The three positions inside the L-corridor offer extremely good long-distance sniping opportunities; you can escape unscathed thanks to the two openings this room offers. The first location gives good ambush points across to Building K, allowing you to cut down foes there and those heading for the Ghost. The other two locations allow you to watch foes coming in from the broiler and tag everyone all the way to the side of Building M! For enemies trying to grab the Overshield, you can ambush them here. The pallet offers extra hiding opportunities.

Broiler

Broiler: Inlet Side

Watch the longer weapons you wield, such as the Sniper Rifle, as the tip of the barrel sticks out, giving away your position. Choose either side of this corner wall, depending on whether you're planning to head out toward the quayside or not. Snipe the entire inlet plant courtyard, much of Building K, and foes entering the courtyard from the hopper or container yard ramp.

Broiler: Quayside

Choose either side of this open garage door to snipe from, which gives you a great view of Building M but leaves you exposed unless you're really hugging the metal walls. From here, you can mount an attack on the base, head up and into the hopper, or fall back into the courtyard. Also check the orange cones for signs of disturbance. Remember the Grav Lift is in this chamber, too.

Broiler: Garage

This area is more useful during team games, when you have backup who can bring down foes in the quayside area using the Grav Lift as shown. Shoot the Grav Lift so there's no sign of your antics, then crouch on the lip of the garage top, and ambush anyone who heads in or out of the broiler. This isn't even the nastiest surprise in this area!

Broiler: Surprise

The broiler surprise tactic involves you using a Grav Lift in either of the two larger corners inside the broiler; remain floating, scraping your head on the metal lattice ceiling—when foes enter the broiler, you'll be floating a few feet up from their weapon's sight, giving you an advantage to rain down Grenades or cut them down a split second before they can react. This is a great strategy during King-of-the-Hill matches.

Building M and Taco Hut

Building M: Turret Defenses

Both Buildings K and M have Turret defenses. Although Turrets are powerful, it is usually unwise to man one because you're easily sniped. There's just as much to target from either Turret, and the sheer power of the weapon can be enough to counteract the impact on speed and maneuverability you incur if you pick one up.

Building M: Interior

This area offers fewer floors than Building K and has different aiming opportunities, as you can target the broiler exit, the hopper and freezer exits, and all along the quayside. Be wary of the rear entrance, though; you're easily able to be outflanked by a rear attack. Keep moving around here, and use those walls as cover, popping in and out to inspect the thoroughfares you're guarding.

Behind the Taco Hut

Despite the tendency for some overeager players to plummet off the quayside to a terminal swimming session, the rear of the taco hut is an excellent spot to stay. You have a huge number of sniping places to hit, including the ramp up from the lower quayside, the containers, the freezer and hopper entrances, and most of Building M.

Taco Hut Roof

Using the Grav Lift located inside the broiler, you can jump atop the Fish Taco Hut close to Building M. This is one of many large advantage points in Infection matches and a great sniper vantage point in team games. You can keep moving forward and backward, or duck down to avoid incoming enemy fire, although avoiding Grenades can be a problem!

Container Yard

Dinghy Patrol

These two locations, facing different directions in the lower quayside area, allow you to easily protect Building K or the Active Camo and Shotgun, respectively. Expect foes down here for just this reason, and Ghosts usually travel down here, because it's easier to navigate than the container yard. Use the pallet and support columns as cover.

Container Yard Freezer Pipe

This one takes a little time and a lot of skill to master; grab the Grav Lift from the broiler, and run to the container yard, placing the Grav Lift on the corner of the container shown here. Then leap up and land on the rusting pipe just left of the "Fronks" sign. It is possible to stand up at this position and tag foes in the yard, the quayside, or coming out or into the hopper. They all die with a confused expression on their faces....

Container Yard Lamppost

Offering additional height at the expense of additional exposure, you can try to use a Grav Lift and land atop any of the lampposts. In this example, we placed a Grav Lift on the container shown here, and landed on the lamppost, but it's easy to overshoot and land in the water. From here, you can snipe away at Building K, the yard, and the quayside.

Traxus Container

This allows you to maintain a cunning sniping spot from an area you can easily reach: simply shimmy along the narrow edge without falling in the water, and take up a sniping position at either end. All the other containers (or the insides of them) can be accessed, too.

Freezer and Hopper Access

Freezer and Hopper Interior

These two areas are both on the lowest floor of the hopper and show the area between the Energy Sword and the quayside access **R1** and the Freezer itself **R2**; the Rocket Launcher is lying inside, coaxing enemies (usually into a firefight). Expect this to be a cluster of foes and fighting, and take refuge near the barrel pallet close to **R1**, as you're afforded extra protection.

Freezer and Hopper Interior

The remaining locations, all technically inside the hopper chamber that runs between the quayside and plant courtyard, is filled with sniping and ambush positions. The first one **R3** is behind the valves, next to the "Do Not Block" sign. This allows you to tag foes in the busy thoroughfare below. The next one **R4** is only accessible via a Grav Lift (as shown) and allows you to perch above the Energy Sword, ready to pounce or attack from a strange angle. The next location **R5** is in the upper hopper connecting room and allows you to exit onto the exterior areas, with views of Building M and the broiler. Expect heavy fire from here, and thus sniping opportunities. The last location **R6** is atop the second room and leads to the bridge extension. Unless your foes are using a Grav Lift, there's no way they can attack you from the bridge, making this sniping spot very beneficial.

Bridge Extension

These two sniping positions on the bridge half span the inlet plant courtyard and Building K, directly above the Energy Sword. These positions are close to each other but require completely different maneuvers to reach. Stand at the first location by accessing the gate atop the hopper. Access the bridge support **S2** by using a Grav Lift from Building K. Both locations offer fantastic ambush and sniping positions and quick and easy retreating or fleeing. The first position allows you to pull back, using the underside of the bridge as protection.

NARROWS

PMS Ruin, PMS Dark Ivory

Without cooling systems such as these, excess heat from the Ark's forges would render the construct uninhabitable.

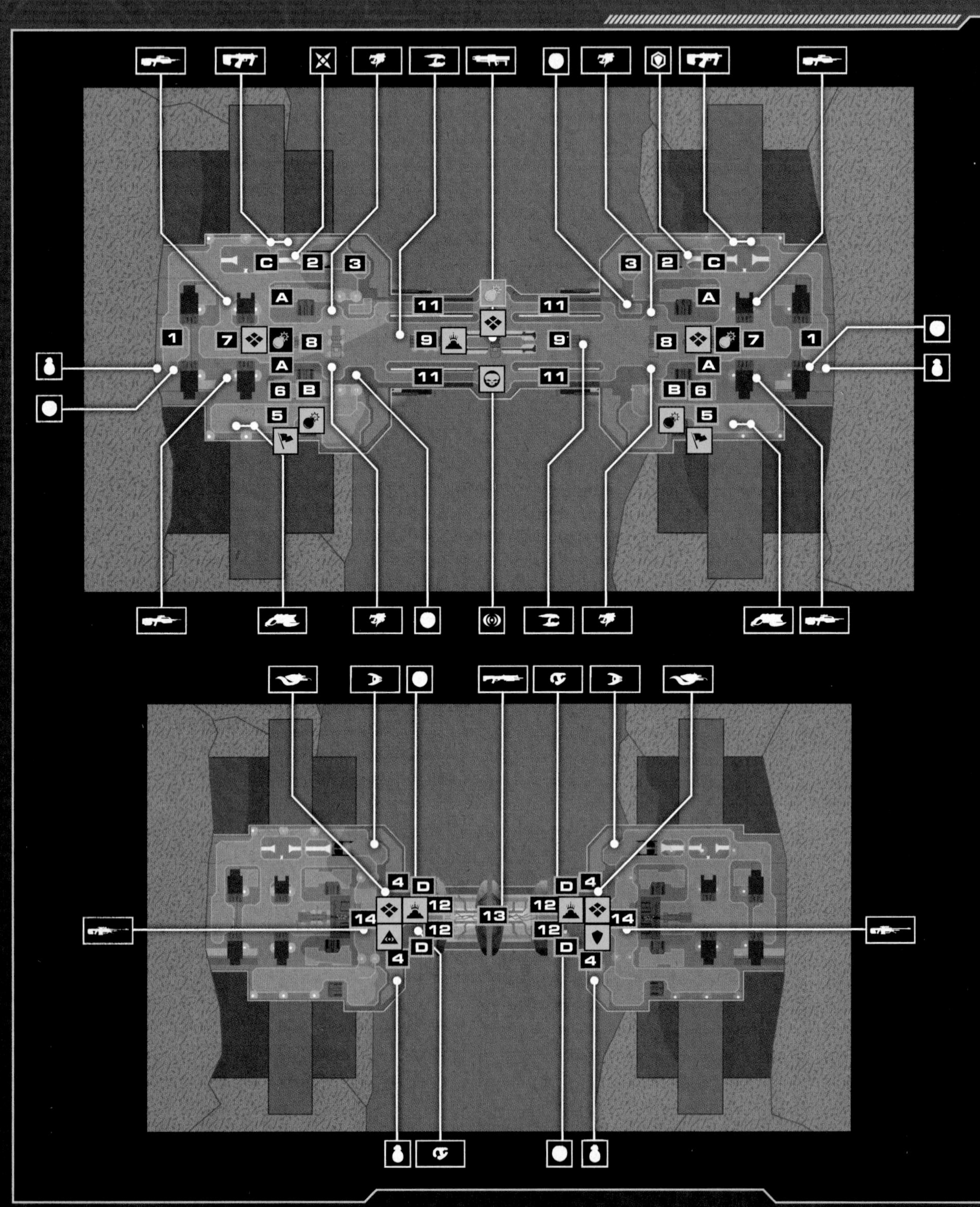

DATA STREAM

Recommended Game Variants: Team Slayer, Team Swat, Team Sniper, Capture the Flag, Assault, King of the Hill

Recommended/Maximum Number of Players: 4-8/10

Advantageous Equipment: Sniper Rifle, Rocket Launcher, Mauler, Shotgun, Bubble Shield, Power Drain

●○○○○ = Slow   ●●●●● = Fast

Weapons	
Battle Rifle	●●●●○
Brute Shot	●●●○○
Grenade, Frag	●●●●●
Grenade, Plasma	●●●●●
Mauler	●●●●○
Needler	●●●○○
Plasma Pistol	●●●○○

Weapons	
Plasma Rifle	●●●●●
Rocket Launcher	●○○○○
SMG	●●●●○
Shotgun	●●○○○
Sniper Rifle	●○○○○
Spiker	●●●●○

Equipment	
Active Camo	●○○○○
Bubble Shield	●●●○○
Overshield	●○○○○
Power Drain	●●●○○
Radar Jammer	●●●○○

Topographical Overview

Call-out Locations

Narrows is a long series of two bridges connecting a blue base to a golden red base. Besides the two bridges, there are two Man Cannons, one on each side. Bright blue jet streams will launch your Spartan into the air into your enemies' base. Narrows is a symmetrical map with only a few variations on each side. The Red Base has a golden beam of light shooting out from it, and the Blue Base has a flowing waterfall.

Narrows has become popular simply because of its mathematically smooth layout. When spawning in the Red Base, all call-outs are opposite those of the Blue Base. Instead of flowing right from Stage into Man Cannon, you'll take the ramp left. The only other variation is the Active Camo present (making this nicknamed "Invis Tunnel") instead of an OS Tunnel wrapping around the bottom of Man Cannon to the flag spawn.

Red Stage/Blue Stage

Other names: N/A

The Stage is a lighted step up onto a platform on the very back of each base.

Man Cannon

Other names: N/A

Going right from Blue Stage, there is a ramp heading to the double-paned glassy floors where you will find the Man Cannon.

Landing Zone

Other names: Needles

Past the Man Cannon, on the small avenue to the right, hang left as you drop down and pass through the Landing Zone/Needles.

Power-up Tunnel

Other names: Overshield Tunnel, OV Tunnel, OS, Camo Tunnel

Follow through the glassy path to a small tunnel with open beams, and you'll cross an Overshield. This is known as the Power-up Tunnel. One base has an Overshield, the other Active Camo.

Flag Spawn

Other names: N/A

Continue until the tunnel opens up onto another ramp. This leads you to the area known as Flag Spawn. In all flag Objective games, this is where your team's flag will spawn. You'll pass a small ledge on your left that hides two fusion cores.

Flag Attic

Other names: N/A

To your right is an archway from the base that has a small, climbable ledge. This ledge is known as Flag Attic.

Base

Other names: N/A

There are two paths from flag to base separated by a large chunky pillar. Take either path into Blue Base. "Base" is categorized as the area in front of Stage, the completely flat place between the two pillars. Blue is the darker-colored base and Red is the golden-colored base.

Lobby

Other names: N/A

As you head forward out of the base, the incline leads you into Lobby. Immediately after the horizontal structure, to the left and right of you, there are two smaller wedges on the floor. This is known as "L3" on the left side and "R3" on the right.

Mohawk

Other names: N/A

Moving forward from Lobby, you pass a large, pyramid-shaped structure known as Mohawk. Standing at Mohawk, you'll see two small curbs that open up to a pocketlike drop into the bottom level. Being pocketlike, these areas are nicknamed Pockets. The right-side pocket closest to you is R1, followed by R2, which heads into Red Base. The left side is known as L1 and L2.

Top Mid

Other names: N/A

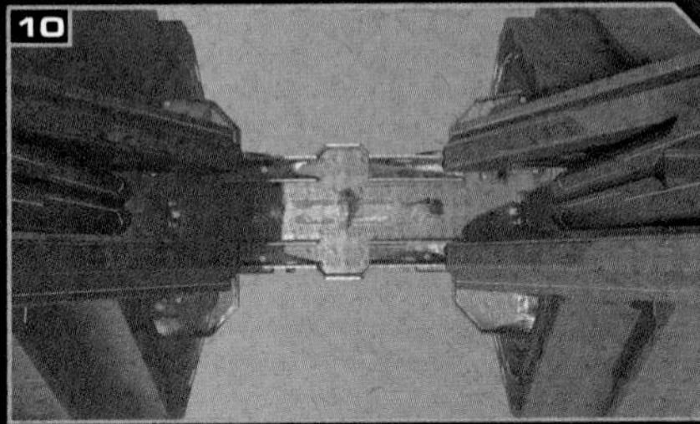

Since Narrows is symmetrical, the call-outs for both sides are essentially the same. Heading forward out of the Lobby from either base, you'll see a horizontal structure in front a fusion coil. This marks the exact middle of Narrows, commonly called Top Mid. From your base, the short platform between L1 and L2 on the top level is Left Mid. R1 and R2 is Right Mid.

Pockets

Other names: R1/R2 and L1/L2

Standing at Mohawk, there are two small curbs that open up to a pocketlike drop into the bottom level. Being pocketlike, they are nicknamed Pockets. The right-side pocket closest to you is R1, followed by R2, which heads into Red Base. The left side is known as L1 and L2.

Bumpers

Other names: N/A

Take the ramp down (L1) to the bottom level. Facing your base, you'll see another pair of wedges to your right and left known as Bumpers. Throughout the game, keep in mind that all call-outs concerning right and left are made when you spawn and look toward Top Mid, even as you come down L1 into Bottom Mid and turn back toward Blue Base. The Bumper to your right is Left Bumper; the same goes for the one on your left. This may seem confusing at first; the trick is only remembering where you initially spawn. You will always drop down to L1 and approach Left Bumper. If you move left from L1, you will head into Bottom Mid.

Bottom Mid

Other names: N/A

This is easily designated by the force-field bridge that crosses from the Red Base to the Blue Base. Turning right from L1, passing the Bumpers, you head back to your Sniper Rifle spawn.

Sniper Room

Other names: Sniper

This open, medium-sized room is nicknamed Sniper, because the only feature in the room is the Sniper Rifle, which is leaning against the back wall. Facing the Sniper Rifle, move left and you'll approach a small walkway leading back into the room with the Man Cannon.

Enhanced Knowledge

Narrows is one of the most versatile maps in Matchmaking; you'll find 14 different game types. Given its symmetrical layout, Narrows is fair game for any objective. Here are the game variants available:

FFA Games: Slayer, Oddball, Krazy King, and Juggernaut

Team Games: Team Slayer, Team Swat, One Flag CTF, Multiflag CTF, Assault, One Bomb, Neutral Assault, Team Oddball, Team King, and Team Snipers

The game variants can be further separated into five categories for an in-depth approach to each: FFA, Team, One Side Objective, Neutral Objective, and Classic Objectives.

FFA: Slayer, Juggernaut, Oddball, Krazy King

- For all FFA game types, the basic strategy is load up on power-ups, power weapons, and equipment. Using Rockets to clear out the Objective field makes acquiring points easy. Do not sit back and snipe. You have to maintain a very aggressive play style to win in FFAs.
- One you have the Oddball, it's best to have a power weapon and a Bubble Shield. Move forward to pick up whichever power-up you're closest to, with OV being the obvious choice. Because the Oddball is a one-hit kill, the Power-up Tunnel makes a great vantage point if you put your back to the wall. If you're carrying the Bubble Shield, another great position with the Oddball is the Cubby on Stage. Basically, any nook in which you can put your back to a wall is goal for Oddball
- In Juggernaut games, it's good to have a long- and short-range weapon. Narrows offers a Battle Rifle and a Shotgun. As the Juggernaut, you can escape larger groups with the Man Cannon, which allows you to focus on more one-on-one combat. Power Drains and rocketing at the Juggernaut is a quick way to eliminate it. Don't forget—you're next, so save some Rockets and flee the scene.
- Krazy King Hill moves every 30 seconds, so always keep an eye on the clock. The hill is random, so people generally don't know which way to run when that 30 seconds is winding down.

Team: Team Slayer, Team Swat, Team Sniper

- There are two ways to approach Narrows while playing Team Slayer games. Depending on your team's ability to attain quick kills, you may play very offensively or defensively. At one point in the game, your team may have to employ both approaches.
- During Team games, an optimal approach for any style is sending two players to Bottom Mid and two to Top Mid. The two players going Bottom Mid will each grab a power weapon—one grabs the Sniper Rifle, and the other takes the Shotgun. Then, the sniper should head to Attic or Stage, and the player with the Shotgun should head to Top Mid. The two players going Top Mid should head toward Rockets. One player grabs Rockets while the other supports them with a Battle Rifle. Drawing the opposing team to your base is an optimal defensive approach.
- If the opposing team isn't rushing your base, your team should move to Top Mid to try to bring them out of their base. Once you bombard your opponent with longer-range BR shots and plenty of thrown Grenades, they should attack forward to push you back.
- A good tactic for playing an offensive game is to have one player, ideally with a Sniper Rifle, hold down the area directly behind the rest of the group. Then two players should locate themselves in the Mid and actively shoot together and fall back when weakened. To minimize deaths, have only one scout head toward the opposing base. This person should always be a main slayer and usually the strongest player. The two players in the back can shoot forward to back up your main slayer and can turn to defend your sniper.
- Use the same offense/defense style of play with Team Slayer, Team Swat, and Team Sniper; however, don't put a sniper in the Attic. It's the first place foes with Sniper Rifles check.

One Side Objective: One Flag, One Bomb

- With any Objective game, frequent and accurate call-outs and communication are more important than a strong BR team.
- In defense mode, keep two players with BRs on your flag or bomb while the other two rush for power weapons. Your sniper should run to Bottom Mid, picking up the Sniper Rifle. Use the Sniper Rifle to clear out anyone on Bottom Mid so that you can then advance to pick up the Shotgun. The sniper should then head to Top Mid to shoot enemies approaching from their base and trying to rush over from the Man Cannon. The second player running out should have grabbed Rockets. Due to this weapon's ability to wipe out larger groups of people, possibly with one round, it's possible your team will survive if you get outnumbered. After obtaining Rockets, take the L1/R1 jump to Flag while a supporting teammate with the BR heads to Top Mid to back up and defend the sniper.
- In offense mode, use the same strategy as far as power weapons go. Pairing up while on offense will help your team grab power weapons; even though the defensive team is trying to grab them as well, they are also defending a flag. Deciding which player grabs what before the match starts is necessary to avoid confusion. Paired in teams, rush to kill the opposing team to obtain the flag or bomb. The sniper should stop rushing at Top Mid so they can shoot down into their flag and clear the objective. The flag/bomb carrier route consists of two choices. The first involves taking the Man Cannon to your destination. This is risky and quick and can entail resetting your flag/bomb if you die. The second choice is to run back-to-back with a teammate down to Sniper; the person not carrying the flag/bomb acts as a meat shield and support cover. Running through Pockets aids in dashing from attacks on Bottom and Top, as you can bounce between the two; however, be warned—this is a longer route. Advance to R2/L2 and make the jump to your flag. Arm the bomb and defend or capture the flag.
- Remember, it takes 15 seconds to completely fuse the bomb; however, it takes only 5 seconds to disarm it. Your team must defend the bomb for at least 11 seconds! A good tip for keeping the bomb armed is throwing a Power Drain on it. While the enemy tries to disarm, you then simply shoot them. *Never* throw a Bubble Shield over it. That will only give your foe cover and time to disarm. If you drop the bomb/flag because you die or need to defend yourself, you and your teammates have 30 seconds to pick it back up before it respawns to the enemy base.

Neutral Objectives: Neutral Assault, Oddball, Team King, King of the Hill

- When playing Neutral Assault and Oddball, follow the same defense and offensive mechanisms as when playing One Flag and One Bomb. The only offensive detail to change is to have one person rush for the Sniper Rifle, clearing Bottom Mid to obtain the Shotgun. Then have three teammates rush Top Mid, with one player grabbing the ball/bomb while the other two support him with BRs.
- In Neutral Assault, after you arm the bomb and have four seconds before the fuse goes off, players can rush back to Top Mid to grab the freshly spawned bomb.
- During King of the Hill matches, run three players to power weapons and one into the hill. The three power-weapon players then position themselves around the hill to kill opponents attempting to enter it. The hill moves every 60 seconds, rotating from Top Mid to Red Sniper and Blue Sniper randomly. Always keep an eye on the clock.

Classic Objectives: Multiflag, Assault

- Maintain your team with one person defending and three attacking, ready to grab the flag or bomb. Successful teams will count out the deaths of the opposing team, because the optimal time to rush for the Objective is when three foes are in respawn. This will give you a few seconds' head start on grabbing the flag/bomb and heading back toward your base.
- Your main slayer shouldn't be carrying the flag. However, they should be ready to fall back and kill the opponent carrying your flag back to their base.
- The same routes back to your base as discussed in One Sided Objectives will also be used in Classic.

General Tactics

- You can use the Man Cannon to quickly get from base to base.
- Any equipment can be thrown through the Man Cannon and onto spawning enemies.
- Keep an ear out for the noise the Man Cannon makes; this will alert you to an enemy's approach.
- You are vulnerable in the landing zone off the Man Cannon, as you always land in the same spot. All the enemy has to do is throw one Plasma Grenade and you're history.
- While traveling via Man Cannon, you can deploy a Power Drain on unsuspecting enemies on Top Mid. Caution: Do not Power Drain your teammates!
- Bubble Shields can be deployed on teammates while they are in the Man Cannon.
- Always keep an eye on Top Mid; the main battle is always here.
- Remember, you can throw a Grenade from your base to almost three-quarters of the way across the map.
- Before jumping through the Man Cannon, grab the Needler and lock onto an enemy.
- Your team's Attic is a great vantage point from which to snipe, because your enemy will have a hard time figuring out where the bullets are coming from. Take your time and you'll get headshots.
- While being stormed in the base, use the Pillars to run around and try to confuse your opponent. This buys some time for your shields to go back up.
- Don't load into the Man Cannon if someone is loading in on the opposite side. You will collide and both will die. If this happens on accident with an opponent, make sure you get a kill by getting a shot in!.
- The easiest way to get someone out of the Attic is to shoot a Rocket at them or stick them with a Plasma Grenade.
- Fusion coils aren't just map décor; they can be used as equipment to kill approaching enemies.
- Grenades can be bounced from Sniper to Top Mid off the Pockets.
- The Bumpers on Bottom Mid aid in excellent surprise Mauler kills.
- Cubby Hole is a good hiding spot for snipers; it can buy you a few seconds to regenerate your shield.
- Being chased on Bottom Mid? Drop to OS to lose enemies.
- R3/L3 provides great cover for mid- to long-range weapons.
- It's easy to complete a kill on a "one-shot" opponent when they're jumping up and down trying to retreat. Try not to panic on Narrows while being fired upon. You can always fall back and grab cover; there's plenty.

Advanced Tactics

- You can jump from the ledge at L2/R2 to the Man Cannon or flag.
- If you run the flag from Bottom Mid, drop a Bubble Shield behind you while running for quick cover.
- Run your flag back-to-back with a teammate to absorb bullets and maintain cover fire.
- Use Left and Right Mid to snipe down on respawning enemies.
- Grab the Sniper Rifle and line up behind the Man Cannon. The stream from the Man Cannon gives you cover.
- While getting fired upon on Top Mid, use the Pockets to drop down to Bottom and run away.
- At close range, Plasma Grenades can be effective; stick them onto enemies, then line up your crosshairs on them. Aim for their middle section.

Sniper/Ambush Locations

Left/Right Attic

The Flag Attic/Left Attic provides great vantage points for Objective games. There is a horizontal and vertical structure built into the Lobby that you can use for cover. On each side of the vertical structure, there are ledges that you can climb on. The ledges are tilted at a 45-degree angle, which makes it easy to access without skilled jumping. The attic on the left side is known as Left Attic; the right is Right Attic.

Flag Attic

To your right, you'll approach an archway from the base that has a small, climbable ledge. This is Flag Attic and is a great place to hide while waiting for your team to grab the flag.

Behind Man Cannon

Grab the Sniper Rifle and line up behind the Man Cannon. The stream from the Man Cannon gives you cover.

Behind Bumpers

Use the Bumpers for surprise attacks in Bottom Mid and as a hideout to let your shields recharge in cover.

ORBITAL

PMS Ovaryacting, PMS Eclipse, PMS Dark Ivory, PMS Shadowleet

With a lot of situational awareness, and a little luck, hopefully the only thing you will lose is your luggage.

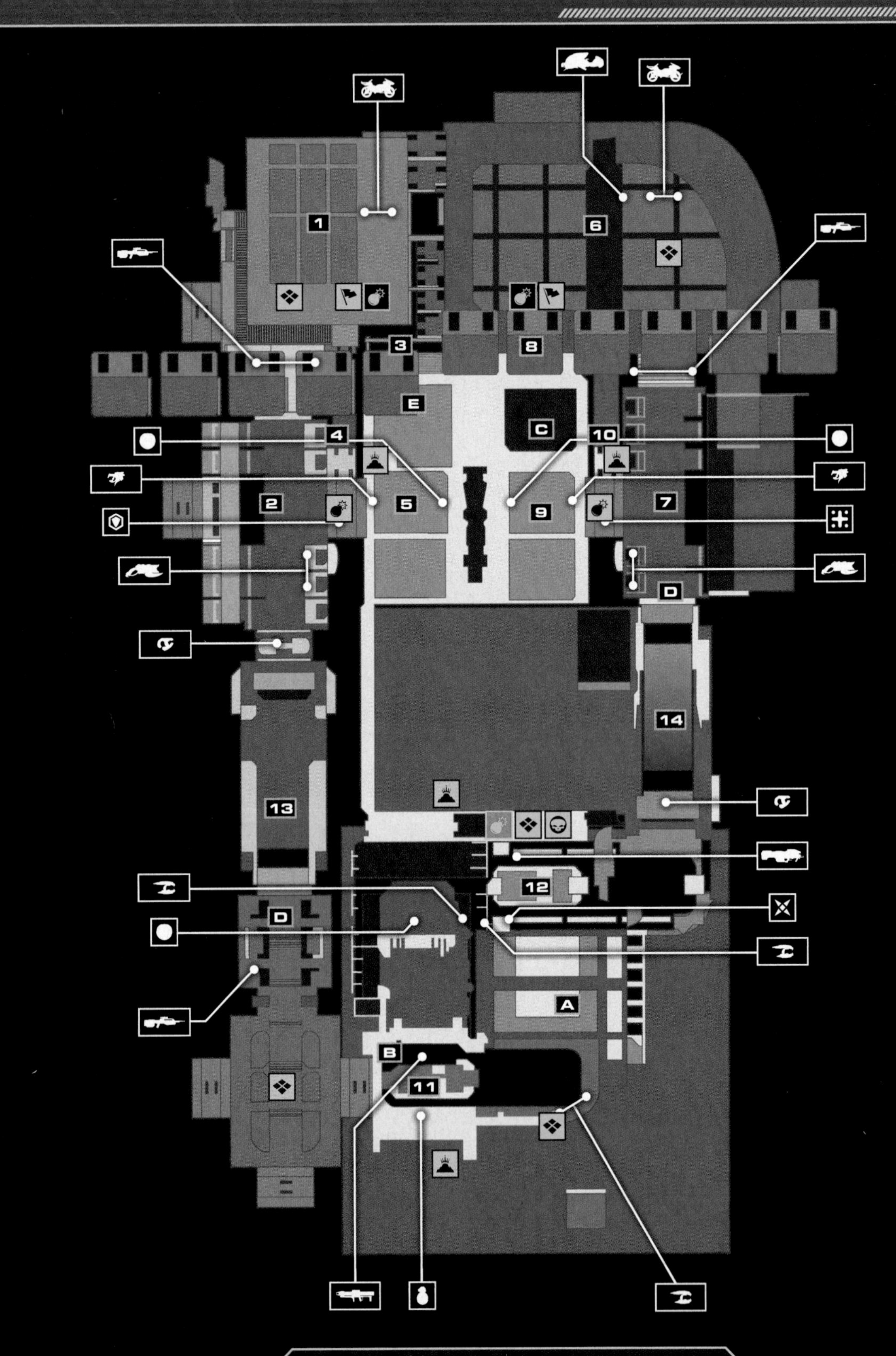

DATA STREAM

Recommended Game Variants: Team Slayer, One Flag, Multiflag, Assault, One Bomb

Recommended/Maximum Number of Players: 4–10/16

Advantageous Equipment*: Rocket Launcher, Sniper Rifle, Ghost (for Objective only)

*Using these weapons will definitely give you the upper hand in any game type on this map. However, the power weapon ammunition is cut in half due to the map's size.

AVAILABLE EQUIPMENT AND GEAR RESPAWN TIMES

●○○○○ = Slow ●●●●● = Fast

Weapons	
Battle Rifle	●●●●●
Grenade, Frag	●●●●●
Grenade, Plasma	●●●●●
Mauler	●○○○○
Plasma Pistol	●●●●○

Weapons	
Plasma Rifle	●●●●○
Rocket Launcher	●○○○○
Sniper Rifle	●○○○○
Spiker	●●●●○
Vehicles	
Ghost	●●●○○

Vehicles	
Mongoose	●●●●○
Equipment	
Bubble Shield	●●●○○
Power Drain	●●●○○
Regenerator	●●●○○

Topographical Overview

Orbital is a small map, featuring two bases linked in a horseshoe shape with overlapping hallways that create a sort of loop. The Red Base is located in the upper level, and the Blue Base is located in the lower level. From Red Base, you can reach Blue Base by taking a staircase that leads down to Sniper Hall or by taking the upper corridor to Rocket Spawn. From Blue Base, you can reach Red Base by going up the staircase to Rocket Spawn or by taking Bottom Corridor to Sniper Hall. Both connect in the middle and are separated by a drop-off. Falling here will kill you. You can jump from Rocket Spawn (the upper level) to Sniper Hall (the lower level); however, if you want to go from the lower level to the upper level, you must take a Grav Lift.

Call-out Locations

Blue Base/Blue Flag

Other names: N/A

1

This base features two main entrances/exits. One leads to the Lobby's doorway, and the other leads to Lower Hallway (Dark Hallway) through the gate door. In Slayer games, this gate remains open. In Objective games, the gate is closed but can be opened.

Blue Lobby

Other names: N/A

2

The Blue Lobby has the same layout as Red Lobby, but the staircase leads upward, and the walls are blue.

Blue Gate Door

Other names: N/A

3

This is located in Dark Hall/Lower Corridor.

Blue Maintenance Hallway/Secret Hall

Other names: N/A

4

This connects the Lobby with Lower Corridor and Gate Door. Secret Hall is a small, single-player pathway; try not to have a lot of people in here, because you are closed in and will probably die if a foe tosses Grenades here.

Blue Sniper Hall

Other names: N/A

This connects Blue Gate Door to the Sniper Hall.

Red Base/Red Flag

Other names: N/A

This base features two main entrances/exits. One leads to the Lobby's doorway, and the other leads to Lower Hallway (Dark Hallway) through the gate door. In Slayer games, this gate remains open. In Objective games, the gate is closed but can be opened.

Red Lobby

Other names: N/A

The layout of Red Lobby is the same as Blue Lobby; however, the staircase leads downward, and the walls are red.

Red Gate Door

Other names: N/A

This is located in Upper Corridor/Crate Hall.

Red Rocket Hall

Other names: N/A

This connects Red Gate Door to the Sniper Hall.

Red Maintenance Hallway/Secret Hall

Other names: N/A

This connects the Lobby with Upper Corridor and Gate Door. Red Maintenance Hall is a small, single-player pathway; try not to have a lot of people in here, because you are closed in and will probably die if a foe tosses Grenades here.

Rocket Spawn/Rocket Hall

Other names: N/A

Rocket Hall has three elevator doors (numbered 1, 2, and 3) and links with Rocket Stairs and Upper Corridor.

Sniper Spawn/Snipe Spawn/Sniper Hall

Other names: N/A

This is located on the lower level.

Rocket Stairs/Escalators

Other names: N/A

These lead up to the Rocket Launcher and Upper Corridor.

Sniper Stairs/Escalators

Other names: N/A

These lead down to Sniper Hall and Lower Corridor.

Enhanced Knowledge

On the gate side of Red Base, there are two Mongooses and a one Ghost (which spawns only in Objective games for the attacking team). In Red Base, you can go through the left door, which leads to Red Lobby, the gate door, or the secret walk at the top. In the secret walk is a Regenerator. Go through the gate door and locate the Mauler and some Plasma Grenades, then head straight and get the Rockets around the corner by the elevator shaft. If you go through the left door, you will find two Battle Rifles and a pair of Brute Spikes. After grabbing these items, run down the escalators at the bottom of the steps, where you find a Plasma Pistol. A little farther around the corner to the right is the Sniper Rifle. Then on your left is a Power Drain. In Sniper Hall, grab the pair of Plasma Rifles, and take the Plasma Grenades located by the crates in front of the railing. Continue on to Blue Base.

In Blue Base, go through the gate door, where there are two Mongooses. Straight ahead are two Plasma Grenades in the loading area. To your right is the Mauler and Bubble Shield and a secret path back into Blue Base. If you run down the hallway near where you picked up the Mauler, it will take you back to where you found the Sniper Rifle. This hall will lead you back to Red Base. Through the right door are two Battle Rifles; beyond that, to your left and right, are two Brute Spikers. At the base of the escalators is a Plasma Pistol, and up the stairs, in the doorway on the right, is another Battle Rifle. Outside the gate room to the left, next to railing by the drop-off, are Rockets. On the right, next to door number 3, are two Frag Grenades. A bit farther down are two Plasma Rifles beside the window. Around the corner, down the hallway, you will run into Red Base. There is also a Battle Rifle right around this corner, perched up against a window.

■ One Flag, Multiflag, One Bomb, Assault

Defense

- Place your players wisely on the map. Do not completely desert the base to capture the power weapons, but do not have everybody hide in the base waiting for the eventual attack from the opposing team. Because the flag spawns in the base behind the gate door, keep this door closed. Have two people rush toward the Rockets (grab a BR if it is not a BR start game).
- Watch out for the attacking team's Mongooses and Ghosts. Use Rockets and Sniper Rifles to take them out, and protect the gate controls to prevent vehicles from driving into your base.
- If your flag is taken down below, and it probably will be, try to reach Rocket Hall or cut off your opponent at their Lobby. Remember, you will not be able to see the enemy's bomb or your stolen flag when the other team picks them up, so communicate with your team about the direction the carrier is going.

Offense

- Never try to take the flag or plant the bomb by yourself. Coordinate an attack with your teammates. Have your sniper attempt to take out the defense team and gain control of Rockets.
- Do not drive the Mongoose with your bomb carrier or flag holder in the passenger seat, as you won't get very far in Orbital's small hallways without being attacked. The lower corridor has fewer obstacles, so use the Ghost to splatter enemies there. Also taking the Ghost through the opponent's base and lobby can damage your foe, as you will catch them in a small area.
- Crouch-walking makes you invisible to enemy radar. While storming the base, use this technique to sneak in undetected with the bomb or to grab the flag when the other team is not looking. Crouch-walking also gives you an advantage when going around corners.
- Once you obtain the flag, have your team tell you the location of the enemy team to determine which way is best to walk the flag.
- In Assault, when you plant the bomb, do not desert the area. Stay around and protect the ticking bomb so the other team does not disarm it. Throw Grenades or Power Drains on the bomb when the other team attempts to disarm it. You may leave the base or take cover when the time reaches five seconds, which is the time it will take the enemy to disarm; if they have less than five seconds, they cannot disarm the bomb.

Advanced Tactics

- If you are the bomb carrier or have just stolen the flag, do not hang on to the bomb or flag when someone is trying to kill you. You can get an instant kill with a bomb or flag melee, but if enemies aren't in close quarters with you, it is best to drop your load and fight off the other team with the weapons you have.
- When you have control of the Sniper Rifle, plant yourself in the back of a hallway so no one can sneak up behind you. Use crates for cover or head to Rocket spawn and look down onto the lower corridor.
- Though tempting, don't use Bubble Shields at the immediate sight of danger. Using the Bubble Shield too often will sometimes obscure shots that would have otherwise finished off the opponent.
- Team-shoot as much as you can, and if you are getting shot and your shields are low, find quick cover and have a teammate switch positions with you. Orbital is really good for this technique, since line of sight can be obscured very quickly.
- Be careful not to shoot Rockets near teammates; this can have deadly effects in these small hallways.
- Once you are comfortable with the map, have a teammate stand at one end of Rocket Hall while you, armed with the Mauler or Rockets, are on the railing near the drop-off; or, use melee to get assignations.
- Having your team split up into pairs can help you gain control of the map. Have two teammates go for Rockets, throwing Grenades before entering the hallway. Have two go snipe, also throwing Grenades before going around corners. Try and bounce Grenades off the crate at the bottom of the escalator to hit oncoming foes coming down.
- In Objective games, do your best to keep your gate closed if defending the Lower Hallway and Top Rockets.
- Don't be afraid to camp in this map, and use the element of surprise.
- This map is really about trial and error; see what works and communicate with your team.

Sniper/Ambush Locations

Crate Snipe 1

Use crates for cover down the long hallway (upper corridor).

Rocket Snipe

Snipe from the Rocket Launcher down the long hall.

Crate Snipe 2

Use crates for cover, this time from Lower Base looking into Lower/Dark Hall.

Stair Snipe

Looking down the escalators provides a great advantage.

Rocket Snipe 2

Snipe from Lower Corridor to Rocket spawn, using the crates as cover.

RAT'S NEST

PMS Doom, PMS Disco, PMS Pip Sq3ak

Snowmelt from Kilimanjaro feeds reservoirs every bit as vital as the fuel and ammunition stores.

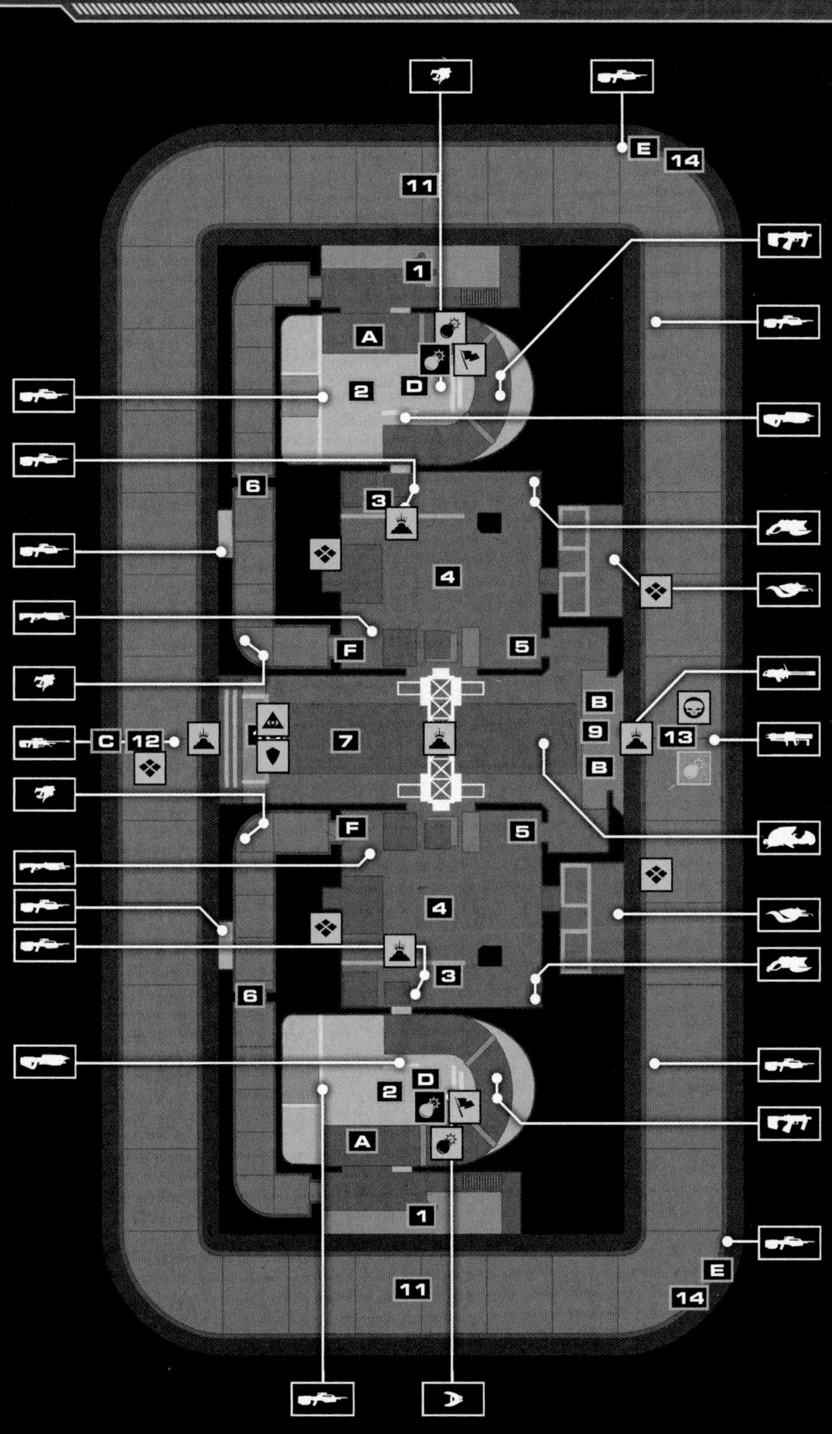

DATA STREAM

Recommended Game Variants: Team Slayer, Multiflag, One Flag, Assault, One Bomb, Neutral Assault, Rocket Race

Recommended/Maximum Number of Players: 8–16/16

Advantageous Equipment: Rockets, Sniper, Shotgun, Warthog, Camo, Gravity Hammer

AVAILABLE EQUIPMENT AND GEAR RESPAWN TIMES

1 skull = Slow; 5 skulls = Fast

Weapons	Respawn (skulls of 5)
Assault Rifle	5
Battle Rifle	4
Brute Shot	3
Grenade, Frag	5
Grenade, Plasma	5
Gravity Hammer	2
Machinegun Turret	3
Needler	4
Rocket Launcher	2
Shotgun	3
SMG	5
Sniper Rifle	1
Spiker	2
Vehicles	
Ghost	3
Mongoose	5
Warthog	4
Equipment	
Active Camo	1
Bubble Shield	3
Regenerator	3
Trip Mines	3

Topographical Overview

Call-out Locations

Hangars

Other names: Red Base, Blue Base, Red Spawn, Blue Spawn

In most game variants, your main spawn is in one of the Hangars. You can tell which base you spawn at by the red or blue markings on the walls inside your base. Include these in your call-outs (e.g., Blue Hangar). Two Warthogs, two Mongooses, a Trip Mine, and two Frag Grenades spawn in each Hangar.

Objective

Other names: Flag, 1st BR, Home

When you spawn, walk straight from Hangar and you will enter Objective. This location is comprised of two different levels. Lower Objective serves as the home for your flag in Capture the Flag (CTF) and for your bomb in Neutral Assault, Assault, and One Bomb. A Battle Rifle spawns on the right wall (aka, 1st BR), a Needler spawns alongside the left wall, and an Assault Rifle spawns on the floor when you enter. Upper Objective is horseshoe-shaped and is accessible by the stairs that run along the inside of the room. Two SMGs spawn in Upper Objective.

Brick

Other names: N/A

If you continue walking straight through Objective to the next room, you will enter Brick. This area got its name because the section is made of bricks. On the left side in Lower Brick, you will find 2nd BR. Two Spikers spawn to the right. Connected to Upper Objective is Upper Brick, where a BR spawns.

Garage

Other names: N/A

Brick comprises a small section of the Garage, which is made of two levels (Upper and Lower). Upper Garage has three doors (Middle Bridge, Ops Center, Halls), and Lower Garage has one main/large door that connects to Mid (middle of map). The stairs on the left lead to Upper Garage; the Brute Shot spawns on the stair landing. If you continue up the stairs, you will find a Regenerator. Down the stairs, the Shotgun spawns on the left and a Bubble Shield on the right. This door connects to Mid.

Ops Center/Turret

Other names: N/A

Through the left door in Upper Garage is Ops Center. Here you'll find the Turret, which rests above Mid. If you continue walking across Turret, you will enter the enemy's Upper Garage.

Halls

Other names: N/A

The door across from the Ops Center is known as the Hall Entrance. Through this door, you will enter a hall that contains blue or red streaks of paint on the wall, depending on which base you are in. If you exit the hall through the first door you see, you will enter the outer street, which circles the entire map. A BR spawns at this doorway, along with two Frag Grenades. If you continue down the hall, you will end at the Upper Hangar of the Red or Blue Base. Each hall contains two Maulers and two Plasma Grenades.

Middle

Other names: Mid, Connector, Gravity Hammer Street

Mid is the area that connects both bases and has multiple sections. These include Turret, Bridge, Gravity Hammer, and Camo.

Bridge

Other names: N/A

This is the only bridge on the map. Bridge connects Upper Red and Upper Blue Garage. Below the bridge on Mid Street, the Warhammer and two Plasma Grenades spawn.

Camo

Other names: Cloak

On the opposite side of Turret, the Camo spawns in the middle of the area with a Grav Lift on each side. On one side of Camo is a set of pipes; on the other side is a group of boxes. Use either of these to jump onto the ledge above Camo to grab the Sniper Rifle.

Blue Street

Other names: Blue Track

This street runs outside the Blue Base and connects to Sniper Street and Main Street. This also connects to an entrance to Blue Hall.

Red Street

Other names: Red Track

This street runs outside of Red Base and connects to Sniper Street and Main Street. You may enter Red Hall through the entrance on this street.

Sniper Street

Other names: Sniper Spawn, Ghost Spawn

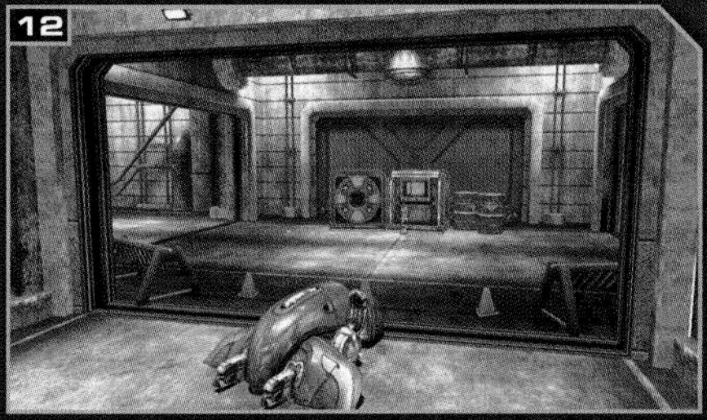

This is the street on which the Sniper Rifle and Ghost spawn. It is accessible from Camo or Blue/Red Street.

Main Street

Other names: Rocket Street, Rocket Spawn, Open Street

Rockets spawn on this street, along with a BR and two Frag Grenades at each light pole. This street is connected to the large entrance to Lower Mid, below Turret.

BR Ramp and Platform

Other names: N/A

Blue Street and Red Street each contain a platform between the base's Hangar and Main Street. This platform is made of two sets of stairs and spawns one BR and two Plasma Grenades. This is also considered a secondary spawn.

Tactical Knowledge

Rat's Nest is basically a giant circle, consisting of an outer street surrounding the entire map, two main bases, and a large open area in the map's middle, where Gravity Hammer and Camo are located. The map is symmetric in that both bases contain the same weapons and structure. Because the map is basically streets and bases, players must choose whether to risk playing in the open streets or to use the levels and terrain of their respective bases to their advantage.

Both bases are also equipped with an adequate set of vehicles, while the middle of the map (Middle/Sniper Street) houses a neutral Ghost, given to whoever reaches it first. This vehicle allows for fast and efficient maneuvering around the map.

The Middle is a highly traveled spot on the map, as it has both Camo and the Gravity Hammer, with a detachable Turret above the Hammer. With no place for cover, traveling in this section is dangerous but is necessary, as it houses power spots and weapons.

As the map is symmetrical, both team's bases are identical. Each base consists of two rooms complete with multiple ramps and stairs housing many different weapons. The most important weapons in the bases include the Shotgun and the BR. Both bases also include a Hangar with two Mongooses and two Warthogs, giving you more than enough opportunity to get your fill of vehicular manslaughter.

Along with a bottom level, the bases have a separate top level, which is the preferable vantage point, as you can see enemies below and ahead. You can use the top level to reach various places on the map that the bottom level does not have access to (i.e., Turret and Bridge) and to reach a Regenerator (located on the route to Turret) that can be very useful in-game. The bottom level, while a little more risky to be in, contains the Needler; the BR; and, most importantly, the Shotgun and Bubble Shield.

General Tactics

- Exploit the various tactical hideouts on Rat's Nest (i.e., doorways, pipes, etc.).
- Achieving the "high ground" is of greater importance on Rat's Nest than on other maps because of the use of vehicles.
- One teammate should rush for the Shotgun and Bubble Shield (opposite from each other), while another rushes for Camo and the Sniper Rifle.
- The rest of the teammates should rush for Rockets, as these are the most important weapons on the map.
- If your team has Rockets, utilize the vehicles around the map. If not, use the "high ground" on the map.
- If a vehicle is approaching, use the boxes and barriers scattered throughout the map for cover.
- Avoid leaving yourself exposed while on open streets, as you will surely die.
- Useful sniping spots include Ghost Spawn, Bridge, Overhead Pipes, and Turret.
- In vehicles, attempt to control the main streets, but be wary of enemies camping with Plasma Grenades along the outside walls.
- Avoid camping in Bottom Middle, as you are vulnerable in every direction.

Game Variant Strategies

General Slayer Tips

- Weapon control is more important in Slayer-based games rather than in Objective games, as the sole objective is to kill.
- Players should utilize the vehicles on the map, especially in Big Team Slayer, because there are many targets and many roadways for you to drive on.
- Do not put the player with Rockets into a vehicle, as it is harder to shoot a target while moving, and losing or wasting Rockets can seriously affect your game.
- Take advantage of the high grounds of this map, as there are many chances for one to jump down from the high ground and assassinate an unsuspecting player.

General Assault Tips

- Because there are two bombs in Assault, deciding whether to be offensive or defensive is crucial. Offensive play and defensive play differ immensely, but in the end, you can succeed using either style.
- Both team's bombs are located in their respective lower section of Objective. The bombs are marked by an icon above it that states how far away the bomb is from you.
- An enemy bomb takes four seconds to disarm, so once your team has successfully planted the bomb, and it reaches that four-second mark, have your team return to your base and escort the new bomb carrier (your teammate who should already have the new bomb) back to the enemy base for a quick second cap. Doing this in sync can win you the game in a ridiculously short amount of time.

Neutral Assault Tips

- In Neutral Assault, the single bomb is located directly in front of Rockets, which can be very dangerous.
- Because there is only one bomb in this game type, an offensive setup is favored over a defensive one.
- Being the first team to arrive at the bomb is crucial, as you want to quickly gain control over the Rockets after you obtain the bomb.

- If you are the first team to arrive and the opposing team is nowhere to be found, have one player get Rockets while the rest of the team escorts the bomb carrier to the opposing base. Camp in the upper levels of Middle, as the opposing team might arrive on the scene late and will be blown to bits by the deadly Rockets.
- Camo is very important in Neutral Assault, as a single player with both Camo and the bomb can annihilate the opposing team's chance at a defense.
- An enemy bomb takes four seconds to disarm, so once your team has successfully planted the bomb, and it reaches that four-second mark, have your team return to your base and escort the new bomb carrier (your teammate who should already have the new bomb) back to the enemy base for a quick second cap. Doing this in sync can win you the game in a ridiculously short amount of time.

General Multiflag CTF Tips

- Multiflag is a lot like Assault except it is faster paced. Once your flag hits the opposing team's flag point, you score, so it is quite possible to win the game in less than two minutes.
- Instead of going directly through the Middle, as one might in Assault, have your team utilize either the Mongoose or the Warthog and drive to the map's opposite side. Because these vehicles are fast, the opposing team will have a harder time both finding and killing your team.

Offensive Plays

- In an offensive setup, the entire team (or at least three of the four teammates) will escort the bomb carrier or flag holder. The strategy is to take the fastest route to the opposing team's base—which means going straight through Middle—with teammates gathering the power weapons and equipment (i.e., Rockets, Bubble Shields, Camo, Shotguns) in the shortest amount of time and helping to ambush the opposing team's Objective.
- In Assault or Neutral Assault, have a single player get the Shotgun and the Bubble Shield; they will be the one to camp in the opposing team's Objective while the bomb is being armed. When attacked, this player will throw the Bubble Shield on top of the bomb and camp inside it with the Shotgun. This can be a deadly combination. Also, if possible, have another player attempt to steal the opposing team's Shotgun and Bubble Shield; controlling these weapons is crucial.
- After scoring the first time, have a player (preferably one with the Shotgun), camp inside the opposing team's base, eliminating the opposing team's chances of establishing a defense.

Defensive Plays

- In some ways, defensive play is closely related to offensive play. Have two players rush Rockets, while one player grabs the Shotgun, Bubble Shield, and Camo. All players should return to Objective.
- Instead of rushing out to find enemies, wait until the opposing team makes the mistake of entering the base, where they will be ambushed.
- The player in possession of Rockets should crouch above a doorway or somewhere on the upper level of their team's Objective.
- Have all players rotate between positions, making sure to cover all openings and doors into the base; this ensure no one can sneak in undetected.
- If your team is *not* able to grab Camo, be on the lookout for an enemy player sneaking in with the bomb or the flag, as they can do this easily.
- If your team is successful in thwarting the opposing team's attempt to arm their bomb or capture the flag, have one player stay inside the Objective (preferably with a Shotgun and Bubble Shield) while the other players escort the bomb carrier through the middle of the map.
- Be sure to switch up the ways your team delivers the bomb or tries to capture the flag, as your opponent will quickly catch on to your strategies if you use them to excess. An example of this is if your team has carried the bomb directly through the Middle for two out of three successful bomb plants and is getting killed before even exiting your base, try getting into a Mongoose and driving through the back streets and tagging the opposing team from an unexpected position.

Advanced Tactics

- As this map has a lot of edges that stick out and random pieces of architecture, it allows for multiple hiding spots, which you can access via jumping.
- You can access the green tubes that run along the top edges of the streets by jumping on the red tubes (located to the left and right of Sniper Spawn), and then crouch-jumping onto the green tubes. You can walk along these tubes as far as the beginning of Rocket Street. This can be very helpful to your team, as you have the higher vantage point and can detect any unsuspecting walking enemies.
- Crouching atop the multiple doorways and entrances to the bases can be very helpful in a sneak attack. Not many players look on top of doorways or even think of the possibility of an aerial attack. You can jump onto nearly every doorway or entrance on the map. Take advantage of this, and you can have your enemies running for their lives.
- Jumping to bridge pillars can be difficult to get used to and is not recommended if you cannot accomplish it at least 80 percent of the time, as it will reveal the position of those who can manage to reach it. Only do this jump if your team has control of the Turret, as getting shot from behind is never pleasant. Jump from the bridge to the pillar located to the left or right. You can stand on this pillar to escape an oncoming enemy or to ambush any unsuspecting foes crossing the bridge. Also, this spot is invisible to any enemies located at Camo or Sniper Spawn.
- Located to the back left and right of Camo, Camo Pillars allow you to remain unseen by an enemy at Sniper Spawn. Camping here with Rockets is both valuable and dangerous. Be sure that your team has control of Turret and Bridge before trying to sneak attack an enemy coming from Sniper Spawn.

Sniper/Ambush Locations

Brick

Sitting atop this small brick wall can be very helpful to any player in possession of the Sniper Rifle. You can see any player coming in from both the bottom and top of Middle, and if you turn around, you can see any players coming from inside the Objective.

Turret

With Camo located directly on the ground in front of you, as well as access to the Ghost and Sniper Rifle, sitting atop this location with Rockets can be deadly for your opponent. You have a wide view of any enemies beneath and in front of you who try to grab the Ghost or Camo. Securing this position is very useful. This is also a great place for any player in possession of the Sniper Rifle.

With a teammate camping out on Sniper Spawn, this is an extremely advantageous position. With access to both bases, you can easily enter the enemy's base unseen, as enemies frequently ignore the Turret area. In addition, any foes coming through Middle will frequently ignore the Turret, leaving them open to an attack. These strategies will allow you to defend the sniper and take a great deal of pressure off him or her. As the sniper is in a safer position and must defend only themselves from two directions instead of three, your team will get more kills. If your position is compromised, remember that the Turret is detachable. You will be able to obtain easy kills on approaching enemies who underestimate the power of the Turret. Happy killing!

Sniper Spawn

Be cautious of camping in this spot, as it is easy for the enemy to tag you with Grenades and Rockets and can be targeted from five different spots. While at this spot, grab the Camo, the Shotgun, and the Bubble Shield to allow for both close- and long-range combat.

While vulnerable in this location, you are given a slight chance at cover, as the Sniper Rifle rests on two metal crates, which can be vital to your survival in an enemy attack. This section of the map receives a lot of traffic, because it houses the Sniper Rifle and looks straight toward the Rockets, Gravity Hammer, Camo, and Turret. You also have a view of both sides of the streets (Red Street and Blue Street) and of Middle. You will have an advantage over any unsuspecting player rushing for the Ghost, Camo, Turret, Gravity Hammer, and Rockets.

This spot is a great location from which to establish map control. Also, because this area is so vulnerable, have a teammate watch your back while you are sniping. While you're scoped in, it is impossible to see an enemy approaching from your blind spots (anywhere not in your scope); a teammate can warn you and help you attack the approaching enemy, and you can still hold down the position.

TIP

If you have low shields or if the other team has discovered you but you do not want to lose sight of possible approaching enemies, try some jumping techniques. Facing the wall, jump onto the metal crates that the Sniper Rifle rests on, then crouch-jump onto the doorway's ledge. From this point, you can either crouch here to recover your shields or turn toward the green metal tube in front of you and crouch-jump atop that.

Bottom and Top Objective

These spots are great for any player in possession of the Shotgun. As these areas are small, the player will encounter close-quarter combat, and the player with the Shotgun is sure to beat out a surprised defenseless Assault Rifle wielder.

BR Ramp and Platform

With the ability to see Main Street and Red Street or Blue Street, sitting atop this platform perched with a Sniper Rifle is a great way to gain control over weapons. You can see any approaching vehicles and the spawn of Rockets. This is also a dangerous position, as you have zero cover to protect you from oncoming enemies.

Shotgun Spawn

With a Shotgun in hand, crouching in this spot gives you the gift of cover. Players rushing for Ghost, Shotgun, Rockets, Camo, or Gravity Hammer will get an unpleasant surprise if you come at them when they pass you. Be wary, though, as this spot does not provide full cover.

PMS Jezabelle, Righty Is Law, Strawberry Boo, PMS Soli

endless wasteland still holds many secrets. Some of them are held more deeply than others.

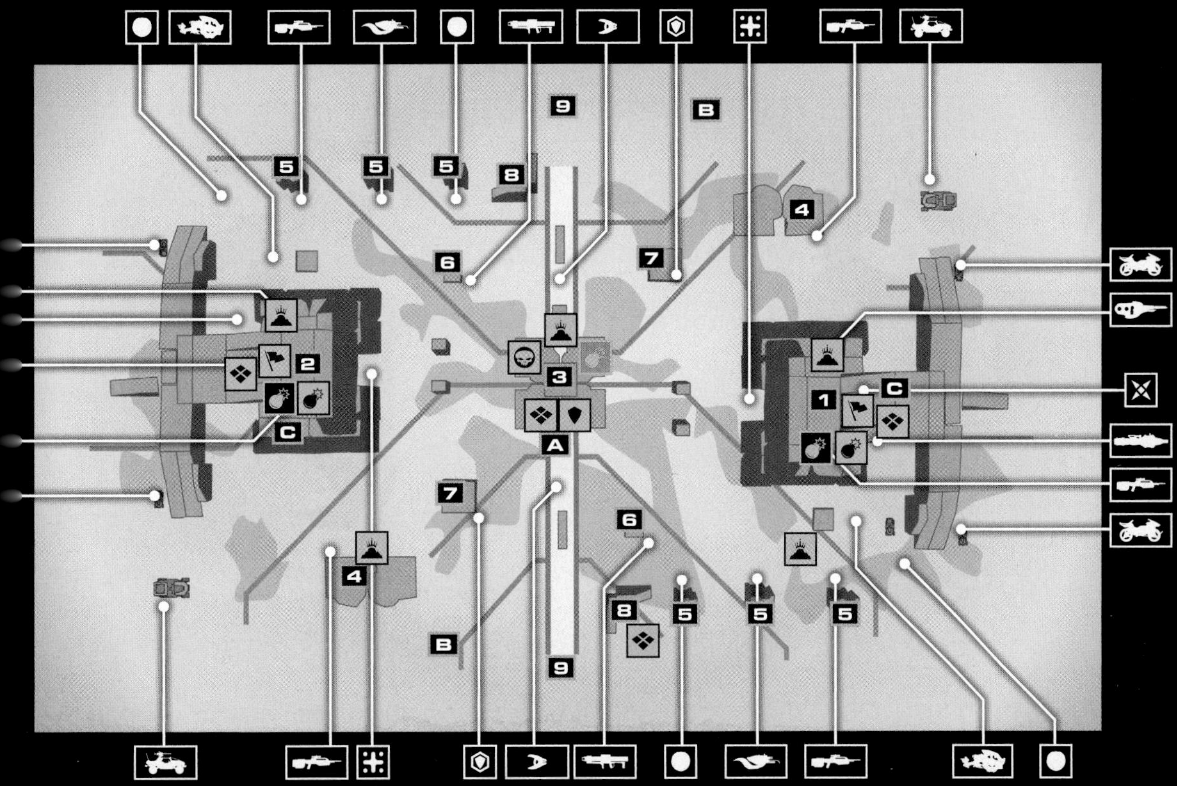

DATA STREAM

ommended Game Variants: Team Slayer, Capture the Flag, One Flag, Assault, Neutral Assault, VIP

ommended/Maximum Number of Players: 4–12/16

antageous Equipment: Rockets, Overshield, Regenerator, Warthog

AVAILABLE EQUIPMENT AND GEAR RESPAWN TIMES

●○○○○ = Slow ●●●●● = Fast

Weapons	
Battle Rifle	●●●●●
Brute Shot	●●●●○
Carbine	●●●●●
Grenade, Plasma	●●●●○
Missile Pod	●○○○○
Needler	●●●○○

	Weapons	
	Rocket Launcher	●●○○○
	Vehicles	
	Brute Chopper	●●○○○
	Mongoose	●●●○○
	Warthog	●●○○○

	Equipment	
	Bubble Shield	●●○○
	Gravity Lift	●●●●
	Overshield	●○○○
	Power Drain	●●●●
	Regenerator	●●○○

Call-out Locations

Blue Base

Other names: N/A

Blue Base is identified by the glowing blue orb located above it.

Red Base

Other names: N/A

Red Base is identified by the glowing red orb located above it.

Grav Lift Spawn

Other names: N/A

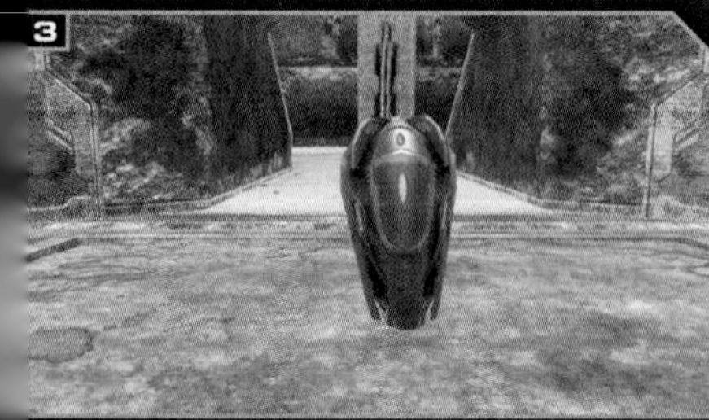

The Grav Lift spawns in the bottom middle of map. Here a player can access a semienclosed enclave to locate the Grav Lift. This area has four entrances: two facing the Red and Blue bases and the other two facing the sides of the map.

Ant Hill

Other names: N/A

Located on the right side of each base are low-rising, sand-buried structures known as Ant Hills. These are great

Obelisks

Other names: N/A

Rising from the sand to create the "edge" of Sandbox's playing field are several areas known as "Obelisks." Several weapons rest against and in front of these pillars. Depending on which side of the map you are located, you'll find a Battle Rifle or a Brute Shot.

Rocket Block

Other names: N/A

Always a coveted location, the Rocket Block contains the Rocket Launcher, which is a power weapon. Rush this location to ensure stealth attacks on the opponent's vehicle.

Bubble Shield Block

Other names: N/A

The Bubble Shield Block is located on the front side of each base. Here, the Bubble Shield stands ready to protect the masterchief from harmful gunfire and Grenade attacks.

Corners

Other names: N/A

Along the "edge" of Sandbox, you'll find what are known as the Corners. These odd-shaped stone corners provide ample cover for ducking in and out of gunfire.

Dunes

Other names: N/A

Sandbox is surrounded by sand. On the outskirts of the map, the players will see the Dunes, fortified by forerunner structures of years past.

Enhanced Knowledge

- For Slayer games, it is best to get control of both sets of Rockets. Do this by running to the ones that spawn closest to your base and throwing the Power Drain over the Rockets. Quickly take out opponents who rush for their Rockets.
- Controlling Rockets and using the Warthog is an easy and quick way to win a match. The only weapon that is really dangerous is the Missile Pod.
- If the other team has a Warthog, stay in the base, because most of the map is fairly open and the Warthog can easily take you down.
- To take out an enemy Warthog, use the Missile Pod or Rocket Launcher. Two Sticky Grenades will also destroy this vehicle.
- If the opposing team has an Overshield, use the Needler to take them out.
- Use the Grav Lift located in front of the base to quickly reach the top of the base, where you can confront opponents.
- When playing Capture the Flag, have one person stay in the base to toss the flag off the base and help keep the opposing team from returning it.
- A quick way to get into a base is by using the jump block that is located on the base's left side.
- You can use the Power Drain to keep your opponent off the objective, such as the flag or bomb.
- Utilize vehicles for faster travel across the map when you're trying to capture the flag or plant the bomb.
- The Chopper is great for splattering recently spawned foes and flipping Warthogs with the Chopper's guns.
- A new Chopper will always win in a collision with a new Warthog and will kill everyone in the Warthog.
- The angled blocks can serve as great cover while in a heated battle.
- When under heavy fire, deploy the Regenerator to regain shields and jump back into fire. Putting the Regenerator behind some cover will almost always guarantee you a win in the fight.
- If the other team has shorter-ranged weapons, a good place to camp is on the sand dunes, but do not forget to watch your ammo.
- When Rockets or a Missile Pod aren't handy, you can use the Brute Shot to flip a Warthog.
- While driving the Warthog, it is best to stay toward the outside of the map and kill off the spawn, because there are a lot of obstacles to avoid on the main part of the map.
- Tossing the Power Drain over the base's top and toward the map's other side can bring down many players' shields.
- Try to steal the opponent's Warthog; without one of these vehicles, your foe doesn't stand a chance with the respawns. Drive a Mongoose or a Warthog to the back of the enemy base to steal their Warthog.
- If the other team is using a Regenerator, the Needler is a quick and easy solution. The Needler quickly kills even full-health players and reloads very fast.

Advanced Tactics

- Timing the Overshield will give your team a good advantage. The Overshield spawns three minutes after it has been last picked up.
- Crouch-jumping on the base's side will enable you to slide up the side without having to use the jump box.
- Because the Battle Rifle and Carbine spawn atop the base, camping the other team's base with these weapons makes for easy killing, as they will spawn out in the open with shorter-range weapons.
- The Bubble Shield can be used for both offensive and defensive purposes. If an enemy is chasing you into a Bubble Shield, toss a Grenade inside the Bubble Shield and jump out. Doing so will severely hurt your enemy and will make an easy kill.
- It can be easy to trick your enemy in Capture-the-Flag games. Throw the flag to the bottom of the opponent's base so they attempt to return it. Have one person behind the base in a Warthog or Mongoose and another person waiting for the returned flag. The enemy will be so preoccupied with the previous flag that it will almost make capturing their flag seem easy.

- To rush the other base, one strategy is to grab the Grav Lift from Bottom Mid and place it in front of the opponent's Regenerator spawn. With the Grav Lift deployed, grab the Regenerator and throw it near the base of the Grav Lift. To take out several enemies without dying, just float up and down on the Grav Lift and let the Regenerator heal you when your shields drop.
- Throwing a Bubble Shield can be an excellent lure for enemy Warthogs. Stay in the Bubble Shield as the Warthog drives toward you; when the vehicle is close enough to jump over, jump and throw a Sticky Grenade on it. You can also easily assassinate the Warthog gunner while they drive by.
- Timing the enemy's Missile Pod is essential if your team has a Warthog. When the Missile Pod respawns, just waste all of its shots because they're not very accurate unless they're targeting a vehicle. This will allow your team to keep spawn-killing the other team.
- When in a Regenerator and if an opponent is rushing you, switch to a shorter-range weapon. Six on-target Assault Rifle shots and a beatdown will kill the opponent.
- Strafing behind the Obelisks and Corners is a good way to distract the opposing team; then your teammates can kill the players who chase you!. It is also easy to bank Grenades off the Obelisks if the other players are hiding as well.

Sniper/Ambush Locations

Grav Lift Spawn Ambush

As you rush for the Grav Lift, hide within the small corridors of the Grav Lift Spawn so you can melee your opponents as they rush in. Also, while in a gunfight, you can easily duck and cover within the four entrances to this area.

Sand Dunes

Most players will take to the sides and center of the map to attack their opponents. Knowing this, rush the outskirts of the map—either on foot or in a warthog—to take out the opposing team as they rush. They won't notice you until it's too late!

Back/Top Base

This area is often the best place from which to snipe at your opponents. In doing so, you have the back of your base to take cover in. Starting from the top, if you are fired upon, you can drop back, take cover, and snipe off the sides.

MULTIPLAYER

SANDTRAP

PMS Ruin, PMS Dark Ivory

Although the Brute occupiers have been driven from this ancient structure, they left plenty to remember them by.

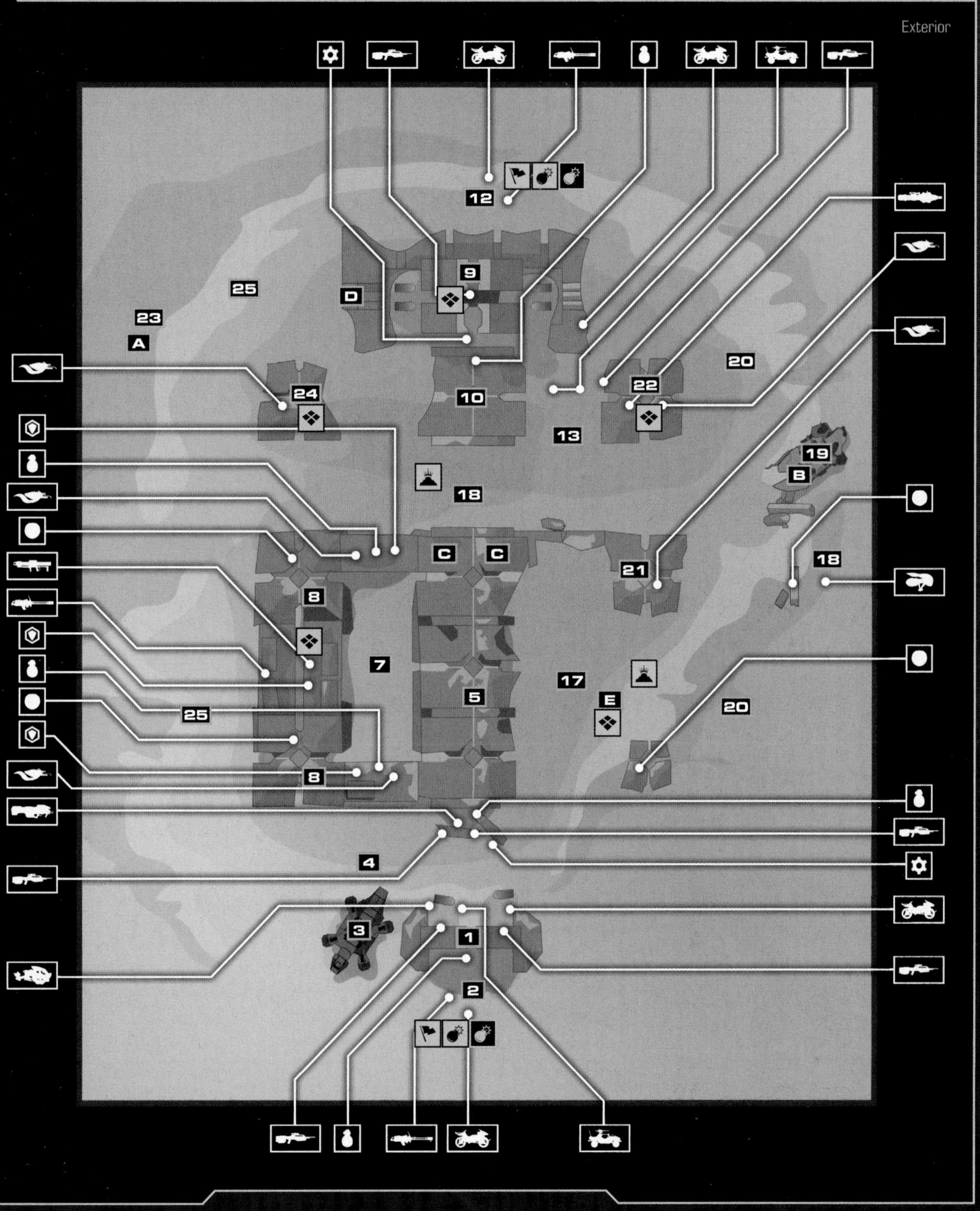

Exterior

12

9

25

D

23

A

24

10

22

20

13

19

B

18

C C

21

18

8

7

17

E

5

25

20

8

4

3

1

2

Data Stream

Recommended Game Variants: Big Team Slayer, Capture the Flag, Team Snipers, Land Grab

Recommended/Maximum Number of Players: 8/16

Advantageous Equipment: Rocket Launcher, Missile Pod, Spartan Laser, Banshee, Warthog, Power Drain

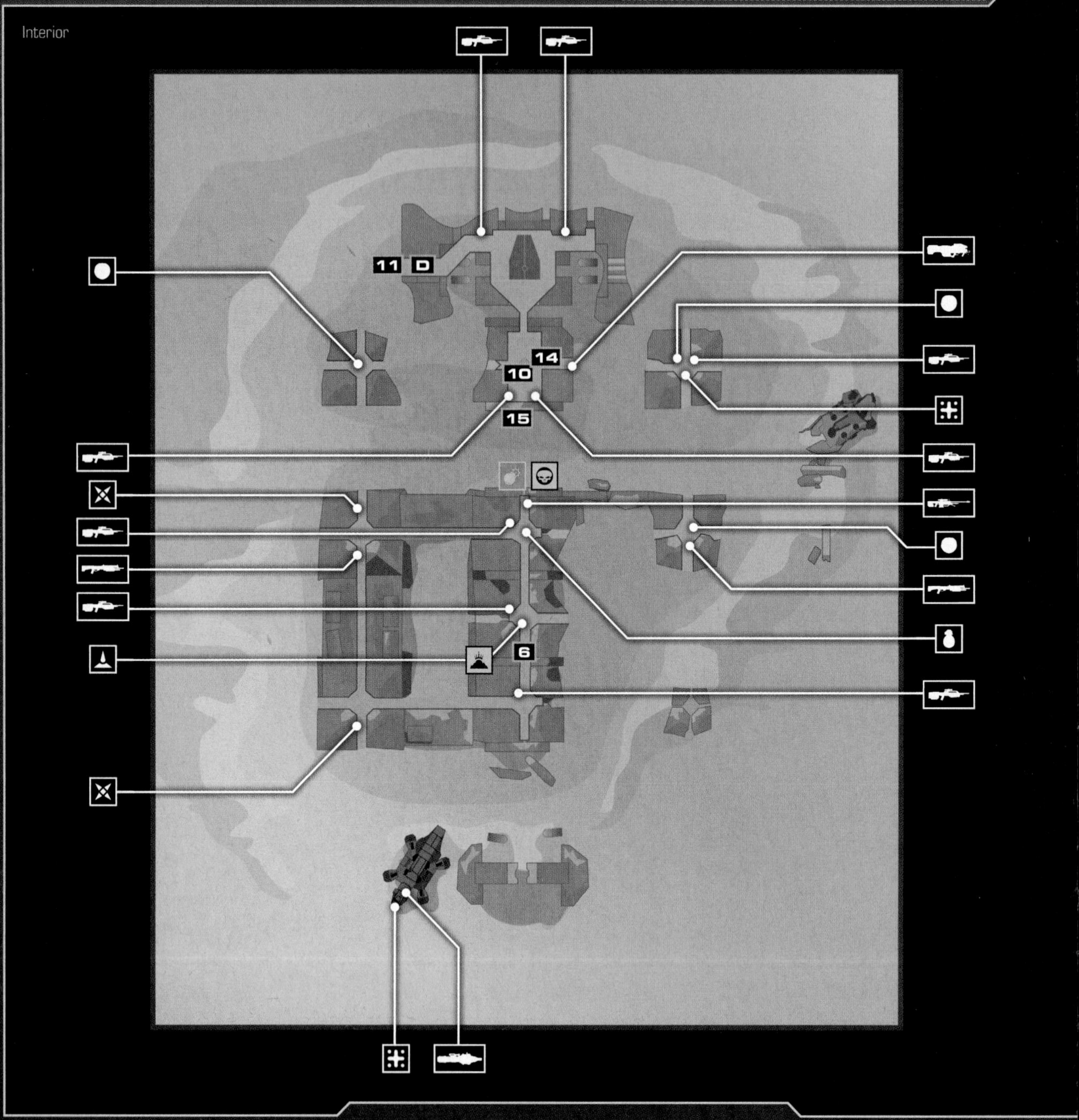

Interior

11 D 14 10 15 6

AVAILABLE EQUIPMENT AND GEAR RESPAWN TIMES

	Weapons	
	Battle Rifle	●●●●●
	Brute Shot	●●●●○
	Gravity Hammer	●●○○○
	Grenade, Frag	●●●●●
	Grenade, Plasma	●●●●●
	Machinegun Turret	●●●●○
	Missile Pod	●○○○○

	Weapons	
	Rocket Launcher	●●○○○
	Shotgun	●●●●○
	Sniper Rifle	●●○○○
	Spartan Laser	●○○○○
	Vehicles	
	Banshee	●○○○○
	Brute Chopper	●●●●●

	Vehicles	
	Mongoose	●●●●●
	Warthog	●●●●●
	Equipment	
	Bubble Shield	●●●○○
	Grav Lift	●●●●○
	Power Drain	●●●●○
	Regenerator	●●●●○
	Trip Mine	●●●○○

Call-out Locations

Red Base

Other names: N/A

You start out in the back of Red Base, standing near/under a large golden archway. In front of the arch are two smaller broken pillars. There are two Warthogs, a Chopper, and a Mongoose in Red Base. The edges of the base are surrounded with barricades and sandbags you can use as cover.

Elephant

Other names: Red Elephant, Behemoth

Behind you is the Behemoth, also known as the Red Elephant. The Elephant is a large mobile base that can hold vehicles and teammates. Its sloped ramp allows any vehicle to board. One Elephant can house every vehicle spawned at each base, plus your entire team. In Capture the Flag, each Elephant acts as a base, and your flag will spawn here.

Pelican

Other names: N/A

To the left of the Red Base is the downed Pelican. Here you will find a Missile Pod and a Regenerator.

Red Drive

Other names: N/A

The path that stretches across Red Base to the Pelican is known as Red Drive. The Red Drive begins at Long Base and ends where Rocket Street begins (at Pelican).

Long Base

Other names: N/A

In front of Red Base are a few broken rocks; one is buried in the sand, and one is leaning against a building. This building is Long Base. Climb the leaning rock to access the top of Long Base, where you'll find an entry point to the area known as Long Hall.

Long Hall

Other names: N/A

Long Hall contains three corridors to the right or left that you can take to exit. All exits left lead you to Underpass; any exits right take you to Long Walk.

Underpass

Other names: N/A

Underpass is the open path between Long Base and a series of bridges. The parallel bridge is known as Rocket Bridge.

Red Jet and Mid Jet

Other names: N/A

8

If you move across Underpass to the bottom side of Rocket Bridge, you'll notice two air shafts. You can take either to access the top of the bridge. The air shaft closest to Red Base is Red Jet; the other is Mid Jet.

Blue Base

Other names: N/A

9

Blue Base is marked by the vast archways much like Red Base. It is located behind Small Base.

Small Base

Other names: N/A

10

Standing on top of Plasma Bunker with your back to Rocket Street, you'll face Small Base, which is also connected to Blue Base. Much like Red Base, Blue Base is marked by vast archways.

Side Door

Other names: N/A

11

Moving toward the end of Rocket Street, you'll notice a small door on your right. This is a side entrance to Blue Base and is known as Side Door.

Elephant

Other names: Blue Elephant, Leviathan

12

At the rear of Blue Base are a series of three underground doorways. All lead you to Blue Base. Also in front of you will be the Leviathan, or the Blue Elephant. The small mound in the Blue Base is an objective field. The rear of Blue Base is sloped at a climbable angle. The topside of Blue Base and Small Base is easily accessible from this area.

Blue Driveway

Other names: N/A

13

Along the top of Blue Base is a barricade. If you look down to your right, you'll see Plasma Bunker. To your left is another spawn point for vehicles. This area is known as Blue Driveway. Red Base and Blue Base have the same amount of spawning vehicles.

Shortcut

Other names: N/A

14

Looking down toward Blue Driveway from Blue Base, you'll see a small patch of darkened sand next to a Warthog. This marks an additional entrance to the Blue Base known as Shortcut.

Front Door

Other names: N/A

15

When entering Shortcut, you'll see a small room with a single golden pillar; this is known as Small Base. On your left is a walkway leading you out to Open Street. This is known as Front Door. To your right, a small doorway leads you back into Blue Base.

Mid Street

Other names: Open Mid, Mid Map, Open or Mid

Mid Street is the large sandy avenue separating the Small Base from the Long Base and stretches from Rocket Street to Missile Street.

Long Walk

Other names: N/A

From Banshee, you'll see Missile Street wrap around to Red Drive and a plateau of sand that has covered a bunker. The plateau is known as Long Walk, as taking this route is very time-consuming without a vehicle.

Banshee

Other names: N/A

In front of the Phantom, running along Missile Street, is a small ledge with two supply cases and two Plasma Batteries perched around it. To the ledge's left is the Banshee. This small area has only one feature—the Banshee—and is very active.

Phantom

Other names: N/A

Cross Missile Street into a purple, destroyed craft. This mangled piece of metal was once a Phantom. It still has its uses as one of the few carney holes in Sandtrap.

Missile Street

Other names: N/A

Taking Shortcut back toward Blue Drive, you'll pass the Missile Bunker and see another pathway that stretches back around to Red Base. This is known as Missile Street, because it begins at Missile Bunker.

Shotty Bunker

Other names: N/A

To the left of Blue Driveway are two more bunkers. The first is known as Missile Bunker; the second (across Open Street) is Shotty Bunker. Both are named for the main spawning weapons on each.

Missile Bunker

Other names: N/A

To the left of Blue Driveway are two more bunkers. The first is known as Missile Bunker; the second (across Open Street) is Shotty Bunker. Both are named for the main spawning weapons on each.

The Dune

Other names: N/A

There's a large wall of sand running along the left of Rocket Street. You can climb up the wall from an entrance point in front of Open Street. This top area is known as the Dune, as it's simply a large sand dune.

Plasma Bunker

Other names: N/A

Rocket Street stretches across the middle of the map (Mid Street) to Blue Base. After crossing the Open, you'll approach a single bunker. The bunkers resemble smaller pyramids with entries on all sides and from the top. This bunker is known as the Plasma Bunker. Every bunker, including this one, has a Brute Shot on top, but Plasma Bunker also has Plasma Grenades.

Rocket Street

Other names: N/A

The vast area to the left of Rocket Bridge is known as Rocket Street and is a very active path for vehicles.

Enhanced Knowledge

Big Team Slayer and Objective

- One of the main game variants played on Sandtrap is Big Team Slayer. This map is designed with heavy Slayer options, which is fruitfully supported with Warthogs, Choppers, and a Banshee. Regardless of which base your team spawns at, you want to first determine which teammates will control the vehicles and which will run for power weapons.
- With rampaging vehicles stalking every avenue, it's difficult to get a sniper in position to put up the big kills. While equipped with the Sniper Rifle, take a Mongoose and try to reach the Dune. This area is high on the map, giving the sniper a vast view of the battle. You'll also remain practically unnoticed as long as you don't create a ruckus getting up there. From the Red Base, you can walk up from the beginning of the Dune and creep all the way across.
- The team spawning at Blue Base doesn't have this advantage, because the only other entrance to the top of the Dune is in the middle of the map at Rocket Street. They'll have to avoid many vehicular attacks before reaching the Dune.
- You do have the option of posting your sniper on top of Long Base/Small Base, but their view will be limited. Vehicles can drive to the top of both and easily splatter a sniper who is stuck in their scope, unaware of the enemy's approach.
- Although it seems the Warthog would be first to achieve quick kills, your opponents are securing the same items as well. Grabbing the Missile Pod and blasting away at their Warthog can clear the field for your team to push an assault through.
- You can also set up with the Spartan Laser on any of the bunkers. Make sure you have a Battle Rifle equipped along with laser; that way if you're fired upon, you can drop into the bunker and let your shields regenerate. When setting up, keep in mind the Missile Bunker has a Regenerator.
- Many players will want to pilot the Banshee. Consider one or two players only when using the Banshee to your advantage. A skilled pilot can easily maneuver around missiles and bombarding rockets. They can also support any teammates on foot who need cover fire. In extreme situations, the Banshee can hover low enough to the ground and Boost to splatter an opponent.
- The distance to the Banshee from each base is pretty much the same. Since the Mongoose is the fastest vehicle in the game, use this reach the Banshee. Although the Chopper is fast, it's an assault vehicle and shouldn't be burned just to acquire another assault craft. Save the Chopper for another teammate; the Mongoose isn't considered a big loss.
- The Warthog is one of the most useful vehicles because it can steal kills without requiring much skill. The mounted Turrets are easy point-and-shoot weapons that don't need to be reloaded and don't ever run out of ammunition. This saves time and leaves opponents frantic to escape your path. Having a skilled driver will achieve more kills, as they can smoothly operate the Hog and keep it from rolling out of control while driving rugged terrain. The less time you spend flipping an overturned Warthog the better. When flipping a Warthog, you are blind to rushing attacks, as you are focusing your attention on getting it back to its feet and on the road.
- In addition to being an armored killing machine, the Warthog can carry an extra person in the passenger seat. When playing Objective games, this vehicle is crucial. Although it isn't the fastest passenger craft, it's hard to take down and supplies endless cover fire. Throwing your flag carrier in and heading back to your base is the ultimate strategy for any Objective game.
- If your team succeeds in controlling the attack in an Objective game, push a few teammates forward to the opposing team's Elephant. These are considered moving bases during flag games. Have two players drive their Elephant back around your base and push it into yours. To win the game from here on out, your team simply provides the cover fire needed to keep rushing opponents from taking back their Elephant while your team grabs their flag and scores easily.
- The Elephant isn't often used in attack, because it's slow and awkward to operate. It's also easy to board, since you can walk faster than it moves. Keep that in mind when sneaking to your opponent's base to steal it. You'll succeed more easily if you send a small group, as the nondriving teammates can use the Turrets to wipe out the approaching team.

Team Snipers

- While the Dune is a great sniping position during Objective and Slayer games, it is a little too obvious and leaves you wide open during Team Snipers. This map is large, so the approach on Sandtrap is to sit and wait. Minimize your time spent in the open. You may spawn here, so remember to advance to cover as quickly as possible.
- Acquiring sniping position is normally difficult. Try to be patient, because this game may actually end by the time clock. While camping it out, if you aren't getting any kills, reconsider your position. The opposing team may be settled and waiting for your team's movement. Try to use the bases to keep from getting picked off. Basically, any position in which you have cover and can see a broad range of the map is where you want to be.

Here are some ideal positions for your team:

The Phantom: This is a great carney hole. You can move in and out of it as needed without much effort.

The ridge between Long Walk and Missile Street: You'll have a view of any movement between Red Base and in and out of Long Base, and you'll have a partial view of Open Street, Shotgun and Missile Bunkers, Shortcut, and the back of Blue Base. Use the ridge separating Long Walk and Missile Street as cover.

Small Base: Utilizing Shortcut and Side Door, you can peek out to two different sides of the map with cover. From Shortcut, you can view Blue Driveway, the Missile and Shotgun Bunkers, the Phantom, the Banshee, and Missile Street. From Side Door, you can see Plasma Bunker, a partial view of Open Street, and Rocket Street. You can also see the topside of Mid Jet, with a partial view of the topside Rocket Bridge and Bubble Bridge.

Weapons Tactics

- Sandtrap is one of the largest maps in the game, making it a perfect place to wage an all-out vehicular war. With that in mind, most weapons have been created to destroy vehicles and shoot with accuracy at a long range.
- Although the Rocket Launcher is not the heat-seeking round it was in *Halo 2*, it still has the ability to destroy any ground vehicles in one shot. You can use the Rocket Launcher to destroy a Banshee, but it must be low flying and at a closer range.
- Use the Missile Pod to destroy any vehicle, land- or sky-based. The heat-seeking round means that you have to aim only in a general area of a boarded opponent and fire. Be careful when firing, because the Missile Pod alerts your opponent's radar, which gives them opportunity to escape. The missile will not bend corners at steep angles. The only downsides are it may take two missiles to destroy vehicles, and it has poor accuracy on people.
- The Spartan Laser is one of the ultimate power weapons because it can take out any vehicle with a single shot. The only real downside to the Laser is charge time and accuracy. You need to allow yourself enough time to fire while keeping steady aim.

Sniper/Ambush Locations

Dune

You can use the Dune's distance from the bases as a disguise when sniping.

Phantom

This is a great carney hole. You can move in and out of it as needed without much effort. The Phantom has many nooks and hiding spaces to snipe from.

Pillars

Use the pillars atop Long Base to give you a height advantage on moving players and cover from return fire.

Small Base

Shortcut and Side Door give you cover while you peek out to two different sides of the map. From Shortcut, you can view the Blue Driveway, the Missile and Shotgun Bunkers, the Phantom, the Banshee, and Missile Street. From Side Door, you can see Plasma Bunker, a partial view of Open Street, and Rocket Street. You can also see the topside of Mid Jet, with a partial view of the topside of Rocket Bridge and Bubble Bridge.

The Ridge

This is the ridge between Long Walk and Missile Street. From here, you can see any movement between Red Base and in and out of Long Base, and you have a partial view of Open Street, Shotgun and Missile Bunkers, Shortcut, and the rear of Blue Base. Use the ridge separating Long Walk and Missile Street as cover.

SNOWBOUND

PMS Ruin, PMS Dark Ivory

Hostile conditions did not prevent the Covenant from seeking salvage on this buried Forerunner construct.

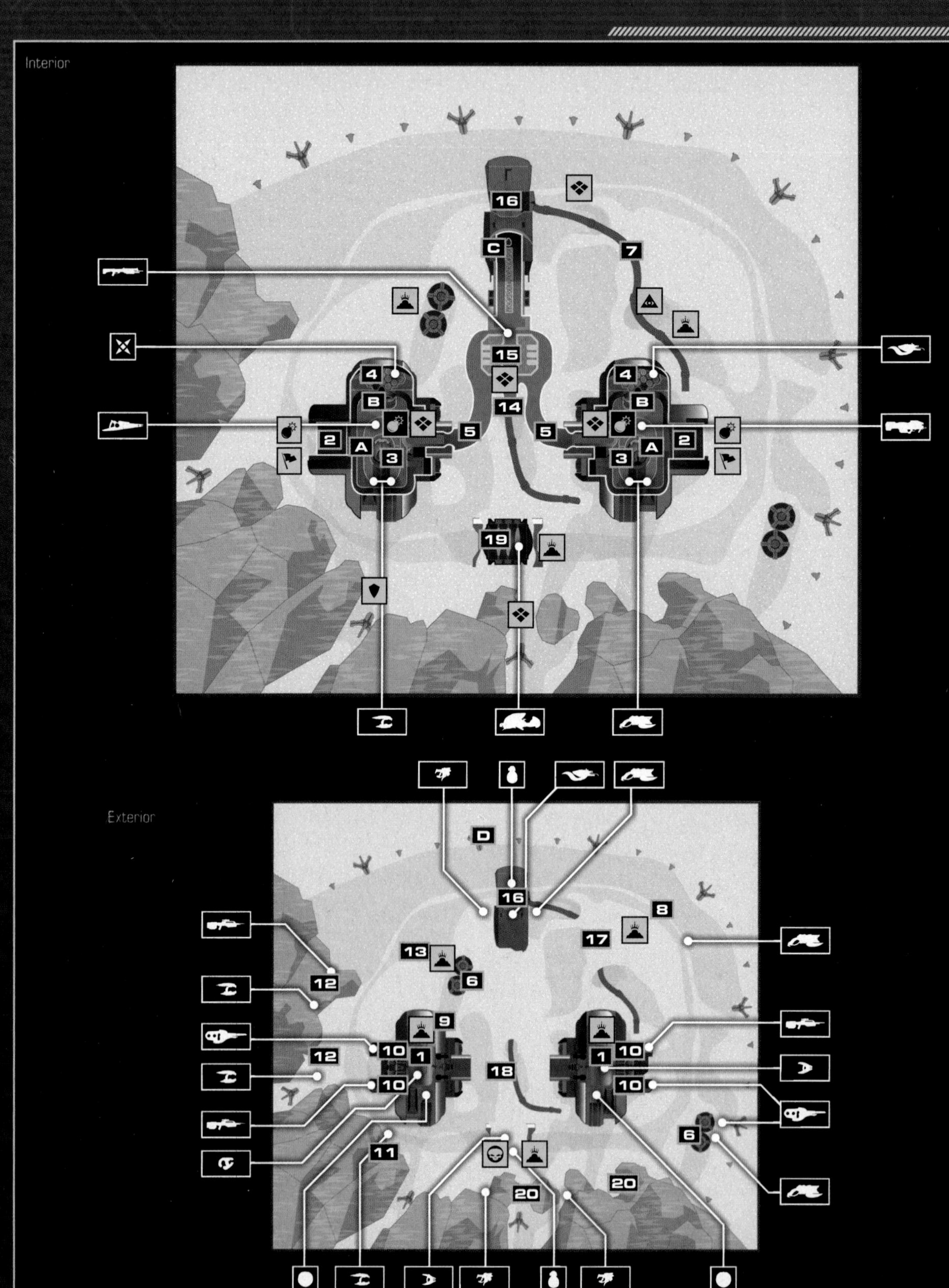

DATA STREAM

Recommended Game Variants: Team Slayer, Team Snipers, Oddball, King of the Hill, Team Swat, Capture the Flag

Recommended/Maximum Number of Players: 4–10/10

Advantageous Equipment: Mauler, Beam Rifle, Spartan Laser, Ghost, Shotgun

AVAILABLE EQUIPMENT AND GEAR RESPAWN TIMES

1 of 5 skulls = Slow 5 of 5 skulls = Fast

Weapons	Respawn (skulls)
Battle Rifle	4/5
Beam Rifle	1/5
Brute Shot	2/5
Carbine	4/5
Grenade, Frag	5/5
Grenade, Plasma	5/5
Mauler	4/5

Weapons	Respawn (skulls)
Needler	3/5
Plasma Pistol	3/5
Plasma Rifle*	5/5
Shotgun	1/5
Spartan Laser	1/5
Spiker*	5/5

** These weapons have longer spawn times when located inside each base.*

Vehicle	Respawn (skulls)
Ghost	1/5
Equipment	
Active Camo	1/5
Bubble Shield	2/5
Overshield	1/5
Power Drain	2/5

Topographical Overview

Snowbound is a well-balanced map as far as the bases are designed. It is bilevel with an underground cave system connecting the two bases. .

Call-out Locations

Blue Base

Other names: N/A

The Blue Base is identified by two horned structures atop glowing blue. The Red Base has a similar structure with exception that the horns aren't glowing.

Back Door

Other names: N/A

Moving forward into Blue Base, you'll see a large shield door. This is Back Door. Go through here and you'll walk right into a

Ball

Other names: N/A

To your left, you'll see a large blue glowing orb named Ball.

Stage

Other names: N/A

On your right is the Stage, noted by a stepped, lighted barrier and a pane of honeycombed glass.

Blue Pass

Other names: N/A

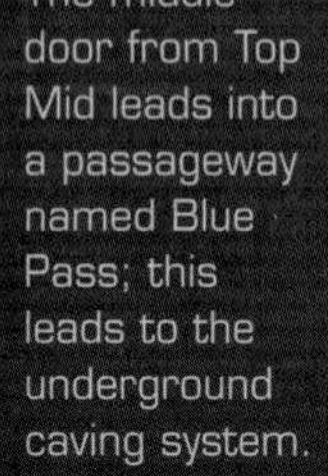

The middle door from Top Mid leads into a passageway named Blue Pass; this leads to the underground caving system.

Purple Stack (Blue Base)

Other names: Blue Stack, Blue Crates, Batteries, Cylinder

To your left are two cylinders piercing the ground. These are nicknamed Purple Stack, but when in the Blue Base, they're referred to as Blue Stack.

Rabbit Hole

Other names: Power-up Tunnel, Camo

As you look right, you'll see a small hill with a tunnel and an Active Camo. The tunnel is known as the Rabbit Hole.

Tundra

Other names: N/A

The area to your left has a randomly placed Spiker and is lined with Turrets. This is Tundra. The Tundra looks like a beaten path you can follow back to Blue Base.

Glass

Other names: Blue Glass

Stepping off the mound, you cross over a small ground pipe that leads back to Blue Base. If you approach from the side, you can see it is tilted an angle that makes it easy to climb. Honeycombed glass comprises the exterior of this part of Blue Base, which easily identifies this area as Glass. Walk up the Glass onto the base's top.

Back Ramp

Other names: N/A

This slight incline down to the back entrance located on each base is known as Back Ramp.

Purple Stack (Red Base)

Other names: Red Stack, Batteries, Crates, Cylinders

Two cylinders pierce the ground and are nicknamed Purple Stack. The stack located near the Red Base is identified as "Red Stack."

Red Pass

Other names: N/A

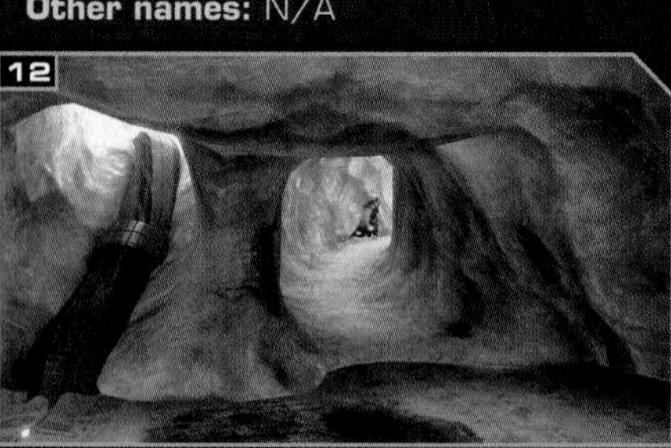

If you take Mid Pass down, Red Pass will be to your left and Blue Pass will be on your right while facing the Main

OS Rock

Other names: OV Rock

To the right of Red Base is an Overshield sitting atop a smaller, flattened rock known as OS Rock.

Red Rocks

Other names: N/A

Moving forward from OS Rock, you'll encounter a Plasma Rifle that marks the next set of rocks. This area, which is located behind the Red Base, is known as Red Rocks. The first rock, which is set with a Plasma Rifle, is known as Plasma Side. The next rock is known as BR Side, because a Battle Rifle spawns against the back of it.

The Flat

Other names: N/A

Entering from BR Side, you'll see a flattened area of the map. This is the flattest area of Snowbound and is divided by a beaten path from Red Stack. This area, due to its geography, is known as the Flat. Heading across the Flat, you'll make your way to the Main Entrance of the Cave.

Back Door (Red Base)

Other names: N/A

Moving through the larger shield door into Red Base, you will enter what's known as the Back Door.

Mid Pass

Other names: N/A

About halfway across Top Mid, a ridge forms. At the beginning of this ridge is an entrance into the Cave. Since this is at Top Mid, this tunnel is known as Mid Pass. If you take Mid Pass down, you'll have Red Pass directly to your left and Blue Pass on your right while facing the Main Entrance.

Cave

Other names: Basement, Shotty Room, Bat Cave

Following Blue Pass, you enter the main lobby of the Cave. Staying along the right side of Cave, you'll notice a larger sized shield door armed with fusion coils and a Shotgun. This is the Main Entrance into the Cave.

Main Entrance

Other names: Big Door

Walking through Main Entrance from Cave, you'll notice a single pillar followed by a radio tower and two Plasma Batteries. This area is known as Main Entrance.

Mound

Other names: N/A

The entirety of the hill forming the tunnel known as Rabbit Hole is named the Mound. Once you're standing on the Mound, you will have the Blue Base back in your sights.

Top Mid

Other names: N/A

The middle path from the Basement leads to Top Mid, which is located in the middle of the map and offers little to no cover. This area stretches from the beginning of each base, to the Ghost, and back to the Cave.

Ghost Hangar

Other names: The Ghost, Top Ghost

Moving forward over the Ghost, you will approach a radio tower with two empty crates.

Rockside

Other names: Rocks

Jumping down from the Plasma Batteries located atop each base, you'll spot a series of rocks. These stretch from the edge of Blue Base to behind Red Base. The series that starts here and extends into the top of the Ghost Hangar is known as Rockside.

NOTE **In Snowbound, as in all symmetrical *Halo* maps, your base is the one in which you spawn at the beginning of the match. With this in mind, you can use your base's landmarks as your call-outs, rather than specifying their color; for example, if you spawn in Blue Base and two enemies are approaching from the Mound toward Blue Glass, instead of saying, "Two coming from Mound running up toward Blue Glass," try, "Two rushing our Glass from Mound." This makes calling out locations on a difficult map more efficient and will allow your teammates to respond to you quickly rather than wasting time trying to decode your call-out.**

Enhanced Knowledge

With Snowbound being a smaller map, you won't play one-sided objectives very often. Although the map is very symmetrical, it doesn't have the proper space for all game types. Here are some game types you may run into playing on Snowbound:

FFA Game Types: Slayer, Oddball, and Krazy King

Team Games: Team Slayer, Team Swat, Multiflag CTF, Team Oddball, Team King, Team Snipers, and Territories

On this map, the game variants can be further separated into four categories for an in-depth approach to each: FFA, Team, Neutral Objective, and Classic Objectives.

FFA: Slayer, Oddball, Krazy King

- For all FFA games, the basic strategy is load up on power-ups, power weapons, and equipment. Make every attempt to rush for these items. You must maintain a very aggressive play style to win in FFAs.
- When playing Oddball and King of the Hill, you can clear out opponents easier if they have the hill/ball by lowering their shields first with Grenades. While carrying the ball, back yourself into the Cave and use the Bubble Shield and shield doors to your advantage. Remember that the ball gives you a one-hit melee kill. You can also keep moving for a more aggressive approach to point scoring.
- The hill in Krazy King moves every 30 seconds, so always keep an eye on the clock. The hill's new location is random, so people generally don't know which way to run when that 30 seconds is winding down.

Team: Team Slayer, Team Swat, Team Sniper

Players often mistake a smaller map as being easier than bigger maps. Spawning and running out into the open are beginners' mistakes that should be avoided. The key to this map is defense. With very little cover to choose from, running around with lowered shields can be costly.

There are two ways to approach team games on Snowbound. We'll discuss a general strategy and a strategy used by more seasoned players.

General Approach

When playing Slayer, each of the players will rush for power weapons and power-ups. If you spawn in Red Base, one player should run to pick up OV, then the Ghost. The other three players should rush Cave via Red Pass. On the way to Cave, there are three weapons that you should grab: the Beam Rifle, Carbine, and Shotty. The three players then hold down the Cave while your Ghost runs perimeters around the map, easily killing any freshly spawned opponents. Your Ghost can also call out which direction your opponents are fleeing to ready you in the Cave. This should consistently push players down into the bases and Cave to escape.

If you spawn in Blue Base, then the player rushing for Ghost will not pick up equipment right away. Instead, you'll have one person run out from Back Door to Rabbit Hole, picking up Camo on the way. That player then heads to Shotgun and holes up in the Cave. The other two players will take Blue Pass to Cave; one will pick up a BR and the other will grab the Spartan Laser. Both will help hold down the Cave.

Seasoned-Player Approach

Another strategy is to acquire and control the Blue Side of the map. This is a more seasoned approach because you need only a BR or Carbine to succeed. There should be one player each positioned in these locations: at Rockside, behind Blue Stack, at Tundra/Mound, and at Back Ramp (Blue Base)/Top Mid. The level of importance for these positions is equal, as they all play a main role in survival.

Assign your main slayer—your strongest player—to Tundra/Mound. This is an active rush point for the opposing team, meaning this player may often be approached my multiple opponents at a time. Your slayer can seize the Rabbit Hole as a route to escape damage while teammates offer cover fire.

The player positioned at Rockside is the main communicator for the team. Use Rockside as a vantage point from which to see most of the map, and you can begin firing on rushing opponents from here. Patrolling from front to back, Rockside can fire onto Mound, Tundra, Blue Base, Top of Red Base, back of Red Base, Red Stack, and parts of Cave.

The two players at Blue Stack and Back Ramp provide supporting fire. They will be able to complete, assist, and clean up any kills called out to them. If all four players remain at their posts, the opposing team will always spawn on the map's opposite side. The key here is to stay defensive at all times. Use the same defensive style of play with Team Slayer, Team Swat, and Team Snipers.

■ Neutral Objectives: Oddball, Team King/King of the Hill, Land Grab

- While playing Oddball, two players should defend the player running for the ball. The fourth player should rush for the Shotgun. After the ball and Shotgun are obtained, all teammates should return back to their base. Use the base as a retreat from enemy attacks, because shield doors protect every entrance.
- Two players without the ball or Shotgun act as scouting and supporting fire for each other. They work together to obtain kills via team-shooting, and the Shotgun can clean up any stragglers who make it through. During King of the Hill, use the same strategy to clear out the hill as you would playing FFA. Leave one person on the hill, with three supporting players positioned outside. The player getting time on the hill should have a Bubble Shield to protect them from launched Grenades. The hill spawns at Ghost, Red Stack, Top Blue Base, and Top Red Base. It moves randomly every 60 seconds, so keep an eye on the clock.
- The five Land Grab positions are as follows: behind Red Base, behind Blue Base, in Rockside, in front of Rabbit Hole, and in Cave at the bottom of Mid Pass. Leave the territory closest to your base for last, as this is the easiest to capture. Have the main slayer equip Grenades and power-ups, then head to the enemy's base. The other three players then rush Rabbit Hole, Rockside, and Mid Pass independently. There should be only one opponent on each, if that, because some are attempting to capture their base while your slayer is busy distracting them. If they figure out your approach and double up on territories, then send two at a time to each area.

■ Classic Objectives: Multiflag

The team should advance as three, with one person defending your team's flag at Red Rock/Blue Stack (depending on which side you spawn). Your flag carrier can run one of two routes, depending on which is clear. If your team is successful in removing the opponents, they can run Rockside back to your base seemingly unnoticed. If your team is cut short, you may run the flag over the base and onto Top Mid as an emergency. This leaves you open for all fire, but you can jump off the base and toss the flag, launching it close to your base. Spawning teammates can grab the flag and return through the base, where shield doors will protect them from long-range Grenades and enemy fire. Whoever is covering your flag should never move from their post.

General Tactics

- If you've secured the Shotgun and are controlling the Cave, you can wait for enemies at shield doors and kill them easily as they pass through.
- Pay attention to your teammates. There isn't a lot of cover on Snowbound, and they'll need coverage while passing through.
- Try not to chase an opponent into the Cave. They are probably running you into their team.
- If your team isn't actively using the Ghost, destroy it so your foe can't use it against you.
- Always secure the Spartan Laser if your team is using the Ghost as its primary equipment.
- You can always use Plasma Grenades as a last resort to stop a Ghost on a splatter spree.
- Top Mid has absolutely no cover. Try to stay out of it even while traveling base to base.
- Use the Mauler when hiding around corners in the base for quick kills.
- There are three times more Maulers than Shotguns on Snowbound. Try to equip these often over the Shotty. It means more ammo and a much faster reload.
- If you're attempting to storm the Cave, make sure to equip the Overshield to minimize damage.
- Back in and out of the shield doors to avoid damage from Grenades.
- Watch your back in the Cave. There's a wall of fusion coils lining the entrance that can be used against you. They respawn every three minutes, so destroy them as often as they spawn.
- You can squat next to the Turrets and remain unnoticed.
- The BR Rock makes an efficient sniping position, as you can reach many spawn points without much pivoting.
- If you spawn on top of the base, immediately move, as you are an easily spotted target.
- The Plasma Battery on each base makes killing any enemies on the bases quicker. Just destroy the pack, then move to shooting the opponent.
- The glass on the top and side of the bases is a one-way mirror; if someone is creeping over, you can see them while undetected on your radar.
- Don't grab Camo and Laser thinking your invisible. Lasers have long charge times, and you will appear visible the duration of the charge.
- Good weapon and equipment combinations include Snipe Rifle plus Camo or Shotgun plus Camo.
- If you need to travel across the map, going Rockside is a good route when sneaking around. This is the one location on Snowbound with adequate cover.
- Beware of Mound: People often spawn here and sneak down Tundra to Blue Base, using the Mound as cover.
- Help your team control the Cave by equipping a person with the Shotgun and another with the Sniper Rifle. Both can eliminate the worry of an opponent traveling through the passes to make an attack.
- Grenades are easily tossed into Cave via Mid Pass.
- If sniping from the Red Base, keep an eye on the Cave Entrance. Most activity on this map happens in the Cave.
- You can drive the Ghost down into Cave from Mid Pass. This can be a great source for an ambush.
- You can also ride Ghost up Glass to the top bases.
- Remember, from Blue Base, Top Mid can only be jumped from Mid Pass or Ghost.
- Any attempt to pass Turrets from behind will mostly result in death. Stay away.
- Don't follow your teammates too closely into passes. They are extremely narrow, and you both can be easily killed with Grenades. You will also block your teammates' attempt at backing up to escape continuous fire.

Sniper/Ambush Locations

Ball Camper

While carrying the ball in Objective games, you can jump atop the ball in each base for an optimal hideout.

Ledge Camper

While carrying the ball in Objective games, you can jump atop the Stage in each base for an optimal hideout.

Shotty Ledge

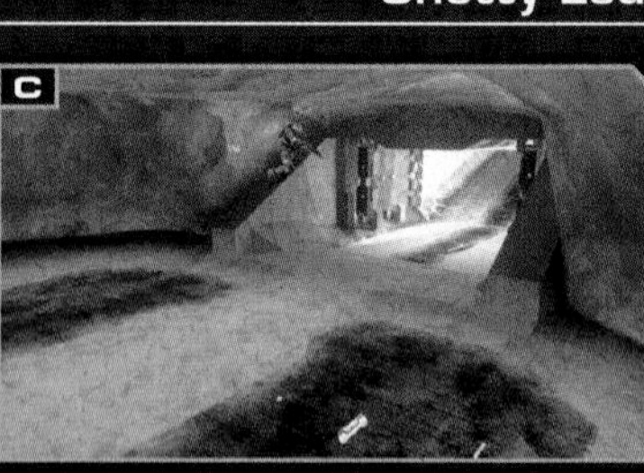

Climb on the Entrance ledge in Cave. Post up here and drop down for a surprise attack.

Turret Hideout

You can squat next to the Turrets and remain unnoticed.

STANDOFF

PMS Deception, PMS Eclipse, PMS Shadowleet, PMS Ovaryacting, PMS Mrs Lulu

Once, nearby telescopes listened for a message from the stars. Now these silos contain our prepared response.

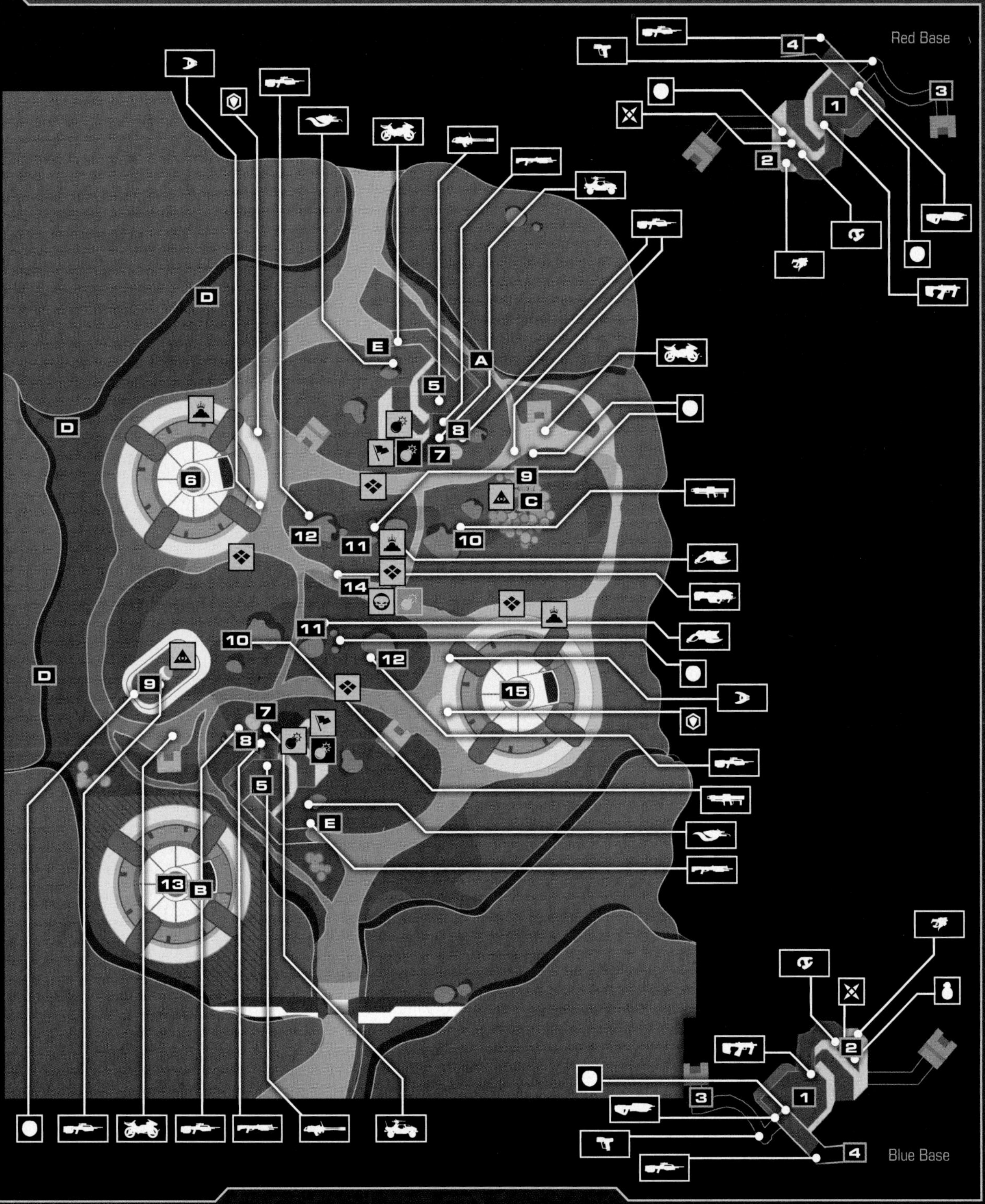

Red Base

Blue Base

DATA STREAM

Recommended Game Variants: Team Slayer, Big Team Slayer, One Flag, Multiflag, Assault, One Bomb, Snipers, Standoff Heavy (BTB)

Recommended/Maximum Number of Players: 8–16/16

Advantageous Equipment: Spartan Laser, Rocket Launcher, Machinegun Turret, Active Camo, Warthog

Weapons	
Assault Rifle	●●●●●
Battle Rifle	●●●●○
Brute Shot	●●●○○
Grenade, Frag	●●●●●
Grenade, Plasma	●●●●●
Machinegun Turret	●○○○○
Magnum	●●●●●

Weapons	
Mauler	●●●●○
Needler	●●○○○
Plasma Pistol	●●●○○
Rocket Launcher	●○○○○
Shotgun	●●○○○
Spartan Laser	●○○○○

Vehicle	
Mongoose	●●●●●
Warthog	●●●○○
Equipment	
Bubble Shield	●●●○○
Power Drain	●●●○○

Topographical Overview

Call-out Locations

Both Red and Blue Bases are identical in layout, weapons, and equipment. To determine which base you are in, look at the coloring within the bases. The bases will be your main spawn point in all game types. Your base will also house your flag in Capture the Flag (CTF), and you will arm the bomb in the enemy's base in Assault. Each base can be broken up into categories and have their own call-outs. When calling out areas, simply add "red" or "blue" to the location (e.g., Top Blue, Blue Turret).

Main Room/Flag Room

Other names: Red Flag/Blue Flag

1

There is an SMG by the front door here, and you'll find an Assault Rifle and two Plasma Grenades in the corner of the room. This room also houses your flag in CTF and is where you will arm the bomb in Assault. There are four ways to exit the base from here.

Red/Blue Control Room

Other names: Red Control/Blue Control

2

In this room, you will find two Frag Grenades, a Plasma Pistol, a Power Drain, and a Mauler. There is a switch inside

Red/Blue Camo/Invis Door

Other names: Red Camo Door/Blue Camo Door

3

This door leads into a hallway where you can locate a Magnum. Follow the hall to Camo Spawn.

Red/Blue Back Entrance/Back Door

Other names: Red Back Door/Blue Back Door

4

If you take the Back Door to each base, you will find a Battle Rifle up against the outside wall.

Red/Blue Top Base

Other names: Top Red/Top Blue

5

This is the upper, outside level of the base. The Machinegun Turret is located by sandbags and fusion coils.

Missile Silo 1

Other names: Launch Pad 1, Silo 1, Territory 3

6

In front of the side door of Red Base, near the Missile Silo, you will find a Bubble Shield and a Needler.

Red/Blue Warthog/Shotgun Spawn

Other names: N/A

7

You have quick access to a Warthog out in front of Base. The Shotgun is outside the base, propped against the left wall.

Red/Blue First BR

Other names: N/A

8

The first Battle Rifle is located next to the cylinder outside the front door.

Red Camo

Other names: N/A

9

The Red Active Camo is located between a tree and a rock, which also has a BR leaning up against it and two Plasma Grenades. The Blue Camo is a flat surface with a cylinder and an antenna. There's a BR and two Plasma Grenades here, too.

Rocket Launcher Spawn

Other names: Rocket Spawn, Rockets, Territory 4

10

The Rocket Launcher Spawn is located on the outer left of the rock formation that protects the base, nearest Camo Spawn.

Middle Rocks

Other names: Mid Rocks

11

This is a cluster of three smaller boulders where a Plasma Grenade, a Frag Grenade, and a Spiker are located.

Red/Blue Battle Rifle Rock

Other names: Red BR Rock, Blue BR Rock

12

This is the large boulder located on the right of the rock formation that protects the base, nearest Missile Silo 1.

Missile Silo 3

Other names: N/A

13

Located in Upper Back Blue, Missile Silo 3 is where players will spawn. A Mongoose is located here.

Mid Map/Laser Spawn

Other names: N/A

The Spartan Laser spawns in Mid Map, which is also a good pathway for vehicles.

Missile Silo 2

Other names: Launch Pad 2, Silo 2

In front of the side door to Blue Base, you will find a Bubble Shield and a Needler.

Enhanced Knowledge

Advanced Tactics for Team Slayer

- With Standoff's small size, it is easy to take control of the map by simply controlling the Spartan Laser and keeping enemy vehicles at bay. If your team is controlling the Laser, use your Warthog to cause some major damage; however, try to take the outside paths to steer clear of Power Drains and Plasma Grenades.
- Work with your team to hold a base or position wherever you may spawn. Do not run out in the middle of the map with no cover. You will probably get team-killed.
- Generally, do not rush into the middle of the map. You will die. Hold back, wait for better weapons such as the BR to spawn, and use the cover to your advantage.
- Controlling the map on the opposing team's boulders is extremely advantageous for Team Slayer and Objective games. Also, using the boulders for cover allows you to see almost every spot on the map, every vehicle driving by, and every person on either team. Use the Spartan Laser or Machinegun Turret to support your team.
- Short-range weapons usually come in handy for enclosed areas such as within Blue and Red Base.
- Have no more than two people in the Warthog at one time. Unless you are using the Warthog as transportation, do not use that third seat. You are unable to fire accurately from that seat, and if the Warthog is destroyed, you give the opponent a triple kill! Use the Power Slide ability for quick turns without rolling.
- As soon as the match begins, Grenade where you think the enemy Warthog is. This will flip their Warthog and possibly destroy it.
- Grab the Power Drain to take out Warthogs whenever you have the chance. Also work as a team—you won't win on this map by yourself.
- If you are on one side of the ample rocks on this map and your enemy is on the other side, throw a Grenade to take out their shields, then run in the opposite direction of your throw and kill your opponent when you meet them coming around the rock.

Tactics for One Flag, Multiflag, One Bomb, and Assault

Defense

- Place your players wisely on the map. Do not completely desert the base to capture the power weapons, but do not have everybody hide in the base waiting for the eventual attack from the bomb carrier or flag bandit. Obtain the Spartan Laser so you can take out incoming vehicles, and use the Machinegun Turret to kill footmen before they get into your base. Leave a few teammates inside the base to protect the exits. Inside the base, use short-range power weapons such as the Shotgun or use dual-wielding Plasmas Pistols with Spikers and Maulers.
- For Multiflag games, try to balance the number of players between those who are protecting your flag and those who are capturing the other team's flag.
- Watch out for Mongooses and Warthogs coming from the map's outer edges; use the Spartan Laser, Power Drain, and Plasma Pistols on them.
- If your opponent steals your flag, consider taking a Mongoose to cut off the other team before they make with the flag.
- Remember, you cannot see the enemy's bomb or your stolen flag when the other team has possession of them. An optional and amusing tactic for protecting your base from being bombed or your flag from being stolen is to pile a bunch of vehicles on your flag or bomb region. This will make capturing the flag or planting the bomb complicated, because the other team will not be able to find it through the mess of vehicles!
- Have your team grab the Shotgun, Maulers, and Power Drain to protect your flag or base from bombing groups hiding near doorways.

Offense

- Never try to take the flag or plant the bomb by yourself. Coordinate an attack with your teammates. Have a team member or two attempt to take control of the defending team and use the Spartan Laser effectively.
- Drive the Warthog or Mongoose with the flag or bomb in the passenger seat. If driven correctly, the Warthog and Mongoose can get your team into the opponent's base, capture the flag or plant the bomb, and get out within minutes. All three seats in the Warthog should be full (a driver, a Turret operator, and a footman to plant the bomb or capture the flag).
- Depending on your team's size, you may also want to take a fully loaded Mongoose with your Warthog so you may overwhelm the other team.
- Crouch-walking makes you invisible to enemy radar. When storming the base, use crouch-walking to sneak in undetected with the bomb or to grab the flag when the other team is not looking.
- If you have possession of the bomb or flag, do not hang on to it for dear life when someone is trying to kill you. You can get an instant kill with a bomb or flag melee, but sometimes it is best to drop your load and fight off the other team with your weapons on hand. You can pick up your load after.
- When playing Assault or One Bomb, do not abandon your planted bomb. Stay around and protect it so the other team does not disarm it. If necessary, stay until the bomb detonates. Throw Grenades or Power Drains on the ticking time bomb when the other team attempts to disarm it.
- For CTF games, when you have just snatched the flag, determine whether you will proceed on foot or take the Warthog. If your team has control of the Spartan Laser, consider taking the Warthog. If the other team controls the Laser, you may want to go on foot. Send a vehicle as a decoy.
- If you are going on foot, try to "hop" from cover to cover. Take the outside path, going from Side Door to Missile Silos, covering yourself from place to place.
- Camo is great for sneaking with the bomb into bases and taking out enemy Rockets. Camo is also useful for defense if the opposing team has control of the Spartan Laser.

■ Sniper/Ambush Locations

Boxes

On top of Red Base is a series of crates and boxes. This makes a great sniping position, as it gives a complete view across the map and hosts enough room for a few players to snipe from. Strafe in and out of sight between the crates.

Blue Silo

On top of Blue Base is an elevated silo. It gives no cover as a sniping position, but you can evade very easily by dropping off and hiding behind the arms of the silo or dodging into the base. The elevation gives you the ability to snipe anyone trying to gain position on your base.

Red Invis

The Invis located on the Red Side is planted between a rock and a tree. Strafe in between the rock and tree while sniping and waiting for Invisibility to spawn. The tree is located on a small hill, which you can also use to your advantage as cover.

Side Walls

The sides of the map are very shaded and dark. Use this path to snipe from while traveling from base to base. With your back against the wall, you will be slightly camouflaged in the environment. It's best to use this area only while traveling and for short durations, because your foe can easily spot you here.

Mongoose

On the right side of each base is a Mongoose spawn. There is also a tunnel that leads back into the base. If you stand in the tunnel exit, you can peek your head out next to the Mongoose and snipe across the map. Strafe behind the Mongoose to protect yourself.

THE PIT

PMS Jezabelle, Righty Is Law, Stawberry Boo, PMS Dark Ivory, PMS Eclipse

Software simulations are held in contempt by the veteran instructors who run these training facilities.

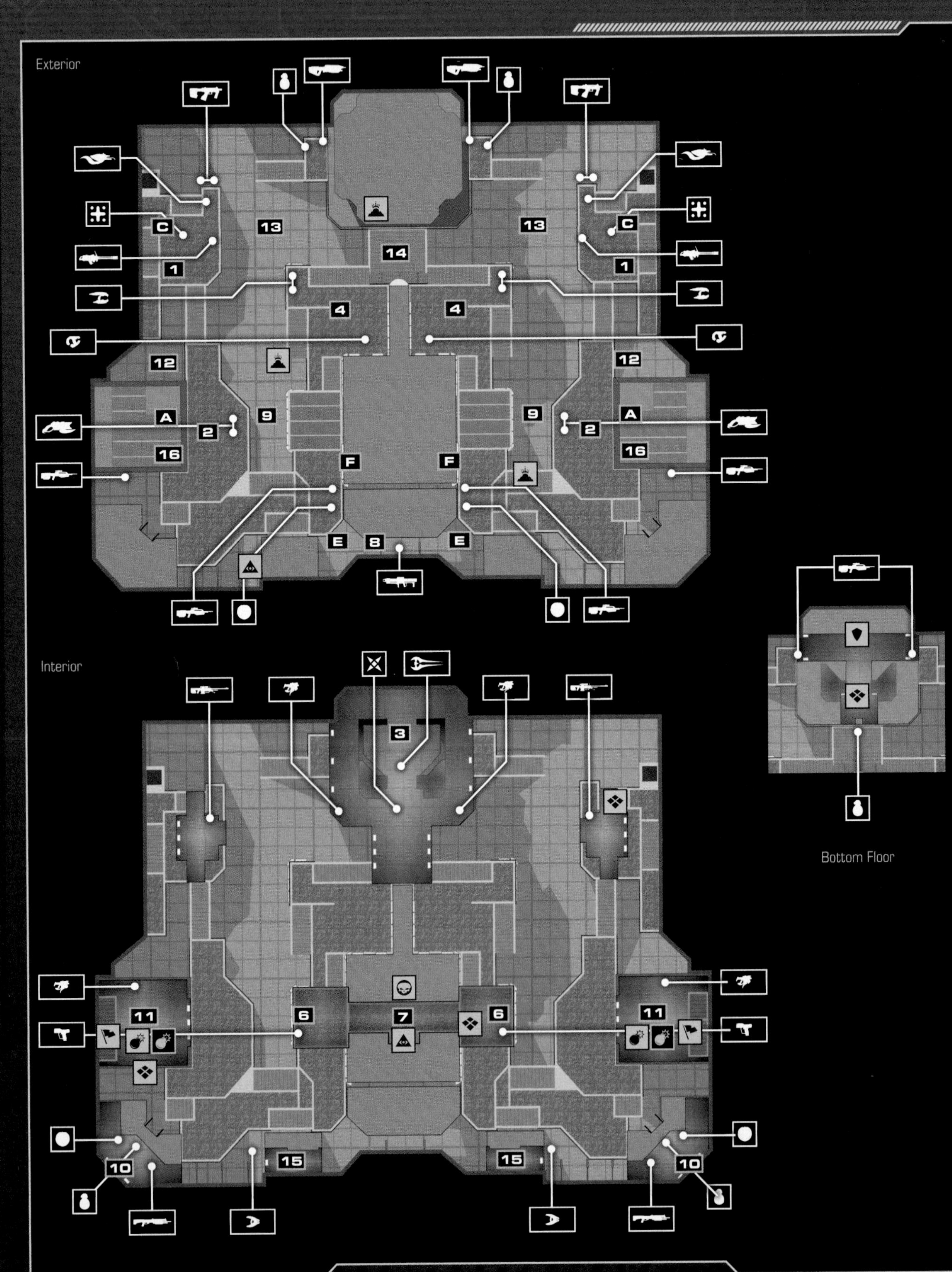

DATA STREAM

Recommended Game Variants: Team Slayer, Capture the Flag, One Flag, Assault, Neutral Assault, Free-for-All, Land Grab, Territories

Recommended/Maximum Number of Players: 4–10/16

Advantageous Equipment: Rockets, Overshield, Active Camo, Sniper, Energy Sword, Shotgun

AVAILABLE EQUIPMENT AND GEAR RESPAWN TIMES

1 of 5 skulls = Slow 5 of 5 skulls = Fast

Weapons	Respawn
Assault Rifle	5 of 5
Battle Rifle	4 of 5
Brute Shot	2 of 5
Energy Sword	2 of 5
Grenade, Frag	5 of 5
Grenade, Plasma	5 of 5
Machinegun Turret	1 of 5
Magnum	5 of 5

Weapons	Respawn
Mauler	4 of 5
Needler	2 of 5
Plama Pistol	3 of 5
Plasma Rifle	4 of 5
Rocket Launcher	1 of 5
Shotgun	2 of 5
SMG	4 of 5

Weapons	Respawn
Sniper Rifle	2 of 5
Spiker	4 of 5
Equipment	
Active Camo	1 of 5
Overshield	1 of 5
Power Drain	3 of 5
Regenerator	3 of 5

Topographical Overview

Call-out Locations

Sniper Tower

Other names: Snipe 1 and Snipe 2

On each side of the map, across from one another at Blue Base and Red Base, is the Sniper Tower. This tower consists of several areas. On the bottom is where the Sniper Rifle spawns. To the side, facing the open air outside, is the Grav Lift, which takes you to the second level, known as Snipe 2. Snipe 2 contains the Regenerator, along with a cornered barricade behind which you can take cover. Leading from Top Snipe or Snipe 2 toward the back of the tower is the Snipe Ramp. This ramp leads to the area known as "the Cut." Also leading from Top Snipe or Snipe 2 is the Snipe Bridge. This bridge takes you to the Platform, or "Plat."

Platform

Other names: Plat

Platform is located in the open spawn area on either side of the map. From here, you

Sword Spawn

Other names: Sword

Hidden within this area's bunker is a Covenant Sword. Accessing this area from either Red Base Courtyard or Blue Base Courtyard (the area directly in front and to the side of the Sniper Tower) via the Sword Ramp will allow entrance to the Side Sword areas. One can also access the Sword via Sword Bridge. This area is shrouded by low light and is a secured stronghold against enemies.

Training

Other names: N/A

Positioned between the Sword Bridge and the base, Training is designated by the training poster that appears on

OS Tunnel

Other names: Runway

Beneath Sword Spawn is a tunnel that connects the Sniper Towers at both bases. This area is also accessible via the area directly beneath Sword Bridge.

Green Box

Other names: N/A

The Green Box of either base is positioned directly in front of the area known as the Green Hall. This is centered between Needles Hallway and the Training area and is shielded on one side (the side facing the platform) by a tall, green, sheet-metal wall.

Green Hall

Other names: Camo Hall

Green Hall is located directly in the map's center and is connected on either side to each base's Green Box. This area is always a hotbed of activity, as it contains the coveted Active Camo, which provides a stealth-attack option for gaining quick access to the opponent's base.

Rocket Hall

Other names: Dark Hall, Long Hall, Black Hall

Another hallway that is always active is the Rocket Hall, or Black Hall. This area connects the Needles areas on both sides

Pit

Other names: N/A

your way through this area. Leading from t
to the Sniper Tower courtyard, the Pit is a
to get caught, as your opponent will have t
advantage.

Shotgun Tunnel

Other names: Shotty Tunnel

positioned between the Needles Hall and th
area, Shotgun Tunnel is a death trap.

Flag Spawn

Other names: Objective

Shotgun Tunnel and the shortcut of Sniper
ramp located against the exterior wall of th

Shortcut

Other names: Cut

Courtyard

Other names: N/A

Sniper Courtyard is an open, flat area located in front of and on the side of Sniper Tower.

Sword Bridge

Other names: N/A

Connecting the Sword Room and the Training areas of the bases, the Sword Bridge is located directly in the middle of the bases. The area under Sword Bridge is known as "Under Sword Bridge."

Needles

Other names: N/A

Aptly named for the weapon within its corridor, Needles is located on the path between the Shotgun Tunnel and Long Hall. This area is great for duck and cover and features a pit in which you can trap your opponent.

The Apartment

Other names: The Attic, Upstairs

This small room is located above the flag and has a walkway leading out to Shortcut and Shotgun Tunnel. It also has a window looking out toward the Platform. Getting into the Apartment can be difficult. To access the Apartment, you can team-jump, Grenade-jump, or use the Brute Shot to propel yourself up there.

Enhanced Knowledge

- When the game starts, obtaining Rockets should be a very high priority. One of the best tactics is to grab the Needler and needle the rushing opponents through Rocket Hall. It is a quick rush tactic that has a high success rate.
- In the beginning of the match, the sniper should guard the Overshield, preventing the opponent from sniping it from their runway.
- A sniper can camp their own Sniper Tower and take out the other team to stop rushes from Sword Room and Sword Bridge. Also, a Regenerator respawns at Snipe 2, so it is difficult to flank the sniper.
- When rushing Camo, it is easy to bounce a Grenade to explode the fusion coils on the other side of Green Tunnel. This can drop the shields of other enemies and sometimes will score a lucky kill.
- Another good place to snipe is near Needler Spawn and Shotgun Spawn. Both spots provide enough cover and enable an average sniper to rack up the kills. When at Shotgun Spawn, you can fall back to your objective; when at Needler Spawn, it is easy to fall back to Needle Pit, which is a safer position.
- Crouching atop the yellow mats is an easy way to surprise your enemy. It is harder to aim high quickly and accurately, but being up here allows you to get at least one kill without being noticed or killed. However, don't do this too often in the same match or you will become an easy target.
- The detachable Machinegun Turret that is located at Snipe 2 can be used as a power weapon if the enemies have shorter-ranged weapons like the Assault Rifle or Sword. Detaching the Turret is a good way to weaken the enemies so that your team can get easy kills.
- The Rocket Launcher can be deadly, especially in close quarters like Rocket Hall, Camo Hall, and the Training area. It is better to stay in more covered areas to increase the damage done by a single Rocket; the enemy won't have much room to move around and dodge the Rocket.
- Use the Sword and Shotgun as flanking weapons to get a pesky sniper off their Sniper Tower, even if they are in a Regenerator.
- When playing Capture the Flag, it is best to take the flag through Rocket Hall, because it is the shortest distance with the most cover.
- It is very easy to control the Training areas by rushing with a Plasma Rifle; this weapon lowers an enemy's shield and you can then kill them in one shot with the Battle Rifle.
- Using the SMG in one hand and a Spiker in another makes for quick kills from short to medium range.
- If you have a Regenerator, it is best to use closer-range weapons to draw opponents into your Regenerator for an easy kill.
- When camping in close quarters, one or two Brute Shot blasts and a beatdown will quickly kill an opponent.
- Because this is a short- to medium-range map, it is best to stay near your teammates so that you do not get caught by yourself.
- When rushing Camo or Rockets, it is best to bank your Grenades off the inside walls so that it takes your opponent's shields down.
- If the other team has the Overshield, use the Plasma Pistol and Needler to quickly take down all their shields.
- When you have Camo, it is best to crouch-walk if you know that there are nearby enemies.
- The flag and bomb are great melee weapons, as one melee hit with these items will kill opponents.

Advanced Tactics

- It is possible to send a Grenade into Sword Spawn by bouncing a Grenade through the small gaps at the tops of the walls that run parallel to the entrances. This can get rid of enemies who are camping with the Sword or who are hiding.
- With the help of another person or with Grenade-jumping, you can get into the attic above the Flag Spawn to snipe people from a lot of cover.
- On top of Sniper Tower and at Training, you can jump over the walls to confuse opponents. To jump over them, you need to crouch at the peak of your jump.
- On a few panels, like in the Pit and the Cut, it is possible to jump onto the higher platform by crouch-jumping and then jumping again.
- Throwing Grenades over the middle structures near Shotgun Tunnel or between Shotgun Tunnel and Flag Spawn can destroy an enemy spawn.
- When playing CTF, the fastest way to run the flag is by juggling it. Do this by either pressing ↗ or pushing the Grenade Throw button and then picking up the flag and repeating. Do not do this on Assault, because it shows where the bomb is.
- If you put a sniper on top of the opposing team's Sniper Tower and put one person by the opposing team's Training area and one person between Green and the enemy's side of Long Hall, you will probably force the enemy to respawn in their Shotgun Hall. Beware, though: they can respawn at the bottom of their Sniper Tower as well, trapping you in their tower.
- When trying to sneak up on a sniper atop a tower, stand near the snipe lift and bounce a Grenade off the back wall. It typically lands by the shorter wall on the top of Sniper Tower.
- The wall atop Sniper Tower has little holes through which you can snipe. These holes provide a good view of the Training area, and most opponents will not realize where they have been shot from until it is too late.
- While standing on a Training area, you can Grenade the other Training area by bouncing a Grenade off the wall above the Sword Bridge.

Sniper/Ambush Locations

The Apartment

This provides an excellent sniping point and good cover unless enemies begin throwing Grenades up at you or launching Rockets. Don't stand on the floor grating, or you'll be seen—and shot at—from the base below. From the Apartment, you have sight of Long Hall, Green Hall, Training, Sword Bridge, Sniper Tower, and parts of your Pit.

Shotty Snipe

Shotgun Tunnel provides a great sniping location, because it looks down your Needles, into Long Hall, and into your opponent's flag ramps. Because of the narrow opening here, you can strafe between the wall and Shotgun with enough cover to dodge approaching snipers.

Snipe 2

The upper Turret location has aluminum L-walls to hide behind, while the walls underneath are excellent for darting in and out of. There are excellent views across to the opposite Sniper Rifle location. This can also be used to protect players running into your flag area and can assist in killing any enemy flag carriers.

Sword Snipe

With direct views of both side's Green Box, partial views of Long Hall and Training, the Sword Room provides plenty of cover for ample sniping. You can also perch out on the ramps to assist teammates who are being swarmed.

Long Hall Sniping

Just as with sniping from Shotty Snipe, you can stand at the beginning of Long Hall and strafe between the wall and Rocket Spawn; however, from this location, you can also snipe any players entering through your Training area and Green Hall and from their Shotgun Tunnel.

Yellow Ledge

In front of Sword Bridge is a yellow ledge called "Top Yellow." This area of the map is often overlooked by players in Matchmaking games. Positioning yourself atop the yellow protruding wall will give you the height advantage to take our your enemy below. You can also perch on the yellow ledge next to Long Hall to attack any players entering through Long Hall and Green Hall.

▪VALHALLA

PMS Ovaryacting, Athena AzMADEUS, PMS Serenity yo

The crew of V-398 barely survived the unplanned landing on this gorge...this curious gorge.

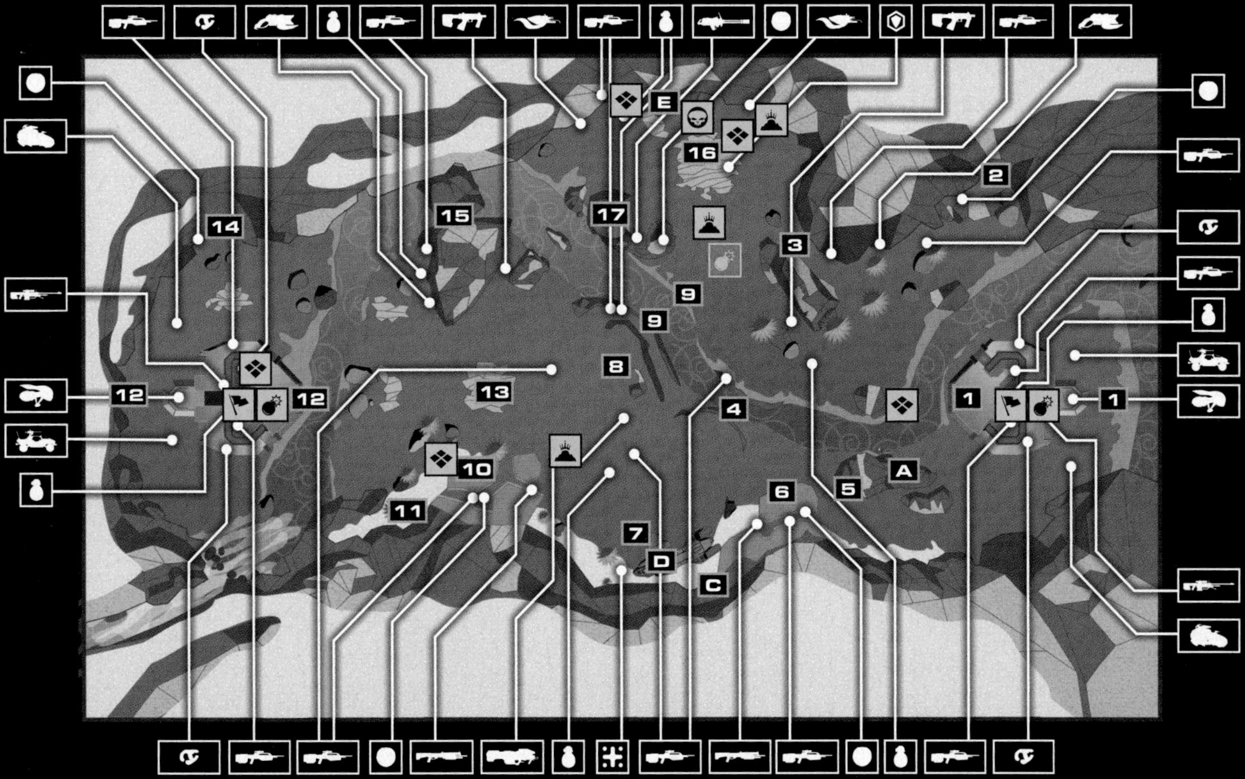

Lake Base

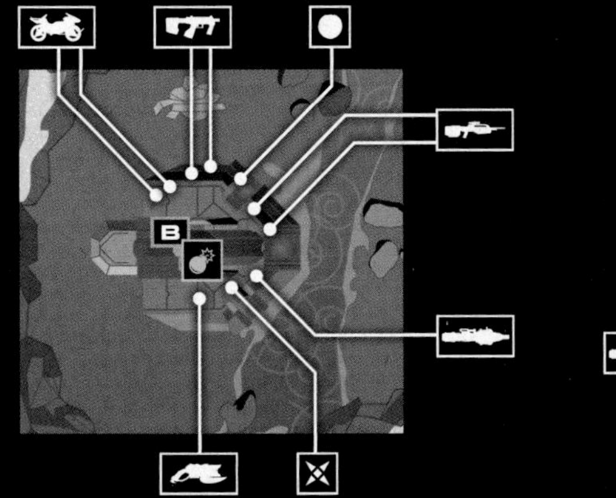

Waterfall Base

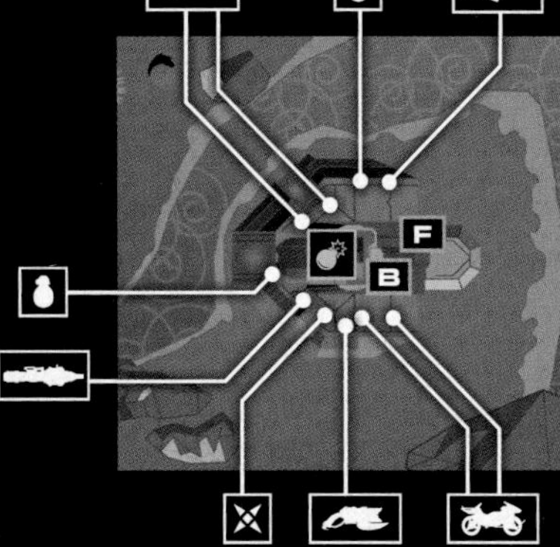

DATA STREAM

Recommended Game Variants Team Slayer, One Flag, Multi-Flag, One Bomb, Assault, Territories, VIP

Recommended/Maximum Number of Players: 6–16/16

Advantageous Equipment: Spartan Laser, Sniper Rifle, Missile Pod, Machinegun Turret, Banshee, Warthog

Basic Training
Arms & Equipment
Know Your Enemy
Campaign
Firefight
Halo 3 Multiplayer
Appendices

(1 skull) = Slow (5 skulls) = Fast

Weapons		
	Battle Rifle	4
	Brute Shot	4
	Grenade, Frag	5
	Grenade, Plasma	5
	Machinegun Turret	3
	Missile Pod	1
	Plama Pistol	4

Weapons		
	Shotgun	2
	SMG	4
	Sniper Rifle	1
	Spartan Laser	1
	Spiker	5
Vehicles		
	Banshee	1

Vehicles		
	Mongoose	5
	Warthog	2
	Wraith (Forge only)	1
Equipment		
	Bubble Shield	3
	Power Drain	4
	Regenerator	3

Topographical Overview

Call-out Locations

Red Base

Other names: Top Base, Bottom Base, Top Red, Bottom Red, Red Flag, Flag Spawn, Territory 5

Red Base is one of two identical bases located on the map. They are the spawn locations for Red and Blue teams for Team Slayer and Objective game types. Red Base is located next to the beach and has two levels, Top Red and Bottom Red. Behind Red Base, you will find a landing pad, called Red Banshee Pad. A Banshee is resting on this pad, and there's a small beach behind the pad called Back Red. To the side of the Banshee sits a Warthog. Red Base also is the Territory 5 for Territory games.

Top Red

Other names: N/A

Top Red features two Man Cannons. Stepping on the Man Cannon positioned at an angle will take you to a group of rocks and trees. Resting next to the Man Cannon are two Battle Rifles, two Plasma Grenades, and two SMGs. Stepping on the center Man Cannon will push you forward to the midpoint of the creek flowing before you. There is a fusion coil sitting atop the center Man Cannon. Top Red also has two Mongooses, one Spiker, one Power Drain, one Missile Pod, and one exploding barrel, and it houses the flag in Capture the Flag (CTF) games.

Bottom Red

Other names: N/A

There are three entrances into Bottom Red. One entrance is located in the back of the base in front of Red Banshee Pad. There is one Sniper Rifle and two Frag Grenades next to this entrance. The other two entrances are located on either side of the back entrance. A Battle Rifle and Plasma Pistol appear next to each of these entrances. Bottom Red is also the location for planting the bomb in Assault and One Bomb games.

Red Cliff Side Spawn

Other names: Side Spawn

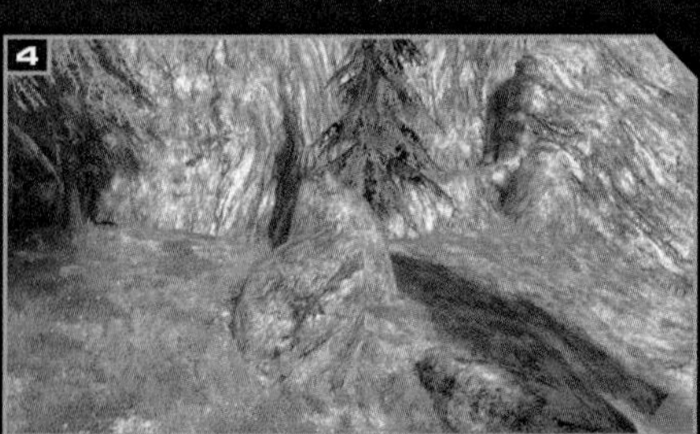

If you step on the angled Man Cannon, it will land you next to a group of trees and rocks. Searching around this area, you will find a Battle Rifle and a Spiker. The cliffs to the far right of these trees and rocks are known as Red Cliff Side Spawn, and they contain two Plasma Grenades.

Turret Cave

Other names: Territory 3

Next to those trees and rocks, you will see a large pathway through the mountain known as Turret Cave. There is a Battle Rifle inside the pathway. On the path's left side, next to the river, is an opened Drop Pod with an SMG and two Frag Grenades. Turret Cave also is the Territory 5 for Territory games.

Mid Creek

Other names: Mid River, Red Man Cannon Landing

Mid Creek is the area to the left of the opened Drop Pod in the middle of the creek. If you step onto the center Man Cannon back in Red Base, it will take you to Mid Creek and land you almost exactly on top of a Battle Rifle.

Sniper Rock

Other names: N/A

If you follow the creek back to Red Base and move to the creek's other side (to your right), you will find a large flat rock called Sniper Rock. This is a popular sniping location because of the vantage point and good visibility of the map.

Pelican Cave

Other names: Territory 4

Scaling the side of the cliff next to Sniper Rock, you will approach a small cave housing a Shotgun, two Plasma Grenades, and one Battle Rifle. This cave is known as Pelican Cave and is Territory 4 for Territory games.

Pelican

Other names: Territory 2

Travel through the cave to approach a downed Pelican. This area is simply known as Pelican and provides excellent cover during battles. Near the cockpit of the Pelican is a Regenerator lying on the ground. The area next to the Regenerator is also Territory 2 of Territory games.

Top Mid

Other names: Laser Spawn, Mid Map

Next to the Pelican is a large hill with the many tall trees; this is called Top Mid. Controlling Top Mid is essential in Team Slayer and in most Objective games. Top Mid provides the best vantage point for the entire map; you can see almost every section on the map from here. Mid Map also has the only Laser and contains a Battle Rifle and two Frag Grenades. The Battle Rifle is located just below the large rock on the lower side of Top Mid, facing the other base. This rock is known as BR Rock.

Mid Cliff Side

Other names: Mid Cliff

Located to the side of Top Mid, just above the creek, is a little cliff or nook called Mid Cliff Side. You will find a Battle Rifle and two Frag Grenades on it.

Shotgun Cave

Other names: N/A

To the left of Top Mid and in front of Pelican is a little cave called Shotgun Cave. It houses a Battle Rifle, two Sticky Grenades, and one Shotgun.

Snow Side

Other names: N/A

On the other side of Shotgun Cave is a snowy area hidden by landscape called Snow Side. From Snow Side, you can see the waterfall and the second base.

Blue Base

Other names: N/A

The other base is known as Blue Base and is identical to Red Base in structure, weapons, and equipment. The Banshee Pad is called Blue Banshee Pad and the area behind it is Back Blue.

Mid Cannon Landing

Other names: N/A

The center Man Cannon on Blue Base will take you to a bald patch or flat rock surface in front of BR Rock. This surface is known as Man Cannon Landing.

Blue Spawn

Other names: Blue Rocks, Blue Cliff Side Spawn

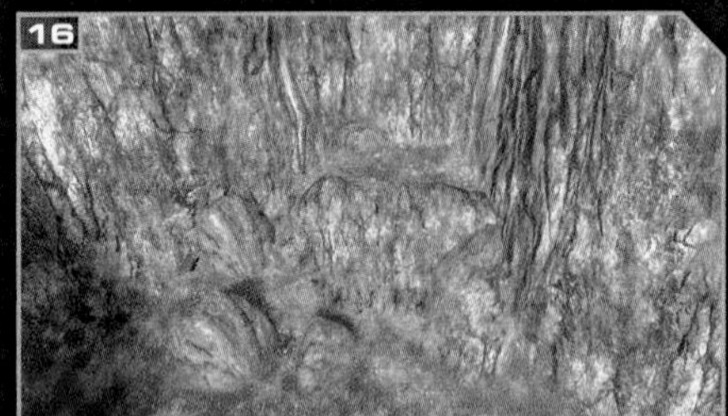

The rocks at the far left side of Blue Base (opposite the waterfall) are called Blue Rocks. Two Plasma Grenades are located there.

Water Rocks

Other names: Water Cave, River Cave, Territory 1

Following the creek away from the waterfall, you will approach a passage situated between a large rock and the cliff side. There is a smaller rock leaning against the larger rock, splitting the passage in two. This area is known as Water Rocks. Alongside the large rock is a Battle Rifle, two Frag Grenades, and a Spiker. The area next to these weapons is Territory 1 for Territory games. On the other side of the passage to the right is an SMG lying against a small rock. To the left of the passageway against the Forerunner Wall (large metal wall) is an opened Drop Pod with a Brute Shot, Battle Rifle, and two Frag Grenades. Looking directly in front of the passage is a large antenna and a Turret.

Radio Antenna

Other names: Turret Side, Antenna

The radio antenna has a Mongoose and one Bubble Shield. Just beyond the antenna, against the Forerunner Wall opposite the opened Drop Pod, is a Brute Shot.

Turret

Other names: Turret Rock

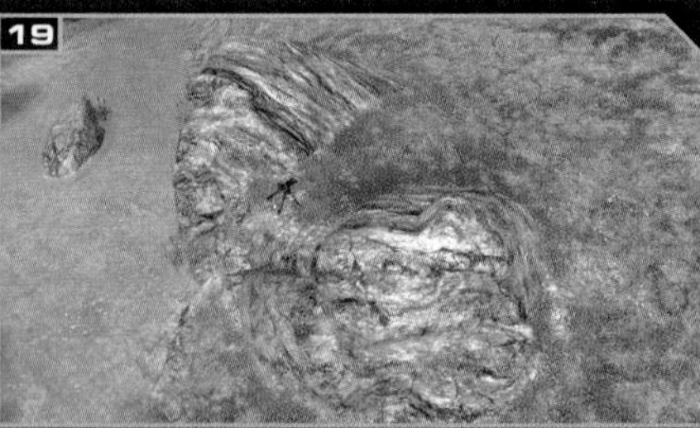

The area where the Turret is positioned is simply known as Turret. To the Turret's left are two Plasma Grenades. From the Turret and radio antenna, you will see the other side of Turret Cave.

Enhanced Knowledge

Team Slayer Tactics

- Work with your team to hold a base or position wherever you may spawn. For example, if your team spawns near the Pelican Cave, stay there and hold that area, using Pelican Cave as cover. If you spawn later, in Top Mid, stay in that area and hold it, firing at the enemy. Also, stay under cover. Do not run out in the middle of the map with no cover. You will be picked off immediately.
- Controlling Top Mid is extremely advantageous for Team Slayer and Objective games. You will be able to see almost every location on the map, every vehicle, and every person on the other team. While holding Top Mid, use the Spartan Laser or Sniper Rifle to support your team.
- Short-range weapons mostly come in handy for enclosed areas such as Blue and Red Base or Shotgun Cave and Pelican Cave.
- Have no more than two people in the Warthog at one time. Unless you are using the Warthog as transportation, do not use that third seat. You are unable to fire accurately in that seat, and if the Warthog is destroyed, you give the opposing team a triple kill! Use the Power Slide ability to execute quick turns without rolling.
- During Team Slayer games, you will frequently spawn in your base. If you notice your team has been spawning outside the base instead of inside, there is probably a member of the other team hiding out in your base.
- The Banshee is excellent for Team Slayer. It can be a devastating attack for the other team. If your team can control the Spartan Laser and the Banshee operator can evade the Missile Launcher, you will be on your way to winning the match.
- Remember, the other team has a Banshee, too, so try to destroy their Banshee with your Banshee immediately. If a Banshee is not available, destroy the enemy Banshee with the Spartan Laser, Missile Pod, Power Drain, Warthog Turret, or Machinegun Turret. You can even effectively use the Battle Rifle or Plasma Pistol. If you are a footman and notice your Banshee is sparring with the enemy Banshee, help your Banshee with these weapons as well.

One Flag, Multiflag, One Bomb, and Assault Tactics

Defense

- Place your players wisely on the map. Do not completely desert the base to capture the power weapons, but do not have everybody hide in the base waiting for the eventual attack from the bomb carrier or flag bandit either. Send a few to patrol the area. Get the Spartan Laser to take out approaching vehicles, and use the Sniper Rifle to take out footmen before they get into your base. The Turret can also help quickly destroy a group of footmen. Leave a few teammates inside the base to protect the exits. Preferably, use short-range power weapons inside the base, such as the Shotgun or dual-wield SMGs or Spikers.
- For Multiflag games, try to balance the number of players who are protecting your flag versus the number of players who are capturing the other team's flag.
- Watch out for Mongooses and Warthogs coming from the outer edges of the map. Use the Spartan Laser, Power Drain, and Plasma Pistols on them.
- If the opposing teams grabs your flag, consider taking a Mongoose or Man Cannon to cut them off before they make with the flag.
- Remember, you cannot see the enemy's bomb or your stolen flag when the other team has possession of them. The Banshee is excellent for instantly spotting and stopping your captured flag or the bomb carrier. Keep in mind that the other team has a Banshee, so try to help destroy that Banshee with the Spartan Laser or Missile Pod.
- An optional and amusing tactic for protecting your base from bombings or flag captures is to pile a bunch of vehicles on your flag or bomb region. This complicates capturing the flag or planting the bomb, because the other team will not be able to find it through the mess of vehicles!

Offense

- Never try to take the flag or plant the bomb by yourself. Coordinate an attack with your teammates. Have a team member or two attempt to capture Top Mid, where they can use the Spartan Laser effectively. Have someone from your base use the Sniper Rifle to take out any footmen trying to gain Top Mid. Once Top Mid is captured, the sniper may want to sit on this location while supporting your bomb carrier or helping your flag man while he escapes with the flag.
- Driving the Warthog or Mongoose with the flag or bomb in the passenger seat is the best strategy. The Warthog and Mongoose can get your team into the base, where you can capture the flag or plant the bomb and then get out within minutes. All three of the seats in the Warthog should be full (a driver, a Turret operator, and a footman to plant the bomb or capture the flag). Depending on your team's size, you may also want to take a fully loaded Mongoose with your Warthog so you can overwhelm the other team.
- Crouch-walking makes you invisible to enemy radar. While storming the base, crouch-walking can be an excellent method for sneaking in undetected with the bomb or grabbing the flag when the other team is not looking.
- If you have possession of the bomb or flag, do not hang on to it for dear life when someone is trying to kill you. You can get an instant kill with a bomb or flag melee, but sometimes it's best to drop your load and fight off the other team with your weapons on hand. You can pick up your load after.
- When playing Assault or One Bomb, do not abandon your planted bomb. Stay around and protect the ticking time bomb so the other team does not disarm it. If necessary, stay until the bomb detonates. Throw Grenades or Power Drains on the bomb when the other team attempts to disarm it.
- For CTF games, when you have just snatched the flag, determine what course you should take—for example, go on foot or take the Warthog. If your team has control of the Spartan Laser, consider taking the Warthog. If the other team controls Top Mid with the Laser, you may want to go on foot.
- If you are going on foot, try to "hop" from cover to cover (such as going to the Turret Cave, the Antenna, the Water Rocks, and then to Blue Base) instead of running down the middle of the map (such as running from Mid Creek to Top Mid to Man Cannon Landing to Blue Base).

■ Territories

There are two main tactics you can use for Territory game types:

First Tactic: Try sending a couple of small groups (in sizes of 2 or 3) to take two territories at the same time. This will hopefully confuse the other team and cause disarray. In addition, the other team will probably split up into small groups and defend each territory at once, giving you even chances of surviving an encounter. The Regenerator will be an effective tool for maintaining your shields while capturing territories.

Second Tactic: Instead of sending out two small teams, consider going as one large unit and taking each territory one at a time. If your teammates are better marksmen than the other team, then you may outshoot them. Also, your larger numbers may overwhelm the other team.

■ VIP

- Gaining control of Top Mid is not as important for VIP games. Usually the VIP is hidden inside bases, and it is useless to use long-range weapons such as the Spartan Laser or Sniper Rifle. However, just because your target is hidden does not mean you want to sacrifice map control as well.
- Disperse your players wisely on the map. Send out your team to attack the other VIP, but do not leave your team's VIP defenseless. Use short-range power weapons such as the Shotgun or dual wield weapons.

Attacking and Defending the VIP

- The popular method for VIP games is to let your VIP camp in a protected area such as Red Base or Blue Base. Since the VIP is usually hiding, use powerful short-range weapons to kill or protect the VIP. Use Plasma Grenades or Shotguns, or dual wield weapons.
- Give your VIP the best weapons with which to protect himself, such as the Shotgun.
- Opposing VIPs probably should not hunt each other down. Remember, the target for both teams is the other VIP. Placing the two VIPs together will cause both teams to converge in one large catastrophe.
- An opposite method for VIP games is to make the VIP a constant moving target. Have the VIP get on the back of a Mongoose and ride like crazy, never stopping. This may work, depending on which team has the Missile Pod, Spartan Laser, or Sniper Rifle.

■ Sniping

Red Base/Blue Base

Use the Banshee to reach the top of Red or Blue Base. Stand on top of the base or on a ledge near the top and snipe from there. The vantage point is great!

Turret Wall

Try sniping in the small nook at the back of the Turret Wall/Forerunner Wall.

Red Base Ledge

To reach a ledge midway up the base, use Grenade-jumping or team-jumping up the back of Red Base on the slanted, smooth side (while continuously jumping up the smooth side). However, vision is limited.

Territory 1

The Pelican and Territory 1 is an optional sniping position.

Sniper Rock

Sniper Rock is far enough away from enemy fire and allows a quick retreat into the rocks for cover from Grenades or long-range weapons.

APPENDICES

In this section, you'll find the breakdowns for scoring during Campaign and Firefight missions, all the medals you can obtain in Firefight missions and *Halo 3* multiplayer mode, how unlockable characters and Firefight missions are awarded, and advice and information on every ODST Achievement.

Scoring and Multipliers

Scoring is automatically awarded during Campaign, Firefight, and *Halo 3* multiplayer modes. The following tables show exactly what actions constitute points or multiplication of points. Points involving the defeat of Covenant enemies are not applicable to *Halo 3* multiplayer. You can also refer to the "Know Your Enemies" chapter for additional enemy information.

General Multipliers

Skull Multipliers

Icon	Name	Multiplier Value
	Black Eye	1.5
	Thunderstorm	1.5
	Iron	3.0
	Tough Luck	1.5

Skull Multipliers

Icon	Name	Multiplier Value
	Catch	1.5
	Famine	2.0
	Tilt	2.0
	Mythic	2.0

Difficulty Multipliers

Icon	Mode	Multiplier Value
	Easy	.25
	Normal	1.0
	Heroic	2.0
	Legendary	4.0

Time Multipliers (Campaign Only)

Each Campaign mission has a multiplier that decreases depending on how long you take to complete the mission. The longer you take, the lower the multiplier.

Multikill Multipliers

Icon	Name	Consecutive Kills	Multiplier Value
	Double Kill	2	2.0
	Triple Kill	3	3.0
	Overkill	4	4.0
	Killtacular	5	5.0
	Killtrocity	6	6.0

Multikill Multipliers

Icon	Name	Consecutive Kills	Multiplier Value
	Killamanjaro	7	7.0
	Killtastrophe	8	8.0
	Killapocalypse	9	9.0
	Killionaire	10	10.0

Set Multipliers (Firefight Only)

Set#	Multiplier Value
1	1.0
2	1.5
3	2.0

Set Multipliers (Firefight Only)

Set#	Multiplier Value
4	2.5
5	3.0
6	3.5

Set Multipliers (Firefight Only)

Set#	Multiplier Value
7	4.0
8	4.5
9	5.0

Style Multipliers			
Icon	Name	How to Achieve	Multiplier Value
	Headshot	Kill enemy with headshot with Carbine/Sniper Rifle/Magnum	1.5
	Needler Super Detonation	Kill enemy with Needler such they die from the explosion.	1.5
	EMP	Kill an enemy who lost his shields to a Plasma Pistol overcharge within a short time period	1.5
	Beatdown	Kill enemy with melee attack	1.5
	Assassination	Kill enemy with melee from behind	1.5
	Stick	Stick enemy with Plasma/ Spike Grenade	1.5

Style Multipliers			
Icon	Name	How to Achieve	Multiplier Value
	Incineration	Kill enemy with Flame Grenade/Flamethrower	1.5
	Laser	Kill enemy with Spartan Laser	1.5
	Splatter	Kill any enemy by running them over with vehicle	1.5
	Death from the Grave	Kill any enemy a short time after you are killed	1.5
	Vehicle Jack	Steal an enemy vehicle	1.5
	Sky Jack	Steal an enemy aerial vehicle	1.5

Multiple Kills (Spree) Point Awards

Regular Sprees			
Icon	Name	Kill Streak	Scripted Points Value
	Killing Spree	10	50
	Killing Frenzy	20	150
	Running Riot	30	250

Regular Sprees			
Icon	Name	Kill Streak	Scripted Points Value
	Rampage	40	500
	Untouchable	50	750
	Invincible	100	1,000

Custom Sprees				
Icon	Name	Weapon Used	Kill Streak	Scripted Pts. Value
	Shotgun Spree	Shotgun	5	500
	Open Season	Shotgun	10	1,000
	Stick Spree	Sticky/Spike Grenades	5	500
	Sticky Fingers	Sticky/Spike Grenades	10	1,000
	Splatter Spree	Any vehicle collision kill	5	500

Custom Sprees				
Icon	Name	Weapon Used	Kill Streak	Scripted Pts. Value
	Vehicular Manslaughter	Any vehicle collision kill	10	1,000
	Hammer Spree	Hammer/Hammer Melee	5	500
	Dream Crusher	Hammer/Hammer Melee	10	1,000
	Sniper Spree	Sniper	5	500
	Sharpshooter	Sniper	10	1,000

Point Values

Player Events	
Event Name	Point Value
Betrayal	-75
Suicide	-25
Dying	-25
Revert to last save	-25

Enemies		
Name	Classification	Point Value
Brute	Infantry	20
Brute Bodyguard	Specialist	30
Brute Captain	Leader	50
Brute Chieftain Armor	Hero	150

Enemies		
Name	Classification	Point Value
Brute Chieftain Weapon	Hero	150
Brute Jump Pack	Specialist	30
Brute Jump Pack Major	Specialist	30
Brute Jump Pack Ultra	Specialist	30
Brute Stalker	Specialist	30
Bugger	Infantry	10
Grunt	Infantry	10
Grunt Heavy	Specialist	10
Grunt Spec Ops	Specialist	10
Hunter	Specialist	150
Jackal	Infantry	15
Jackal Sniper	Specialist	20

Allies		
Name	**Classification**	**Point Value**
ODST	Infantry	100
Marine Pilot	Infantry	50
Marine Sgt	Infantry	100
Marine Sgt Hero	Infantry	100
Marine Wounded	Infantry	50
Naval Officer	Infantry	50
Worker	Infantry	50
Worker Wounded	Infantry	50

Vehicles		
Name	**Classification**	**Point Value**
Scarab	Heavy Vehicle	500
Phantom	Heavy Vehicle	0
Banshee	Standard Vehicle	100
Chopper	Light Vehicle	100
Ghost	Light Vehicle	100
Shade Turret	Light Vehicle	50
Wraith	Heavy Vehicle	200
Scorpion	Heavy Vehicle	200

Other		
Name	**Classification**	**Point Value**
Engineer	Infantry	50

Medals

Medals are awarded in both Firefight and *Halo 3* multiplayer modes after you complete certain tasks. The following data reveals all the medals in Firefight and in *Halo 3* multiplayer, and how to obtain each one. Medals are simply worth more points than normal actions and are shown in the Postgame Carnage Report.

NOTE

Medals are listed in rank order. "Rank" simply indicates how difficult it is to obtain a specific medal consistently; for example, a Rank 5 medal is generally more difficult to obtain than a Rank 1, 2, 3, or 4 medal.

ODST Firefight Medals

Rank F1: Role Sprees		
Icon	**Medal Name**	**Description**
	Sniper Spree	Kill 5 opponents in a row with a sniper weapon without dying.
	Sharpshooter	Kill 10 opponents in a row with a sniper weapon without dying.
	Shotgun Spree	Kill 5 opponents in a row with the Shotgun without dying.
	Open Season	Kill 10 opponents in a row with the Shotgun without dying.
	Splatter Spree	Splatter 5 opponents in a row using a vehicle without dying.
	Vehicular Manslaughter	Splatter 10 opponents in a row using a vehicle without dying.

Rank F2: Standard Sprees		
Icon	**Medal Name**	**Description**
	Killing Spree	Kill 10 opponents in a row without dying.
	Killing Frenzy	Kill 20 opponents in a row without dying.
	Running Riot	Kill 30 opponents in a row without dying.
	Rampage	Kill 40 opponents in a row without dying.
	Untouchable	Kill 50 opponents in a row without dying.
	Invincible	Kill 100 opponents in a row without dying.

Rank F3: Multikills		
Icon	**Medal Name**	**Description**
	Double Kill	Get 2 kills in the blink of an eye.
	Triple Kill	Get a third kill moments after your second.
	Overkill	Get a fourth kill moments after your third.
	Killtacular	Get a fifth kill moments after your fourth.
	Killtrocity	Get a sixth kill moments after your fifth.
	Killamanjaro	Get a seventh kill moments after your sixth.
	Killtastrophe	Get an eighth kill moments after your seventh.
	Killapocalypse	Get a ninth kill moments after your eighth.
	Killionaire	Get a tenth kill moments after your ninth.

Rank F4: Heroics of Circumstance		
Icon	**Medal Name**	**Description**
	Vehicle Jack	Board a vehicle by removing and then quickly killing its driver.
	Assist	Wounded an enemy, but a teammate killed it.
	Hero	As the last player alive, single-handedly bring your team into the next wave.

Rank F5: Kill Finesse		
Icon	Medal Name	Description
	Sniper Kill	Get a headshot with the Sniper Rifle or the Beam Rifle.
	Splatter	Hit and kill an opponent with your vehicle.
	Beatdown	Hit and kill an opponent with a melee attack.
	Assassin	Hit and kill an opponent with a melee attack from behind.
	Grenade Stick	Kill an opponent by sticking it with a Plasma or Spike Grenade.

Rank F5: Kill Finesse		
Icon	Medal Name	Description
	Laser Kill	Kill an opponent by using the Spartan Laser.
	Incineration	Kill an opponent with a flame-based weapon.
	Headshot	Kill an opponent with a headshot.
	EMP Kill	Kill a shielded opponent shortly after using an overcharged Plasma Pistol blast to neutralize their shields.

■ *Halo 3* Multiplayer Medals

Rank MP0: Special		
Icon	Medal Name	Description
	Extermination	Wipe out an enemy team with at least an Overkill.
	Perfection	Win a Slayer game without dying and with at least 15 kills.

Rank MP1: Role Sprees		
Icon	Medal Name	Description
	Sniper Spree	Kill 5 opponents in a row with a sniper weapon without dying.
	Sharpshooter	Kill 10 opponents in a row with a sniper weapon without dying.
	Shotgun Spree	Kill 5 opponents in a row with the Shotgun without dying.
	Open Season	Kill 10 opponents in a row with the Shotgun without dying.
	Splatter Spree	Splatter 5 opponents in a row using a vehicle without dying.
	Vehicular Manslaughter	Splatter 10 opponents in a row using a vehicle without dying.
	Sword Spree	Kill 5 opponents in a row with the Energy Sword without dying.
	Slice 'n Dice	Kill 10 opponents in a row with the Energy Sword without dying.
	Hail to the King	Kill 5 opponents in a row from inside the hill before it moves.
	Juggernaut Spree	Kill 5 opponents in a row as the Juggernaut without dying.
	Unstoppable	Kill 10 opponents in a row as the Juggernaut without dying.
	Infection Spree	Kill 5 humans in a row as the Zombie without dying.
	Mmmm Brains	Kill 10 humans in a row as the Zombie without dying.
	Zombie Killing Spree	Kill 5 Zombies in a row as the human without dying.
	Hell's Janitor	Kill 10 Zombies in a row as the Human without dying.

Rank MP2: Standard Sprees		
Icon	Medal Name	Description
	Killing Spree	Kill 5 opponents in a row without dying.
	Killing Frenzy	Kill 10 opponents in a row without dying.
	Running Riot	Kill 15 opponents in a row without dying.
	Rampage	Kill 20 opponents in a row without dying.
	Untouchable	Kill 25 opponents in a row without dying.
	Invincible	Kill 30 opponents in a row without dying.

Rank MP3: Multikills		
Icon	Medal Name	Description
	Double Kill	Kill 2 opponents within 4 seconds of each other.
	Triple Kill	Kill 3 opponents within 4 seconds of each other.
	Overkill	Kill 4 opponents within 4 seconds of each other.
	Killtacular	Kill 5 opponents within 4 seconds of each other.
	Killtrocity	Kill 6 opponents within 4 seconds of each other.
	Killamanjaro	Kill 7 opponents within 4 seconds of each other.
	Killtastrophe	Kill 8 opponents within 4 seconds of each other.
	Killapocalypse	Kill 9 opponents within 4 seconds of each other.
	Killionaire	Kill 10 opponents within 4 seconds of each other.

Rank MP4: Objective Heroics		
Icon	Medal Name	Description
	Bomb Planted	Plant the bomb in an Assault game.
	Killed Bomb Carrier	Kill an opponent bomb carrier in an Assault game.
	Flag Score	Complete a scoring flag capture in a Capture the Flag game.
	Killed Flag Carrier	Kill an opponent flag carrier in a Capture the Flag game.
	Flag Kill	Kill an opponent with a melee attack using the flag.
	Killed VIP	Kill an opponent's VIP in a VIP game.
	Killed Juggernaut	Kill the Juggernaut in a Juggernaut game.
	Oddball Kill	Get a melee kill while swinging the oddball.
	Last Man Standing	Be the last human in an Infection game.

Rank MP5: Heroics of Circumstance		
Icon	Medal Name	Description
	Skyjacker	Board an aircraft by forcibly removing the opponent in it.
	Carjacker	Board a land-based vehicle by forcibly removing the opponent in it.

Rank MP5: Heroics of Circumstance		
Icon	Medal Name	Description
	Killjoy	End an opponent's killing spree.
	Death from the Grave	Kill an opponent after you have died.
	Bulltrue	Without using a sword, kill an opponent that is in the act of a sword lunge.

Rank MP6: Kill Finesse		
Icon	Medal Name	Description
	Sniper Kill	Get a headshot with the Sniper Rifle or the Beam Rifle.
	Splatter	Hit and kill an opponent with your vehicle.
	Melee Kill	Hit and kill an opponent with a melee attack.
	Assassin	Hit and kill an opponent with a melee attack from behind.
	Grenade Stick	Kill an opponent by sticking him with a Plasma or Spike Grenade.
	Laser Kill	Kill an opponent by using the Spartan Laser.
	Incineration	Kill an opponent with a flame-based weapon.

Unlockables

This shows the unlockable Firefight characters and maps that are not initially available, and how to obtain them.

Firefight Character: UNSC Sergeant Avery Johnson

How to Obtain: Preorder Halo—ODST to receive token to unlock this character.

Firefight Character: Buck

How to Obtain: Complete "Mission 02: Tayari Plaza" on Normal difficulty or harder.

Firefight Character: Dutch

How to Obtain: Complete "Mission 03: Uplift Reserve" on Normal difficulty or harder.

Firefight Character: Mickey

How to Obtain: Complete "Mission 04: Kizingo Boulevard" on Normal difficulty or harder.

Firefight Character: Romeo

How to Obtain: Complete "Mission 06: NMPQ Headquarters" on Normal difficulty or harder.

Firefight Character: Dare

How to Obtain: Complete Campaign on Legendary difficulty.

Firefight Mission: Alpha Site

How to Obtain: Complete "Mission 05: ONI Alpha Site" on Normal difficulty or harder.

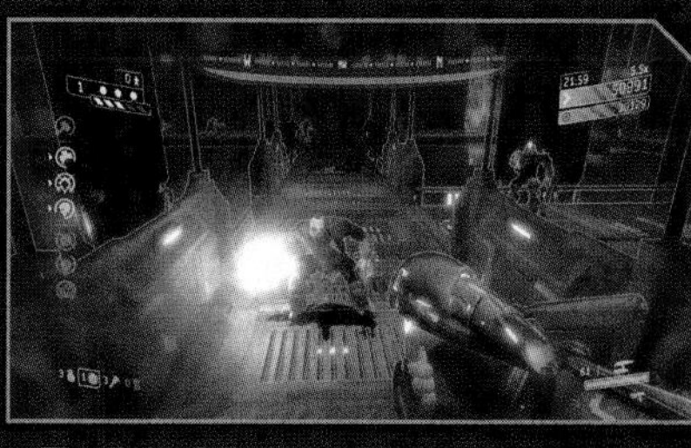

Firefight Mission: Chasm Ten

How to Obtain: Complete "Mission 08: Data Hive Site" on Normal difficulty or harder.

Firefight Mission: Last Exit

How to Obtain: Complete "Mission 09: Coastal Highway" on Normal difficulty or harder.

Achievements

There's a wide variety of Achievements available, ranging from the easily obtainable to the downright improbable. Use the following information to help you achieve some of these antics. Every Achievement is divided into categories based on how you unlock them. Within each category, the following information is provided: the Achievement's name, the points it is worth, the difficulty of obtaining the Achievement (out of ten), the Achievement's description, and notes on how to obtain it.

Campaign Achievements (24 Achievements/675 Pts.)

The following are directly related to missions in the ODST Campaign. Tactics for completing them are shown, where applicable.

Name: Campaign Complete—Normal

Points: 100

Difficulty: 5/10

Description: Completed the Campaign on Normal difficulty.

Notes: Play through the entire campaign on Normal. See the walkthrough for details on each mission.

Name: Campaign Complete—Heroic

Points: 100

Difficulty: 7/10

Description: Complete the Campaign on Heroic difficulty.

Notes: Complete this Achievement, and you automatically receive the Campaign Complete: Normal Achievement as well. Play through the entire campaign on Heroic. See the walkthrough for details on each mission.

Name: Campaign Complete—Legendary

Points: 100

Difficulty: 9/10

Description: Complete the Campaign on Legendary difficulty.

Notes: This unlocks the character Dare in Firefight missions. Complete this Achievement and you automatically receive the Campaign Complete: Normal and Campaign Complete: Heroic Achievements as well. Play through the entire campaign on Legendary. See the walkthrough for details on each mission.

Name: Tayari Plaza

Points: 30

Difficulty: 5/10

Description: Complete Tayari Plaza on Normal, Heroic, or Legendary to unlock a new Firefight character.

Notes: This unlocks the character Buck in Firefight missions. You'll get this Achievement during the Campaign. You will not receive this Achievement on Easy.

Name: Uplift Reserve

Points: 30

Difficulty: 5/10

Description: Complete "Mission 03: Uplift Reserve" on Normal, Heroic, or Legendary to unlock a new Firefight character.

Notes: This unlocks the character Dutch in Firefight missions. You'll get this Achievement during the Campaign. You will not receive this Achievement on Easy.

Name: Kizingo Boulevard

Points: 30

Difficulty: 5/10

Description: Complete Kizingo Boulevard on Normal, Heroic, or Legendary to unlock a new Firefight character.

Notes: This unlocks the character Mickey in Firefight missions. You'll get this Achievement during the Campaign. You will not receive this Achievement on Easy.

Name: ONI Alpha Site

Points: 30

Difficulty: 5/10

Description: Complete ONI Alpha Site on Normal, Heroic, or Legendary to unlock a new Firefight mission.

Notes: This unlocks the Firefight Mission "Alpha Site." You'll get this Achievement during the Campaign. You will not receive this Achievement on Easy.

Name: NMPD HQ

Points: 30

Difficulty: 5/10

Description: Complete NMPD HQ on Normal, Heroic, or Legendary to unlock a new Firefight character.

Notes: This unlocks the character Romeo in Firefight missions. You'll get this Achievement during the Campaign. You will not receive this Achievement on Easy.

Name: Kikowani Station

Points: 30

Difficulty: 5/10

Description: Complete "Mission 09: Coastal Highway" on Normal, Heroic, or Legendary.

Notes: You'll get this Achievement during the Campaign. You will not receive this Achievement on Easy. There are no characters or Firefight missions to unlock when this is completed.

Name: Data Hive

Points: 50

Difficulty: 5/10

Description: Complete "Mission 08: Data Hive" on Normal, Heroic, or Legendary to unlock a new Firefight mission.

Notes: This unlocks the Firefight mission "Chasm Ten." You'll get this Achievement during the Campaign. You will not receive this Achievement on Easy.

Name: Coastal Highway

Points: 50

Difficulty: 5/10

Description: Complete "Mission 09: Coastal Highway" on Normal, Heroic, or Legendary to unlock a new Firefight mission.

Notes: This unlocks the Firefight mission "Last Exit." You'll get this Achievement during the Campaign. You will not receive this Achievement on Easy.

ame: Wraith Killer

oints: 5

fficulty: 4/10

escription: Kill all Wraiths in Uplift Reserve.

otes: During "Mission 03: Uplift Reserve," you must destroy (at least partially) all six Wraiths instead of running past each one. If Marines are firing on the Wraiths, you must at least damage the Wraith for the Marine's kill to be counted toward this Achievement. The same is true if playing on Cooperative mode; each player interested in this Achievement needs to hit the Wraith.

ame: Laser Blaster

oints: 5

fficulty: 4/10

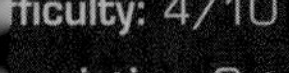

escription: Get 10 Spartan Laser kills on ONI Alpha Site.

otes: In Campaign "Mission 05: ONI Alpha Site," you begin with five shots with your starting Spartan Laser. An easy way to complete this is to aim at several enemies lined up behind each other on the bridge at the start of the mission. Each Wraith you hit (which takes only one direct shot) counts as three kills. If you run out of ammunition, a second Spartan Laser is available on a bench at the raised top end of the stepped courtyard.

ame: Both Tubes

oints: 5

fficulty: 4/10

escription: Get 10 Rocket kills on Kizingo Boulevard.

otes: In Campaign "Mission 04: Kizingo Boulevard," you have a limited number of Rockets, so use them against large clusters of enemies. Better yet, give your Rocket Launcher to a UNSC Marine, and make sure he's sitting on your Scorpion. Any kills he makes (with a Rocket Launcher that has infinite ammunition as long as the Marine holds it) are added to your total.

ame: Dome Inspector

oints: 5

fficulty: 4/10

escription: Get 15 headshot kills on NMPD HQ.

Notes: During Campaign "Mission 06: NMPD HQ," tagging any foe in the head with a Sniper Rifle, Beam Rifle, Magnum, or Carbine counts toward this Achievement. Take your time when picking targets with the Sniper Rifle. With the Magnum or Carbine, Grunts are the obvious and easy targets. Remember to work on the Boom, Headshot! Achievement at the same time.

Name: I Like Fire

Points: 5

Difficulty: 4/10

Description: Kill 10 enemies with the Flamethrower on Data Hive.

Notes: During "Mission 08: Data Hive," look for the Flamethrower in the corner at the far end of a corridor encased in ice, just after the Brute Chieftain with the Plasma Turret but before you find Dare. This is the only mission in which you find the Flamethrower. Immediately use it on the next ten enemies, frying them in short, controlled bursts to conserve your ammunition, as there's no other Flamethrowers or ammunition available.

Name: Tourist

Points: 5

Difficulty: 1/10

Description: Access and download the city map to your VISR.

Notes: The first time you open your PDA in Campaign or Firefight, you receive this Achievement. You have the opportunity to do this during "Mission 01: Prepare to Drop."

Name: Headcase

Points: 5

Difficulty: 1/10

Description: Finish any level with at least one Skull activated.

Notes: Unlike *Halo 3*, you immediately have access to all the Skulls from the Main menu. Simply activate one before beginning the Campaign to unlock this Achievement very quickly. The Skull you switch on doesn't need to be Gold; you can turn on a "fun" skull (such as the always-entertaining Grunt Birthday Party) instead of a Difficult skull.

Name: Junior Detective

Points: 10

Difficulty: 2/10

Description: Find the first clue unraveling the mystery.

Notes: These are awarded automatically as the Campaign story line progresses, even on Easy difficulty.

Name: Gumshoe

Points: 10

Difficulty: 3/10

Description: Find the third clue unraveling the mystery, alone or with another ODST.

Notes: These are awarded automatically as the Campaign story line progresses, even on Easy difficulty.

Name: Super Sleuth

Points: 10

Difficulty: 4/10

Description: Find the final clue unraveling the mystery, alone or with another ODST.

Notes: These are awarded automatically as the Campaign story line progresses, even on Easy difficulty.

Name: Trading Down

Points: 5

Difficulty: 1/10

Description: Trade weapons with a fellow character.

Notes: During any Campaign mission, go up to a UNSC Marine or ODST squadmate and swap weapons with them. The first time you can try this is during "Mission 02: Tayari Plaza."

Name: Good Samaritan

Points: 20

Difficulty: 6/10

Description: Killing things that are new and different is bad, alone or with another ODST.

Notes: During Rookie's missions, do not kill any Engineers in the city at night, throughout the entire campaign. However, Engineers found on Kikowani Station do not count against this Achievement. Aside from simply ignoring Engineers, there are times when their protection makes combat with Brutes much more difficult, so use the Plasma Pistol overcharge on

the Brute controlling the Engineer; it won't affect this Achievement. In Cooperative games, you can shoot an Engineer, as long as a teammate finishes them. If they don't or if you kill an Engineer, you need to play through the entire Campaign again, so work on the Naughty Naughty Achievement instead.

Name: Naughty Naughty

Points: 5

Difficulty: 4/10

Description: Killing things that are new and different is good, alone or with another ODST.

Notes: During Rookie's missions, kill ten Engineers in the city throughout the entire Campaign. Engineers found on Kikowani Station do not count toward this Achievement. There are more than ten Engineers in the city, but they appear randomly, so this Achievement takes a while: Simply wander around the city until one appears. Note that any progress toward this Achievement prevents you from obtaining the Good Samaritan Achievement on this play-through. However, this doesn't cross over in Cooperative games, so one player can obtain Naughty Naughty while the other attempts Good Samaritan.

■ COMM Terminal Audio Log Achievements (4 Achievements/125 Pts.)

The following can be completed only during Rookie's Campaign missions. Tactics for completing them are shown, where applicable.

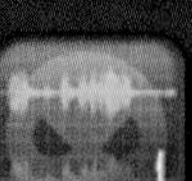

Name: Listener

Points: 5

Difficulty: 2/10

Description: Find the first Audio Log.

Notes: Access the first of the 29 terminals found throughout Mombasa Streets.

Name: Tuned In

Points: 15

Difficulty: 2/10

Description: Find 3 Audio Logs, alone or with another ODST.

Notes: Access any three of the 29 terminals found throughout Mombasa Streets.

Name: All Ears

Points: 30

Difficulty: 4/10

Description: Find 15 Audio Logs, alone or with another ODST.

Notes: Access any 15 of the 29 terminals found throughout Mombasa Streets.

Name: Audiophile

Points: 75

Difficulty: 6/10

Description: Find all Audio Logs, alone or with another ODST.

Notes: Access all 29 terminals found throughout Mombasa Streets (this can be done before or after you finish the Campaign the first time), plus the one extra terminal you can find in "Mission 08: Data Hive" after accessing all the others.

■ Firefight Achievements (9 Achievements/90 Pts.)

The following are directly related to missions in the ODST Firefight mode. Tactics for completing them are shown, where applicable.

Name: Be Like Marty

Points: 10

Difficulty: 4/10

Description: In Firefight, finish a full round without killing a single enemy.

Notes: This Achievement is impossible unless you are playing a Cooperative game. Simply sit back, away from combat and let your teammates handle all aggressive responsibilities. No friends? Then start a split-screen Firefight game; keep one player inside the spawning room, and use only one controller to get the job done.

Name: Firefight—Crater

Points: 10

Difficulty: 6/10

Description: Score over 200,000 points in Firefight mission "Crater."

Notes: Simply continue to play Firefight on this mission map until you have accumulated 200,000 points. Use combo-kill bonuses (the points and multipliers are listed earlier in this chapter) for rapid point gains. This is a team score; it is much easier in a Cooperative, four-player game.

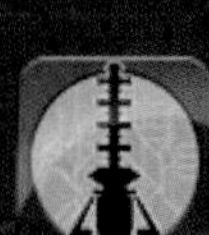

Name: Firefight—Lost Platoon

Points: 10

Difficulty: 6/10

Description: Score over 200,000 points in Firefight mission "Lost Platoon."

Notes: Simply continue to play Firefight on this mission map until you have accumulated 200,000 points. Use combo-kill bonuses (the points and multipliers are listed earlier in this chapter) for rapid point gains. This is a team score; it is much easier in a Cooperative, four-player game.

Name: Firefight—Rally Point

Points: 10

Difficulty: 6/10

Description: Score over 200,000 points in Firefight mission "Rally Point."

Notes: Simply continue to play Firefight on this mission map until you have accumulated 200,000 points. Use combo-kill bonuses (the points and multipliers are listed earlier in this chapter) for rapid point gains. This is a team score; it is much easier in a Cooperative, four-player game.

Name: Firefight—Alpha Site

Points: 10

Difficulty: 6/10

Description: Score over 200,000 points in Firefight mission "Alpha Site."

Notes: Simply continue to play Firefight on this mission map until you have accumulated 200,000 points. Use combo-kill bonuses (the points and multipliers are listed earlier in this chapter) for rapid point gains. This is a team score; it is much easier in a Cooperative, four-player game.

Name: Firefight—Chasm Ten

Points: 10

Difficulty: 6/10

Description: Score over 200,000 points in Firefight mission "Chasm Ten."

Notes: Simply continue to play Firefight on this mission map until you have accumulated 200,000 points. Use combo-kill bonuses (the points and multipliers are listed earlier in this chapter) for rapid point gains. This is a team score; it is much easier in a Cooperative, four-player game.

Name: Firefight—Security Zone

Points: 10

Difficulty: 6/10

Description: Score over 200,000 points in Firefight mission "Security Zone."

Notes: Simply continue to play Firefight on this mission map until you have accumulated 200,000 points. Use combo-kill bonuses (the points and multipliers are listed earlier in this chapter) for rapid point gains. This is a team score; it is much easier in a Cooperative, four-player game.

Name: Firefight—Windward

Points: 10

Difficulty: 6/10

Description: Score over 200,000 points in Firefight mission "Windward."

Notes: Simply continue to play Firefight on this mission map until you have accumulated 200,000 points. Use combo-kill bonuses (the points and multipliers are listed earlier in this chapter) for rapid point gains. This is a team score; it is much easier in a Cooperative, four-player game.

Name: Firefight—Last Exit

Points: 10

Difficulty: 6/10

Description: Score over 200,000 points in Firefight mission "Last Exit."

Notes: Simply continue to play Firefight on this mission map until you have accumulated 200,000 points. Use combo-kill bonuses (the points and multipliers are listed earlier in this chapter) for rapid point gains. This is a team score; it is much easier in a Cooperative, four-player game.

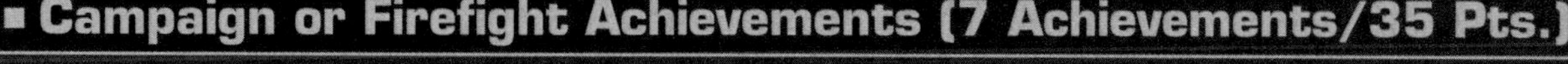

■ Campaign or Firefight Achievements (7 Achievements/35 Pts.)

The following can be completed in either ODST Firefight or Campaign modes. Tactics for completing them are shown, where applicable.

Name: Boom, Headshot

Points: 5

Difficulty: 3/10

Description: Get 10 Magnum headshot kills in any level.

Notes: Despite the description, you can gain this Achievement using the Sniper Rifle, Beam Rifle, or Carbine. Bullets to the head are mandatory, so target Grunts, as they are slow-moving and don't have shields. If Campaign mode is presenting a challenge to you, switch to Firefight instead, where you'll have more time and an infinite number of foes to target.

Name: Stunning!

Points: 5

Difficulty: 3/10

Description: Stun a vehicle with an overcharged Plasma Pistol and quickly kill the driver.

Notes: Find a Plasma Pistol near the corpse of a fallen Covenant, and in either Campaign or Firefight, approach a vehicle and shoot it with an overcharged Plasma Pistol shot. There's no need to fiddle with small arms afterward; simply lob a Grenade (or a highly damaging weapon shot) at it immediately afterward. Try this out in "Mission 02: Uplift Reserve"; kill the Grunts at the start of the mission, picking up a Plasma Pistol, then shoot the nearby Wraith before quickly destroying it with your Spartan Laser.

Name: Dark Times

Points: 5

Difficulty: 2/10

Description: Kill 5 enemies while using VISR mode.

Notes: Press ⊗ to activate your VISR in a dark area (or a light one, although the glare causes problems with your vision) and kill any five enemies in either Campaign or Firefight. This is almost always obtained during "Mission 01: Prepare to Drop."

Name: Ewww, Sticky

Points: 5

Difficulty: 3/10

Description: Get five Sticky Grenade kills in any level.

Notes: Use either Plasma or Spike Grenades to do the job; if you're having problems with enemies dodging your Grenades, locate a Plasma Pistol: Shoot Brutes with an overcharged Plasma shot to bring down their shields, and stun them for a few moments. This gives you the perfect opportunity to lob a Sticky Grenade. Not enough Grenades? Then switch from Campaign to Firefight, where there's an almost infinite number of Grenades to scavenge.

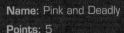

Name: My Clothes!

Points: 5

Difficulty: 4/10

Description: Plasma Pistol overcharge and quickly kill 10 Brutes.

Notes: By now, you should be consistently using the combination of the Plasma Pistol and Magnum; hit a Brute with an overcharged Plasma shot before switching to the Magnum to tag it with a headshot while it is stunned. This is the way to complete this Achievement, although you can have a friend assist you; let them strike the Brute with the overcharged Plasma shot, then take the headshot yourself (this still counts!). Also make sure you complete the Boom, Headshot! Achievement while working on this one.

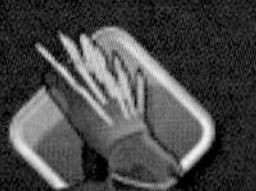

Name: Pink and Deadly

Points: 5

Difficulty: 3/10

Description: Get 10 Needler supercombine kills on any Covenant.

Notes: This attack simply means you arm yourself with a Needler and rapidly unload it on a single enemy until the needles explode. Preferred targets are Brutes, as they are tougher than Grunts or Jackals, who can die before you can supercombine them. If you're having problems locating ammunition in Campaign, switch to Firefight, as there are far more enemies that drop Needlers.

Name: Heal Up

Points: 5

Difficulty: 1/10

Description: Find the first Optican Kiosk and heal yourself.

Notes: Simply pick up any Health Pack in Campaign or Firefight. There's one at the very start of "Mission 01: Prepare to Drop." If you start Firefight, you'll need to take some damage first, but the Health Packs are usually in the spawning area.

Vidmaster Achievements (3 Achievements/75 Pts.)

The following are extremely difficult Achievements for the professional Orbital Drop Shock Trooper. Tactics for completing them are shown.

Name: Vidmaster Challenge—Classic

Points: 25

Difficulty: 6/10

Description: Finish any level solo on Legendary, on LIVE, with no shots fired or Grenades thrown.

Notes: You can attempt this on any Campaign mission, but "Mission 03: Uplift Reserve" is the easiest by far. Simply obtain a Warthog at the start of the mission, and allow the UNSC Marines to board your vehicle and do the fighting for you. Retreat whenever your Stamina is compromised; this allows you to rest until it is restored. Note that "shots fired" also includes e-braking (whether into foes or not) and honking your horn, so refrain from these actions, too.

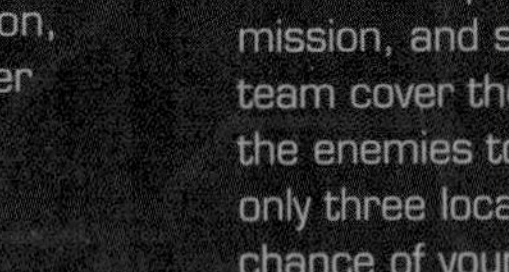

Name: Vidmaster Challenge—Endure

Points: 25

Difficulty: 9/10

Description: In any Firefight mission, pass the fourth set on four-player Heroic LIVE co-op.

Notes: Even Heroic difficulty is a real challenge, and surviving to the fifth set can be a problem. It is wise to choose either "Mission 02: Lost Platoon" or "Mission 06: Windward," which are the two Firefight maps you can most easily accomplish this Achievement on.

For "Lost Platoon," the wide-open spaces can be initially difficult to master, which leaves players exposed to fire from multiple directions. Two players should stay in or on the central building, using the Spartan Laser to eliminate Wraiths quickly and using Sniper Rifles to tag all other foes. The other two teammates should man vehicles (ideally Brute Choppers), and use this machine's superior firepower and ramming ability to cut down or splatter any remaining foes.

For "Windward," you should stay inside the spawning lobby building as often as possible throughout the mission, and simply have all your team cover the doors. This forces the enemies to enter from one of only three locations and lessens the chance of your team being outflanked or hit from a direction they aren't aware enemies are in. Conserve your ammunition by picking up Plasma Pistols and comboing them with Magnums. Conserving lives is far more important than gaining points, so abandon reckless tactics and pull back, getting assistance from teammates if the action heats up.

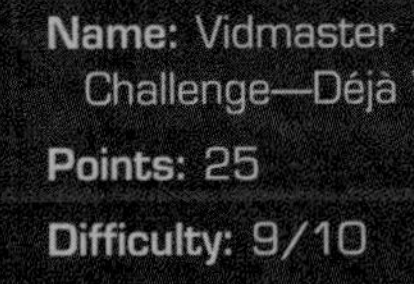

Name: Vidmaster Challenge—Déjà Vu

Points: 25

Difficulty: 9/10

Description: Complete "Mission 09: Coastal Highway" on four-player Legendary LIVE co-op, with Iron Skull active, and no Warthog or Scorpion.

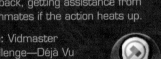

ODST Achievement Totals

Campaign Achievements: 24 Achievements/675 points

COMM Terminal Audio Log Achievements: 4 Achievements/125 points

Firefight Achievements: 9 Achievements/90 points

Campaign or Firefight Achievements: 7 Achievements/35 points

Vidmaster Achievements: 3 Achievements/75 points

Grand Total: 47 Achievements/1,000 points

BUNGIE CREDITS

Keep it Clean

Halo3: ODST

Story and Design by Bungie, LLC.

ODST : DESIGN

Design Director: Paul Bertone Jr.

Creative Director, Writer: Joseph Staten

Designers: Lars Bakken, Dan Miller, Alex Pfeiffer

Cinematics Director: CJ Cowan

ODST : ENGINEERING

Engineering Leads: Charlie Gough, Andrew Solomon, Ben Wallace

Engineering: David Aldridge, Max Dyckhoff, Brad Fish, Bob Glessner, Yaohua Hu, Damián Isla, Petar Kotevski, Eamon McKenzie, Mat Noguchi, Chris Tchou, Luke Timmins, Luis Villegas, Xi Wang

Additional Engineering: Tam Armstrong, Mike Baldwin, Chris Butcher, Jon Cable, Hao Chen, Christian Diefenbach, Paul Lewellen, Adrian Perez, Brian Sharp, Brendan Walker

Tools Engineering: Aaron Lieberman, Tristan Root, Sean Shypula

Online Engineering: Tom Gioconda, Chris Gossett, Michael R. Williams, Roger Wolfson

ODST : ART

Environment Art Leads: Justin Hayward, Michael Wu

Additional Art Direction: Christopher Barrett

Art Department Manager: Dave Dunn

Environment Artists: Matt Bennier, Mike Buelterman, Vic DeLeon, Samuel Jones, Blake Low, Michael Means, Mike Milota, Cameron Pinard, Paul Russel, Jason Sussman, Kentarou Taya, Jason Keith (Aquent)

3D Art Leads: Scott Shepherd, Shi Kai Wang

Effects Art Lead: Steve Scott

Effects Artist: Chad Foxglove

3D Artists: Chris Alderson, Travis Brady, Milton Cadogan, Tom Doyle, Eric Elton, Raj Nattam, Paul Brandl (Two Degrees), Loren Broach (Aquent), Ray Broscovak (Filter), Roger Campbell (Filter), Kevin Dalziel (Filter), Matt Lichy (Aquent)

Visual Design Lead: James McQuillan

Visual Design Artists: Aaron Lemay, Lorraine McLees, Erik Bertellotti (Perhapsatron), Kris Hamper (Filter), Brian Hargrave (Infusion)

Content Coordinator: Carlos Naranjo (Aquent)

Concepts and Skies: Dorje Seattle Bellbrook, Mark Goldsworthy, John Gronquist, Isaac Hannaford, Steve Chon (Two Degrees)

User Interface Lead: David Candland

User Interface Artist: Andrew G Davis

Animation Lead: Roberta Browne

Animators: Jeremy Fones, Richard Lico, Bill O'Brien, Jason Robertson, Drew Shy, Mike Hoffman (Aquent)

Cinematics Animation: Pat Jandro, Kurt Nellis

Tech Art Lead: Paul Vosper

Tech Artists: Javier Burgos, Seth Gibson, James Haywood, David Hunt, Steve Theodore

ODST : AUDIO

Audio Director & Composer: Martin O'Donnell

Audio Lead & Sound Design: Jay Weinland

Sound Design & Additional Music: C Paul Johnson

Additional Music: Stan LePard (Panther Modern), Michael Salvatori (TotalAudio)

ODST : PRODUCTION

Director of Production: Jonty Barnes

Production Lead: Curtis Creamer

Producers: Sam Arguez, Matthew Burns, Matthew Priestley, Matt Richenburg, Dave Lieber (Aquent)

ODST : PRODUCTION ENGINEERING & TEST

Production Engineering Lead: Graham Bartlett

Production Engineers: Josh Rodgers, Tim Williams, Cullen Bradley (Excell), Nathan Rodland (Xversity), Ben Wommack (Volt)

Test Manager: Jamie Evans

Test Leads: David Gasca, Domenic Koeplin

Testers: Nicholas Gerrone, Andrew Harrison, Jon Weisnewski, Michael Axworthy (Excell), David Bai (Volt), Carlos Cardona (Comsys), Richard Chen (Comsys), John Comstock (Volt), Chris Daltas (Excell), Joel Day (Volt), Michael Durkin (Volt), Justin Ewert (Excell), Luana Gullo France (Volt), Chris Garrett (Volt), Doug Gorman III (Comsys), Andrew Hopper (Comsys), Gerry Jackson (Volt), Kenny Jackson (Comsys), Rob Kehoe (Volt), Tomonori Kinoshita (Excell), JA-IL Koo (Volt), Judith Kriess (Volt), Jonathan Kubo (Excell), Justin Lakin (Xversity), Paul Morris (Volt), Andra Ion Niculescu (Comsys), Eddie Nuñez (Volt), Michael Sechrist (Volt), Joe Sifferman (Volt), Joon Sim (Volt), Misao Tidd (Volt), Mark Uyeda (Volt), Lionel Ward (Excell), Chris Wilson (Volt),

BUNGIE.NET

Head of Infrastructure & bungie.net: Zach Russell

Bungie.Net Writer: Luke Smith

Bungie.Net Community: Eric Osborne (Xversity)

Web Design: Stosh Steward (Two Degrees)

BUNGIE

President: Harold Ryan

Director of Marketing: Pete Parsons

Marketing/PR/Community: Brian Jarrard

Business Development and Finance: Brent Abrahamsen, Ondraus Jenkins, Shawn Taylor, Renae Wetsig

Administration: Davina Chan Gallagher, Christine Edwards (Two Degrees)

HR: Gayle Chonzena, Shauna Sperry, Kari Erickson (Independent)

IT Lead: Steve Lopez

IT Team: Alex Bezman, Jae Parks, Douglas Patrick, James Phillips, Claw Kelsay (Volt), Sergey Mkrtumov (Comsys)

Security Lead: Jerry Simpson

Security: Philip Kauffman; Arturo (Adam) Gutierrez Jr. (Kelly Services)

HALO 3 CONTRIBUTORS...: David Allen, Chad Armstrong, Frank Capezzuto, Christopher Carney, Steve Cotton, Tyson Green, Jaime Griesemer, Jason Jones, Marcus Lehto, Robert McLees, Allen Murray, Christopher Opdahl, Niles Sankey, Joseph Tung, Lee Wilson, Michael Zak

...AND THE REST OF THE BUNGIE CREW: Robert Adams, Christian Allen, Noah Bordner, Tom Burlington, Derek Carroll, Glenn Israel, Jaime Jones, Sage Merrill, Patrick O'Kelley, Thomas Saville, Matthew Segur, Joseph Spataro, Natalya Tatarchuk, Benjamin Thompson, Michael Tipul

ODST : CINEMATIC ANIMATION PARTNERS

Animation Supervisor: Emilio Ghorayeb

Production Coordinator: Nabil Yared

Animators: Adrien Annesley, George Banks, Dana Boadway, Cristinel Bostan , Jason Clarke, Frédéric Côté, Marco Foglia, Cameron Folds, Benoît Gagné, Brent George, Mike Kitchen, Bartek Kujbida, Chris Lam, David Lam, Velislava Nikolova, Andrew Ogawa, Brett Paton, Ryan Pickering, Peter Reynolds, Scott Slater, John Velazquez, Ryan Yee, Philippe Zerounian

ODST : CAST

Buck: Nathan Fillion

Dare: Tricia Helfer

Dutch: Adam Baldwin

Mickey: Alan Tudyk

Romeo: Nolan North

Sgt. Johnson: David Scully

Firefight Announcer: Jeff Steitzer

Marines: Nika Futterman, Mikey Kelley, Andy McKaige, Debra Wilson Skelton, Pete Stacker, David White

Police Officers: Todd Licea, Mark Lund, Pete Stacker

Brutes: Ken Boynton, John DiMaggio, David Scully, Fred Tatasciore

Grunts: Chris Edgerly, Joseph Staten

Superintendent: Joseph Staten

ODST : "SADIE'S STORY"

Writing & Design: Fourth Wall Studios

Artwork: Ash Wood

Cast

Sadie Endesha: Masasa Moyo

Dr. Endesha: Hakim Kazim

Commissioner Kinsler, Additional Voices: John Patrick Lowrie

Mike Branley, Additional Voices: Dave Wittenberg

Duty Officer, Additional Voices: Carol Roscoe

Marshall, Additional Voices: Gavin Cummins

Stephen, Additional Voices: Don Brady

Tom, Additional Voices: Dennis Bateman

Jim, Additional Voices: Ken Boynton

Crone, Additional Voices: Laura Kenny

Jonas, Additional Voices: Richard Ziman

Crowd, Additional Voices: Gin Hammond

Crowd: The Bungie Auxiliary Players

Casting & Voice-Over Production Services: Blindlight

COMMUNITY

Let our special thanks crash against these rocks from our Community (in alphabetical order):

7th Column - Bungie's Underground Army

Ascendant Justice (www.ascendantjustice.com)

Claude Errera

GhaleonEB

Good Game Network

Halo.Bungie.Org

Major League Gaming (www.mlgpro.com)

Red vs Blue (www.redvsblue.com)

Ryan Wheeler

SPECIAL THANKS TO

Clifford Garrett, Eric Neustadter, Victor Tan, Stephen Toulouse, New Zealand, and The makers of Gauss Ammunition

MICROSOFT GAME STUDIOS

Executive Producer: James Veevaert

Lead Producer: Chris Lee

Producers: Alex Cutting, Brett Gow

Director of Art: Ben Cammarano

MGS : BUSINESS DEVELOPMENT

Senior Director: Rich Wickham

Director: Steve Schreck

Business Lead: Dennis Ries

MGS : USER EXPERIENCE

Editing Leads: Kevin Grace, Brent Metcalfe

Manual Design Leads: Ginny Baldwin, Dana Ludwig

MGS : USER RESEARCH

User Research Lead: Eric Schuh

User Research Engineers: John Hopson, Jun Kim

MGS : ENGINEERING

Engineering Leads: Greg Hermann, Aaron Nicholls, Kutta Srinivasan

MGS : AUDIO

Additional Sound Design: Peter Comley, Mark Yeend

MGS : MARKETING & PUBLIC RELATIONS

Ryan Crosby, Jamie Davies, Craig Davison, Aaron Elliot, Chad Hodge, Josh Kerwin, Chris Lee, Caroline McNiel, Brandy O'Briant, Carol Ragolski, Nancy Ramsey, Taylor Smith, Kevin Unangst

MGS : TEST

Test Manager: Jimmy Bischoff

Test Lead: Chris Shaules

SDETs: Tony Bradley, Alex Emmet, Paul H. Gradwohl, Eric Helbig, Peter Kugler, Lewis Liaw, Desmond Murray, Johnney Nguyen

Excell Data Corporation: Josiah Bolek, Anthony Bryan, Paul Conrad, Dan Hitchcock, Scott Kankelborg, Bryan Link, Travis Pijut, Jai Salzwedel, Shay Sanders, Derek Shefveland, Mitch Sullivan, Mike Toyama

Volt: Jake Jarvis, Sally Kayl, Jeffrey Kleinman, Cameron Laborde-Zank, Nelson Lavin, Xhavar Strothers, Craig Swanson, Kyle Symonds, Tristan Yolton

MGS : LOCALIZATION

Dublin Localization Team

Program Manager: Ian Walsh

Software Engineer: Michael Ivory

Audio Producer: Jason Shirley

Japan Localization Team

Program Manager: Masato Ishida

Content Editor: Tomoko Kometani

Software Test Engineers: Go Komatsu, Souichiro Shimano

Korea Localization Team

Program Manager: Jae Youn Kim

Localization Program Manager: Young Hoon Shim

Software Test Engineer: In Goo Kwon

Taiwan Localization Team

Program Manager: Robert Lin

Localization Program Manager: Eva Lin

Software Test Engineer: Andy Chen An Liu

MGS : SPECIAL THANKS

Alicia Brattin, Paul Chavez, Keith Cirillo, Jill Eppenberger, David Figatner, Dana Fos, Alicia Hatch, David Holmes, Greg B. Jones, Shane Kim, Jason Mangold, Don Mattrick, Oliver Miyashita, Yasmine Nelson, Bruce Phillips, Kyle Pullman, Bonnie Ross, Kevin Salcedo, John Schappert, David Shaw, Phil Spencer, Lief Thompson, Arthur Tien, Matt Whiting, JoAnne Williams

Love, Bungie

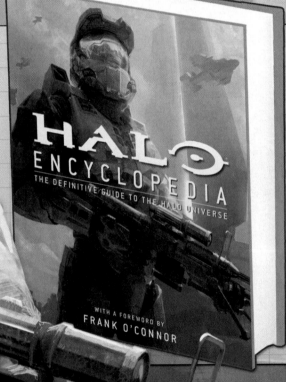

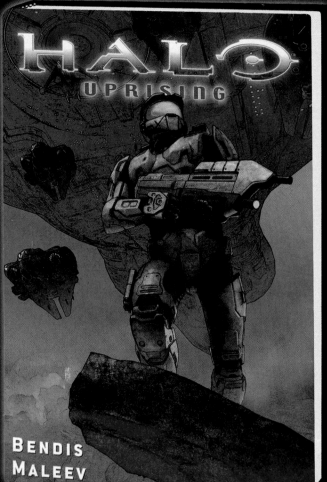

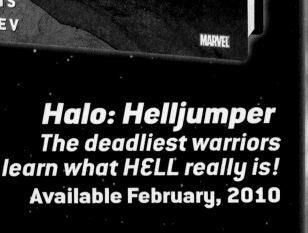

HALO
WAYPOINT